Straussophobia

Straussophobia

Defending Leo Strauss and Straussians against Shadia Drury and Other Accusers

Peter Minowitz

LEXINGTON BOOKS

A division of
ROWMAN & LITTLEFIELD PUBLISHERS, INC.
Lanham • Boulder • New York • Toronto • Plymouth, UK

Published by Lexington Books
A division of Rowman & Littlefield Publishers, Inc.
A wholly owned subsidary of The Rowman & Littlefield Publishing Group, Inc.
4501 Forbes Boulevard, Suite 200, Lanham, Maryland 20706
http://www.lexingtonbooks.com

Estover Road, Plymouth PL6 7PY, United Kingdom

British Library Cataloguing in Publication Information Available

Library of Congress Cataloging-in-Publication Data

Minowitz, Peter, 1955–
  Straussophobia : defending Leo Strauss and Straussians against Shadia Drury and
other accusers / Peter Minowitz.
    p. cm.
  Includes bibliographical references and index.
  ISBN 978-0-7391-1951-8 (cloth : alk. paper) — ISBN 978-0-7391-1952-5 (pbk. : alk.
paper) — ISBN 978-0-7391-4019-2 (electronic)
  1. Strauss, Leo—Criticism and intepretation. 2. Strauss, Leo—Political and social
views. 3. Political science—Philosophy. I. Title.
JC251.S8M56 2009
320.53092—dc22
                                                                    2009014497

Printed in the United States of America

This one's for Debbie and Joan

Contents

Abbreviations

ABBREVIATIONS FOR WORKS BY LEO STRAUSS

AAPL *The Argument and Action of Plato's Laws.* Chicago: University of Chicago Press, 1975.

CM *The City and Man.* Chicago: Rand McNally, 1964.

Epilogue "An Epilogue." In *Essays on the Scientific Study of Politics*, edited by Herbert J. Storing, 307–27. New York: Holt, Rinehart, and Winston, 1962. Reprinted in *LAM* 203–23.

FP "Farabi's *Plato.*" In *Louis Ginzberg Jubilee Volume*, 357–93. New York: American Academy for Jewish Research, 1945.

GN "German Nihilism." *Interpretation* 26, no. 3 (Spring 1999): 353–78. Lecture written in 1941.

GS *Gesammelte Schriften, Band III: Hobbes politische Wissenshaft und zugehörige Schriften—Briefe.* Edited by Heinrich and Wiebke Meier. Stuttgart, Germany: Verlag J. B. Metzler, 2001.

HPP *History of Political Philosophy*, 2nd ed. Edited by Leo Strauss and Joseph Cropsey. Chicago: Rand McNally, 1972.

LAM *Liberalism Ancient and Modern.* New York: Basic Books, 1968.

MITP "The Mutual Influence of Theology and Philosophy." In *Faith and Political Philosophy: The Correspondence between Leo Strauss and Eric Voegelin, 1934–1964*, edited by Peter Emberley and Barry Cooper, 217–33. University Park: Pennsylvania State University Press, 1993. Originally published in *Independent Journal of Philosophy* 3 (1979): 111–18.

NCS "Notes on Carl Schmitt, *The Concept of the Political.*" In Heinrich Meier, *Carl Schmitt and Leo Strauss: The Hidden Dialogue*, translated by J. Harvey Lomax, 91–119. Chicago: University of Chicago Press, 1995.

NRH   *Natural Right and History*. Chicago: University of Chicago Press, 1953.

OT   *On Tyranny. Revised and Enlarged*. Ithaca, NY: Cornell University Press, 1975. First published 1963. For Kojève's essay, for the Strauss-Kojève correspondence, and for my discussions of Nicholas Xenos's *Cloaked in Virtue*, I cite the *OT* edition edited by Victor Gourevitch and Michael S. Roth (New York: The Free Press, 1991); a second edition, which I have not consulted, was published in 2000.

PAW   *Persecution and the Art of Writing*. Chicago: University of Chicago Press, 1952.

PL   *Philosophy and Law: Contributions to the Understanding of Maimonides and His Predecessors*. Translated by Eve Adler. Albany: SUNY Press, 1995. German original published in 1935.

PPH   *The Political Philosophy of Hobbes: Its Basis and Its Genesis*. Translated by Elsa M. Sinclair. Chicago: University of Chicago Press, 1963. First published in 1936.

RCPR   *The Rebirth of Classical Political Rationalism: Essays and Lectures by Leo Strauss*. Selected and Introduced by Thomas L. Pangle. Chicago: University of Chicago Press, 1989.

SA   *Socrates and Aristophanes*. Chicago: University of Chicago Press, 1966.

SCR   *Spinoza's Critique of Religion*. Translated by Elsa M. Sinclair. New York: Schocken Books, 1965. German original published in 1930.

SPPP   *Studies in Platonic Political Philosophy*. Introduction by Thomas L. Pangle. Chicago: University of Chicago Press, 1983.

TM   *Thoughts on Machiavelli*. Seattle: University of Washington Press, 1969. First published in 1958.

TWM   "The Three Waves of Modernity." In *Political Philosophy: Six Essays by Leo Strauss*, edited by Hilail Gildin, 81–98. Indianapolis: Bobbs-Merrill/Pegasus, 1975.

WIPP   *What Is Political Philosophy? And Other Studies*. New York: The Free Press, 1959.

WWRJ   "Why We Remain Jews: Can Jewish Faith and History Still Speak to Us?" In *Leo Strauss: Political Philosopher and Jewish Thinker*, edited by Kenneth L. Deutsch and Walter Nicgorski, 43–79. Lanham, MD: Rowman & Littlefield, 1994. Lecture delivered in 1962.

XS   *Xenophon's Socrates*. Ithaca, NY: Cornell University Press, 1972.

XSD   *Xenophon's Socratic Discourse: An Interpretation of the "Oeco-*
                 nomicus." Ithaca, NY: Cornell University Press, 1970. Includes
                 a translation of Xenophon's *Oeconomicus* by Carnes Lord.

ABBREVIATED WORKS BY SHADIA DRURY, JOHN LOCKE, CARNES LORD, ANNE NORTON, ANDREW PAYTON THOMAS, NICHOLAS XENOS, AND CATHERINE AND MICHAEL ZUCKERT

AK   Shadia B. Drury. *Alexandre Kojève: The Roots of Postmodern
                 Politics.* New York: St. Martin's Press, 1994.

AM   Shadia B. Drury. *Aquinas and Modernity: The Lost Promise of
                 Natural Law.* Lanham, MD: Rowman & Littlefield, 2008.

CTB   Andrew Payton Thomas. *Clarence Thomas: A Biography.* San
                 Francisco: Encounter Books, 2001.

CV   Nicholas Xenos. *Cloaked in Virtue: Unveiling Leo Strauss and
                 the Rhetoric of American Foreign Policy.* New York: Rout-
                 ledge, 2008.

LSAR   Shadia B. Drury. *Leo Strauss and the American Right.* New York:
                 St. Martin's Press, 1997.

LSPAE   Anne Norton. *Leo Strauss and the Politics of American Empire.*
                 New Haven, CT: Yale University Press, 2004.

MP   Carnes Lord. *The Modern Prince: What Leaders Need to Know
                 Now.* New Haven, CT: Yale University Press, 2003.

PILS   Shadia B. Drury. *The Political Ideas of Leo Strauss.* New York:
                 St. Martin's Press, 1988.

PILS-05   Shadia B. Drury. Introduction to the updated edition of *PILS*. New
                 York: Palgrave Macmillan, 2005.

RC   John Locke. *The Reasonableness of Christianity: As Delivered in
                 the Scriptures.* Edited by George W. Ewing. Washington, DC:
                 Regnery Gateway, 1965.

ST   John Locke. *The Second Treatise of Government.* Edited by
                 Thomas P. Peardon. Indianapolis: Bobbs-Merrill, 1952.

TALS   Catherine H. Zuckert and Michael Zuckert. *The Truth about Leo
                 Strauss: Political Philosophy and American Democracy.* Chi-
                 cago: University of Chicago Press, 2006.

TC   Shadia B. Drury. *Terror and Civilization: Christianity, Politics, and
                 the Western Psyche.* New York: Palgrave Macmillan, 2004.

Note to the Reader

Unless otherwise noted, emphases and italics were in the original. (When I have added italics to one word or phrase, I typically abbreviate "emphasis" as "emph."; when I have added italics to separated words, I write "emphases added.")

To avoid adding clutter to a long manuscript, I have not routinely specified the dates on which I accessed various websites; I did check almost all of the links in the fall of 2007 or later. To find an online piece, in any case, it will often be easier to plug a quoted phrase into a Google search than to enter the web address I provided.

Acknowledgments

My debts are numerous and deep. First and foremost, I must thank the readers who plowed through drafts of the entire manuscript: Christopher Bobonich, Murray Dry, Janet Flammang, Eric Hanson, Timothy J. Lukes, Jeff Zorn, and two anonymous referees selected by Rowman & Littlefield. Each of these readers broadened my thinking, each diagnosed a variety of errors and stylistic glitches, and each supplied encouragement along with constructive advice. Regarding the defects that remain, furthermore, they can all summon "plausible deniability": each offered sensible suggestions that I refused to heed.

I also received useful feedback from Dennis Gordon, Kenneth Faulve-Montojo, Josh Hayes, Carol McNamara, Laurie Mylroie, and Shannon Vallor, who graciously responded to my requests for assistance concerning specific portions of the manuscript. For help with translations, I am indebted to Christopher Bobonich, John Dunlap, Mark and Nina Homnack, Timothy J. Lukes, Therese Mathis, Gudrun Tabbert-Jones, Joan Robins, and Anthony Soldato (the last two were amazingly generous with their time). I would also like to thank Terri Peretti and Janet Flammang for the institutional support they provided, successively, as chairs of the Santa Clara University political science department; our administrative assistant, Julie Wong, was a key enabler during the past two years. Joseph Parry and Julia Loy at Rowman & Littlefield, finally, deployed their experience and expertise to assist me in a variety of useful ways.

Introduction

Persecution and the Art of Writhing

Correct a wise man, and he will be your friend.

—Proverbs 9:8

Rarely have personalities, ideas, institutions, and events collided to produce a conflagration as perplexing as the Iraq War.

Consider the following sequence of developments. A Jewish scholar (Leo Strauss) fleeing from Nazi Germany draws upon a medieval Muslim (Farabi) to rediscover hidden depths in Western philosophy. Roughly sixty years later, his American disciples are blamed for manipulating the United States into a "preemptive" invasion of a major Arab country. While the majority of those disciples toil away in the ivory tower, the most widely heralded interpreter of that scholar (Shadia B. Drury) accuses him of establishing a "covert tyranny" that would keep the Western world "mired in perpetual war." The *New York Times* and the *New Yorker* bequeath flagrant errors to the discussion, respected journals (e.g., the *New York Review of Books*, *Harper's*, *Political Theory*, *International Politics*, and *Christianity Today*) convey the most heinous accusations, Yale University Press offers a citation- and bibliography-free book (*Leo Strauss and the Politics of American Empire*) that further muddies the waters, and Netflix is distributing the filmed version of a 2003 play by Tim Robbins in which the president's inner circle abase themselves before Strauss's image as they orchestrate death and destruction.

While Robbins was writing his play (*Embedded*), I was an unabashed but unassuming Straussian professor at a Catholic university, attempting to write a book about the use and abuse of the term "diversity." I was impelled mostly by the way that other forms of difference tend to be ignored or depreciated when diversity is equated with the presence (in sufficient numbers) of women, racial/ethnic minorities, and comparably disadvantaged and/or underrepresented

1

groups. The puzzle is especially complex for institutions that embrace Jesus's claim that anyone "who does not dwell in me is thrown away like a withered branch" (John 15:6).[1]

I scrutinized court cases from *Weber* and *Bakke* to *Hopwood, Gratz,* and *Grutter.* I absorbed the work of numerous friends of diversity, including Mary Frances Berry, Richard Delgado, Troy Duster, Michael Eric Dyson, Henry Louis Gates, Lani Guinier, Patricia Gurin, Ian Haney-Lopez, bell hooks, Sylvia Hurtado, Glenn Loury, Michael Omi, Miranda Oshige, Ronald Takaki, Cornel West, Patricia Williams, and dozens of other scholars. Among other things, I equipped myself to dispute Nicholas Xenos's suggestion that Straussians only write about "a depressingly small, and distressingly repetitive, range of authors, texts, and themes."[2] But nothing prepared me for the explosion of "Straussophobia" that I shall address in subsequent chapters. Sensitized by years of diversity research to the subtlest manifestations of racism, sexism, classism, ableism, and other forms of prejudicial stereotyping and marginalization, I was stunned by the vilification I was increasingly encountering about Strauss and Straussians.[3] I decided to write a chapter in the book about my "diversity" as a Straussian after I watched the DVD of *Embedded,* the play in which members of a Bush administration "cabal" regularly chant to Strauss while scheming to initiate and prosecute the Iraq War. That chapter swelled into this book.

Who was Leo Strauss? All informed parties—but not all parties who offer confident pronouncements—agree about some basic facts: Strauss lived from 1899 to 1973; he produced eleven stand-alone books (including *Natural Right and History*), three essay collections (including *Persecution and the Art of Writing*) published in his lifetime, and various articles, chapters, and reviews; he founded an informal political-philosophy "school" as a political scientist at the University of Chicago (along with his colleague Joseph Cropsey he edited a widely used textbook, *The History of Political Philosophy*[4]); and he had a transformative impact on Allan Bloom, Harry V. Jaffa, William Kristol, Harvey C. Mansfield Jr., and other influential authors.

To many of his students, and to many individuals who encountered him second hand by studying with those students, he was a towering reader and thinker who rediscovered esoteric writing (e.g., writing "between the lines") as he attempted to plumb "the theological-political problem"—particularly the centuries-long encounter between Jerusalem and Athens—and to revive appreciation of classical political philosophy against modern alternatives (e.g., "permissive egalitarianism" [*LAM* 222]) that emerged along a winding path he traced back to Machiavelli.[5] Among Strauss's chief targets were nineteenth- and twentieth-century scholars who invoked science or history to deny that individual lives can be rationally guided and that human societies can be rationally ranked.

To someone who approached him via his critics, however, Strauss would represent a variety of ominous prospects. Was he an "obscurantist authoritarian" (Sidney Blumenthal) who conveys "a pervasive and obfuscatory theoretical dogmatism" (Richard Wolin) that exudes "German windbaggery" (Arthur Schlesinger Jr.)? An "utterly mad historian of political thought" who unleashed "paranoid theories of textual interpretation" upon the academic world (Robert Paul Wolff)? The "éminence grise" who inspired neoconservatives to "forfeit no deceit, no calumny, no subterfuge" in opposing "every sign of postcolonial political autonomy" in Latin America, Asia, and the Middle East (Stanley Aronowitz)? A "sworn enemy of freedom and democracy" who dwelled in "the most fearful depths of depravity" and promoted the "fascistic glorification of death and violence" (Shadia Drury)? A "right wing fundamentalist seeking to undermine liberal freedoms in the U.S. and instigate an old world 'war culture' at the core of U.S. foreign policy" (Jim George)? Or an enthusiast for acquisitiveness who believed that "unlimited appropriation without concern for the needs of others is true charity" and who opposed "any restraint on individual liberty" (Will Hutton)? A fanatical elitist who declared that "the entire Western world" (except for himself) was "depraved and diseased" and that the lives of most people are "utterly valueless and unjustifiable" unless they serve to "make philosophers more comfortable and secure" (Stephen Holmes)? An ex-Trotskyite devotee of "Jewish Bolshevism" (David Duke) who insisted that "religion is nothing more than a lie that 'breeds deference to the ruling class'" (David Luban)? Or a believer who "viewed the status quo as an expression of divine will" (Brent Staples)?[6]

Reading about Straussians too, I have had to ask myself some awkward questions. Are we exemplars of "antisocial myopia" (Joe Klein) and "grandiose ambition" (Sheldon Wolin) who tend to practice "unrestrained persecution" of Arabs and Muslims (Anne Norton)? "An intolerable sect of true believers" (John Pocock) who represent "the surrender of the critical intellect" (Myles Burnyeat)? Scholars who exude "a sanctimonious sense of privilege" even though we possess "no conception of the process of history" (Gordon Wood) and we "write as though Freud had never lived" (Richard H. King)? "Power-mad propagandists" who believe that everyone who dissents from our guru must be "crushed or eliminated" (Thomas J. DiLorenzo) and who are destroying "the conditions that make thinking and critique possible" (Joseph Buttigieg)? "Intellectual poseurs and frauds, purveyors of shoddy scholarship and arguments (when there are arguments at all)" (Brian Leiter)? A "cabal of sycophants and mediocrities" (Eugene McCarraher) who exercise "a near monopoly on interest in the history of political theory" and who use "helping friends and hurting enemies" as their moral compass (Nicholas Xenos)? "Neo-Nazis" (Francis A. Boyle) or "Platonic fundamentalists" who controlled U.S. foreign policy in President Bush's first term (Douglas Massey)? A "whole class of compulsive and self-righteous deceivers" who are "ill equipped to handle philosophical debate" and who "will imagine that they are gods entertaining themselves with the mutual slaughter of the mortals on their television screens" (Shadia Drury)?[7]

Most of the statements I quote in the above two paragraphs have issued from the hands of nationally or internationally celebrated scholars and journalists. A Google search will quickly yield accusations that are no less distressing. In his blurb for Xenos's new book, Professor Stephen Eric Bronner of Rutgers nevertheless characterizes it as the first political analysis of Strauss/Straussians that "doesn't mince words."

Formidable Straussians—Nasser Behnegar, David Janssens, Heinrich Meier, Thomas Pangle, Steven B. Smith, Daniel Tanguay, and Catherine and Michael Zuckert—have entered the recent fray and offered lucid, informed, and thoughtful overviews of Strauss. Their books are invaluable, but none has attempted a systematic and detailed reply that focuses on the shortcomings of the diatribes.[8] In responding to attacks on Strauss, especially to the escalations inspired by the Iraq War, I shall complement these books in at least five additional respects: I'll do more to combat both intemperate attacks on *Straussians* and the indiscriminate identification of prominent conservatives (e.g., Richard Perle and Clarence Thomas) as Straussians; I'll provide a more thorough discussion of Paul Wolfowitz, the highest ranking Bush-administration official who studied with Strauss; I'll say more about Iraq; I'll address Xenos's *Cloaked in Virtue*, a weighty critique of Strauss that was not published until 2008; and I'll incorporate reflections on multiculturalism and affirmative action. Among the above-mentioned authors, the Zuckerts do the most to relay and rebut criticisms, but they neither convey the extent of the assault nor expose its bigotry and buffoonery. We live in strange times. And now a Straussian is playing the diversity card.

In the decades that have elapsed since Straussian-related polemics began, the American academic world has come to equate *diversitas* with *veritas*. Yet Straussians continue to be the object of heinous stereotyping—and we have graduated to the rank of scapegoats. To borrow a phrase from Al Gore, people increasingly speak of us "with the kind of dripping contempt and virulent hostility that used to be associated with racism and sectarian religious strife."[9]

I would not shock anyone if I suggested that academic freedom is coming under siege. Let me quote Jonathan R. Cole, former provost and dean of faculties at Columbia University: a chill wind blows on campuses from a "rising tide" of intolerance; professors are "publicly savaged for their ideas, often by outside groups"; and "challenges to reigning academic dogma" are considered "off limits."[10] Let me quote Ellen Willis: there are "serious internal obstacles to intellectual freedom and diversity on the contemporary campus," in part because debates are "too often settled, or stifled, by the ubiquitous tendency of academic departments to exclude or marginalize scholars whose approach diverges from prevailing orthodoxy."[11] Let me invoke Corey Robin's protest against the "fear that stifles political options," Zbigniew Brzezinski's against the fear-mongering that "generates its own momentum," and Joe Conason's against the authoritarian rhetoric that employs "innuendo and lies to transform political opponents into soft-minded dupes and potential traitors."[12] Let me cite a letter signed by Derrick Bell, Noam Chomsky, Juan Cole, Richard Delgado, Richard Falk, Rashid Khalidi, Immanuel Wallerstein, and Howard Zinn: the "most honorable calling of institutions of higher learning" is "to provide a safe haven for unpopular and distasteful views."[13]

In the spirit of the landmark book (*Faces at the Bottom of the Well*) that Derrick Bell wrote before he left Harvard Law School for Stanford and New York University, I shall pose the first of my thought experiments. Imagine a Michigan State University student writing a personal statement while applying to graduate schools in philosophy or political science. Which of these nonobvious facts would a prudent student trumpet, and which would she conceal: My mother is Mexican? Or my mentor is Melzer?[14] These days, I submit, the boost the mother provides would often be eclipsed by the ill-will the mentor arouses.[15] Given what people are willing to write about Straussians, one can only imagine what they *say*—and what they would *do* in tester studies where they can freely act upon their shadiest thoughts.

Straussians of course differ from "minorities," women, gays, and so forth, in not confronting a long history of social repression. We differ from minorities because we rarely if ever inherit disadvantage or even identity; no one is born a Straussian, and we can easily "pass" in the larger community (outside of academia, the identity has typically been too obscure to be disadvantageous). It is also possible to offer legitimate criticisms of Straussians as one could of Marxists, libertarians, and so on, but not of Chicanas. Straussianism, however, routinely becomes an immutable identity—in Xenos's words, our "cult" has spawned "schisms, sects, and heretics" but few if any apostates (*CV* 10)—and there are circumstances that dramatically amplify the sting of Straussophobia. We are a tiny minority, we are routinely excoriated, and we have become the scapegoat de jour in the eyes of prominent individuals from both ends of the political spectrum.[16] Like members of the GLBQT (gay, lesbian, bisexual, questioning, and transgender) community, furthermore, Straussians sometimes confront the possibility of "coming out" to colleagues, students, or family members. Certain Straussians are affluent and powerful, but so are numerous women, homosexuals, blacks, and Latinos. And whereas a racist is typically a fool who hates or devalues people on the basis of superficial traits, a Strauss-basher is impugning things in which a Straussian is deeply invested.

Innumerable critics of President Bush and his neoconservative advisors are outraged by the falsehoods his administration conveyed about weapons of mass destruction and the linkages between Al-Qaida and Saddam Hussein. Yet the accusers of Straussians have been profusely lying, or at least erring, as they complain about deceptive Straussian theory and practice. And our accusers, typically, are not politicians acting under the pressure of events and constituents; they are scholars, professors, and journalists who are supposed to model rigor and reliability.

Despite the allegations that Straussians dress alike, one cannot *see* Straussian identity. There remains a crucial overlap with the standard diversity categories, however. The sheer variety of the accusations contributes to the air of chauvinism: "we" know "they" are repulsive, and maybe someday we can offer evidence. As with myriad forms of racism, sexism, homophobia, and ethnocentrism, people presume they are well-informed about Straussians based on scant familiarity. And people, despite their ignorance, are willing to pronounce the most scathing judgments, as they sometimes are about religions or political orientations that appear alien.[17]

The iconoclastic Walter Been Michaels, who offers a proudly left-wing critique of the diversity *Zeitgeist*, might cavil at my complaints about bias and bigotry. Michaels emphasizes the difference between prejudice—which "involves the unjustified assumption that your identity is somehow better than someone else's identity"—and disagreement, which "involves the absolutely justified— indeed unavoidable—assumption that your belief is better than someone else's."[18] But insofar as individuals are inclined to condemn Straussians without making a serious effort to ascertain our opinions—and to promulgate generalizations that are extremely silly or offensive—I am confident in speaking of prejudice. The carelessness with which so many people apply the "Straussian" label does distinguish it from claims about sexual and racial/ethnic identity— though individuals are still flippantly accused of being gay or lesbian—and link it with the way that liberals in decades past were called "commies" and people throughout the centuries have been called heathens, heretics, or atheists.[19] In his 2004 BBC documentary, "The Power of Nightmares" (aired in the United States by PBS), Adam Curtis is skeptical about the existence of a terrorist *organization* run by Osama bin Laden. Yet Curtis intones constantly about both "the neoconservatives"—among other things, he holds them responsible for the *American Spectator*'s hounding of President Clinton—and Straussians as if they were conspiratorial monoliths.[20]

My agenda centers on the earliest stages of diversity training: smoking out the ignorance and rage that suffuse stereotypes, and encouraging people to accept the "differences" that distinguish Straussians from academia's hegemonic mainstreams. Although I would not join Kenji Yoshino in characterizing "covering"—when someone is pressured "to tone down a disfavored identity to fit into the mainstream"—as a "hidden assault on our civil rights,"[21] I am calling for consciousness-raising.[22]

Although any self-respecting American university would be appalled if it lacked feminists, queer theorists, or ethnic studies scholars, it would be absurd to put Straussians in such company. Among other things, hardly any incoming undergraduates identify themselves as Straussians, so there is little if any need for role models, and Straussians have not been around long enough to produce centuries of unacknowledged viewpoints and experiences. Affirmative action would be inappropriate, but discrimination studies might be illuminating. And although our numbers fall way short, much could be gained by the presence of a "critical mass" of Straussians—female and male, gay and straight, Democrat and Republican, fourth generation and first generation, Jewish and Catholic, East Coast and West Coast, and so on—at some leading universities.

Apart from centuries-old patterns of intolerance, the hyper-rapid communication of the past fifty-plus years leaves Straussians facing a challenge that diversity scholars have identified only in the last decade or two: stereotype threat. According to Claude M. Steele, the Stanford psychologist who has immortalized the term, stereotype threat arises in people from the prospect of "being viewed through the lens of a negative stereotype, or the fear of doing something that would inadvertently confirm that stereotype."[23] Here is a longer definition from a more scholarly setting:

> the social-psychological threat that arises when one is in a situation or doing something for which a negative stereotype about one's group applies. This predicament threatens one with being negatively stereotyped, with being judged or treated stereotypically, or with the prospect of conforming to the stereotype.[24]

Defenders of affirmative action now routinely invoke this phenomenon as a way of minimizing the relevance of the test-score gaps between targeted minorities (especially African Americans) and whites/Asians. In the package of supporting material that the University of Michigan submitted to various courts in the *Grutter* and *Gratz* cases, the university included a nine-page single-spaced essay from Steele "to establish the basis for the University's argument that there is a compelling need for diversity in higher education."[25]

Steele and his coworkers conducted clever experiments about the performance of high-achieving black students on difficult verbal examinations: if students were told in advance that they were being tested for *ability*, they performed substantially worse (compared to a similarly high-achieving group of white students) than students who were told that the experimental agenda was to examine their approaches to problem-solving.[26] The researchers found similar results with talented female students taking math tests. In connection with Straussian "performance," there is of course nothing comparable to an SAT test that could be affected. Steele, however, emphasizes that the phenomenon might exist in any "group about which negative stereotypes exists" ("Thin Ice" 46). The effect, furthermore, can be "cued by the mere recognition that a negative group stereotype could apply to oneself in a given situation," it can happen even when the person is alone, and it can affect someone who *rejects* the stereotype.[27]

All of these circumstances apply to an individual who is addressing, via writing or speech, any audience that could perceive her or him as a Straussian. Whereas a speech or a job interview would fall into the "domain performance" threat that subsumes test performance, the writing process could qualify as the "chronic" threat that Steele illustrates with the example of the woman who spends "considerable time in a competitive male-oriented math environment."[28] Stereotype threat must of course be distinguished from long-recognized forms of stigmatization in which negative evaluations are internalized pervasively rather than activated by specific triggers or situations.

As we think about Leo Strauss in connection with diversity, additional ironies leap to mind. First, although people increasingly regard the "noble lie" as the defining feature of Straussianism, the term can also be applied to diversity. As numerous commentators on both the right and the left have complained, the relevant vocabulary is pervaded by distortion as arbitrary decisions are made about which forms of human difference will be recognized as "diverse" and which will be temporarily forgotten or concealed.[29] Even Justice Ruth Bader Ginsburg, while defending the admissions plan that Michigan's College of Literature, Science, and the Arts had employed, acknowledged the "winks, nods, and disguises" that often accompany the practice of affirmative action (focusing on the twenty-point bump that the college automatically allocated to every member of a targeted minority group, the court's majority held that the plan violated the Equal Protection clause).[30] In the eyes of many critics, diversity is merely a euphemism for affirmative action, which, apart from outreach programs and antidiscrimination measures that are widely embraced, is in turn a euphemism for racial/ethnic preferences (if not quotas); all of these policies dance perilously on the distinction between practicing discriminating and preventing or counteracting it. If the case for diversity is so compelling, why do people routinely dress it up with slogans? I concede that Straussians who appeal to diversity might be hypocritical insofar as they protest nihilism more than they protest racism, sexism, or classism. Although Strauss invokes "the exhilaration deriving from the beholding of diversity" (*SPPP* 149) and laments the prospect of the "universal and homogeneous state,"[31] furthermore, he suggests that the persecution of dissidents and philosophers is natural, so perhaps Straussians should be prepared to endure demonization and sporadic blacklisting. But insofar as dominant sectors of U.S. society—political, corporate, legal, medical, and academic—are rapturous in celebrating diversity, Straussians too are entitled to grouse. Within our natural habitat, our numbers are miniscule and our orientation is heterodox.

Although I found myself fretting about presidential contenders from both major parties—Congressman Ron Paul, the prodigious fund-raiser who squawked about Strauss on the House floor in 2003, and John Edwards, the ex-senator who welcomed Tim Robbins onto the "Main Street Express" in December, 2007[32]—I do not wish to exaggerate the plight of contemporary Straussians. No senator has conducted press conferences and summoned hearings, the American Political Science Association continues to grant the Leo Strauss Award annually to the best dissertation in political philosophy, and Bill Kristol lasted a full year as a *New York Times* columnist.[33]

There is a huge body of serious scholarship on Strauss that I shall address only intermittently, since my focus is on the spreading hostility. I object neither to responsible criticism of Strauss nor to speculation about how he might address policy issues, but the discussion needs to rise from the gutter. I'll denounce exaggerations, and I'll avoid issuing them except when it's obvious that I am trying to add humor; with a view to our dour image and other matters, I shall periodically attempt what Steele calls "cracking the stereotypic lens."[34]

Although this book will not present a comprehensive overview of Strauss, I hope that my detailed expositions of sections from *On Tyranny*, *The City and Man*, *Natural Right and History*, *Thoughts on Machiavelli*, and various essays will both highlight fundamental themes and promote appreciation of Strauss's meticulousness, imagination, depth, breadth, and eloquence.

By far the largest portion of my apologetics will be directed against Shadia Drury. After spending over two decades at the University of Calgary, Drury in 2003 became the Canada Research Chair in Social Justice at the University of Regina, where she directs the master's program in social and political thought. For most of her career, her primary scholarly enterprise was to reveal the grave dangers posed by Strauss and Straussians. Her books and essays have been translated into Chinese, Korean, Arabic, and Italian.[35] Her work is also highlighted in major encyclopedias and lauded by contemporary critics of Strauss, from the dregs of the Internet to illustrious scholars such as Stephen Holmes. By assigning Drury a tier 1 chair, the Canadian government has included her among the "outstanding researchers acknowledged by their peers as world leaders in their fields."[36]

I shall do to Drury something analogous to what she attempted to do to Strauss, although I shall not address her work as comprehensively as she addressed his. I am awed that she took on so much, but there is insufficient space for me to reconstruct her entire argument (fortunately, her seminal work—*The Political Ideas of Leo Strauss*—is sharply focused and highly readable), and "diversity" obliges me to illuminate the corners that the chief accuser has cut. Drury writes as a scholar, but as I shall demonstrate, her work on Strauss and Straussians is plagued by exaggerations, misquotations, contradictions, factual errors, and defective documentation.

I shall endeavor throughout this book to be scrupulous in identifying Drury's views and in refuting them. I shall even offer what I regard as sensible restatements of several of her wilder pronouncements. I shall not assert, moreover, that Drury is a "compulsive liar," that she is "poorly trained," that she is "ill-equipped to handle philosophical debate," that she "completely subverts what the ancients are about," that she represents "the largest academic movement in the twentieth century," that she feels "comfortable only when preaching to the converted and consorting with the like-minded," that she hates ancient Athens because of its "philosophical love of truth," that her interpretations of the great books reveal more about herself than about their authors, or that her influence threatens "the meaningful exchange of ideas in the academy." And I would not even dream of suggesting that she is a "Jewish Nazi," that she is a "callous ruffian," that she has fallen into "the most fearful depths of depravity," that she makes Dostoevsky's Grand Inquisitor look "compassionate and humane in comparison," that she displays animosity toward "freedom, justice, and equality before the law," that she belittles liberal democracy as "a spineless regime . . . ruled by the rabble as represented by Hitler," that she regards European peoples as "mystical purebreds," that she harbors "a fascistic glorification of death and violence," or that she would welcome "perpetual war." These quotations appear either on the list I made of the top ten most *foolish* things Drury has said about Strauss (or Straussians) or on the list I made of the top ten most *demonizing* things she has said (the two categories often overlap).[37] Now that Mitt Romney has apologized for describing Boston's Big Dig as a tar baby,[38] perhaps Drury will be inspired to show some contrition.

The opening chapter, "All Hate Leo Strauss," presents my most concentrated survey of Straussophobic discourse. After critiquing the lively but warped portrayal of Strauss in Tim Robbins's *Embedded*, I offer a definition of Strauss-ianism, describe the real-world Office of Special Plans, and then scrutinize Paul Wolfowitz, the only member of *Embedded*'s "cabal" who has any significant connection to Strauss. I here correct a batch of commentators, including Seymour Hersh and James Atlas, who have broadcast misinformation about Wolfowitz (and related matters) that professors at prominent institutions have incorporated into musings about Straussian conspiracies; in addition, I highlight Albert Wohlstetter, the Chicago political scientist whose protégés and writings played important but often underappreciated roles in connection with Iraq. After unmasking a sampling of additional slanders and errors that Atlas's *New York Times* travesty helped inspire, I show how irrelevant Strauss appears to be for Richard Perle, another member of the *Embedded* cabal who is widely labeled a Straussian (I also comment on Rice, Rumsfeld, and Cheney). My next section appraises the sources that Tim Robbins draws upon—one of whom invokes Hannah Arendt's alleged spurning of Strauss's romantic advances—after which I respond to other frivolous insults that trace Arendt's rebuffing of Strauss to his allegedly Nazi-like political orientation. The final section of the chapter addresses some "classic" assaults on Strauss and Straussians that occurred in major academic and journalistic settings.

In the second chapter, "'Careless Scholarship and a Tendency to Quote out of Context': Early Drury on Strauss, Locke, and Xenophon," I begin my deconstruction of the world's best-known critic of Leo Strauss. After a quick exploration of how Shadia Drury underestimates Strauss's scholarship and overestimates the prevalence of his disciples, the chapter criticizes the way her 1988 blockbuster (*The Political Ideas of Leo Strauss*) approaches Strauss's interpretations of Locke and Xenophon (regarding Xenophon, I also discuss her 1994 book on Alexandre Kojève). Because Drury highlights her own mentor, John Yolton, to bolster her pervasive and hasty dismissals of Strauss's merits as a scholar, I defend Strauss's Locke against Yolton's critique (I also respond to Will Hutton's pathetic attempt to recruit Locke into a campaign against Strauss). After condemning the amazing condemnation with which Drury ends *PILS*, I turn to Xenophon. In this section, I expose exaggerations and outright errors in Drury's discussions of *On Tyranny* and *Xenophon's Socratic Discourse*. I show that Drury misreads both Strauss and Kojève in attempting to argue that the quest for honor/glory would impel Straussian "philosophers" to injure other human beings; I respond to her charges that Strauss encourages "tyrannical government" and "casts a shadow on the noble life"; and I make a detour to assess Xenos's Xenophon. After refuting Drury's accusation that Strauss in *On Tyranny* was attempting to summon a nihilistic global revolution, the chapter concludes by examining Strauss's 1941 lecture, "German Nihilism."

The third chapter, "The American Right, Pious Frauds, and Secret Kingship," introduces Drury's 1997 book, *Leo Strauss and the American Right* (*LSAR*). Initially, I impugn several alarming insults and exaggerations—for example, that Strauss failed to appreciate "the inner dimension of faith" and that he was undeniably "phallocratic." Focusing on William Bennett, Clarence Thomas, and Robert Bork, I next address the book's unsound and embarrassingly lazy specification of Straussians in power. The chapter then offers a detailed critique of how Drury (starting with a 1985 article) attempts to marshal Strauss's writings on Farabi and on Plato's *Laws* in arguing that he endeavored to equip his students to rule "behind the scenes with no risks to themselves or to philosophy." The Nocturnal Council of Plato's *Laws*, Drury adds, "ensures the secret rule of the philosopher in the real city."

Chapter 4 is titled: "'A Great Enemy of Democracy'? Strauss on Plato's *Republic*, Germany, and Empire." This chapter starts by rebutting Drury's claim in the *Routledge Encyclopedia of Philosophy* that, according to Strauss, the savage

Thrasymachus was Plato's "true spokesman." When Drury elsewhere presents Strauss as an enemy of democracy, she treats *Socrates* as Plato's mouthpiece—and she relies heavily on the proposition that Strauss, inspired partly by the *Republic*'s cycle of regimes, "abhorred" liberal democracy because he associated it with Weimar. In responding to this momentous charge, I draw on Strauss in correcting Drury's sketch of the cycle. I proceed to elaborate Strauss's critique of Weimar—and to attack Drury's claim that, for Strauss, liberal democracy is "a regime ruled by the rabble as represented by Hitler." The chapter's next section argues that subtle endorsements of democracy emerge from Strauss's appeals to Hesiod's "golden age" in connection with Plato, Nietzsche, and Weimar (along the way, I address Drury's attempt to portray Strauss as a Nietzschean). I then turn to confront the scandalously right-wing paragraph Strauss composed as an epithet for Weimar in a 1933 letter to Karl Löwith, a paragraph that grounds Xenos's radical new interpretation of Strauss. Commenting upon the Virgilian passage ("to subdue the proud and spare the vanquished") that Strauss quotes later in the letter, I also examine some lesser-known texts in which he seems to disparage imperialism in the name of freedom, civilization, and peace. The chapter concludes with a critique of Daniel Flynn, a strident right-wing critic of Strauss, who states that Strauss regarded the pursuit of empire as "proof of health in nations."

The fifth chapter, "'Mired in Perpetual War': A Confrontation with Cyber-Age Intolerance," begins by discussing a long and widely cited 2003 interview in which Drury asserts that Strauss harbored a "fascistic glorification of death and violence" that prompted him to regard perpetual war as the remedy for the ills of modernity. Because Drury on this point links Strauss with Carl Schmitt, I also show how Drury distorts Schmitt's *The Concept of the Political* and Strauss's 1932 commentary upon it (this commentary is likewise crucial for Xenos's efforts to portray Strauss as "an extreme right-wing antimodernist" agitating against "the evil nature of human beings"). I proceed to address analogous distortions in the recent writings of Justin Raimondo (at www.antiwar.com), Earl Shorris (in *Harper's* and elsewhere), and Jim George (in *International Politics*). Next, I explain the ways that a memorable scene from *Gulliver's Travels*—in which Gulliver urinates over the Lilliputian castle to extinguish a fire—has been linked to Strauss and appropriated by Drury, *Embedded*, journalist Jim Lobe, and political scientist John Mason in a cascading chorus of erroneous claims about Straussian elitism and militarism. To show how Drury abuses *The Brothers Karamazov* in a similar polemic, I deconstruct her article about Dostoevsky's Grand Inquisitor. The chapter concludes by exposing the slanders that Anne Norton directs against Straussians, particularly Carnes Lord, in a confused, careless, and caustic book (*Leo Strauss and the Politics of American Empire*) that was published in 2004 by Yale University Press.

The sixth chapter is titled, "'Untold Mischief' and 'Enigmatic Works': Appreciating Strauss on Machiavelli and Modernity." I begin by refuting the snide but ill-informed attacks by Daniel Flynn on Strauss's interpretations of Machiavelli (and Spinoza). The rest of the chapter defends Strauss's controversial approach to Machiavelli against Drury's critique of it. Working from the assumption that Machiavelli was a blunt and straightforward writer, Drury argues that Strauss's elaborate discussions use Machiavelli as camouflage for *Strauss's* political agenda. I show that Drury misrepresents and underestimates Machiavelli as well as Strauss, and I provide examples of the Machiavellian subtleties Strauss illuminates that have been overlooked by generations of interpreters. Turning to rebut Drury's claim that, for Strauss, Machiavelli founded modernity by abandoning esoteric writing, I sketch Strauss's treatment of Hobbes, Locke, and Rousseau. From here, I respond to Drury's claim that, according to Strauss, Machiavelli was thoroughly "under the spell of Christianity."

The seventh and final chapter, "From the Peloponnesus to Iraq—and Michigan," returns foreign policy to center stage, initially focusing on the introduction Drury wrote for the 2005 reprinting of *PILS*. First, I use Strauss's account of Thucydides in *The City and Man* to demolish two absurd statements by Drury: that Strauss was a Spartanist who hated the frankness that allegedly prevented the Athenians from relying upon "sacred myths"; and that he had "antipathy" for Athens because of its "philosophical love of truth." I proceed to illustrate a bevy of new misquotations, factual mistakes, and unconscionable accusations that the new introduction offers in connection with the Iraq War, for example, that members of Strauss's "monstrous" elite welcome "catastrophe and carnage" so that they "will not lack for entertainment" (*PILS*-05 li). I then turn to Drury's criticisms of a foreign-policy document published in 2000 by the Straussian-led Project for a New American Century. By comparing Drury's critique to the original, I demonstrate one final time how untrustworthy she is as a commentator.

In my concluding remarks, which constitute the second part of the final chapter, I reflect on the unusual puzzles we confront regarding Leo Strauss and his legacy. Among other things, I emphasize how remote most of Strauss's writings are from the realm of policy-making, I argue that he did not use the classroom to convey a secret teaching, and I appraise the two Iraq War controversies (regime change and WMDs) that have become widely associated with Straussianism. To illuminate the "cave"-like aspects of politics that render philosophy a permanent challenge to human society and that prompted various philosophers to write between the lines, I also expose certain "noble lies" that suffuse the jurisprudence of affirmative action.

We should blame Straussians, and innumerable others, who champion policies despite their grossly deficient knowledge of the relevant circumstances. But we must also blame those Strauss-bashers who have abandoned intellectual rigor while demonstrating the persistence of bigotry in the Age of Diversity.

NOTES

1. The distinguished historian Wilson D. Miscamble, C.S.C., laments that at the University of Notre Dame only 53 percent of the faculty are Catholic and that even this figure is inflated by those who checked the "Catholic" box on the questionnaire but "for whom the practice of the faith appears nominal at best" (Miscamble, "The Faculty 'Problem,'" *America*, 10 September 2007, 26–27). Catholic colleges and universities were instructed in the 1990s by Pope John Paul II and the United States Conference of Catholic Bishops to bolster the representation of "faithful Catholics" among their faculties and staffs.

2. Nicholas Xenos, *Cloaked in Virtue*: *Unveiling Leo Strauss and the Rhetoric of American Foreign Policy* (New York: Routledge, 2008), ix; I shall subsequently refer to this book as *CV*. Xenos, who was once the managing editor of *Political Theory*, the flagship journal in political philosophy, elsewhere complains that Straussians write "the same books on the same themes over and over again" (Xenos, "Leo Strauss and the Rhetoric of the War on Terror," *Logos* 3.2 [Spring 2004], http://www.logosjournal.com/xenos.pdf, 11).

3. I concede that Straussophobia is not a perfect term to characterize anti-Straussian sensibilities. Phobia typically involves a visceral reaction; in its most frequently used instantiation (homophobia), it is presumably fueled by elements of latency, etc. People are increasingly denouncing Islamophobia, however, although the alleged hostility obviously arises much more from fear of slaughter than from revulsion at differences in clothing, prayer, rituals, theology, or sex roles.

4. For a concise and highly informed summary of Strauss's thought, see the epilogue Thomas L. Pangle and Nathan Tarcov wrote for the third edition of this textbook (Leo Strauss and Joseph Cropsey, eds., *The History of Political Philosophy* [Chicago: University of Chicago Press, 1987], 907–38); I would also recommend the Wikipedia entry on Strauss. Good bibliographies of Strauss are available in Wikipedia and at the conclusion of *SPPP* (the posthumously published collection of Strauss's essays).

5. For the record, my primary undergraduate mentors were Murray Dry and Paul Nelson at Middlebury College; both were University of Chicago PhDs who took courses with Strauss but wrote their dissertations under Straussians (e.g., Herbert Storing and Joseph Cropsey). I earned my PhD at Harvard, where my primary advisor, for a dissertation about Adam Smith, was Harvey Mansfield (Judith Shklar served as my second advisor). I certainly belong to what Harold Bloom describes as the "plague of his [Strauss's] disciples' disciples" (Harold Bloom, "The Heretic Jew," *New York Times*, 18 June 2006). I have wrestled with aspects of Strauss's legacy on two prior occasions: "Machiavellianism Come of Age? Leo Strauss on Modernity and Economics," *Political Science Reviewer* 22 (1993): 157–97 (I apologize for the missing "one" in the epigraph from *WIPP* 49); and "Political Philosophy and the Religious Issue: From the Ancient Regime to Modern Capitalism," in *Educating the Prince: Essays in Honor of Harvey Mansfield*, ed. Mark Blitz and William Kristol (Lanham, MD: Rowman & Littlefield, 2000), 142–75.

6. Here are the citations for the comments I shall *not* address later: Sidney Blumenthal, "Paul Wolfowitz's Tomb," *openDemocracy*, 30 May 2007, http://www.opendemocracy.net/paul _wolfowitzs_tomb.jsp; Stanley Aronowitz, "Considerations on the Origins of Neoconservatism: Looking Backward," in *Confronting the New Conservatism: The Rise of the Right in America*, ed. Michael J. Thompson (New York: New York University Press, 2007), 57.

7. Here are the citations for the comments I shall not address later: Xenos, *CV* ix and "Leo Strauss" 14; Richard H. King, "Rights and Slavery, Race and Racism: Leo Strauss, The Strauss-

ians, and the American Dilemma," *Modern Intellectual History* 5, no. 1 (2008): 72; Thomas J. DiLorenzo, "The Ivy League Dissects the Neocon Cabal" (http://www.lewrockwell.com/dilorenzo/dilorenzo80.html) and "Moronic Intellectuals" (http://www.lewrockwell.com/dilorenzo/dilorenzo81.html); Joseph A. Buttigieg, "Straussism and the 'Habits of Civilized Discourse,'" *Boundary 2* 33, no. 1 (Spring 2006): 5. *Boundary* is published by Duke University Press, and Buttigieg is the William R. Kenan Jr. Professor of English at Notre Dame. DiLorenzo is professor of economics at Loyola College of Maryland. The website on which DiLorenzo's pieces were posted is run by Llewellyn H. Rockwell Jr., who was the chief of staff for Congressman Ron Paul from 1978 to 1982 and who wrote the foreword for Paul's 2007 book, *A Foreign Policy of Freedom: "Peace, Commerce, and Honest Friendship"* (Lake Jackson, TX: Foundation for Rational Economics and Education, 2007), i–iv.

8. Peter Berkowitz, who has contributed several shorter pieces that defend Strauss, came up with the phrase "Tabloid Scholarship" to categorize the tendencies that both he and I are protesting. See his review of Anne Norton's *Leo Strauss and the Politics of American Empire* in the *New York Post*, 3 October 2004; he has posted the review at http://www.peterberkowitz.com/tabloid scholarship.htm.

9. Al Gore, *The Assault on Reason* (New York: Penguin Press, 2007), 66.

10. Jonathan R. Cole, "The New McCarthyism," *Chronicle of Higher Education*, 9 September 2005, B7–8. Despite Cole's warning about the "scorn, ridicule, sanctions, and ostracism" that may greet someone who is "challenging shoddy evidence and poor reasoning on politically sensitive topics," I shall soldier on. Cole's article is also available at http://www.columbia.edu/cu/univprof/jcole/NewMcCarthyism.pdf.

11. Ellen Willis, "The Pernicious Concept of 'Balance,'" *Chronicle of Higher Education*, 9 September 2005, B11.

12. Corey Robin, *Fear: The History of a Political Idea* (Oxford: Oxford University Press, 2004), 163; Zbigniew Brzezinski, "Terrorized by the War on Terror," *San Jose Mercury News*, 3 June 2007, 6P; Joe Conason, *It Can Happen Here: Authoritarian Peril in the Age of Bush* (New York: Thomas Dunne Books/St. Martin's Press, 2007), 25.

13. *New York Review of Books*, Ad/Open Letter on Ward Churchill, 12 April 2007, 65. Perhaps some Straussians could profit even from Wendy Brown's campaign to "open liberal regimes . . . to the possibility of being transformed by their encounter with what liberalism has conventionally taken to be its constitutive outside and its hostile Other" (Wendy Brown, *Regulating Aversion: Tolerance in the Age of Identity and Empire* [Princeton, NJ: Princeton University Press, 2006], 174).

14. Arthur Melzer, professor of political science at Michigan State University, is a Mansfield student who recently published a splendid article on Strauss in the *American Political Science Review*.

15. Also imagine the positive reactions, in a typical job search conducted by an American or British university, that would follow from learning the following facts about an applicant: one of the applicant's parents is African American; despite an "Anglo" name, the applicant is Latino; or the applicant has a same-sex partner. Now imagine the reaction if the applicant were suspected of being a Straussian.

16. Prominent intellectuals occasionally say nasty things about postmodernists or even feminists. But the position of these groups in a typical university is far more secure, since each probably outnumbers Straussians by twenty or thirty to one.

17. By the time this book is published, I hope to have launched a website, www.straussophobia .com, that will allow visitors to protest abusive remarks and actions (directed against Strauss or Straussians) that this book does not address. If you are unable to post pertinent materials on the site, you may send them to me via e-mail (pminowitz@scu.edu).

18. Walter Benn Michaels, *The Trouble with Diversity* (New York: Metropolitan Books, 2006), 178. For a poignant exploration of the *connections* between identity and ideology, see Dorothy A.

Austin, "The Cloistered Closet," in *One Nation under God? Religion and American Culture*, ed. Marjorie Garber and Rebecca L. Walkowitz (New York: Routledge, 1999), 60–71.

19. "Communist" at least had a precise meaning insofar as communists belonged to a revolutionary party that was allied (during most of the twentieth century) with a belligerent superpower.

20. An abridged DVD of the documentary is available, and the full transcript is posted online. According to Curtis (who supplies the voiceover) and author Jason Burke, the United States in effect created Al-Qaida so that the perpetrators of the 1998 embassy bombings in Kenya and Tanzania could be prosecuted under RICO-type statutes. See part III, "The Shadows in the Cave" (http://www.daanspeak.com/TranscriptPowerOfNightmares3.html). To his credit, Curtis lets prominent Straussians, including Mansfield and Bill Kristol, speak for themselves about Strauss's legacy.

21. Kenji Yoshino, *Covering: The Hidden Assault on Our Civil Rights* (New York: Random House, 2006), ix, xi. On the pitfalls of drawing analogies between racism and the "failure to tolerate nonmainstream norms and practices," see Richard Thompson Ford, *The Race Card: How Bluffing about Bias Makes Race Relations Worse* (New York: Farrar, Straus, and Giroux, 2008), 20, 104–6, 120–21, 143–44, 154–55, 158–61, 174–77.

22. Iris Marion Young diagnoses "oppression" whenever there are "institutionalized social processes which inhibit people's ability to play and communicate with others or to express their feelings and perspectives on social life in contexts where others can listen" (*Justice and the Politics of Difference* [Princeton, NJ: Princeton University Press, 1990], 38). Drawing on feminism to redraw the lines between public and private, Young likewise touts a "heterogeneous" public in which "no persons, actions, or aspects of a person's life should be forced into privacy" and "no social institutions or practices should be excluded a priori from being a proper subject for public discussion and expression" (120).

23. Claude M. Steele, "Thin Ice: 'Stereotype Threat' and Black College Students," *Atlantic Monthly*, August 1998, 46.

24. Claude M. Steele, "A Threat in the Air: How Stereotypes Shape Intellectual Identity and Performance," *American Psychologist* 52, no. 6 (June 1997): 614.

25. In another seminal work, Steele and a coauthor provide the statistical analyses and additional details about how they conducted their experiments: see Claude M. Steele and Joshua Aronson, "Stereotype Threat and the Intellectual Test Performance of African Americans," *Journal of Personality and Social Psychology* 69, no. 5 (1995): 797–811. On the lavish funding of recent research on stereotype threat, see John Gravois, "Making a Living on Choking under Pressure," *Chronicle of Higher Education*, 2 September 2005, A10–12, and http://sbs.arizona.edu/development/2005/depts/depts.html (concerning the work of Toni Schmader). On the impact the 2008 election may have in reducing stereotype threat, see Sam Dillon, "Study Sees an Obama Effect as Lifting Black Test-Takers," *New York Times*, 23 January 2009.

26. Several other experimental manipulations that accentuated awareness of racial identity had a similar effect on student performance.

27. Steele, "Threat," 617, 618. According to Professor Becca Levy of Yale, stereotype threat is something that "you don't outgrow," and the stereotype, "at least in the short run, overwhelms long-held beliefs" (quoted in Sharon Begley, "The Stereotype Trap," *Newsweek*, 6 November 2000, 67).

28. Steele, "Threat," 614. Cf. Steele, "Thin Ice," 51, on the possibility that stereotype threat compromises performance by inducing the afflicted to try too hard, particularly by striving to avoid mistakes; in speculating about the mechanisms of the performance problem, Steele and Aronson mention the diverting of attention onto "task-irrelevant worries," the development of overcautiousness, and the development of an "interfering self-consciousness" (Steele and Aronson, "Stereotype Threat," 799).

29. See, for example, Peter H. Schuck, *Diversity in America: Keeping Government at a Safe Distance* (Cambridge, MA: Harvard University Press, 2003). Also invaluable is Peter Wood, *Diversity: The Invention of a Concept* (San Francisco: Encounter Books, 2003); make sure to

absorb Wood's hilarious multilevel typology on pp. 88–97. Although Sanford Levinson's sweeping endorsements of affirmative action distinguish him from Schuck and Wood, he too laments the obfuscations that mar contemporary diversity discourse (Levinson, *Wrestling with Diversity* [Durham, NC: Duke University Press, 2003], 3–5, 16–18, 35–52, 68–69, 97–121). Geoffrey Nunberg censures Wood's zeal, but concedes that diversity has become "a vague and elastic symbol"; although conservatives have "scored points with their calls for 'color-blind' policies," they have failed to make any "serious inroads in the power of the counter-symbol 'diversity,' which most Americans accept uncritically as a social good" (Geoffrey Nunberg, *Talking Right: How Conservatives Turned Liberalism into a Tax-Raising, Latte-Drinking, Sushi-Eating, Volvo-Driving,* New York Times–*Reading, Body-Piercing, Hollywood-Loving, Left-Wing Freak Show* [New York: Public Affairs, 2006], 239n157).

30. Justice David Souter, another dissenter, noted that "Equal Protection cannot become an exercise in which the winners are the ones who hide the ball."

31. *OT* 223–24, *NRH* 23; Cf. *OT* 26–27, *RCPR* 41–42, *PAW* 56, *WIPP* 38, and *CM* 5. In discussing the universal and homogenous state in the preface to *LAM*, Strauss notes the relatively superficial diversity that resides in "language, folk songs, pottery, and the like" (*LAM* viii). He later commends Herodotus for illuminating "the mysterious unity of oneness and variety in human things" (*LAM* 23).

32. On Edwards, see http://www.youtube.com/watch?v=lXBQIH2QWGw&feature=related.

33. On the consternation that Kristol's hiring caused, see Clark Hoyt, "He May Be Unwelcome, but We'll Survive," *New York Times*, 13 January 2008, and Gabriel Sherman, "The Fifth Columnist: How Kristol Landed that *TIMES* Gig," *New Republic*, 13 February 2008, 12–13. According to Eric Alterman, the paper "insult[ed] its readers, and itself," by adding a columnist so renowned for, among other things, "impugning the honesty, integrity and patriotism of anyone who refuses to join his jihad" (Alterman, "The Lies of Quinn-Broderville," *Nation*, 28 January 2008, 11). In the pages of the allegedly neoconservative *New Republic*, ironically, the *TRB* column had previously invoked Kristol's "belief in [*sic*] the philosopher Leo Strauss" before ridiculing Kristol's "knucklehead slogans" and claiming that his "good standing in the Washington establishment depends on the wink-and-nod awareness that he's too smart to believe his own agitprop" (Jonathan Chait, "Substandard: The Thuggery of William Kristol," *New Republic*, 27 August 2007, 5).

34. Steele, "Threat," 622.

35. Shadia B. Drury, *Aquinas and Modernity* (Lanham, MD: Rowman & Littlefield, 2008), 169n5. I shall occasionally abbreviate this book's title as *AM*.

36. See http://www.chairs.gc.ca/web/program/index_e.asp. In 2005, Drury became a fellow of the Royal Society of Canada.

37. The acknowledgments of Drury's 1997 book (*LSAR*) start by crediting John Gunnell, who, like Drury, thinks that Strauss's political agenda—for example, his concern to "explain and evaluate the present"—fatally compromises his efforts as an interpreter (John G. Gunnell, "The Myth of the Tradition," *American Political Science Review* 72 [March 1978]: 130). The two critics differ, however, because Gunnell only rarely distorts what Strauss writes—and because none of Gunnell's accusations is foolish or demonizing. Other pertinent statements by Gunnell about Strauss can be found in the following pieces: "Political Theory and Politics: The Case of Leo Strauss," *Political Theory* 13, no. 3 (August 1985): 358; "Strauss before Straussism: The Weimar Conversation," *Vital Nexus* 1, no. 1 (May 1990): 74; and *Between Philosophy and Politics* (Amherst: University of Massachusetts Press, 1986), 21–22, 95–98, 108, 113, 115. For a sharp but measured reply to Gunnell's early work, see Nathan Tarcov, "Philosophy and History: Tradition and Interpretation in the Work of Leo Strauss," *Polity* 16 (Fall 1983): 5–29.

38. David Abel, "Governor Apologizes for Use of Expression," *Boston Globe*, 31 July 2006, http://www.boston.com/news/local/articles/2006/07/31/romney_apologizes_for_use_of_expression/.

Chapter One

All Hate Leo Strauss

To accuse, requires lesse Eloquence (such is man's Nature) than to excuse.

—Thomas Hobbes

I. "AS LEO STRAUSS WOULD SAY": THE IGNOBLE LIES OF TIM ROBBINS

Tens of thousands of Americans have now gazed upon a photo of Leo Strauss while watching caricatures of President George W. Bush's inner circle invoke Strauss's ideas in order to justify and execute the U.S. invasion of Iraq.

Embedded was originally a play written and directed by Tim Robbins and performed by The Actors' Gang. It opened on 15 November 2003, in Los Angeles, and later moved on to New York, London, Chicago, and other locales. A filmed version, which is the version I shall comment upon, is called *Embedded Live*. The ninety-seven-minute film, which has been shown on the Sundance Channel, is available via Netflix, Amazon.com, and The Actors' Gang.[1] In a telephone interview with a newspaper reporter, Robbins noted that, from the start, he had been "aiming for DVDs and television," not for a theatrical run.[2]

The play, which covers the period from October 2002 to June 2003, begins with a screen presentation of a wordy quotation from Irving Kristol about "different kinds of truths for different kinds of people." The focus soon turns to Leo Strauss. While his visage is projected above the stage and gradually fills the screen, we read that he is the "guiding light of the neo-conservatives, who are forging America's new foreign policy." Specific linkage to Iraq is provided by *Embedded*'s next posted text, an altered quotation from an article by two professed Straussians, Bill Kristol and Steven Lenzner: "President Bush's advocacy

19

of 'regime change' is a not altogether unworthy product of Strauss's rehabilitation of the notion of regime."[3]

As the play unfolds, Strauss figures prominently in a series of scenes displaying a "cabal" that meets at the Pentagon's Office of Special Plans to plot the invasion of "Gomorrah."[4] The cabal is a lively chorus comprised of six masked individuals: Woof (i.e., Paul Wolfowitz), Pearly White (Richard Perle), Rum-Rum (Donald Rumsfeld), Dick (Dick Cheney), Gondola (Condoleezza Rice), and Cove (Karl Rove, played hilariously by an almost unrecognizable Tim Robbins). In their initial appearance (scene 2: "Let's Have a War"), after arguing about which rationales would best define and advance the mission, they select a date for the invasion and then offer their first "Incantation" to Leo Strauss. As the camera displays photos of Strauss projected above each side of stage rear, Rum-Rum suggests a bland chant, which he enunciates slowly and ominously. Other members then try to formulate incantations to their "intellectual sovereign" that would be more poetic and that would better capture "the Straussian philosophy," for example, the "the noble lie for the greater good." After Woof agrees to compose a superior incantation for their next meeting, Dick starts their termination ritual by saying "All Hail Leo Strauss." The others then stand up—with their right hands raised—and repeat the chant.[5]

When we next encounter the cabal (scene 4: "Chomping at the Bit"), the members become sexually aroused as they discuss the imminent invasion. The scene then reverts to the play's pseudoscholarly mode. The candles come out, the visage returns, stringed instruments play eerily, and Woof shares a Latin incantation to convey their adoration of "Leonardo Strauss." Woof repeats the Latin chant and is quickly joined by the group, who speak with increasing intensity—and sexual excitement, as they masturbate and ejaculate. After a remark from Dick about philosopher-kings and gentlemen-warriors leading the world to stability, we get a peek at the classic postcoital mode of Straussians. Rum-Rum announces, in a halting and soft voice, that the operation will commence tomorrow, and then leads them in a variation of their termination chant (their right hands again rise).

Although the cabal members and even Iraq appear under pseudonyms, nothing dilutes the play's rendition of Strauss. When Tim Robbins boasted to an interviewer for the *Nation* (Abby Aguirre) that he was "telling this story before any of these facts came out," furthermore, he said nothing about the fanciful character of Strauss's role.[6] Robbins also told Aguirre that "[m]ost of the material is sourced material. I made up some things, some of the lines that the journalists say." But what about the things that the cabal members say? Given the salience of Strauss's role, it is amazing that the play never quotes anything he actually wrote.

The cabal returns in scene 6 ("The Road to Babylon"), where their discussion of civilian casualties prompts Pearly White to describe, inaccurately, how Gulliver urinated to put out a fire in Lilliput. Soon after, Pearly attributes arrogant and disturbing words to Strauss:

> Moral virtue has no application to the truly intelligent man, the philosopher. As Leo Strauss would say, "moral virtue only exists in popular opinion where it serves the purpose of controlling the unintelligent majority."

As Terry Teachout first confirmed via a Google search,[7] Strauss did not write these phrases about moral virtue; the source is rather an article by Tony Papert in *Executive Intelligence Review*—the "news" weekly of Lyndon H. LaRouche Jr.[8] It turns out that Papert here cites the report Shadia Drury provides in *PILS* of the dispute between Thomas Pangle and Harry Jaffa, two well-known Straussians. The phrases quoted above about moral virtue and the philosopher, according to Papert, represent Drury's interpretation of Pangle's interpretation of Strauss; although Papert might seem to be paraphrasing what Drury wrote (on *PILS* 183), the phrases are his. His skill as a scholar is undermined, however, when he cites Drury for the proposition that "Pangle implied that for Strauss, philosophy had disproved religious faith." Drury in fact asserts the opposite: for Strauss as interpreted by Pangle, "philosophy cannot refute revelation . . . and as a result must show respect for faith and accord it a status equal to that of reason and philosophy" (*PILS* 186). From Strauss to Pangle to Drury to Papert to Robbins to Pearly to Minowitz to you.[9]

The Papert article ("The Secret Kingdom of Leo Strauss") is accessible in a clean PDF format as part of a document, *Children of Satan*, that LaRouche released for his 2004 presidential campaign. LaRouche has since published at least two sequels, and I was offered one of these pamphlets on the Seattle waterfront in the summer of 2007.[10] LaRouche's essay ("Insanity as Geometry") for *Children of Satan*, part I, offers a critique of the cabal that Robbins might want to incorporate in a follow-up to *Embedded*: like Caligula, Nero, Hitler, and Hegel, Strauss, Allan Bloom, and the Rumsfeld-Cheney cabal are "collectively insane"; they are, moreover, "equivalent to a species whose very existence is morally, and functionally worse than that of naturally determined lower forms of life" (21). LaRouche extends his list of "systematically insane" thinkers to include Galileo, John Locke, Adam Smith, Bertrand Russell, and . . . Al Gore (at least regarding "economic and military matters") (13).[11]

The *Embedded* cabal makes its final appearance in scene 9 ("Where to Now?"). After they congratulate themselves for the success of the military operation, engage in a variety of amusing banter, and address difficulties that an Iraqi election would pose, it falls to Woof to conjure up what "Leo Strauss would say"; the actress shifts to her real voice, which adds emphasis to a clunky pronouncement about how "those that are smarter" are obliged to educate the populace in an emerging democracy. The cabalists agree that election plans should be drawn up, and they proceed to present a frenzied and highly humorous barrage of suggestions about "what's next" to conquer. Discussion of the challenge posed by the insurgents sets up the scene's denouement, which starts with portentous words from Woof ("It's predestined") and Rum-Rum, who touts the courage that will be required during "the times of the philosopher kings." After the group considers the need to raise the color of the terror threat from yellow to orange, Dick commences the concluding incantations by highlighting the timeless utility of terror, and various characters note its usefulness for justifying military spending, stifling dissent, and narcotizing the populace. The scene culminates in an exchange in which three of the characters solemnly invite the cabal, and perhaps the audience, to "bless" (Pearly), "honor" (Rum-Rum), and "love" (Gondola) terror. Because the members finish by saying (in unison) "End terror," some viewers might infer that the cabal would rather eliminate terror than exploit it. But when we contemplate the rest of the play—particularly the preceding invocations to bless, honor, and love terror—and the sources Robbins relies upon, we should favor a different interpretation: that, for Robbins, "End terror" is merely the *rationalization* Straussians use to empower themselves, militarize the masses, and squelch debate. Apart from the last two words, in any case, viewers have witnessed a concluding paean to terror from a group that previously spent much of its time chanting incantations to Leo Strauss.

II. CALLING NAMES

It is conceivable that at the time the war was launched a full half of *Embedded*'s cabal (Rumsfeld, Cheney, and Rove) did not know anything about Leo Strauss. Francis Fukuyama, who has abundant firsthand knowledge of Straussians as well as the Bush administration, speaks similarly about Rumsfeld, Cheney, and Bush.[12]

It is very difficult to specify what makes someone a Straussian, and this difficulty should itself counteract the tendency to describe Straussians as either cultists or conspirators. There may be only a handful of Straussians who think that they understand Strauss "as he understood himself," and their interpretations might clash. When we turn our focus to the much larger group of individuals who regard themselves as Straussians, moreover, we would doubtless struggle to identify any two who would align completely in specifying either what Strauss thought or what (if any) societal changes he intended to engineer. Among the accusers for whom "Straussian" denotes a warmongering elitist liar, finally, few have carefully studied Strauss, his followers, and the history of political philosophy.

I would suggest, provisionally, that we should *not* designate people as Straussians unless at least the following conditions obtain. They have studied an assortment of Strauss's major books (e.g., *On Tyranny, Natural Right and History, Thoughts on Machiavelli,* and *The City and Man*) and articles/chapters (e.g., "Persecution and the Art of Writing," "On Classical Political Philosophy," "What Is Political Philosophy?" "An Epilogue," and the *SCR* preface). They are impressed, and often dazzled, by the power of his reasoning. Having also scrutinized several of the texts he wrote about, they find him to be a dexterous if not virtuosic interpreter; and before venturing to publish an article or book about one of those texts, they would scrutinize the relevant commentary by Strauss. They are convinced that certain philosophers of the past wrote energetically "between the lines," they think that silences can speak loudly, and they have spent hundreds of hour trying to extract buried teachings. They believe that both "the quarrel between the ancients and the moderns" (*SPPP* 168, *NRH* 323) and the relationship between Jerusalem and Athens warrant profound reflection. They have serious interest in, and respect for, Plato and Aristotle. They are not Marxists, and they do not regard *A Theory of Justice* as a "great book." They are dissatisfied with historicism (e.g., the doctrine that human thought is merely the "mysterious dispensation of fate" [*WIPP* 26]) and positivism (e.g., the doctrine that "objective value judgments are impossible" [*NRH* 62]), they are familiar with Strauss's criticisms of these doctrines, and they admire the philosophical life.

Special Plans

The Office of Special Plans (OSP) was the name assigned to a bureau within the Pentagon's Office of Near East and South Asia Affairs when Douglas J. Feith (undersecretary of defense for policy) and his deputy William J. Luti expanded that bureau—between August and October of 2002—to promote interagency planning about Iraq.

To direct the OSP, which included up to eighteen staffers, Feith and Luti selected Abram Shulsky, a Straussian who left academia for government work in the 1970s. In an account that has been widely cited, echoed, and amplified, Seymour Hersh blames a Strauss-inspired "Cabal" of policy advisors and analysts within the OSP for equipping Cheney, Rumsfeld, Wolfowitz, Feith, and others with dubious intelligence reports alleging Iraqi weapons of mass destruction (WMDs) and linkages to Al-Qaida.[13] Neither Feith nor Luti has any Straussian leanings that I have been able to unearth, and the only other individual Hersh associates with the Cabal is Wolfowitz, whose "orientation" I'll discuss below.

Hersh seems to have confused the OSP with a smaller Feith-founded operation, the Policy Counterterrorism Evaluation Group (PCTEG); when Hersh was writing in 2003, reliable information about both outfits was difficult to acquire. Encouraged by Wolfowitz, Feith created the PCTEG after 9/11 to analyze intelligence reports about "links between terrorist groups and host countries." The group started out with two members, David Wurmser and Michael Maloof.[14]

George Packer claims that its work was "absorbed" into the OSP and then "piped by Luti and Shulsky directly to the White House";[15] according to Alan Weisman, reporting generated by the OSP suffused the forty-eight-page report Lewis Libby (Cheney's chief of staff) gave Colin Powell to prepare Powell's UN speech of 5 February 2003.[16]

Several recent and more thorough accounts exonerate the OSP concerning both cherry-picking and stovepiping.[17] The report issued in February of 2007 by the deputy inspector general for intelligence—*Review of the Pre-Iraqi War Activities of the Office of the Under Secretary of Defense for Policy*—does chastise Feith's office for promulgating PCTEG-generated assessments about Iraq's relationship to Al-Qaida that were "inconsistent with the consensus of the Intelligence Community" (15–16). But it concludes that the OSP had nothing to do with these "inappropriate" intelligence maneuvers (1, 16).[18] As far as I can determine, there were no Straussians among the four or five individuals who passed through PCTEG.[19]

The compendious study that RAND recently completed for the U.S. Army likewise denies that the OSP was involved in intelligence activities or that it was linked to PCTEG (26); the OSP focused on postwar planning issues such as "coalition building, troop deployments, government reorganization, de-Ba'athification, maintaining the oil sector, training a police force, and war crimes prosecution" (24).[20] In the 2008 document that names both groups—*Report on Intelligence Activities Relating to Iraq Conducted by the Policy Counterterrorism Evaluation Group and the Office of Special Plans within the Office of the Under Secretary of Defense for Policy*—the Senate Select Intelligence Committee quotes the above-mentioned criticisms of Feith's office from the deputy inspector general's report. But roughly 90 percent of the SSCI's main report (i.e., the report issued by the committee's Democratic majority) focuses on several 2001 Rome gatherings in which a man (Harold Rhode) who later joined the OSP engaged in discussions about . . . Iran (3–34).[21]

Wolfowitz, Wohlstetter, Shulsky

As an undergraduate at Cornell, Paul Wolfowitz came under the influence of Strauss's student, Allan Bloom, and later took two courses with Strauss—one on Plato's *Laws* and one on Montesquieu's *Spirit of the Laws*—at the University of Chicago. But with his doctoral thesis, which invoked proliferation concerns to oppose proposals for nuclear powered desalinization-plants in the Middle East, Wolfowitz established himself as a specialist in international relations rather than political philosophy, and his primary mentor was the hawkish number-cruncher Albert Wohlstetter (1913–1997), not Strauss or Bloom. Fukuyama, who worked for Wolfowitz in two different jobs—at the Arms Control and Disarmament Agency and at the State Department—and who likewise studied with Bloom at

Cornell, maintains that Wolfowitz *"never* regarded himself as a Strauss protégé" (emph. added) and that his views on foreign policy were "much more heavily" influenced by Wohlstetter.[22] Alex Abella, in his compendious study of RAND, depicts Wolfowitz's debt to Wohlstetter in still stronger terms: "All the different skeins that would eventually weave through Wolfowitz's career (the fact-based approach to problem solving; the belief in America's messianic role in the world; the sub-rosa Zionism that predicates the survival of Israel as essential to the survival of mankind—all joined to a bedrock conviction that democracy can grow vigorous roots anywhere in the world) were beliefs that were encouraged by Wohlstetter."[23]

Professor Anne Norton of the University of Pennsylvania, a Straussian-basher who did her undergraduate and graduate work at Chicago, leavens her account of Wolfowitz with obfuscation. After belittling the significance of Wolfowitz's dissertation-connection with Wohlstetter, Norton adds, erroneously, that Wolfowitz "spent a good deal of his undergraduate life studying with Allan Bloom."[24] In fact, Wolfowitz took only a single course with Bloom, though Bloom helped motivate Wolfowitz to pursue his graduate studies at Chicago rather than at Harvard or MIT.[25] In her book, Norton is willing to concede that Wolfowitz was "as much a student of Wohlstetter as a student of Strauss" (*LAPAE* 183). Elizabeth Drew rightly identifies Wohlstetter as the key mentor for both Wolfowitz and Richard Perle.[26]

In his well-known *Vanity Fair* interview (10 May 2003) with Sam Tanenhaus, Wolfowitz confirmed that he did sometimes speak with Bloom when their school days were over (Tanenhaus asked Wolfowitz about the scene in Saul Bellow's *Ravelstein* in which Ravelstein spoke on the telephone with Phil Gorman): "Bloom loved to talk to any students of his who were in government, and even though I wasn't his closest student I was probably one at the highest level in government so it gave him the most bragging rights."[27] For the record, Wolfowitz here denied he was a Straussian, as he did in a 2003 interview with *Newsweek*.[28] Alan Weisman, a former producer for *60 Minutes* and several CBS news programs, nevertheless includes Wolfowitz among both the "proud Straussians" and the individuals who are "unapologetic in their allegiance to Strauss's writings and teachings, at least as they interpret them."[29] Wolfowitz presumably has retained some of the flavorings, but he is, at most, a Straussian "in recovery."

It is bad enough that an actor (Tim Robbins) inflates Strauss's influence beyond all proportion, but what excuse does Pulitzer Prize winner Seymour Hersh have for proclaiming that both Wolfowitz and Shulsky "received their doctorates under Strauss in 1972" at Chicago?[30] One wonders what happened to the vaunted fact-checkers at the *New Yorker*, especially since it has been widely publicized that Strauss left Chicago in *1968*. Hersh's error about Wolfowitz's doctorate is repeated verbatim in his 2004 book, *Chain of Command*.[31]

The mistake is particularly significant because, unlike Strauss, Wohlstetter publicly agitated against Saddam Hussein. A week after Iraq invaded Kuwait in 1990, he wrote in the *Wall Street Journal* that Saddam was "a murderous neighborhood bully bent on expanding indefinitely the neighborhood he terrorizes"— and that he "needs to be thrown out of Iraq as well as from Kuwait."[32] More than two years before the first issue of the *Weekly Standard* appeared, indeed, Wohlstetter was articulating regime-change arguments regarding Iraqi WMDs: "Nothing less than replacing the dictatorship with a government that gives its people a voice and protects its citizens from terror can assure an end to Iraq's programs to acquire nuclear, chemical, and biological weapons." Wohlstetter here also assures his readers that Iraqi dissidents, specifically the Free Iraqi Movement, had "achieved an impressive consensus for a democratic structure representing all segments of the disparate population, protecting them 'from all sectarian, ethnic, or political discrimination'" (30–32).[33] One can even trace a path from Wohlstetter's promotion of precision targeting to Rumsfeld's agendas for Pentagon reform and "shock and awe."[34]

Like Wolfowitz, Shulsky started out at Cornell (and in Telluride) as a math major and later earned his PhD in political science at Chicago. Unlike Wolfowitz, Shulsky remained on a Straussian "track" by writing his dissertation on Aristotle's *Politics*, advised (I believe) by Joseph Cropsey. Shulsky, furthermore, later coauthored a brief but widely cited article about Strauss and intelligence-analysis (it will be discussed below). Michael Isikoff and David Corn begin their massive exposé with a character list that includes over 100 names, but Shulsky's is not among them, and the book never mentions him.[35] One of Shulsky's major steps along the path to power, incidentally, was his service on the staff of Democratic Senator Daniel P. Moynihan.

Hersh's error about Wolfowitz's training has proliferated wildly both on and off the web. Congressman Ron Paul of Texas (R)—the eleven-term member whom John McCain once described as "the most honest man in Congress"— announced on the House floor (or, at least, in the Congressional Record) that Wolfowitz "actually got his PhD under Strauss."[36] The mistake also appears in SourceWatch,[37] where it picks up associations with some truly wild and crazy critics. (My Google search for "Leo Strauss" on 15 July 2007 yielded almost half a million hits, and the SourceWatch entry was listed fourth; fortunately, Wikipedia's sensible entry was listed first.) For further information about the OSP, the SourceWatch entry on Strauss provides two paragraphs that it credits to an *Ether Zone* article by Al Cronkrite. In this article, "Judeo-Christian Decadence: At the Fount of Power," Cronkrite highlights the Hersh article, repeats the error about Wolfowitz, and proceeds to fault the "strongly Zionist" OSP—it indeed has "an overweening Zionist persuasion"—for being "tainted with the Pharisaical Jewish notion of superiority"; Cronkrite also quotes a Muslim suicide bomber who complained that "Jews in America have the money and the newspapers to tell the Crusader Presidents what to do."[38] A link to Cronkrite's article is in turn highlighted by the article on Leo Strauss in dKosopedia, the brainchild of Markos Moulitsas.[39]

In assimilating the error about Wolfowitz's doctorate, Joel Bleifuss, the publisher and editor of *In These Times*, butchers Hersh's account by claiming that it depicted an eight to nine person cabal united by its "worship of Leo Strauss."[40] In a speech that Hersh delivered to the ACLU roughly a year after his *New Yorker* article appeared, however, he did assert that eight or nine neoconservative "cultists" had "taken the government over" and muzzled a wide range of powerful institutions—press, bureaucracy, military, Congress. He also suggested that Wolfowitz was "the greatest Trotskyite of our time."[41] None of this would surprise David Duke, who identifies Strauss as the "former Trotskyite" who founded neoconservatism.[42]

The mental decay that infects many current commentators on Strauss is displayed even in the pages of the *New York Times*. James Atlas, the "model biographer" (Joyce Carol Oates) who once published an illuminating article about Allan Bloom, correctly identifies Wolfowitz and Perle as protégés of Wohlstetter, but he goes *completely* astray in describing Wohlstetter as a "Straussian" professor of mathematics and military strategist.[43] It does not take much research to establish that Wohlstetter's scholarship, teaching, and educational background were worlds apart from Strauss's; as a titan at RAND, as an advisor to the Kennedy administration, and as author in journalistic venues (the *New York Times*, the *Washington Post*, the *Wall Street Journal*, the *New Republic*, *National Review*, and *Commentary*), furthermore, Wohlstetter also engaged with policy-making vastly more closely than Strauss did. Describing the "illuminati of the foreign policy establishment" who attended Wohlstetter's détente-denouncing presentation to the California Arms Control Seminar in June of 1974, Abella says that "they all knew him as the most prominent nuclear analyst in the country, the one college professor whose calls were returned not just by his former students at the Pentagon but by the secretary of defense, the secretary of state, and the president's national security adviser, when not by the president himself."[44] In 1985, Albert and his wife Roberta were awarded Presidential Medals of Freedom by Ronald Reagan.

Although Norton denies that Albert Wohlstetter was a Straussian, she claims that he had "a certain cadet line relation to the lineages of the Straussians who came to power" (*LSPAE* 182). What could she mean by this? Apart from the two men she discusses who were shaped by both Strauss and Wohlstetter (Fukuyama and Wolfowitz), her main evidence is that alleged Straussians within RAND and Republican "networks" allegedly recommended Wohlstetter's writings (183). She also claims to have heard that Strauss and Wohlstetter became closer during the Vietnam War (9).[45] In fact, Wohlstetter and Strauss overlapped at Chicago for only four years (1964–1968) and apparently had a cool relationship. When listing the Chicago faculty with whom Strauss had significant contact, neither George Anastaplo nor Cropsey mentions Wohlstetter.[46] Wohlstetter is the dominating figure in *Soldiers of Reason*, and Abella says nothing to suggest that he had any kind of relationship with Strauss.

Three remaining matters should be considered in appraising Wohlstetter's relevance for Iraq. First, his influential protégés include not only Wolfowitz, Perle, and Zalmay Khalilzad, but William Luti (the cofounder of the OSP)—and Ahmad Chalabi.[47] With Wohlstetter's help, Chalabi published a 1991 op-ed piece in the *Wall Street Journal*, titled "A Democratic Future for Iraq."[48] Among the subsequent developments that bear Chalabi's fingerprints are the failed Kurdish uprising in 1995, the passage of the Iraq Liberation Act in 1998, the WMD articles by Judith Miller in the *New York Times* from 2001 to 2003, the disbanding of the Iraqi army in 2003, and the implementation of de-Ba'athification in 2003. According to Hersh and many other commentators, Chalabi and the Iraqi National Congress also provided unreliable intelligence that filtered through Douglas Feith's office; in an interview with Frontline, Michael Maloof stated that PCTEG had reached out for information to Chalabi.[49]

Second, Wohlstetter appears to have been a formidable networker. The renowned Joseph Wilson, who describes the neoconservatives as "a small pack of zealots," claims that W. Patrick Lang (then an officer in the Defense Intelligence Agency) was once "recruited for possible membership in the group." At the suggestion of Wolfowitz, then undersecretary of defense for policy, Lang allegedly received an unannounced visit in 1992 from . . . Albert and Roberta Wohlstetter, who chatted with Lang to assess his suitability; in his published account of the incident, Lang adds that the Wohlstetters similarly checked out other individuals.[50] Third, when Donald Rumsfeld distributed books, behind closed doors, to the members of the House Armed Services Committee in May 2001, he selected Roberta's *Pearl Harbor: Warning and Decision*[51]—not *On Tyranny*.

"The Best Brains in Our Country"

However egregiously James Atlas errs in making Wohlstetter a Straussian, it does not compare to the frivolity he displays when he invites his readers to consider the tribute President Bush paid (in February 2003) to the following individuals:

> the cohort of journalists, political philosophers and policy wonks known—primarily to themselves—as Straussians. "You are some of the best brains in our country," Mr. Bush declared in a speech at the American Enterprise Institute, "and my government employs about 20 of you."

> "Employs" is too weak a verb. To intellectual-conspiracy theorists, the Bush administration's foreign policy is entirely a Straussian creation.

It is hard to decide which paragraph reveals a more pathetic level of ignorance. That Bush would appear before, and praise, a group of Straussians, is itself highly unlikely, as is the prospect that his administration would include twenty of them. A little snooping on the Web suffices to unearth the entire speech,[52] and a quick glance at the speech reveals that Bush was singling out not Straussians, but AEI employees.[53] How can an internationally celebrated journalist who possesses some expertise concerning Straussians not grasp that AEI is more oriented toward policy analysis and free markets than toward the history of political philosophy? When Atlas in the second paragraph claims that the verb "employs" is too weak he only compounds the farce since the number has been so overstated. Joshua Muravchik, himself a Resident Scholar, estimated that same year (2003) that only two or three of AEI's fifty-six scholars/fellows were Straussians.[54]

Let me borrow a question from Ian Buruma: "How could some of the best, most fact-checked, most reputable news organizations in the English-speaking world have been so gullible?"[55] Let me borrow an answer from David Kay, the UN weapons-inspector who later headed the Iraq Survey Group: "The most dangerous thing you can do is connect the dots when you haven't collected the dots."[56]

Atlas attributes the thesis that "the Bush administration's foreign policy is entirely a Straussian creation" to "intellectual-conspiracy theorists," but it has become a commonplace. William Pfaff, who is widely published in *Foreign Affairs*, the *New Yorker*, the *New York Review of Books, Harper's, Commonweal*, and other prestigious venues, wrote in 2003 that Strauss's "followers" were "in charge of U.S. foreign policy." In addition to Wolfowitz, Shulsky, and Bill Kristol, Pfaff seems to include Perle, Elliot Abrams, and Robert Kagan on a list of "radical neoconservatives" who were acting with "arrogance and intolerance" and upon whom Strauss was the "main intellectual influence." Pfaff, in any case, presumably drew on Hersh in maintaining that both Wolfowitz and Shulsky "took doctorates under" Strauss.[57] Sweeping language also issued from the impressively credentialed Tom Ashbrook, a long-time foreign correspondent for the *Boston Globe* who rose to the rank of deputy managing editor and who won the Livingston Prize for National Reporting in 1989. As the host of NPR's "On Point," Ashbrook began his 15 May 2003 show by pronouncing that a "remarkable number of the men who have President Bush's ear right now . . . are staunch followers of one Leo Strauss."[58] Unless the president forgave Bill Kristol for supporting John McCain (in the primaries leading up to the 2000 election) and commenced a regular dialogue with him, it is highly unlikely that *any* "staunch" followers of Strauss have—or ever had—Bush's ear.

Even Douglas Massey, the exalted diversity scholar and the former president of the American Sociological Association, ridiculed "the Platonic fundamentalists who controlled our foreign policy in Bush's first term, the followers of Leo Strauss who have a bizarre notion that truth was revealed through the ancient classics and that careful study of those works will lead to enlightenment so that you can lead the masses."[59] Massey mentions no names, and it seems obvious that *none* of the most powerful figures in the administration's first term—Bush, Cheney, Rumsfeld, Rice, Rove, and Andrew Card (chief of staff)—had engaged in "careful study" of "the ancient classics." Were Shulsky and Bill Kristol (a journalist), who did engage in such study, calling the shots? Did Massey carefully study even the introduction to Strauss's broadest treatise on classical political philosophy, *The City and Man*, where Strauss suggests that classical political philosophy *cannot* provide "recipes for today's use" (*CM* 11)? Massey certainly did not consult Strauss's long essay, "On a New Interpretation of Plato's Political Philosophy," which was published just a few months after George W. Bush was born. Strauss here emphasizes his emphatically *anti*-fundamentalist reading of Plato:

> Plato composed his writings in such a way as to prevent for all time their use as authoritative texts. . . . His teaching can never become the subject of indoctrination. . . . No social order and no party which ever existed or ever will exist can rightfully claim Plato as its patron.[60]

These claims, incidentally, would apply still more directly to Strauss, who never wrote a book like the *Republic* or the *Laws* which could be misconstrued as providing a political blueprint.

When Massey elaborates his campaign against fundamentalisms, alas, he again displays the polemical distortions for which he chastises the Vast Right-Wing Conspiracy. Among other things, he alters a quotation from Irving Kristol in order to exaggerate Strauss's responsibility for neoconservative foreign policy.[61] I nevertheless agree wholeheartedly with Massey that "[r]eal journalism"—and I would add, real scholarship—"requires a relatively intelligent, educated person finding a story and digging up facts—both of which are necessarily time-intensive."[62]

I was at first exhilarated to read the criticism of James Atlas penned by Brian Leiter, the professor at the University of Chicago law school—and director of the university's new Center for Law, Philosophy, and Human Values—who produces a highly touted annual ranking of graduate programs in philosophy. On a prominent philosophy website, Leiter commences with a sharp protest of "the mainstream media's long-standing *fraudulent* portrayal of Leo Strauss" (emph. added) and of several disciples (Fukuyama along with Allan Bloom and Harry Jaffa). But what Leiter condemns as fraudulent is that they are characterized as being "serious political philosophers and scholars." How could the *New York Times* call him a "classicist and political philosopher," Leiter asks, without "noting that he could not have been appointed in any serious classics or philosophy department because of the poor quality of both his scholarship and philosophical argumentation"?[63] Leiter not only celebrates Myles Burnyeat's well-known claim in the *New York Review of Books* that "surrender of the critical intellect is the price of initiation into the world of Leo Strauss's ideas"; Leiter pronounces that this assessment is "of course, uncontroversial outside the Straussian coterie." I assume a philosopher of Leiter's stature would not thus amplify ("of course") an empirical claim unless that claim were both true and well grounded. The stereotype-threat index here rises to the fieriest red.

Leiter goes on to depict Straussianism as a pathology centered in U.S. political science departments. The *Times*, Leiter laments, describes it as a "movement" of political philosophers even though it is "universally shunned by political philosophers," and the public is being tricked into believing that "non-philosophers like Strauss and Fukuyama . . . represent our field"; the *Times* should explain that Strauss is viewed by "actual scholars" as "a politically motivated and unreliable scholar, whose philosophical competence is minimal at best." A few days later (15 May 2003), Leiter added further denunciations on his own website, identifying his earlier complaints with "what almost all philosophers believe about Straussians." Consistent with his above-recounted expulsion of Straussians from the ranks of "actual scholars," Leiter here puts "scholarship" in quotation marks—and adds a *sic*—when describing Straussian writing. Leiter is drawing partly on the Straussian materials he has encountered in his own studies of Nietzsche. With "a rare exception (an article here, a chapter there), the work is of very poor quality . . . by reference to the *de minimus* requirements for sound scholarship in any humanistic arena—requirements like fidelity to the texts, logical argumentation, clarity, command of the relevant philosophical issues, and so on."[64] I remain puzzled that Leiter said nothing about the dramatic errors in Atlas's piece. Despite his standing as a philosopher and the sweeping knowledge of Strauss and Straussians he proclaims for himself, Leiter concluded that the only urgent task was to correct the validation implied by Atlas's designation of Strauss as a "classicist and political philosopher." I nevertheless join my voice to Leiter's in touting "the *de minimus* requirements for sound scholarship."

Atlas's twenty-Straussian estimate is proliferating among leftish blogs in the version regurgitated by Francis A. Boyle for *Counterpunch* (an online magazine presided over by *Nation* columnist Alexander Cockburn). "According to his own public estimate and boast before the American Enterprise Institute, President Bush Jr. hired about 20 Straussians to occupy key positions in his administration." With references to a "public . . . boast," the reader would feel confident Bush had actually mentioned Straussians or at least Strauss.[65] In an interview, Boyle upped the estimate to twenty-five, and clarified that "Straussians are really neo-Nazis."[66] Boyle is professor of law at the University of Illinois, and served on the Amnesty International Board of Directors from 1988 to 1992. In addition to his undergraduate degree from Chicago, Boyle earned two graduate degrees from Harvard: a JD in Law (1976) and a PhD in political science (1983); his thesis advisor was Stanley Hoffmann.

Even Richard Wolin has been suckered by Atlas. It is old news that one cannot trust the White House for the truth; now we must routinely suspect the *New York Times*, the *New Yorker*, the *Chronicle of Higher Education*, the *International Herald Tribune*, and various world-renowned scholars. In the first paragraph of his article for the *Chronicle Review*, Wolin invokes "the vast number of his [Strauss's] disciples occupying positions of influence in Washington." Climbing up the absurdity ladder, Wolin adds that "[t]he paranoia of conspiracy theorists was no doubt stoked" by the 2003 AEI speech in which President Bush "volubly praised Strauss's followers" and boasted that his government employs twenty of them. "What more proof could be needed?" Wolin asks, perhaps facetiously, but without awareness of the irony caused by his reliance on Atlas's hallucination;[67] maybe Wolin should take epistemology lessons from Brian Leiter. Although Wolin accuses Strauss of "a pervasive and obfuscatory theoretical dogmatism," he admits Strauss's worth as an interpreter along with Strauss's "prodigious achievements as a thinker."[68]

Platonic Fundamentalists? Perle, Rice, Rumsfeld, Cheney

Let us finally turn our attention to Richard Perle, another instigator of the invasion—and member of the *Embedded* cabal—who is routinely described as a Straussian.[69] As reported by Alan Weisman, his biographer, Perle "insists" he is not a Straussian, and Weisman—who insists that Wolfowitz is a Straussian—believes him.[70] Every Straussian whom I have queried also denies that the label applies to Perle.[71] As an undergraduate majoring in international politics at the University of Southern California, Perle was profoundly shaped by Hans Morgenthau's book, *A Realistic Theory of International Politics*: "I grew up with Morgenthau."[72] While earning his master's degree at Princeton later in the 1960s, Perle did take a political philosophy seminar with Robert Faulkner, a Straussian who received his PhD at Chicago in 1964 and eventually settled at Boston College. In response to an e-mail query I sent him, Professor Faulkner on 4 September 2005 suggested that the focus of the seminar was John Locke, and offered the following assessment: "I have never thought that I had any formative impact, Straussian or otherwise, on Richard Perle." Faulkner added that "we've never talked since the seminar, to my knowledge, and I actually recall no conversations with him outside of class during the seminar." I am tempted to equate Faulkner's impact with that of "Miliband the Militant," the Marxist with whom Perle later studied at the London School of Economics, where Perle commenced (but did not complete) a doctoral program; in 1976, amazingly, Vice President Nelson Rockefeller accused Perle of harboring communist sympathies.[73] Although Perle has doubtless heard of Strauss, he seems to have received minimal training in political philosophy.

Perle's enchantment with Albert Wohlstetter began while Perle was in high school (he was a friend of Wohlstetter's daughter).[74] Wohlstetter, furthermore, was responsible for introducing Perle to Wolfowitz, and indirectly responsible for Perle's abandonment of academic life. In 1969, when Perle was a PhD student, he traveled to Washington, DC, at Wohlstetter's request to join Wolfowitz and interview Senators about ballistic missile defense. One of the interviewees was Henry "Scoop" Jackson. Senator Jackson suggested that Perle's understanding of politics would benefit from some experience in DC, and Jackson offered him a one-year job, during which Perle could have continued to work on his thesis: "But there was never any spare time working for Scoop, and I was there for eleven years."[75]

A key text that has enhanced Perle's infamy is his coauthored book, *An End to Evil: How to Win the War on Terror*.[76] Perle dedicates the book to the "memory of my friend and mentor, Albert Wohlstetter and the many dedicated officials and thinkers he encouraged and inspired." In a 280-page work titled *An End to Evil*, a Straussian might manage to mention Strauss or at least some authors Strauss highlighted. The longest chapter of Perle's and Frum's book is titled "The War of Ideas," but the book nowhere mentions Strauss or even *one* of the authors about whom Strauss wrote a book, article, chapter, subchapter, or review: for example, Aristophanes, Thucydides, Plato, Xenophon, Aristotle, Lucretius, Maimonides, Farabi, Marsilius of Padua, Machiavelli, Hobbes, Spinoza, Locke, Rousseau, Burke, Nietzsche, Weber, Freud, Heidegger, Carl Schmitt, and Isaiah Berlin. *An End to Evil* mentions hundreds of diverse twentieth-century figures—including John Maynard Keynes, George Patton, Michel Foucault, H. Rap Brown, Doo Hwan Chun, Jacques Poos, Hasan Karim Akbar, and Julia Roberts—but the only one who even approaches being a Straussian is Wolfowitz, who appears twice (128, 136). Although the book refers once to the "ancient Aztecs" (134), it does not otherwise speak of ancients, antiquity, classics, or the classical.[77]

Steven Smith laments the title (*An End to Evil*), noting that Strauss "would have been deeply skeptical"; Strauss, adds Smith, would have similarly rejected Bush's "Axis of Evil" speech and his second inaugural. Smith even quotes Patrick Buchanan: "If God accepts the existence of evil in the world, how is it that Perle and Frum propose to end it?"[78] In fairness to Frum and Perle, however, we must acknowledge that their book (apart from the title) does not suggest anything like an "end to evil."[79] They do label terrorism as "the *great* evil of *our time*" and claim that the outcome for America in confronting it will be "victory or holocaust" (6).[80] In the same spirit, they liken the "war against extremist Islam" to the Cold War (125) and criticize those who thought that hopes for victory in the Cold War were "dangerous delusions" (172). Since my focus is Straussophobia, I shall not take the time to convey the distortions Norton employs in attacking *An End to Evil*, although in several of her many occluded passages she seems to label Perle a Straussian (*LSPAE* 17, 210–12); suffice it to say that, contra her assertion, the authors nowhere employ "the language of blood libel" (*LSPAE* 211) to describe the world's Muslims.[81]

Outside of *Embedded*, I have not encountered references to Condoleezza Rice as a Straussian, although—unlike most of the *Embedded* cabal—she has a PhD and has been employed as a political science professor.[82] From the start, her post-piano academic studies focused on Russia, Soviet Politics, Eastern Europe, and international relations rather than the history of political philosophy. Her undergraduate mentor at the University of Denver was Josef Korbel, Madeleine Albright's father.[83] Rice later received her doctorate from Denver's Graduate School of International Studies in 1981, writing a thesis under Jonathan Adelman comparing the Soviet and Czech militaries (*The Politics of Client Command: The Case of Czechoslovakia, 1948–1975*).[84] Her primary exposure to political philosophy came at Denver, courtesy of Professor Alan Gilbert, with whom she took eight courses (some of these addressed comparative communism and were apparently cotaught by Korbel). Gilbert, highlighting the "basically leftist" character of various papers Rice wrote for his classes, has assured Elisabeth Bumiller that Rice displayed no conservative views during their Denver days.[85] Starting in 1982, Rice taught at Stanford, a Straussian-free environment, where she served as provost from 1993 to 1999. In 1989, Rice was lured into her first government position (director of Soviet and East European affairs at the National Security Council) by Brent Scowcroft, her primary political mentor. Scowcroft was a protégé of Henry Kissinger, whose realism-based policies of détente were *opposed* by Wolfowitz and Perle.[86] It goes without saying, finally, that Rice, compared to Wolfowitz, was and is much closer to George W. Bush.[87]

Richard Perle was not even a governmental employee when the Iraq War was launched.[88] Vice President Cheney and Secretary of Defense Rumsfeld may have matched his eagerness in pushing the war, and they certainly dwarfed his influence. According to Andrew Cockburn, indeed, it was Rumsfeld whose bond with Bush enabled him "to change the president's mind on issues in public, to ignore decisions that he found inconvenient, and to survive repeated attempts by powerful enemies seeking to bring him down."[89] And if Perle was among the small number of individuals whom Rumsfeld "accepted . . . as his intellectual equal" and "to whom he was prepared actually to defer," Rumsfeld was "always uneasy" with Wolfowitz,[90] the administration official who had (in his teens and early twenties) actually studied with Bloom and Strauss.[91]

The lives of Rumsfeld and Cheney have been dominated by Republican politics and big business, not the revival of classical rationalism using Farabi and Maimonides as intermediaries. Although Cheney earned a master's degree in political science from the University of Wyoming and commenced a PhD program at the University of Wisconsin, his primary focus was U.S. politics; the article he published with one of his Wisconsin professors used cluster analysis, multiple regressions, and interscale correlations to analyze Congressional roll-call voting.[92]

Although the arch-accuser Drury, in her 1997 book (*Leo Strauss and the American Right*) does briefly discuss Wolfowitz, she does not here mention any other member of the *Embedded* cabal. Drury subjects Wolfowitz to more extensive scrutiny in the introduction she composed for the 2005 reprinting of her first book (*PILS*), but, as we shall later explore, she errs on basic facts and she presumptuously calls Wolfowitz a "self-proclaimed" Straussian.

III. "LEADING THE STUPID MASSES"

On the website and in its program, *Embedded* attempts to provide documentation for its provocative allegations and insinuations; recall Robbins's pride in the amount of "sourced material." Via the Internet, I accessed the program that accompanied a 2004 performance at Saint John's University in Minnesota.[93] The program concludes with roughly a page of information and misinformation. The only scholarly book about Strauss it mentions is Drury's *PILS* and it quotes Drury at length. The bulk of the program's discussion about Strauss is taken, with attribution, from a 2003 article by Kitty Clark in the September/October issue of *Adbusters*.[94] The program cites Gordon Wood, the world-renowned historian, for the proposition that Straussians were "the biggest phenomenon in 20th-century academia." I infer that the program and Clark are here borrowing a flagrant error from the introduction to Drury's 1997 book, which claims that Wood identified Straussianism as "the largest academic movement in the twentieth century" (*LSAR* 2). When I first read this, I was stunned. Could someone as learned and sober as Gordon Wood possibly think that Straussianism is a larger "academic movement" than feminism, postmodernism, multiculturalism, behaviorism, or Marxism? Of course not.[95] In the cited passage from an article in the *New York Review of Books*, Wood was actually addressing Strauss's influence within academic *conservatism*: "at least one of them sees the Straussians as 'the most powerful *conservative* intellectual force in the academy' today" (the "them" apparently refers to conservatives, not Straussians).[96] By here quoting the judgment of another scholar (Charles Kesler), Wood only partially endorses the proposition that Straussians form the most powerful *conservative* movement in academia. Yet Drury, Clark, and now the *Embedded* program cite him on behalf of the preposterous thesis that Straussianism rules the academic world.[97] Jeffrey Steinberg, in his *Executive Intelligence Review* profile—"Leo Strauss, Fascist Godfather of the Neo-Cons" (21 March 2003)—offers a more modest, yet still unhinged, estimate when he says that Straussians "dominate most undergraduate political science and philosophy departments." This article was listed sixth in my 15 July 2007 Google search for Strauss.

The *Embedded* program invokes and quotes Drury via Clark to explain how the allegations about Iraq's WMDs might have been regarded as noble lies: "you are the wise few, the elite, who are leading the stupid masses, and the stupid masses aren't going to agree to sacrifice their lives for nothing—for the glory of the nation—unless their own survival is at stake." The quotation, which I am guessing came from an interview that Clark did with Drury, does not explain *why* the wise would want the masses to "sacrifice their lives for nothing," or even for national glory.

Portions of the Clark article that are not incorporated into the program also contain nuggets of nuttiness. According to Clark, many of "the major players occupying the White House are descendants of the Jewish-American New York intellectuals who veered from the radical left (anti-Stalinist Trotskyitism of the 1920s and 1930s) to the radical right (hence the 'neo')." Apart from the issue of whether Irving Kristol is part of "the radical right," none of his descendants was "occupying the White House" in 2003. Have *other* "Jewish-American New York intellectuals who veered from the radical left" produced such descendants?[98] If you find this question juvenile, consider the one Clark poses to launch an appendix that sketches fourteen individuals whom she regards as major players: "If the brilliant and beautiful Hannah Arendt, the German-Jewish intellectual who famously described the 'banality of evil' at work in Nazi Germany, had not spurned a young suitor named Leo Strauss, would Americans be killing and dying in Iraq?"

IV. HANNAH AND HER BROTHERS

The relationship between Strauss and Arendt has surfaced in other contexts. The key original source appears to be Elisabeth Young-Bruehl's landmark 1982 biography of Arendt. Here is the tale as recounted briefly by Young-Bruehl. At some point in the early 1930s—before 1932, when Strauss left Germany for England, one presumes—he courted Arendt at the Prussian State Library and received a "curt rejection." When she "criticized his conservative political views and dismissed his suit, he became bitterly angry." The feud lasted decades and grew worse when they were together at the University of Chicago in the 1960s. Strauss, concludes Young-Bruehl, was "haunted" by the "rather cruel way in which Hannah Arendt had judged his assessment of National Socialism: she had pointed out the irony of the fact that a political party advocating views Strauss appreciated could have no place for a Jew like him."[99]

Needless to say, it is the last sentence that has contributed the most to today's feeding frenzy. Via e-mail (18 July 2006), Professor Young-Bruehl graciously revealed to me that the main sources for her discussion of the relationship were interviews she conducted with three now-dead individuals; she does not know of any "primary written sources" or of any other interview sources.[100] Catherine Zuckert is quite dismissive regarding Arendt's report: "It is hard to find any basis for her accusation except his qualified sympathy for critics of liberalism like Nietzsche and Schmitt."[101] Sheppard regards the courtship account as "plausible, but unsubstantiated."[102]

As Young-Bruehl's account has been absorbed by other scholars—and by poseurs such as Kitty Clark—it has morphed ever closer to absurdity. The baton has even been picked up by Luc Ferry, who served as France's Minister of Education from 2002 to 2004 under President Jacques Chirac. From Young-Bruehl's account, Ferry unsoundly infers that Arendt's humor "hits home" on "the neoconservative tendency to sacralize natural inequalities, even to inscribe them, in fact and in law within the social and political hierarchy."[103] Via the imagination of Eugene McCarraher, both the humor and the vitriol explode:

> Besides rebuffing his amorous advances (what minor nightmares they must have been!), Arendt saw in Strauss' careful attitude toward the Nazis all the signs of a sniveling opportunist, especially when, as a Jew, he could hardly expect any favors. . . . Having seen the Master in action, Arendt would have known what to make of the Straussian cabal of sycophants and mediocrities.

The claims about "nightmares" and the "sniveling opportunist" are pure embellishments by McCarraher, as are the depiction of Straussians as a "cabal of sycophants and mediocrities" and the prediction that Arendt would perceive them as such. Has an article in *Christianity Today* described any other scholarly school as "a cabal of sycophants and mediocrities"?[104] Regarding the master, Arendt wrote in a 1954 letter to her close friend, Karl Jaspers, that Strauss was a "truly gifted intellect" although she did not like him.[105]

Never has a spurned date generated such political invective sixty years later. In commenting on the irony Arendt allegedly perceived in Strauss's politics, neither Ferry nor Young-Bruehl note a greater irony: although Arendt apparently spurned Strauss, she had previously yielded body and soul to Martin Heidegger, a married man (with two sons) who in 1929 complained that Germany faced "the choice between sustaining our *German* intellectual life through a renewed infusion of genuine, *native* teachers and educators, or abandoning it once and for all to *growing Jewish influence [Verjudung]*."[106] Soon thereafter, moreover, Heidegger spent eleven years as a member of the Nazi Party.[107] As is well known, he also served for roughly a year under the Nazis as the Rector of Freiburg University. In this capacity, he both extolled the Nazi agenda and mistreated Jewish faculty and students.[108] Heidegger even retained a reference to "the inner truth and greatness" of National Socialism in a 1953 book, *An Introduction to Metaphysics*, that was based on lectures he had given in the summer of 1935.[109] Arendt herself fled Germany in the 1930s because of her Jewish background, but she maintained a close friendship with Heidegger after the war,[110] and she continued to extol his work.[111] Is it possible that Strauss's alleged bitterness was fueled by Arendt's embrace of Heidegger rather than by her alleged rebuke of Strauss's conservatism?[112]

V. "TAINTED WITH CERTAIN SPECIFIC VICES": CLASSIC STRAUSSOPHOBIA AT THE INTELLECTUAL SUMMIT

Before Allan Bloom's 1987 book, *The Closing of the American Mind*, popularized many of Strauss's ideas, the disparagements of Strauss and Straussians were sometimes tempered by the scholarly settings in which they typically appeared. At other times, however, lines were crossed.[113] While I was still an undergraduate, the premiere political-theory journal published harsh words from the world-renowned John Pocock. Pocock could not get through a brief exchange with Harvey C. Mansfield about Strauss's *Thoughts on Machiavelli* without offering ad hominem attacks on Straussians. According to Pocock, "the combination of a belief that nobody but themselves cares for moral truth with a belief that nobody but themselves knows how to read a text has gone too far towards turning the followers of Leo Strauss into an intolerable sect of true believers"; they "possess a private gnosis which they expound—publicly, it is true, but always to those already faithful—with the zeal of converts, the prolixity of scholastics and the angry infallibility of hierarchs." From here Pocock proceeds to impugn their collegiality: "One is constantly hearing that they work hard to see that only the enlightened are appointed to vacancies; that the students of Straussian professors avoid the classes of non-Straussian professors because the latter are teachers of evil."[114]

We condemn teachers of evil or we are teachers of evil; we're the ones who care for moral truth or we're the ones who reject it. As with many racial/ethnic and sexual stereotypes, the accusations contradict each other but the hatred is a constant.

Based on the events at Yale University recounted by Robert Kagan, we can hypothesize that Pocock's attitude was somewhat widespread in the 1970s. Yale's decision to turn down Thomas Pangle's application for tenure in 1979 was initially overturned because of a remark that Professor Douglas Rae made as part of the ad hoc/review committee. Potentially disturbed by Pangle's diversity—that is, about his distance from the "mainstream of contemporary political theory"—Rae also stated that "academic freedom is one thing. But there are two types who should never be allowed to teach here—Leninists and Straussians."[115] Leninists and Straussians! Perhaps even the ACLU would defend us.

Drawing on Pangle's petition (to Dean Horace Taft) that challenged the original denial of tenure, a later piece by Kagan describes a prereview meeting with

Pangle in which Charles Lindblom, the department chair, mentioned the "fear of Straussians" that "crops up frequently in political science departments." As here reported, Lindblom also said that several members of the senior faculty were "convinced that any scholar associated with the outlook, or coming under the influence, of Leo Strauss was necessarily 'tainted with certain specific vices' which made him 'unacceptable' as a tenured colleague."[116] After Pangle launched his appeal, Yale's president (Bartlett Giametti) appointed an investigative committee chaired by Edmund Morgan. Based entirely on Rae's comment, the committee overturned the original department decision and recommended the formation of a new committee that would consider the case afresh. Because Pangle's other objections were ignored or dismissed, however, he terminated the appeal and accepted a tenured position at the University of Toronto.[117] Skeptics who do not trust the account of Rae's remark by Kagan—who is sometimes called a Straussian—should first consult Kagan's article, "I Am Not a Straussian."[118]

Hostility was also evident at Harvard. Reviewing Steven Smith's book, Professor Allan Nadler, professor of religious studies and director of the Jewish studies program at Drew University, reports that he was "warned about the treachery of the 'Straussians' almost three decades before Strauss became demonically associated with the architects of the war in Iraq." The source of the warnings was Professor Isadore Twersky of Harvard, who "regularly warned his students against Strauss's methods and ideas." This "academic anti-Straussianism to which we were exposed in the mid-1970s" had nothing to do with foreign policy; Twersky apparently focused his ire on Strauss's effort to elevate Maimonides' *Guide for the Perplexed* at the expense of the *Mishneh Torah*, which Strauss portrayed as a primarily "exoteric" work, that is, a work designed for public consumption.[119]

Am I paranoid when I harp on the disparagement of Straussians? Consider what Robert Paul Wolff, the famous philosopher, wrote when reviewing *The Closing of the American Mind* within the stuffy confines of *Academe*, the journal of the American Association of University Professors. Wolff did not confine his ridicule to Bloom, but asserted that Strauss was "a brilliant, learned, utterly mad historian of political thought who spawned, nurtured, reared, and sent out into the world several generations of disciples dedicated to his paranoid theories of textual interpretation."[120]

Just a few years before Bloom's book appeared, the *New York Review of Books* published a lengthy assessment of Strauss. The author was Myles Burnyeat, the distinguished classicist-philosopher at UC–Berkeley. Although Burnyeat eschewed personal invective, he did proclaim audaciously that "surrender of the critical intellect is the price of initiation into the world of Leo Strauss's ideas."[121] A few years later, the *Review* turned to mega-historian Gordon Wood for the verdict that Straussians, despite their "sanctimonious sense of privilege," possess "no conception of the process of history."[122]

The editorial page of the *New York Times* entered the fray in 1994. Reacting to the election that brought Newt Gingrich and the Contract with America into Congressional predominance, the paper printed a hysterical op-ed piece by Brent Staples, who has been on the Editorial Board since 1990. Here are Staples's chief accusations: Strauss told students that Hitler had "sprung full blown from the Enlightenment presumptions that all people were created equal and that society was better governed by reason than slavish devotion to tradition"; Strauss maintained that "the Philosopher Kings (himself included) were born to rule" and that "servants were born to serve"; he was "unapologetically elitist and anti-democratic"; he "viewed the status quo as an expression of divine will"; and he appealed to "political ideologues because he provided 'wedge issues' that pit the electorate against itself, specifically the privileged against the poor."[123] There's room for debate about elitism and democracy, as I'll elaborate in subsequent chapters, but the other charges are ridiculous.

NOTES

1. To purchase the DVD directly from The Actors' Gang, go to http://www.embeddedlive.com or http://www.theactorsgang.com.

2. Elaine Dutka, "Tim Robbins Is Showing His Independent Streak," *Los Angeles Times*, 24 May 2005, http://articles.latimes.com/2005/may/24/entertainment/et-embedded24.

3. Here is the complete quotation from Lenzner's and Kristol's article, "What Was Leo Strauss Up To?" *Public Interest* 153 (Fall 2003): "President Bush's advocacy of 'regime change'—which avoids the pitfalls of a wishful global universalism on the one hand, and a fatalistic cultural determinism on the other—is a not altogether unworthy product of Strauss's rehabilitation of the notion of regime" (38).

4. The cabal episodes are interspersed with scenes (mostly set in Iraq or Kuwait) that focus on several soldiers and a batch of "embedded" journalists. On the real Office of Special Plans, see pp. 23–24.

5. On the dangers that "the science of social perception" reveals about such visual and auditory associations, see Mahzarin R. Banaji, "The Science of Satire: Cognition Studies Clash with 'New Yorker' Rationale," *Chronicle of Higher Education* 54, no. 31 (1 August 2008): B13. Banaji is the Harvard professor whose Implicit Association Test (https://implicit.harvard.edu/implicit/) is now a landmark in diversity studies.

6. The "Download Press" link (click on PDF2) at http://www.embeddedlive.com includes the interview, "The War on Center Stage," which was originally posted on 13 June 2005 at http://www.thenation.com/doc/20050627/aguirre.

7. I believe that Teachout reported this finding in the 16 March 2004 *Wall Street Journal*. See Brent Bozell, "'Embedded' Gets Shredded," http://www.cnsnews.com/bozellcolumn/archive/2004/col20040323.asp.

8. Pearly changes Papert's version by using the present tense and by substituting "truly" for "really."

9. Papert's lines about moral virtue and "controlling the unintelligent majority" appeared in the *Guardian* courtesy of Geoffrey Wheatcroft, who writes regularly for the *New York Times* and who was previously the literary editor of the *Spectator*, the prestigious British weekly. In the spirit of *Embedded*, Wheatcroft uses quotation marks, as if *Strauss* had written about "control-

ling the unintelligent majority"; Wheatcroft supplies no citations. Wheatcroft also confidently but mistakenly includes Richard Perle among Strauss's "disciples." See Geoffrey Wheatcroft, "Blair Still Took Us to War on a Lie," *Guardian*, 5 March 2005, http://www.guardian.co.uk/comment/story/0,3604,1431009,00.html.

10. Professor Mark Lilla was more aggressively confronted on the campus of the University of Chicago by LaRoucheans armed with a sound truck ("Leo Strauss: The European," *New York Review of Books* 51, no. 16 [21 October 2004]: 58).

11. These citations are from a document on a website sponsored by the LaRouche PAC. The document includes all three versions of *Children of Satan* (http://www.larouchepac.com/files/pdfs/child_satan_book.pdf); the first (2004) version was previously posted as a separate pamphlet. LaRouche's article opens the pamphlet, and Papert's runs from pp. 47–55. Papert's article ("The Secret Kingdom of Leo Strauss") originally appeared in the 18 April 2003 issue of *Executive Intelligence Review*; one can easily access any issue of this magazine via http://www.larouchepub.com/eirtoc/index.html. Stefan Halper and Jonathan Clarke, amazingly, draw a list of Straussians from this article (Halper and Clarke, *America Alone: The Neo-Conservatives and the Global Order* [Cambridge: Cambridge University Press, 2004], 67); the list is manifestly flawed.

12. Francis Fukuyama, *America at the Crossroads* (New Haven, CT: Yale University Press, 2006), 21.

13. Seymour A. Hersh, "Selective Intelligence," *New Yorker*, 12 May 2003, 44–45, 48–49. Hersh commences by asserting that the members "call themselves, self-mockingly, the Cabal" (44).

14. James Risen, "How Pair's Finding on Terror Led to Clash on Shaping Intelligence," *New York Times*, 28 April 2004; Douglas J. Feith, *War and Decision: Inside the Pentagon at the Dawn of the War on Terrorism* (New York: HarperCollins, 2008), 116–18, 293–94, 386n, 606–7n. Feith told Eric Schmitt that the PCTEG was disbanded in August, 2002, but other sources told Schmitt that it continued into the fall (Eric Schmitt, "After the War: Prewar Intelligence; Aide Denies Shaping Data to Justify War" [*New York Times*, 5 June 2003]).

15. George Packer, *The Assassin's Gate* (New York: Farrar, Straus, and Giroux, 2005), 107.

16. Alan Weisman, *Prince of Darkness: Richard Perle* (New York: Union Square Press, 2007), 179; cf. Bob Woodward, *Plan of Attack* (New York: Simon & Schuster, 2004), 289–92.

17. Among intelligence professionals, "stovepiping" means recommending an action "directly to higher authorities . . . without the information on which it is based having been subject to rigorous scrutiny" (Seymour M. Hersh, "The Stovepipe," *New Yorker*, 27 October 2003).

18. See http://www.dodig.mil/fo/Foia/pre-iraqi.htm.

19. In a 1999 book, Wurmser sounds several Strauss-compatible refrains about the evils of modern utopianism (David Wurmser, *Tyranny's Ally: America's Failure to Defeat Saddam Hussein* [Washington, DC: AEI Press, 1999], 42–43, 46, 49–51, 55–57, 67–71, 86, 127–29, 132–35, 137). But Wurmser never here cites Strauss, Straussians, or classical authors, and he relies instead on historians such as Michael Ledeen and Paul Johnson (xxii, 6); on Ledeen and Strauss, see pp. 252n29, 256n64 below. Wurmser and Maloof were replaced in PCTEG by Christopher Carney, a Penn State political scientist who was elected to Congress as a Democrat in 2006, and Christina Shelton, an analyst at the Defense Intelligence Agency. On PCTEG, also see Michael Isikoff and David Corn, *Hubris: The Inside Story of Spin, Scandal, and the Selling of the Iraq War* (New York: Crown Publishers, 2006), 101–14, 176–78; on its relationship to the OSP, see Dana Priest, "Pentagon Shadow Loses Some Mystique," *Washington Post*, 13 March 2004; Jeffrey Goldberg, "A Little Learning," *New Yorker*, 9 May 2005; and Jason DeParle, "Faculty's Chilly Welcome for Ex-Pentagon Official," *New York Times*, 25 May 2006.

20. Nora Bensahel, Olga Oliker, Keith Crane, Richard R. Brennan Jr., Heather S. Gregg, Thomas Sullivan, and Andrew Rathmell, *After Saddam: Prewar Planning and the Occupation of Iraq* (Santa Monica, CA: RAND Corporation, 2008), http://www.rand.org/pubs/monographs/MG642/.

21. Also attending these Rome meetings were Ledeen, Larry Franklin, and several Iranians, including the notorious Manucher Ghorbanifar. See http://intelligence.senate.gov/080605/phase2b .pdf; pp. 35–56 convey protests and suggestions from four members of the Committee's Republican minority (Senators Bond, Chambliss, Hatch, and Burr). For an overview of the report, see John Walcott, "Did Iranian Agents Dupe Pentagon Officials?" *McClatchy Newspapers*, 6 June 2008, http://www.mcclatchydc.com/reports/intelligence/story/40080.html.

22. Fukuyama, *America*, ix, 21. David Bolotin, a Straussian professor at St. John's, roomed with Wolfowitz freshman year and likewise emphasizes the detachment Wolfowitz maintained from the hard-core Straussians (David Dudley, "Paul's Choice," *Cornell Alumni Magazine* 107, no. 1 [July/August 2004], http://cornellalumnimagazine.com/Archive/2004Julaug/features/ Feature.html). Clifford Orwin, an "out" Straussian at the University of Toronto (and a registered Democrat) who has known Wolfowitz for four decades, provides a similar assessment: "Bloom impressed him at Cornell, but he also kept his distance from Bloom, as he did during his graduate years at Chicago, too" (Clifford Orwin, "The Straussians Are Coming!" *Claremont Review of Books* [Spring 2005]: 15).

23. Alex Abella, *Soldiers of Reason: The RAND Corporation and the Rise of the American Empire* (Orlando: Harcourt, 2008), 199.

24. Norton issued these remarks during her 25 October 2004 appearance on Neal Conan's "Talk of the Nation" (National Public Radio); one can listen to the segment, "Leo Strauss's Lasting Influence on U.S. Policy," at http://www.npr.org/templates/story/story.php?storyId=4125689 (the transcript, available for purchase, bears the title "Analysis: Understanding Leo Strauss"). In her book, Norton in two short pages describes Wolfowitz three times as a Straussian (*LSPAE* 16–17), and throws in Robert Kagan, who is clearly not a Straussian.

25. Wolfowitz had been accepted at MIT to pursue a PhD in biophysical chemistry (Dudley, "Paul's Choice"). Embellishing Norton's exaggeration, Richard H. King reports, incorrectly, that Wolfowitz took "several courses" with Bloom ("Intellectuals and the State: The Case of the Straussians," *Comparative American Studies* 4, no. 4 [2006]: 402). In Norton's book, the key evidence is the time Wolfowitz spent in Telluride, where Bloom was a resident faculty member: "For any Straussian, the mention of Telluride House signals a more intense relation with Allan Bloom. At Telluride House, Wolfowitz turned from mathematics to political theory, and to Bloom's Strauss" (*LSPAE* 59). Both Fukuyama and Orwin have remained in contact with Wolfowitz and also resided at Telluride, so their assessments should carry much more weight than that of Norton, who does not even claim to know Wolfowitz; he apparently left Chicago before she arrived (*LSPAE* 183).

26. Elizabeth Drew, "The Neocons in Power," *New York Review of Books*, 12 June 2003, 20.

27. See http://www.defenselink.mil/transcripts/2003/tr20030509-depsecdef0223.html. In a more recent discussion with Eric Alterman, Wolfowitz adds that he does not find political philosophy "all that exciting and Allan Bloom found him to be a disappointment in this regard, but a 'successful disappointment,' which appealed to Bloom"; when Wolfowitz gathers with "real Straussians" he becomes "impatient with the level of abstraction of the discussion." See Eric Alterman, "Wolfowitz on the Record/My Tuna Sushi Canapés with Paul," *Altercation*, 8 March 2005, http://www.msnbc.msn.com/id/7127721/#050308. On Bloom's time-consuming devotion to telephone conversations, see Werner J. Dannhauser, "My Friend, Allan Bloom," *Weekly Standard*, 9 October 1995, 43. Although Xenos acknowledges the strong influence of Wohlstetter and therefore hesitates in labeling Wolfowitz—the "full extent of his actual Straussianism is not easy to discern"—Xenos also offers the slightly chilling claim that Wolfowitz has already been "*identified* in journalistic accounts of the Straussians" within the Bush administration (emph. added). See Nicholas Xenos, "The Neocon Con Game: *Nihilism Revisited*," in Thompson, ed., *Confronting the New Conservatism*, 244n7; cf. *CV* 5, 161n24.

28. Michael Hirsh, "Welcome to the Real World," *Newsweek*, 23 June 2003, 32.

29. Weisman, *Prince of Darkness*, 25.

30. Hersh, "Selective Intelligence," 48. Reviewing the above-sketched BBC documentary by Adam Curtis ("The Power of Nightmares"), Andrew Billen has Wolfowitz—and Francis Fukuyama—imbibing "fanaticism" and "rubbish" in Chicago from Strauss in the *1940s* (Andrew Billen, "Hard to Believe," *New Statesman*, 25 October 2004, http://www.newstatesman .com/200410250044). Wolfowitz was born on 22 December 1943; Fukuyama was born in 1952, and never studied with Strauss.

31. Seymour M. Hersh, *Chain of Command* (New York: HarperCollins Publishers, 2004), 219. Having retired from the University of Chicago, Strauss commenced his sixteen-month stint at Claremont as early as January of 1968 (David Janssens, *Between Athens and Jerusalem: Philosophy, Prophecy and Politics in Leo Strauss's Early Thought* [Albany: SUNY Press, 2008], 233n2).

32. Albert Wohlstetter and Fred Hoffman, "Confronting Saddam: A Model Danger," *Wall Street Journal*, 9 August 1990, A10. Years earlier, Wohlstetter had warned about the danger that Iraqi might invade Kuwait (Albert Wohlstetter, "'Lesser' Excluded Cases," *New York Times*, 14 February 1979, A25).

33. Albert Wohlstetter, "High Time," *National Review*, 15 February 1993, 30–32. This is not the only article in which Wohlstetter expressed the sort of optimism that the Bush administration absorbed from the Iraqi National Congress, Ahmad Chalabi, and Kanan Makiya. Roughly a year earlier, he wrote that the three major population groups in Iraq had "intermarried extensively and have developed educated professional and business classes"; he added that various exiles—that is, "free Iraqis" who were "issuing newspapers and newsletters and holding conferences in several foreign cities"—were seeking a "free" Iraq that would respect the rights of minorities, the rule of law, and other democratic institutions (Wohlstetter, "Wide Open Secret Coup," *National Review*, 16 March 1992, 36). On Wohlstetter's commitment to containing and even transforming nuclear-armed tyrannies, also see Anthony David, "The Apprentice," *American Prospect*, 5 June 2007, http://www.prospect.org/cs/articles?article=the_apprentice. For an excellent bibliography, see http://www.albertwohlstetter.com/archives/albert_wohlstetter_bibliography.html. In their pitch for the U.S. invasion, Kristol and Kaplan mention neither Strauss nor Wohlstetter, but on many points they seem to echo Wohlstetter (Lawrence F. Kaplan and William Kristol, *The War over Iraq: Saddam's Tyranny and America's Mission* [San Francisco: Encounter Books, 2003], 79, 94, 99, 105, 124).

34. Although Sheldon Wolin includes Wolfowitz among the Straussian "initiates" who were "principal architects of the invasion," and later speaks very broadly in blaming Straussians (along with neocons) for their "decisive role in deceiving the public about the reasons for attacking Iraq," he provides no citations or evidence on either occasion (Sheldon S. Wolin, *Democracy Incorporated: Managed Democracy and the Specter of Inverted Totalitarianism* [Princeton, NJ: Princeton Univ. Press, 2008], 169, 264). Had Wolin appreciated Wolfowitz's debts to Wohlstetter, he might have been less surprised that Wolfowitz became the deputy secretary of defense under Rumsfeld (169).

35. Isikoff and Corn, *Hubris*, ix–xii. Shulsky also fails to earn recognition in the following blockbusters: *Circle in the Sand: Why We Went Back to Iraq* (New York: Doubleday, 2006), by Christian Alfonsi; *Rumsfeld: His Rise, Fall, and Catastrophic Legacy* (New York: Scribner, 2007), by Andrew Cockburn; *Dead Certain: The Presidency of George W. Bush* (New York: The Free Press, 2007), by Robert Draper; *Cheney: The Untold Story of America's Most Powerful and Controversial Vice President* (New York: HarperCollins, 2007), by Stephen F. Hayes; and *Angler: The Cheney Vice Presidency* (New York: Penguin Press, 2008), by Barton Gellman. Xenos refers repeatedly to "Schulsky" ("Leo Strauss" 1, *CV* xiii, *CV* xv), before offering the correct spelling at *CV* 15. According to George Packer, Shulsky and Zalmay Khalilzad wrote the hawkish 1992 Defense Planning Guidance that was commissioned by Cheney (then secretary of defense) and "overseen" by Wolfowitz (Packer, *Assassin's Gate*, 13). Khalilzad's role is universally acknowledged, but other sources include Lewis Libby rather than Shulsky among the authors. See James Mann, *Rise*

of the Vulcans: The History of Bush's War Cabinet (New York: Viking, 2004), 209–13; Lewis D. Solomon, *Paul D. Wolfowitz: Visionary Intellectual, Policymaker, and Strategist* (Westport, CT: Praeger Security International, 2007), 50–53; and Jacob Weisberg, *The Bush Tragedy* (New York: Random House, 2008), 168. Khalilzad wrote his PhD thesis with Wohlstetter at Chicago and subsequently served (nonsimultaneously) as the U.S. ambassador to Afghanistan, Iraq, and the United Nations. On allegations that Libby is a Straussian, see p. 217n62 below.

36. See "Neo-CONNED!" 10 July 2003, http://www.house.gov/paul/congrec/congrec2003/cr071003.htm. The seventeen planks Congressman Paul provides in his "brief summary of the general understanding of what neocons believe" include these three: neoconservatives "agree with Trotsky on permanent revolution, violent as well as intellectual"; they "hold Leo Strauss in high esteem"; and they have "a close alliance with the Likud Party." Paul has included this speech in his recent book, *A Foreign Policy of Freedom*, where the above-quoted remarks appear on pp. 261–62.

37. See http://www.sourcewatch.org/index.php?title=Leo_Strauss. SourceWatch is a project of the Center for Media & Democracy; according to its website (http://www.prwatch.org), the Center is a "non-profit, public interest organization that strengthens participatory democracy by investigating and exposing public relations spin and propaganda, and by promoting media literacy and citizen journalism."

38. See http://etherzone.com/2003/cron051503.shtml.

39. See www.dKosopedia.com/wiki/Leo_Strauss. Beyond the Daily Kos, Moulitsas's influence pervades the YearlyKos convention, which every major candidate seeking the Democratic nomination for the 2008 presidential election attended.

40. Joel Bleifuss, "Isn't That Special," 28 May 2003, http://www.inthesetimes.com/comments.php?id=203_0_3_0_M; the piece is also available at http://www.inthesetimes.com/article/450/isn_that_special/.

41. Seymour Hersh, ACLU Keynote Speech, 8 July 2004, http://informationclearinghouse.info/article6492.htm. On the Soviet angle, Sidney Blumenthal claims that Wolfowitz's "notion of politics was essentially Bolshevik, but less democratic in practice than Lenin's." At least Blumenthal concedes that Strauss's "influence on him at the University of Chicago was decidedly minor." See Sidney Blumenthal, "Wolfowitz's Tomb," *Salon*, 24 May 2007, http://www.salon.com/opinion/blumenthal/2007/05/24/wolfowitz_aftermath/.

42. David Duke, "To My Fellow Academics, Walt and Mearsheimer: Act Like Real Men! Stop Cowering to the Jewish Supremacists!" 25 October 2006, http://www.davidduke.com/general/david-duke-responds-to-statement-by-walt-and-mearsheimer_1205.html#more-1205. Writing in the *American Muslim*, Dr. Habib Siddiqui credits Strauss for introducing Trotskyite-spawned neoconservatism to America in the 1960s (Siddiqui, "Neo-conservatism: The Cult of American Ascendancy or Moral Bankruptcy?" 20 November 2005, http://www.theamericanmuslim.org/tam.php/features/articles/neo_conservatism_the_cult_of_american_ascendancy_or_moral_bankruptcy/). In a later essay, Siddiqui highlights the role of Strauss's "foot soldiers" among the "the ultra-nationalist, racist bigots" of Myanmar who are attempting to "de-legitimize any non-Buddhist connection to this historical landmass" ("What's in a Name—Discovering Leo in Arakan?" 17 February 2008, http://theamericanmuslim.org/tam.php/features/articles/whats_in_a_name_discovering_leo_in_arakan/).

43. James Atlas, "A Classicist's Legacy: New Empire Builders," *New York Times*, 4 May 2003. This mistake (Wohlstetter was a "protégé" of Strauss) is echoed by Craig Unger, contributing editor at *Vanity Fair* and a fellow at the Center for Law and Security at NYU Law School (Craig Unger, *The Fall of the House of Bush: The Untold Story of How a Band of True Believers Seized the Executive Branch, Started the Iraq War, and Still Imperils America's Future* [New York: Scribner, 2007], 42). Unger, despite the copious documentation he offers elsewhere in the book, links Wohlstetter to Strauss without offering any evidence. When Stefan Halper and Jonathan Clarke

describe Wohlstetter as Strauss's "protégé," they seem to cite an article from LaRouche's *Executive Intelligence Review* that links Wohlstetter with Wolfowitz but *not* with Strauss; Halper and Clarke make additional mistakes when they trust Drury for a list of Straussians in governmental positions (Halper and Clarke, *America Alone*, 62).

44. Abella, *Soldiers of Reason*, 231–32. To appreciate the gulf that separates Wohlstetter from Strauss, one may contemplate the personal along with the political. Wohlstetter originally entered college on a modern dance scholarship, he and his wife were known for their "dazzling dinner parties featuring experimental ethnic cuisine," and they would provide "elaborate instructions on the optimal ratio of fondue dipping" (Neil Swidey, "The Mind of the Administration, Part One: The Analyst," *Boston Globe*, 18 May 2003, http://www.boston.com/news/globe/ideas/ articles/2003/05/18/the_analyst/; Unger, *Fall*, 42). For additional perspectives on Wohlstetter, see Khurram Husain, "Neocons: The Men Behind the Curtain," *Bulletin of the Atomic Scientist* (November/December 2003): 62–71; Abella, *Soldiers of Reason*, 67–87, 93–94, 117–21, 128–31, 172, 195–200, 219–20, 230–44, 249–55, 278–86, 302–3; Jacob Heilbrunn, *They Knew They Were Right: The Rise of the Neocons* (New York: Doubleday, 2008), 98–106, 119–20, 132, 148–49; Fukuyama, *America*, 31–36; Gary Dorrien, *Imperial Designs: Neoconservatism and the New Pax Americana* (New York: Routledge, 2004), 43–50; Mann, *Rise of the Vulcans*, 29–32, 53; Halper and Clarke, *America Alone*, 63, 90, 92, 220; and Solomon, *Paul D. Wolfowitz*, 12–17.

45. Citing Norton, Richard H. King pronounces that Wohlstetter was "fairly close to Strauss" (King, "Intellectuals," 402).

46. See the following two articles from Kenneth L. Deutsch and John A. Murley, eds., *Leo Strauss, the Straussians, and the American Regime* (Lanham, MD: Rowman & Littlefield, 1999): George Anastaplo, "Leo Strauss at the University of Chicago," 24n7; Joseph Cropsey, "Leo Strauss at the University of Chicago," 39.

47. Perle believes that it was Wohlstetter who (in 1985) introduced Perle to Chalabi (Weisman, *Prince of Darkness*, 155). Although there is widespread agreement that Wohlstetter paved the way for Chalabi's political maneuverings in the United States, the origin of their relationship is obscure. Most sources claim that they met at Chicago, where Chalabi received his mathematics PhD in 1969. Several sources even credit Wohlstetter for introducing Chalabi to Wolfowitz (Heilbrunn, *They Knew*, 258; Unger, *Fall*, 44, 123; W. Patrick Lang, "Drinking the Kool-Aid," *Middle East Policy Journal* 11, no. 2 [Summer 2004], http://www.mepc.org/journal_vol11/0406_lang.asp; and John Dizard, "How Ahmed Chalabi Conned the Neocons," *Salon*, 4 May 2004, http://archive.salon.com/ news/feature/2004/05/04/chalabi/). As reported via e-mail by Chalabi to Alex Abella, however, Wohlstetter and Chalabi were introduced in Wolfowitz's office after Chalabi left Chicago (Abella, *Soldiers of Reason*, 287, 289, 341n4; Abella specifies neither the year nor the city). As reported to me in an e-mail from Abella on 19 June 2008, the account Abella had derived from Chalabi was confirmed by Perle and by Wohlstetter's daughter, Joan.

48. Aram Roston, *The Man Who Pushed America to War: The Extraordinary Life, Adventures, and Obsessions of Ahmad Chalabi* (New York: Nation Books, 2008), 69.

49. Unger, *Fall*, 227, 368n60; for additional details, see Risen, "How Pair's Finding," A19; David Wurmser, the second original member of PCTEG, had extolled Chalabi and the INC in his 1999 book (*Tyranny's Ally*, xxi, 14–17, 22, 25, 42, 65, 80, 88, 90–91, 128–29, 137). On Chalabi's contributions before, during, and after the U.S. invasion of Iraq, also see Roston, *The Man Who Pushed*; Unger, *Fall*, 124–26, 148–49, 160–61, 242, 252–53, 264, 278, 313; Thomas E. Ricks, *Fiasco: The American Military Adventure in Iraq* (New York: Penguin Press, 2006), 31, 56–57, 91, 107, 154, 163–64, 315–17, 382–83, 463, 470; Michael R. Gordon and General Bernard E. Trainor, *Cobra II: The Inside Story of the Invasion and Occupation of Iraq* (New York: Pantheon Book, 2006), 18, 476–77, 482–85; Drew, "Neocons," 20–22; Packer, *Assassin's Gate*, 36, 78–79, 108, 115, 127–28, 140–41, 168, 178–79, 191–92, 195, 391, 408; Feith, *War and Decision*, 189–92, 196–97, 239–45, 254–58, 277, 279, 281, 364–65, 372, 380, 397–401, 404, 413, 431, 444. 481–82, 486–90; Weisman,

Prince of Darkness, 158–59, 161–63, 174–75, 206–9; Lang, "Drinking the Kool-Aid"; Gellman, *Angler*, 246–49, 332–33; James Risen, *State of War: The Secret History of the CIA and the Bush Administration* (New York: Free Press, 2006), 73–76, 133–36; Dexter Filkins, "Where Plan A Left Ahmad Chalabi," *New York Times Magazine*, 5 November 2006; and Patrick E. Tyler, "U.S. and Iraqis Tell of a Coup Attempt against Baghdad," *New York Times*, 3 July 1992.

50. Joseph Wilson, "The Cult That's Running the Country," *Salon*, 3 May 2004, http://dir.salon .com/story/books/feature/2004/05/03/accuse/index2.html; Lang, "Drinking the Kool-Aid."

51. Leila Hudson, "The New Ivory Towers: Think Tanks, Strategic Studies and 'Counterrealism,'" *Middle East Policy* 12, no. 4 (Winter 2005): 126; Bob Woodward, *Bush at War* (New York: Simon & Schuster, 2002), 22.

52. See http://www.aei.org/include/news_print.asp?newsID=16197. The transcript of the speech, accompanied by a video, was posted by the White House at http://www.whitehouse.gov/ news/releases/2003/02/20030226-11.html. The Zuckerts note the absurdity of Atlas's claim that the Bush administration is "rife with Straussians," but fail to point out the humongous AEI gaffe (*TALS* 3).

53. Amir Butler, executive director of the Australian Muslim Public Affairs Committee, identifies Wohlstetter as a Straussian and states that *sixty* Straussians worked for the Bush administration. In writing to oppose neoconservative "demonization of Muslims and Arabs," Butler concludes his short, error-ridden essay by lamenting the American and allied troops sent to Iraq "to kill and be killed on the wings of a Straussian lie" ("There Are No Neocons in Foxholes," 31 December 2003, http://www.antiwar.com/orig/butler2.html).

54. Joshua Muravchik, "The Neoconservative Cabal," *Commentary*, September 2003, 28. Atlas also joins the herd of commentators who mislabel Perle as a Straussian. I read Atlas's piece on-line, but Robert L. Bartley reports that it included a photo-essay highlighting several of the usual suspects, including Wohlstetter, Clarence Thomas, and Perle (Bartley, "Joining LaRouche in the Fever Swamps," *Wall Street Journal*, 9 June 2003, http://www.opinionjournal.com/columnists/ rbartley/?id=110003602). In offering reflections that will "appeal to those who enjoy speculating about secret cliques that rule the world," Professor Peter Singer of Princeton claims that Straussians are "cultish" and attained "extraordinary influence" in the Bush administration; for figuring out who is a Straussian, Singer commends both Atlas and Hersh (along with Jeet Heer). See Peter Singer, *The President of Good & Evil: The Ethics of George W. Bush* (New York: Dutton, 2004), 220–21, 268. Singer further elaborates the conspiracy hypothesis in connection with a July 2003 press conference during which Bush highlighted Saddam Hussein's alleged refusal to admit UN inspectors. Because it is so unlikely that Bush was drunk—"or had ingested mind-altering substances, or was having a psychotic episode"—Singer again raises the possibility that "on Iraq, he really was someone's puppet" (223).

55. Ian Buruma, "Theater of War," review of *The Greatest Story Ever Sold*, by Frank Rich, *New York Times*, 17 September 2006.

56. Quoted in Ivo H. Daalder and James M. Lindsay, *America Unbound: The Bush Revolution in Foreign Policy*, rev. ed. (Hoboken, NJ: John Wiley & Sons, 2005), 155.

57. William Pfaff, "The Long Reach of Leo Strauss," *International Herald Tribune*, 15 May 2003.

58. See http://www.onpointradio.org/shows/2003/05/20030515_a_main.asp. The guests Ashbrook interviewed were Shadia Drury, Harvey Mansfield, and Jack Beatty. Beatty, senior editor at the *Atlantic Monthly* and previously the literary editor at the *New Republic*, errs by describing Perle and Feith as Straussians; Drury concludes the discussion by jumping in—"he's destroyed discourse!"—to protest Ashbrook's concluding description of Strauss as a philosopher.

59. "Return of the 'L' Word: An Interview with Douglas Massey," *Mother Jones*, 13 May 2005, http://www.motherjones.com/news/qa/2005/05/douglas_massey.html. In the corresponding book—*The Return of the "L" Word* (Princeton, NJ: Princeton University Press, 2005)—Massey

likewise speaks with unwarranted confidence: "It is thus very much a Straussian perspective that underlies the militant, unilateralist foreign policy of George W. Bush" (130).

60. Leo Strauss, "On a New Interpretation of Plato's Political Philosophy," *Social Research* 13, no. 3 (September 1946): 351.

61. Massey, *Return*, 128–30; see p. 269 below.

62. Massey, *Return*, 165.

63. See http://www.ephilosopher.com/article441.html. When Leiter wrote the material I am quoting, he was the Hines H. Baker and Thelma Kelley Baker Chair in Law at the University of Texas–Austin.

64. See http://utexas.edu/law/faculty/blieter/moreleostrauss.html. In another subsequent posting, Leiter describes us as "intellectual poseurs and frauds, purveyors of shoddy scholarship and arguments (when there are arguments at all)" (http://leiterreports.typepad.com/blog/2003/08/leo_strauss_red.html).

65. Francis A. Boyle, "My Alma Mater Is a Moral Cesspool," *Counterpunch*, 2 August 2003, http://www.counterpunch.org/boyle08022003.html. The quotations also appear in Boyle's book, *Destroying World Order: U.S. Imperialism in the Middle East Before and After September 11* (Atlanta: Clarity Press, 2004), 140–43.

66. To watch a high-quality video of this interview, "A Conversation with Professor Francis Boyle," see http://radiofreesilver.com/programs/070523_fab.shtml. Boyle adds the completely preposterous claim that the political science department at Chicago was "all Straussians" when it arranged for Robert McNamara to receive a peace award. Boyle's book provides these details: at the behest of its "Straussian Neo-Con Political Science Department," the university gave McNamara the first "Albert Pick Jr. Award for Outstanding Contributions to International Understanding" in 1979 (Boyle, *Destroying World Order*, 143).

67. Richard Wolin, "Leo Strauss, Judaism, and Liberalism," *Chronicle of Higher Education*, 14 April 2006, B13. If Wolin casts aspersions on the "conspiracy theorists," he does so quite delicately.

68. Richard Wolin, "Leo Strauss," B14, B13.

69. Many of the individuals associated with OSP and PCTEG—including Feith, Maloof, Shulsky, and Wurmser—had worked at some point under Perle, who also wrote the introduction for *Tyranny's Ally*.

70. Weisman nevertheless adds, moronically, that Wolfowitz and "most other proud Straussians" are Perle's "friends and colleagues" (Weisman, *Prince of Darkness*, 25–26). Perhaps Weisman intended to say that *many* of the *professed* Straussians in *Washington* are Perle's friends/colleagues. When he is not discussing the Straussian things, Weisman's writing is informed, precise, temperate, and eloquent. Here, as elsewhere, I wonder if I am confronting corruptions introduced by a gremlin.

71. For published denials, see Muravchik, "Neoconservative Cabal," 28; Orwin, "Straussians," 15; and David Lewis Schaeffer, "The Ass and the Lion," review of *Leo Strauss and the Politics of American Empire*, by Anne Norton, *Interpretation* 32, no. 3 (Summer 2005): 288. In *America*, our country's oldest Catholic weekly, an editorial titled "Noble Lies?" includes Perle along with Wolfowitz among the "students" and "alumni" of Strauss (7–14 July 2003, 3); *America* is produced by the Society of Jesus (a.k.a. the Jesuits), the largest religious order in the Catholic church. Perle and Wolfowitz are also two of the five "self-described" Straussians that Arthur Goldwag identifies in *-Isms and -Ologies* (New York: Vintage Books, 2007), 60. Project Censored, despite its commitment to speaking truth to power and its emphasis on the threat neoconservatism poses, carves out a unique error for itself by identifying Perle as a student of Allan Bloom (Peter Phillips and Project Censored, *Censored 2007: The Top 25 Censored Stories* [New York: Seven Stories Press, 2006], 11, 308). In attempting to convey how "the lineage is usually described in the media," Weisman approaches the summit of absurdity in stating that Bloom "begat" *Irving Kristol* before Bloom and

Strauss hatched the "tribe of true believers who would dominate the George W. Bush administration and bring about the Iraq War" (Weisman, *Prince of Darkness*, 25).

72. Quoted in Weisman, *Prince of Darkness*, 19–20.

73. See Weisman, *Prince of Darkness*, 22 (on Ralph Miliband) and 41 (on Rockefeller).

74. Weisman, *Prince of Darkness*, 16–19; Abella, *Soldiers of Reason*, 131, 199; Dorrien, *Imperial Designs*, 46–47.

75. "Richard Perle: The Making of a Neoconservative," http://www/pbs.org/thinktank/transcript1017.html. The material here is a transcript of the 14 November 2002 session of "Think Tank with Ben Wattenberg." Also see Weisman, *Prince of Darkness*, 29–31.

76. David Frum and Richard Perle, *An End to Evil: How to Win the War on Terror*, with a new afterword by the authors (New York: Ballentine Books, 2004).

77. Frum and Perle provide one or more intelligent discussions about the transition to "the modern world" (*End to Evil* 129), but they never use the term "modernity." Nor do they mention philosophy, philosopher, historicism, or "the city."

78. Steven Smith, *Reading Leo Strauss* (Chicago: University of Chicago Press, 2006), 199, 200.

79. In his remarks at the National Cathedral on 14 September 2001, by contrast, President Bush stated that America's responsibility to history required us to answer the attacks of 9/11 and to "rid the world of evil" (http://www.whitehouse.gov/news/releases/2001/09/20010914-2.html). Stephen Holmes likewise exaggerates by associating Perle with a campaign "to end evil" (Holmes, *The Matador's Cape* [Cambridge: Cambridge University Press, 2007], 202).

80. Emphases added. Although Xenos denies that a Straussian conspiracy has propelled the Bush administration, he faults the allegedly Straussian impetus that has caused "[s]erious" writers to "ponder the presence of evil in political affairs" (*CV* xi).

81. On Perle's efforts to protect the Muslims of Bosnia, see Weisman, *Prince of Darkness*, 128–33. For a more thorough rebuttal of Norton's line on Frum and Perle, see Schaeffer, "Ass and the Lion," 292–93, and p. 221n119 below.

82. Karl Rove, who never graduated from college, is likewise free of Straussian taint.

83. Elisabeth Bumiller, *Condoleezza Rice: An American Life* (New York: Random House, 2007), 57–69, 72–74; Antonia Felix, *Condi: The Condoleezza Rice Story* (New York: Pocket Books, 2002), 86–89, 93, 103–31.

84. Adelman arrived at Denver in early 1979; he was hired to replace Korbel, who had died in the summer of 1977. At roughly the same time, Denver also hired Catherine Kelleher, who combined general expertise about defense/security studies with knowledge of Russia. Kelleher joined Adelman in advising Rice; George A. Brinkley, a Soviet specialist with whom Rice had studied while picking up a 1975 master's degree in government and international studies from Notre Dame, also helped Rice with her PhD thesis. See Bumiller, *Condoleezza Rice*, 73–74, 66, 83, and Felix, *Condi*, 111, 117–18, 125, 129.

85. Bumiller, *Condoleezza Rice*, 67. Gilbert, whose leftist credentials are beyond reproach, is writing a book-length attack on Strauss titled *Worse Than Any of Us Could Imagine*; see p. 211n3 below.

86. Bumiller, *Condoleezza Rice*, 83–84, 93–95, 98, 110–12, 187–88; Felix, *Condi*, 6–7, 158–63, 200–201, 259–61.

87. According to Robert Draper, "[h]er swoon for him was such that she announced her resignation from Stanford in December 1998, making herself available for a presidential candidacy that had not yet been officially determined" (Draper, *Dead Certain*, 286). In the words of Jacob Weisberg, their views merged so closely while Bush was first pursuing the presidency that eventually "there was no saying where his ended and hers began"; they'd speak roughly eight times a day in the White House (Weisberg, *Bush Tragedy*, 148; cf. 188, 206). Also see Bumiller, *Condoleezza Rice*, xxvii, 125–29, 134–38, 151–52, 168–69, 188–90, 197–98, 212, 219–20, 225, 228–29, 300.

88. Perle's closest connection came as a member of the Defense Policy Board (DPB), an "assembly of unpaid consultants" who met roughly four times each year to offer recommendations to the secretary of defense. Reappointed by both of the men (William Perry and William Cohen) who served as secretary of defense under President Clinton, Perle had served continuously on the DPB since 1987, the year he resigned his position as an assistant secretary of defense. Rumsfeld appointed him chair of the DPB after 9/11; the DPB then included Henry Kissinger, James Schlesinger, Harold Brown, Tom Foley (Weisman, *Prince of Darkness*, 164), and other well-known non-Straussians. Perle resigned as chair on 28 March 2003, and left the DPB in February of 2004 amidst accusations of financial impropriety (Weisman, *Prince of Darkness*, 195, 204; Cockburn, *Rumsfeld*, 180). On Perle's use of the DPB to agitate for the Iraq War, cf. Gordon and Trainor, *Cobra II*, 17–19, and Heilbrunn, *They Knew*, 250–51.

89. Cockburn, *Rumsfeld*, 98; also see 127–28, 135–36, 140–41, 177–78.

90. Cockburn, *Rumsfeld*, 103, 102. On Perle, also see 124–25, 149, and Heilbrunn, *They Knew*, 252. On Wolfowitz, see the following accounts: Cockburn, *Rumsfeld*, 149, 167; Heilbrunn, *They Knew*, 231, 234, 254; and Weisman, *Prince of Darkness*, 170.

91. One of Rumsfeld's closest aides, however, was Stephen A. Cambone, who had earned his PhD at Claremont Graduate School with a Straussian-sounding thesis: "Noble Sentiments and Manly Eloquence: The First Continental Congress and the Decision for American Independence" (http://research.history.org/files/JDRLibrary/Microforms.pdf); I assume that the thesis was advised by Harry Jaffa. Cambone is not mentioned by Drury, Norton, or Xenos; nor did Deutsch and Murley include him in 1999 when they listed twenty-seven Straussians who had held "significant positions" in DC (Deutsch and Murley, *Leo Strauss*, xiii, xivn4). According to Andrew Cockburn and other sources, Maloof and Wurmser of the PCTEG reported to Cambone weekly in the fall of 2001 while he was Feith's chief deputy, and he quarreled with Wolfowitz as well as Feith over Ahmad Chalabi and other matters (Cockburn, *Rumsfeld*, 102, 107, 167). Seymour Hersh describes Cambone as a Straussian (Hersh, "Selective Intelligence," 48), and holds him partly responsible for the abuses at Abu Ghraib (Hersh, "The Gray Zone," *New Yorker*, 24 May 2004). After receiving his PhD in 1982, when academic jobs were scarce, Cambone went to work at Los Alamos National Laboratory and commenced his shift to defense-related work (Victorino Matus, "Who Is Steve Cambone?" *Armed Forces Journal*, April 2006, http://www.afji.com/2006/04/1813786).

92. Aage R. Clausen and Richard B. Cheney, "A Comparative Analysis of Senate and House Voting on Economics and Welfare Policy: 1953–1964," *American Political Science Review* 64, no. 1 (March 1970): 138–52. Under the auspices of a Joe Davies Fellowship awarded by the American Political Science Association, Cheney did an internship with Representative Bill Steiger (R) of Wisconsin in 1969, hoping that it would help him write a PhD thesis on Congress. Cheney first met Rumsfeld, then a Republican representative from suburban Chicago, when Rumsfeld spoke at the orientation session for the Davies program (Hayes, *Cheney*, 43–45, 47, 51–54). Although Cheney had "dabbled in consulting" during the gaps in his governmental service, his corporate involvement was unremarkable until he became CEO of Halliburton in 1995 (265–68). Rumsfeld, by contrast, served as president and CEO of G. D. Searle, the pharmaceutical giant, from 1977 to 1985; he ran General Instrument, whose main product was cable TV equipment, from 1990 to 1993, and he later spent ten years on the board of directors for Asea Brown Boveri (ABB), the Swiss construction firm (Cockburn, *Rumsfeld*, 55–70, 88–90).

93. Based on Lawrence F. Kaplan's discussion of the play's New York production, the programs are quite similar ("Devious Plot," posted 10 March 2004 at http://www.tnr.com/doc .mhtml?i=online&s=kaplan031004; as I write, the *TNR* site is being revamped). When I rechecked on 17 November 2007, the program was no longer available on the Saint John's University website.

94. For a while, the Clark article could be accessed on line at http://www.adbusters.org/ magazine/49/articles/leo_strauss/noflash.html. Although this link is no longer functional, a slightly

expanded version of the article appears in *Adbusters* 71 (May–June 2007), posted at http://adbusters.org/the_magazine/71.php?id=285.

95. I doubt we even outweigh libertarianism, critical legal studies, queer theory, or "rational choice." As historian Allan J. Lichtman has observed, Straussians are simply "the most notable body of conservatives outside of economics, business, and law to emerge as a force on college campuses" (Lichtman, *White Protestant Nation: The Rise of the American Conservative Movement* [New York: Atlantic Monthly Press, 2008], 285–86).

96. Wood was here quoting from Charles R. Kesler, "Is Conservatism Un-American?" *National Review*, 22 March 1985, 28, http://www.findarticles.com/p/articles/mi_m1282/is_v37/ai_3691622/pg_4. See Gordon S. Wood, "The Fundamentalists and the Constitution," *New York Review of Books* 35, no. 2 (18 February 1988): 34. Wood does include one sweeping estimate about Straussians: they are "everywhere in government and academia, in both high and low places, in conferences, in symposiums, in books and journals" (33).

97. Professor Klaus J. Milich, writing in a peer-reviewed journal published by the University of Minnesota Press, likewise credits Wood with identifying "Strauss's impact" as "the largest academic movement in the twentieth century." See Milich, "Fundamentalism Hot and Cold: George W. Bush and the 'Return of the Sacred,'" *Cultural Critique* 62 (Winter 2006): 199n14. Although Milich's article elsewhere draws on Drury, he provides no reference for the Wood/Strauss claim, as if a claim so completely absurd could count as common knowledge.

98. One encounters similar nonsense from the Robert Walton Goelet Professor of French History at Harvard University: in attempting to explain Strauss's responsibility for neoconservative duplicity, belligerence, and Manichaeanism, Patrice Higonnet asserts that many neocons were "brought" to America by Weimar's collapse (Higonnet, *Attendant Cruelties: Nation and Nationalism in American History* [New York: Other Press, 2007], 304).

99. Elisabeth Young-Bruehl, *Hannah Arendt, for Love of the World* (New Haven, CT: Yale University Press, 1982), 98.

100. McCormick thus appears to err in describing the report as an "assessment of young Strauss's political predilections that Hannah Arendt conveyed to her biographer" (John P. McCormick, "Fear, Technology, and the State: Carl Schmitt, Leo Strauss, and the Revival of Hobbes in Weimar and National Socialist Germany," *Political Theory* 22, no. 4 [November 1994]: 651–52n59). Young-Bruehl's biography does not specify interviewees, but such details are available in her notes, which are archived at Wesleyan University. Perhaps some East Coast Straussian can investigate further.

101. Catherine H. Zuckert, *Postmodern Platos* (Chicago: University of Chicago Press, 1996), 301n18. Zuckert may have been unaware of the 1933 letter in which Strauss appeals to the "fascist, authoritarian, and imperial" principles of the right; see pp. 154–58 below for a detailed discussion.

102. Eugene R. Sheppard, *Leo Strauss and the Politics of Exile: The Making of a Political Philosopher* (Waltham, MA: Brandeis University Press, 2006), 177n13.

103. Luc Ferry, *Political Philosophy 1: Rights—the New Quarrel between the Ancients and the Moderns*, trans. Franklin Philip (Chicago: University of Chicago Press, 1990), 20–21.

104. Eugene McCarraher, "The Incoherence of Hannah Arendt: Breaking the Marriage between Heaven and Earth," *Christianity Today*, March–April 2006, http://www.christianitytoday.com/bc/2006/002/8.32.html. McCarraher seems to equate the "cabal" with Strauss's "intellectual spawn"; they "occupy" editorial offices and university faculties as well as the Bush administration, and they possess a "reckless lust for power." McCarraher is a professor at Villanova and a fellow of the American Council of Learned Societies. His core humanities seminar, "Progress and Its Discontents," asserts that the seminar program "aims to cultivate critical intelligence, clarity and civility in argument, and moral sophistication" (http://www21.homepage.villanova.edu/eugene.mccarraher/syllabus.html). One wonders how he would criticize Strauss and Straussians if he were not so committed to critical intelligence, moral sophistication, and civility. I should add that

McCarraher responded promptly and quite politely to an e-mail query from me on 17 July 2006 concerning the sources of his comments about Strauss and Arendt. When I later pointed out the discrepancies between his account and its apparent source in Young-Bruehl, he did not reply.

105. Arendt to Jaspers, 24 July 1954 (#158), *Hannah Arendt-Karl Jaspers Correspondence, 1926–1969*, eds. Lotte Kohler and Hans Saner, trans. Robert and Rita Kimber (New York: Harcourt Brace Jovanovich, 1992), 244. Roughly a decade later, Arendt stated to Jaspers that Strauss was the "only person here on the campus who is agitating against me" because of her book, *Eichmann in Jerusalem* (24 November 1963 [#343], 535).

106. Wolin, *Heidegger's Children: Hannah Arendt, Karl Löwith, Hans Jonas, and Herbert Marcuse* (Princeton, NJ: Princeton University Press, 2001), 11. On Heidegger's family, see Young-Bruehl, *Hannah Arendt*, 50, 53. For informed and fair-minded overviews of Arendt's evolving assessments of Heidegger, see Young-Bruehl, *Why Arendt Matters* (New Haven, CT: Yale University Press, 2006), 7–8, 20–25, and Dana Villa, "Arendt and Heidegger, Again," in *Heidegger's Jewish Followers: Essays on Hannah Arendt, Leo Strauss, Hans Jonas, and Emmanuel Levinas* (Pittsburgh: Duquesne University Press, 2008), ed. Samuel Fleischacker, 43–82.

107. Wolin, *Heidegger's Children*, 10; also see Michael Andre Bernstein, "Being and His Time," *New Republic*, 26 October 1998, 33.

108. Wolin, *Heidegger Controversy*, 11, 26–27, 148, 179–80. Heidegger's own words suffice to demonstrate his enthusiasm. See the *Rektoratsrade* on pp. 29–39 and the "Political Texts" on pp. 40–60.

109. Martin Heidegger, *An Introduction to Metaphysics* (New Haven, CT: Yale University Press, 1959), trans. Ralph Manheim, 199. Strauss calls attention to the passage at *SCR* 4/*LAM* 227.

110. See, for example, Arendt's 10 February 1950 (#49) letter to Heidegger's wife, Elfride, in *Letters 1925–1975: Hannah Arendt and Martin Heidegger*, trans. Ursula Ludz (Orlando: Harcourt, 2004), 61. At some point Heidegger had confessed the affair and a three-way friendship developed.

111. For Arendt's overview of Heidegger's philosophy and life, see her letter to him of 26 September 1969 (#116), in *Letters 1925–1975*, 148–62; she drew on this letter for the radio talk she recorded the previous day to celebrate his eightieth birthday. An earlier translation was published in the *New York Review of Books*, 21 October 1971 (*Letters 1925–1975*, 269n116).

112. According to Anastaplo, Strauss both told various students traveling to postwar Germany that they should avoid Heidegger and broke off relations with a Jewish friend because that friend reconciled with Heidegger (George Anastaplo, "On Leo Strauss: A Yahrzeit Remembrance," *University of Chicago Magazine* 67 [Winter 1974]: 38n3).

113. As will be touched on in succeeding chapters, Strauss's books received numerous hostile and/or dismissive reviews. As early as 1963, Schaar and Wolin in the pages of the flagship political science journal complained that *Essays on the Scientific Study of Politics* created "a scholarly atmosphere charged with accusations of atheism, venality, conspiracy, and treason" (Strauss had written the Epilogue; his students Walter Berns, Herbert J. Storing, Leo Weinstein, and Robert Horwitz wrote the remaining chapters). See John H. Schaar and Sheldon S. Wolin, "*Essays on the Scientific Study of Politics*: A Critique," *American Political Science Review* 57, no. 1 (March 1963): 150.

114. J. G. A. Pocock, "Prophet and Inquisitor," *Political Theory* 3, no. 4 (November 1975): 399.

115. Robert William Kagan, "God and Man at Yale—Again," *Commentary* 73, no. 2 (February 1982): 51.

116. Robert Kagan, "Yale & the Pangle Case," *Commentary* 74, no. 2 (August 1982): 11. The Lindblom letter to which Kagan replies is on pp. 4–5; Kagan's original article provides a briefer account of the "specific vices" remark (Kagan, "God and Man," 51).

117. Kagan, "God and Man," 51; Richard Vigilante, "Communism, Sí; Straussianism, No," *National Review*, 12 March 1980, 350.

118. Robert Kagan, "I Am Not a Straussian," *Weekly Standard*, 6 February 2006, 16–17. Kagan here situates himself at a great distance from Strauss: "I have never understood a word the political philosopher wrote. . . . Nor have I been very good at understanding his disciples, really, and Pangle, from whom I once took two courses, can back me up on this." Kagan also agrees with his father, Donald, that Straussians are ahistorical and that Bloom misunderstood Plato. For those who nevertheless think that Kagan is a brazenly lying Straussian under deep cover, the letter that Lindblom wrote in response to Kagan's article illuminates some key issues. Lindblom discusses the tenure process in detail and disputes various things (including Kagan's rendering of Lindblom's preliminary conversation with Pangle). But Lindblom says *nothing* about the comment attributed to Rae, and he thus implicitly confirms Kagan's account of it ("Yale & the Pangle Case," 4, 8). Cf. Heilbrunn, *They Knew*, 214–16, on Kagan's role in shaping Bill Kristol's endorsement of a "neo-Reaganite" approach to U.S. foreign policy; Kagan has a PhD in U.S. history from American University.

119. Allan Nadler, "Who Owns Leo Strauss?" *Forward*, 21 July 2006, 15.

120. Robert Paul Wolff, "Book Reviews," *Academe*, September–October 1987, 64.

121. Myles Burnyeat, "Sphinx without a Secret," *New York Review of Books* 32, no. 9 (30 May 1985): 31.

122. Wood, "The Fundamentalists," 33, 36.

123. Brent Staples, "Undemocratic Vistas," *New York Times*, 28 November 1994, A14. In an interview with James Ring Adams of the Jewish *Forward*, Staples claimed that his piece stirred up abundant discussion within the *Times* and that the response of his colleagues was overwhelmingly favorable. Staples admitted to Adams, however, that he had never studied with Strauss or Strauss's students and that his "main sources" were critiques of Strauss in the *New York Review of Books* (Myles Burnyeat, I presume) and the *Times Literary Supplement* (Stephen Holmes, I presume). See James Ring Adams, "New 'Cause of the Holocaust' Found," *Forward*, 2 December 1994, 1–2. When calling attention to this interview, Steven Smith exaggerates Staples's irresponsibility and incompetence: according to Smith, Staples confessed that he never studied Strauss's "works" and that he drew "entirely" on the above-mentioned sources (Smith, *Reading*, 217n7). For the record, Stephen Holmes published an article in the *Times Literary Supplement* ("Truths for Philosophers Alone?" 1–7 December 1989) that was later absorbed into his chapter on Strauss in *The Anatomy of Antiliberalism* (Cambridge, MA: Harvard University Press, 1993).

Chapter Two

"Careless Scholarship and a Tendency to Quote out of Context"

Early Drury on Strauss, Locke, and Xenophon

There is no royal road to science, and only those who do not dread the fatiguing climb of its steep path have a chance of gaining its luminous summits.

—Karl Marx

I. DETHRONING DRURY

Shadia Drury, the Strauss critic who helped inspire *Embedded* and many of its sources, entered the fray roughly a decade before Brent Staples with a 1985 article in *Political Theory*.[1] The article was more or less absorbed into her 1988 book, *The Political Ideas of Leo Strauss* (*PILS*), which appeared a year after Bloom's *The Closing of the American Mind*;[2] Drury is now the world's most widely read and cited commentator on Strauss and Straussians. *PILS* even gets high billing from the entry on Strauss (written by Stephen Hayward) in the new encyclopedia, *American Conservatism*.[3]

In *PILS*, Drury establishes the package of ingredients—the insight, creativity, and eloquence one expects of a scholar combined with the vilification, sloppiness, and paranoia one expects of a third-rate blogger—that she deploys in her later treatments. Regrettably, it is the blogger side that has prevailed in more recent years, enthralling Internet denizens and inspiring Tim Robbins to write, produce, film, and distribute a play that portrays Bush's inner circle as terror-loving Strauss-worshipers. Straussians have subjected her work to many penetrating criticisms, but Drury never apologizes, corrects, or retracts. In my opinion, the critics have been too gentlemanly, and their efforts to publicize Strauss's virtues have left many of Drury's vices in the shadows. In response to a question during a 2005 interview on the *Progressive Radio Show*, Drury insists that she has *not* been "assailed" by Straussians ("No, no, not enough") and that she would "love to get more assailed by them." If and when she is done reading this book, I doubt that she will invite a second assailing.[4]

I am happy to laud Drury for presenting some imaginative and important interpretations of Strauss that warrant a patient and detailed examination. But given the way that Straussophobia has spread, partly via her impetus, I shall mostly confine myself in this and succeeding chapters to clearing away the trash and demonstrating that Drury often accuses so irresponsibly—especially in her more recent pronouncements—that *everything* she says must be read skeptically. Ironically, this is one of the messages—"Readers/students, beware!"—that she is trying to spread about Strauss and Straussians as she boasts of her own scholarly competence and integrity. Rarely has an authority so cried out for deflating. Early in her first book, Drury tries to distinguish herself from the duplicitous Strauss: "In writing this book I will be adhering to the biblical principle that 'the truth will set you free'" (*PILS* 15). She nevertheless proceeds to present an embarrassing array of errors and contradictions. Drury also complains that "[t]he Straussians are characterized by an overwhelming self-confidence that often bespeaks an embarrassing lack of modesty" (206n21). In her long new introduction to the 2005 reprinting of the book, she goes still further, describing us as a "class of compulsive and self-righteous deceivers" (*PILS*-05 xvi). My task is to demonstrate that *Drury* is a "self-righteous" and energetic (but not "compulsive") deceiver, and I shall let you draw your own conclusions about her modesty.

On the very first page of *PILS*, Drury tries to hook readers with the implausible claim that Strauss's "followers" (a.k.a. Straussians) "occupy high positions in almost all the universities in North America." Given the roughly 4,000 institutions of higher education in the United States alone—I do not think Drury intended to exclude colleges—I doubt that there are enough PhD-holding Straussians to provide extensive coverage. Well, let us forget temporarily about the more obscure locations. In the San Francisco Bay Area, where I teach, I am apparently the only Straussian with a full-time academic appointment (let alone a "high position"). I know I am the only one on the roughly 500-member faculty of my university, and I cannot locate *any* on the faculties of San Jose State, Stanford, UC–Berkeley, UC–Santa Cruz, the University of San Francisco, and San Francisco State, to mention only the major institutions within fifty miles of me.[5]

One may presume that Drury both heard and read complaints about this obvious exaggeration concerning the prevalence of Straussians. When she returned to the subject nine years later in her second book, she cites an august authority, Gordon Wood, for her diagnosis. She also extends the scope of her warning from North America to the world, claiming that Straussianism is "the largest academic movement in the twentieth century" (*LSAR* 2). As we have seen, however, Drury had to butcher what Wood actually wrote—that one conservative regarded Straussianism as "the most powerful *conservative* intellectual force in the academy"—to arrive at her completely preposterous formulation. In the 2005 introduction to *PILS*, Drury invokes our "staggering numbers within the academy." What is staggering, however, is her subsequent claim that her initial purpose in writing the book was to discredit a school/movement "so prevalent that it threatened the meaningful exchange of ideas in the academy" (*PILS*-05 ix).

Returning to the original introduction of her first book, one can only marvel at the dramatic contrast Drury establishes between the impact of the movement and its lack of substance. She quickly declares her sympathy for the reviewers of Strauss's commentaries who found themselves "genuinely perplexed as to how such rubbish could have been published"; on the whole, she found Strauss's books "arid, insipid, tedious and repetitive," and she has no hesitation in concluding that, "[j]udged solely as a historian of ideas, Strauss deserves much of the contempt that has been heaped upon him" (*PILS* 4). His "method of interpretation," she adds, is "notoriously lacking" in both "clarity and rigor" (10).[6] To explain his impact, she thus emphasizes the "cult that revolves around his personality," a cult that has been extended by his students as they deal with *their* students:

> They too attempt to establish "intimate ties" with their students by socializing with them, spending a great deal of time eating, drinking, and talking together. This practice allows the professor to enter the lives of the students and to shape their character in its most minute details. (*PILS* 2)

Via the word "too," Drury implies that Strauss spent "a great deal of time" establishing intimate ties by eating and drinking with his students. Drury provides little evidence for these sweeping generalizations, and she mishandles one of the two articles she cites. To document Strauss's behavior, Drury merely reports George Anastaplo's brief reference to the "intimate ties" a younger Strauss established with his students, ties that Strauss during his later years did *not* establish (*PILS* 206n22). The claim from Anastaplo—who does not mention eating, drinking, or time devoted to conversation—must carry great weight because her second source (Werner Dannhauser), as Drury correctly reports, emphasizes Strauss's "formality and aloofness" (*PILS* 206n22).[7]

Regarding the mode in which Strauss's *students* taught, Anastaplo is silent and Drury relies completely on Dannhauser. While contrasting his style to Strauss's, Dannhauser does indeed highlight his own belief in "entering the life" of his students by "socializing" as well as by mental engagement. Dannhauser, however, does not extend this judgment to any other Straussians. In fact, Dannhauser states that like many Straussians, he favors a "somewhat severe" pedagogy (Strauss, by contrast, was "most permissive, demanding almost nothing one did not feel like doing").[8] Earlier in his article, Dannhauser mentions having "talked and ate and drank together"—but he is here describing what he had done, while studying at Chicago, with *other graduate students* who were taking

Strauss's classes.[9] Drury doubtless absorbed this image and then spun it into her ungrounded scenario of Straussians "eating, drinking, and talking" with their students. If you studied with a Straussian and allowed him or her to shape your character "in its most minute details"—or if you suspect that Strauss exercised such domination over Harry Jaffa (b. 1918), Joseph Cropsey (b. 1919), Muhsin Mahdi (1926–2007), Herbert Storing (1928–1977), Allan Bloom (1930–1992), or other early disciples—please write to me.[10]

Despite her contempt for cultishness and for Strauss's efforts as an interpreter, Drury says she began to find his work "fascinating, captivating and even bewitching" (*PILS* 4–5) once she identified the somewhat hidden teachings that render him "a philosopher in the rich and meaningful sense of having a most comprehensive view of the world: of life and death, morality and religion, politics and society, justice and injustice." Although she disdains the prospect of scrutinizing Strauss's works the way he scrutinized the writers of the past (e.g., by counting paragraphs), she claims to have uncovered a political philosophy "behind what appeared to be mundane commentaries" (4). Her key shortcut is that she "will attribute to Strauss the ideas he attributes to the wise ancients" (15). In her 1990 "Reply to My Critics," Drury provides a subtly but decisively different account of her "method": she assumes it is "eminently reasonable to attribute to Strauss the ideas he attributes to *the wise* or ancients."[11] Although she was presumably attempting to accommodate critics (e.g., David Schaeffer) who emphasized how *PILS* violated the shortcut by trumpeting Strauss's alleged debt to the non-ancient Machiavelli and Nietzsche, she fails to acknowledge the alteration—and how it invites cherry-picking.[12] In any case, Drury proclaims on the first page of the *PILS* Preface that she will "under no circumstances reverse what Strauss actually says. . . . Everything I will attribute to Strauss is directly there, not between the lines or behind the lines, but *in the lines*" (ix). She even credits Strauss's "sound advice" when she boasts of her own commitment to "reading very carefully" (15).[13]

It is crucial to Drury's argument that Strauss's scholarly efforts fail conspicuously, and that they are valuable or rather, that they are even more damnable, because they are primarily verbiage within which he can present a distinctive but menacing political philosophy that celebrates atheism, elitism, brutality, treachery, and perpetual war. In her 2005 interview with Matthew Rothschild, she says that Strauss's "bizarre" interpretation of texts was "meant to conceal what he was about," to confuse readers "so that people focused on the wrong things"; she concedes that she has "*never* taken him seriously as an interpreter," and insists that he "completely subverts what the ancients are about."[14] With her brusque dismissal of the antihistoricist efforts by Strauss (and Straussians) to free "great books" from their "contexts" by uncovering elaborate esoteric messages, Drury caters to hostile anti-Straussian sentiments that have long been widespread in the academy. In her later writings, Drury is still more heavy-handed in dismissing Straussian scholarship.

Fortunately, Drury's efforts to demonstrate both the failed scholarship and the sinister teaching are doomed because of *her* numerous shortcomings in "rigor" (*PILS* 10). Drury does *not* consistently succeed in "reading very carefully" (15); and her claim that everything she attributes to Strauss is "directly there, not between the lines or behind the lines, but *in the lines*" (ix) is hilarious in light of the frequency with which she both exaggerates shamelessly and makes blatant errors in quoting, paraphrasing, and citing. Given the magnitude of the accusations she levels, it is stunning that she did so little to check her citations and quotations before her 1988 book was published—and before it was reprinted in 2005. As we shall see, her later discussions are even more warped.

II. "DEVASTATING REVIEWS" AND
THE BATTLE FOR LOCKE

To back up her quick dismissal of Strauss's merits as a scholar, Drury in *PILS* provides a footnote that, when scrutinized, loses much of its force. She starts by citing the "devastating reviews" of Strauss's books by Terence Irwin (Strauss just succeeds in reminding us of how "unexciting Xenophon can be"), Trevor J. Saunders (Strauss sails "serenely across the surface of the text, skirting obvious rocks and crashing on submerged ones without knowing he is doing so"), and John Yolton, who "points to innumerable examples of careless scholarship and a tendency to quote out of context." Before proceeding to invoke Burnyeat's above-discussed critique, she immediately instructs us to "see also" an article by Gourevitch in which "the list of errors occurs on pp. 326–8" (*PILS* 204n3). Her wording hints that Strauss is so incompetent that commentators routinely provide a "list of errors" when discussing him. I had a copy of Gourevitch's articles, but I did not recall anything that would justify their being included among "devastating reviews." Upon seeing Drury's reference to a *three-page* "list of errors," I felt stereotype threat welling up to monumental proportions. It turns out that Gourevitch does provide an appendix that discusses errors in Strauss's book *On Tyranny*. But he attributes only three errors to *Strauss*, and they would strike most readers as trivial.[15] I have no problem admitting Strauss's fallibility, but Gourevitch's criticisms fall almost entirely on the translations of the two texts (Xenophon's *Hiero* and the essay by Kojève discussing Strauss) that *accompany* the two essays by Strauss (Strauss's original interpretation plus his "Restatement on Xenophon's *Hiero*"). The errors Gourevitch protests were thus made by the two translators, Marvin Kendrick (Xenophon) and Michael Gold (Kojève), not by Strauss; some blame should also fall on Allan Bloom, the general editor of

the Agora series, who presumably helped to commission these essays and to ar-
range for their inclusion in the volume.[16] Gourevitch's appendix starts with the
claim that "Strauss is unsparingly critical of editors and scholars who take liberties with a text." My guess is that Drury wrote this down, rushed through the rest
of the appendix—she often strikes me as a scholar in a hurry—and assumed that
Gourevitch was about to provide an indignant three-page list of passages where
Strauss had taken undue "liberties" with *Xenophon's* text. It is Drury's works,
not Strauss's, that summon the reader to compose errors lists.

Yolton versus Strauss on Locke and Hobbes

Drury's appeal to the condemnation of Strauss—"innumerable examples of
careless scholarship and a tendency to quote out of context"—that Yolton issued in his 1958 *Philosophical Review* article has special relevance for two
reasons. First, Drury places this article among the "most devastating critiques of
Strauss's methods of interpretation" (*PILS* 251).[17] Second, her book's acknowledgments commence with her stating that she is "first and foremost" indebted
to Yolton, "who has been a constant source of encouragement and inspiration"
(*PILS* xv).[18] An examination of the cited article by Yolton supports this assessment. In critiquing Strauss's subchapter on Locke in *Natural Right and History*, Yolton deploys a level of hyperbole that sometimes approaches Drury's:
Strauss's interpretation of the law of nature is "violently distorted"; his reading
fails because of its "obvious incorrectness"; it is "startling to discover the flimsi-
ness of the pretended support and the unscholarly nature of Strauss's analysis"
(478); concerning roughly the first half of Strauss's discussion, in "many cases,
the references are quite irrelevant to the point Strauss has been arguing," and in
"all cases, Locke is quoted out of context, the context being ignored or carefully
covered up" (483n10); Yolton later complains of Strauss's "perversity" (490).[19]
Unlike Drury, Yolton avoids misquoting Strauss, and most of his criticisms connect directly with specific passages.

   Yolton's criticisms address important matters and I think they deserve a
response, despite their excesses. Strauss's Locke subchapter in *NRH*, clearly,
presents a radical thesis and addresses, in a highly compressed fashion, works
by Locke that fill more than a thousand pages. Strauss here does *not* provide the
methodical, detailed, and lengthy analysis he elsewhere offers of Plato, Xenophon, Thucydides, Aristophanes, Lucretius, Maimonides, Machiavelli, Spinoza,
or Hobbes. Although there are obvious mistakes in Yolton, he launched a serious debate on several key points, for example, the degree to which one should
associate Locke's state of nature with "the first ages," "the beginning," penury,
or war; Strauss at times applies to the "state of nature" traits (e.g., penury) that
Locke attributes, sometimes implicitly, to nature generally.

Even if Yolton offers legitimate criticisms of Strauss's attempt to summarize Locke's massive corpus in forty-nine pages, however, there is no excuse for the errors in Yolton's twenty-one-page critique of Strauss.[20] While attempting to refute selected portions of Yolton's critique, I shall also attempt to demonstrate some of the "clarity and rigor" (*PILS* 10) that Drury is unable to discern in Strauss's endeavors as a scholar.

Yolton spends roughly two pages responding vociferously to Strauss's effort to equate Locke's state of nature with Hobbes's,[21] especially Strauss's claim that for Locke too "the state antedating civil society is the state of war" (*NRH* 225). Clearly, Strauss's thesis here clashes with a wide variety of passages in which Locke depicts the state of nature in anti-Hobbesean terms. Yolton provides an unobjectionable overview of the anti-Hobbesean Locke. Along the way, however, he has trouble providing adequate documentation of Strauss's view; since Yolton earlier denounced Strauss's footnoting practices in the harshest of terms, he has earned the right to have his own documentation assessed. And the passages Strauss cites, when scrutinized, actually provide additional manifestations of a Hobbesean ethos in Locke. To the extent that Locke agrees with Hobbes that nature "dissociates" human beings by planting them in an amoral "war of all against all," of course, one might come to question Locke's commitment to liberty, piety, and human rights.

After providing a footnote (*NRH* 225n86) full of citations to document his claim that "the state antedating civil society is the state of war," Strauss continues his paragraph by offering the following elaboration:

> This is either the cause or the effect of the fact that the state of nature is a state not of plenty but of penury. Those living in it are "needy and wretched." Plenty requires civil society. (*NRH* 225)

In assessing these statements, Yolton criticizes *NRH* 225n87, which cites seven paragraphs from the *Second Treatise* (32, 37, 38, 41–43, 49):

> Strauss also claims that Locke's state of nature was a condition of penury. But his reference to T II, 32 (the chapter on property) speaks of a period of plenty. T II, 37–38 also talk of plenty, not of penury.[22]

Yolton's complaint in the second sentence is both lazily worded and wrong. If we look ahead to Yolton's statement about what paragraphs 37–38 "talk of," his objection must be this: Strauss's thesis loses support because *Locke* in §32 (not "Strauss's reference" to this paragraph) "speaks of" plenty (rather than penury). Yolton is wrong because Locke in §32 mentions "penury," not "plenty"; the penury of the human condition is what compels us to labor.

Locke does mention "plenty" in §37, but his theme remains the natural penury that only human *labor* can remedy. In the paragraph's first reference to plenty, Locke argues that in "the beginning," one could appropriate all one could use without diminishing "the plenty"—the abundance of "the things of nature"—which was left to others. When the paragraph refers for the second time to "plenty," however, it does so in developing the *contempt* for nature's spontaneous gifts that infuses the rest of the chapter: he who "encloses" and cultivates ten acres of land will produce a "greater *plenty* of the conveniences of life" (emph. added) than would be produced by "a hundred left to nature." Locke proceeds to suggest that the ratio is closer to a hundred to one, contrasting what a thousand acres "left to nature" in "the wild woods and uncultivated waste of America" provide for "the needy and wretched inhabitants" with what ten acres of equally fertile land in Devonshire provide (*ST* 37). The initial "plenty" in §37 thus evokes a "needy and wretched" life of penury, for example, a diet of acorns and water as opposed to bread and wine (42); the second "plenty" evokes the prosperity that, in Locke's account, results from proto-capitalistic values and institutions (private property, money, greed, exchange, the division of labor, etc.). Yolton also errs in saying that §38 speaks of plenty (the word is never mentioned). On Yolton's behalf, we should note that the paragraph does address the historical process whereby possessions increased as "families increased and industry enlarged their stocks." Even here, however, Locke defends private "possession" of land (not just the enclosure discussed in §37), and explains how the *scarcity* of land that accompanies the aforementioned increase of families and herds impels the fixing of ownership via cities, domestic laws, and territorial borders.[23] Locke's invocation of cities, laws, and borders reinforces the association of "plenty" with civil society rather than the state of nature.

Strauss proceeds on *NRH* 225 to assert that society and civil society are "synonymous terms," and Yolton—although conceding that Locke sometimes says "society" when he means civil society (e.g., at *ST* 131)—again lashes out: "Strauss is confused about these terminological distinctions."[24] Strauss actually prepares this claim quite carefully; and despite Yolton's general complaints about footnoting, the footnote on *NRH* 225 makes it very easy for the reader to track down the relevant passages. Strauss's first paragraph on *NRH* 224 highlights the obviously anti-Hobbesean passages in which the law of nature is "effective" in the state of nature and the latter is peaceful;[25] Strauss also quotes the anti-Hobbesean formulation, "God has given us all things richly," from the Pauline letter that Locke quotes in *ST* 31. In his next paragraph (*NRH* 224), Strauss quotes from the later paragraph in which Locke describes men without a government as comprising "one society" ruled by the law of nature (*ST* 128).[26] Strauss is obviously aware that the society Locke mentions here is *not* "civil" or political society in which people are "united into one body and have a common established law and judicature to appeal to, with authority to decide controversies between them and punish offenders" (*ST* 87).[27] Even Drury and Yolton, furthermore, might concede that Locke was self-consciously exaggerating when he added that "were it not for the corruption and viciousness of degenerate men, there would be no . . . necessity that men should separate from this great and natural community and by positive agreements combine into smaller and divided associations" (*ST* 128).[28]

Such exaggerations are the focus of Strauss's next paragraph: "After having drawn or suggested this picture of the state of nature especially in the first pages of the *Treatise*, Locke demolishes it as his argument proceeds" (*NRH* 224). After quoting and citing numerous passages, and offering the above-discussed claim that "[p]lenty requires civil society," Strauss says the following:

> Being "pure anarchy," the state of nature is not likely to be a social state. In fact, it is characterized by "want of society." "Society" and "civil society" are synonymous terms. The state of nature is "loose." For "the first and strongest desire God planted in man" is not the concern with others, not even concern with one's offspring, but the desire for self-preservation. (*NRH* 225)

It is the third sentence that most offends Yolton. Yet Strauss's footnote (225n88) specifies passages that document *all* of the claims Strauss makes in the above-quoted extract. Regarding the identification of society with civil/political society, Strauss cites the following passages, for which I shall specify the relevant language from Locke (the emphases are added): to avoid the state of war, men leave the state of nature "by putting themselves into *society*" (21); because the state of nature is "an ill condition," human beings are "quickly driven into *society*" (127); every one enters "society" the "better to preserve himself, his liberty and property" (131); and when individuals first unite into "society," the whole power of the community is "naturally" vested in the majority (132). These are only some of the pertinent passages Strauss cites.[29]

Although Yolton claims that the state of nature "pertains to many complex political units organized on principles other than those of Locke's civil polity,"[30] the only type of society that the *Treatise* clearly distinguishes from civil/political society is the family.[31] Before Strauss asserts the equivalency of "society" and "civil society," he carefully assesses what Locke calls "[t]he first society" (*ST* 77): the "conjugal society" created by "a voluntary compact between man and woman" (78); the relationships that comprise the family (male/female, parent/child, master/servant) indeed "came short of political society" (77). It is hard to dispute Strauss's interpretation that according to Lockean "natural law, conjugal society is not necessary for life"; its procreative and educative ends merely require that "the male and female in mankind are tied to a longer conjunction than other creatures."[32] The primal human "society," which often but not always emerges via a lifelong bond, is thus the fruit of human convention, not nature;[33] yet Yolton confidently proclaims that, for Locke, "Man is by nature social."[34]

Although Locke initially identifies "man and wife" as the participants in "[t]he first society" (*ST* 77), he shifts to the "[c]onjugal society" of "man and woman" (78) before providing a flurry of biology-infused references to the "conjunction" between "male and female" among humans, "beasts of prey," and "viviparous animals which feed on grass" (79, 80). When Locke here traces the relatively long bond among *human* mates to "the wisdom of the great Creator," he emphasizes that human "industry" is thereby encouraged (80).

As early as the chapter on the state of war, moreover, Locke often uses the term "society" as the equivalent of what he will later describe as civil or political society. He opposes "the state of nature" to "commonwealth" or "the state of society" (*ST* 17); he argues that a state of war can emerge even against an aggressor who is "in society" and "a fellow subject" (19); he highlights the relatively speedy termination of the "state of war" once actual violence has ceased among individuals who are "in society" (in the state of nature, war is likely to continue much longer) [20]; and he infers that avoiding the state of war is "one great reason" that people leave the state of nature by putting themselves "into society" (21). The next chapter ("Of Slavery"), furthermore, begins by opposing the "natural liberty" we enjoy in the state of nature with the liberty of "man in society" (i.e., being subject to "no other legislative power but that established by consent in the commonwealth") [22].[35] In both of the *Treatises*, finally, Locke uses "society" as synonymous with "civil society" vastly more times than he specifies a society that *cannot* be described as a civil society.[36]

Yolton is correct in denying that Locke ever said that "plenty requires civil society."[37] These words of Strauss, however, are a summary statement; unlike Drury, Strauss does not routinely abuse quotation marks. As we have seen, however, in many passages Locke does link nature with penury, equate society with civil society, and paint society as a remedy for war.[38] In chapter V, furthermore—just a few pages after he had presented his basic framework involving the state of nature, the state of war, and the different terms he uses to describe the community (society, commonwealth, "civil government," "body politic") people form when they leave the state of nature—Locke disparages nature in additional ways that conjure up the penurious and precarious plight of human beings in Hobbes's state of nature.

In chapter V, Locke repeatedly couples the words "nature" and "state" to designate the condition of material things (e.g., "fruits," venison, acorns, apples, grass, ore, and fish) that nature produces without human intervention. For example, he speaks of such things being in their "natural state" (26), "the state that nature has provided" (27), "the state nature leaves it in" (28), "the state of nature wherein she [the hunted hare] was common" (30), and "the state nature had put it in" (46). Locke's initial state of nature, likewise, is a condition into which nature has placed human beings, and humanly created "compacts" are required to lodge us in societies (especially political/civil and conjugal society). Only after chapter V does Locke do full justice to the disadvantages of the state of nature compared to civil society, and he prepares that shift in chapter V with his widely discussed economic disparagements of nature, "the common mother of all" (28). Nature even falls short regarding basic material needs: the king of a "large and fruitful territory" in America "feeds, lodges, and is clad" worse than the English day laborer (41), and "in the beginning all the world was America" (49). Labor is necessary because of the "penury" of the human "condition" (32); Locke repeatedly describes uncultivated land as "waste" (37, 42, 43, 45); the diet nature serves up for immediate consumption is acorns and water (42); despite the land, the plants, and the innumerable raw materials that contribute to the production of a loaf of bread, "nature and the earth" have furnished "only the almost worthless materials" (43); human labor contributes ten, a hundred, or perhaps even a thousand times the amount of "value" or human "benefit" that nature does (37, 40, 43). The Machiavellian and Hobbesean strands in chapter V—which also include the disappearance of God and the Bible after §39—can thus sensitize reader to the echoes of "those justly decried names" in the political doctrines that the *ST* subsequently conveys.[39]

The presence of a king, of course, suggests that the Indians were living in some type of civil society. On the other hand, one might want to refine Strauss's equation of society and civil society in order to incorporate Locke's claim that absolute monarchy is simply "inconsistent with civil society"; because there is no authority to which subjects may appeal concerning an injury or "controversy," the absolute monarch is in a state of nature "in respect of those who are under his dominion" (*ST* 90).[40] Locke proceeds to describe this condition as an "unrestrained state of nature": when the subject's property is invaded by the monarch, the subject lacks even the "liberty to judge of or to defend his right" (91). Yolton is wise to cite this passage, but he distorts Locke by saying that "even very complex political units, such as monarchy, are in a state of nature."[41] Locke only criticizes *absolute* monarchy in these terms. Although Locke suggests that civil society does not emerge until legislative authority is "placed in collective bodies of men"—and that no one "can be exempted from the laws of it" (*ST* 94)—his chapter on the forms of government allows individuals to vest legislative authority in a monarch.[42] The limited authority of Native American kings/chiefs, in any case, distances them from the "unrestrained state of nature" (91) of the absolute monarch; although they "command absolutely in war," when they are "at home and in time of peace they exercise very little dominion" and the decision to wage war ordinarily lodges in "the people or in a council" (108).[43] Locke stresses, finally, that the paternal monarchies that prevailed in "the beginning of things" were defined by a "simple, poor way of living" (107). They were thus characterized by the penury Strauss associates with the state of nature.[44]

A Declaration of Incompetence: Will Hutton and
Joe Klein Join the Anti-Strauss Campaign

When it comes to interpreting Strauss and Locke's *Second Treatise*, Yolton represents a paragon of integrity and skill compared to Will Hutton, the distinguished English author and political economist who has entered the ranks of the Straussophobes. Hutton comes with exemplary credentials: for example, he has written over ten books, he is a governor of the London School of Economics, he serves on the governing council of the Policy Studies Institute, and for four years he was the editor in chief of the *Observer* and director of the *Guardian National Newspapers*. In his nonfiction best-seller, *A Declaration of Interdependence: Why America Should Join the World*, alas, Hutton comically attributes the capitalist celebration of "the emancipation of acquisitiveness" to Strauss himself, oblivious to the fact that in the relevant paragraph on *NRH* 242–43—as in the immediately surrounding paragraphs—Strauss is expounding the views of *Locke*.[45] Anyone, friend or foe, who has seriously studied Strauss knows how far he was from thinking that "unlimited appropriation without concern for the needs of others is true charity";[46] Strauss even highlights *Locke*'s reservations or equivocations about acquisitiveness.[47] Strauss elsewhere characterizes Lockean acquisitiveness as a "degradation of man" (*WIPP* 50) that accelerated the Machiavellian endeavor to find "an immoral or amoral substitute for morality" (*WIPP* 49).[48] Even when Strauss lambastes communism or the Soviet Union, he places little if any emphasis on private property, free markets, or economic growth.[49]

Hutton, however, wants to condemn Strauss and other "conservative successors" for abandoning both Locke's concern that "too much acquisitiveness might lead to hoarding and avarice" and Locke's specification of limits to initial appropriation. Hutton even struggles to convey an accurate account of Locke. He attempts to quote from the *Second Treatise* to show that, for Locke, the right of appropriation was subject to there being "enough and as good left in common—(of what God had given to the Earth to the Children of Men in common) for others."[50] To produce this gibberish, Hutton patched together passages from *two* different paragraphs in Locke's book (25 and 27) and badly misquoted one of them (25). Hutton does not even provide a citation.[51] Hutton elsewhere cites Drury's *LSAR* to explain Strauss's "core idea"—"the most influential of our times"—in these terms: that "just states must be run by moral, religious, patriotic individuals and that income redistribution, multilateralism and any restraint on individual liberty are mortal enemies of the development of such just elites."[52] Hutton in his book displays additional ignorance by describing John Ashcroft as a "convinced" and "committed" Straussian (62, 75)—I'll bet even Drury would bristle here—and by stating that "almost every strand in current American conservative thought . . . can trace its lineage back to him." When someone as learned as Hutton feels entitled to unmask Strauss's "lethal legacy"

(75) while knowing so little about Strauss and his students, we are entitled to invoke Straussophobia.[53] Joe Klein, the renowned author and columnist (*Time*), may have been infected by Hutton during their European travels in June, 2002. Although Klein offers some serious complaints about *The World We're In*—the earlier, English version of *A Declaration of Interdependence*—Klein *credits* the book for what it does to "criticize the antisocial myopia of conservative thinkers such as Leo Strauss, who have had an influence on some of the more extreme sorts lurking in the shadows of the Bush administration."[54]

Yolton versus Strauss on Christianity and Circumlocutions

Let us now focus our attention on a Yolton-Strauss clash that reverberates loudly for Drury's general denunciations, especially given her tendency to dismiss Strauss's efforts at uncovering esoteric/hidden teachings, her condemnation of his doubts about the degree to which rationality can make everyone "perfect in ethics" (Locke's phrase), and her presumptuous invocation of the Bible's claim that the truth will set you free.

Yolton quickly runs into trouble when he addresses *The Reasonableness of Christianity: As Delivered in the Scriptures* (hereafter, *RC*) to show the "lengths to which Strauss will go in making Locke say what Strauss wants him to say" in *NRH* 207–9.[55] Regarding the question of whether Locke might write esoterically, Strauss concludes that in Locke's view "cautious speech is legitimate if unqualified frankness would hinder a noble work one is trying to achieve or expose one to persecution or endanger the public peace." After quoting these words, Yolton protests Strauss's attempt to document them with passages from *RC* that elaborate the way Jesus delayed revealing his identity as the Messiah. For Yolton, the matter appears to be trivial: "Locke's point is that Christ did not come right out and say 'I am the Messiah' simply because he knew he had to fulfill his mission of preaching the Gospel." Contra Strauss, Locke "in no way generalizes from this very special situation to a theory of the art of writing under persecution."[56]

We must first note that Strauss thoroughly incorporates what Yolton regards as "Locke's point." In the portion of his paragraph that immediately precedes the above-quoted generalization about "cautious speech," Strauss quotes Locke's claims that premature revelation would have prevented Jesus from going through with "the work which he came to do," for example, because the Roman authorities would have "hindered the work he was about" (*NRH* 208).[57]

The major flaw in Yolton's critique, however, is the way he distorts the context (recall how Drury highlights Yolton's complaint that Strauss pervasively quotes Locke "out of context"). First, Yolton ignores what Strauss said, *within the same paragraph,* to establish or at least prepare the generalization concerning "cautious speech." Strauss begins with Locke's remarks about ancient philosophers who concealed their monotheistic views. Locke alludes to the price Socrates paid for having "opposed and laughed at their polytheism." Plato and "the soberest of the philosophers" thus proceeded differently; whatever they "thought of the nature and being of the one God, they were fain, in their outward professions and worship, to go with the herd, and keep to their religion established by law" (*NRH* 208, quoting *RC* 238). After quoting these passages, Strauss offers the following, eminently reasonable, inference: "It does not appear that Locke regarded the conduct of the ancient philosophers as reprehensible." Strauss then suggests that this conduct "might be thought to be incompatible with biblical morality." Strauss asserts bluntly that Locke "did not think so." To back up *this* judgment, Strauss quotes extensively from what *RC* says to explain the caution, "prudent carriage and reservedness" (*RC* 108), and other forms of self-concealment that *Jesus* employed (e.g., Jesus "so involved his sense, that it was not easy to understand him" [*RC* 115]). In addition to passages that illustrate Yolton's sketch of the purpose of such concealment—to enable Jesus "to fulfill his mission of preaching the Gospel"—Strauss also quotes what Locke said about the "manifest danger of tumult and sedition," and so on (*NRH* 208, *RC* 74).

Strauss's extensive discussion of Locke's elaboration of Jesus's caution thus does justice to the "special situation" Yolton emphasizes. Contra Yolton, Strauss does not allege that Locke "generalizes from this very special situation to a *theory* of the art of writing under persecution" (emph. added). In connection with Jesus, indeed, Strauss further generalizes by incorporating what *Locke* said about the danger of sedition (for Yolton, it seems, Jesus only concealed to prevent direct threats to "his mission of preaching the Gospel"). Strauss's larger generalization, moreover, starts with the portion of the paragraph that Yolton simply ignores, where Strauss states that Locke did not condemn ancient philosophers who concealed their religious unorthodoxy. Strauss invokes the accommodations Jesus made to show that Locke would not condemn, on *biblical* grounds, the accommodations the ancient philosophers made. Let us consult the concluding sentence of Strauss's paragraph in its entirety:

> We see, then, that, according to Locke, cautious speech is legitimate if unqualified frankness would hinder a noble work one is trying to achieve or expose one to persecution or endanger the public peace; and legitimate caution is perfectly compatible with going with the herd in one's outward professions or with using ambiguous language or with so involving one's sense that one cannot easily be understood.[58] (*NRH* 208–9)

In the portion that Yolton quotes, there are three goals that can legitimate cautious speech: promoting a "noble work," avoiding persecution, and endangering "the public peace." It seems obvious, however, that each of these three goals is compatible with everything Locke says in the *Second Treatise* to specify the law of nature, particularly its concern for "the peace and preservation of mankind."

It likewise seems that each goal is potentially relevant to Jesus as well as to the ancient philosophers. In the conclusion of the sentence, which Yolton does not quote, the first action (going with "the herd") strongly evokes what Strauss had quoted from Locke about the ancient philosophers, while the third ("involving one's sense") strongly evokes what Strauss had quoted from Locke about Jesus; the second ("ambiguous language") less strongly evokes what Strauss had quoted from Locke about Jesus. Regarding ambiguous language, Strauss quotes Locke's claim that Jesus used "obscure and doubtful" words (*RC* 105). Although Locke in *RC* did not use the word "ambiguous," he offered numerous equivalents beyond "obscure and doubtful": "circumlocutions" (59), "mystical and parabolical" (120), "prophetical or parabolical" (136), "a mystical and involved way of speaking" (156).

The huge amount of space that Locke devotes to Jesus's evasions itself casts doubt on Yolton's claim that Locke "in no way generalizes from this very special situation."[59] Insofar as Jesus could deploy miracles to promote *his* "noble work," moreover, one might infer that he needed to employ "cautious speech" even less than the all-too-human philosophers did. Locke addresses this angle when he points out that, if miracles were overused, they would "lose their name and force" (*RC* 143).[60]

In passages that Strauss does not quote, Locke elaborates the situation of Socrates in a way that further strengthens Strauss's case that Locke sympathized with esotericism. Locke observes that there was only one Socrates among the Athenians, even though "[t]here was no part of mankind who had quicker parts or improved them more, that had a greater light of reason or followed it farther in all sorts of speculation" (*RC* 238). In the ancient world, we may infer, even the most intellectually advanced society could not tolerate a great philosopher who impugned its polytheism. If reason, "speaking ever so clearly to the wise and virtuous, had never authority enough to prevail on the multitude" (238), philosophers might be *compelled* to "go with the herd," at least to a degree.

There are thus many reasons to reject Yolton's attempt to belittle Strauss by presenting the rhetorical situation of Jesus as an idiosyncratic case. Yolton's argument further weakens—in a way that also counteracts Drury's efforts to present Strauss as a uniquely menacing teacher of deceit—because Locke in *RC* (especially at the end) puts so much emphasis on the insurmountable obstacles that philosophy confronts in trying to spread moral enlightenment. In addition to the above-quoted material from *RC* 238, consider the following passage from which Strauss quotes at different places in his chapter:

> Philosophy seemed to have spent its strength and done its utmost, or if it should have gone farther, as we see it did not, and from undeniable principles given us ethics in a science like mathematics, in every part demonstrable—this yet would not have been so effectual to man in this imperfect state, nor proper for the cure. The greatest part of mankind want leisure or capacity for demonstration, nor can carry a train

of proofs. . . . And you may as soon hope to have all the day laborers and trades-
men, the spinsters and dairymaids, perfect mathematicians, as to have them perfect
in ethics this way. Hearing plain commands is the sure and only course to bring
them to obedience and practice. The greatest part cannot *know*, and therefore they
must *believe*. . . . And were all the duties of human life clearly demonstrated, yet
I conclude, when well considered, that method of teaching men their duties would
be thought proper only for a few, who had much leisure, improved understandings,
and were used to abstract reasonings. But the instruction of the people were best still
to be left to the precepts and principles of the gospel. The healing of the sick, the
restoring sight to the blind by a word, the raising and being raised from the dead,
are matters of fact, which they can without difficulty conceive, and that he who does
such things, must do them by the assistance of a divine power.[61] (*RC* 243)

To anyone without firm Christian faith—and perhaps even to many Christians
who cannot accept the *RC* in its entirety—Locke's book provides abundant
reasons that one could employ to justify the use of noble lies on behalf of moral
causes. And any philosopher who doubted the miracles, or doubted that the New
Testament provides a perfect and complete articulation of natural law, could still
be persuaded of the need for cautious speech.

III. "THE MOST FEARFUL DEPTHS OF DEPRAVITY"

One might wonder what an author who launches her books on Strauss with insult
(Strauss's interpretations are basically "rubbish"), hyperexaggeration ("the largest academic movement in the twentieth century"), and distortion (the garbled
quote from Gordon Wood) will come up with for conclusions. Drury rises to the
occasion. Her first book ends with a bang, not a whimper:

> His idea of philosophy as *eros* is a splendid excuse for being one of the Hugh
> Hefners of the philosophical set. The transition from "shameless" or "intoxicated"
> thoughts to shameless deeds is almost natural. It is an understatement to say that
> Strauss's conception of nobility lends itself to vulgarization. It is impossible for
> men who harbor Strauss's contempt for morality not to fall into the most fearful
> depths of depravity. This is most unfortunate, for it serves to undermine Strauss's
> contribution to political philosophy. (*PILS* 202)

The concluding mention of a contribution hardly compensates for the initial
ferocity. How, moreover, would Drury distinguish the view of *eros*, shame-
less thoughts, nobility, and morality that she here demonizes from the "comprehensive view" that she earlier invoked to explain what in Strauss could be
"fascinating, captivating and even bewitching" despite the "arid, insipid, tedious
and repetitive" character of his scholarship (*PILS* 4–5)? If by "contribution to
political philosophy" Drury means a neo-Nietzschean pitch for lying, militarism,

and tyranny, both she and I would want to see that "contribution" *rejected*. As we shall continue to explore, Drury consistently disparages the core of Strauss's scholarship—his interpretations of the history of political philosophy—and of late she has been even more dismissive.

The accusation about Hefnerism seems to be original, and is perhaps unintentionally funny in light of the oft-ridiculed stodginess of Straussians. Thoroughly repulsive, however, is Drury's inquisitorial posture. In the second sentence, as elsewhere, Drury is willing to condemn Strauss for things she *thinks* that he *thought*, apart from things that he wrote or did. Consider likewise her claim in the penultimate sentence about "Strauss's contempt for morality." Whatever Strauss really thought about morality, I hasten to point out, he obviously had to "harbor" his own views. One therefore cannot escape the inference that, according to Drury, *Strauss* fell into the deepest depravity. To back up such an accusation, one needs to cite heinous deeds. One should at least cite unambiguously heinous words (e.g., those of Hutu leaders who used the radio to provoke extermination of Tutsis).[62]

Although Anastaplo once proclaimed in public that Strauss was "obviously the most law-abiding . . . of men," he does not shrink from relaying Strauss's dark side: Strauss's "manner was gentle and courteous, yet sometimes so firmly efficient as to border on a callous selfishness"; through much of his life he was "a physically timid man, perhaps unduly so"; the wife of a former student accused him of being "both over-anxious and indifferent to the conditions of the material world"; and he confessed to Anastaplo that he had sometimes displayed "contempt" for certain colleagues and administrators at Chicago.[63] According to another admiring student, Werner Dannhauser, Strauss "could be tight with money," he sometimes feared imaginary dangers, he was not free of malice, and "one suspects that under the threat of economic privation he occasionally succumbed to opportunism."[64] On the other hand, Strauss abstained from assault, embezzlement, adultery, and substance abuse; he married once, he never divorced, and he even adopted his orphaned four-year-old niece who is now a classics professor (at the University of Virginia) eager to defend her father's legacy.[65] Given the massive atrocities committed by twentieth-century intellectuals such as Stalin, Khieu Samphan, Radovan Karadzic, and Nikola Koljevic, I would hesitate to accuse even Michel Foucault, Timothy Leary, Norman Mailer, Alfred Kinsey, or Herbert Aptheker of depravity.

IV. STRAUSS'S XENOPHONIC DISCOURSE: HARMING, TYRANNY, SLAVISHNESS, REVOLUTION?

As we have seen, Drury both opens and closes *PILS* with alarmist and poorly grounded statements about Strauss's influence and character. In the body of the book, perhaps her largest departures from scholarly rigor come when she addresses Strauss's interpretations of Xenophon. Three of her denunciations are particularly inflammatory: that Straussian philosophers are easily impelled to hurt their fellow creatures, that Strauss embraces tyranny, and that he "casts a shadow on the noble life." Because all three examples concern Xenophon, they have special significance for the shortcut Drury uses—attributing to Strauss whatever he attributes to the wise ancients—in attempting to unmask Strauss's sinister agenda. Strauss indeed published more about Xenophon than about any other ancient author.

To facilitate comparisons with Drury, I shall mostly be citing the Agora edition of *On Tyranny*, which is still in wide circulation. When quoting Kojève's portion of that text, however, I'll cite the much-improved Gourevitch and Roth translation from 1991 (Drury in *PILS* never cites specific pages of Kojève's essay, in any case). I'll also cite the Gourevitch and Roth version of the *Hiero* (using section numbers, so that the reader can consult any edition), in which the original translation by Kendrick was revised by Seth Benardete. My attention shall reside mostly on the original Strauss manuscript, whose pagination is very similar to the 1991 edition.[66]

"Motivated to Harm"

After reminding the reader of her alarm concerning Strauss's elevation of philosophy at the expense of moral virtue, Drury paraphrases Strauss's comforting claim (articulated in various texts) that "the philosopher, unlike the city, has no reason for harming anyone, for he has little regard for the things that other men hotly contest."[67] To dismiss this claim, Drury offers the following observations about the exchange between Strauss and Kojève in *OT*:

> But as Alexandre Kojève has shown, in Strauss's own account the philosopher seeks not simply the pleasure of contemplation, but immortality. He wishes to be admired by a "competent minority," which means that in spite of what Strauss says, the philosopher too seeks honor and glory. Since this is the case, he will be motivated to harm those who would stand in his way, and his "wisdom" is ill-equipped to provide him with reasons for self-restraint. (*PILS* 198)

After the second sentence Drury provides a footnote that cites the entirety of Kojève's forty-five-page essay ("Tyranny and Wisdom") about Strauss's original 1948 essay/book on Xenophon's *Hiero*. By invoking what Kojève has "shown" about the issue, she implies that Kojève has provided some kind of demonstration or proof; she does not simply invoke what Kojève had argued or alleged. Her formulation, however, fails even to provide an accurate statement of Kojève's thesis. It turns out that nowhere in Kojève's long essay—nor in Kojève's Hegel book, which Strauss discusses in the "Restatement"—does he say that the philosopher seeks either immortality or glory (which is not identical to honor). According to Kojève, Simonides (the speaker in the *Hiero* who touts honor) represents the aristocratic or pagan outlook that Hegel attributes to the "Master"; from this perspective, honor and glory are the defining goals ("specifically and necessarily" characteristic) "only of *born* Masters" (*OT* 140), especially tyrants.[68]

Kojève does argue, against Strauss, that the philosopher is driven to seek *widespread* recognition and/or admiration.[69] But Kojève also offers statements that shatter the inference *Drury* wishes to draw (that the philosopher, in Strauss's view, has a desire for honor and glory that undermines "self-restraint" and motivates harming). The most telling consideration is this: Kojève argues that Strauss (along with Strauss's Xenophon) *rejects* Simonides' exaltation of honor. According to Strauss, says Kojève, Xenophon prefers Socrates—who is "not in the least interested" in receiving recognition, admiration, or praise from other people—to Simonides, and "one has the impression that Strauss agrees with this 'Socratic' attitude" (*OT* 158).[70] Even if she defers completely to Kojève's essay, therefore, Drury is not entitled to deduce from it that "the pleasure of contemplation" is inadequate, that tangible injuries are likely to issue from philosophers seeking immortality, glory, and honor.

Turning to Strauss, one can easily find passages that amplify Kojève's point about Simonides and Socrates. It seems that Socrates is "not at all concerned with being admired or praised by others, whereas Simonides is concerned exclusively with it" (*OT* 105), and Socrates is "*the* representative of wisdom."[71] By seeking "admiration or praise" only from "those who are free in the highest degree" (*OT* 91), indeed, Simonides himself would presumably be less "motivated to harm" (*PILS* 198) when seeking honor.[72] Strauss also suggests that, among the "natural" desires—desires "which 'grow' in human beings independently of any education or teaching"—Simonides exalts honor "because it is the foundation of the desire for any excellence, be it the excellence of the ruler or that of the wise man" (*OT* 90).[73] In the "Restatement," finally, Strauss states that Simonides is "very far from accepting the morality of Masters or from maintaining that honor is the supreme goal of the highest human type"; neither Xenophon nor his Simonides "believe[s] that honor is the highest good" (203).[74] Strauss argues more broadly that "the philosopher as such is free from ambition or from the desire for recognition"; if "the weakness of the flesh" inflames such ambition, one becomes (in "the strict view of the classics") a *sophist* (218).[75]

When Strauss speaks elsewhere about philosophers seeking long-lasting recognition, his focus is on the *writings* they composed—for distant audiences. Because ancient philosophers lived when impiety was a crime, in order to share their views with a majority of the "small number of people who were able and willing to accept these views," they wrote books, which could be read by people "not yet born."[76] The works of "men like the mature Spinoza, which are meant as possessions for all times, are primarily addressed to posterity" (*PAW* 160); Rousseau too "wished to live as a writer beyond his time" (*NRH* 259) and (at least in his *First Discourse*) "wrote for posterity rather than for his own time."[77] To use Drury's language, who exactly "would stand in his way," and how would such a philosopher be "motivated to harm" (*PILS* 198)?

An additional difficulty for Drury's use of *On Tyranny* to impugn philosophers is posed by the threefold "anthropology of human types" she repeatedly attributes to Strauss: the philosophers who "seek wisdom for its own sake," the gentlemen/citizens who are "lovers of honor," and the "ordinary men" who seek security and pleasure. Drury likewise places the few "super-citizens" who seek "greatness and worldly immortality" within the gentleman class (*PILS* 129); in the more detailed threefold scheme she sketches in her widely cited 2003 interview with Danny Postel, Drury simply identifies the gentlemen as "lovers of honour and glory." Both of these typologies undermine her warning that the quest for "honor and glory" will weaken the "self-restraint" of *philosophers* and incline them to inflict injuries (*PILS* 198). Neither of the two typologies, furthermore, coheres with the complex array of human types that Strauss unearths in the *Hiero*: philosophers, sophists, tyrants, gentlemen, "real men," and the vulgar.[78]

"The Innumerable Crimes"

Drury's inflammatory treatment of Strauss and Kojève near the end of *PILS* is prepared by her inflammatory treatment of Strauss and Xenophon in the middle of the book.

Let us start with a dramatic, and manipulative, sentence: "In Strauss's words, 'tyrannical government can live up to the highest political standards'" (*PILS* 96). How many of Drury's readers have realized that Strauss, in this passage quoted from *On Tyranny* (70), is summarizing what he regards as *Xenophon's* view? The quoted sentence concludes a dense paragraph from Drury that begins more carefully: "According to Strauss, Xenophon's message is this." This paragraph—which I shall henceforth label her "tyrannical paragraph"—never again mentions Xenophon. So the concluding invocation of "Strauss's words" would leave most readers with the impression that Strauss is stating his own views rather than his interpretation of Xenophon's. If one looks at the whole sentence from which Drury extracts the most incendiary part, furthermore, one sees that Strauss distances himself even further from the tyrannical teaching with which Drury saddles him: "He [Simonides] thus creates the impression that according to Xenophon tyrannical government can live up to the highest political standards." Strauss is here summarizing an *impression* that the reader would derive about *Xenophon's* views from the words of a *character* in Xenophon.[79] Strauss indicates that Simonides functions within the dialogue as a "wise man"

(*OT* 32, 68, 69, 108), but Strauss also questions his wisdom (37). Xenophon, Socrates, and certainly Strauss, moreover, differ profoundly from Simonides. Consider Simonides' enthusiasm for power, wealth, and food (52, 93), his indifference to "the responsibility of the citizen" (97), and the fact that he "lives as a stranger" (101).[80] Simonides, unlike Socrates, is not a "citizen-philosopher" (79, 108); Drury forgets about Socrates and others when she asserts that, for Strauss, "the philosopher is not a citizen, but a stranger" (*PILS* 198). In the "Restatement," Strauss claims that the philosopher "cannot help being more attached to his family and his city than to strangers" (*OT* 214), and Strauss elsewhere notes that Socrates "led the philosophic life although he was an active member of a political community which he considered very imperfect" (*PAW* 117).[81]

In her tyrannical paragraph, Drury shrewdly emphasizes that Strauss's Xenophon elevates wisdom above "legitimist" or "constitutionalist" (*OT* 76) principles that exalt the role of inheritance or elections. But she nowhere acknowledges that Strauss's Xenophon also regards "tyrannical rule as a radically faulty political order" (60) and "lets it be understood that tyranny even at its best suffers from serious defects" (69). When Strauss begins the key chapter ("The Teaching Concerning Tyranny") by stating that tyranny is "essentially a faulty political order," whose "teaching" involves both "pathology" and "therapeutics" (67), he joins his voice to Xenophon's. Here, as elsewhere, Drury abandons her "intention" to avoid "dismissing what he says repeatedly and in the most obvious places as expressions of salutary myths that have no bearing on his real thought" (*PILS* x).

As Drury elaborates Strauss's account of "Xenophon's message," she offers this citation- and quotation-free assertion: according to Strauss, the wise "do not object . . . to the innumerable crimes" tyrants commit (*PILS* 96). The tyrannical paragraph later cites, but badly misquotes, a passage in which Strauss's Xenophon commends the tyrant who listens to "reasonable men" after having committed "any number of crimes" (*OT* 76–77).[82] Drury, moreover, also fails here to convey the reformist context in which Strauss invokes the crimes.[83] After Hiero caps off his litany of the tyrant's miseries by asserting that he "lives night and day as one condemned by all human beings to die for his injustice" (*Hiero* 7.10), Simonides asks about abdicating (7.11); in replying, Hiero stresses that he could never repay all of the money he had plundered, "suffer in turn the chains" he had imposed on his subjects, or "supply in requital enough lives to die" for those he had killed (7.12).[84] Hiero, Strauss comments, has "thus confessed having committed an untold number of crimes" (*OT* 62) and apparently prefers "heaping new crimes on the untold number of crimes which he has already committed" (58); in trying to edify Hiero, therefore, it would be silly for Simonides to invoke "the noble" (61). In the remainder of the dialogue, Simonides suggests a variety of reforms that would, among other things, enable Hiero to be "loved far more than the private men" (*Hiero* 8.7). For Xenophon, Strauss emphasizes, "a good ruler is necessarily beneficent" (*OT* 76), so Strauss's Xenophon would hardly smile upon a tyrant's "innumerable crimes."[85] We can also infer that, for someone attempting to induce a salutary "conversion" (*OT* 76) in a tyrant, it might be prudent to avoid excessive scolding. Is it unreasonable for Strauss to argue that "[e]ven a perfectly just man who wants to give advice to a tyrant has to present himself to his pupil as an utterly unscrupulous man" (57)?[86]

As previously explained, Drury misleads her readers when she quotes *Strauss* as asserting (on *OT* 70) that "tyrannical government can live up to the highest political standards" (*PILS* 96). And although Strauss attributes this view of tyranny to Xenophon, the preparatory material amplifies the public-spirited concerns I sketched in the preceding paragraph; if Xenophon cares about the welfare of the ruled, we can assume he would "object" to "the innumerable crimes" a tyrant commits, even if he chose not to address them. In the paragraph that precedes the one about the "highest political standards," Strauss clearly indicates that he will be addressing "the broad outlines of Simonides' *criticism* of tyranny *at its best*" (*OT* 69; emphases added), that is, "tyranny as corrected according to Simonides's suggestions" (*OT* 70); Simonides' recommendations conspicuously dominate the final three sections of the *Hiero*. Strauss emphasizes that, even for Simonides, such tyranny, although it remains "absolute" rule insofar as it departs from the rule of law, is "most certainly rule over willing subjects" (70). And as rule over willing subjects, such a regime abandons one of the two criteria that are deployed by Xenophon/Socrates to *define* tyranny.[87] Thus, "tyranny at its best," according to Simonides, would be *kingly* rule without laws.[88] Drury does not mention *any* of the salutary features that Simonides attributes to such tyranny: for example, that the tyrant can be united with his subjects—whom he treats like "comrades or companions," not like small children—by "the bonds of mutual kindness";[89] according to Strauss, indeed, Simonides "makes it clear" that the tyrant's city/subjects "may be very happy" (*OT* 70).[90] Strauss nonetheless provides a sober elaboration of the "serious defects" (69) and other shortcomings of "tyranny at its best" (71–72).[91]

The injustice in Drury's account peaks when she asserts that, for Strauss, "tyranny, or rule in the absence of law, comes closest to the best regime which is absolute tyranny of the wise" (*PILS* 96)—as if Strauss thought that one could find a society superior to Stalin's Russia only in the pages of Plato's *Republic*.[92] I think Drury is propelled to this summit of absurdity mostly by the laziness and haste of her writing, not by paranoia or viciousness; on the next page, she regains her footing when she sketches a "practically best regime" constituted by "the rule under law of 'gentlemen'" who administrate laws framed by "wise legislators" and "freely adopted by citizens" (*PILS* 97). Along the way, however, Drury lobs another bombshell: Strauss "makes it clear that absolute rule without law, if it is wise, is infinitely superior to the rule of law" (96). But who could think that any type of rule is *infinitely* superior to the rule of law? In a society of even modest size and complexity, who could think about trying to rule it by issuing spontaneous decrees about most major decisions?

A few pages after Strauss sketches the beneficent tyranny that might embody "Simonides's suggestions" (*OT* 70), he characterizes the individual who would enact them as "a tyrant who listens to the counsels of the wise" (77). In her tyrannical paragraph, Drury twice invokes the last seven words, slightly misquoting them when she says that for Xenophon and/or Strauss, "[a]ny rule is legitimate only to the extent that it 'listens to the counsel [*sic*] of the wise'" (*PILS* 96). By ignoring the beneficent dimensions of the tyranny that can approach "the highest political standards," Drury's paragraph accentuates both the brutality of the tyrant and the presumption of the wise. More problematically, Drury fails to acknowledge what Strauss says to finish the relevant sentence: Xenophon "seems to have thought that tyranny at its best could hardly, if ever, be realized" (*OT* 77). Strauss thus stresses that nowhere in the entire *Corpus Xenophonteum* does Xenophon make "any reference to beneficent and happy tyrants who actually existed."[93] Strauss proceeds to offer a concrete explanation of the rarity: the tyrant's lack of a "title which is generally considered valid" makes such government "essentially more oppressive and hence less stable than nontyrannical government" (hence the tyrant's need for a bodyguard) (*OT* 77). Strauss concludes his paragraph as follows: "Reasons such as these explain why Xenophon, or his Socrates, preferred, for all practical purposes, at least as far as Greeks were concerned, the rule of laws to tyranny and why they identified, for all practical purposes, the just with the legal" (*OT* 77–78).[94] Strauss even claims that, for Xenophon, "the aim of a good ruler is *much more likely* to be achieved by means of laws" than by absolute rule (*OT* 74; emph. added).

In the "Restatement," Strauss stresses that Cyrus remained "a legitimate ruler" and that Xenophon appreciated "the blessings of legitimacy" (*OT* 195).[95] Strauss also quotes Xenophon's observation that Cyrus's sons "immediately quarreled" after Cyrus died, and observes in his own name that "the good order of society requires stability and continuity" (193); he subsequently invokes the distinction between William III and Cromwell (195).[96] As Strauss puts it in his essay on the *Anabasis*, Cyrus "achieved what he achieved partly by virtue of his descent, his inheritance." Strauss proceeds to suggest that "knowledge of how to rule" needs "some iron alloy, some crude and rough admixture in order to become legitimate, i.e., politically viable" and nontyrannical (*SPPP* 128).

The "Restatement" begins by likening tyranny to cancer, and concludes with Strauss's chilling warning about the "substitution of suspicion and terror for law" (*OT* 226).[97] Contra Drury, it is anything but "clear" that Strauss regarded even wise absolutism as being "infinitely superior" to the rule of law. Could Strauss have thought that the predictability ensured by the rule of law was *less* precious in the gigantic, complex, and hi-tech societies of the twentieth century than it was in Greek cities and empires?[98] As he prudently warns us in restating "the classical

view," what "pretends to be absolute rule of the wise will in fact be absolute rule
of unwise men" (*OT* 206; cf. *NRH* 141). The Zuckerts thus emphasize the clash
between Drury's initial proclamation—"I have no intention of dismissing what
he says repeatedly" (*PILS* x)—and her disregard of Strauss's numerous celebrations of the rule of law.[99] Particularly relevant in *On Tyranny* is the inference
Strauss draws for contemporary politics: "liberal or constitutional democracy
comes closer to what the classics demanded than any alternative that is viable
in our age" (*OT* 207). He elsewhere speaks even more sharply when he depreciates the prospects that the "the liberally educated" can wield political power: the
"grandiose failures" of Marx and Nietzsche, who were both educated on "a level
to which we cannot even hope to aspire," help demonstrate that "wisdom requires
unhesitating loyalty to a decent constitution and even to the cause of constitution-
alism" (*LAM* 24).

Strauss does not mention Orwell's *1984*, which was published the same year
(1948) as the original *On Tyranny*, but it unforgettably conveys how the conquest of nature and "the completely unabashed substitution of suspicion and terror for law" could equip contemporary tyrants with "practically unlimited means
for ferreting out, and for extinguishing, the most modest efforts in the direction
of thought" (*OT* 226).[100] Can any earlier leader even begin to match the evils
that Hitler and Stalin inflicted by virtue of their thoroughly modern tyrannies?
When Strauss wrote *On Tyranny* (and other memorable books) there was a real
possibility that communism would conquer the world by some combination of
bullets and ballots. Strauss in 1941 invoked 2,000 years of experience in arguing that persecution "cannot prevent independent thought" or prevent "even the
expression of independent thinking" to "reasonable friends" (*PAW* 23), but his
language in *On Tyranny* seems more alarmist. In any case, independent thinking would not survive under the conditions of either *Brave New World* or *1984*.
Does it exist today in North Korea?

Even if we decide to blame Strauss for everything we find objectionable
in contemporary neoconservatism, we must still thank him for redeeming
Xenophon. Drury joins the mainstream in dismissing Strauss's merits as an
interpreter, but the research I have undertaken to rebut her attacks has left me
with deep appreciation for the artistry, daring, and subtle humor Strauss has
uncovered in Xenophon. Drury cites Irwin's dismissal of *Xenophon's Socrates*,
and she could have added Vlastos's review of *On Tyranny*. Because Vlastos
clings to the common view that Xenophon's mind was "pedestrian" and that
Simonides was simply his mouthpiece, he proclaims that Strauss's complex
readings "would have astonished the retired colonel who was nothing if not
plain spoken and straightforward."[101] In Drury's words, the *Hiero* is "vintage
Xenophon—which is to say that it is not particularly profound or philosophically
sophisticated" (*AK* 144). Yet Drury accuses Straussians of evading "the weight
of the history of philosophy" (76).[102]

Haze in the Maze: Xenos on Xenophon and Strauss

Nicholas Xenos properly chides Drury for engaging skimpily with the text of *On Tyranny* (*CV* 87–88). Xenos wrestles energetically with both Strauss and Xenophon, and seems to avoid misquoting them. When he attempts to deploy classic esotericism-unmasking strategies to illuminate Strauss's "maze of inferences, references, and references within references" (*CV* 100), furthermore, he illuminates several urgent questions, for example, whether Strauss sometimes exaggerates the practical obstacles to "the tyrannical teaching" (*CV* 113). But in setting out to penetrate the "haze" of references and thereby uncover Strauss's alleged penchant for premodern authoritarianism (*CV* 101), Xenos stumbles early and often. First, Xenos exaggerates when alleging that Strauss has committed an "obvious 'blunder'" in comparing philosophy to gentlemanliness (*CV* 104).[103] Xenos blunders much more seriously when he proceeds to discuss the second *Memorabilia* reference Strauss makes in the key footnote (*OT* 109n27). For Strauss's actual reference (IV.6.7) Xenos substitutes another passage (IV.6.12), which he quotes at length before setting out on a quixotic quest to explain its relationship to Strauss's text (*CV* 104–5). Since the latter (but not the former) discusses tyranny, Xenos can use it to support his thesis that Strauss secreted an authoritarian political agenda between the lines of his post-1930s books (*CV* 70–71, 101). In his chapter's next section, which starts with an epistemological question—"What is it that the philosopher knows?" (*CV* 106)—Xenos reaches the summit of confusion. Xenos begins by correctly quoting Strauss's statement that, for Socrates, "the greatest good is wisdom, whereas education is the greatest good for human beings, and the best possession is a good friend" (*OT* 85). Immediately thereafter, alas, Xenos says that Strauss "refers the reader to a comparison between *Hiero* 4.3 and two passages from the *Memorabilia* in a note following 'human beings'" (*CV* 106); Xenos then quotes from *Hiero* 4.3, and tries to dispel the haze he encounters when comparing the three Xenophon passages to the *OT* 85 quotation about wisdom, education, and friendship. But despite the precision Xenos displays in specifying the location of the footnote in Strauss's text, the actual footnote (*OT* 123n32) incorporates *nothing* about the *Hiero* and fails to cite either *Memorabilia* passage.[104] Xenos has not earned the right to complain that Strauss, with his stream of footnote-housed citations and comparisons, "dogmatically treats all of Xenophon's writings as a single text" (*CV* 100).

"A Shadow on the Noble Life"

As we have seen, Drury flails in invoking *On Tyranny* on behalf of some disturbing allegations, particularly the claim that for Strauss "tyranny, or rule in the absence of law, comes closest to the best regime which is absolute tyranny of the wise" (*PILS* 96). When Drury directs her attention to *Xenophon's Socratic Discourse: An Interpretation of the "Oeconomicus,"* she amplifies an equally vivid accusation that distils Strauss's 500-plus pages of commentary on Xenophon down to a fortune-cookie message: the philosopher is a hedonist who "knows that the life of the citizen and gentleman . . . is indistinguishable from servitude." This message, she maintains, is "the gist of Strauss's commentaries on the writings of Xenophon" (*PILS* 82). Her discussion of *XSD* culminates in another flamboyant denunciation:

> By portraying Isomachus [the wealthy farmer who converses with Socrates in Xenophon's *Oeconomicus*] as the model of the "perfect gentleman," Strauss casts a shadow on the noble life, the morally virtuous life, the honest life of the husband, father and citizen. He believes it to be a life of servitude, coupled with self-deception or the lie in the soul that Plato loathed so much. In other words, the sort of life that has been championed by civilization is a life fit for fools. . . . There is nothing genuinely noble about it. (*PILS* 84)

Because *Socrates* calls Ischomachus a "perfect [ἀπειργασμένον] gentleman" at *Oeconomicus* XI.3, Drury's opening sentence unjustly targets Strauss.[105] When Drury claims that any reader of the *Oeconomicus* "no doubt" will realize that Ischomachus is "an overbearing fool" (*PILS* 83), furthermore, she unwittingly implies that *Xenophon* intended to broadcast a harsh—and very easy to discern—critique of the "perfect gentleman." I myself do not regard Ischomachus as an overbearing fool. One wonders, moreover, how Drury could explain that *Strauss* lived the "honest life of the husband, father and citizen" that he allegedly associated with "servitude" and "self-deception." Did he live frugally, gently, law-abidingly, and hyperindustriously so that his students could fornicate, drink, snort, steal, and rape without inhibition?[106]

In extending her analysis to incorporate Strauss's suggestions that Ischomachus overestimated his success in educating his wife—Strauss concludes by describing an historical Ischomachus whose wife had a scandalous affair with her son-in-law, Kallias (*XSD* 157–58)—Drury makes blatant interpretive mistakes. According to Drury, Strauss "speculates that he is probably the same Isomachus whose daughter married Kallias, son of Hipponikos" (*PILS* 83). Strauss, she concedes, "cannot assert without a doubt that this is the same Ischomachus who was father-in-law to Kallias"; she nevertheless maintains that Strauss was "certain" both that Ischomachus's wife was "not the sweet, devoted wife her husband believed her to be" and that "this fact was known to all who were listening" when Socrates spoke of Ischomachus (*PILS* 84).[107]

Drury accurately summarizes the tale about the doubly adulterous mother-daughter tryst involving Kallias (or Callias), a story Strauss bases on a single source—*On the Mysteries* by Andocides (124–27), "a contemporary orator" (*XSD* 157). Here is the connection as Strauss sketches it between this scandal and the interlocutor Ischomachus (Strauss at *XSD* 131 emphasized Xenophon's failure to provide a patronymic that might identify the specific man, among "the many Athenians called Ischomachus," to whom Socrates was speaking):

> It is impossible to assert that Xenophon's Ischomachus was Kallias' father-in-law or even that Xenophon knew of that scandalous story. But one can safely say that what Xenophon's Socrates reports about Ischomachus and his wife is perfectly compatible with the possibility that that woman proved in later years to be less good than her pedagogic husband expected her to become and that this disappointing truth was known to Socrates and his friends when he gave them his report. (*XSD* 158)[108]

In Drury's formulation, Strauss indicates that the two men named Ischomachus are "probably the same" (*PILS* 83). Strauss, by contrast, states that it is *impossible* to claim that they are the same; Strauss, moreover, says it is *impossible* to claim "even that Xenophon knew" of the scandalous story. According to Drury, Strauss was "certain" that Ischomachus's wife was *not* the standout "her husband believed her to be" and that this "fact" was known to "all who were listening" (*PILS* 84). All Strauss claims, however, is that the treatment of Ischomachus and wife in the *Oeconomicus* is *compatible* with the "possibility" that Ischomachus had been overly optimistic and that the "disappointing truth" was known by Socrates and by the friends Socrates later addressed.[109]

"Warriors and Workers . . . Unite"!

Drury's 1994 book on Kojève includes a chapter on Strauss that introduces a new absurdity—the malicious thesis that Strauss in *On Tyranny* was summoning nihilistic revolution against the modern world, specifically, against "the universal and homogeneous state" toward which "history has been marching inexorably" (*AK* 152–54).

Drury here draws upon the huge forty-fourth paragraph from the final pages of the "Restatement."[110] Roughly a page into the paragraph, Strauss quotes a passage about the end of history from Kojève's *Introduction à la lecture de Hegel*—"There is no longer fight nor work. History has come to an end. There is nothing more to *do* (pp. 385, 114)"—to show why, within Kojève's framework, the end of history would resemble Nietzsche's "last man": for Kojève, "the participation in bloody political struggles as well as in real work" is what "raises man above the brutes."[111] Strauss proceeds to criticize Kojève:

> It is perhaps possible to say that the universal and homogeneous state is fated to come. But it is certainly impossible to say that man can reasonably be satisfied with it. If the universal and homogeneous state is the goal of History, History is absolutely "tragic." . . . For centuries and centuries men have unconsciously done nothing but work their way through infinite labors and struggles and agonies, yet

ever again catching hope, toward the universal and homogeneous state, and as soon as they have arrived at the end of their journey, they realize that through arriving at it they have destroyed their humanity and thus returned, as in a cycle, to the prehuman beginnings of History. (*OT* 223)

Despite Drury's assertion that Strauss too thought that history was "marching inexorably" toward "the universal and homogeneous state" (*AK* 152), the premise here about the "goal of History" is clearly Kojève's, not Strauss's; note too the Hegelian capitalization ("History"). When directly addressing the inevitability of the UHS (the universal and homogeneous state), furthermore, Strauss's wording is equivocal (it is "perhaps possible" to say such a state is "fated to come").[112] The preceding celebration of "bloody struggles" and "real work" also belongs clearly to Kojève (Strauss cites three different places in Kojève's Hegel book). Strauss, I assume, offers his own judgment when he states that the cycle *would be* tragic, but this evaluation is conditional: "if" the UHS is inevitable, then history would be tragic. In *LSAR*, Drury nonetheless cites *On Tyranny*—and directs the reader to her above-discussed account of it in *Alexandre Kojève*—as an example of Strauss's speaking "as if the modernity in which he lived was an intolerable state of affairs that must be destroyed for the sake of man's humanity" (*LSAR* 75 and 192n36). Unlike Anne Norton, however, Drury acknowledges that Strauss and Kojève *differ* about the UHS. In her discussion of *On Tyranny*, Norton asserts that both men feared the UHS and saw in the League of Nations "and other multinational institutions the threat of an imperial totalitarianism" (*LSPAE* 147–48); among other things, Norton is apparently unaware of Kojève's devotion to Stalin.[113] Drury, in any case, fails conspicuously to demonstrate that Strauss agrees with Kojève about "the goal of History." In a publication that appeared just three years after the first English-language version of the "Restatement" (*WIPP* 95–133), Strauss proclaimed, quite reasonably in my view, that "societies still move as if on an uncharted sea and surely without the benefit of tracks toward a future that is veiled from everyone and which is pregnant with surprises" (Epilogue 313/*LAM* 209). If Jacob Weisberg is correct in saying that "[t]he assumption that events will conform to a preconceived model is a failing to which neoconservatives are notably vulnerable,"[114] we can posit another important respect in which the neocons were *not* good students of Strauss. Whether or not he was a Straussian, Strauss was *pas de Marxiste ou Trotskyite*.

After two Latin quotations—*Vanitas vanitatum* ("Vanity of vanities," from Ecclesiastes 1.2) and a modern restatement by Strauss, *Recognitio recognitionum* (*OT* 223)—Strauss proceeds immediately to the passage Drury invokes in arguing that Strauss favors "nihilistic revolution":

Yet there is no reason for despair as long as human nature has not been conquered completely, i.e., as long as sun and man still generate man. There will always be men (*andres*) who will revolt against a state which is destructive of humanity or in which there is no longer a possibility of noble action and of great deeds. They may be forced into a mere negation of the universal and homogenous state, into a negation not enlightened by any positive goal, into a nihilistic negation. While perhaps doomed to failure, that nihilistic revolution may be the only action on behalf of man's humanity, the only great and noble deed that is possible once the universal and homogenous state has become inevitable. But no one can know whether it will fail or succeed. We still know too little about the workings of the universal and homogenous state to say anything about where and when its corruption will start. What we do know is only that it will perish sooner or later (see Friedrich Engels' *Ludwig Feuerbach*, ed. by Hans Hajek, p. 6).[115]

Although, as we have seen, Drury asserts that Strauss shares Kojève's view that "history has been marching inexorably toward the universal and homogeneous state," she claims that Strauss departs from Kojève regarding the permanence of that condition. According to Drury, Strauss "conceives of history in terms of the eternal recurrence of the same"; and although he does not know *how* the universal and homogeneous state will end, he "knows" that "it will 'perish sooner or later'" as the *andres* of the world "plunge us back into history" (*AK* 153). Drury here cites *OT* 224 (*AK* 250n48), and the above-quoted extract from it supports some of her propositions: there would be *andres* who revolt against a dehumanizing state, and they "may be" forced into a nihilistic revolt. As she continues, however, she exaggerates, saying that for Strauss the nihilistic negation "is" the only great and noble deed that remains possible (*AK* 154), whereas Strauss (as quoted above) says only that this negation "may be" the only such deed that remains possible. Needless to say, Strauss's invocation of "the cycle of the seasons" (*OT* 224) hardly vindicates Drury's sweeping assertion that he "conceives of history in terms of the eternal recurrence of the same."

Building on her unsound insistence that Strauss regarded the UHS as inevitable and on her exaggerated claim that nihilistic negation is the only great deed left, Drury then adds additional distortion to produce one of her most inflammatory summaries of Strauss: "Under the abominable conditions bequeathed to us by modernity, where there is nothing to conserve, the only 'noble deed' is 'nihilistic revolt,' which is to say, destruction without any 'positive goal'" (*AK* 154). Modernity has surely arrived, according to Strauss, and he acknowledges the possibility that the UHS, under certain circumstances, might "become inevitable" (*OT* 224). But he *always* situates such a state in the future, not the present, and he conveys a huge hedge about its inevitability when he writes that it is "perhaps possible" to "say" that it is "fated to come."[116] And even if this manifestly hypothetical future comes to pass, furthermore, Strauss says only that the *andres* "may be" forced into a nihilistic revolt that in turn "may be" the only remaining "great and noble deed."[117] Is Strauss convinced that either Jerusalem or Athens would survive nihilistic revolution in a thermonuclear world? Even in twenty-first-century modernity, finally, are there not great books that we are obliged to "conserve," and are not many Straussians, inspired by Strauss's acute interpretation of their depths, diligently helping to vivify them? In his well-known essay on liberal education, Strauss forces us to confront the nightmare that nuclear wars might cause us to regress to the level of "illiterate tribes" (*LAM* 5–6). The *OT* "Restatement" is mostly a response to a Stalinist, as the original introduction is an attack on Stalinism and Nazism ("the horrors of the twentieth century").[118] In 1948, how could Strauss, or anyone, know that the Soviet Union would not prevail, or that modern civilization would not be devastated by the next world war?[119] Given the possible triumph of Stalinism and the pronounced decay of classical education, indeed, perhaps the free world urgently needed instruction about comprehending and producing esoteric writing.

Drury also exaggerates when she says Strauss knows that the UHS "will perish at the hands of the *andres*" (*AK* 153). When Strauss at the end of the passage mentions the knowledge that the UHS will perish, he does not identify what will cause the perishing—the previous sentence indeed highlighted how *little* we know about "the workings of the universal and homogenous state"—and he provides a citation to . . . Friedrich Engels, who was hardly a modern-day Hiero.

In the passage from *Ludwig Feuerbach und der Ausgang der deutschen klassichen Philosophie* that Strauss cites, Engels says nothing about revolution issuing from men, however manly. Engels is rather asserting the impermanence of all societal phases—and the impermanence of the natural environment that supports them:

> Nothing is imperishable except the uninterrupted process of becoming and perishing, of the endless ascent from the lower to the higher. . . . We do not have to consider here the question as to whether this view agrees with the present state of natural science, for at present natural science predicts a possible end to the existence of the earth and a certain end to the inhabitability of the earth. (*RCPR* 238)

Strauss proceeds to complain that Engels and his ilk are able to harp on progress only because they have decided "just to forget about the end, to forget about eternity."[120] In a recently published 1942 lecture, Strauss elaborates this criticism while singling out Hegel and Marx for expecting human beings to "put all their will, hope, faith, and love on something which is admittedly not eternal, but less lasting than this planet of ours."[121]

Engels also figures in the final passage Drury invokes to portray Strauss as a revolutionary nihilist. Strauss concludes the forty-fourth paragraph (*OT* 222–24) with a passage that Drury quotes accurately (except for the two quotation marks that she misplaces):

> Warriors and workers of all countries unite, while there is still time, to prevent the coming of "the realm of freedom." Defend with might and main, if it needs to be defended, "the realm of necessity." (*OT* 224)

Drury, alas, reverts again to incompetence when she says that this passage "can only be described as a revolutionary call to action" (*AK* 154).[122] We have previously explored occasions on which Drury is sloppy and/or vicious; here she just seems frivolous. Although she doubtless recognized the allusion to the *Communist Manifesto*, she seems oblivious to the irony and embellishment that dominate Strauss's words. Did Strauss expect that *On Tyranny* would be read by *either* workers or warriors in "all countries"? Given his horror about the possible emergence of a universal and homogeneous state, furthermore, how eager would he be to summon a *global* revolution? Earlier in the "Restatement," Strauss both notes that "extreme danger" is not something that any "sensible man would create" (*OT* 201), and argues that the philosopher will "not engage in revolutionary or subversive activity" (214). After finishing the forty-fourth paragraph with his parody of Marx and Engels, furthermore, Strauss commences the next paragraph with the word "But" to deliver what sounds like a vastly closer statement of his real views: "But perhaps it is not war nor work but thinking that constitutes the humanity of man" (224). Strauss's subsequent sentence continues his summons to wisdom: "Perhaps it is not recognition (which for many men may lose in its power to satisfy what it gains in universality) but wisdom that is the end of man" (224). Now, Kojève too celebrates the attainment of wisdom that Hegel's books signaled,[123] but Strauss manifestly rejects the historicizing framework of both Hegel and Kojève. Strauss traces man's humanity to wonder and worship, not to war and work, and he illuminates trans-Hegelian peaks in a variety of ancient and medieval thinkers.

V. "BLOOD, SWEAT, AND TEARS"

In a 1941 lecture ("German Nihilism") that was not published until after Drury's Kojève book came out, Strauss identifies nihilistic revolution with . . . Nazism. Nazism, Strauss insists, is the worst form of German nihilism, and the latter is a desire for the destruction of modern civilization without a "clear positive conception."[124] The moral ideals of modern civilization include the relief of man's estate, the safeguarding of human rights, "the greatest possible happiness of the greatest possible number," and internationalism (GN 358). The nihilistic response, however, was triggered more directly by the Marxist vision of the future—the "withering away of the state," a classless society, "a pacified planet, without rulers and ruled," a "planetary society devoted to production and consumption only"—that represents a "world in which everyone would be happy and satisfied . . . in which no great heart could beat and no great soul could breathe, a world without real, unmetaphoric, sacrifice, i.e. a world without blood, sweat, and tears" (GN 360). Apart from the withering of the state, this vision of civilization evokes Kojève's UHS and Nietzsche's "last man."[125]

After noting that many of the German nihilists were "very young" (along with "very intelligent and very decent"), Strauss faults the young nihilists for their fanatical urge to destroy modern civilization: they lacked a "tolerably clear" conception of what would replace it, and they thought that "literally anything"— "the *nothing*, the chaos, the jungle, the Wild West, the Hobbian [*sic*] state of nature"—would be "infinitely" better than "the communist-anarchist-pacifist future." From here, Strauss identifies an obvious "fallacy" in their thinking. Because they accepted the communist thesis that without proletarian revolution and proletarian dictatorship, civilization would perish, they assumed that "all rational argument" favored communism and they resisted in the name of "irrational decision" (GN 360). Had there been "old-fashioned teachers" who grasped their longings, perhaps the young nihilists could have been swayed, but "the belief in old-fashioned teaching declined considerably in post-war Germany" (361).[126] For positive guidance, the youths instead turned to figures (including Spengler, Jünger, Schmitt, and Heidegger) "who knowingly or ignorantly paved the way for Hitler" (362). Strauss's lecture ends with praise of civilization, peace, Churchill, and England.

In a recent article, William H. F. Altman has provided an eloquent, witty, and ingenious interpretation of the lecture that questions its enthusiasm for England and peace. Among other things, Altman emphasizes an ambiguity in Strauss's posture toward England. Strauss's *conclusion*, which celebrates England's struggle against Nazi Germany, maintains that the English were defending both "modern" civilization and "the eternal principles" of civilization against German nihilism (GN 373). Earlier, however, Strauss stated that the "modern" ideal of civilization associated with England was a "debasement of morality" (GN 370–71).[127] Altman's bombshell is his claim that GN reveals Strauss's "secret teaching," a teaching suffused by the principles of the German nihilists; Strauss was apparently "a post-Hitler National Socialist."[128]

Although Altman's article deserves more attention than I can here grant it, I shall attempt to convey its main weaknesses. Most importantly, Altman ignores four aspects of GN that clash with his thesis. First, Strauss sharply criticizes militarism: he complains that Nazi Germany, insofar as it was willing to use "*any* means" in its pursuit of world domination, destroys "everything which makes life worth living for any decent or intelligent being" (GN 368); he suggests that "the business of destroying, and killing, and torturing is a source of almost disinterested pleasure to the Nazis" (369); and after stating that "the natural aim of man . . . is happiness," he chides Hegel and Fichte along with Nietzsche for overemphasizing "the dignity of military virtue" (371).[129] Second, Strauss claims that it was the prospect of a communist global future "at least as much as the desperate present, which led to nihilism"; he also faults the young nihilists for summoning "irrational decision" to oppose communistic determinism (360).[130] Third, Strauss emphasizes the vitality of "the classical tradition" or "the classical ideal of humanity" in England (372). Fourth, the nihilists' insistence on the "constant awareness" of the sacrifices life requires and of "the necessity, the *duty*, of sacrifice of life and all worldly goods" (358) might be matched by versions of every major world religion. Even my irreligious grandmother harped on the toil and torment one must endure to avoid becoming a "good for nothing."

Altman is wise to note the "terse and lively" style in which Strauss temporarily speaks from "the point of view of the nihilists themselves" (GN 363).[131] It is almost impossible, however, to imagine that *Strauss* in 1941 thought that Hitler "will soon be forgotten" and that as "the rather contemptible *tool* of 'History'" Hitler was "the midwife who assists at the birth of the new epoch" (GN 363).[132] Altman similarly falters when he implies that Strauss in GN only condemned Hitler's Germany, as opposed to "an imperialist or even a National Socialist Germany," because Hitler became a "prisoner" of anti-Semitism and did not simply use it as a tool.[133] In elaborating this view, Altman yanks words from their context. In the relevant passage from the 1962 lecture, "Why We Remain Jews," Strauss is addressing "the lesson which Hitler gave Stalin" (Altman ignores this qualifying phrase), not touting the virtues of anti-Semitism:

> The fact that anti-Semitism is the socialism of fools is an argument not against, but for, anti-Semitism; given the fact that there is such an abundance of fools, why should one not steal that very profitable thunder. Of course, one must not become a prisoner of this like that great fool Hitler who believed in his racial theories. (WWRJ 48)[134]

If Altman's interpretation of this passage were correct, Strauss would be endorsing Stalin's anti-Jewish policies despite their notorious brutality, injustice, and ugliness.

Although Altman offers a variety of sparkling observations in attempting to unmask fascistic and imperialistic endorsements in GN, finally, he never pauses to wonder why Strauss, as a New School instructor who had lived less than five years in the United States, would incorporate such a secret teaching into a faculty-seminar talk.[135] The manuscript, furthermore, includes two different outlines, the text is messy because of written as well as typed alterations, and historian Eugene Sheppard, who "inspired" Altman,[136] was unable to find evidence that the talk was ever delivered.[137] Altman nevertheless refers repeatedly to the audience, even suggesting that a certain passage shows Strauss speaking as if he were activating a "sleeper cell of his fellow nihilists."[138] As Altman reminds us, Strauss claimed that "one writes as one reads" (*WIPP* 230), but why would someone in an unrecorded presentation attempt to *speak* as Strauss reads?[139]

With both reaction and proletarian revolution off the table in the twenty-first century—and with radical Islamism, perpetual war, and nihilistic revolt as noxious alternatives—perhaps Straussians should continue to promote the crusade of *our* "old-fashioned teacher" for . . . liberal education, "the counterpoison to mass culture," the "endeavor to found an aristocracy within democratic mass society" (*LAM* 5).[140] Despite the new challenges—for example, *Grand Theft Auto*, *The Jerry Springer Show*, WrestleMania, the Sex Pistols, "Hot in Herre," Internet pornography, Botox, methamphetamines, "Stop Snitching" campaigns, the explosion of single-parent households—it remains true that no one "prevents us from cultivating our garden or from setting up outposts which may come to be regarded by many citizens as salutary to the republic and as deserving of giving to it its tone" (*LAM* 24).

Let me emphasize that I do not regard the current world, or any one that I can imagine emerging unless we enter the terrain of *Brave New World*, as bereft of either the possibility of noble deeds or the necessity of blood, sweat, and tears; among other things, recall that Huxley's dystopia had to eliminate childbirth and parenting.[141] Nor must one be a communist to point out that rivers of human blood, sweat, and tears—not to mention limbs and corpses—continue to flood the world's factories, mines, farms, and construction sites. Unlike the Zuckerts, I would grant to Monday Night Football a meaningful level of striving, sacrifice, and commitment (*TALS* 36), and I would highlight the nobility that countless people manifest in struggling to overcome starvation, disease, handicaps, addiction, orphaning, maiming, and sexual abuse. There are infinite ways to sweat without making other people bleed.

Not even universal immersion in *Orientalism*, *A Theory of Justice*, and *The Vagina Monologues* would stop technology, industrialism, fanaticism, and population growth from generating practical crises that will stretch our theoretical horizons.[142] In his 1941 lecture, Strauss notes that although the English proclivity for "muddling through" or for "crossing the bridge when one comes to it" might have harmed "the radicalism of English thought," it proved to be "a blessing to English life" because it helped them avoid "those radical breaks with traditions which played such a role on the continent" (GN 372).[143] If Strauss's books and ideas survive whatever catastrophes lie ahead, they will augment the diversity of intelligible political orientations, including several that favor "small but beautiful" societies that are less environmentally toxic. Even if ambitious leaders derive benefits from invoking and/or creating crises, the rest of us have no excuse for impatience.

NOTES

1. Shadia B. Drury, "The Esoteric Philosophy of Leo Strauss," *Political Theory* 13, no. 3 (August 1985): 315–37.

2. *PILS* also absorbed these two articles by Drury: "The Hidden Meaning of Strauss's *Thoughts on Machiavelli*," *History of Political Thought* 6, no. 3 (Winter 1985): 575–90; and "Leo Strauss's Classic Natural Right Teaching," *Political Theory* 15, no. 3 (August 1987): 299–315.

3. The Strauss entry cites only two secondary sources, and Drury's is one of them. See Bruce Frohnen, Jeremy Beer, and Jeffrey O. Nelson, eds., *American Conservatism: An Encyclopedia* (Wilmington, DE: ISI Books, 2006), 821. In the article on Straussians, written by Mark C. Henry, *PILS* is one of only three cited sources (826).

4. The interview was conducted by Matthew Rothschild, the editor of *The Progressive* magazine; in response to an e-mail query, I was told by Elizabeth DiNovella that the interview took place on 30 September 2005. One can download the interview from Drury's home page (http://phil.uregina.ca/CRC/). On 12 January 2006, I was able to download it at http://progressive.org/radio_drury05, but it is no longer available on this site (for a list of available interviews, see http://www.progressive.org/radio).

5. Although Peter Berkowitz is now a senior fellow at the Hoover Institution, a think tank based at Stanford University, he is not a member of the Stanford faculty (roughly twenty Hoover fellows do have joint appointments). Berkowitz apparently operates out of the Hoover office in Washington, DC, and the two of us have never met or spoken. I sent him an e-mail about Adam Smith in 2000, when he was a professor at George Mason University Law School, and I sent him one in the summer of 2008 with some questions about this book. On neither occasion did he reply.

6. When she concedes later that however "bizarre his commentaries on the Great Books might be, they are nevertheless full of valuable insights" (*PILS* 193), perhaps she would allow that these commentaries convey insights about the authors he discusses. But the remark about "valuable insights" is a rare concession, and one she probably wishes to disown given the escalation in the levels of Straussian evil and incompetence she has recently alleged.

7. Dannhauser points out that Strauss "almost never called a student by his first name, and it was unthinkable for us to call him by his first name, even after we had ourselves become teachers" (Werner J. Dannhauser, "Becoming Naïve Again," *American Scholar* 44, no. 4 [Autumn 1975]: 641). For the material from Anastaplo, see "On Leo Strauss," 32–33; a revised version of this article appears in Anastaplo, *The Artist as Thinker: From Shakespeare to Joyce* (Chicago: Swallow Press, 1983), 249–72.

8. Dannhauser, "Becoming Naïve Again," 641.

9. Dannhauser, "Becoming Naïve Again," 639.

10. As recounted by Heilbrunn, Bloom operated intrusively with some of his students: "He found jobs for them, screened their friends, and, in some cases, played matchmaker" (Heilbrunn, *They Knew*, 97).

11. Emph. added. Titled "To My Critics," Drury's essay was initially published in *Vital Nexus* 1, no. 1 (May 1990): 119–34; the quotation above appears on page 2 of the Internet version. The critics whose pieces were included in the journal include Anastaplo, Peter Emberley, Ernest L. Fortin, and Clifford Orwin. Drury has posted her "Reply" at http://phil.uregina.ca/CRC/vitalnexus.html.

12. The terrain is further cluttered by her twice-issued claim that "the ancients to whom Strauss appeals have been transfigured by Nietzsche" (*PILS* 170, 181). Drury elaborates this view in the "Reply": "According to Strauss, the mature Socrates, the Socrates of Plato and Xenophon, is the quintessential representative of the wise ancients. However, an examination of Strauss's account of the Platonic and Xenophontic Socrates reveals a postmodern Socrates, one who has been transfigured by Nietzsche, and is fully cognizant of the crisis of modernity. This postmodern Socrates is Strauss" (p. 2 of the Internet version). On Strauss and Nietzsche, see pp. 83–86 above and 151–53 below. On the analogy between Drury's shortcut and Strauss's remarks about how Farabi deployed "the specific immunity of the commentator" (*PAW* 14), see *PILS* x–xi, 24, 27 and p. 120 below.

13. She also once concedes that "his advice to interpreters contains elements that are sound and invaluable" (*PILS* 12–13).

14. Professor Claude Polin of the Sorbonne amplifies Drury's criticism beyond all sanity by claiming that, because of his relative indifference to "what the philosophers actually say or try

to say," Strauss "*never* quotes them precisely" (emph. added). See Claude Polin, "The Enigmatic Professor Strauss, Part I," *Chronicles*, July 2007, 47.

15. Victor Gourevitch, "Philosophy and Politics II," *Review of Metaphysics* 22 (1968): 326–28. Space does not permit a full discussion, but here is a quick summary: there was an erroneous citation that was later corrected in the paperback edition; in one quotation, a Greek letter was switched for a similar-looking one; there is a phrase in Strauss's reply to Kojève ("current thought, i.e., heedless or running") that was much more clearly expressed in French as "pensée courante" (the 1954 edition of *On Tyranny* was first published in French, and included both an essay by Kojève and Strauss's well-known "Restatement"). There is a fourth error diagnosed by Gourevitch that I would blame on the editor[s] who assembled the texts of the expanded English version that was published in 1963: a footnote reference to another page in the volume had not been changed to reflect the repagination of the second edition. This mistake was corrected by the 1975 printing.

16. Regarding the Xenophon translation, the first page of Bloom's foreword states that "Mr. Strauss is not responsible for it," and Strauss of course had nothing to do with the translation of Kojève (it is the translation of Kojève that receives Gourevitch's harshest condemnation). Gourevitch has coedited a revised and expanded edition of *On Tyranny* that provides improved translations of both Xenophon and Kojève. In her 1994 book on Kojève, Drury was happy to use Gold's error-ridden translation—instead of the heavily revised 1991 version by Gourevitch and Roth—because the original was more accessible (Shadia B. Drury, *Alexandre Kojève: The Roots of Postmodern Politics* [New York: St. Martin's Press, 1994], 220).

17. In the annotated bibliography of her 1997 book, Drury again summons Yolton's article: it "illustrates the careless nature of Strauss's scholarship, and his habit of quoting out of context" (*LSAR* 234).

18. Drury dedicates *LSAR* to Yolton, and the acknowledgments reiterate her admiration: "as always, he sets the scholarly standard to which I continue to aspire."

19. The above citations are to J. W. Yolton, "Locke on the Law of Nature," *Philosophical Review* 67 (1958): 477–98; Xenos joins Drury in touting Yolton's complaints about Strauss's references (*CV* 158n19). In a review four years later, Yolton dismissed *Locke on War and Peace*, a book written by Strauss's student Richard H. Cox, with Druryite gusto: "There is nothing of value here for the philosopher, the historian of thought, or the political scientist unless it be a lesson in how not to read a text" (*Philosophical Review* 71, no. 2 [April 1962]: 271). Ironically, Yolton provides a lesson in how not to read a *title* when he here refers to *NRH* as *Natural Law and History* (270).

20. For Strauss's other long statement on Locke, see his review of the von Layden edition of Locke's *Essays on the Law of Nature* (*WIPP* 197–220). This review was first published in the 1958 *American Political Science Review*, and would be relevant for other criticisms by Yolton that deserve a careful reply.

21. Yolton, "Locke," 494–96.

22. Yolton, "Locke," 494n24.

23. As Strauss emphasizes later, there was indeed a "plenty of natural provisions" when the world was "sparsely populated"; Strauss cites §31 for the former phrase (*NRH* 238). For the *Second Treatise*, I am quoting from the version edited by Thomas P. Peardon (Indianapolis: Bobbs-Merrill, 1952).

24. Yolton, "Locke," 493n23.

25. The *Second Treatise* provides multiple specifications of the "law of nature," but Locke generally orients it around human peace and preservation.

26. This claim comes shortly after an earlier paragraph—from the same chapter—in which Locke provides his most extreme descriptions of the *defects* of the state of nature: the enjoyment of our freedom and "empire" in the state of nature is "very" uncertain and "constantly" exposed to invasion; the enjoyment of property, correspondingly, is "very unsafe, very unsecure"; the state of

nature is "full of fears and continual dangers" (*ST* 123). Strauss quotes the last comment on *NRH* 224–25.

27. Although Locke is often elliptical in defining the state of nature—as he is with other fundamental concepts such as the law of nature—it designates a condition in which individuals or groups are not subject to a higher worldly authority. Putting together two key paragraphs, one may claim that in the state of nature individuals possess the "freedom to order their actions and dispose of their possessions and persons" constrained by the law of nature but independent of "the will of any other man" (*ST* 4); such individuals lack the "established law and judicature" that would judge and punish (87).

28. Locke's formulation encompasses a fundamental ambiguity. Since Locke refers to "degenerate men" rather than to "some" or "the" degenerate men, he could be construed as signaling a universal human depravity; cf. *ST* 92 on "the baseness of human nature," and Yolton, "Locke," 495 on pravity in Locke's *Letter on Toleration*. Nowhere in the *Second Treatise*, of course, does Locke invoke "fallen" man or original sin, as Strauss illuminates when he carefully compares Locke's state of nature with the biblical chronology (*NRH* 215–16). Yolton, by contrast, speaks in a more facile manner: "the perversity of men was for Locke a deviation from the norm"; hence "the state of war was sharply and carefully differentiated from the state of nature" (495).

29. Strauss in a later footnote (*NRH* 232n100) addresses Locke's contradictory statements and indications about whether society can exist without government; to dispel the contradiction, Strauss suggests that, for Locke, "society exists, and acts without government only in the moment of revolution." See *ST* 149, 243; cf. 212, 227.

30. Yolton, "Locke," 495.

31. For example, it seems that the American tribes that are ruled by councils and that use kings as temporary generals would qualify as civil societies (*ST* 108).

32. *NRH* 217; in the last phrase, Strauss is quoting *ST* 80. Strauss emphasizes the degree to which Locke here abandons the New Testament's focus on the permanence of marriage and the related prohibitions of polygamy and incest (*NRH* 217–18). Among the passages Strauss cites concerning polygamy is one (§65) from the chapter that precedes Locke's account of conjugal society.

33. In the same chapter, Locke denies that the "voluntary submission" people make to a government by inheriting their fathers' estates counts as a *natural* tie or engagement" (*ST* 73; emph. added). Later, after describing paternal/parental government as "natural" (170), he characterizes nature and "compact" as contrasting sources of power (172); whereas parental power comes from nature, political power comes from "voluntary agreement" (173; cf. 116–17).

34. Yolton, "Locke," 492.

35. In chapter III ("Of the State of War"), Locke also contrasts the state of nature with "commonwealth"; he likewise contrasts the law of nature with "the positive laws of commonwealths" (*ST* 12). He later argues that a robust family—a grouping in which the "master"/husband presides over servants and slaves in addition to children and wife—is "very far" even from a "little" commonwealth regarding their "constitution, power, and end" (*ST* 86). The political salience of "commonwealth" is further enhanced when Locke highlights it in his chapter—"Of the Forms of a Commonwealth" (chapter X)—about the three forms of government. Yolton thus errs in claiming that Locke used the term "commonwealth" when he wished to *avoid* discussing civil societies "under their political rubrics" (Yolton, "Locke," 492–93).

36. In the *First Treatise of Government*, Locke seems to equate society with civil society in sections 3, 6, 65, 83 (societies, not society), 92, 93, 106, and 156 (societies, not society); the only clear exception comes at 131, where he speaks of "voluntary Societies" that are temporary; cf. 144 on the Indian tribes. My quotes from the *First Treatise* are taken from the Peter Laslett edition of the *Two Treatises of Government* (New York: Mentor Books, 1963).

37. Yolton, "Locke," 494–95n24.

38. Also see *ST* 101 on the essential contributions civil society makes to "safety, ease, and plenty."

39. Strauss posits such an evolution between the two treatises and between the opening words of the *ST* chapters VII (God) and VIII (Men); he likewise emphasizes the parallel in the *Essay Concerning Human Understanding*, where the only chapter that opens with "God" (III.1) is followed by the only chapter that opens with "Man" (III.2). See *NRH* 217n74.

40. As early as §12 of the *ST*, in any case, Locke had argued that absolute monarchy is worse than the state of nature.

41. Yolton, "Locke," 495. When Yolton adds that "[i]n all forms of the state of nature explicit and specific consent of the governed is absent" (494), he may have forgotten that "express" consent is not routinely incorporated into civil societies (*ST* 119–22).

42. The "majority," who initially have "the whole power of the community naturally in them," may "put the power of making laws . . . into the hands of one man" and thus constitute a monarchy, which can be either hereditary or elective (*ST* 132). Elsewhere, of course, Locke pushes for lawmaking to be done by "diverse persons" (143) or authorized "persons" (212); cf. 135 and 243 on solitary legislators and 159 on "moderated" monarchies in which the supreme executive has only a share in the legislative authority.

43. Drawing on Josephus Acosta, a Jesuit missionary, Locke says that parts of America appeared to have "no government at all" because, in Acosta's words, they lacked kings and commonwealths and lived in "troops" that simply chose "captains" as the occasion warranted (*ST* 102); a bit later, Locke implies that these people retained their "natural freedom" despite the presence of such kings (105). Cf. 109 on the captains, generals, judges, and "first kings" of Israel.

44. If space permitted, we could profitably explore how Drury struggles to convey Locke's terminology about both property and "civil society" in her early article about Locke and Nozick (Shadia B. Drury, "Locke and Nozick on Property," *Political Studies* 30, no. 1 [1982]: 28–41). When she later cites this article on behalf of the proposition that her understanding of appropriation "differs considerably from Strauss's" (*PILS* 234–35n33), she is again unreliable: although the article does not stoop to mention Strauss, it follows him on many key points.

45. According to Locke, argues Strauss, "the exercise of all the rights and privileges of the state of nature" would give the English "day laborer" (*ST* 41) less wealth than he gets by receiving subsistence wages: "Far from being straitened by the emancipation of acquisitiveness, the poor are enriched by it. . . . Unlimited appropriation without concern for the needs of others is true charity" (*NRH* 242–43). When Strauss casually invokes "[t]he superiority of communism" in interpreting Plato's *Republic* (*CM* 115), it should likewise be obvious that he is not articulating his own view.

46. Will Hutton, *A Declaration of Interdependence: Why America Should Join the World* (New York: W. W. Norton & Company, 2003), 37.

47. While elaborating how Locke proceeds in "concealing the revolutionary character of his doctrine of property" and in "occasionally mentioning and apparently approving the older view" (*NRH* 246), Strauss notes a key contrast between the *Treatises*: whereas I.42 states that "it will always be a sin" for an affluent man "to let his brother perish for want of affording him relief out of his plenty," the property chapter of the *ST* is "silent about any duties of charity" (*NRH* 248).

48. Cf. Minowitz, "Machiavellianism Come of Age?" and *OT* 205, where Strauss contrasts "the strict moral demands made by both the Bible and classical philosophy" with the modern tradition of Machiavelli, Hobbes, and Adam Smith that "emancipated the passions and hence 'competition'"; in opposing this tradition, Strauss seems to insist that "man as man" is *not* "thinkable as a being that lacks awareness of sacred restraints." For his respectful consideration of C. B. Macpherson's critique of "possessive individualism," see *SPPP* 229–30 (cf. *NRH* 234n106 and Xenos, *CV* 133–34). One should also note Strauss's observations that "whether men are rich or poor depends as much on chance as on natural inequality" (*SA* 280) and that economic inequality can "disturb the natural order" (*SA* 302).

49. *CM* 3–6, *LAM* vi–viii; cf. *LAM* 271, *RCPR* 40, *OT* 202, *WIPP* 38. As Tarcov notes when discussing the introduction to *CM*, "Strauss distinguishes communism with respect to moral and political, not social and economic differences. He does not mention private property or free enterprise or the godless character of communism. In these respects he differed from much of the anti-communism of his time, in particular from conservative anti-communism in contradistinction to liberal or even social democratic forms." See Nathan Tarcov, "Will the Real Leo Strauss Please Stand Up?" *The American Interest* 2, no. 1 (September/October 2006), http://www.the-american -interest.com/ai2/article.cfm?Id=166&MId=5. On other occasions, Strauss does express or imply a critique of communism's godlessness (*LAM* 271, *TWM* 97).

50. Hutton, *Declaration*, 36.

51. A few pages earlier, Hutton garbles another key passage (§27) from chapter V (Hutton, *Declaration*, 34).

52. Will Hutton, "Time to Stop Being America's Lap-Dog," *Guardian Unlimited*, 17 February 2002, http://observer.guardian.co.uk/worldview/story/0,,651674,00.html. Hutton's book cites *LSAR* in its bibliography, but does not mention Drury in the text or the notes.

53. Professor Mazin Qumsiyeh, a geneticist and administrator at Yale Medical School, has an equally vivid imagination. Writing before the 2004 election, he maintained that both John Kerry and George W. Bush "display classic Straussian characteristics," including an unwillingness to "tackle the global environmental threats for which the U.S. bears special responsibility"; Qumsiyeh identifies the "Straussian model" with "believing and acting based on the worst elements of human history." See Mazin Qumsiyeh, "Their Dog-Eat-Dog World," *Al-Ahram Weekly* #706, 2–8 September 2004, http://weekly.ahram.org.eg/2004/706/op60.htm.

54. Joe Klein, "Neither Here nor There," *Guardian Unlimited*, 3 July 2002, http://www .guardian.co.uk/eu/story/0,,748364,00.html.

55. Yolton, "Locke," 478n5. I shall be quoting from the edition of *RC* edited by George W. Ewing (Washington, DC: Regnery Gateway, 1965).

56. Yolton, "Locke," 478n5.

57. Strauss is quoting from *RC* §108, 62; cf. *RC* 120 on "the work which he came for."

58. Drury accurately quotes this passage, and concedes that Locke "seems to endorse Strauss's own view of the differences between Socrates and Plato, and to follow Strauss in admiring the caution of the latter" (*PILS* 144).

59. For Locke's attributions of the words "caution" and "cautious" to Jesus, see *RC* 62, 72, 120, 128, 131, 136, 139. Other passages about Jesus that echo the ones Strauss quotes are 108 (on "the seemingly doubtful and obscure way of speaking"), 145 (on the "admirable wariness of his carriage"), and 155 (on his "prudent and wary carriage").

60. Jesus could also count upon a "promise of assistance"—"If we do what we can, he will give us his Spirit to help us to do what and how we should" (*RC* 246)—that could not help the ancient philosophers in their efforts as teachers.

61. Strauss draws on these passages at *NRH* 205n51, 221, and 225–26.

62. In elaborating his indignation against Drury's accusations on this score, Anastaplo draws on his extensive contact with Strauss—he seems to have audited Strauss's classes for over a decade at Chicago—to offer some eminently sensible reflections. Regarding morality, "the testimony of those who know a teacher personally and well, and over many years of intimate contact in the classroom and out, can be almost conclusive." Drury, furthermore, fails to provide "revelations of previously unknown thoughts and deeds on his part" (George Anastaplo, "Shadia Drury on Leo Strauss," *Vital Nexus* 1, no. 1 [May 1990]: 11).

63. Anastaplo, "On Leo Strauss," 32, 34, 37.

64. Werner J. Dannhauser, "Leo Strauss in His Letters," in *Enlightening Revolutions: Essays in Honor of Ralph Lerner*, ed. Svetozar Minkov (Lanham, MD: Lexington Books, 2006), 361.

65. See Jenny Strauss Clay, "The Real Leo Strauss," *New York Times*, 7 June 2003. I am baffled that Xenos, who addresses the secondary literature on Strauss sparingly, devotes so much energy to denouncing this letter. In elaborating the proposition that her father would have been proud of how "masterfully deceptive" she is, Xenos erroneously denies that a well-known article by Jeet Heer used the word cabal (*CV* 6, 146n20); Heer in fact asked whether Strauss was an elitist who wanted society to be "ruled by a secretive cabal" (Jeet Heer, "The Mind of the Administration, Part One: The Philosopher," *Boston Globe*, 11 May 2003, H1, http://www.boston.com/news/globe/ideas/articles/2003/05/11/the_philosopher/).

66. In the concluding "Restatement on Xenophon's *Hiero*," however, the gap between the two editions is at least ten pages. The "Restatement" is also available in *WIPP* 95–133. For an expanded version, which attempts to restore the entire manuscript that was included (in French translation) in the first published version from 1954, see Emmanuel Patard, "'Restatement' by Leo Strauss (Critical Edition)," *Interpretation* 36, no. 1 (Fall 2008): 29–78.

67. Within *OT*, note Strauss's claims that "the specific function of the wise man is to understand" (93), that what the philosopher seeks "can never become private or exclusive property" (213), and that the philosopher "will not hurt anyone" (214). Cf. *OT* 94 on the wise man's lack of "malevolence or hatred" and 214 on the philosopher's freedom from "the delusions bred by collective egoisms." Also see *CM* 115 and Seth Benardete, "Leo Strauss's *The City and Man*," *Political Science Reviewer* 8 (1978): 7–8.

68. Cf. Xenos, *CV* 117, 122, and Aakash Singh, *Eros Turannos: Leo Strauss and Alexandre Kojève Debate on Tyranny* (Lanham, MD: University Press of America, 2005), 44, 50–54, 56. Regarding Kojève's and Hegel's perspectives on pagan aristocracy, also see Smith, *Reading*, 142–43, and Francis Fukuyama, *The End of History and the Last Man* (New York: Free Press, 2006), 155, 161, 200–201, 402n2. The last passage is one of several places that demonstrate the absurdity of Drury's claim, articulated twice in the space of three pages, that Kojève's is "the only Hegel he [Fukuyama] knows" (*AK* 184, 187).

69. *OT* 155, 156, 157–58, 160, 162n6, 163.

70. Kojève also claims that although Simonides "believes he is a wise man," for Strauss he is "only a poet" (*OT* 138); cf. Gourevitch, "Philosophy and Politics I," *Review of Metaphysics* 22 (1968): 66, 69; and "Philosophy and Politics II," 309–11. When Kojève argues that Simonides overestimates the importance of honor, furthermore, he draws closer to Strauss's critique by touting self-sufficiency (*OT* 140; cf. 159, 161).

71. *OT* 85, emph. in original. Cf. 133n43 on how love of honor may motivate "those wise men who converse with tyrants," and 55 on how Xenophon's Simonides seems to crave "tyrannical power" (55). Strauss, moreover, claims that only a "momentary illusion"—the prospect of a virtuous/beneficent tyrant's attaining happiness without being envied—could lead a wise man even "for a moment" to "wish to be a ruler" (85–86). But envy directed against the wise does not impair their "happiness or bliss" (86), and from this Strauss seems to infer that "[t]he wise man sits leisurely upon the very goal toward which the ruler is blindly and furiously working his way and which he will never reach" (89).

72. Unlike Hiero, furthermore, Simonides seems to lack "strong warlike inclinations" and the propensity to take "delight in war or killing" (*OT* 93). Strauss quotes the phrase about the "highest degree" of freedom from *Hiero* 1.16. In the above-quoted passage from Drury about the philosopher's wish to be admired by a "competent minority" (*PILS* 198), Drury seems to be combining passages in which Strauss emphasizes the approval of a "small *minority*" (91, 210) with passages in which he refers to "*competent* judges" (101, 217; emphases added). Although Kojève quotes the first phrase ("small minority") on 154 and 155 (Gourevitch and Roth; in the Agora edition, see 163 and 165), neither he nor Strauss uses the phrase "competent minority" in *On Tyranny*. Drury here provides no citation from Strauss; as previously mentioned, she cites the entire essay by Kojève.

73. Cf. *OT* 93 on how "[t]he desire for praise and admiration" provides "the natural foundation for the predominance of the desire for one's own perfection."

74. For "the classics" in general, Strauss adds, the highest good is "a life devoted to wisdom or to virtue" and honor is just "a very pleasant, but secondary and dispensable reward" (*OT* 203–4).

75. A sophist, likewise, is someone who "prostitutes wisdom for base purposes" (*OT* 42); the historical Simonides was a sophist, assuming that a sophist is someone who "uses his wisdom for the sake of gain and who employs arts of deception" (*OT* 97). Strauss elsewhere states that sophistry, in "the classical view," is "the use of philosophy for non-philosophic purposes by men who might be expected to know better, that is, who are somehow aware of the superiority of philosophy to all other pursuits" (Strauss, "New Interpretation," 342). Also see Thomas L. Pangle, "A Platonic Perspective on the Idea of the Public Intellectual," in *The Public Intellectual*, ed. Arthur M. Melzer, Jerry Weinberger, and M. Richard Zinman (Lanham, MD: Rowman & Littlefield, 2003), 15–26.

76. Strauss, "The Spirit of Sparta or the Taste of Xenophon," *Social Research* 6, no. 4 (November 1939): 534. In his 1963 synoptic chapter on Machiavelli, Strauss strikingly observes that Machiavelli "thought or wrote only a short while ago, about 500 years ago" (*HPP* 272). Also see "Spirit of Sparta" 536 on Xenophon's "escape to immortality"; *PAW* 34–35, 58–59 on oral transmission; and Gourevitch, "Philosophy and Politics I," 78n53, 81–82.

77. Strauss, "On the Intention of Rousseau," *Social Research* 14, no. 4 (December 1947): 471.

78. *OT* 29, 40, 42, 47, 52, 55, 90, 91, 93, 105, 133–34n45, 218. Also see Nathan Tarcov, "Preface to the Japanese Translation of *On Tyranny*," *Perspectives on Political Science* 33, no. 4 (Fall 2004): 221–26.

79. Cf. Strauss's claim on *OT* 60–61: it is "certain that Simonides' praise of tyranny in the second part of the *Hiero* was considered by Xenophon even more rhetorical than Hiero's indictment of tyranny in the first part."

80. The previously discussed statement that Simonides is "concerned exclusively" with gaining admiration and praise (*OT* 105) also suggests that he is vain. According to Pippin, Simonides for Strauss represents a "poet-businessman-sophist-perhaps-wise-man" (Robert B. Pippin, "Being, Time, and Politics: The Strauss-Kojève Debate," *History & Theory* 32, no. 2 [May 1993]: 141).

81. Cf. Xenos, *CV* 107–9.

82. *PILS* 96. By leaving out thirteen words (plus an "i.e."), Drury makes the passage seem more disparaging to "elected magistrates" than it is. In using *OT* 76–77 to provide the epigraph for his chapter, "Intellectual Elites against Democracy," Sheldon Wolin reproduces Drury's errant version (Wolin, *Democracy Incorporated*, 159).

83. *OT* 58, 61, 62, 76, 77.

84. In his "Restatement," Strauss chides Kojève for using the word "unpopular" to describe actions that Hiero himself had called "criminal" (*OT* 198, quoting Kojève from *OT* 137). I assume that Kojève was alluding to *Hiero* 7.12 along with the following passages: 4.10 (tyrants are "compelled by their need to live by contriving something bad and base"); 4.11 (tyrants are "compelled most of the time to plunder unjustly both temples and human beings, because they always need additional money to meet their necessary expenses" and they'll perish unless they maintain an army); 5.2 (fear sometimes lead them to kill secretly the brave, the wise, and the just). Kojève distorts Xenophon by limiting the nasty deeds to ones the tyrant did "in order to *come* to power" (*OT* 137; remember that I am citing the Gourevitch and Roth version of Kojève).

85. Citing *Memorabilia* IV.8.11, Strauss links the claim about a ruler's beneficence with Xenophon's claim (paraphrased by Strauss) that "the just man is a man who does not hurt anyone, but helps everyone who has dealings with him" (*OT* 76; cf. *SPPP* 120). Six paragraphs (and two full pages) before her tyrannical paragraph, Drury does state that Simonides showed Hiero that if the tyrant is to "lead a pleasant life free from fear of violent death, he must become a good tyrant, or a tyrant who is a benefactor of his city" (*PILS* 94). This thesis could be expressed more accurately, and it is placed too far from the tyrannical paragraph to soften the blows of the latter (Drury's

intervening discussion addresses dense material from *NRH*). In her book on Kojève, furthermore, Drury's discussion of *On Tyranny* in effect retracts the pardon by claiming that, for Strauss, the best that philosophers can do in "influencing tyrants" is to make the world "safe for *philosophy*" (*AK* 146; emph. added). Xenos, in any case, clearly incorporates the "good" tyrant's beneficence into his critique of *OT* (Xenos, "Leo Strauss," 15; cf. *CV* 88 on "the interest of the ruled").

86. Cf. *OT* 65 on the "rule of tact" that explains the absence of the word "king" from the *Hiero*.

87. See, for example, *Memorabilia* IV.6.12; Xenophon's Ischomachus makes a similar distinction at *Oeconomicus* XXI.11–12. Strauss returns to the topic of willing subjects at the end of *Xenophon's Socratic Discourse*: whereas the *Oeconomicus* closes with "strongly worded blame of the tyrant who rules over unwilling subjects," the *Hiero* closes with "strongly worded praise of the tyrant who rules over willing subjects" (*XSD* 209). On the difficulty of extracting a definition of tyranny from *On Tyranny*, see Tarcov, "Preface."

88. *OT* 70; cf. Xenophon, *The Education of Cyrus* VIII.1.21; I shall also refer to this work as the *Cyropaedia*.

89. Xenophon, *Hiero* 9.6–11, 10.2–7, 11.1–8, 11.14.

90. These remarks on *OT* 70 about the salutary measures prepare the paragraph's conclusion, which Drury quotes to demonstrate "Strauss's words" about tyranny's fulfilling "the highest political standards" (*PILS* 96).

91. In responding to Kojève's objection that Simonides displayed a poor understanding of the danger the mercenaries would pose should Hiero attempt to implement Simonides' reforms, Strauss suggests that Simonides either "regarded the good tyranny as a utopia" or "rejected tyranny as a hopelessly bad regime." Perhaps the "best one can hope for," Strauss concludes, is improvement whereby "the tyrannical rule" will be "exercised as little inhumanely or irrationally as possible" (*OT* 200). Responding to Kojève's claim that "the Simonides-Xenophon utopia has been *actualized* by modern tyrannies," including Portugal's António de Oliveira Salazar (139), Strauss concedes that Salazar's regime might qualify as a "good tyranny" and adds that he had not "denied that good tyranny is possible under very favorable circumstances" (201).

92. From this outrageous "top ten" slander, Drury further escalates the menace by proceeding immediately to the sentence I have criticized above: "*In Strauss's words*, 'tyrannical government can live up to the highest political standards'" (*PILS* 96; emph. added).

93. When Strauss acknowledges a possible exception—the references in the *Cyropaedia* to "a tyrant who was apparently happy"—he notes first that Xenophon did *not* describe that tyrant as either beneficent or virtuous. Even more decisive is the fact that this tyrant was not Greek: "the chances of tyranny at its best seem to be particularly small among Greeks" (*OT* 77). The note about the happy tyrant (129n48) cites *Cyropaedia* I.3.18. This passage clearly establishes that Astyages, the grandfather of Cyrus, is a tyrant, but one must look elsewhere in the book for evidence of Astyages' happiness. Because Astyages' rule ended over a century before Xenophon was born in 431 B.C., finally, this example amplifies the breadth of Strauss's claim about the absence from Xenophon's writings of any beneficent and happy tyrants "who actually existed."

94. Strauss also invoked the silence in the *Corpus Xenophonteum* about "happy tyrants who actually existed anywhere in Greece" a few pages earlier (*OT* 60). On the just and the legal, cf. *XS* 114: "while the identification of the just with the legal is theoretically wrong, it is practically as a rule correct."

95. Since Xenophon clearly presents Cyrus as being both "beneficent and happy," Strauss's above-quoted claim—that Xenophon never refers to "beneficent and happy tyrants who actually existed" (*OT* 77)—apparently requires Strauss to note that Cyrus remained "a legitimate ruler" (195). Thus "Cyrus is not a tyrant strictly speaking" (108). Cyrus was the son of the Persian King, Cambyses, the grandson of the Median King, Astyages, and the nephew of the son (Cyaxares) who succeeded Astyages; he became heir to the Median throne only after marrying a close relative of

Cyaxares (*Cyropaedia* VIII.5.18–19). Even after Cyrus acquired immense power via the conquest of Babylon, furthermore, both Cambyses and Cyarxes retained their titles along with their heads (VIII.5.17–28), and they seem to have retained their authority despite Cyrus's subsequent conquests (VIII.6.19–21). On the legitimacy of Cyrus, also see II.1.13.

96. For a Straussian perspective on how Xenophon conveyed the shortcomings of Cyrus that produced the succession catastrophe, see W. R. Newell, "Tyranny and the Science of Ruling in Xenophon's 'Education of Cyrus,'" *Journal of Politics* 45, no. 4 (November, 1983): 889–906.

97. Strauss also starts the book by including "present day tyranny" among "the horrors of the twentieth century" (*OT* 21–22); cf. *WIPP* 171 on "the contemporary tyrants whose rule rests on obscurantism and beastiality." In the discussion of legitimacy in the "Restatement," Strauss is responding to Eric Voegelin's defense of Caesarism as a "postconstitutional" adaptation to "the final breakdown of the republican constitutional order" (*OT* 190–91).

98. In a prominent essay, Strauss emphasizes the difficulty that even "intelligent men" face in acquiring sufficient political knowledge or understanding in contemporary societies "characterized by both immense complexity and rapid change" (*WIPP* 15).

99. The Zuckerts focus on the conclusion, where Drury claims that he "may have paid lip service to the rule of law" but "in reality his esoteric philosophy subverts it" (*PILS* 200). The Zuckerts exaggerate in stating that Strauss defended the rule of law in "nearly everything he ever said or wrote" (*TALS* 119).

100. Whereas Strauss here sketches a world state ruled by "the Universal and Final Tyrant" (*OT* 226), the plight of Big Brother's Oceania in Orwell's dystopia is aggravated rather than mitigated by the wars with Eurasia and Eastasia. As many commentators have noted, Strauss's introduction sketches two contrasting paths whereby "man, or human thought" could be "collectivized": by "one stroke and without mercy" or by "slow and gentle processes" (*OT* 27). Although the first path suggests communism and fascism, the second suggests Western democracies.

101. Gregory Vlastos, review of *On Tyranny*, by Leo Strauss, *Philosophical Review* 60, no. 4 (October, 1951): 592–94.

102. Also recall Drury's claim that Strauss "completely subverts what the ancients are about" (Rothschild interview).

103. Xenos here focuses on the references Strauss provides at *OT* 109n27 (to facilitate comparisons with Xenos, I am now citing the Gourevitch and Roth edition), and fails to note that one of the two passages Strauss cites from Xenophon's *Memorabilia* (I.1.16) discusses the knowledge that "makes one a gentleman [*kalos kagathos*]." I'm guessing that Xenos, who almost never employs a Straussian translation, here failed to check the Greek text.

104. To comprehend how Xenos could make such a massive error, I pored over the *OT* notes and eventually found the trio of references (*Memorabilia* II.3.2 and II.1.13–15 plus *Hiero* 4.3) in the notes from a *different chapter* (*OT* 129n32), where they relate directly to what Strauss says in the text (*OT* 97–98). The final mishap comes when Xenos at *CV* 158n24 corrects "what is obviously a misprint" and offers I.1.13–15 as the passage Strauss presumably meant to cite; in his text, Xenos spins his wheels yet again when he struggles to connect I.1.13–15 with the other materials (Strauss's text in *OT* 85, *Hiero* 4.3, and *Memorabilia* II.3.2). But there is no misprint. Although the Gourevitch and Roth typeface, compared to that of the Agora edition, makes it hard to distinguish Roman from Arabic numerals, Strauss's use of periods suffices to reveal that *OT* 129n32 is citing *Memorabilia* II.1.13–15 (the "II" carries over from the prior citation, II.3.2).

105. Drury never cites the *Oeconomicus*. When first describing Ischomachus (Drury uses an alternate spelling) to the interlocutor Kritoboulos, Socrates says that he was someone "to whom the name of gentleman is justly applied" (VI.12); he was "named a gentleman by everyone—by men and women, foreigners and townsmen alike" (VI.17). Cf. *Oeconomicus* VII.2, XI.1, XII.2; *XSD* 144, 164, 184; *OT* 42, 203; *XS* 158, 177. For Strauss's discussion of the Greek phrase (*kalos te kagathos aner*) and its "ordinary" English translation as "perfect gentleman," see *XSD* 127–29.

Although Strauss (in his books on Xenophon) usually appends "perfect" to the relevant nouns—gentleman, gentlemen, gentlemanship—he sometimes omits the adjective (e.g., at *XSD* 99, 105, 161, 176 and *XS* 97, 152, 154, 157).

106. Drury proceeds to claim that Strauss "sought to cultivate two different types of men," one type being "statesmen and gentlemen" (e.g., Jaffa) who would cherish morality, religion, honor, and nobility as "necessary components of genuine human excellence that are good by nature"; he taught the other type (e.g., Pangle) to be Nietzschean philosophers who would fathom the "artificial" character of the Jaffa-like orientation (*PILS* 188, 191; cf. *LSAR* 99–100 on Jaffa and 80 on "Strauss's liars who fancy themselves gods playing pranks"). Drury abandons the distinction in her later writings when she suggests that Straussians as such are "compulsive liars," "callous ruffians," and so on.

107. To assess the comments and speculations Strauss offers about Ischomachus's wife, one should contemplate a wide range of considerations that Drury ignores. For example, in the sections of the *Oeconomicus* that depict his pedagogy (VII.4–X.13), Ischomachus states that his wife was younger than fifteen when the instruction began (VII.5) and that her successful management of the household enabled him to spend all of his time outdoors (VII.3); Strauss stresses the contribution of "outdoor life" to Ischomachus's manliness (cf.. IV.2–4, VII.22–25, 30, 39–40, X.1), the eagerness Socrates displays (at VII.4 and VII.9) for learning about the wife's education (*XSD* 132), the manliness of the wife's mind (*XSD* 153–55), the relationship Socrates had with Xanthippe (*XSD* 110–11, 158, 166, 177, 195), and the relevance of Ischomachus for the Socratic turn (*XSD* 147–50, 160–61, 163–64, 184, 194–96). Note also that Socrates discusses the education of wives at III.10–15, well before he first mentions Ischomachus at VI.17.

108. The "friends" are Xenophon, Kritoboulos, and unnamed others (*Oeconomicus* I.1, III.1, III.12; cf. *XSD* 89–90, 107, 110, 118, 153). For the record, Andocides was on trial for a capital offense, and his recent translator, M. J. E. Edwards, believes that his speeches "are biased and selective in the details they provide, and may simply be lying or deceitful." See *Greek Orators IV: Andocides* (Warminster, England: Aris & Phillips Ltd., 1995), 3, 14–15. Andocides, apparently, is also the unnamed informant Thucydides disparages in *Peloponnesian War* 6.60.

109. It turns out that in a lecture published in 1989 (a year after Drury's book came out), Strauss provides a discussion closer to the one Drury claims to draw from *XSD*. Ischomachus's wife, according to the lecture, later "would have a love affair with their son-in-law Callias" (*RCPR* 149). This lecture was delivered in 1958 (*RCPR* xxxii), twelve years before the publication of *XSD*. I would speculate that, before committing himself to describe the matter in print, Strauss investigated the source, and, based on the evidence he found, formulated the more tentative wording of *XSD*. Even in the lecture, Strauss does not insist that Xenophon knew of the story (contra Drury).

110. As previously noted, the "Restatement," which concludes the 1963 Agora edition of *OT*, was first published in 1954.

111. *OT* 223, with additional citations to Kojève. Here, and for the rest of the chapter, I am again quoting/citing Strauss (but not Kojève) from the Agora edition, as Drury does throughout.

112. Stephen Holmes speaks more carefully on this issue, saying merely that, according to Strauss, a world society is a "dream," propagated by universalistic ideologies, that "could lead to a world tyranny where philosophers would find no refuge from oppression" (Holmes, *Anatomy*, 67–68). Strauss does elsewhere state that if we were forced to choose between "a communist world society" and "the destruction of modern civilization," we would need to *consider* "which alternative is preferable"; he proceeds to suggest, however, that our willingness to risk the latter would diminish the prospects of the former (*WIPP* 69). To speak crudely, proclaiming "better dead than Red" might reduce the chances of ending up either Red or dead.

113. On Kojève's important work for France's Ministry of Economic Affairs in preparing the EEC and GATT, see Lilla, "End of Philosophy," 3; Singh, *Eros Turannos*, 36; and *OT* 219. The contemporary "tyrant" Kojève praises obliquely and does not name would seem to be Stalin (*OT*

169, 173), as Strauss protests (*OT* 201); Kojève even claims to detect "'Stakhanovite' emulation" in Xenophon's *Hiero* (*OT* 138–39), to which Strauss responds by protesting the NKVD and gulags (*OT* 202). On Kojève and Stalin, see Singh, *Eros Turannos*, 36–37, 64–65n3; and Mark Lilla, "The End of Philosophy," *Times Literary Supplement*, 5 April 1991, 3–5. On Kojève's attitude toward the UHS, cf. *OT* 146, 168–70, 172–73, 175 (Gourevitch and Roth edition); and Kojève, *Introduction to the Reading of Hegel*, trans. James H. Nichols (New York: Basic Books, 1969), 89–90, 95–96, 231, 237. Although Kojève's oft-discussed pair of footnotes (a huge note from the second edition, written in 1959 or later, critiquing a much shorter note written in 1946) suggests defects in the UHS (*Introduction* 158–62), Strauss's opposition to the UHS is obvious throughout *OT* and in many other writings.

114. Jacob Weisberg, "Occupational Hazards: How the Pentagon Forgot about Running Iraq," *Slate*, 6 November 2003, http://www.slate.com/id/2090852/.

115. *OT* 223–24. Whereas the "it" in the sentence that begins with "But" apparently refers to the "nihilistic revolution," the "its" and the "it" in the final two sentences unambiguously refer to the UHS.

116. Also recall Strauss's statement that the future is both "veiled from everyone" and "pregnant with surprises" (Epilogue 313).

117. In a 1952 review of R. G. Collingwood, Strauss suggests that "'defeatist' withdrawal" might be the only sane course of action within an age of "unqualified decay" in which "virtuous political action is impossible" (Strauss, "On Collingwood's Philosophy of History," *Review of Metaphysics* 5, no. 4 [June 1952]: 577). Would nihilistic revolution be virtuous? Xenos speaks more temperately than Drury when he says that Strauss, confronting the "flattening out of experience" that modernity tends to produce, "held out the hope . . . for some rebellion, for acts of courage or honor to reverse this trend, this so-called tyranny" (Xenos, "Leo Strauss," 15).

118. As the Zuckerts memorably observe, late-modernity has yielded "political ambition on a grand scale, much grander than the kind of ambition Plato and Aristotle attempted to tame. We have here not merely an ambition to rule (to be the tyrant), but a political idealism with no discernable limits, which leads to one political horror after another in the name of the highest goals: the terror of the French Revolution, the gulags of the Soviet regime, the 'racial purification' of the Nazis, the 'great leap forward' and cultural revolution of the Chinese, the Pol Pot regime's effort to cleanse itself of all corrupted forces by means of the killing fields" (*TALS* 67). In the eloquent words of Thomas Pangle, we have "witnessed in the very bosom of the West horrifying totalitarian police states based on slave labor and on mass exterminations—all engineered by a science under the tutelage of fantastic ideological faiths and dreams" (Pangle, *Leo Strauss*, 9). For sober reflections by Drury on such matters, see *PILS* 161–62, 168–69.

119. Strauss elsewhere suggests that a "political philosopher," unlike "a philosopher of history or a pseudo prophet," must acknowledge that the world might "go through a period of atomic wars" (*WIPP* 309).

120. Strauss quotes the Engels passage (in German) on *NRH* 176n10, and elsewhere translates it (*RCPR* 238); Drury accurately paraphrases part of it at *PILS* 160. In his essay on Nietzsche's *Beyond Good and Evil*, Strauss cites the passage to illustrate that Engels and others were "deceptively and deceivingly appeased" by the realm of freedom: because that realm is "destined to perish," it will "abound in 'contradictions' as much as any earlier age." In his next paragraph, Strauss discusses eternal return (*SPPP* 180); elsewhere, he suggests that Nietzsche articulated this doctrine in order to prevent "the longing for the equality of all men when man is at the peak of his power"—a longing that would prevent the emergence of the "Over-man" (TWM 97; cf. *SPPP* 185–86, 189–90).

121. "To mistake eternity for a time of very long duration," Strauss adds, would be "the mortal sin for a man who claims to be a philosopher." Strauss prepared the lecture for delivery at the New School's General Seminar in July, 1942. See Leo Strauss, "What Can We Learn from Political

Theory?" *Review of Politics* 69, no. 4 (Fall 2007): 526. According to Nathan Tarcov, who edited the lecture, the manuscript can be found in box 6, folder 12 of the Leo Strauss Papers at the University of Chicago (Special Collections, Regenstein Library).

122. Drury errs more flagrantly when she asserts that Strauss with this passage "ends his reply to Kojève" (*AK* 154; Drury cites *OT* 224 on *AK* 250n53). In fact, Strauss provides three additional paragraphs (all of them robust), two of which mention Kojève (*OT* 224–26); and then comes the concluding paragraph about Being that Gourevitch and Roth restored in their 1991 edition.

123. Kojève, *Introduction*, 62, 164–68.

124. Leo Strauss, "German Nihilism," *Interpretation* 26, no. 3 (Spring 1999): 357. Also consult the corrections Wiebke Meier provided in a subsequent issue (*Interpretation* 28, no. 1 [2000]: 33–34). According to David Janssens and Daniel Tanguay, who edited and published the manuscript, internal evidence suggests that Strauss prepared the lecture to be delivered on 26 February 1941 to the general seminar of the New School's graduate faculty. The original version of the manuscript can be found in box 8, folder 15 of the Strauss Papers (GN 353).

125. For both Nietzsche and "the typical Continental European conservative," Strauss elsewhere states, communism represented "the completion of democratic egalitarianism and of the liberalistic demand for freedom which is not a 'freedom for' but only a 'freedom from'" (*SPPP* 32–33; cf. *RCPR* 40). This article was originally published (in Hebrew) in 1969 (*SPPP* 256).

126. Strauss associates the desired approach to teaching with "the old and noble educational system" founded by "great liberals" in the early 1800s; the "inroads" made by Kaiser William II were enlarged under Weimar (GN 361).

127. Altman, "Leo Strauss on 'German Nihilism': Learning the Art of Writing," *Journal of the History of Ideas* 68, no. 4 (October 2007): 594–95.

128. Altman, "Leo Strauss," 607, 608. Altman argues that Strauss refrained from publishing GN because the secret teaching was too easy to detect; Strauss's deceptions were better executed in subsequent writings (611–12; cf. 589).

129. In his 1943 *Social Research* review of John's Dewey's book, *German Philosophy and Politics*, Strauss similarly criticizes German philosophy's propensity to forget "the natural aim of man, which is happiness" (*WIPP* 280); he suggests, moreover, that "moralism unmitigated by sense of humor or sense of proportion" is a characteristic vice of "German thought" (280–81). Although Hermann Rauschning, whom Strauss examines in GN, pulls few if any punches in denouncing Nazi brutality and ruthlessness, he asserts that Hitler's "will to peace is an undeniable fact" and that "[t]he German nation," lacking any desire for war, "wants peace and quiet" (Rauschning, *The Revolution of Nihilism: Warning to the West* [New York: Alliance Book/Longmans, 1939], 181, 270). Sheppard reports that the New School faculty seminar had been reading this book (Sheppard, *Leo Strauss*, 96).

130. Strauss proceeds to blame historicism—specifically, its "depreciation" and "contempt" of reason—for undermining the prospect that human beings can guide themselves by "a *known* and *stable* standard" (GN 364; on the differences between knowing a stable standard and merely believing in it, see Altman, "Leo Strauss," 608–10). For Altman, anticommunism was a "central element" in Strauss's "attempt to make these young nihilists attractive" (Altman, "Leo Strauss, 589); cf. 595 on "anti-Communist Nietzscheanism" and 611 on the error in their "rational argument."

131. Altman, "Leo Strauss," 603.

132. Cf. *WIPP* 55 and pp. 152–54 below on Weimar as "the golden age." It is likewise difficult to imagine that Strauss thought that "literally anything" would be "infinitely" better than the communist future (GN 360). Altman is silent about this passage.

133. Altman, "Leo Strauss," 598–99.

134. Cf. Altman, "Leo Strauss," 603 on Hitler's connection with "vulgar" rather than "honorable" nihilism. Altman is citing a different reprinting of WWRJ, but the text is the same.

135. Before becoming a lecturer in philosophy at the New School in 1938, Strauss was an "itinerant" scholar in France and England from 1932 to 1938 (Kenneth Hart Green, ed., *Jewish Philosophy and the Crisis of Modernity: Essays and Lectures in Modern Jewish Thought* [Albany: SUNY Press, 1997], 4–5).

136. Altman, "Leo Strauss," 587n.

137. Sheppard, *Leo Strauss*, 169n79.

138. Altman, "Leo Strauss," 606; on the alleged listeners, also see 598, 600, 602, 607, 610, 611.

139. Altman insightfully notes the redundancy in Strauss's climactic criticism at GN 364 of people who "are not guided by a known and stable standard: by a standard which is stable and not changeable, and which is known and not merely believed" (Altman, "Leo Strauss," 607). But we need to be cautious about diagnosing "an addition disguised as repetition" ("Leo Strauss" 609) in words intended for *verbal* delivery.

140. Strauss had previously stated that democracy is "meant to be an aristocracy which has broadened into a universal aristocracy" (*LAM* 4).

141. Cf. *RCPR* 21 on "the realm of homunculi produced in test tubes by homunculi." Like Drury, I do not regard the modern world as "an egalitarian nightmare of uniformity and homogeneity" (*AK* 85; cf. *PILS*-05 xx on our "age of super-athletes, super-heroes, and supermodels"). I would also commend her emphasis on the contemporary prevalence of "war, Islamic fundamentalism, nationalism, and ethnic cleansing" (*AK* 209; cf. 43, 64, 190, 208–12). In my mind, using science to prevent mankind from being annihilated by comets, asteroids, and other natural catastrophes would also qualify as a great and noble deed, although I concede the likelihood that "unlimited technological progress" will prove "destructive of humanity" (*OT* 223).

142. Fukuyama, who studied with Paul de Man and Derrida along with Bloom and Mansfield, readily concedes that contemporary liberal democracies face "serious problems, from drugs, homelessness, and crime to environmental damage and the frivolity of consumerism." He can still argue for the end of history insofar as "these problems are not obviously insoluble on the basis of liberal principles, nor so serious that they would necessarily lead to the collapse of society as a whole, as communism collapsed in the 1980s" (Fukuyama, *End of History*, xxi). On the dangers posed by environmental problems and high-tech weaponry, see 83, 114, 127, 278, 328, 335–36, 353; Fukuyama apparently assumes that neither nuclear terrorists nor the population explosion will ever pose a grave challenge to liberal principles.

143. In responding to these passages, Altman glibly quotes Strauss's well-known suggestion (from *WIPP* 32) that although moderation should shape a philosopher's "speech," it is "not a virtue of thought" (Altman, "Leo Strauss," 601). Would Altman deny that immoderate words and actions made the twentieth century home to "[c]atastrophes and horrors of a magnitude hitherto unknown" (*SPPP* 168)? As Altman acknowledges (600, 610), Strauss also states that the English "almost always had the very un-German prudence and moderation . . . to conceive of the modern ideals as a reasonable adaptation of the old and eternal ideal of decency, of rule of law, and of that liberty which is not license, to changed circumstances" (GN 372). As mentioned above, Strauss once wrote that "wisdom" itself requires "unhesitating loyalty" to a "decent" regime (*LAM* 24).

Chapter Three

The American Right,
Pious Frauds, and Secret Kingship

Coarse and erroneous interpretations give birth to unintelligent and shameful actions.

—Stephen Holmes

I. INTERPRETING THE INTERPRETERS

Drury's second book, *Leo Strauss and the American Right*, was published in 1997. Since the "American Right" is now a predominant theme, one would expect her to maintain her alarmist and dismissive hostility. She does not disappoint.

As before, Drury's powers of hyperbole are immense: "After reading Leo Strauss and Allan Bloom, and wallowing in all the gloom of modernity, one is likely to conclude that the world in which we live does not contain a *single* redeeming attribute, that life in the modern world is *not worth living*."[1] This exaggeration is crucial because of her effort to tar Straussianism with the promotion of both nihilistic revolt and perpetual war. For evidence of Strauss's exasperation with modernity, Drury at one point summons the exasperation of . . . Heidegger. To illustrate that Strauss "could not have been more sympathetic to Heidegger's despair in the face of the modern predicament," Drury attributes to Strauss phrases that his lecture (at *RCPR* 42) clearly presents as paraphrases of Heidegger: "In the modern world human life is 'nothing but work and recreation' and 'complete emptiness!'" (*LSAR* 72).[2] Drury compounds the distortion by adding the exclamation point.

Perhaps even more arrogantly and contemptuously than she did in 1988, Drury in 1997 rejects the core of Strauss's scholarly and pedagogical enterprises: "Strauss's interpretations of Plato, Aristotle, Xenophon, Alfarabi, Averroës, Maimonides, and the other greats, tells [*sic*] us more about Strauss than about the thinkers in question" (*LSAR* 49). This statement is a preposterous reversal. Although Strauss's writings incorporate pronouncements and arguments he makes in his own name, he is first and foremost a thinker whose ideas were shaped by the books he studied so assiduously. Given his relentless focus on past writers, one cannot escape the conclusion that *he* learned from *them*. And no one deeply committed to learning could seriously insist that books such as *Natural Right and History*, *The City and Man*, *Thoughts on Machiavelli*, *Socrates and Aristophanes*, *On Tyranny*, and *The Political Philosophy of Hobbes* fail to convey sharp and comprehensive insights into the primary authors they discuss: for example, Thucydides, Aristophanes, Xenophon, Plato, Aristotle, Machiavelli, Hobbes, Locke, Rousseau, Burke, and Weber. Strauss's attention to their texts is so careful, methodical, detailed, and precise that they should tell an open-minded reader more about the authors than about him, even if he sometimes buried "teachings" within his commentaries.[3] Inspired by Strauss, a typical Straussian begins from the assumption not commonly made by contemporary scholars that the "canonical" authors might be wiser than contemporary readers. By continuing their painstaking dissections of the canonical works, Straussians continue to be educated by individuals other than Strauss.[4] Insofar as Straussians are perpetual students, of course, they cannot be Leninists, Nazis, or conspiratorial cultists.

No one could confuse Machiavelli's treatment of Livy—the long stretches of silence, the constant misquoting and reversals, the absence of citations—with what Strauss wrote concerning the above-named figures. Nor, as will be elaborated below, should one confuse Farabi's palpably—and pervasively—quirky commentaries on Plato with Strauss's meticulous reconstructions. It is hard to escape the thought that Drury attempts to pry Strauss from *his* teachers so that she can more easily traduce him and his students.[5] The travesty is augmented by *Drury's* numerous errors, distortions, and inconsistencies. Had she delved more deeply into most of the books Strauss examines, she would have been better equipped to tackle Strauss.

Drury can easily cite disparagements of Strauss's scholarship. His approach was radical. He often wrote dialectically rather than linearly, and, except in his book reviews, he rarely directed sustained attention to the "secondary literature." He exudes a certain antiegalitarian spirit, and he leaves abundant work for his readers.[6] By devoting extreme attention to a relatively small number of texts, furthermore, we Straussians may occasionally stumble because we do not know more about history, anthropology, economics, the natural sciences, and other disciplines.

Even someone who has not scrutinized every word Strauss wrote and/or who is unwilling to suppose that she or he understands Strauss as he understood himself—that is, even someone who cannot confidently specify the multiple levels (exoteric and esoteric) of what Strauss intended to communicate—can plunge, with Strauss's help, ever deeper into the history of political philosophy. And that plunge can promote the "critical intellect" the student brings to the issues themselves. I am inclined to agree with Strauss that "probably the most disastrous form of dogmatism is that which proceeds from the belief in continuous progress; if that belief is sound . . . no passionate interest in earlier views, no serious willingness to submit to the teaching of earlier thinkers, no serious effort at liberation from the prejudices of the present, no progress, can develop" (*WIPP* 266).

Many authors who demonize Strauss, I submit, allow their alarm about political consequences to preempt their openness to Strauss's interpretations. These critics might say that they are fighting dangerous lies, but insofar as they subject *truths* to friendly fire they qualify as persecutors who may induce esoteric writing. Strauss's writings, in my opinion, should be confronted by any serious student of Western culture. I would in no way insist, however, that Strauss's efforts to remedy—and perhaps merely to diagnose—the "crisis of the West" should be treated with similar deference. He stated in 1963 that the crisis was "obvious" to the meanest capacities, but that is an assertion rather than an argument.[7]

Drury's attempts to read Strauss's agenda *into* his interpretations of the dead white males makes it easier to dismiss *their* wisdom, and thus fuels the historicist, positivist, deconstructivist, feminist, multiculturalist, and careerist agendas with which most academic Straussians periodically contend. Commentaries can be vehicles for secret teachings, but Strauss's interpretations have their own acute force. Among other things, his works convey the depths of the insights that the old guys could acquire—without Google, Wikipedia, or classes in women's studies—and the care with which they could write via quill and parchment.

II. DRURY AND LUBAN ON THE INNER DIMENSIONS OF RACE AND RELIGION

How potent are the powers of imagination that, in Drury's opinion, Strauss employs as he misinterprets authors in order to communicate his own perverse views? Anemic, it would seem. After arguing, with limited success, that his rejection of assimilation for Jews signals his rejection of America's liberalism and "melting pot," Drury says "[i]t does not occur to him that the 'peoples' of Europe are not some mystical purebreds that have sprung from rock and oak" (*LSAR* 43).[8] Beyond attributing to Strauss a conspicuously foolish view—that entire peoples can qualify as "mystical purebreds"—she is claiming that the sober alternative never even crossed Strauss's mind. In his 1962 lecture, "Why We Remain Jews"—from which Drury quotes extensively in the same chapter—Strauss explicitly states that human beings "are not descended from rocks or oaks (to quote an old poet)" (WWRJ 72). Strauss adds the prescient observation that "'[r]ace' as it is used in any human context is not a subject about which biologists can say anything" (WWRJ 71).

The eagerness Drury displays in belittling Strauss's brain is also evident in her brusque declaration that he had "little or no appreciation of the inner dimension of faith that is at the heart of religious experience."[9] Drury is entitled to emphasize, as many responsible scholars have done, Strauss's agnostic inclinations, but this claim about "the inner dimension of faith" is ludicrous. Has she seen into his soul and found it wanting compared to what *she* presumes to know of the religious experience?

Strauss's respectful, captivating, and abundant descriptions of piety cannot be construed simply as a mask. Let me share a few of the many examples that would illustrate the same point. Could passages such as the following have been penned, let alone published, by someone who had "little or no appreciation of the inner dimension of faith"?[10]

If miracles are denied, then the relation of God to the corporeal world, to nature, the sovereign power of God over nature becomes suspect. Yet the efficacy of God in and over the natural course of events is the pre-condition that man in his human existence can know that he is truly in the hands of God. Trust in God, obedience to Him, discerns in each cosmic process (not only in the stirrings of the human heart), the hand of God at work. (*SCR* 212–13)

God's revealing Himself to man, His addressing man . . . is genuinely known through present experience which every human being can have if he does not refuse himself to it. This experience is not a kind of self-experience . . . but of something undesired, coming from the outside, going against man's grain; it is the only awareness of something absolute which cannot be relativized in any way as everything else, rational or nonrational, can; it is the experience of God as the Thou, the father and king of all men; it is the experience of an unequivocal command addressed to me here and now as distinguished from general laws or ideas which are always disputable and permitting of exceptions. Only by surrendering to God's experienced call which calls for one's loving Him with all one's heart, with all one's soul and with all one's might can one come to see the other human being as one's brother and love him as oneself. (*SCR* 8–9)[11]

Recent theology has become inclined to deny that divine punishment is more than the misery which is the natural or necessary consequence of the estrangement from God or of the oblivion of God, or than the emptiness, the vanity, the repulsive or resplendent misery, or the despair of a life which is not adherence to God and trust in God. (*TM* 197)

Human suffering from evil presupposes human knowledge of good and evil and *vice versa*. Man wishes to live without evil. The Bible tells us that he was given the opportunity to live without evil and that he cannot blame God for the evils from which he suffers. By giving man that opportunity God convinces him that his deepest wish cannot be fulfilled. The story of the fall is the first part of the story of God's education of man. This story partakes of the unfathomable character of God. (*SPPP* 157)

Prayer is the language of the correlation of man with God. As such it must be a dialogue while being a monologue. It is this because it expresses man's love of God as an actual experience of the soul, for the soul is given by God and hence is not exclusively the human soul; therefore it can speak to God and with God. Love of God is the highest form of human love; it is longing for God, for nearness to Him. This must not make one forget that man's longing for God is longing for his redemption, for his moral salvation—a longing that originates in anguish. But man is not merely his soul; all human cares and sorrows become legitimate themes of prayer. Above all, the dangers to intellectual probity are impenetrable for man; if all other purposes of prayer could be questioned, its necessity for veracity, for purity of the soul cannot: God alone can create in man a pure heart. (*SPPP* 245)

In the first extract, it is clear that Strauss is speaking entirely for himself. Strauss also appears to be speaking for himself in the second extract; the paragraph begins with Strauss's invoking both present experience and "inherited opinions" to explain why efforts to portray traditional Judaism as "the religion of reason"—efforts that would culminate in the assertion that God is a "product of the human mind"—"suddenly lost all their force."[12] The third extract comes from Strauss's discussion of Genesis in his famous essay, "Jerusalem and Athens: Some Preliminary Reflections"; although the relevant paragraph begins with a sentence about what the Bible "intends" to teach, Strauss's own voice clearly surfaces. The fourth extract comes from his introduction to Hermann Cohen's *Religion of Reason out of the Sources of Judaism*. Although Strauss here draws on Cohen's chapter about prayer, particularly Cohen's repeated remarks about man's "correlation" with God,[13] the sequencing and the specific wording belong to Strauss, who goes through the entire paragraph without even mentioning Cohen.

Drury's crudity in alleging that Strauss was oblivious to "the heart of religious experience" (*LSAR* 56) is matched by a prominent American academic, David Luban, the Frederick Haas professor of Law and Philosophy at Georgetown University. For Strauss, implies Luban, "religion is nothing more than a lie that 'breeds deference to the ruling class'" (and philosophers are simply "those who understand" this thesis).[14] No, religion is a fundamental alternative that philosophy would at best struggle to refute (*NRH* 74–75); "philosophy and the Bible are the alternatives or the antagonists in the drama of the human soul" (MITP 223); and the vitality of western culture lies in the fertile tension between Jerusalem and Athens. Based on her meticulous study of "Jerusalem and Athens" (*SPPP* 147–73), Susan Orr argues that several of the essay's early tilts toward Athens were *not* "meant to be taken seriously."[15] Because the possibility of continued search or questioning "appeals to our modern souls more immediately than the life demanded by the Bible," and because atheism was "the reigning academic

fashion," Strauss's strategy enables the "lost souls" of both Judaism and Christianity "to consider what the Bible has to say openly, without feeling threatened
by the idea of God, especially by that God which we thought we had outgrown
and left behind in childhood." As Strauss's essay unfolds, its "exacting exegesis
. . . brings the text to life, and the text itself demands that we respect it."[16]

According to Strauss, "all assertions of orthodoxy" rest on "the *irrefutable
premise* that the omnipotent God whose will is unfathomable, whose ways are
not our ways, who has decided to dwell in the thick darkness, may exist" (*SCR*
28/*LAM* 254; emph. added). It is clear that Strauss is here speaking in his own
name, as he is in this memorable sequel: "The genuine refutation of orthodoxy
would require the proof that the world and human life are perfectly intelligible
without the assumption of a mysterious God; it would require at least the success
of the philosophic system: man has to show himself theoretically and practically
as the master of the world and the master of his life; the merely given world must
be replaced by the world created by man theoretically and practically" (*SCR* 29/
LAM 254–55).[17] As far back as 1963, two of America's most illustrious political philosophers were outraged because Strauss both criticized "sociological or
psychological theories . . . which exclude, without considering, the possibility
that religion rests ultimately on God's revealing Himself to man" and protested
that "the dogmatic exclusion of religious awareness proper renders questionable
all the long-range predictions concerning the future of societies" (Epilogue 322).
To John Schaar and Sheldon Wolin, these two passages from Strauss exude
"the violent language . . . of the fanatic" and are thus "beneath the contempt of
philosophy."[18] Surely, the behaviorist/empiricist political scientists Strauss cri-
tiqued typically failed to predict our current problems with Islamism.

One can scrutinize the many hundreds of published pages on which Strauss,
over the course of roughly fifty years, discusses religion, and not find him utter or even imply a formulation as crude as Luban's. Luban would also have
to explain why so many Straussians are observant and devout Jews, Catholics,
Protestants, Mormons, or Muslims.[19] Apart from passages I discuss elsewhere, I
would emphasize Strauss's claim that "[n]o one can be both a philosopher and a
theologian. . . . But every one of us can be and ought to be either the one or the
other, the philosopher open to the challenge of theology or the theologian open
to the challenge of philosophy" (MITP 217).[20] I think Strauss believes this—I
know that I do—and Strauss did more than any other author to open my eyes
and my heart to the claims of theology. Strauss, moreover, demonstrated through
five decades of scholarship that even if his primary orientation was philosophical, he could not have been more "open to the challenge of theology." How
many of the critics who condemn Strauss for reducing religion to a political tool
are open to that challenge?

The phrase Luban quotes about deference comes from *Thoughts on Machiavelli*, where Strauss is merely inferring that *Machiavelli* held such a view. Even

if one leaves out Strauss's surrounding references to Machiavelli, to quote the entire sentence would demonstrate that Strauss is not speaking for himself: "Religion as reverence for the gods breeds deference to the ruling class as a group of men especially favored by the gods and reminiscent of the gods" (*TM* 230–31).[21] Does Luban think that Paul Wolfowitz's primary agenda is not neoconservativism but neopaganism? In attempting to sketch Strauss's views about religion, Peter Singer cites the same pages of *TM* when thanking Luban for the quotation ("breeds deference to the ruling class").[22] Luban wrote his letter in response to Atlas to show that Strauss's "views were more peculiar than Mr. Atlas suggests." Like Brian Leiter, Luban says nothing about the peculiar, nay ridiculous, errors that pervade Atlas's article.

Drury's crudity regarding religion in Strauss also surfaces in her discussion of his treatment of Maimonides. If, as Drury asserts, his "reverence for Judaism, as for any religion," is "little more than a veneer adopted for political purposes,"[23] why did Strauss examine religious topics at such great length and with such great penetration throughout his career? When Drury in *LSAR* proceeds to invoke Strauss's early book, *Philosophy and Law: Contributions to the Understanding of Maimonides and His Predecessors*, she articulates an outright fabrication. According to Drury, Strauss "says explicitly that medieval philosophers such as Maimonides, 'did not believe in Revelation properly speaking. They were philosophers in the classical sense of the word: men who would hearken to reason, and to reason only'" (*LSAR* 51). Even though she here accentuates her quotation marks with the prior claim about what Strauss says "explicitly," I could not find the quoted words—or anything that would qualify even as a paraphrase—on the page she cites (*LSAR* 187n65 cites *PL* 47) or on any other page of Strauss's book. One instead finds Strauss explicitly saying opposite things about how Maimonides and his Islamic predecessors understood revelation. For them, "the *fact* of revelation is certain" (*PL* 128). The following elaboration is likewise crucial:

> Even if, after assuring themselves of the permittedness or commandedness of philosophizing as such, they can explain the possibility of the revelation philosophically, and can ultimately regard reason as sole judge of the truth or falsehood of revelation, nevertheless, *before* all endeavors and convictions of this kind, before *all* philosophizing, the fact of the revelation stands firm. (*PL* 81)[24]

In a passage that focuses only on Maimonides, Strauss asks whether revelation conveys "truths that reason cannot contradict because these truths are not accessible to reason?" Strauss says the "answer of Maimonides is beyond doubt: human intellect has a limit which it cannot cross; for this reason man is obliged, for the glory of his Lord, to halt at this limit and not to reject the teachings of revelation that he cannot comprehend and demonstrate" (90–91).[25]

III. THE SEXIST STRAUSS

When Drury complains that Strauss assumed that European peoples were "mystical purebreds" (*LSAR* 43), she links him with racism. Regarding sexism, she accuses much more vigorously. In attempting to demonstrate the "misogyny" that she diagnoses at the heart of neoconservativism's "intellectual lineage," Drury emphasizes the "phalocratic" [*sic*] character of "Strauss's philosophy" (167).[26] Although Drury regards this verdict about Strauss as "undeniable," she defends it with undeniable feebleness when she appeals to his chapter in *Socrates and Aristophanes* about *The Assembly of Women*. Although she is wise to observe that he highlights the repellent character of scenes in which "the 'old hags' pursue young men in the streets," she exaggerates in declaring that he found the whole play "repulsive." She errs more seriously when she traces Strauss's ire to the play's "inversion of what he regards as the natural order of things—the rule of men over women" (*LSAR* 168). The page she cites says nothing about the inferiority of women. Strauss instead observes that "conventional equality"—the new law that forces young men to have sex with the hags—is subverting a "natural inequality" regarding both "age and beauty" (*SA* 272), and he later highlights the injustice done to the young *girl* deprived by the hags of her lover, Epigenes (275–77); Strauss even proclaims that Praxagora, the woman who conceived and led the revolution, is "the living refutation of egalitarianism" (280) who "surpasses by far all men and women" (281).

Drury proceeds to assert that the play ends without dramatizing the defects of Praxagora's scheme because Aristophanes "does not assume, as does Strauss, that the old order is natural" (*LSAR* 168). Strauss indeed states that the ending is "unsatisfactory" (*SA* 278), even "repulsive or nauseating." Here too, however, he is reacting to the plight of nobility and beauty, not to a critique of patriarchy's naturalness: the men of Athens, says Strauss, have been led "to sacrifice all concern with the noble or beautiful," lured by "the prospect of being lavishly fed and otherwise taken care of by the women" (*SA* 279). When Drury adds that Strauss "cannot understand" why Aristophanes didn't "condemn the triumph of the women at the end of the play" (*LSAR* 168), she again reveals the limits of her own understanding. Unlike Drury, Strauss assesses the conclusion by comparing it with the conclusions of Aristophanes' other plays, where "we see at the end whether the character responsible for the design that animates the action has succeeded or failed or partly succeeded, and therewith whether and to what extent the poet approves of the design" (*SA* 278). Highlighting the problems that envy poses regarding both sex and wealth (269, 276, 280)—and highlighting the characters' recurring invocations of democratic procedures and principles (264, 270, 271–72, 274, 276)—Strauss argues that *The Assembly of Women* was meant to satirize egalitarianism.[27]

IV. STRAUSSIANS IN WASHINGTON

As in her first book, Drury concludes with alarmism. The "Strauss-inspired" neoconservative elite is "ready, willing, and able to use almost any means to achieve its end"; neocons "identify their political opponents as the enemy, and therefore introduce into domestic politics a friend/foe mentality that transforms the political contest into a life-and-death struggle against diabolical forces"; having established itself as "the dominant ideology of the Republican party," neoconservatism "threatens to remake America in its own image" (*LSAR* 177–78). Would Drury concede that Straussians are less than "diabolical"?

Given the magnitude of her accusations about Straussians in power and about the deep-seated Straussian commitment to dishonesty, Drury is obligated to identify us reliably in a book titled *Leo Strauss and the American Right*. Here too she falls embarrassingly short, paving the way for Tim Robbins, James Atlas, and other incompetent investigators of the Vast Straussian Conspiracy. In her opening chapter, "Straussians in Washington," Drury provides a list of "Strauss's students and their students" who played important roles in the Republican Party and/or in the administrations of Ronald Reagan and George H. W. Bush. We can reasonably characterize some of those individuals as Straussians: John T. Agresto, Seth Cropsey, Alan Keyes, Bill Kristol, and Carnes Lord. Drury also includes William Bennett, Robert Bork, and Clarence Thomas (*LSAR* 3), who are certainly more powerful and better known than Agresto, Cropsey, and Lord. But I have not been able to unearth *any* evidence that Bennett, Bork, or Thomas took a single course with a student of Strauss, let alone with Strauss himself, or that any of them had studied Strauss's writings. Is Drury willing to call Bennett a "student" of Kristol because Kristol worked for Bennett? Would any Straussian agree with Bennett that Rush Limbaugh was "very serious intellectually" and might be "our greatest living American"?[28] According to Nina Easton, Bennett "claimed never to have read a word of Strauss"; in Bennett's words, "I have no idea what the man ever wrote. All I was told was that I should never go to a Straussian party because all they do is talk."[29] What, no poker? Bennett attended a Jesuit high school, did his undergraduate work at Williams College and earned his PhD in philosophy at the University of Texas; he also picked up a law degree from Harvard. But it does not appear that he studied with *any* Straussians along the way.[30]

Anyone who has paid serious attention to Clarence Thomas knows that his thinking is difficult to pigeonhole. Thomas presumably encountered Strauss's influence by reading Jaffa's *The Crisis of the House Divided*.[31] Thomas was particularly swayed by Jaffa's efforts to appeal beyond the Constitution, which sanctioned slavery, to the principles of natural equality conveyed by the Declaration of Independence;[32] arguing along these lines in a 1989 article, Thomas

cites a *National Review* article in which Jaffa attacked Robert Bork.[33] Although
Thomas was also impressed by Bloom's *The Closing of the American Mind*, he
complained that the book's middle section was boring (*CTB* 298); most Straussians, I assume, find this section exhilarating compared to, say, *The Argument
and Action of Plato's Laws*.

In a 1987 speech, Thomas had the temerity to say that an article by Lewis
Lehrman about the Declaration and the "meaning of the right to life" was "a
splendid example of applying natural law." Specifically, grounding a political
regime in natural law

> allows us to reassert the primacy of the individual, and establishes our inherent
> equality as a God-given right. This inherent equality is the basis for aggressive
> enforcement of civil rights laws and equal employment opportunity laws designed
> to protect individual rights. (*CTB* 302)

What several Democratic senators and many other people found so disturbing
about these words was their implications for *Roe v. Wade*, which Lehrman had
criticized—not their implications for Strauss's critique of Locke.

In his second term (1986–1990) as chairman of the Equal Employment Opportunity Commission (EEOC), Thomas hired as speechwriters two students
of Harry Jaffa: Ken Masugi and John Marini.[34] According to Andrew Peyton
Thomas, Thomas's prime motivation in hiring Masugi and Marini was to provide more ideological balance to a staff that already included many liberals and
people of color (*CTB* 286).[35] In Thomas's words, Masugi served as "a docent of
prevailing conservative thought and a sort of connoisseur of periodical literature"
(*CTB* 287). Thomas had long valued ongoing learning, and scheduled regular
staff meetings for open-ended discussions during his second term (289–90).

Thomas has condemned racism in America more sharply than Straussians
and Republicans typically do. As EEOC chair, he criticized the Reagan administration for its "blatant indifference" to blacks (*CTB* 293–94), including its
interventions on behalf of Bob Jones University;[36] because of the unfair impact
on racial/ethnic minorities, he protested the tax deduction for mortgage-interest
payments (300); and he has said, of white Americans, that from "the first drop of
the venom of racism to the slave codes to the Jim Crow laws, they broke God's
law" (591). In 1972, he voted for George McGovern (143).

Thomas has never called himself a Straussian, and I feel compelled to follow
his lead. I have found no evidence that Thomas ever cracked one of Strauss's
books, and I have found abundant evidence that his intellectual development
was shaped by various twentieth-century authors—particularly Thomas Sowell,
Ayn Rand, Malcolm X, Friedrich Hayek, and Richard Wright—whose agendas
are hardly "Straussian."[37] In a 1987 interview, when he was chair of the EEOC,
Thomas described his debts to Sowell and Wright in dramatic terms. Sowell's
1975 book, *Race and Economics*, was "manna from heaven," like "pouring half

a glass of water on the desert"; Sowell was "not only an intellectual mentor, but my salvation as far as thinking through these issues." When asked about writers who had swayed him in his youth and who were still very influential, however, Thomas invoked Richard Wright: "I would have to put him number one, numero uno. Both *Native Son* and *Black Boy* really woke me up."[38] Thomas's favorite movie is *The Fountainhead* (based on the novel by Ayn Rand). While director of the EEOC, he frequently showed this 1949 film over lunch; as a Supreme Court Justice, he makes his four clerks at the start of each term watch it.[39] Looking over his whole educational odyssey, finally, I am struck by its Catholic components. Thomas attended Saint Benedict the Moor School through eighth grade, Saint Pius X for high school, Holy Cross for college, and proceeded to enroll in two different seminaries (Saint John Vianney Minor Seminary and Conception Seminary College).[40] In a recent interview, Father Jerome Fasano of St. Andrew the Apostle Church in Clifton, Virginia, described him as "an exemplary Catholic."[41] For Drury, Luban, Singer, and countless other critics, Fasano's verdict, if accurate, would almost guarantee that Thomas is no Straussian.

Turning to Robert Bork, we must first note his letter to the *New York Times* — responding to Brent Staples (28 November 1994) and Richard Bernstein (29 January 1995) — that emphatically denied that he was even "influenced" by Strauss. Bork declares that he had never met Strauss or read *any* of his writings.[42] The *Times* printed a correction of Bernstein, apparently on the same day, for having "included a name incorrectly in citing former students and other followers of Professor Strauss."

Bork cut his teeth in the "law and economics" movement, and his thoroughgoing legal positivism has prompted sharp criticisms from Jaffa, who places him among the "Confederate jurists" (*CTB* 308).[43] Another set of hilarious claims can be found in the *Journal of Blacks in Higher Education*, which maintains that Strauss was "the intellectual mentor" to various "law and economics" scholars at Chicago, including Richard Posner, Antonin Scalia, Ralph K. Winter, and Richard A. Epstein.[44]

In playing up Strauss's political influence, Drury claims that the *New York Times* "has dubbed Leo Strauss the godfather of the Republican Party's 1994 Contract with America" (*LSAR* 3). As happens so often, the source Drury cites (on 180n5) said something much less sweeping: in the relevant op-ed article, Richard Bernstein merely stated that Strauss's "ghost" had become a "sort of intellectual godfather" to the Republicans. Here's the full, spectrally wrought sentence: "Embraced by prominent conservatives in the context of the 1994 campaign, the ghost of Professor Strauss emerged from his cloister transformed, now a sort of intellectual godfather to the Contract with America." Whatever one concludes about Bernstein's metaphor — the ghost who emerges via embrace and becomes a godfather — one must fault his sloppiness in designating Bennett, Bork, and Thomas as Straussians.[45] Bernstein's and Drury's errors have spread like wildfire.[46] Will Hutton offers additional detail, claiming that Gingrich admitted that the Contract with America was "inspired by Strauss."[47] I cannot bring myself to peruse Gingrich's vast body of writing and speeches, but I would hypothesize that Hutton, who provides no citation, has just embellished (directly or via a web intermediary) Drury's claim about godfathering. Or maybe he was subliminally influenced by the photo of Gingrich that joins the photos of Strauss and Clarence Thomas on the cover of *LSAR*.

One of Drury's nastier accusations about Washington Straussians concerns Bill Kristol and Colin Powell. Kristol and the *Weekly Standard* endorsed Powell as the Republican nominee in 1996, even though, according to Drury, Kristol "admitted that he did not agree with Powell on anything—but no matter, Powell looked like a winner." Once the election is won, Drury continues, "the candidate can always be reconstructed" (*LSAR* 179–80n3). A comparable extrapolation is issued by John Walsh on a website coedited by Alexander Coburn, columnist for the *Nation*. Current neoconservatives, Walsh asserts, "go beyond Strauss and leave nothing to chance. It would even appear that they look for the stupid, gullible or those who are mentally compromised." Hence Kristol becomes Quayle's chief of staff, and Lewis Libby "the right hand man to the addled Cheney as well as assistant to the Quayle-like Bush." Walsh's judgment that Drury's books provide a "superb account" of Strauss's ideas is belied by the ignorance he displays when he asserts that Strauss was "mainly interested in foreign policy."[48]

In an embarrassing display of Straussophobia combined with professorial egotism, Klaus J. Milich pronounces that the "list of Strauss's students or students of his students" who held important Washington positions is "too long to be mentioned here," but in the list his footnote provides, he includes six "disciples"—Clarence Thomas, William Bennett, Norman Podhoretz, Robert Bork, Perle, and Wolfowitz—only one of whom (Wolfowitz) is even arguably a Straussian.[49] The sources Milich here cites—Devigne and Deutsch/Murley—include *none* of the six, and not even Drury (whom Milich elsewhere cites) includes Perle or Podhoretz. As previously mentioned, Milich's article appeared in a peer-reviewed journal (*Cultural Critique*) published by the University of Minnesota Press.

V. FARABI AND THE SECRET KINGSHIP

Strauss now appears to be wielding his hegemony both beyond the grave and behind the scene. In the first paragraph of her introduction to the 2005 reprinting of *PILS*, Drury asserts that the book "showed" that Strauss was "a sworn enemy of freedom and democracy who believed that the best form of government is the absolute but covert rule of a 'wise' elite independent of law" (*PILS*-05 ix). Drury has here supplied the most egregious of her contradictions. In the conclusion of this very book, Drury *denies* that Strauss is an enemy of democracy, let alone a sworn enemy: "Strauss makes it *clear* that he is *not* an enemy of democracy" (emphases added); he is "elitist, but he is not anti-democratic." She even admits his attachment to freedom: "For Strauss, democratic society provides the sort of freedom that is necessary to the unhampered pursuit of the philosophical life" (*PILS* 194). How can Drury interpret Strauss and the giants of political philosophy when she fails so patently in interpreting herself? As elsewhere, the impact of her error is multiplied because it appears in such an inflammatory accusation. Based on the chronology of the reprinting, and the accusations she offers in later settings (*LSAR, AK,* and recent articles/interviews), one would infer that Drury came to abandon the above-quoted concession from the conclusion of *PILS*. But she should be ashamed of what she wrote in 2005 about her thesis in 1988.

To support her case regarding what the new introduction labels "The Covert Rule of the Wise" (xiii–xviii), Drury emphasizes how Strauss, initially stimulated by Farabi, interpreted Plato's *Laws*.[50] One can trace this agenda back to a 1985 article, where she builds to an insinuation of real-world conspiracy: that the secret advice and influence, nay "rule," of philosophers as conceived by Strauss is "not unlike the sort of influence that we find neoconservatism exerting on contemporary politics."[51] A careful examination of how Drury over this twenty-year period tries to ground her allegations in the texts of Plato, Farabi, and Strauss, reveals a by-now-too-familiar pattern whereby she formulates an intriguing hypothesis but then contaminates it with misquotation, exaggeration, contradiction, and paltry documentation.

Here is the key passage from the 1952 introduction to *Persecution and the Art of Writing* (17) that Drury attempts to quote in her 1985 article (on 319):

> We may say that Farabi's Plato eventually replaces the philosopher-king who rules openly in the virtuous city, by the secret kingship of the philosopher who, being "a perfect man" precisely because he is an "investigator," lives privately as a member of an imperfect society which he tries to humanize within the limits of the possible.[52]

The secret kingship, according to Drury's article, means that "philosophers can rule the city behind the scenes with no risks to themselves or to philosophy."[53] Because Drury pays no attention to *Farabi*'s text, she does not appreciate the light Strauss casts on it, and her grave assertion about risk-free "behind the scenes" hegemony is not supported by the relevant texts of either Strauss or Farabi.

Strauss's statement about secret kingship, a phrase I have not encountered in Farabi, provides a climax to his delicate discussion of several profound puzzles that Farabi's *Philosophy of Plato* poses about the philosopher's relationship to the city. While working through the *Phaedrus*, the *Republic*, and other Platonic dialogues, Farabi provides diverse elaborations of how philosophy, for example, "the theoretical art that supplies the knowledge of the beings" (§19), is complementary and/or identical to the "princely and political art" that in practice "guides souls toward happiness" (§21–22).[54] His concluding section, however, seems to emphasize that, according to Plato, "the perfect man, the man who investigates," can exist even in flawed cities lacking philosopher-kings (§38).[55]

Anticipating his subsequent interpretation of the *Republic*, Strauss highlights the *Philosophy of Plato*'s movement from the city to the individual. Strauss argues that Farabi's earlier elevations of the royal art, including his quasi-identifications of it with the philosophical life, were intended partly to soften the deeper message that complete happiness is available only to philosophers. The philosopher nevertheless remains engaged with politics insofar as he "tries to humanize"—within "the limits of the possible"—an imperfect society (*PAW* 17). By identifying philosopher and king, Farabi implies that philosophy "does not need to be supplemented by something else, or by something that is thought to be higher in rank than philosophy, in order to produce happiness"; Farabi thus demotes religion (*PAW* 12–13). But by retaining the distinction between philosophy as "the highest theoretical art" and the royal art as "the highest practical art," Farabi accommodates "the orthodox view according to which philosophy is insufficient for leading man to happiness" (*PAW* 15). In "Farabi's *Plato*" (hereafter, FP) a 1945 essay by Strauss that the *PAW* introduction made "free use" of (*PAW* Preface) and that Drury freely cites, Strauss states that "philanthropy" also required Farabi to soften a doctrine that would basically eliminate "the very prospect of happiness to the large majority of men" (FP 378).[56]

Citing *PAW* 15, Drury attempts to explain the religious angle when she adds that, for Strauss, Farabi "replaces religion with politics" and therefore

> lays the foundation for the secular alliance between philosophers and princes friendly to philosophy. In so doing, he "initiates the tradition whose most famous representatives in the West are Marsilius of Padua and Machiavelli." Strauss silently omits Plato. ("Esoteric Philosophy," 320)

Drury here has both misquoted and embellished. In the *PAW* paragraph from which she draws her quotation, Strauss did not write that Farabi "initiates" the tradition of Marsilius and Machiavelli; he wrote that Farabi "may be said . . . to initiate" that tradition (and to "lay the foundation for the secular alliance between philosophers and princes friendly to philosophy").[57] And why does Drury conclude her paragraph by saying that Strauss "omits Plato" ("Esoteric Philosophy" 320)? To answer this question, we must turn to the comparable discussion she provides in 1988. After repeating the material from the above block-quotation about the secular alliance, she adds that "the tradition that Strauss describes belongs equally to Plato as to Machiavelli" (*PILS* 29). If this is true, Strauss would be a moron to suggest that Farabi, who lived more than a millennium after Plato, initiated that tradition. And why should Plato be included among the philosophers who sought a *secular* alliance with princes (*PAW* 15) or who replaced "religion with politics" ("Esoteric Philosophy" 320)?

In the much longer statement that Strauss provided in "Farabi's *Plato*," he highlights considerations that reflect the *post*-Plato emergence of Christianity, Islam, and their emphatically universalizing agendas. Strauss boldly asserts here that Farabi "uses the identification of philosophy with the royal art as a pedagogic device for leading the reader toward the view that theoretical philosophy by itself, and nothing else, produces true happiness in this life, i.e. the only happiness which is possible" (FP 370).[58] In a footnote, Strauss highlights that Farabi's identification of philosopher and king occurs in "what appears to be" Farabi's summary of Plato's *Statesman* even though that dialogue is "based on the explicit thesis that philosopher and king are not identical."[59] For Plato to trumpet in pagan Greece that philosophy produces "the only happiness which is possible" might have been dangerous. But broadcasting such a claim in a medieval community dominated by any of the Abrahamic religions would certainly be dangerous.

Let us return to Drury's insinuation that Strauss in *PAW* was concealing that Plato as much as Marsilius and Machiavelli had sought a "secular alliance" with friendly princes (*PAW* 15). That Plato's situation differed from the situation of Farabi, Marsilius, and Machiavelli is suggested in the sentences that immediately follow Strauss's invocation of the latter two men. Farabi, says Strauss, "speaks of the need for the virtuous city which he calls 'another city.' He means to replace the other world or the other life by the other city" (*PAW* 15).[60] Plato, we may infer, did *not* encounter the same threat from "the other world or the other life," despite the threats that philosophy faced in his time.[61]

In the relevant paragraph from *PAW* 15, Strauss's Farabi maintains that, to achieve happiness, one must combine philosophy with "the royal art."[62] When Strauss proceeds quickly to say that "the supplement to philosophy" is "not religion or Revelation but politics, if Platonic politics" and that Farabi thus prepares "the secular alliance" (*PAW* 15), he seems to be reiterating or elaborating Farabi's worldly orientation.[63] In any case, he is *not* inviting the reader to group Plato with Marsilius—who harped on the "one singular and very obscure cause" that Aristotle (like every other "philosopher of his time or before") could not have "known" or anticipated.[64] Nor is Strauss—in either the *PAW* introduction or FP—inviting the reader to group Plato with Machiavelli, whom Strauss playfully likens to the Antichrist (*TM* 171). Regarding Marsilius, moreover, Strauss in his *HPP* chapter (first published in 1963) accentuates the gap between Marsilius and Plato when he uncharacteristically highlights historical context. According to Strauss, Marsilius regarded his "anticlerical policy" as "by far the most urgent task for his age" (*LAM* 195/*HPP* 262), and Strauss proclaims that Marsilius's "venture" aimed at "the eradication of papal plenitude of power and everything reminding of it" (*LAM* 193/*HPP* 260).

The circumstances that distance Plato from what Strauss called the "secular" alliance between philosophers and "princes friendly to philosophy" are also addressed by Strauss's essay on Farabi ("How Fārābī Read Plato's *Laws*") in *WIPP*. Strauss here writes that Farabi "may have rewritten the *Laws*, as it were, with a view to the situation that was created by the rise of Islam or of revealed religion generally" (144).[65] In the FP paragraph immediately following the one claiming that for Farabi "theoretical philosophy by itself, and nothing else, produces true happiness," furthermore, Strauss points out that Aristotle was "free to state that doctrine without much ado since he was under no compulsion to reconcile it with the belief in the immortality of the soul or with the requirements of faith" (FP 371).[66] When Strauss proceeds to identify the "real remedy" and Farabi's "last word on the subject," his Farabi drifts even further from Drury's:

> Farabi makes it absolutely clear that there can be, not only philosophers, but even perfect human beings (i.e., philosophers who have reached the goal of philosophy) in imperfect cities. Philosophy and the perfection of philosophy and hence happiness do not require—this is Farabi's last word on the subject—the establishment of the perfect political community: they are possible, not only in this world, but even in these cities, the imperfect cities. But—and this is the essential implication—in the imperfect cities, i.e. in the world as it actually is and as it always will be, happiness is within the reach of the philosophers alone. (FP 381)[67]

As we have seen, a compressed version of this pattern appears in the *PAW* paragraph that mentions the "secular alliance" and that immediately precedes the paragraph addressing "secret kingship"; Farabi, by contending that the "royal art" must be included for philosophy to produce happiness, accommodates the orthodox/religious view that would reject philosophy's self-sufficiency.[68] Strauss proceeds immediately to observe that the "supplement" philosophy would need to produce happiness is *not* "religion or Revelation," but politics. It is by thus substituting "politics for religion" that Farabi may prepare the *secular* alliance between princes and philosophers such as Marsilius and Machiavelli (*PAW* 15). For Plato, one might hypothesize, philosophy would not bind itself to the authority of either church or state.[69] Despite her emphasis on whispering, not even Drury accuses Straussians and neoconservatives of attempting to "replace[s] religion with politics" or to establish a "secular alliance" with "princes."

In asserting that the secret kingship means that philosophers will "rule the city behind the scenes with no risks to themselves or to philosophy" ("Esoteric Philosophy" 319), Drury also fails to address the more limited agenda that both Farabi and Strauss emphasize: rescuing philosophy from extinction. Drawing on *Attainment* §63, Strauss identifies the "origin" of the whole tripartite work as "concern with the restoration of philosophy 'after it has been blurred or destroyed'" (*PAW* 12, 18); when Strauss adds that the work is "more concerned with the purpose common to Plato and Aristotle" than with the compatibility of "the results of their investigations" (*PAW* 12), one is likewise reminded of *his* efforts to restore "classical political philosophy" as a whole against the challenges that historicism and other modern developments pose. Strauss also highlights Farabi's comment about the "grave danger" that philosophy and philosophers faced in Plato's time from "the multitude of the citizens of cities and nations."[70] Strauss in *PAW* elaborates that in Plato's time "there was no freedom of teaching and of investigation" (*PAW* 16). When Strauss invokes the danger facing philosophers in "any actual society" because of "the naturally difficult relations between the philosopher and the non-philosophic citizens" (FP 382), he might seem to join his voice to Farabi's. In attempting to revive, promote, and preserve philosophy in twentieth-century liberal democracies, Strauss articulated thoughts that push the envelope of diversity. But I cannot conceive that his philosophical agendas would require anyone to "rule the city behind the scenes," or to experiment with regime change.

Drury not only distorts Strauss's texts in the ways just described. She refers three times in her 1985 article to the "secret kingship" without raising, let alone answering, five obvious but important questions (nor does she address them in her later discussions). First, to what extent can a secret king approach the status of an unsecret legislator or founder? In his 1945 essay, "On Classical Political Philosophy," Strauss celebrates "the higher kind of political understanding" exercised by the "true legislators" (e.g., "the fathers of the Constitution") who "establish, as it were, the permanent framework within which the right handling of changing situations by excellent politicians or statesmen can take place" (*WIPP* 83); he elsewhere faults Burke for denying that "the best social order can be or ought to be the work of an individual, of a wise 'legislator' or founder" (*NRH* 313).[71] Plato's *Laws*, furthermore, teaches that the best way to combine wisdom with freedom and consent is by mixing "the rule of wise laws framed by a wise legislator"—and "administered by the best members of the city"—with "the rule of the common people" (*HPP* 56).[72] Interpreting what the Eleatic stranger says in *Statesman* 293a–303b, Strauss concedes that the "true king," unlike other rulers, may "justly change the laws or act against the laws"; but in the absence of the true king, "the stranger would probably be satisfied if the city were ruled by a code of laws framed by a wise man, one which can be changed by the unwise rulers only in extreme cases" (*HPP* 50). As interpreted by Catherine Zuckert, "[t]he best practical solution to the division between the wise and the unwise presented in the *Statesman* would seem to be for the philosopher to convince a legislator to enact a code of law, including provisions for the education of other wise men to administer the laws once enacted." Although this philosopher-initiated enterprise might seem to resemble what the Athenian does in the *Laws*, Zuckert insists that for Strauss the *Laws*'s city is no more realizable than the *Republic*'s.[73] Annabel Patterson, by contrast, provides a subtle but brief discussion of *AAPL* in order to support a sweeping conclusion: that Strauss extracts from the *Laws* "an authoritative model not only for the anti-Enlightenment society he recommended, but also for Straussianism itself, as a mode of communication and social practice exempted from the rules that apply to others."[74]

We must also wonder about the degree to which secret authority can be kingly, let alone "absolute" (*PILS*-05 ix). Strauss emphasizes that classical political philosophy is "guided by the question of the best regime" and that a regime is "a specific manner of life" that "depends decisively on . . . the *manifest* domination of society by human beings of a certain type" (*WIPP* 34, emph. added). Speaking for himself in 1962, Strauss wrote that the states of the world differ "above all in their regimes and hence in the things to which the preponderant part of each society is dedicated or in the spirit which more or less effectively pervades each society" (Epilogue 313); "[t]hat which at least everyone who counts politically is supposed to look up to . . . gives a society its character; it constitutes and justifies the regime" (318). Strauss further develops this notion in his 1964 essay on Aristotle: "the character of a given city becomes clear to us only if we know of what kind of men its preponderant part consists" (*CM* 46); "every political society derives its character from a specific public or political morality, from what it regards as publicly defensible, and this means from what the preponderant part of society (not necessarily the majority) regards as just" (48).[75] Especially in the second passage, Strauss seems to be speaking as much (and perhaps more) for himself as for Aristotle.[76] Regime change, for Strauss, would require much more than shifting the advisors who whisper in the ears of the president. Nor will it suffice to conquer, occupy, and de-Ba'athify.

My three remaining questions about secret kingship can be presented more succinctly. First, to what degree can a group—Drury once refers to "the secret kingship of the philosophers" ("Esoteric Philosophy" 321) and often refers to ruling done by philosophers (rather than by one philosopher)—have kingly authority?[77] Second, even if someone succeeds in influencing a powerful individual, how often does the power of the influence approach kingly power? And isn't it plausible, finally, that a philosopher who "lives privately" might try to "humanize" a society by speaking to individuals who are not "princes" or by penning salutary texts that, for example, combat racism and militarism or turn certain citizens away from bread and circuses—hot-dog eating contests and *Fear Factor*—to higher pursuits?[78]

Just a few sentences before *PAW* invokes the secret kingship, Strauss attributes to Farabi the following interpretation of Plato's "virtuous city in speech": to avoid the persecution that Socrates experienced because of his "intransigent" challenges to the defective opinions and "way of life" of the Athenians, Plato abandoned "the revolutionary quest for the other city" (16) and instead promoted "the gradual replacement of the accepted opinions by the truth or an approximation to the truth" (17).[79] The type of whispering that Drury, Robert Pippin, Claes Ryn, and others harp upon can have momentous political effects, but we must not overlook the impact of published writings.[80] In FP, but not in *PAW*, Strauss offers the following elaboration *immediately* after the sentence about secret kingship: "That kingship is exercised by means of an exoteric teaching which, while not too flagrantly contradicting the accepted opinions, undermines them in such a way as to guide the potential philosophers toward the truth" (FP 384). Guiding a smattering of readers or listeners to the truth hardly counts as "ruling" a society, openly or covertly.[81] Consider the overview of political improvement Strauss elsewhere offers in elaborating the anti-utopianism he traces to classical political philosophy: "if you do not believe that the perfect condition can be brought about by political action, you cannot hope for more than that one or the other of those in power might be induced, by moral appeal, by advice, by exhortation, by *sermons*, to do his best in his station along the lines of decency and humanity."[82] As Christopher Colmo points out concerning Strauss's account of Farabi's Plato, ordinary political reform (e.g., altering the tax code) typically requires "the kind of open, public participation in political affairs that Strauss's philosopher eschews." As a "secret king," Colmo infers, the philosopher "will do his best publicly to promote the accepted opinions with respect to morality and religion while esoterically working through his books to destroy the hold of those opinions over the minds of potential philosophers."[83] In reflecting upon "the heart of Strauss's political vision," even Eugene Sheppard adopts a nonconspiratorial interpretation: the philosopher "should accommodate to the particular regime under which he lives, yet always retain a hidden loyalty to the secret kingship of philosophy."[84]

VI. SECRET KINGSHIP AND PLATO'S *LAWS*

For additional evidence concerning secret kingship, Drury's 1985 article turns lamely to Plato's *Laws*. In Farabi's view, Drury insists, the *Laws* "fulfills" (rather than "violates") the *Republic* ("Esoteric Philosophy," 319) by implementing a secret kingship. As elsewhere, Drury neither quotes nor cites any texts of Farabi's, and she seems to be drawing entirely on Strauss's interpretation.[85] But nowhere in his writings on Farabi does Strauss say that the *Laws* (according to either Farabi or Strauss) fulfills the *Republic*. Perhaps the most pertinent passage occurs in "Farabi's *Plato*," though Drury nowhere cites it:

> Rejecting both the assimilation of philosophy to the vulgar and the withdrawal from political life, he [Plato as interpreted by Farabi] had to seek a city different from the cities which existed in his time: the city completed in speech in the *Republic* whose results are supplemented in various ways by the *Timaeus*, the *Laws*, the *Menexenus* and other dialogues. The final question which he raised, concerned the way in which the cities of his time could be gradually converted to the life of the perfect city. (FP 362)

"Fulfilling" and "supplementing" may harmonize, but they are not synonyms, and the *Laws* here is given no special status vis-à-vis three other named dialogues and additional ones that Strauss does not name. Strauss, furthermore, highlights the "extreme brevity" with which Farabi's *Philosophy of Plato* (§34) addresses the *Laws* (*WIPP* 153); it is not certain that Farabi's sentence about the *Laws* even invokes the *Republic* (*WIPP* 152).[86] Farabi's description of the *Laws* here (34), finally, is markedly briefer than his description of the *Timaeus* (33) and the *Menexenus* (37).

Drury's indifference toward such intricacies of Farabi's Plato illuminates an important weakness in her attempts to expose the true Strauss allegedly hiding behind the "immunity of the commentator." I concede that her above-described shortcut, however erratically she employs it, applies a lesson Strauss draws from the story (in Farabi's *Summary*) of the pious ascetic, whose general reputation shielded him from the fallout of speaking a dangerous truth (*WIPP* 135–37).[87] In addition, the following remarks about Farabi are doubtless pertinent to the prospect of identifying Strauss's views within his commentaries (especially his later ones): Farabi's *Summary* appears to be "pedantic, pedestrian and wooden writing which abounds in trivial or insipid remarks" (*WIPP* 140); "it is frequently impossible to say where Farabi's alleged report of Plato's views ends and his own exposition begins" (*WIPP* 143); and history can provide a "playful garb" for a Platonist's philosophical teaching (FP 377).[88] Strauss, however, differs from Plato and Farabi insofar as he regards his world as a cave—one *beneath* the "natural" cave—in which we need "elaborate historical studies . . . which would have been superfluous and therefore harmful in more fortunate times" (*PAW* 155).[89] Strauss also departs from Plato (and perhaps Farabi) when he directly addresses *What is* questions and on the numerous occasions when he appears to say "explicitly and unambiguously what he thinks" (*WIPP* 137). Strauss's commentaries, moreover, are intimately tied to the texts, whereas Farabi takes astounding liberties with his Plato. In Strauss's words, Farabi's *Philosophy of Plato* provides "apparently fanciful remarks on the purport of various dialogues" (FP 377), and tacitly imparts a "flagrant deviation" regarding the soul and the afterlife;[90] Farabi's *Summary* appears to reveal "an amazing lack of comprehension of Plato" (*WIPP* 140); there is "a great divergence" between "what Plato explicitly says in the *Laws* and what Farabi explicitly says in the *Summary*" (*WIPP* 142); and in more than half of the places that Farabi (in the *Summary*) says "he [Plato] said" something, Plato did *not* say it (*WIPP* 143).[91] In conclusion, Strauss does *not* invent speeches the way that Plato invents Socratic speeches or even in the way that Farabi invents Platonic speeches.[92]

One additional, and particularly vexing, flaw mars Drury's account of Strauss's Farabi. Consider this attempt to marshal the Nocturnal Council on behalf of her thesis that Strauss appropriated a vision of secret kingship from what Farabi maintained about the relationship between the *Laws* and the *Republic*:

Later, when Strauss studies Plato's *Laws* for himself, he comes to the same conclusion as did Farabi. The Nocturnal council is cleverly introduced only in the twelfth book of the *Laws,* where it is likely to be missed. It ensures the secret rule of the philosopher in the real city. (Drury, "Esoteric Philosophy," 320)

This remark is even more fanciful than her claim that for Farabi and/or Strauss the *Laws* "fulfills" the *Republic* (319). Not once in his published writings on Farabi does Strauss even *mention* the Nocturnal Council.[93] Nor, as far as I know, does Farabi ever mention it. Had Drury consulted the preface to the excerpts from the *Summary* that Lerner and Mahdi provide (83), she would have noticed that Farabi only comments on the first nine books of the *Laws*; and even if she never read a page of Farabi, the opening of Strauss's key *WIPP* essay—"How Fārābī Read Plato's *Laws*"—highlights Farabi's statement that he had seen only the first nine books (*WIPP* 134).[94] As evidence for her claim about the Nocturnal Council, Drury's footnote lazily cites the entirety of Strauss's posthumously published book, *The Argument and Action of Plato's Laws*,[95] a dense 186-page commentary that never mentions Farabi. In this book, furthermore, Strauss never states or even hints that Plato delayed discussing the council until the final book so that lazy readers would fail to notice it. With a view to defusing the conspiratorial miasma that surrounds so many current discussions of Strauss, I must also highlight Christopher Bobonich's comment that "Dawn Council" would be superior to "Nocturnal Council" as a translation of *nukterinos sullogus*;[96] the council meets "from dawn until the sun has risen" (951d) rather than at night. Think joggers.

As everyone knows, Strauss typically suggests that *central* locations rather than beginnings or endings are more suitable for muting controversial teachings.[97] Even a hasty reader of the *Laws*, furthermore, is unlikely to overlook that, based on the initial description by the Athenian, the Nocturnal Council will have a variety of philosophical features: for example, it will hear reports from citizens who travel to "observe the affairs of the other human beings at greater leisure" (951a–b); it will include the supervisor of education (951e); it will dilute the status of the old by linking each elder with a "young" (ages 30–40) associate (951e, 961b); it will focus on "laws and their own city, and anything they may have learned elsewhere that is different and pertains to such matters, as well as whatever branches of learning might seem to contribute to this inquiry" (952a); and it will invite discussion of utterances concerning "the laying down of laws, or education, or upbringing" (952b). Does Drury think that these prominent considerations are "likely to be missed" because they are presented in the dialogue's last book? And why would readers struggle to perceive that the council's authority will be robust?[98]

These philosophical features, however, do not come close to establishing Drury's concluding claim that the council "ensures the secret rule of the philosopher in the real city." First, as Strauss emphasizes, the Athenian does not definitively specify the composition of the council.[99] How then could it "ensure" what goes on in *any* "real city"? Second, the council itself will be the site of negotiation if not struggle between the more philosophically inclined members and unphilosophical but powerful men such as the interlocutor Kleinias. In Strauss's words, the two Dorian interlocutors (Megillus and Kleinias) are "not even tainted by philosophy" (*AAPL* 128), and yet "men of Kleinias' kind will form no insignificant part" of the council (180); Strauss later highlights Kleinias's philosophical shortcomings to illuminate the council's "heterogeneous composition" (185). Kleinias, furthermore, is "only one of the ten men commissioned to draft the laws for the new city" (75) at the behest of the Cretans (702c). Strauss thus concludes that although "the rule of the philosophers is excluded by the character of the second best regime" (see *Laws* 739a on the "second-best city"), even the "most successful compromise" that Kleinias could make with the other nine would drop the regime from second best to third best (*AAPL* 75).[100] We also might wonder if any institutions could ensure that enough genuine philosophers are on hand so that philosophy can play even a subordinate role in the council; Strauss elsewhere states that even in the *Republic* "there may very well be only a single philosopher in the city and surely never a herd or a platoon" (*CM* 114).[101] So it is ridiculous for Drury to claim that the Nocturnal Council "ensures" philosophical rule.

Equally troubling is Drury's reference to "the real city" as the arena where the philosophers will rule secretly. How many societies similar to the one presented in the *Laws*, with its distinctive combination of laws (including the "preludes") and institutions, have ever existed?[102] Strauss, however, does elsewhere make comments that might provide a modicum of support for the case Drury struggles to make. When Strauss discusses the *Laws* in *HPP*, he calls its city the "best possible regime" and positions it between the city of the philosopher kings and the Spartan/Cretan-flavored "timocracy" that Socrates in book VIII depicts as second best. As he proceeds, he emphasizes the resemblance between the city of the *Laws* and the "ancestral regime" of Athens:

> In the *Laws* the Athenian stranger attempts to correct timocracy, i.e., to change it into the best possible regime which is somehow in between timocracy and the best regime of the *Republic*. That best possible regime will prove to be very similar to "the ancestral regime," the predemocratic regime, of Athens. (*HPP* 53)[103]

It remains very difficult to conceive, however, how the *Laws* can provide a general model for "the secret kingship of the philosopher" in "the real city" given how far most actual societies have been from any of the three cited ones (the city of the philosopher-kings, Spartan/Cretan timocracy, and the predemocratic regime of Athens). And how would one adapt a secret kingship to the contemporary United States, whose population and territory are over a thousand times larger?[104] We must also wonder whether ancestral Athens incorporated any institution that even remotely resembles the Nocturnal Council. Strauss emphasizes, finally, that at the conclusion of the *Laws*, two old men who have the power and opportunity to start a colony exhort each other to found the city they have just created in speech; they are not thinking about smuggling *philosophical* authority into any existing community.

For Strauss, clearly, it is the *Republic* rather than the *Laws* (or any other writing by Plato or anyone else) that provides "the broadest and deepest analysis of political idealism ever made."[105] As was mentioned above, Strauss argues that Farabi's Plato abandoned "the revolutionary quest for the other city" (*PAW* 16). And while the politically quiescent strands of the *Republic* are capped off by Socrates' concluding invocation about faring well in the afterlife, an antirevolutionary ethos also suffuses the conclusion of *AAPL*: regarding Megillos's agreement to help Kleinias found the city and persuade the Athenian to join them, Strauss asserts that "[t]he Athenian 'naturally' does not respond" (186).[106]

VII. THE CITY IN SPEECH AND PERVERSE HIERARCHIES

In the second chapter of her 1988 book (*PILS*), Drury incorporates most of the above-summarized material (from her 1985 article) about Plato, Strauss, and Farabi. Her documentation regarding Strauss's account of the *Laws* is equally thin.[107] She does provide a more detailed comparison of the *Laws* and the *Republic*, but not without introducing a major howler. Her main new effort is to undermine Straussian recourse to the propositions that philosophers prefer the private life, escaping the cave, etc., and that the communistic regime of the philosopher kings is merely a "city in speech":[108]

> In Strauss's view, Marx's communist utopia is impossible; it depends on a radical change in the nature of human things. In contrast, Plato's "city in speech" is only improbable. It depends on the chance coincidence of philosophers and princes friendly to philosophy who are willing to listen to their advice. The "city in speech" becomes a reality when the philosophers win the ear of the powerful. In this way, philosophers can rule the city behind the scenes with no risk to themselves or to philosophy. The solution can be found in the difference between Plato's *Republic* and his *Laws*. The *Laws* fulfills rather than violates the intention of the *Republic*. (*PILS* 28)

After repeating her skimpily documented claim that the Nocturnal Council "ensures the secret rule of the philosopher in the real city," Drury adds that "[t]he actualization of the 'city in speech' is therefore *highly probable*" (28–29, emph. added). But where has a city that even approximates the *Republic* or the *Laws* existed during the past 2,500 years? Is a society transformed whenever a philosopher whispers seductively into a ruler's ear? Based on what Socrates says at the end of the *Republic*'s ninth book, where he brings to a close the long and intricate conversation about cities (from the founding of the "city in speech" through the final comparison of the philosopher king with the tyrant), the city in speech would exist only in heaven as "a pattern . . . for the man who wants to see and found a city within himself on the basis of what he sees" (592b). Strauss suggests elsewhere that this city exists metaphorically among philosophers who are, as a rule, separated by both space and time. As long ago as 1939, Strauss addressed the matter quite memorably: in Xenophon's era, philosophers seeking out the "small number" of individuals "able and willing" to accept their views had to write books because "the larger part of that small number . . . was not yet born."[109] According to Daniel Tanguay, likewise, secret kingship involves "the community of solitaries (*solitaires*) who transcend all frontiers of time and space."[110] Strauss's discussions of the *Republic* in *CM* and *HPP* harp on the obstacles to the best regime, including the reluctance of philosophers to sacrifice their wisdom-quest to rule in such a city, let alone to found it. Expelling the adults (*Republic* 540e–541a) would require a huge army, such an army would only exist *within* this city, and Socrates had to be coerced (327b–328b) merely to spend a night speaking about these matters.[111] Not even the *Laws* ends with an enterprise of founding.

Damon Linker, despite his PhD in political science, displays a Drury-like blindness to institutional considerations when he asserts that Strauss presents a "shocking vision of the ideal human society," marked by "the steepest of hierarchies. At the very top is a tiny group of apolitical, amoral, atheistic philosophers who devote their lives to endless questioning of everything under the sun." But in what sort of real-world community could a tiny group engaged in "endless questioning of everything" reside at "the very top"? When Linker returns to this theme, he adds an insult that blasts even academic Straussians who mind their own business: "in nearly every case, the Straussians' pedagogy presupposes their teacher's distinctive—and distinctively perverse—view of modern society: extramoral philosopher-supermen at the top, moral and religious simpletons in the vast middle, and at the very bottom, leading their fellow citizens into bondage in the cave beneath the cave, the nation's non-Straussian academics and intellectuals."[112] Does the *New Republic* routinely include dismissive portrayals of Strauss and Straussians in order to *disguise* its notoriously neoconservative orientation?[113]

Immediately after asserting that actualization of the best regime is "highly probable," Drury links this proposition to a passage from Harry Jaffa that she both misquotes and takes out of context. Here is Drury's version of the quotation:

No one who has experienced the magic of Strauss's teaching can doubt that the best regime not only is possible, but that it has been actual. Nor can he doubt that whatever amelioration of our condition is possible will come about by the influence of those who exercise political power by its spirit. (*PILS* 29)[114]

Jaffa actually ends the second sentence by saying that "whatever amelioration of our condition is possible will come about by the influence *upon* those who exercise political power *of* its spirit."[115] According to Jaffa, that is, amelioration could occur only when the spirit of the best regime influences "those who exercise political power."[116] Drury's most serious distortion, however, involves the context. From her assertion that the Nocturnal Council "ensures" the secret rule of the philosopher in "the real city," Drury infers that the actualization of the city in speech is "highly probable" (*PILS* 28–29) and she proceeds to invoke Jaffa. In the sentences that *immediately* precede the two sentences about "Strauss's teaching," however, Jaffa emphatically denies that the city in speech can be actualized, or made real, in any political setting:

> Statesmanship informed by the awareness of ignorance is not likely to aim at final, much less universal solutions. . . . The best regime is not a political regime; it lives in speech and not in deed. But it *is* the best and we need not transform the world to live there—we need only transform ourselves.[117]

As articulated here, the best regime is a *nonpolitical* community of thinkers/writers and students/readers, and that is why Strauss was able to create it in the *classroom*.

Strauss concludes one of his most famous essays by suggesting that only education can solve the ultimate political challenge: "how to reconcile order which is not oppression with freedom which is not license" (*PAW* 37). As Michael Frazer observes, Strauss, by encouraging readers of texts by Plato (and other authors) to consider "deeds" as well as "speeches," encourages his own readers to escape the torment of seeking ever-deeper levels of esoteric teachings in *Strauss*: his "often hyperbolic odes" to "the philosophical vocation" are validated by his own pursuit of "the life of a teacher and a scholar."[118] In other words, Strauss's real views about the best life are expressed by his lifelong immersion in reading, thinking, writing, speaking, and listening; his disengagement from politics stands out even when compared to the lives led by many of the individuals he wrote about.[119] In addition, almost all of his best known "first-generation" students—for example, George Anastaplo, Seth Benardete, Walter Berns, Allan Bloom, Joseph Cropsey, Werner Dannhauser, Martin Diamond, Robert Faulkner, Ernest Fortin, Victor Gourevitch, Hilail Gildin, Harry Jaffa, Richard Kennington, Ralph Lerner, David Lowenthal, Muhsin Mahdi, Roger Masters, and Herbert Storing—likewise led academic lives.[120] The major exception would appear to be Robert A. Goldwin, who spent a portion of the 1970s in Washington after completing academic stints at the University of Chicago, Kenyon College, and St. John's College in Annapolis.[121]

The "secret kingship" theme is even more prominent in the new introduction of *PILS*, which features a subsection titled "The Covert Rule of the Wise" (xiii–xvii), and Drury adds still higher levels of vitriol. But in the intervening seventeen years, I am pleased to report, Drury has generated . . . a page citation. On behalf of the proposition that, according to Strauss, Plato's "real solution is for the wise to rule behind the scene" (xiv–xv), Drury provides a footnote (liii–liv note 14) that cites two pages of *AAPL*. After stating that Strauss "points to the 'nocturnal council' in Plato's *Laws* and to Xenophon's discussion of 'gentlemen,'" Drury instructs the reader to see *AAPL* 177–78. Although Strauss discusses the council, he says *nothing* here about hidden rule of any sort. As Drury elaborates the *AAPL* citation, she goes further astray by adding this interpretation: "the Council is to the city what intellect is to the body of man. Strauss suggests that in comparison to the Council, the citizens are hardly distinguishable from animals." Her opening claim is only a bit imprecise.[122] But nowhere on the cited pages, or anywhere else in his book, does Strauss "suggest[s] that in comparison to the Council, the citizens are hardly distinguishable from animals." In the pages Drury cites, Strauss does *mention* animals. Beyond the paraphrasing he does of Plato's text, however, Strauss simply asks why—given that "all animals with the exception of man lack intellect"—the Athenian had claimed that "the salvation of every animal" requires intellect (*nous*).[123] Strauss suggests this answer: the Athenian might here blur "the distinction between man and the other animals" in order to accentuate "the indispensable contribution" (to "the salvation of man and the city") available from "sense perceptions which are common to all animals" and from "other things common to animals."[124] The pages Drury cites from *AAPL* make no additional mention of "animal," "animals," or any specific animal. Drury again seems to be dabbling in free association: while discussing the council, Strauss addresses soul, head/intellect, and how man differs from animal, and we know he's an elitist, so he's obviously equating the citizens with beasts.

Drury concludes the paragraph with an accentuated indictment. Earlier, as was previously discussed, she repeatedly accused Strauss of trying to promote "the secret kingship of the philosopher," a phrase Strauss does employ. Now she substitutes tyranny for kingship: "the real Platonic solution as understood by Strauss is the *covert tyranny of the wise*" (*PILS*-05 xv). If only George Carlin could have added "covert tyranny" to his marvelous riff on jumbo shrimp! Hiding and keeping secrets reflects a lack of strength that might repulse most tyrants, not to say the "real men" Drury loves to ridicule.[125] Did any of the subjected inhabitants not know that Mussolini, Hitler, Stalin, Mao, Idi Amin, and Saddam Hussein were firmly in charge? Such tyrants were of course skilled in accusing their scapegoats of "covert" manipulation and domination.

NOTES

1. *LSAR* 140, emphases added. In a similar spirit, Stephen Holmes includes Strauss on his list of "[c]ontentious writers who . . . declare the entire Western world except for themselves to be depraved and diseased" (Holmes, *Anatomy*, xvi).

2. At *LSAR* 48, Drury reiterates her previously discussed strategy (first sketched at *PILS* 15) of identifying Strauss's views with those he attributes to "his wise ancients." Surely Strauss did not regard Heidegger as a wise ancient.

3. Strauss's Farabi imitates Strauss's Plato in employing "ambiguous, allusive, misleading, and obscure speech" (*WIPP* 145), and we can apply such adjectives to some of Strauss's sentences.

4. As Harvey Mansfield notes, Strauss differed from scholars such as Rawls, Oakeshott, and Voegelin by refusing to "encourage or even permit his students to write about him" (Mansfield, "Timeless Mind," review of *Leo Strauss and the Politics of Exile*, by Eugene Sheppard, and *Leo Strauss: An Intellectual Biography*, by Daniel Tanguay, *Claremont Review of Books* 8, no. 1 [Winter 2007/2008]: 25).

5. Recall again her interview accusation that he "completely subverts what the ancients are about." As Fortin explains, Drury's rejection of the need for esoteric writing distinguishes her from many of the above figures, not to mention authors such as Clement of Alexandria and Origen, so that Strauss becomes a scapegoat. See Ernest Fortin, "Between the Lines: Was Leo Strauss a Secret Enemy of Morality?" *Crisis*, December 1989, 23. A slightly longer version was published later as "Dead Masters and Their Living Thought: Leo Strauss and his Friendly Critics," in *Vital Nexus* 1, no. 1 (May 1990): 61–71.

6. Cf. G. R. F. Ferrari, "Strauss's Plato," *Arion* 5, no. 2 (Fall 1997): 36–38, 58, 64.

7. See pp. 276–77 below for a more detailed discussion.

8. The exaltation of diversity and multiculturalism within the contemporary American university, needless to say, makes this "top ten" accusation even more threatening. In her 1994 book on Kojève, Drury conveys similarly inane mind-readings of Francis Fukuyama, whom she describes as a "hapless victim" of Strauss's (*AK* 198): "It does not occur to Fukuyama that there can be distinctions among people on the basis of their character" (the "only distinction he recognizes is between those who flirt with death and those who opt for slavery") [192]; "[f]or all his preoccupation with recognition, Fukuyama has not thought about what it is that people admire" (195). Even a rapid reading of *The End of History and the Last Man*, the focus of Drury's discussion, would suffice to refute both of these risible slanders.

9. *LSAR* 56. Drury's indignation here—she also complains that Strauss "ignores the miracle of the direct relation with the infinite" and "reduces religion to irrational prejudice, fear, and superstition"—is further discredited by the sweeping disparagements of religion that she voices in her latest book. Religion is not "merely a collection of harmless nonsense"; "[m]ore often than not, it is very dangerous nonsense" (*AM* 41); and the Biblical God is "vicious" (107) or "pathological" (180n19). Although *AM* once acknowledges that politics can be "destructive of the dignity and sublimity of religious life," it devotes more attention to explaining "why religion is destructive of political peace, order, and justice" (163–64; cf. 57, 127).

10. To borrow a phrase from *PAW* 24 that Drury highlights, one might say that Strauss here writes in that "terse and lively style" that could attract energetic young readers to controversial views. See Drury, "Esoteric Philosophy," 323 and *PILS* 26–27; her block quotation on *PILS* 26 contains two minor errors ("the statement" should be "that statement," and "giving" should be "give").

11. In the *LAM* version of the *SCR* preface, the quoted passage ends with "himself" rather than "oneself" (*LAM* 232–33). Another difference is that the *SCR* version has fewer paragraphs.

12. Later in the paragraph, however, Strauss links such criticisms of the "religion of reason" approach with a type of "new thinking" that his next paragraph traces to Franz Rosenzweig. The above-quoted phrases about "the religion of reason" and God's being a "product of the human mind" are from the *prior* paragraph on *SCR* 8/*LAM* 232.

13. Hermann Cohen, *Religion of Reason out of the Sources of Judaism*, trans. Simon Kaplan (New York: Frederick Ungar, 1972), 374, 376, 381, 398. Anne Norton quotes passages from the same *SPPP* essay to argue, unsoundly, that Strauss "turns away" from the desire "to establish a

homeland for the Jews"; she fails to perceive that the relevant passages apply initially, and primarily (if not exclusively), to Cohen (*LSPAE* 216–17). Norton's sin is aggravated because here, as elsewhere, she provides no page citations.

14. Letter to the *New York Times*, 11 May 2003, Week in Review, 12. Even in the pages of an environmental law journal, one can now read that "Straussians, like their arch-enemy Karl Marx, generally have considered religion to be a mindless opiate of the people." See Zygmunt J. B. Plater, "Dealing with Dumb and Dumber: The Continuing Mission of Citizen Environmentalism," *Journal of Environmental Law and Litigation* 20 (2005): Section IIIC. Not surprisingly, the relevant footnote (97) quotes Drury.

15. Susan Orr, *Jerusalem and Athens: Reason and Revelation in the Work of Leo Strauss* (Lanham, MD: Rowman & Littlefield, 1995), 49, 56. Although Leora Batnitzky is skeptical about Orr's Jerusalem-leaning Strauss (217n6), she could hardly do more to demonstrate Strauss's respect for revelation (Batnitzky, *Leo Strauss and Emmanuel Levinas: Philosophy and the Politics of Revelation* [Cambridge: Cambridge University Press, 2006]). Meier, who appears to be unfamiliar with Orr's work, claims that Strauss on occasion has deliberately exaggerated the case for revelation (Heinrich Meier, *Leo Strauss and the Theologico-Political Problem*, trans. Marcus Brainard [Cambridge: Cambridge University Press, 2006], 16). But in doing so, Meier argues, Strauss was attempting to promote "self-examination" and "the justification of philosophy" (15) by reviving concern for "the most important question, the question of the right or the best life," a question that revelation vigorously poses (16). In a similar spirit, Strauss also attempts to restore "the dignity of the political life," confronting an increasingly prosperous world in which "the demands of politics are rejected with the same matter-of-factness as those of religion" (109). According to Batnitzky, the key modern prejudice Strauss attacked is "the dogmatic view that the important questions about human life have been settled once and for all or, what amounts to the same things, are irrelevant" (Batnitzky, *Leo Strauss*, 209). Also see Janssens, *Between Athens and Jerusalem*, 74–76, 103–4, 173, 178; Meier, *Leo Strauss*, 2–11, 20, 23–24, 28, 100; and Michael P. Zuckert, review of *Political Philosophy and the God of Abraham*, by Thomas Pangle, *Perspectives on Political Science* 36, no. 3 (Summer 2007): 168–70. Xenos, by contrast, worries that the "theological-political feint" is "diverting attention from the actual, real-life influence" of Strauss's writings (*CV* xv).

16. Orr, *Jerusalem and Athens*, 149, 150. Because the Bible presents "a purely moral understanding of human excellence that can and does compete" with the ancient exaltation of the philosophical life, argues Catherine Zuckert, Strauss departs from the Averroistic and Machiavellian attempt to "treat[s] biblical religion merely as civil theology" (Zuckert, *Postmodern Platos*, 197). In the words of Daniel Tanguay (my translation), Strauss departed from Averroism because of its "refusal to consider (*s'interroger*) the intrinsic value of religion," and he departed from Socrates by having "lived in his heart the combat between Athens and Jerusalem"; hence "the serenity of his Socratic piety can occasionally be troubled by fear and trembling" and his "Socratic laughter cannot make him forget the tears of repentance." See Tanguay, *Leo Strauss: Une biographie intellectuelle* (Paris: Grasset & Fasquelle/Brodard & Taupin, 2003), 373, 346, 348. Tanguay even argues that, for Strauss, Buber and Rosenzweig were more coherent than Nietzsche and Heidegger (291); on how Strauss departs from Nietzsche's and Heidegger's "atheism from probity," see Janssens, *Between Athens and Jerusalem*, 92–94, 100, 132, 171, 191–92. Reviewing the 2007 English translation of Tanguay, Mansfield helpfully explains that, on the Socratic or zetetic conception favored by Strauss, philosophy is "a friendly critic and rival of religion"; it both "justifies our love of the perfect" and "respects the human imperfection that comes with our freedom" (Mansfield, "Timeless Mind," 26). On Averroës, also see Clark A. Merrill, "Leo Strauss's Indictment of Christian Philosophy," *Review of Politics* 62, no. 1 (Winter 2000): 96–100. On Jerusalem and Athens, also see *WIPP* 9–10, *CM* 1, *RCPR* 72–73, and the Strauss essay on Machiavelli in *HPP*.

17. Two paragraphs later in the *SCR* version, Strauss offers his striking reference to "[t]he victory of orthodoxy through the self-destruction of rational philosophy" (*SCR* 30/*LAM* 256).

18. Schaar and Wolin, "*Essays*," 126, 128. For an overview of how Strauss in the 1920s grappled with "the inner dimension of faith" (Drury's phrase), see David N. Myers, *Resisting History: Historicism and Its Discontents in German-Jewish Thought* (Princeton, NJ: Princeton University Press, 2003), 117–29. Myers, however, exaggerates Strauss's affinity for "radical historicism" (118). Xenos, who draws on Myers (*CV* 127), soon thereafter errs by attributing to Strauss a position—"the impossibility of genuine knowledge of 'Ought'" (*CV* 131)—that Strauss on *NRH* 41 is attributing to *Max Weber* (the "belief that there cannot be any genuine knowledge of the Ought"). Xenos sometimes falters when addressing the early chapters of *NRH*, and might have profited from consulting Behnegar's book on Strauss and Weber.

19. According to one reviewer of *TALS*, the Zuckerts originally intended to present a section on "Faith-Based Straussians" to supplement their discussion of the Western, Eastern, and Midwest types, but gave up to save space (Michael P. Foley, "Helpful Agnostics," *Touchstone* [July/August 2007]: 43–44). On Strauss's respect for religiosity, also see Kim A. Sorensen, *Discourses on Strauss: Revelation and Reason in Leo Strauss and His Critical Study of Machiavelli* (South Bend, IN: University of Notre Dame Press, 2006), 10, 45, 46, 78, 109, 111, 129, 139, 162–66. On Strauss's posture toward Judaism, see Kenneth Hart Green, *Jewish Philosophy and the Crisis of Modernity: Essays and Lectures in Modern Jewish Thought* (Albany: SUNY Press, 1997), xiii–xvii, 1–84, which also provides a fine guide to the secondary literature.

20. Strauss repeats the claim verbatim on the last page of his "Progress or Return" lecture (*RCPR* 270). Cf. Batnitzky, *Leo Strauss*, 12–13, 124, 138, 187, 189, 207, 213.

21. Luban also offers the bizarre assertion that, according to Strauss, the gentlemen "sons of prominent families run the government."

22. Peter Singer, *President of Good and Evil*, 221, 267. The "deference to the ruling class" phrase from *TM* 231 is likewise the only passage that Stephen Holmes invokes in trying to answer this question: "why is religion 'socially useful,' according to Strauss?" (Holmes, *Anatomy*, 63–64).

23. *LSAR* 48. Drury highlights similar accusations in her Web interviews, freely incorporating the term "pious fraud." In *PILS*, she asserts that "[t]he existence of God and His immutable Law is one of the most pious frauds that the philosopher can perpetuate" (34); a few pages earlier, she asserts that, for Strauss, religion *and morality* are "two of the biggest but most pious swindles ever perpetrated on the human race" (20). As happens so often, her claim has been further inflated as it works down the food chain. Professor John Mason says that Strauss called organized religion a "pious fraud," which he does not, whereas Drury confines herself here to describing what Strauss allegedly thought. See John Mason, "Leo Strauss and the Noble Lie: The Neo-Cons at War," *Logos* 3.2 (Spring 2004), http://www.logosjournal.com/mason.htm. In her latest book, Drury opines that "[t]he Straussians are closet atheists" who believe that reviving faith or "the pretense of faith" would cure "all the ills of modernity" (*AM* 128).

24. I am quoting from p. 81 of the translation of *PL* by Eve Adler (Albany: SUNY Press, 1995). In checking Drury's quotations, however, I used the earlier translation (by Fred Baumann) that she cited (Philadelphia: The Jewish Publication Society, 1987).

25. For Maimonides, likewise, "the revelation is *simply* binding" (*PL* 103); "the philosopher does not occupy the highest rank in the human race" (131) since that place is occupied by the prophet.

26. Drury elsewhere asserts that Strauss subtly imparted "a prejudice in favour of pederasty while overtly promoting contempt for the female sex" (Shadia Drury, "The Making of a Straussian," *Philosophers' Magazine* 25, 1st quarter 2004, 25); she even uses the word "glorification" to characterize his attitude toward pederasty (*AK* 248n19). Anne Norton highlights the "persistent rumors of homosexual rites and rituals among the Straussians" at Cornell (*LSPAE* 62), and claims that Allan Bloom longed for "a world without women" (67). Martha Nussbaum was so incensed by Harvey Mansfield's last book, *Manliness*, that she posed this appalling question about his career:

"How did someone whose every paragraph is a stake in Socrates's heart come to be an exemplar of philosophical seriousness?" (Nussbaum, "Man Overboard," *New Republic*, 26 June 2006, 30).

27. Recall Praxagora's status as the "refutation of egalitarianism" (*SA* 280). This is the only play, Strauss adds, in which Aristophanes attacks, not a specific institution (e.g., the jury system), demagogue, or policy associated with Athens, but "the very principle of democracy;" when he ends the play without signaling any defects in Praxagora's scheme, Aristophanes is proceeding ironically (279). In interpreting the "humdrum" *Plutos*—an "old men's play" (305) that nevertheless incorporates a sexual relationship between a hag and a young man—Strauss invokes *The Assembly of Women* as he assesses a "victorious" scheme, initiated by Chremylos, which abolishes economic inequality (*SA* 295, 301–4). For comments by Strauss about outcomes in other plays, see *SA* 11–12, 46–48, 50, 158, 193–94, 247.

28. Quoted in David Brock, *Blinded by the Right* (New York: Crown Publishers, 2002), 57. The latter phrase is also quoted in Terry Eastland, "Rush Limbaugh: Talking Back," *American Spectator* 25, no. 9 (September 1992): 23.

29. Nina Easton, *Gang of Five* (New York: Simon & Schuster, 2000), 180; Easton does not indicate when Bennett said this. In a brief appendix, "Intellectual Influences," Easton recommends both of Drury's books (435), so she cannot be accused of whitewashing.

30. For a brief overview of Bennett's career, see http://www.ashbrook.org/events/memdin/bennett2/home.html.

31. Andrew Payton Thomas, *Clarence Thomas: A Biography* (San Francisco: Encounter Books, 2001), 308. To avoid confusion concerning the two Thomases, I shall hereafter designate this book as *CTB*.

32. Ken Foskett, *Judging Thomas: The Life and Times of Clarence Thomas* (New York: HarperCollins, 2004), 189–91; on Thomas's praise of Jaffa, see *CTB* 558.

33. Clarence Thomas, "The Higher Law Background of the Privileges or Immunities Clause of the Fourteenth Amendment," *Harvard Journal of Law and Public Policy* 12 (Winter 1989): 63–64. In the annotated bibliography of *LSAR*, Drury accurately summarizes this article until she concludes that Thomas "[s]hares Jaffa's high regard for Oliver North" (*LSAR* 231–32); the article never mentions or alludes to Oliver North.

34. The Zuckerts are too dismissive of Thomas's indirect connections to Strauss. After denying that there is "a shred of merit" in the claim that Bennett (along with Bork and Perle) is a Straussian, they turn to Justice Thomas: "We believe that Thomas once had someone on his staff at the Equal Employment Opportunity Commission who had studied with a student of Strauss" (*TALS* 264). They believe, but perhaps they do not know, although the information is not hard to gather. Thomas's staff included *two*, they were not gophers or administrative assistants, and they were students of Jaffa—the wily founder and ruler of West Coast Straussianism, "the most overtly political of the various Straussian camps" (*TALS* 252; cf. 217–27, 239–53).

35. As late as 1986, Thomas hired Pamela Talkin, a liberal Democrat, as his chief of staff (*CTB* 289). On Masugi and Marini, also see Foskett, *Judging Thomas*, 187–89; under their tutelage, Thomas read Tocqueville, the Federalist Papers, Madison, and Jefferson. For a statement of Thomas's that sketches his appreciation of the American constitution/regime, see the speech ("We Hold These Truths . . .") he delivered on 15 March 2001 at James Madison University in Virginia, posted at http://www.ifapray.org/NewsletterHTML/IFANL2001/JulyPg1_2001.htm. The full speech, including Q&A remarks in which Thomas credits libertarians as well as Straussians as formative influences, was previously posted on the university's website (http://www.jmu.edu), but it has been removed.

36. Foskett, *Judging Thomas*, 197; also see Clarence Thomas, "Higher Law Background," 68.

37. On Thomas's debt to these authors, see *CTB* 162–65, 180–81, 230, 245, 290–91; Foskett, *Judging Thomas*, 142–45; Kevin Merida and Michael A. Fletcher, *Supreme Discomfort: The Divided Soul of Clarence Thomas* (New York: Doubleday, 2007), 141–45, 163, 226, 267, 291–92, 371.

38. Bill Kauffman, "Clarence Thomas," *Reason*, November 1987, http://www.reason.com/news/show/33217.html.

39. *CTB* 468; Foskett, *Judging Thomas*, 179, 280.

40. Foskett, *Judging Thomas*, 54–59, 70–91.

41. Merida and Fletcher, *Supreme Discomfort*, 337–38.

42. Robert Bork, "Not a Straussian," *New York Times*, 3 February 1995.

43. The Bork-Jaffa feud reached a climax in the following articles: Robert Bork, "Mr. Jaffa's Constitution," *National Review* 46, no. 2 (7 February 1994): 61–64; and "Jaffa v. Bork: An Exchange," *National Review* 46, no. 5 (21 March 1994): 56–59.

44. "The University of Chicago's Underpowered Campaign to Achieve Racial Diversity," *Journal of Blacks in Higher Education*, Autumn 2000, 36–37. The article's author is not specified.

45. Richard Bernstein, "A Very Unlikely Villain (or Hero)," *New York Times*, 29 January 1995, E4.

46. In its unsigned "Hot Type" celebration of Drury's *LSAR*, the *Chronicle of Higher Education* opens by specifying that Clarence Thomas is among the "disciples" of Strauss who have entered politics in "droves" as commentator and candidates. The piece does not even mention Drury until its second paragraph and thus seems to present its initial claims as obvious facts. See "New Book Renews Attack on Political Theories of Leo Strauss," *Chronicle of Higher Education*, 24 October 1997, A15. Norman Kelley cites *LSAR* and—in a chapter entitled "Notes on the Niggerati: Or, Why Dead White Men Still Rule"—identifies Bork, Bennett, Thomas, and Perle as Straussians; according to Kelley, "Strauss and his disciples are the individuals who have brought the American people the war in Iraq" (Kelley, *The Head Negro in Charge Syndrome: The Dead End of Black Politics* [New York: Nation Books, 2004], 158). Michiko Kakutani does not mention Drury, but lists both Thomas and Bennett among the "followers" of Strauss ("How Books Have Shaped U.S. Policy," *New York Times*, 5 April 2003, D7). Aakash Singh, who invokes the current "infestation" of American government by influential Straussians (Singh, *Eros Turannos*, 130), follows the herd by including Clarence Thomas. Singh, however, carves out a unique and gargantuan error by adding Antonio Negri (33n9), the militant Marxist who was finally released from Italian prison in 2003.

47. Will Hutton, *Declaration*, 75. As recounted in the *Weekly Standard*, by contrast, Gingrich "has made no secret of his intellectual mentors: futurists Alvin and Heidi Toffler, management gurus Peter Drucker, W. Edwards Deming, and Joseph M. Juran; and a shelf-full of military theorists. Gingrich's published writings are a condensed soup of all these thinkers" (Matthew Continetti, "Scenes from the Gingrich Campaign," *Weekly Standard*, 19 March 2007, 22). On 31 July 2007, the Recommended Reading List on Gingrich's website started with *Revolutionary Wealth* by the Tofflers; it specified the *Federalist Papers* and *Democracy in America*—along with *Moneyball*, *Gone with the Wind*, and *The Godfather*—among the twenty-three listed books, but included no book authored by Strauss or a Straussian. (This list was previously easier to find, and the 3.0 beta version of the site used a monstrous address for it: http://newt.org/EditNewt/NewtNewsand OpinionDB/tabid/102/ArticleType/ArticleView/ArticleID/657/PageID/684/Default.aspx.) I hypothesize that, in days past, the book Gingrich most often recommended to students and practitioners of politics was Frans de Waal's *Chimpanzee Politics: Power and Sex among Apes* (1982), which was on the reading list Gingrich distributed to new House Republicans in the pivotal year of 1994 (Michael Crowley, "The Way We Live Now: Questions for Newt Gingrich," *New York Times*, 22 June 2003; David Berreby, "Are Apes Naughty by Nature?" *New York Times*, 26 January 1997). According to Franklin Foer, Bill Kristol filled the "intellectual guru" function for Gingrich for a period in the early 1990s, whispering into the ear of "the aspiring House speaker" (Franklin Foer, "Great Escape: How Bill Kristol Ditched Conservatism," *New Republic*, 28 May 2001, 17). Since Foer crudely describes neocons as "followers of Strauss," and pronounces that the latter's "preferred antidote to relativism" is "the secular religion of the state" (19), I am not convinced by his allegation of whispering.

48. John Walsh, "The Philosophy of Mendacity," *Counterpunch*, 2 November 2005, http://counterpunch.org/walsh11022005.html. Strauss provides an explanation of why the classical political philosophers, whose cause he revived, were *not* "guided by questions concerning the external relations of the political community": the "ultimate aim of foreign policy"—the "survival and independence of one's political community"—is "not essentially controversial" (*WIPP* 84; cf. *CM* 239).

49. Milich, "Fundamentalism," 103, 119n15.

50. *PILS*-05 xiv–xv and lii–liv, note 14. Consistent with Strauss's practice, I shall use the name Farabi rather than Alfarabi (Drury uses both spellings), though I shall omit the accent marks (Fārābī or Fârâbî) he typically provides.

51. Drury, "Esoteric Philosophy," 332–33.

52. Strauss is quoting from the second part (*The Philosophy of Plato, Its Parts, the Ranks of Order of Its Parts, from the Beginning to the End*) of Farabi's tripartite *Philosophy of Plato and Aristotle*. In the edition that I shall be citing—*Alfarabi: Philosophy of Plato and Aristotle*, translated and with an introduction by Muhsin Mahdi (Ithaca, NY: Cornell University Press, 2001), including a foreword by Charles E. Butterworth and Thomas L. Pangle—the phrases Strauss quotes come in §38. The first part, which I shall be discussing below, is *The Attainment of Happiness*. The translation was initially published in 1962, so Drury could have consulted it. Mahdi's paragraphs do not correspond with the paragraphs from the Arabic/Latin text Strauss specifies at *PAW* 11n6. In *PAW*, Strauss indicates uncertainty about the tripartite work when he says it was "apparently" titled, *On the Purposes of Plato and of Aristotle* (*PAW* 11).

53. Drury, "Esoteric Philosophy," 319. By leaving out the ten words between the second "who" and "lives privately" in the block-quotation from *PAW* 17, Drury errs—she provides no ellipsis marks—in a way that we have encountered on multiple occasions. She repeats the doctored quotation in her book (*PILS* 28).

54. Farabi also offers striking equations of king and philosopher in the *Attainment of Happiness* (§54, 56–58). On the differences between the two figures, consult these passages from Farabi: *Attainment* 57 ("the name *philosopher* signifies primarily theoretical virtue"); *Philosophy of Plato* 19 (although the "theoretical art . . . supplies that knowledge of the beings," the "practical art . . . supplies man with that desired way of life"); and *Philosophy of Plato* 21 (the "princely and political art" is "practical").

55. Farabi here does not link his summary with any specific works of Plato. The prior section (§37) addresses the *Menexenus* and the third sentence of §38 commences the discussion of Plato's *Letters* that concludes the *Philosophy of Plato*.

56. Leo Strauss, "Farabi's *Plato*," in *Louis Ginzberg Jubilee Volume* (New York: American Academy for Jewish Research, 1945), 357–93. Cf. Catherine Zuckert: "*The* secret Strauss thought he discovered by studying Farabi's *Plato* was that Socrates represented the only fully satisfying form of human existence—that is, the attainment of happiness in *this* world" but that "the open presentation of that fact was apt to provoke popular envy" (Zuckert, *Postmodern Platos*, 148); cf. Tanguay, *Leo Strauss*, 168, 176, and Christopher Colmo, "Theory and Practice: Alfarabi's *Plato* Revisited," *American Political Science Review* 86, no. 4 (December 1992): 969–72.

57. In order to remove the qualifying phrase, "may be said," Drury had to convert "to initiate" into "initiates."

58. As in the previously discussed passage from *PAW* 17, the linkage of philosophy with royalty has an educative and privatizing thrust rather than the hyperpolitical one—the philosopher will "rule the city behind the scenes" ("Esoteric Philosophy" 319)—that Drury presents. In his well-known 1959 commencement address, Strauss moved from reprising the Platonic notion that human virtue and happiness will "always be imperfect" to stating that the philosopher, who is *not* "simply wise, is declared to be the only true king," that is, someone who exemplifies "all the excellences

of which man's mind is capable" (*LAM* 6–7). Also see Janssens, *Between Athens and Jerusalem*, 129–31, 189–90.

59. FP 369n29. Strauss here also cites *Sophist* 217a3–b2, *Phaedrus* 252e1–2, and *Phaedrus* 253b1–3. Let me elaborate Strauss's reservation about whether Farabi is summarizing the *Statesman*. In *Philosophy of Plato* 22, where Farabi states that Plato "explained that the man who is philosopher and the man who is prince are the same," Farabi departs from his common practice of concluding with a clear specification of the relevant dialogue. Farabi concludes §21, however, by saying that Plato "explained the idea of the Prince and the Statesman"; the work nowhere else even alludes to the *Statesman*.

60. See Farabi, *Philosophy of Plato* 30 (section vii) and 31 (section viii).

61. Farabi, *Philosophy of Plato* 38.

62. In the corresponding discussion in FP, Strauss adds that Farabi, by distinguishing *perfection* from the *happiness* that "the science of the beings" yields, implies that philosophy as a "theoretical art" (what Farabi at §3 identifies as man's "final" and "highest" perfection) must be "supplemented by the right way of life," that is, the politics that brings happiness to non-philosophers (FP 378).

63. On the crudeness with which FP conveys Farabi's "rejection of revelation," see the second section of Steven Lenzner's article, "Strauss's Fârâbî, Scholarly Prejudice, and Philosophic Politics," *Perspectives on Political Science* 28, no. 4 (Fall 1999): 194–202.

64. Marsilius of Padua, *Defensor Pacis* (Gewirth translation) I.1.3; cf. I.1.7.

65. Cf. Laurence Lampert, *Leo Strauss and Nietzsche* (Chicago: University of Chicago Press, 1996), 137–40. Despite the gravity of Drury's charges about "secret kingship," she fails to cite Farabi directly, or even to mention the title of any of his works. The *WIPP* essay was first published in 1957. Strauss's focus here is on a work by Farabi that Strauss calls the *Summary*; Muhsin Mahdi titles the same work, *Plato's Laws*, and translates the introduction along with Farabi's summaries of the first two of the nine books that Farabi addresses. See Ralph Lerner and Muhsin Mahdi, eds., *Medieval Political Philosophy* (Ithaca, NY: Cornell University Press, 1972), 83–94. Strauss's earlier discussions (1945 in FP and 1952 in *PAW*) focus on Farabi's previously discussed *Philosophy of Plato*.

66. In "The Harmonization of the Two Opinions of the Two Sages: Plato the Divine and Aristotle," Farabi highlights the "surface" difference between Plato and Aristotle concerning "the issue of the two abodes." See *Alfarabi: The Political Writings*, trans. Charles E. Butterworth (Ithaca, NY: Cornell University Press, 2001), 129.

67. Strauss does not exaggerate when he describes the sweeping claim in *Philosophy of Plato* §22—that according to Plato, the skill/faculty of both the philosopher and the prince can produce true happiness in its possessor and in "all others"—as an "extravagantly philanthropic remark" (FP 378). In *Attainment* §56, Farabi states that possessing the theoretical virtues would enable the philosopher to create them in "all others according to their capacities."

68. In *Attainment* §57–58, 62, Farabi goes so far as to identify the philosopher with the *Imam*, as Strauss notes at *PAW* 12. Cf. Muhsin S. Mahdi, *Alfarabi and the Foundation of Islamic Political Philosophy* (Chicago: University of Chicago Press, 2001), 189–93.

69. Cf. Meier, *Leo Strauss*, 12–14, 59–60, 99, 108–9.

70. Farabi, *Philosophy of Plato* 38; *PAW* 17, 21. Also see *PAW* 19 on "the eventual collapse of philosophic inquiry" in the Islamic world. According to Lampert, Strauss uses "secret kingship" merely to denote the shaping of societal opinions by philosophers that enables "the rational investigation of the whole" to continue (Lampert, *Leo Strauss*, 18). To her credit, Drury acknowledges the acute danger that philosophy faced in the Islamic world when philosophy became "a suspect pursuit and philosophers a suspect group of men" (*PILS* 21; cf. "Esoteric Philosophy" 321 on "the predicament of philosophy" for both Plato and Farabi).

71. Cicero, by contrast, did not "abandon the notion that civil societies are founded by superior individuals" (*NRH* 322); cf. *CM* 139 on "the charm of the greatness of the founder and legislator."

72. I have broken up Strauss's sentence to remove the challenge posed by the seven appearances of the word "of." In a 1958 lecture, Strauss states, apparently in his own name, that the rule of the wise could at most be "very indirect," consisting in "the rule of laws, on the making of which the wise have had some influence." But because laws "must be applied, interpreted, administered, and executed," the "best solution of the political problem is then the rule of men who can best complete the laws" (*RCPR* 146). Also see *NRH* 141–42.

73. Zuckert, *Postmodern Platos*, 156. Cf. *AAPL* 46–47, 51–52, 61, 85–86, 180. Drury elsewhere touches on the connections Strauss draws between Plato, legislating, and prophecy in *PL*, his early book on Maimonides (*LSAR* 53–54), and she should have pursued such matters further while addressing secret kingship. See *PL* 71, 119, 124.

74. Annabel M. Patterson, *Reading between the Lines* (Madison: University of Wisconsin Press, 1993), 25. Despite being a professor of English at Yale, Patterson ignores everything Strauss says here and elsewhere about the *pedagogical* and *antidogmatic* essence of Plato's dialogues; and she escalates her poorly grounded insult when she adds that Strauss presents the *Laws* as "an essay on political hypocrisy and double-speak."

75. In a recently published 1943 lecture (delivered to the Conference on Jewish Relations) about the prospects for reeducating Germans after the war, Strauss raised similar issues when considering whether one can distinguish the Nazis from "Germany." A nation in "the political sense of the term," Strauss claims, is "the politically relevant, the politically efficient *part* of the nation: when in a free election, about 45% of the Germans voted for Hitler, and the other 55% were in a condition of utter confusion and helplessness, then the 45% *are* the Germans—from any political point of view." See Leo Strauss, "The Re-education of Axis Countries Concerning the Jews," *Review of Politics* 69, no. 4 (Fall 2007): 535. Strauss of course acknowledges that particular laws could be "deceptive, unintentionally and even intentionally, as to the true character of the *politeia*" (*NRH* 136). On the impact of ruling a society "in broad daylight," also see *NRH* 137, *CM* 34, and *LAM* 13. When Xenos describes regime as "an Aristotelian category" (Xenos, "Leo Strauss," 12), he seems to forget that *Politeia* is the title of Plato's *Republic*.

76. Speaking for Thucydides and presumably also for himself, Strauss once claimed that a "sound" regime is one in which a robust group "united by civic virtue" rules "in *broad daylight*" (*CM* 153; emph. added).

77. This puzzle of course originates with the philosopher kings of the *Republic* (445d, 499b, 503b, 540a–b, 587d); cf. *CM* 114 and "New Interpretation" 359. In *The Political Regime*, Farabi claims that if a group of the supremely qualified rulers "happens to reside in a single city, in a single nation, or in many nations, then this group is as it were a single prince because they agree in their endeavors, purposes, opinions, and ways of life. If they follow one another in time, their souls will form as it were a single soul, the one who succeeds will be following the way of life of his predecessors, and the living will be following in the way of the ones who have died" (I am quoting from the Fauzi M. Najjar translation provided in Lerner and Mahdi, *Medieval Political Philosophy*, 37–38). In the next two paragraphs, however, Farabi speaks of perfected souls freeing themselves from matter and becoming incorporeal; having achieved "salvation," such souls unite and increasingly experience each other's pleasures, yielding the "true and supreme happiness, which is the purpose of the Active Intellect" (38). On how Farabi wrestles with the need for plural rulers and the problem of succession, see Mahdi, *Alfarabi*, 131–39. On Farabi's greater frankness in works where he employs "the specific immunity of the commentator," see *PAW* 13–15, FP 374–75, and p. 120 above.

78. Cf. *SA* 311, where Strauss speaks of the philosophic effort "to humanize" by "counteracting the waspishness of the city." Perhaps Strauss's model for a secret prince is Machiavelli, and the most far-reaching of Machiavelli's plans, according to Strauss, was to recruit future *authors* who

would create "a change of *opinion*" (*WIPP* 45, emph. added; cf. *TM* 168, 297). See pp. 241–43 below. After praising Strauss's "brilliant commentary" and quoting the "secret kingship" passage from *PAW* 17, Sari Nusseibeh, the president of Al-Quds University in Jerusalem, states that this wisdom of Farabi "would become a permanent fixture in my later life—especially the bit about quietly doing your best to humanize an 'imperfect society'" (Sari Nusseibeh, with Anthony David, *Once Upon a Country: A Palestinian Life* [New York: Farrar, Straus & Giroux, 2007], 145–46).

79. Strauss is addressing Farabi, *Philosophy of Plato* 38. In three different discussions of Farabi's Plato—*PAW* 16–17, FP 383, and *WIPP* 153—Strauss highlights the contrast Farabi draws between "the way of Socrates," which is "intransigent," and the more accommodating "way of Thrasymachus." Farabi's discussion comes in the final section of his *Philosophy of Plato* (§36). In the final section of "Strauss's Fârâbî," Lenzner observes that FP, by abetting the gradual replacement of accepted scholarly opinions, actually "paints a picture of the process it describes." On the ways Strauss might depart from Farabi's interpretation of Plato concerning "intransigent" rhetoric, see Zuckert, *Postmodern Platos*, 158, 163.

80. Here is Ryn's catchy overview of Straussian philosophers: "Having gained access to the ruler through dissimulation, sycophancy, and general craftiness, they are in a position to whisper in the ruler's ear, making him their instrument" (Claes G. Ryn, *America the Virtuous: The Crisis of Democracy and the Quest for Empire* [New Brunswick, NJ: Transaction Publishers, 2003], 33). Ryn is professor of political science at the Catholic University of America, where he has served as chair and assistant dean; he is also an adjunct professor at Georgetown. Although Xenos offers many insightful interpretations of Strauss's writings in attempting to highlight their impact upon the rhetoric in which neoconservative policies have been "couched" (*CV* xi, xv, 126, 139–44), he too plays the whisper card. Preparing his observation that various journalistic accounts had portrayed Wolfowitz as "the front man for a group of Straussians" who were using a "somewhat dim-witted" president as their "compliant foil," Xenos pronounces—without offering *any* evidence—that Wolfowitz, four days after the towers fell, was "whispering in the ear of George W. Bush" about Iraqi involvement in the attack (*CV* x). None of the accounts I have read of the 15 September 2001 meeting at Camp David says anything about whispering. According to Bob Woodward, Wolfowitz initially addressed the entire group, stressing the military difficulties that Afghanistan would pose; Saddam's regime was "brittle," there was a 10 to 50 percent chance he was involved in the 9/11 attacks, and the war on terror would eventually require the United States to confront him. During a morning break, Bush did join "a side discussion" that included Cheney and Libby (Cheney's chief of staff), and Wolfowitz elaborated his Iraq-Afghanistan military comparison in response to a query from the president. After Wolfowitz interrupted Rumsfeld during a later session of the entire group, Bush sent Andrew Card, his chief of staff, to scold Wolfowitz ("The President will expect one person to speak for the Department of Defense"); before lunch, Bush informed everyone that he had heard enough about Iraq (Woodward, *Bush at War*, 83–85; cf. 87–88, 99, 167). According to Condoleezza Rice, Wolfowitz overstepped his role as a deputy by speaking so vigorously at this meeting of "principals" (Bumiller, *Condoleezza Rice*, 165–66, 359n11,13; Bumiller interviewed Card as well as Rice). Tanenhaus credits an unnamed source for the proposition that Wolfowitz "engaged Bush much more directly over coffee than has been reported" (Sam Tanenhaus, "Bush's Brain Trust," *Vanity Fair*, July 2003, 168).

81. There are many differences between the statements in FP and *PAW* about the secret kingship, but neither version supports Drury's edifice.

82. Strauss, "What Can We Learn," 522–23; cf. *OT* 201 on the reform of "inhuman or irrational practice." Also see Ivan Kenneally, "The Use and Abuse of Utopianism: On Leo Strauss's Philosophic Politics," *Perspectives on Political Science* 36, no. 3 (Summer 2007): 141–47. In the course of explicating the comparison Strauss makes in this lecture between ancient and modern utopianism, Kenneally helpfully speculates about the meanings Strauss attached to the term "political philosophy"; cf. Meier, *Leo Strauss*, xi–xiii, 23n32, 91–111.

83. Colmo, "Theory and Practice," 973.

84. Sheppard, *Leo Strauss*, 105.

85. Drury apparently draws on Strauss to make this controversial pronouncement about Farabi despite her claim that Strauss's interpretation of Farabi reveals more about Strauss than about Farabi (*LSAR* 49).

86. Strauss also notes "the silence of that passage about the obvious and guiding theme of the *Laws*, namely, the laws." Regarding Farabi's claim that Plato in the *Laws* presented "the virtuous ways of life which are followed by the people of this city" [Mahdi's translation is "the virtuous ways of life that the inhabitants of this city should be made to follow"], Strauss says that Farabi "means in all probability" the city of the *Republic* because the *Laws* passage "follows immediately" after the summaries of the *Republic* and the *Timaeus* (*WIPP* 152–53); cf. FP 365.

87. *PILS* x–xi, 24, 27. Marked for arrest by the oppressive ruler of his city, the man escaped by acting like a drunken fop when approaching the gates; he identified himself to the guard as the ascetic, but was not believed. See p. 56 above and Lampert, *Leo Strauss*, 11.

88. Insofar as those whom Drury would classify as "converts" to Strauss are likely to sweat in extracting Strauss's views from beneath such Farabian masks, Drury needs to retract her complaint that Strauss offers the converts "ready-made answers to all the difficult questions" (*PILS* 193).

89. Cf. *PAW* 155–58; *PL* 57–58, 135–36n2; *WIPP* 71, 73–77; "On Collingwood's Philosophy of History," 585–86; Janssens, *Between Athens and Jerusalem*, 102–8, 115–18, 127–32; Lilla, "Leo Strauss," 59; Robert B. Pippin, "The Modern World of Leo Strauss," *Political Theory* 20, no. 3 (August 1992): 454–57; Ted V. McAllister, *Revolt against Modernity: Leo Strauss, Eric Voegelin, and the Search for a Postliberal Order* (Lawrence: University Press of Kansas, 1996), 190–98, 204, 213; and Nathan Tarcov, "On a Certain Critique of 'Straussianism,'" *Review of Politics* 53, no. 1 (Winter 1991): 13–17.

90. *PAW* 14–15, FP 372; cf. p. 136n94 below.

91. Cf. Strauss's above-discussed suggestion that Farabi "may have rewritten the *Laws*" to accommodate "the rise of Islam" (*WIPP* 144); also recall what FP at 369n29 suggests about Farabi's odd treatment of the *Statesman*.

92. Cf. *WIPP* 153 and FP 376; the latter cites *Phaedrus* 275b3–4.

93. Apart from the above-discussed texts, see *PL* and Strauss's 1936 article that was translated by Robert Bartlett as "Some Remarks on the Political Science of Maimonides and Farabi," *Interpretation* 18, no. 1 (Fall 1990): 3–30.

94. Drury displays similar carelessness toward both Farabi and Strauss regarding immortality and the afterlife. From Farabi's silence in the *Philosophy of Plato* about the soul's immortality, Strauss *infers* Farabi's skepticism; as Strauss emphasizes, this work summarizes dialogues (*Phaedo, Republic, Phaedrus, Gorgias*) in which Socrates presents arguments for immortality, and the full title of Farabi's work specifies that it will address Plato's philosophy from "the beginning to the end" (*PAW* 13–15; cf. FP 371–72, 374–75). Drury correctly notes that Strauss regards Farabi's posture as a flagrant departure from "the letter of Plato's teaching" (*PAW* 14; cf. p. 115 above and *TALS* 135 on how Strauss "shucks off Platonic Ideas and Platonic immortality of the soul as mere exotericism"). But Drury distorts Strauss's argument when she states that in Farabi's commentary on Plato Farabi "denies" that Plato believed in "the immortality of the soul or in the life beyond" ("Esoteric Philosophy" 319; Drury provides no citations). In *PILS*, she repeats this misleading formulation and then drifts even farther from the texts of Farabi and Strauss by adding this pretentious and citation-free formulation: "Strauss notes that Farabi makes *this remark* at the *precise point* where Plato maintains the very opposite" (*PILS* 22; emphases added). Drury initially *imagined* that, according to Strauss, Farabi had issued a denial; later, apparently, she imagined further that this denial was a statement that Farabi had carefully placed within his commentary.

95. Drury, "Esoteric Philosophy," 336n10.

96. Christopher Bobonich, *Plato's Utopia Recast: His Later Ethics and Politics* (Oxford: Oxford University Press, 2002), 383, 570n41.

97. For examples concerning centralism in Strauss's writings on Farabi, see *WIPP* 150 and *FP* 371, 372.

98. The institution is initially described as "the council of those who keep watch over the laws" and "shall be compelled to meet each day" at dawn (*Laws* 951d). The prominence of the members whom the Athenian proceeds immediately to specify—priests who won the "prizes for excellence," the eldest ten Guardians of the Laws, and the supervisor of education (951d-e)—provides another obvious signal of the council's authority.

99. *AAPL* 155, 171, 174–81, 184–85. Needless to say, non-Straussian experts such as Morrow and Bobonich place less weight on what distinguishes the different descriptions the Stranger provides of the Council (Bobonich, *Plato's Utopias*, 570n42, citing Glenn R. Morrow, *Plato's Cretan City* [Princeton, NJ: Princeton University Press, 1960], 503–4).

100. On philosophy's place in the city of the *Laws*, also see *AAPL* 33, 38, 46–48, 106. Catherine Zuckert suggests that "the elder members of the Council would finally react to the disruptive effects of the activities of a philosopher among them very much the way the Athenian fathers eventually did to Socrates" (Zuckert, *Postmodern Platos*, 163). Although Bobonich is less exclusionary than Strauss in designating philosophers, he freely concedes that "not every member of the Nocturnal Council will have a full philosophical education" (Bobonich, *Plato's Utopias*, 392). Drawing on Morrow, however, Bobonich wisely emphasizes that the young associates, who must retire from the council at age 40 (951e), would help the council's spirit infuse the city as a whole; the council thus differs from "the tiny philosophical elite of the *Republic* separated by a gulf from the rest of the citizens" (Bobonich, *Plato's Utopias*, 393).

101. See p. 134n77 above.

102. Did Drury instead want to suggest that the city of the *Laws* is meant to *evoke* the "imperfect society" that the philosopher (as described in *PAW* 17) "tries to humanize within the limits of the possible"?

103. Cf. *AAPL* 78–79: "The Athenian tries to introduce into a Dorian community, if not philosophy, at least an important ingredient of the best polity of the city which came to be the home of philosophy, just as he had tried to introduce symposia"; the Athenian has come to Crete "to introduce into Crete new laws and institutions," to "civilize an uncivilized society" (*WIPP* 30, 32). For brief sketches by Strauss of the predemocratic regime in Athens, see *SA* 103–5, 135; also see *AAPL* 51–53 and *RCPR* 97 on book III of the *Laws*. In explaining why Strauss did not want to restore the polis, Pangle claims that, because of his reservations about "imperialistic, growth-oriented Periclean democracy," Strauss maintained a "Platonic preference for the older, quieter, more moderate Athens that Pericles deliberately (if unavoidably) had to destroy" (Pangle, *Leo Strauss*, 76–77).

104. Because of the restrictions on citizenship, the Athenian citizen-body might be 10,000 times smaller than that of the United States.

105. *CM* 27; cf. 65. Also cf. *AAPL* 38: "In the *Republic*, reason or intellect guides the foundation of the city from the beginning, and eventually rules the city in broad daylight without any dilution or disguise. Such a city is something to be prayed or wished for rather than something which can arouse the spontaneous and passionate concern of experienced political men."

106. Mark Blitz concludes his illuminating analysis of the ways in which Strauss imparts his own views into *AAPL*—amidst the sequential paraphrasing—with these remarks about Strauss's conclusion: "This terse statement, not a conclusion in the usual sense, caps Strauss's work. This is fitting. For his legacy is the examination of the political problem as a whole in all its varieties. His legacy is not a series of dogmas" (Mark Blitz, "Strauss's Laws," *Political Science Reviewer* 20 [1991]: 222).

107. *PILS* 214n52 cites all of *AAPL*.

108. Here are the most pertinent passages from the *Republic*: let's "watch a city coming into being in speech" (369a), and "let's make a city in speech from the beginning" (369c); we were "making a pattern in speech of a good city," but is it "possible to found a city the same as the one in speech"? (472e); "the regime we have now described in speech" (473e); "the regime about which we tell tales in speech" (501e); "the one that has its place in speeches" (592a).

109. Strauss, "Spirit of Sparta," 534; cf. pp. 71–72 above. In an article about *CM*, Seth Benardete offers this elegant overview: "The problem of justice is the problem of the common good: is there anything which by nature is common? The only possible answer to this question—knowledge—fixes the limits of the city, for even the community of the best city is grounded in the noble lie." Benardete also touts the *search* for knowledge, and suggests that "the *Republic* as a conversation about justice is itself the model of the best city." He adds, however, that the obstacles represented by the three major interlocutors of book I—Polemarchus (force is deaf to argument), Cephalus (the sacred is "an irreduceable surd in the city"), and Thrasymachus (*thymos* will not always ally with reason)—entail "not only that the best city be in speech and only in speech but that even in speech it is self-contradictory" (Seth Benardete, "Leo Strauss's *The City and Man*," 7–8). Drury's line about *chance* coincidence draws on *Republic* 473c11–e5, *CM* 122, *CM* 125, and perhaps *HPP* 274. The *Republic*, however, refers to coinciding, not whispering, and Strauss at *CM* 125 describes this coinciding as being "extremely improbable." As was explained above, Strauss traces to Farabi, not to Plato, the "secular alliance" that includes "princes friendly to philosophy."

110. Daniel Tanguay, "Neoconservatisme et religion democratique," *Commentaire* 29, no. 114 (Summer 2006): 323. In his book, Tanguay argues at greater length that Farabi (according to Strauss) equates philosopher and king to establish that "*la philosophie seule est suffisante pour procurer la félicité recherchée*" (157). The secret kingship "exercises itself in a city in speech" (159), and "*[o]n chercherait en vain chez Strauss de grands projets, de grandes réformes ou de grandes espérances politiques*" (160).

111. Although Simon Blackburn, professor of philosophy at Cambridge, recognizes the chicken-and-egg problem concerning philosopher-kings, he embarrassingly overlooks the examples of Socrates and Plato when he states that "[t]he philosopher can only grow in the ideal community" (Simon Blackburn, *Plato's Republic: A Biography* [New York: Atlantic Monthly Press, 2006], 96).

112. Damon Linker, "The Philosopher and Everyone Else," *New Republic*, 31 July 2006, 32, 33. Kelley implies that, in Strauss's mind, all of antiquity embodied the inegalitarianism Strauss favored: "the ancient world was based on a natural hierarchy of aristocrats and subordinates who knew their stations . . . guided by those who understood the wisdom of the ancients" (Norman Kelley, *Head Negro*, 160).

113. In addition to Linker, see Louis Menand, "Mr. Bloom's Planet," *New Republic*, 25 May 1987, 38–41; Charles Larmore, "The Secrets of Philosophy," *New Republic*, 3 July 1989, 30–35; and Nussbaum, "Man Overboard," 28–33.

114. Drury quotes the passage correctly on *PILS* 17, a place where she does *not* discuss secret kingship. Jaffa's essay—"The Achievement of Leo Strauss," *National Review* 25, no. 49 (December 1973): 1353–55—also appears as the first chapter of his book, *The Conditions of Freedom* (Baltimore: Johns Hopkins University Press, 1975), 3–8.

115. Jaffa, "Achievement," 1355; emph. added.

116. In Drury's less lucid version, by contrast, it seems that amelioration can occur only when those who exercise political power "by" the spirit of the best regime exert their influence.

117. Jaffa, "Achievement," 1355. Still earlier in his essay, needless to say, Jaffa highlighted the common Straussian complaint that the major modern political philosophers, inspired by Machiavelli, could attempt to "guarantee the actualization" of their regimes only because they were simultaneously "lowering the goal of political life" (1353).

118. Michael L. Frazer, "Esotericism Ancient and Modern: Strauss Contra Straussianism on the Art of Political-Philosophical Writing," *Political Theory* 34, no. 1 (February 2006): 45, 49.

119. Recall Plato's journeys to Syracuse, Xenophon's campaigns, Aristotle's tutoring of Alexander, Cicero's political offices and party maneuvers, Machiavelli's career as a diplomat and militia organizer, Hobbes's and Bacon's work as secretaries, Locke's authorship of the Carolina constitution and his service on England's Board of Trade and Plantations, Montesquieu's work as a judge, Burke's and Mill's service as MPs, Rousseau's authorship of a constitution for Poland, Marx's communism, and Heidegger's Nazism. Cf. TWM 82 on political philosophy as an "academic pursuit."

120. Blackburn, by contrast, suggests that *CM* has inspired Strauss's followers to attain "the superiority of the life of both dictators and plutocrats" (Blackburn, *Plato's Republic*, 157). According to the Zuckerts, Jaffa was heavily involved in Barry Goldwater's 1964 presidential campaign (*TALS* 197).

121. From 1974 to 1976, Goldwin was a special consultant to President Ford. In the words of Stephen F. Hayes, Goldwin was "the administration's in-house academic" who brought "leading intellectuals" to the White House for "long, freewheeling discussions with the president and his senior staff" (Hayes, *Cheney*, 73); for additional details, see Sean Wilentz, *The Age of Reagan: A History, 1974–2008* (New York: HarperCollins, 2008), 62, 468n62, 469n64. From 1973 to 1974 Goldwin was an advisor to Donald Rumsfeld, who was the U.S. ambassador to NATO; Goldwin also advised Rumsfeld in 1976, when he was secretary of defense; according to the Zuckerts, Goldwin served as the campaign manager for Illinois senator Charles H. Percy before joining the Ford administration (*TALS* 197; see p. 279 below on the memo that Strauss wrote to Percy in 1961). More recently, Goldwin spent over two decades as a resident scholar at AEI. For an overview of Goldwin's career, see the AEI profile at http://www.aei.org/scholars/scholarID.23,filter.all/scholar.asp.

122. Strauss, carefully quoting and paraphrasing Plato (961d), does liken the council to some combination of soul, head, intellect/intelligence (*nous*), and senses (especially sight and hearing). Paraphrasing both the Athenian and Kleinias (961e, 962c), Strauss goes on to describe the council as "[t]hat part or pursuit of the city which provides . . . the desired fusion of intellect and sense perception" and which must possess "every virtue of the soul and of the head" (*AAPL* 178).

123. *AAPL* 178. At 961d, the Athenian had included *nous* among the faculties needed for the salvation of animals. He proceeds to ask about the sort of *nous* that, when "mixed with senses, would become the salvation of ships"; the pilot and the sailors would "mix the senses with the intelligence (*nous*) of the piloting art" (961e).

124. *AAPL* 178. Cf. 180–81 on the city's need for "subrational" or "animal" virtue, especially courage.

125. Cf. p. 118 above on "broad daylight."

Chapter Four

"A Great Enemy of Democracy"?

Strauss on Plato's Republic, *Germany, and Empire*

Once everything is shaken, one ought to preserve the trunk at the expense of the branches.

—Jean-Jacques Rousseau

I. "A WILD BEAST": DRURY IN THE ROUTLEDGE *ENCYCLOPEDIA*

Although I have been emphasizing her shortcomings, I regard Shadia Drury as a brilliant woman whose observations are often elegant, insightful, and highly imaginative. So I was not surprised that the Routledge online *Encyclopedia of Philosophy* selected her to write the entry on Leo Strauss.[1] But I am amazed that such an irresponsible article was published in this setting.

The entry commences with five sensible paragraphs. Things start to deteriorate in the sixth paragraph, however, where Drury asserts what she admits is an iconoclastic view: "Strauss denied that Socrates was Plato's mouthpiece. He thought that in the *Republic* Thrasymachus, not Socrates was Plato's true spokesman." When, in an interview with Danny Postel, she says that (according to *CM*) Thrasymachus is "Plato's real mouthpiece,"[2] she goes still farther, presenting Thrasymachus as Plato's generic spokesman (i.e., not just Plato's voice within the *Republic*). In the interview, Drury continues to escalate the indictment when she offers the following claim: Strauss himself "shares the insights of the wise Plato (alias Thrasymachus) that justice is merely the interest of the stronger; that those in power make the rules in their own interests and call it justice."[3]

What kind of evidence does Drury supply for these assertions? Her account in the *Encyclopedia*, where one might hope to find only easily established and

141

strongly supported interpretations, is laughable. To document her claim about what Strauss "denied" and "thought" concerning Plato's "true spokesman," she cites a single page (77) from Strauss's eighty-eight-page essay on Plato in *CM* (Drury's paragraph provides no additional citations). But there is only one passage on page 77 that conveys *any* sympathy for Thrasymachus. After suggesting that the exchange between Thrasymachus and Socrates resembles a lawsuit in which Thrasymachus accuses Socrates, Strauss says the following:

> It is a demand of justice that "the other party," i.e., Thrasymachus, also receive a fair hearing. Everyone listens to what Socrates tells us about Thrasymachus. But we must also pay attention to what Thrasymachus thinks of Socrates. Socrates thinks that Thrasymachus behaves like a wild beast; Socrates is entirely innocent and on the defensive. Thrasymachus has met Socrates before. His present exasperation is prepared by his experience in his earlier meeting or meetings with Socrates. He is sure that Socrates is ironic, i.e., a dissembler, a man who pretends to be ignorant while in fact he knows things very well; far from being ignorant and innocent he is clever and tricky; and he is ungrateful. (*CM* 77)

It seems obvious that Strauss is here alluding to two complaints that Thrasymachus issues. First, Thrasymachus protests that Socrates conducted his conversation with Cephalus and Polemarchus by asking questions and "refuting whatever someone answers" rather than by "clearly and precisely" elaborating a definition of justice (336c–d). When Socrates responds that he would not willingly err in searching for justice any more than he would in searching for gold, which is much less precious than justice (336e), Thrasymachus laughs scornfully and tries to ridicule "that habitual irony of Socrates": "I predicted to these fellows that you wouldn't be willing to answer, that you would be ironic and do anything rather than answer if someone asked you something" (337a). Second, in passages that correspond closely to what Strauss wrote about the prospect that Socrates is clever, tricky, and ungrateful (rather than ignorant and innocent), Thrasymachus goes on to complain that Socrates typically refuses to provide answers and only refutes those that others provide (337e); being "unwilling himself to teach," Socrates "goes around learning from others, and does not even give thanks to them" (338b).

Although Strauss agrees with Thrasymachus that Socrates is often ironic, Drury's encyclopedia entry fails conspicuously in attempting to supply evidence for its shocking thesis that Strauss regarded Thrasymachus as Plato's "true spokesman." Drury nonetheless proceeds to offer a wild elaboration for which she offers *no* textual evidence: "Strauss surmised that Socrates must have taken Thrasymachus aside and explained to him that his views were true, but too dangerous to express publicly."[4] According to the rigorous epistemological standards of a twenty-first-century encyclopedia of philosophy, how could anyone know that Socrates "must have" taken Thrasymachus aside? And even if someone might sanely conclude this, how could Drury know what *Strauss* here "surmised"?

In the above-quoted passage, Strauss articulates a thoroughly sensible exhortation to "pay attention to what Thrasymachus thinks of Socrates" and a thoroughly sensible reminder of Socratic irony. How could we infer from these suggestions by Strauss that he regarded the nasty Thrasymachus as Plato's "true spokesman"? Strauss begins the relevant essay by stressing the difficulties of regarding any speech as a direct expression of Plato's ideas: "We cannot ascribe to Plato any utterance of any of his characters without having taken great precautions" (*CM* 59). In the last nine of the *Republic*'s ten books, moreover, Thrasymachus speaks only twice—one fifteen-word sentence at 450a and one twenty-one-word question at 450b (on both occasions, indeed, he is simply encouraging Socrates to continue speaking). Who would regard Thrasymachus as Plato's "true spokesman" in this long and engrossing dialogue when he says so little?

There are at least three additional obstacles to Drury's elevation of Thrasymachus. First, if Strauss thought that Thrasymachus was Plato's spokesman, Strauss would have thought that Plato held a variety of obviously flawed opinions that Thrasymachus expresses in book I: that the just man "everywhere" has less than the unjust man (343d); that when partnerships/contracts between a just man and an unjust man dissolve, the latter will "always" have more (343d); and that "the best city" is one that enslaves the most cities (351b). Strauss, furthermore, emphasizes the exchange between Cleitophon and Polemarchus in which Cleitophon interprets Thrasymachus to mean that justice is what the stronger *believes* to be his advantage (340a–b), while Drury overlooks the difficulties herein posed for Thrasymachus's view.[5] Second, Drury ignores the criticisms that Strauss conveys when he argues that Thrasymachus's thesis, by implying that justice "consists in obeying the law" (*CM* 75), is "the thesis of the city"—a thesis that "destroys itself" (*CM* 76).[6] Third, Drury nowhere addresses the obvious respects in which Glaucon at the start of book II improves on Thrasymachus's critique of justice, in effect replacing it with the view that "justice is the advantage of the *weaker*" (*CM* 87).[7] As Strauss elaborates the comparison, he baldly states that "Glaucon's dissatisfaction with Thrasymachus's attack on justice is justified" and that Glaucon was able to "surpass" Thrasymachus (86); Strauss does at one point imply that Thrasymachus's view is "truer, more sober, more pedestrian" than Glaucon's (87).

Drury's neglect of Glaucon also contributes to her misguided attempt in *PILS* to damn Strauss by citing his reference to "the cleverness with which Socrates argued badly on purpose" while confronting Thrasymachus in book I (*CM* 84). For Drury, this confirms that Strauss regards Thrasymachus as Plato's spokesman (*PILS* 77). In his very next paragraph, however, Strauss suggests a different reason: that Socrates argued poorly "in order to provoke the passionate reaction of Glaucon" (*CM* 85). We here witness one tiny example of Strauss's sensitivity to the dramatic forms Plato utilizes in composing and arranging the speeches in his dialogues (59); Strauss later highlights "the duty of a genuinely just man like Socrates" to guide individuals like Glaucon—"who, by virtue of their inclinations, their descent, and their abilities, may have some public responsibility"—so that they will promote "order and decency in human affairs" (137). Strauss highlights Glaucon, finally, when he confidently encapsulates the dialogue: "Certain it is that the *Republic* supplies the most magnificent cure ever devised for every form of political ambition" (65).[8] How could a book that provides the definitive cure for every form of political ambition use Thrasymachus as its mouthpiece?

After its paragraph on Thrasymachus, Drury's encyclopedia entry presents this remarkable conclusion:

> The devotion of Strauss' followers, coupled with his esotericism, has made him a figure of some controversy. But one thing is clear, Strauss' followers regard U.S. liberalism as the embodiment of the legacy of modernity and its attendant dangers, and their aim is to rescue the USA from such modernity. Strauss taught them that this would be possible if they could win the ear of the powerful, hence their interest in government and public policy. Some find Strauss' elitism disconcerting. An elite that is radical, secretive and duplicitous, an elite that exempts itself from the moral principles it deems applicable to the rest of humanity, cannot be trusted with political power.

I must again appropriate the words of John Schaar and Sheldon Wolin: "What is the relevance, or the propriety, of such a charge in a work which presents itself as an academic and professional discussion of academic and professional work?"[9] What kind of encyclopedia, furthermore, would publish a short article on a major scholar that spends so little time expounding that scholar's writings and concludes with a dire warning that his followers "cannot be trusted with political power"? The Routledge articles on Leon Trotsky, Carl Schmitt, Frantz Fanon, Michel Foucault, and Islamic fundamentalism provide no such warning or criticisms, and the encyclopedia discusses several minor twentieth-century authors (e.g., Petr Berngardovich Struve) in more detail than it discusses Strauss. Marx and Marxism are examined at vastly greater length than Strauss is: there are subarticles on Marx himself, Chinese Marxism, Western Marxism, Russian and Soviet Marxist philosophy, Marxist philosophy of science, and Marxist thought in Latin America. If the *Encyclopedia* incorporates warnings about followers gaining power, perhaps the philosopher who was intimately involved in revolutionary politics—and whose name was invoked to help justify the slaughter of millions of Russians, Chinese, and Cambodians—should receive a harsher scolding than Strauss. The last sentence in the long section on "Marxism, Western," however, is nonchalant: "Radical critics see analytic

Marxists as engaged in a bourgeois academic pastime. But they can also be seen as conservationists, preserving the valid residue of Marxism for a post-Marxian world."

I presume that readers of the *Routledge Encyclopedia* who are persuaded that the "elite" inspired by Strauss "cannot be trusted" with political power are likely to infer that such an elite should also not be trusted with the education of college-age students, nor granted the professorial leisure to communicate their poisonous ideas in writing.[10] In her 2003 interview with Danny Postel, Drury moves beyond her general warning, bemoaning that the "ominous tyranny" of "the Straussian cabal in the administration" has come "so close to being realized."[11] If she truly believes—and regrets—that Strauss convinced his "acolytes" that they are "the persecuted few," then why is she working so hard, and committing so many scholarly transgressions, to demonize us?[12] To conclude her 1990 *Vital Nexus* "Reply," Drury provides a more amusing condemnation of Straussian elitism: "what could be more comical than the specter of a philosopher trying to convince himself and his students that they are gods? And what could be more laughable than their believing it?"[13] I doubt, however, that Drury was trying to be funny when she wrote "specter" in place of "spectacle."

II. "HOW DEMOCRACY GIVES WAY TO TYRANNY"

In order to portray Strauss as an enemy of *morality*, Drury clumsily claims that, for Strauss, Thrasymachus is Plato's "true spokesman" (*Routledge Encyclopedia*). In order to portray Strauss as an enemy of *democracy*, however, Drury treats *Socrates* as Plato's spokesman, and she does so quite crudely. In her 1997 book (*LSAR*), she offers this superficial synopsis:

> Strauss's experience in Germany confirmed the political teaching of his beloved Plato. A great enemy of democracy, Plato described it as the second worse [*sic*] form of government, and was convinced that it inevitably leads to tyranny. (*LSAR* 4)

Drury adds that Strauss "understood both Weimar and America in terms of Plato's analysis of how democracy gives way to tyranny" (*LSAR* 5). For both Plato and Strauss, democracy is "a licentious state of affairs in which a multiplicity of conflicting and irreconcilable appetites compete for dominance" (4).[14] In the footnote she provides to document her claim about Plato (180n8), she cites book VIII of the *Republic*. But it was Socrates, and not Thrasymachus (or Plato), who here presented democracy as the second worst form of government (and described its decline into tyranny). So if Strauss thought that Thrasymachus were Plato's spokesman, Strauss would hardly identify Plato's "political teaching" with all of the political claims that *Socrates* makes.

Even if we treat Socrates simply as the leading character in the dialogue, moreover, it is hard to imagine that he believed all of the statements he made in book VIII. Democracy here appears before tyranny in the preposterous one-way cycle of decay that begins with the communistic regime of the philosopher-kings and proceeds through timocracy (rule by an honor-loving warrior class), oligarchy, democracy, and tyranny. Would even Myles Burnyeat insist that what Socrates says here reflects what Socrates or Plato really thought was an inexorable path of political decline from a best regime that never even existed?[15] The discussion begins in a *hypothetical* mode: Socrates will "tell the way in which a timocracy *would* arise from an aristocracy" (545c; emph. added), but he soon suggests that the best regime previously existed when he uses the past tense at 545e (like Homer, the interlocutors will pray to the Muses to learn how "faction first attacked") and at 547b (the Muses say that the iron and bronze races "pulled" the regime away from communism).[16] The hypothetical tone is also supplemented by a comical one, as Socrates explains why the philosopher kings would, at some point, come to assign matings among the guardians at the wrong moment (546b–d) and would thus trigger the regime's demise:

> For a divine birth there is a period comprehended by a perfect number; for a human birth, by the first number in which root and square increases, comprising three distances and four limits, of elements that make like and unlike, and that wax and wane, render everything conversable and rational. Of these elements, the root four-three mated with the five, thrice increased, produces two harmonies. One of them is equal an equal number of times, taken one hundred times over. The other is of equal length in one way but is an oblong; on one side, of one hundred rational diameters of the five, lacking one for each; or, if of irrational diameters, lacking two for each; on the other side, of one hundred cubes of the three. This whole geometrical number is sovereign of better and worse begettings. And when your guardians from ignorance of them cause grooms to live with brides out of season, the children will have neither good natures nor good luck.

Does the whimsical tone of this passage—not to mention the appeal to the Muses at 545e, where Socrates suggests that they would be "playing and jesting" with the interlocutors "like children"—fail to color some of the subsequent discussion, which includes the well-known critique of democracy and sketch of its decay into tyranny? Because Blackburn overlooks Socrates' use of the past tense at 545e and 547b, he falls more easily into the trap of thinking that Plato "seems to have been entirely serious" about the eugenic arithmetic of 546b–d.[17]

Beyond claiming that Strauss understood Weimar and the United States via the framework that book VIII of the *Republic* articulates (*LSAR* 5), Drury asserts that he "abhorred liberal democracy because he associated it with the Weimar Republic" and that he regarded Weimar as "the paradigm of liberalism—weak, spineless, and stupid" (4, 88); she attributes similar views to Allan Bloom (*LSAR*

114–16, *AK* 168). On the first page of his 1965 preface to *SCR*, Strauss does assert that Weimar was "weak," that "[o]n the whole, it presented the sorry spectacle of justice without a sword or of justice unable to use the sword." But in the aftermath of World War II, to say nothing of the Trail of Tears and the Civil War, who would say that the United States was similarly unarmed as it pursued what it regarded as just causes? During Strauss's lifetime, the United States incinerated Dresden and Tokyo along with Hiroshima and Nagasaki, carried off the largest amphibious invasions in history, dropped 21 million gallons of defoliants on Vietnam, and put a man on the moon. In his 1973 *National Review* article, Jaffa anticipated Drury when he wrote that Weimar embodied the "resolution of the human problem that modernity at its best had promised" and that Strauss "never failed to see the weakness of the Weimar regime as a paradigm of the weakness not merely of German liberal democracy, but of modernity."[18] But if its modernity made Weimar weak, why didn't modernity also weaken Weimar's Nazi and Communist enemies?

Perhaps Weimar's primary weakness, for Strauss, was how it confronted the challenges from both left-wing and right-wing extremes. After lamenting Weimar's deficiency regarding the sword, Strauss proceeds to state that Weimar had a "moment of strength" in its "strong reaction" to the murder of Walter Rathenau, its Minister of Foreign Affairs (*SCR* 1). Strauss is alluding here to the Law for the Protection of the Republic (*Gesetz zum Schutz der Republik*), which was passed after Rathenau—a Jewish man of diverse accomplishments as a physicist, industrialist, author, painter, and civil servant—was assassinated by right-wing nationalists on 22 June 1922.[19] The law criminalized membership in organizations, for example, the Nazi Party, that encouraged or approved of anti-Weimar violence; even mocking of the flag was prohibited. In a widely touted Reichstag speech promoting the law, Chancellor Joseph Wirth concluded with the following words: "There stands the enemy, where Mephisto drips his poison into a nation's wounds; there stands the enemy and there can be no doubt about it: the enemy stands on the Right."[20] Although a special court was set up in Leipzig to conduct trials under the law, enforcement proved spotty and Communists ended up being its primary victims.[21]

Weimar was frail, but Strauss nowhere belittled the *strength* of the nation that did so much to defeat its militaristic enemies in World War II, obliterating cities all over Japan and Germany. According to the well-known introduction to *Natural Right and History*, America had become the world's "most powerful and prosperous" country—assisted by its dedication to the self-evident truths that the Declaration of Independence proclaimed (*NRH* 1). But let us not conclude that Strauss praised liberal democracy only for the wealth and military power that it sometimes generated. Strauss appreciates even its kinder and gentler side: in explaining the failure of Weimar, Strauss also invokes the harshness of the Treaty of Versailles, whereby "the victorious liberal democracies discredited

liberal democracy in the eyes of Germany by the betrayal of their principles"
(*SCR* 2/*LAM* 225).

III. "RULED BY THE RABBLE"? STRAUSS, HITLER, AND CONTROVERSIES ABOUT INEQUALITY

Drury makes other statements about Strauss's views on Germany that are bizarre
even by her standards. For example, she wrote in the 2005 introduction to *PILS*
that "Strauss assumed that liberal democracy is a spineless regime without any
firm beliefs—a regime ruled by the rabble as represented by Hitler" (xx). Yes,
Drury is claiming that, for Strauss, *Hitler* represented the *rabble* who rule in a
liberal democracy that lacks "firm beliefs." On the first page of the preface to
SCR, however, Strauss conveys a very different assessment of Hitler, arguing
that the Nazis triumphed in Germany because Hitler possessed, among other
things, "the strongest will or single-mindedness," and "the greatest ruthlessness,
daring, and power over his following."[22] Even a superficial reading of *Mein
Kampf* should suffice, furthermore, to convince even a superficial reader that
Hitler was not lacking in "firm beliefs." As Drury proceeds, she introduces additional absurdity, asserting that Strauss

> surmised that when the rabble reigns supreme, the superior few will inevitably
> be persecuted. For Strauss, the plight of the Jews in Germany and the plight of
> Socrates and Alcibiades in Athens represented the fate of the superior at the hands
> of the inferior. (*PILS*-05 xx)

Drury first staked out this terrain in her 1994 book on Kojève: Strauss believed
that the nightmare of the last man and the "universal and homogenous state" had
arrived, and that there was "no place in this world for men like Simonides or Hiero" (*AK* 156). Strauss, Drury adds, "regarded Hitler's regime as the democratic
regime par excellence, and Hitler as the personification of the mass man. . . .
Armed with technological might, the rule of the mob aims at the global extermination of the higher types" (*AK* 156).[23]

Although Drury supplies no citations for any of her above-quoted proclamations about how Strauss regarded Weimar, Hitler, and the Germany-Athens
comparison, she pauses in the 2005 introduction to offer smug criticism of
the perspective (on persecution) she attributes to Strauss: "Surely, one moment's reflection reveals that this analysis is seriously flawed" because Athens
was not a liberal democracy and Alcibiades (perhaps also Socrates) was a
"scoundrel" (xx). Drury's claim about Germany and Athens is manifestly and
deeply flawed, moreover, insofar as Strauss would never attribute to collective
Jewry—or any other human group numbering in the millions—the superiority he attributes to Socrates. Also outlandish is Drury's assertion that Strauss

traced Nazi racism to an egalitarian spirit of leveling. Does Drury think Strauss was ignorant of the zealous and resolute Nazi effort to slaughter or sterilize not only Jews but Gypsies, homosexuals, cripples, and mental patients? Could Strauss have thought that the Nazi extermination of Jews in Poland and the Ukraine was animated by envy rather than contempt?[24] When readers encounter the claim that Strauss held such an inane—and self-serving ("We German Jews are the heirs of Socrates . . .")—view of the Nazis, they might infer that Strauss was an ignoramus. Those who reject the latter inference could instead hypothesize that Drury was just throwing out another momentous but half-baked accusation and/or that *her* knowledge about Hitler is scanty. Had she studied *Mein Kampf*, or scrutinized a major study of Hitler, she presumably would have noticed the exaltation of social Darwinism, blood purity, and *Führerprinzipien* that separates Hitler from what she calls "the democratic regime par excellence" (*AK* 156). No esoteric study of Hitler is needed to unearth these messages, and Hitler even offers a religious framework for his obsession about racial purity.[25]

Let us peruse merely a sampling of the passages scattered throughout *Mein Kampf* in which Hitler champions "the superior" and "the higher types" to prevent them from being further "persecuted" by the Jewish "rabble" and its Marxist-"democratic" principles (these phrases are from *PILS*-05):

> The Jewish doctrine of Marxism rejects the aristocratic principle of Nature and replaces the eternal privilege of power and strength by the mass of numbers and their dead weight. . . . Hence today I believe that I am acting in accordance with the will of the Almighty Creator: *by defending myself against the Jew, I am fighting for the work of the Lord.* (*Mein Kampf* 65)

> [T]he parliamentary principle of majority rule sins against the basic aristocratic principle of Nature. (*Mein Kampf* 81)

> Confronted with the Jewish-democratic idea of a blind worship of numbers, the army sustained belief in personality. (*Mein Kampf* 281)

> With satanic joy in his face, the black-haired Jewish youth lurks in wait for the unsuspecting girl whom he defiles with his blood. (*Mein Kampf* 325)

> Bear in mind the devastations which Jewish bastardization visit on our nation each day, and consider that this blood poisoning can be removed from our national body only after centuries, if at all. (*Mein Kampf* 562)

If the world placed even minor emphasis on physical beauty, Hitler adds, "the seduction of hundreds of thousands of girls by bow-legged, repulsive Jewish bastards would not be possible" (412), and he adamantly promotes eugenic regulation of procreation.[26] The racial foundation of Hitler's hatred is further accentuated because he avoids the classic complaints about Jewish responsibility for the crucifixion of Jesus. At one point, he even faults Austria's Christian Social Party for relying upon "religious ideas instead of racial knowledge" (119) and thus spreading a "sham anti-Semitism which was almost worse than none at all" (121).

It is Hitler, not Strauss, who complains that "the representatives of the majority, hence of stupidity, hate nothing more passionately than a superior mind" (82). It is Hitler who insists that "the spark of genius exists in the brain of the truly creative man from the hour of his birth" (293), and that "the salvation of mankind has never lain in the masses, but in its creative minds" (446). It is Hitler who exalts "the subordination of the inferior and weaker" races "in accordance with the eternal will that dominates this universe"; it is Hitler who invokes "the basic aristocratic idea of Nature" to condemn "a bastardized and niggarized world" that would eviscerate "all the concepts of the humanly beautiful and sublime" (383). For Hitler, the Jew—not the Nazi—is the one who trumpets "the equality of all men without regard to race and color" (316) and who is bereft of "any true culture" (302). In the political realm, the Jew "drags everything that is truly great into the gutter"; in the cultural realm, the Jew simply "contaminates art, literature, the theater, makes a mockery of natural feeling, overthrows all concepts of beauty and sublimity, of the noble and the good, and instead drags men down into the sphere of his own base nature" (326). When Hitler uses terms such as vermin, pestilence, spider, chaff, parasite, "noxious bacillus," "the scourge of God," "eternal blood-sucker," rabble, bastard, "international maggot," and "hissing . . . hydra" to characterize the Jews,[27] how could Strauss think they served as stand-ins for Socrates and Alcibiades?

Granted, Hitler does credit the Jews with several talents that might elevate them above the rabble. They are "champions of deceit, lies, theft, plunder, and rapine" (363), parasites who rely on "cunning craftiness" to challenge the "heroic virtue" of the Aryans (153); by virtue of their "thousand-year-old mercantile dexterity," indeed, Jews can monopolize finance and commerce to foment their "blood-sucking tyranny" against the hyperhonest Aryan (309), whom they manipulate via "lying dialectical skill and suppleness" (473).[28] Hitler's assessment, furthermore, is complicated by the way that he condemns Jews simultaneously as Bolsheviks—he often refers to Marx as "the Jew" (215, 382, 391)—and as capitalists.[29] Bizarrely, Hitler extols the campaign to liberate "those masses which had hitherto stood exclusively in the service of the international Marxist Jewish stock exchange parties" (357), and describes Marxism as the "most faithful companion" of "greedy finance capital": because the true kernel of Marxism is "the categorical rejection of the personality and hence of the nation and its racial content," Marxism spawns "the domination of the inferior being—and this is the Jew" (320). More specifically, Marxism "created the economic weapon which the international world Jew uses for shattering the base of the free, independent natural states" and for enslaving mankind to "supra-state world finance Jewry" (600). Hitler even laments how the Bolshevik/Jewish "scum of humanity" killed thousands of Russia's "leading intelligentsia in wild blood lust" (660–61), and provides a general warning about the attempt to "exterminate the national intelligentsia" (326). Hitler's notorious image of the Jewish "wirepuller" (*Drahtzieher*),[30] finally, anticipates certain current accusations about neocons, Zionists, the Lobby, and Straussian whisperers.[31]

In one of her online pieces from 2003, Drury does a better job of conveying Hitler's elitist side: Hitler had a "profound contempt for the masses"; when it was necessary to make the people "comply with the will of the Fürer [*sic*]," Hitler commended "lies, myths, and illusions as necessary pabulum." Her agenda here, however, is to Nazify . . . Strauss and Straussians. According to Drury, the same contempt for the masses is "readily observed" in "Strauss and his cohorts," and Strauss "advocates the same solution"—that is, lies, myths, and illusions—to "the problem of the recalcitrant masses."[32] Whatever one concludes about Straussian rhetoric, however, no minimally objective reader would confuse it with the sort that Hitler recommends in *Mein Kampf*. Whereas Strauss traces the modern world to the books of Machiavelli, Hitler proclaims that "the greatest revolutions in this world have never been directed by a goose-quill" (106). Hitler instead touts the "magic power of the spoken word," especially words that "like hammer blows can open the gates to the heart of a people" (107). Somehow, I cannot envision pet Straussian phrases—for example, the political things, classical political philosophy, noble simplicity, the quest for the best regime, the theological-political problem, the modern project, the love of wisdom, the problem of justice, the ascent from opinion to knowledge, the substitution of freedom for virtue—having such a pulverizing effect. Nor have I witnessed, or read about, a three-hour Straussian lecture that converted its audience into "a surging mass full of the holiest indignation and boundless wrath" (468). Whereas Strauss frequently aligns himself with the *zetetic* or skeptical character of Socratic philosophy, Hitler insists that "*philosophies proclaim their infallibility*" (455). And how could one even begin to equate the notoriously tedious articles and readings issued by Straussians with the leaflets, posters, and "mighty mass demonstrations" integral to the Nazi movement?[33]

IV. NIETZSCHE, WEIMAR, AND THE GOLDEN AGE

Drury's thesis that, according to Strauss, Nazi Germany was the quintessential democracy, Hitler was "the personification of the mass man" (*AK* 156), and the Jews were persecuted as "the superior few" (*PILS*-05 xx), is also difficult to reconcile with certain criticisms Strauss makes of Nietzsche—and with Drury's emphasis on Strauss's debts to Nietzsche. Strauss not only equates Nietzsche's responsibility for fascism with Rousseau's responsibility for Jacobinism (TWM 98), accentuates his lack of moderation, and characterizes his failure[s] as "grandiose" (*LAM* 24); Strauss also condemns him for having "preached the sacred right of 'merciless extinction' of large masses of men" (*WIPP* 54–55; cf. *SA* 7). Strauss faults neither Nietzsche nor the Nazis for being hyperegalitarian. Yet Drury's Strauss is a Nietzschean—Strauss's "greatest intellectual debt is to Nietzsche" (*PILS* 170, 181) and "Strauss's philosopher is modeled after Nietzsche's superman" (180)[34]—who seems to regard egalitarianism as Nazism's chief flaw.

As David Schaeffer has elaborated, Drury's depiction of Strauss as a Nietzschean undermines the shortcut she deploys when she identifies Strauss's views with those he attributes to the wise *ancients* (*PILS* 15, *LSAR* 48).[35] Drury seems to anticipate this objection when she claims that Strauss smuggled Nietzsche into the ancients, that Strauss's ancients have been "transfigured" by Nietzsche.[36] Here too Drury pays a price for underestimating Strauss's contributions as an interpreter.[37] Strauss traced "the crisis of liberal democracy" to Nietzsche's "critique of modern rationalism" (TWM 98), but he worked assiduously to recover and defend *premodern* rationalism. And whereas Nietzsche was often quick to dismiss the pillars of the Western philosophical tradition, Strauss fastidiously reconstructed premodern—and modern—books that offer alternatives to Nietzsche.[38] One must also appreciate the differences between Nietzsche's "creative call to creativity" (*WIPP* 54) and the efforts Strauss made to stimulate his reader's enthusiasm for patient *reasoning* and to cultivate some of the skills such reasoning requires.

In Drury's most recent foray into Nietzsche, her Nietzsche differs sharply from Strauss, even from the sensationalized versions of Strauss that she periodically peddles. In her 2004 book, Drury describes Nietzsche's posture toward Christianity as "a puerile revolt of the child against the parent" (*TC* 122), at least in part because he "merely celebrates whatever Christianity deems to be evil"; Christian assumptions are "so deeply ingrained in his thought, and weigh so heavily upon him that he had to rebel in order to gain an ounce of sanity and self-esteem."[39] When Drury makes condescending and silly pronouncements about Nietzsche, of course, she by implication conveys new insults against Strauss, Nietzsche's alleged disciple.

Despite the gravity of her accusation that Strauss abhorred democracy, Drury conveys no awareness of a prominent passage in which Strauss's hostility to Nazism apparently prompted him not only to chastise Nietzsche but to praise Weimar. At the conclusion of the essay "What Is Political Philosophy?" Strauss faults Nietzsche for having prepared a regime (Nazism, obviously) that made "discredited democracy look again like the golden age" (*WIPP* 55); I presume that "democracy" here refers primarily to the liberal democracy of Weimar. Strauss had mentioned the golden age earlier, in the essay's section on classical political philosophy: although book VIII of the *Republic* provides the "severest indictment of democracy that ever was written," Plato "makes it clear" that democracy is "in a very important respect, equal to the best regime, which corresponds to Hesiod's golden age" (*WIPP* 36). In Hesiod's golden age, you may recall, human beings were mortal but lived like gods without toil, misery, or aging.

When Strauss elaborates Plato's use of Hesiod in *The City and Man*, he again lauds democracy:

> The descending order of regimes is modeled on Hesiod's descending order of the five races of men: the races of gold, of silver, of bronze, the divine race of heroes, the race of iron (546e–547a; Hesiod, *Works and Days* 106ff). We see at once that the Platonic equivalent of Hesiod's divine race of heroes is democracy. (*CM* 130)

Strauss soon elaborates "this seemingly strange correspondence" between democracy and Hesiod's heroic age (which "comes closer to the golden age than any other"): democracy is the only regime, apart from the best regime, in which "the philosopher can lead his peculiar way of life without being disturbed" (*CM* 131).[40] Strauss elsewhere draws on the parallel between Hesiod and book VIII to suggest that democracy is "almost equal" to the best regime.[41] The connection between philosophy and the fourth race/regime is first implied earlier, in book VII, when Socrates says that philosophers would eschew political action because it would remove them from the Isles of the Blessed (*Republic* 519c): Hesiod incorporates the Blessed Isles into the *fourth* stage, not the idyllic first age. Although most of the fourth-stage heroes were killed at Thebes and Troy, Zeus granted some of them "life and habitations far from human beings" at the ends of the earth, where they "dwell with a spirit free of care on the Islands of the Blessed."[42]

When Strauss says that Nazism made "discredited democracy look again like the golden age" (*WIPP* 55), the word "again" alludes to a text that Strauss does *not* mention in this essay. (Other considerations aside, one may therefore infer that Strauss's claim cannot be dismissed as an insincere apology intended for crude public consumption, as Drury or Xenos might allege.) The "again" apparently invokes Plato's seventh letter (324d7–8), which Strauss discusses not in *WIPP* but in *CM*, where he points out that "Plato himself called the Athenian democracy, looking back on it from the rule of the Thirty Tyrants, 'golden'" (*CM* 131). Strauss thus hints at an unusual social cycle whereby philosophical criticisms of democracy, separated by millennia, are followed by postdemocratic nightmares.

Given Drury's frequent warnings about the danger that depraved Straussians pose to American democracy because of their elitism, we must also note that Plato's primary objection to democracy, in Strauss's account, concerns its defects not for philosophers but for the myriad nonphilosophers who would benefit from "a stable political order that would be conducive to moderate political courses" (*WIPP* 36). Although Drury is quick to identify Strauss with Plato's opposition to democracy, she forgets Plato—and the concern for stability and moderation that Strauss emphasizes—when she presents Strauss as the pitchman for nihilistic global revolution. Nonphilosophers are also decisive for the elaboration Strauss gives in *CM*: Plato "held that democracy is not designed for inducing the non-philosophers to attempt to become as good as they possibly can, for the end of democracy is not virtue but freedom" (*CM* 132).[43]

The alarm being expressed or at least felt by current Straussian-bashers concerning the "chill wind," finally, obliges us to fathom Strauss's suggestion that the presentation of democracy in book VIII of the *Republic* deliberately exaggerated both the mildness of the democratic regime—specifically, the Athenian democracy that had engaged in "an orgy of bloody persecution of guilty and innocent alike when the Hermes statues were mutilated"—and the "intemperance of democratic man" (*CM* 132). As usual, Strauss invokes the dramatic context to explain what he regards as a self-conscious distortion by Plato; among the relevant facts is that Socrates is speaking with the "austere" and smugly antidemocratic Adeimantus (*CM* 133). Whatever the differences between Athenian democracy and twentieth-century liberal democracies, Plato's account, by exaggerating the freedom of the former, brings democracy closer to liberal democracy and its protections for individual freedom. And if Plato thought that a philosopher can live "without being disturbed" (*CM* 131) in Athens, he would presumably marvel at the liberty professors, scientists, artists, musicians, journalists, and others enjoy in the United States.

V. "FASCIST, AUTHORITARIAN, AND IMPERIAL": STRAUSS'S 1933 LETTER TO LÖWITH

In arguing that Strauss's mature scholarship is primarily a vehicle for promoting, via esoteric teachings, a "deeply reactionary . . . political position" (*CV* xi) that reflects "a profoundly reactionary penchant for authoritarian forms" (*CV* 88), Xenos ignores book VIII of the *Republic* and Strauss's scattered remarks about the golden age. In fact, a single document "stands . . . at the beginning, center, and conclusion" of Xenos's interpretation (*CV* xvii). That document is the letter that Strauss wrote to Karl Löwith on 19 May 1933 in which he seems to embrace "fascist, authoritarian, and *imperial*" principles. In 2004 Xenos relied upon the letter in arguing that Strauss had "wanted to go back to a previous, pre-liberal, pre-bourgeois era of blood and guts, of imperial domination, of authoritarian rule, of pure fascism."[44] Why, according to Xenos, has the letter been ignored by the "new wave" of Strauss defenders? In trying to dissociate Strauss from "the actual, real-life influence" of his writings on individuals such as Wolfowitz,

Shulsky, Bill Kristol, and Carnes Lord, the recent defenders are guilty of "intentional political myopia" (*CV* xv).

The letter has also been marshaled against Strauss by Joe Conason, Eugene R. Sheppard, Richard Wolin, Larry N. George, and various contributors to the Balkinization blog. Despite the profundity, learning, and eloquence of Pangle, the Zuckerts, Tanguay, Smith, Meier, Janssens, Behnegar, and so on, critics may dismiss their books on Strauss because of their failure to address this smoking gun/mushroom cloud.[45]

Strauss wrote to his friend Löwith from Paris, where Strauss had been residing since leaving Germany in the summer of 1932. The letter begins with two paragraphs about their respective quests for Rockefeller fellowships. After commenting facetiously on the temptation to return to Germany because of the dreadful competition he confronted in Paris from "the entire German-Jewish intellectual proletariat," Strauss initiates the alarming third paragraph by reflecting on the difficulty of exile:

> one does not choose a homeland and, above all, a mother tongue, and in any event I will never be *able* to write other than in German, even if I *must* write in another language-; on the other hand, I see no acceptable/tolerable (*annehmbare*) possibility of living under the swastika, i.e., under a symbol that says nothing more to me than: you and your ilk, you are φυσει[46] subhumans (*Untermenschen*) and therefore justly pariahs. There is here only *one* solution. We must repeat to ourselves: we "men of science"—as our predecessors (*unseresgleichen*) in the Arab Middle Ages called themselves—*non habemus locum manentem, sed quaerimus. . . .*[47] And, concerning that *issue* (*was die* Sache *betrifft*): the fact that the new right-wing Germany (*das rechts-gewordene Deutschland*) does not tolerate us says absolutely nothing against the principles of the right. To the contrary: only from the principles of the right, that is, from fascist, authoritarian and *imperial* principles, is it possible with propriety (*Anstand*), that is without resort to laughable and pitiful appeal (*lächerlichen und jämmerlichen Appell*) to the droits imprescriptibles de l'homme,[48] to protest against this shabby nuisance/monster (*das meskine Unwesen*).[49]

Although Xenos plants the letter at "the beginning, center, and conclusion" (*CV* xvii) of his provocative account of Strauss and quotes the fascist/authoritarian/imperial phrase five times,[50] his approach is marred by carelessness. Let us start with two indisputable mistakes. First, although Xenos states that Sheppard's book provides the German original "in full" (*CV* xvi), Sheppard includes only one of the six paragraphs, the paragraph Sheppard provides is incomplete, and its text is partially garbled.[51] Strauss's surrounding banter, needless to say, might dilute the letter's political venom. Second, and more seriously, on both occasions that Xenos attempts to quote the pivotal sentence (*CV* xv, 16), he omits almost half of it (everything from "with propriety" to "de l'homme").[52] The gremlin has added Nicholas Xenos to its long list of victims.

When Strauss, in the above-quoted extract, insists that Nazi anti-Semitism does not tarnish "the principles of the right," he conveys unmistakable sympathy for those principles.[53] But the more elaborate sentence that follows, which characterizes those principles as "fascist, authoritarian, and imperial," embodies a crucial ambiguity about the degree to which Strauss regards the principles as intrinsically and/or universally attractive. The milder point is the implicit prediction that proper—that is, effective and dignified?—protest against the Nazis within Germany would have to issue from the right rather than from nonrightist principles appealing to the inalienable rights of man. Strauss's previously discussed lecture on German Nihilism, composed roughly eight years after the *Unwesen* letter, likewise invokes conservatism while disparaging Nazism. On the one hand, Strauss suggests that it would be "dangerous" if those who oppose the Nazis "withdraw to a mere conservatism which defines its ultimate goal by a specific *tradition*" (GN 367). But Strauss also states that "simple reaction"— for example, Crown Prince Rupert of Bavaria's plodding reassurance that "the wheel of history" can be "turned back"—had constituted, during the interwar years, the only "articulate" noncommunist alternative to Germany's floundering liberal democracy (359).[54] German nihilism, whose "No" was not "guided by, or accompanied by, any clear positive conception" (357) in its opposition to modern civilization, was *not* "articulate" (359–60). And Nazism was merely the "lowest, most provincial, most unenlightened and most dishonorable form" of German nihilism (357).

Given the possibility that Strauss's 1933 appeal to the trio of rightist principles primarily addresses the prospects for opposing the Nazis, Sheppard should not so quickly pronounce that the piece is a "shocking" letter that "reveals the fusion of the different elements that anchor Strauss's worldview."[55] Richard Wolin too rushes to judgment, finding the letter "hair-raising" and asserting that it is one of the "few occasions when he [Strauss] dared to express his views openly."[56] In addressing a letter David Schaeffer wrote in response to Wolin, Xenos is still more dogmatic. According to Schaeffer, it was not surprising that Strauss believed—given "the failure of the liberal but weak Weimar Republic" either to "preserve public order or prevent the rise of Nazism"—that the "only possible (if unlikely) source of effective resistance" resided in "movements that appealed to conservative German traditions."[57] By proclaiming that this comment is no less "hair-raising" than Strauss's letter (CV xvi), Xenos both belittles the gravity of the letter and makes himself appear intolerant.

Even as rabid a rightist as Erich Ludendorff, who had allied with Hitler in attempting the 1923 Munich *Putsch*, was horrified by Hitler's ascension to the chancellery in 1933. In a letter to President Paul von Hindenburg, Ludendorff lamented that "[y]ou have delivered up our holy German Fatherland to one of the greatest demagogues of all time" and predicted that "this accursed man will cast our Reich into the abyss and bring our nation to inconceivable misery."[58] Since

Strauss begins by denouncing the swastika and concludes the pivotal sentence by dismissing the Nazis as *das meskine Unwesen*, it is silly and offensive for Scott Horton to claim that Strauss "appears alarmingly willing to accept the Nazis as the carriers of Conservatism in May 1933." On the other hand, Horton may be generous to Strauss by translating *Unwesen* as "abomination" (I've instead used "nuisance/monster" above).[59] The word has no equivalent in English. It has a strongly negative connotation. As I have been informed by several highly educated native speakers of German, however, *Unwesen* is typically used to describe mischievous children rather than serial killers. By translating *das meskine Unwesen* as "the dreadful state of affairs" (*CV* xv, 16), Xenos imparts a very different thrust.[60] With Xenos's wording, the *Unwesen* that Strauss would protest via "fascist, authoritarian, and imperial" principles is simply the *anti-Semitism* of the Nazis.[61] Xenos's decision regarding *Unwesen* may appear even more dubious when one considers how he translates the preceding clause: "that the Germany of the Right does not tolerate us absolutely does not follow from the principles of the Right" (*CV* xv, 16). Xenos here creates a double negative, and seems to make Strauss say, quite oddly, that right-wing Germany's anti-Semitism is "absolutely" not the product of right-wing principles.[62] In Xenos's rendition, finally, Strauss also seems to be insisting that only fascism, authoritarianism, and imperialism provide a proper platform for condemning Nazi mistreatment of the Jews.

Who among Strauss's critics thinks that waving the declaration would have slowed down the Brownshirts? Earlier in 1933, the Nazis had crossed many momentous thresholds. Hitler was appointed chancellor by President Hindenburg in January; in the run-up to the March elections, newspapers were censored and various Nazi opponents (especially Communists) were repressed, particularly in Prussia under its minister of the interior, Hermann Goring; capitalizing on the destruction of the Reichstag via arson on 27 February 1933, the Nazis engineered the Reichstag Fire Decree that eviscerated the constitutional protections for civil liberties, they imprisoned and occasionally murdered Communist deputies and officials (along with smaller numbers of Social Democrats, trade unionists, and intellectuals), and they set up the Dachau concentration camp. In the elections of early March, the Nazis produced their strongest electoral performance to date, securing a plurality of 288 seats (out of a total of 647) in the Reichstag. Soon thereafter (in March and April) came the Enabling Act—which allowed Hitler and his cabinet to legislate without the consent of the Reichstag and to ignore various constitutional restrictions—and the first and second *Gleichschaltung* (coordination/alignment) laws, which brought state and local governments, police forces, and a variety of other institutions and organizations under Nazi control. Other onerous developments were also in place by the time of Strauss's letter: Jews were being boycotted, beaten, and plundered all over Germany; in April, several laws, including the "Law for the Restoration of the Professional Civil Service," banned or severely restricted Jews from holding positions in the professions, the universities, and the civil service; on 2 May, the Nazis occupied the facilities and imprisoned the leaders of the ADGB, the national association of trade unions; on 10 May, 20,000 books were burned in Berlin's *Opernplatz*; and the cult of Hitler grew so absurdly that Goebbels had to prohibit the commercial use of his image.[63] Under these circumstances, Strauss conveys an element of patent contempt when he calls the Nazi Party an *Unwesen*, but the circumstances support his judgment that protest based on the "droits impre-scriptibles de l'homme" would have been "laughable and pitiful."[64]

Even when speculating in 1943 about the prospects that, should the Allies win the war, they could subsequently reeducate a defeated Germany, Strauss appeared skeptical about whether liberal democracy could take root there. The Germans would not only have to reject Nazism; they would have to discover liberal de-mocracy. What might be a more feasible alternative, according to Strauss? "A German form of collectivism perhaps—an authoritarian regime of the bureaucracy based on a resuscitated authoritarian interpretation of Christianity perhaps—but not liberalism." A "form of government which is merely imposed by a victorious enemy," Strauss adds, "will not last."[65] There is no reason to think he would have regarded regime change in Saddam Hussein's Iraq as a "cakewalk."

Despite the above-depicted parade of Nazi triumphs and abuses, one could read a remarkably calm assessment of Hitler in the *New York Times* roughly two months after Strauss wrote to Löwith. Reporter Anne O'Hare McCor-mick noted that, because of Hitler's ascension to leadership in Germany, there was "at least one official voice in Europe that expresses understanding of the methods and motives of President Roosevelt"; as Hitler stated to McCormick during an interview, he had "sympathy with President Roosevelt because he marches straight toward his objective over Congress, over lobbies, over stub-born bureaucracies."[66] Having spent time with Hitler, furthermore, McCormick apparently perceived qualities that escaped Strauss: he at "first sight . . . seems a rather shy and simple man," whose eyes are "almost the color of the blue larkspur in a vase behind him, curiously childlike and candid" and whose voice is "as quiet as his black tie and his double-breasted black suit." To confirm that he received "suggestions, praise and objections, not only from friends and party members, but from all sorts of people," Hitler invoked his daily appointment schedule.[67] Will the hairs of Xenos and Richard Wolin rise if they read these words by McCormick, who won a Pulitzer Prize in 1937?

VI. SPARING THE VANQUISHED AND CRAWLING TO THE CROSS

Immediately after the letter's *Unwesen* comment, Strauss invokes Roman authors—and supplies Xenos with additional ammunition. Strauss states that he was reading Caesar's *Commentaries* with deeper understanding.[68] Echoing his earlier appeal to the *"imperial"* principles, Strauss adds that "I think of" Virgil's line, *"Tu regere imperio . . . parcere subjectis et debellare superbos"* (you rule an imperium . . . to spare the vanquished and to crush the proud).[69] Strauss concludes the third paragraph with these memorable words, which echo his earlier reference to the *Hakenkreuz* (swastika):

> There is no reason to submit to the cross (*Es gibt keinen Grund zu Kreuze zu kriechen*), also not to the cross (*Kreuz*) of liberalism, as long as somewhere in the world the spark of *Roman* thought glimmers. And even then: better the Ghetto than any cross (*lieber als jegliches Kreuz das Ghetto*).[70]

There follows a short paragraph that returns to the fate of emigrants and the prospect that "our sort" (*unsereiner*)—presumably the above-mentioned "men of science" (perhaps he is also thinking of the Jews)—are "always" emigrants. Strauss then presents a Latin line—*Dixi, et animam meam salvavi* ("I have spoken and saved my soul")—that provides additional grist for the critics because it alludes to Christian *confession*.[71]

For Xenos, the Virgil quotation—and perhaps also the ultrabrief reference to Caesar's *Commentaries*—"comes as close as Strauss will come" to answering "the fundamental question as to the aim of the State" (Xenos here quotes *PPH* 152). That aim, according to Xenos's Strauss, is "to impose peace on a recalcitrant human nature" and thereby "realize the principles of the political Right" (*CV* 69). In his preface, Xenos blames Straussian rhetoric for masking the transformation of Americans into "imperial citizens who enjoy the benefits of empire while justifying those benefits and the rule over imperial subjects through their self-styled victimization" (*CV* xii). He concludes the book by describing the enterprise "to strengthen imperial power, to 'rule the peoples . . . to spare the conquered and subdue the proud'" as "Strauss's point" (*CV* 144).

The appeal to Roman rather than Greek thought provides an obvious contrast to Strauss's vast written corpus. Strauss, I would suggest, wrote the infamous letter *before* his fateful new explorations of classical thought. According to the Preface of *SCR*, Strauss in the 1920s had shared "the premise, sanctioned by powerful prejudice, that a return to pre-modern philosophy" was impossible; his 1932 article on Carl Schmitt was only the first expression of the "change of orientation" that had "compelled" him to delve more deeply into the tradition of esotericism (*SCR* 31/*LAM* 257).[72] As early as *Philosophie und Gesetz*, which was published in 1935, Strauss stressed that medievals such as Maimonides and Farabi were convinced that philosophy needed to be esoteric (*PL* 102–5, 145n3).[73] But Strauss does not yet seem to link esotericism with *political* philosophy, and he still identifies the *Republic*'s city in speech as "the Platonic state" (*PL* 74, 124), "Plato's ideal state" (77), "the ideal state" (78, 124, 131), "the perfect state" (126, 127), or "the true state" (128), whose "founder" will compel philosophers to be kings (132). Although *PPH* (first published in 1936) extensively invokes Plato and Aristotle to convey Hobbes's departures from "traditional political philosophy,"[74] Strauss here interprets the duo in fairly conventional terms, and he does not discuss esotericism.[75] When Strauss finally produced a publication that focused on a Greek author (the previously discussed 1939 article on Xenophon's Sparta), he offered an innovative explanation of esoteric writing.[76] As late as the above-mentioned 15 August 1946 letter to Löwith, Strauss was willing to announce that an intellectual "shipwreck" compelled him "to begin once again from the beginning."[77]

As was touched on earlier, Strauss in *PAW* emphasizes the difference between the short-term and recipient-specific audience of a letter and the "flight to immortality" that a book could achieve (*PAW* 160). If Strauss had written his paragraph about Caesar and Virgil for a scholarly publication, it would behoove us to specify a strong connection between the principles of the right and the two Roman authors. Given the actual context—a multithemed letter to a close friend—we could instead hypothesize that Strauss was mainly or perhaps even exclusively conveying his reaction to the book by Caesar that he happened to be reading at the time, a book that in turn reminded him of a line from Virgil. At this stage of his career, when struggling to escape the Nazis and to eke out a living, how likely is it that Strauss would have composed a missive whose pores breathed a controversial if not revolutionary political philosophy? As the paragraph ends, in any case, Strauss invokes Roman thought as an alternative, certainly to liberalism, and presumably also to the Christian cross (*Kreuz*) and the swastika (*Hakenkreuz*).[78] The paragraph's concluding endorsement of the ghetto suggests a more specific refusal, by Jews like Strauss and Löwith, to submit to Christianity (and perhaps also to the assimilation associated with "liberalism").[79] Given the enthusiasm Strauss here expressed for "the spark of *Roman* thought," however, one should also note his later celebration of Jewish resistance to the "foreign oppression" and pagan polytheism that ancient Rome had imposed. Battlefield results do not provide "the highest criteria," and the Jewish resistance was "the only fight in the name of an idea made against the Roman Empire" (WWRJ 54).[80] In contemplating the letter's endorsement of *die rechten Prinzipien*, we must likewise acknowledge that Strauss, as one of the naturally homeless "men of science" who was already living in exile, had reason to dread the enhancement of imperial principles in Germany since such a change could result in the conquest of France, England, and/or other places to which Strauss might flee.

To conclude his 1941 lecture on German Nihilism, Strauss both quotes Virgil's Latin and supplies a translation of the passage. After lambasting Hitler's Germany by appealing partly to the English who were "defending the eternal principles of civilisation," Strauss adds that it is they "who *deserve* to be, and to *remain*, an *imperial* nation." Unlike the Germans, they understand that "to *deserve* to exercise imperial rule, *regere imperio populos*, one must have learned for a very long time to spare the vanquished and to crush the arrogant: *parcere subjectis et debellare superbos*" (GN 373).[81] I hasten to add that earlier in the lecture Strauss defined civilization as the process of "making a man a citizen, and not a slave; an inhabitant of cities, and not a rustic; a lover of peace, and not of war; a polite being, and not a ruffian"; civilization is "the conscious culture of humanity"; its "pillars" are science ("the attempt to understand the universe and man") and morals ("the rules of decent and noble conduct") [365]; civilization is "inseparable from *learning*" (366). In the New School lecture from the following year (1942), Strauss claims that it would be "a great achievement indeed if foundations for a peace lasting two generations could be laid," and he contrasts "the tolerably decent imperialism of the Anglo-Saxon brand" to "the intolerably indecent imperialism of the Axis brand." Strauss even asserts that "the existence of civil liberties all over the world depends on Anglo-Saxon preponderance."[82] In his 1949 article, "Political Philosophy and History," Strauss specifically disparages the Roman Empire after invoking the "standards of freedom and civilization" to praise the ancient *polis*. Although the nineteenth-century state might match "the standards of freedom and civilization" that "the Greek city" had attained, the Roman Empire did not (*WIPP* 65).

In his most elaborate praise of ancient *praxis*, Strauss in fact lauds the citizens of democratic Athens—specifically the audience of Aristophanes, or at least its "best or authoritative part"—in a way that he never lauds any group of Romans. The "audience to which Aristophanes appeals," says Strauss, comprises the following:

> free and sturdy rustics in their cups; good-natured; sizing up women, free or slave, as they size up cows and horses; in their best and gayest moments the fools of no one, be he god or wife or glorious captain, and yet less angry than amused at having been fooled by them ever so often; loving the country and its old and tested ways, despising the new-fangled and rootless which shoots up for a day in the city and among its boastful boosters; amazingly familiar with the beautiful so that they can enjoy every allusion to any of the many tragedies of Aeschylus, Sophocles, and Euripides; and amazingly experienced in the beautiful so that they will not stand for any parody which is not in its way as perfect as the original. . . . The audience to which Aristophanes appeals or which he conjured is the best democracy as Aristotle had described it: the democracy whose backbone is the rural population. (*RCPR* 107)

I shall not attempt to excuse the comparison of women with cows and horses.

In his well-known chapter on "Classic Natural Right," Strauss elaborates the classical preference for the city above both anarchy and a "despotically ruled empire": only a city (or perhaps a federation of cities) can provide the mutual trust and the "mutual responsibility or supervision" that are necessary for the pursuit of human excellence. Only the city constitutes a "community commensurate with man's natural powers of firsthand or direct knowledge" (*NRH* 130–31).[83] Strauss speaks similarly in the preface to *LAM*: classical political philosophy maintains that "the society natural to man is the city, that is, a closed society that can well be taken in in one view or that corresponds to man's natural (macroscopic, not microscopic or telescopic) power of perception" (*LAM* x); recall Strauss's opposition to the "universal and homogeneous state." Although the friend/enemy distinction is obviously integral to polis-type societies, the above-quoted passages distinguish Strauss from the "polemical" and statist orientation of Carl Schmitt that privileges "warlike morals" and the prospect of "physical killing."[84]

The Virgil phrase also appears in the "What Is Political Philosophy?" essay, although Strauss neither quotes nor cites the *Aeneid*. Strauss here lauds classical political philosophy because it "reproduces, and raises to its perfection, the magnanimous flexibility of the true statesman, who crushes the insolent and spares the vanquished." In the next sentence, Strauss traces classical political philosophy's freedom from fanaticism to its knowledge "that evil cannot be eradicated and therefore that one's expectations from politics must be moderate";[85] its spirit "may be described as serenity or sublime sobriety" (*WIPP* 28). The permanence of evil, we may infer, requires both of Virgil's poles: there is no excuse for the violence that attempts to eradicate evil, but there will always be evil individuals who must be vanquished. By using "arrogant" (GN) and "insolent" (*WIPP*) rather than "proud" to translate *superbos*, finally, Strauss provides a gentler rending of Virgil's maxim insofar as there are proud individuals who fall short of being arrogant or insolent.

As previously suggested, one could hypothesize that Strauss's letter to Löwith invoked the Romans because he happened to be reading Caesar and because he regarded Roman thought as a serious alternative to both liberalism and Nazism. One could also hypothesize that in the relevant sections of the letter Strauss, during a desperate period of his life, is expressing a possibly fleeting mood that does not well capture the agenda of his mature professorial activities, when he was determined to reopen the quarrel between ancients and moderns with a focus on classical political philosophy.[86] Or one could hypothesize that Strauss has revealed a dastardly secret teaching that would frame the next forty years of his work.

When we look from the letter to the Strauss whose major impact as a scholar and teacher did not take shape for at least another decade, we must also accommodate the somewhat playful remarks with which he introduces the political observations of the third paragraph. At the end of the second paragraph, Strauss complains that the competition he confronts in Paris from the "entire German-Jewish intellectual proletariat" is so dreadful (*furchtbar*) that he'd "rather just run back to Germany" (*am liebsten liefe ich fort nach Deutschland*). The opening of the third paragraph responds to this theme by elaborating the plight of the exile. And the very sentence that introduces the swastika predicts—before the letter has made any mention of the Nazis—that Strauss would *never* "be *able* to write other than in German, even if I *must* write in another language" (*ich jedenfalls werde nie anders als deutsch schreiben* können*, ob ich gleich in anderer Sprache werde schreiben* müssen).[87] According to Richard Wolin, as recounted above, the letter represents one of the "few occasions when he dared to express his views openly." Does Wolin think that Strauss was eager to "run back to Germany" and that he was never able to write in English? I would like to think that Strauss's subsequent ability as an English-language author—not to mention his publications in French and Hebrew—imparts an element of irony if not whimsy to the right-wing endorsement he proceeds to articulate. Let me nevertheless take this opportunity to proclaim my lifelong opposition to the "fascist, authoritarian and imperial principles" of the right.[88]

Roughly a year before he died, Strauss referred to himself as a "hopeless reactionary" (*hoffnungslosen Reaktionär*) in an obviously jocular way before elaborating the physical afflictions—asthma, prostate surgery, pleurisy, and very painful deterioration in his spine—from which he was suffering.[89] Self-deprecating humor pervades the letters. Also pertinent is something Strauss said while answering a question after his WWRJ lecture: I was reared in "a very old fashioned country," and "I know there is a real disproportion between my primitive feelings—which I learned from my wet nurse, as a much greater man put it—and my rational judgment" (WWRJ 75). As Steven Smith notes, Strauss was "born and raised in an observant family in rural Hesse, far from the liberal cosmopolitanism that nurtured contemporaries like Walter Benjamin, Gershom Scholem, and Hannah Arendt."[90]

If some follower of Drury or Xenos manages to lay out a coherent and *compelling* case to support their portraits of Strauss, I would admit that I have been a midlevel or low-level dupe and I would hesitate to call myself a Straussian. Recall the "lukewarm Christians," who, in Strauss's account, helped to make Machiavelli's books "publicly defensible" so that they would "get some hearing" (*WIPP* 45–46); I am surely not the world's most ardent liberal. But I would continue to employ much of Strauss's vocabulary, to contemplate his critique of modern doctrines, and to cherish his interpretations of long-dead authors. There are nevertheless circumstances that might cause me to disavow my Straussian identity. Although my readings of the texts he writes about have overwhelmingly validated what he says about them, perhaps someone could show that he abused sources the way that Drury and Norton do.

VII. FREEDOM AND EMPIRE:
DANIEL FLYNN'S ACCUSATION ABOUT IMPERIALISM

Anti-imperialism is a dominant refrain in current attacks on Strauss and Straussians. Although Strauss-bashing has traditionally issued primarily from the left side of the political spectrum, there is now a growing bipartisanship, from libertarians (the Cato Institute, Halper and Clarke) and isolationists/nativists (Pat Buchanan) to the paleoconservatives (Paul Gottfried, Thomas J. DiLorenzo, Samuel Francis), the polyphobic David Duke, and the polyscrambled LaRoucheans. Among the right-wing commentators, Daniel J. Flynn has recently articulated a sustained, distinctive, and harsh discussion of Strauss that highlights foreign policy.[91]

Flynn's book, *Intellectual Morons: How Ideology Makes Smart People Fall for Stupid Ideas*, comes with glowing blurbs from William F. Buckley Jr. (Flynn has provided "a sophisticated pile driver of a book, guiding us through the wiles of great luminaries of the netherworld") and Thomas Sowell. On many points concerning Strauss, Flynn is fair and balanced. But his title—and his conclusion about the U.S. officials whose "Straussian reading of intelligence" may be responsible for their having drawn "conclusions not warranted by the facts" (141)—invites a spirited reply. For the record, Strauss is also the book's central moron.

Flynn gets off to a poor start when he asserts that Straussians, as well as Objectivists, "function inside a cloistered environment shielded from outside criticism" (3). Despite his six-year stint as the executive director of Accuracy in Academia (1997–2003), he seems to know little about the life of a typical Straussian. Do our articles avoid being refereed by historians, feminists, behaviorists, Marxists, or postmodernists? Are we never outvoted by Rawlsian colleagues, bullied by Weberian administrators, or unmasked by Freudian spouses? An examination of Flynn's chapter-length discussion of Strauss—"A Truth That Lesser Mortals Failed to Grasp: How Ideologues Hijacked U.S. Foreign Policy"—will demonstrate that accuracy is no longer one of Flynn's specialties. I'll also provide additional reasons for rejecting the starkly imperialistic portrait of Strauss that Xenos offers.

Drury's *LSAR* is a primary source for Flynn (133), and he proves to be an apt pupil. Flynn quickly levels a poorly defended charge of obvious urgency in the aftermath of the Iraq War: "Rather than a sign of minding others' business when you should be tending to your own, Strauss regards the pursuit of empire as not only a universal impulse among states but proof of health in nations, as well" (133). For evidence, his footnote (267n29) cites two pages from *The City and Man* (*CM* 209, 239) and one from *What Is Political Philosophy?* (*WIPP* 238). The *CM* pages provide support for the first claim (that there is a universal impulse to empire), but *nothing* in the pages he cites—or in any other pages of which I am aware—supports Flynn's assertion that Strauss regards pursuit of empire as a proof of health.

Flynn's citation to *WIPP* 238 is totally inappropriate. The key phrase is this: a "healthy" nation "always desires to grow." But because the sentence begins with Strauss's attributing this view to *Kurt Riezler*, the subject of the whole long essay, the nonmoronic reader has no reason to attribute this view to Strauss. Riezler (1882–1955) had been a New School colleague,[92] but no one has alleged that Strauss is his disciple, and in the relevant passages Strauss contrasts Riezler with Plato and Aristotle.[93]

Strauss introduces our topic earlier on *WIPP* 238, when addressing a type of sociology that is guided by notions of society and growth. Here is the first sentence of the next paragraph, on which Flynn is presumably relying: "Riezler too spoke of the nation as of a being that, as long as it is healthy, always desires to grow." Strauss goes on to say that, for *Riezler*, a healthy nation thus "has a tendency toward empire." Even Riezler, however, is far from militarism: he differed from "the nationalists proper," including German ones, who overestimated force at the expense of ideas; he feared that extensive growth would yield "disastrous hollowness" if not accompanied and prepared by growth in "intensity, depth, inwardness and consciousness," that is, "culture" (*WIPP* 238); and unlike "official Germany" on the eve of World War I, Riezler's nationalism was "fundamentally republican and at least on the verge of becoming soberly democratic" (238–39). The imperialism he favored was fashioned on the British model: "farsighted, enlightened, sober, patient," and he concluded that the national interest of all the great European powers "required for the foreseeable future the preservation of peace"; he specifically attempted to avert World War I.[94]

In the paragraph preceding the one that introduces growth, we can find still stronger evidence against Flynn's claim that Strauss associates imperialism with the health of nations. Strauss here moves from expounding difficulties in Riezler's anticosmopolitan views to suggesting that "the political philosophy of Plato and of Aristotle" supplies "another alternative to cosmopolitanism" (*WIPP* 237); and *they* taught that "the natural political community is, not the nation, but the city," which makes the nation appear as a "half-way house between the polis and the cosmopolis" (237–38).[95] Thus, Strauss concludes, to bring out "the truth underlying nationalism" would require one to be "guided by the insight embodied in the classical preference for the polis" (238), whose health would be compromised rather than enhanced by the "pursuit of empire" (Flynn's phrase on *Intellectual Morons* 133).

Flynn accurately cites a claim from *NRH* that empire is half of "mankind's great objects" (*Intellectual Morons* 134): in interpreting classic natural right, Strauss states that men are "sensitive to mankind's great objects, freedom and empire" (*NRH* 133). Flynn seems to overlook, however, that freedom consists partly in not being subjected to an empire (*CM* 239), and that Strauss elsewhere identifies "the ultimate aim of foreign policy" (at least for classical political philosophy) as promoting "the survival and independence of one's political community" (*WIPP* 84). More importantly, Flynn ignores the surrounding *NRH* passages that convey a *critique* of empire. As sympathetically recounted here by Strauss, the "classics" favored the city—not the empire—as the type of society best suited for human thriving. The city must be small and "closed" because a society "meant to make man's perfection possible must be kept together by mutual trust, and trust presupposes acquaintance."[96] Such trust is even necessary for *freedom*, partly because "the alternative to the city, or a federation of cities, was the despotically ruled empire (headed, if possible, by a deified ruler) or a condition approaching anarchy" (*NRH* 131).

The paragraph touting freedom and empire as "mankind's great objects," furthermore, begins and ends with claims that both embody and imply objections to imperialism. The conditional language in the opening sentence—"The full actualization of humanity *would then seem* to consist, not in some sort of passive membership in civil society, but in the properly directed activity of the statesman, the legislator, or the founder" (*NRH* 133; emph. added)—establishes that Strauss is articulating a stage in an argument. The provisional character of the passage would be obvious to most students of Strauss, even unfriendly ones, because of his widely known insistence that philosophy transcends politics. Later in the chapter, Strauss states bluntly that, "[a]ccording to the classics, political life as such is essentially inferior in dignity to the philosophic life" (145). Along the way, indeed, Strauss seems to speak for himself when he says that the "selfish or class interest of the philosophers" consists in "being left alone, in being allowed to live the life of the blessed on earth by devoting themselves to investigation of the most important subjects" (143).

Strauss's paragraph about the "full actualization of humanity" touts freedom and empire as it elaborates a compelling, but provisional, case for the dignity of politics:

> It is then something more solid than the dazzling splendor and clamor that attends high office and something more noble than the concern with the well-being of their bodies which induces men to pay homage to political greatness. Being sensitive to mankind's great objects, freedom and empire, they sense somehow that politics is the field on which human excellence can show itself in its full growth and on whose proper cultivation every form of excellence is in a way dependent. (*NRH* 133–34)

Freedom and empire, we may infer, are "mankind's great objects"—at least in the eyes of classical political philosophy—in connection with a high, but not the highest, form of "human excellence." Given his persistent emphasis on *political* philosophy, Strauss can encompass the classical view that even philosophical excellence is "in a way dependent" on politics.[97] But as the paragraph proceeds, and the chapter moves closer to its celebrations of philosophy, Strauss's elaboration presents additional objections to imperialism. The "feelings" that freedom and empire arouse point beyond vanity and bodily satisfaction; they "point to the view that happiness or the core of happiness consists in human excellence." The city is thus "essentially different from a gang of robbers" and "the end of the city is *peaceful activity* in accordance with the dignity of man, and *not war and conquest*."[98]

When we turn again to the 1949 article, "Political Philosophy and History," we see Strauss more directly asserting his agreement with the classical preference for the city. First, Strauss denies that the demise of the city means that classical political philosophy has been refuted. Strauss emphasizes that the classics were familiar with forms of political association differing markedly from the city: the tribe and "Eastern monarchy." Strauss indicates his agreement with the classics' view that the city is "essentially superior" to these alternatives, and specifies that the classical standard was "freedom and civilization" (*WIPP* 65)—not the "freedom and empire" pairing that Flynn summons from *NRH* 133.[99] When Strauss adds that they "consciously *and reasonably* preferred the city to other forms of political association, in the light of the standards of freedom and civilization" (*WIPP* 65), he himself endorses both the city and the standards. The "standards of freedom and civilization," according to Strauss, likewise inspired several "outstanding" political philosophers before the nineteenth century to prefer ("quite justifiably," in Strauss's view) the city to "the modern state which had emerged since the sixteenth century." Even when classical political philosophy "in a sense became obsolete" in the nineteenth century, it was only because the nineteenth-century state—unlike "the Macedonian and Roman empires, the feudal monarchy, and the absolute monarchy of the modern period"—could plausibly claim to be "at least as much in accordance with the standards of *freedom and civilization* as the Greek city had been."[100] In these passages, Strauss exalts classical politics, not just classical philosophy (the more ubiquitous object of his praise). Let us also savor the anti-imperialist words Strauss supplies—speaking for himself—in the introduction to *The City and Man*: "for the foreseeable future, political society remains what it always has been: a partial or particular society whose most urgent and primary task is its self-preservation and whose highest task is its self-improvement" (*CM* 6).[101]

NOTES

1. Shadia B. Drury, "Leo Strauss," in *Routledge Encyclopedia of Philosophy*, ed. E. Craig (London: Routledge, 1998). Retrieved 28 July 2005 from http://0-www.rep.routledge.com.sculib.scu.edu:80/article/S092. The Routledge volume is one of only seven databases listed on the Philosophy subject-section of the Electronic Resources site of my university's library. Drury has posted the entry on her website at http://phil.uregina.ca/CRC/encyc_leostrauss.html.

2. Danny Postel, "Noble Lies and Perpetual War: Leo Strauss, the Neo-Cons, and Iraq," *openDemocracy*, 16 October 2003, http://www.opendemocracy.net/faith-iraqwarphilosophy/article_1542.jsp.

3. Jim George seems to have inferred that Thrasymachus bequeathed written material from which Strauss extracted "a foundational and universally valid meaning associated with . . . modern issues

and problems" (Jim George, "Leo Strauss, Neoconservatism and U.S. Foreign Policy: Esoteric Nihilism and the Bush Doctrine," *International Politics* 42, no. 2 [June 2005]: 178). Joe Conason offers an analogous error when he includes Socrates as one of the "prose" authors to whom Strauss—deploying a theory that is "widely dismissed as crankery"—attributes esoteric messages (Conason, *It Can Happen Here*, 43). Socrates wrote nothing, and he discusses the defects of writing at *Phaedrus* 275d–e.

4. Drury proceeds immediately to the following sentence: "In this way, Socrates managed to silence Thrasymachus without refuting him." Strauss, by contrast, provides detailed arguments about the aspects of the discussion that serve both to silence and "tame" Thrasymachus; he approaches Plato's texts with profound respect and attention, while Drury dreams up an unprovable shortcut (that Socrates must have taken Thrasymachus aside). Drury reiterates her thesis in *LSAR*, where she complains that Jaffa is "quite oblivious to the fact that Strauss regards Thrasymachus and not Socrates as the true spokesman for Plato" (*LSAR* 99; 199n5 cites *CM* 75ff). "Apparently, Socrates tells him (off-stage) that his views are true but too dangerous for public dissemination" (*LSAR* 100; 199n6 is an Ibid.). Drury discusses Thrasymachus at greater length, and with better documentation, in her first book (*PILS* 76–79).

5. For Strauss's perspective, consider *CM* 75, 79–80. Drury at *PILS* 76 is wise to note the originality of Strauss's claim that Thrasymachus's "principle remains victorious" (*CM* 84). That principle—that "the private good is supreme" (*CM* 81)—is indeed vindicated in various ways as the *Republic* unfolds. On the other hand, the three abbreviated arguments Socrates provides *against* Thrasymachus in Book I (350b–c, 351d, 353e) are also vindicated in various ways as Socrates expands and refines them later in the dialogue. For a more detailed discussion, see *TALS* 166–77.

6. Cf. *CM* 78, 124, and *PILS* 87.

7. Emphasis added. Cf. *PILS*-05 xxxiii, *Gorgias* 483a–c, and *NRH* 114–17.

8. Cf. Ferrari, "Strauss's Plato," 47, 52, 55–56.

9. Schaar and Wolin, "*Essays*," 128.

10. According to one recent critic, the influence that "Straussian intellectuals" exert from "their place at the feet of the emperor is less important than the fact that they roam the corridors of the academy." See Thom Workman, "When Might Is Right: Ancient Lamentations, Straussian Ministrations, and American Dispensations," in *The New Imperialists: Ideologies of Empire*, ed. Colin Mooers (Oxford, England: Oneworld Publications, 2006), 139.

11. When Stephen Harper became Canada's prime minister in January 2006, the influence of the "Calgary School" upon him prompted Drury and others to bemoan the impending Straussian takeover of Canada, but the furor seems to have subsided. See, for example, David Beers, "No Bush, Please—We're Canadian," *Salon*, 25 January 2006, http://www.salon.com/opinion/feature/2006/01/25/canada/index.html; Marci McDonald, "The Man Behind Stephen Harper," *The Walrus*, October 2004, http://www.walrusmagazine.com/articles/the-man-behind-stephen-harper-tom-flanagan/; Robert Sibley, "The Making of a Negative Image," *Ottawa Citizen*, 5 February 2006, B3; and John Ibbitson, "Educating Stephen," *Globe and Mail*, 26 June 2004, http://www.theglobeandmail.com/servlet/story/RTGAM.20040626.wxcentre26/BNStory/specialNewTory2006.

12. Danny Postel, "Noble Lies." All of the quoted phrases in the above two sentences come from this interview. For Xenos too, Straussians "revel in the sense of persecution" (*CV* 9).

13. Shadia Drury, "Reply to My Critics," http://phil.uregina.ca/CRC/vitalnexus.html.

14. Recall her recent charge that Strauss was "a sworn enemy of freedom and democracy" (*PILS*-05 ix).

15. For Burnyeat, Socrates leaves Glaucon and Adeimantus ready, "should the day of Utopia come," to persuade some ruling class to adopt the infamous three waves, including philosopher kings and radical communism (Myles Burnyeat, "Sphinx Without a Secret," *New York Review of Books* 32, no. 9 [30 May 1985]: 35).

16. Strauss takes the trouble to formulate an explanation of why Plato presents this obvious falsehood at this specific place in the dialogue: Socrates here wants to increase the anger of his

interlocutors at tyranny, the most unjust regime. Strauss further elaborates that "the possibility of the just city will remain doubtful if the just city was never actual. Accordingly Socrates asserts now that the just city was once actual. More precisely, he makes the Muses assert it or rather imply it. The assertion that the just city was once actual, that it was actual in the beginning is, as one might say, a mythical assertion which agrees with the mythical premise that the best is the oldest" (*CM* 129). In developing this line of analysis, Bloom's "Interpretive Essay" (appended to his translation of the *Republic*) usefully highlights the resemblances between timocracy and Sparta. Adeimantus will perceive in the philosopher "a blessed remnant of the best regime rather than a sign of the corruption of the times"; but because the best regime is "irrevocably in the past" and any changes in the present democracy can only lead to a worse regime, Adeimantus will avoid "committing any follies in attempting to reinstitute the ancestral regime" (413–14). For Glaucon, meanwhile, Socrates' account serves to counteract Glaucon's cynical argument in book II that civil society is a "mere compact between men who prefer to do, rather than suffer, injustice" (416). Both interlocutors are left "moderate without being closed to reason, as respect for what is truly ancestral would make them" (417).

17. Blackburn, *Plato's Republic*, 123–25. When Strauss looks ahead to the nuptial number during his discussion of communism, he argues that infallible guardian reproduction is needed because of the practical difficulties that would obstruct the elevation of lower-class children from their property-owning biological families into the communist collective of the guardians (*CM* 113); Strauss is confident that Socrates wanted "to limit communism and music education to the upper class" (114). When Blackburn says that the classes of the regime are "ossified" into a "caste system" (*Plato's Republic* 80), he forgets that "it sometimes happens that a silver child will be born from a golden parent, a golden child from a silver parent, and similarly all the others from each other" (*Republic* 415b); the rulers must "assign the proper value" to each child and allow its "nature" to dictate its place in the social hierarchy (415c; cf. 423c–d). A silver-level soldier, furthermore, would be "demoted to craftsman or farmer" for cowardly conduct (468a), while one who died nobly would become "a member of the golden class" (468e). For a politically illuminating analysis of book VIII, see Arlene W. Saxonhouse, "Democracy, Equality, and *Eidē*: A Radical View from Book 8 of Plato's *Republic*," *American Political Science Review* 92 (June 1998): 273–83.

18. Harry Jaffa, "Achievement," 1354 (and *Conditions of Freedom* 5). Eugene Sheppard's summary is more precise: for Strauss, the "link between Weimar's weak liberal regime and its authoritarian successor is explained by the collapse of the liberal foundation: belief in modern rationalism" (Sheppard, *Leo Strauss*, 123). According to Ted McAllister's interpretation of Strauss, "the weakness of the Weimar regime was the inability to identify and defend its highest principles" (McAllister, *Revolt*, 166).

19. Alfred Rosenberg, the Nazi theorist and functionary, disparaged the dead Rathenau as "that hero of the international financial spirit" (Rosenberg, *The Myth of the Twentieth Century*, trans. Vivian Bird [Torrance, CA: Noontide Press, 1982], 370).

20. Quoted in Erich Eyck, *A History of the Weimar Republic*, vol. 1 (New York: John Wiley & Sons, 1962), 217.

21. Eyck, *History*, 216–21. Also see Eric D. Weitz, *Weimar Germany: Promise and Tragedy* (Princeton, NJ: Princeton University Press, 2007), 100–101, 332–33; Ian Kershaw, *Hitler: 1889–1936 Hubris* (New York: W. W. Norton, 1998), 663n178; Adolf Hitler, *Mein Kampf*, trans. Ralph Mannheim (Boston: Houghton Mifflin, 1999), 270n2; Michaela W. Richter, *The Verfassungsschutz* (American Institute for Contemporary German Studies), 3–4, www.aicgs.org/file_manager/streamfile.aspx?path=&name=richter.pdf.

22. Drury paraphrases this passage at *LSAR* 5/180n9.

23. Stephen Holmes offers a milder thesis—and thus escapes a "top ten" tainting—in stating that from Strauss's "Platonic perspective," fascism was "excessively democratic and egalitarian"; like Christianity and liberalism, it "wholly neglected 'the best human type,'" the philosopher

(Holmes, *Anatomy*, 77). In the only passage Holmes here cites (at 279n39), however, Strauss says nothing about fascism, and instead emphasizes that "the best human type" can develop freely in a *democracy* (*WIPP* 36). When Drury recently called Strauss a "Jewish Nazi" (Heer, "Mind of the Administration"), she overlooked her assertions that Strauss regarded Nazism as a "rabble" regime. I was unable to find the repulsive "Jewish Nazi" phrase, which has been widely circulated on the Internet, anywhere in Drury's writings or other interviews, so I assumed it was something she said directly to Heer. It turns out that an enterprising blogger (Kat Herding!) e-mailed Heer, who "responded with blinding speed" to confirm that Drury used the phrase in their interview, conducted roughly a week before the article was published in the *Boston Globe*. See http://mysticbourgeoisie .blogspot.com/2006/09/leo-strauss-neocons-jihad.html (accessed 9 September 2007).

24. As I shall shortly discuss, by 1933 Strauss was already faulting the Nazis for labeling the Jews as *Untermenschen*.

25. Hitler, *Mein Kampf*, 65, 214, 249, 327, 383, 402, 430, 562. Although Drury's above-discussed remarks serve to conceal the thoroughly and pervasively racist foundations of Nazism, she elsewhere complains that *Strauss* was unable to comprehend that "the 'peoples' of Europe are not some mystical purebreds that have sprung from rock and oak" (*LSAR* 43). See pp. 103–4 above. Drury does acknowledge Strauss's condemnation of Nazi anti-Semitism and Hiram Caton's condemnation of Nazi eugenics (*LSAR* 6).

26. "The demand that defective people be prevented from propagating equally defective offspring is a demand of the clearest reason and if systematically executed represents the most humane act of mankind" (Hitler, *Mein Kampf*, 255). Also see 132, 402–5. Hitler chillingly suggests that "only six hundred years" of breeding would suffice both to "free humanity from an immeasurable misfortune" and to produce "a recovery which today seems scarcely conceivable" (404–5). In the words of George Frederickson, "[t]he fear of sexual pollution or violation by the allegedly subhuman race is close to the heart of murderous or genocidal racism whenever and wherever it appears" (George M. Fredrickson, *Racism: A Short History* [Princeton, NJ: Princeton University Press, 2002], 120).

27. Hitler, *Mein Kampf*, 169, 193, 296, 304, 305, 310, 332, 412, 556, 637. Although Rosenberg too exalts "the eternal, natural, aristocratic laws of blood" (Rosenberg, *Myth*, 351), his language about the Jews tends to be milder than Hitler's; cf. 119, 273, 307, 313–14, 319, 351, 363–64, 373–74, 421–22.

28. Eerily, Hitler adds that Jews "speak in order to conceal or at least to veil their thoughts; their real aim is not therefore to be found in the lines themselves, but slumbers well concealed between them" (*Mein Kampf* 64).

29. Cf. Rosenberg, *Myth*, 119, 162, 222, 350.

30. Hitler, *Mein Kampf*, 90, 493, 523, 526, 528, 626.

31. Cf. Michael Kinsley, "What Bush Isn't Saying about Iraq," *Slate*, 24 October 2002, http://www.slate.com/id/2073093: "Neither supporters nor opponents of a war against Iraq wish to evoke the classic anti-Semitic image of the king's advisers whispering poison into his ear and betraying the country to foreign interests."

32. Shadia Drury, "Saving America: Leo Strauss and the Neoconservatives," 11 September 2004, http://evatt.labor.net.au/news/254.html. (When I printed this piece on 31 May 2004, I tracked down a posting date of 10 September 2003; the piece is also posted at http://evatt.org.au/publications/papers/112.html.) To "avoid the horrors of the Nazi past," Drury advises, we must not "accept Strauss's version of ancient wisdom uncritically." As she puts it in her 2005 introduction, a mother lode of Top Ten ore, "[i]t is not liberalism, but Strauss's philosophy that invites the horrors of the Nazi past" (*PILS-05* xxi). She does here offer a small concession when she says that "[t]he ghosts of Weimar inform all of Strauss's work" (xx); in the original 1988 introduction, similarly, she reminds us that "the specter of Nazi Germany is always in the back of his mind" (*PILS* xv; cf. 161).

33. Hitler, *Mein Kampf*, 470, 473, 478, 543.

34. Cf. *PILS* 71, 176–77, 188, 191; Drury's later writings are equally insistent.

35. David Lewis Schaeffer, "Shadia Drury's Critique of Leo Strauss," *Political Science Reviewer* 23 (1994): 84.

36. *PILS* 170, 176, 181; cf. pp. 56–57 and 87n12 above.

37. Drury does laud Strauss's essay on *Beyond Good and Evil* (*SPPP* 174–91) for being "one of the most penetrating and most consistent accounts" of Nietzsche (*PILS* 171). Peter Levine follows Drury in characterizing Strauss as an "esoteric Nietzschean" whose commentaries are dominated by "the deliberate misinterpretation of past philosophers" (Levine, *Nietzsche and the Modern Crisis of the Humanities* [Albany: SUNY Press, 1995], 153–55, 161). Although Levine refrains from demonizing Strauss (and Straussians), he falls embarrassingly short when he attempts to convey Strauss's "method of interpreting." According to Levine's Strauss, "the writers of the past . . . always state their sincere views only at the precise center of their books" (153). Levine fares better when he later focuses on the "great philosophers" (rather than on past authors generally), but he absurdly adds that (for Strauss) the truths they "always" reserve for "the exact middle" of their books are "surrounded by great quantities of dry and irrelevant material" (160). Does Strauss ever say or imply that "great quantities of dry and irrelevant material" can be found in the writings of Plato, Xenophon, Aristotle, Lucretius, Machiavelli, Hobbes, Spinoza, Locke, or Rousseau? For an elaboration of Strauss's debts to Nietzsche that is consistently careful, thorough, coherent, and well-documented, see Lampert, *Leo Strauss*.

38. Drury presumably thinks Strauss was being deceptive when he omitted Nietzsche while identifying Plato and Aristotle as "men of the highest excellence" (*CM* 49). On Strauss's departures from Nietzsche's understanding of the ancients, see *SA* 7; *SPPP* 33, 183, 185; and Zuckert, *Postmodern Platos*, 5, 31–32, 105, 116–17, 164, 166–68, 185–90.

39. In addition, Nietzsche "posed as a champion of nature and the instincts against civilization and its repressions" (123), "long[ed] for the healthy gods of the Greeks," and seemed to be "filled with remorse, guilt, and the symptoms of a bad conscience" (124). These citations are from Shadia B. Drury, *Terror and Civilization: Christianity, Politics, and the Western Psyche* (New York: Palgrave Macmillan, 2004). Her discussion of Nietzsche in *PILS* 170–81 includes fewer flights of fancy.

40. In the 1988 conclusion that she subsequently abandoned and probably forgot, Drury admitted that for Strauss, democratic freedom promotes "the unhampered pursuit of the philosophical life, and he is sure that Plato must have recognized this" (*PILS* 194).

41. This last remark comes from the essay—the mammoth review of Eric Havelock's *The Liberal Temper in Greek Politics*—in which Strauss discusses Hesiod and the golden age at greatest length. Whereas the primordial golden age occurred when the heavens were ruled by Cronos, the four subsequent ages reflect the influence of Zeus, and the steady decline to the current—and most lamentable—age of iron is interrupted by the "far superior" fourth stage of heroes/demigods. Strauss then presents the comparison with Plato: "When Plato adapted Hesiod's scheme in the *Republic*, he . . . intimated in what respect the fourth race, or rather the fourth regime, is almost equal to the first regime: the first regime is the rule of the philosophers, and the fourth regime is democracy, that is, the only regime apart from the first in which philosophers can live or live freely" (*LAM* 35).

42. Hesiod, *Works and Days*, 156–73. Cf. *Republic* 468e–469b, 540b–c, 546e–547a, and note the use of the word "blessed" (*makarios*) at 561d to describe the life of democratic man. I am quoting the revised Loeb Library edition of Hesiod: *Theogony, Works and Days, Testimonia*, edited and translated by Glenn W. Most (Cambridge, MA: Harvard University Press, 2006).

43. Strauss's words here about Socrates are particularly poignant: "One could say that he showed his preference for democracy by deed: by spending his whole life in democratic Athens, by fighting for her in her wars and by dying in obedience to her laws" (*CM* 131–32).

44. Xenos, "Leo Strauss," 4–5. Wikipedia's entry on Strauss quotes from the letter and provides a link to an unpaginated html version of Xenos's article (http://www.logosjournal.com/issue_3.2/xenos.htm).

45. I am told that *The Cambridge Companion to Leo Strauss*, edited by Steven B. Smith, will include a chapter by Susan Shell that assesses the 19 May 1933 letter, Strauss's "German Nihilism" lecture, and related topics. This collection will probably be published while my book is in the production pipeline.

46. By nature.

47. "We don't have a lasting place, but seek." The ellipsis is Strauss's.

48. "The imprescriptible rights of man." Strauss is here quoting from Article 2 of the Declaration of the Rights of Man and of the Citizen (adopted by France's National Constituent Assembly in August, 1789); the Declaration's preamble invokes the "natural, inalienable, and sacred" rights of man. Sheppard translates "imprescriptible" as "unwritten" (Eugene Sheppard, *Leo Strauss*, 61).

49. As Scott Horton points out in note 6 of his 16 August 2006 posting (http://balkin.blogspot.com/2006/07/letter_16.html), *meskine* seems to be borrowed from the French word, *mesquin* (or the Italian, *meschino*). The French word suggests "shabby" or "mean" in appearance, but also paltry, petty, or stingy. Here and below, I have used but modified the translation Horton posted; for the original letter, see *GS* 624–25.

50. *CV* xv, 16, 21, 58–59, 70.

51. Sheppard garbles the end of the sentence about "das rechts-gewordene Deutschland" (Sheppard, *Leo Strauss*, 156n25); Xenos ignores "gewordene" and speaks simply of "the Germany of the Right" (*CV* xv, 16).

52. Despite these two howlers, the citation-travesties involving *On Tyranny* (see p. 77 above), other obvious mistakes, and several ill-tempered pronouncements, I would not belittle Xenos's book—as Xenos belittles *TALS*—by describing it as "allegedly" scholarly (*CV* 147n23).

53. Although in his reply of 28 May 1933, Löwith proclaims his distance from the liberal and rights-based version of the free mind/spirit (*die "liberale" und menschenrechtliche "Geistesfreiheit"*), he is more inclined to condemn the principles of the right (*die rechten "Prinzipien"*) insofar as they failed in practice to tolerate Germany Jewry and the spirit of science (*den Geist der Wissenschaft*) [#12, *GS* 627].

54. Strauss here links German nihilism to Nietzsche (GN 359, 361–62, 372), and elsewhere distinguishes Nietzsche—who held that "all merely defensive positions, all merely backward looking endeavors are doomed"—from the "typical Continental European conservative" (*SPPP* 32–33). Cf. pp. 83–85 above.

55. Eugene Sheppard, *Leo Strauss*, 61; later in his book, Sheppard describes a well-known 15 August 1946 letter to Löwith as revealing Strauss's "true political leanings" (104), even though this letter extols Plato, Aristotle, and the "small city-state." Although Joe Conason does not appear to have read *any* of Strauss's published writings, he blithely announces that the 1933 letter provides "[t]he most startling expression of Strauss's moral confusion during that period" (Conason, *It Can Happen Here*, 44). Werner Dannhauser finds Strauss's "principles of the right" passage painful to read, but takes solace from the hypothesis that in the letters Strauss sometimes "takes a slightly unseemly pleasure in taunting Löwith, or at least in being hyperbolically provocative toward him" (Dannhauser, "Leo Strauss," 359). Steven Smith, in reviewing Sheppard, finds it "entirely conceivable that the young Leo Strauss was a conservative authoritarian" who saw the renewal of imperial rule as "the only practical antidote to Hitler's national socialism." Smith thus suggests that *WIPP*'s retrospective remark about the golden age "should be read as a possible self-criticism and rejection of Strauss's own earlier flirtation with 'fascist, authoritarian, imperial' principles" (Smith, "A Skeptical Friend of Democracy," *New York Sun*, 14 March 2007, http://www.nysun.com/article/50399); cf. Perry Anderson, *Spectrum: From Right to Left in the World of Ideas* (London: Verso, 2005), 26. In his book, however, Smith assured us that Strauss had "*always* considered

modern liberal democracy with its constitutional separation of state and society the best practicable solution to the theologico-political problem" (Smith, *Reading*, 127; emph. added).

56. Richard Wolin, "Leo Strauss, Judaism, and Liberalism," *Chronicle of Higher Education* 52, no. 32 (14 April 2006): B14. Wolin arrives at the memorable conclusion that Strauss's "esoteric political philosophy . . . was conceived not in order to strengthen liberalism but to supersede it."

57. David Lewis Schaeffer, "The Legacy of Leo Strauss," letter to *Chronicle of Higher Education* 52, no. 38 (26 May 2006): B17. In the introduction he provided for the letter's posting on the Balkinization blog, Horton emphasizes that liberalism in Middle Europe then "looked exhausted and unable to function," and warns us that we "should be cautious about projecting postwar sensibilities back into the thirties." See http://balkin.blogspot.com/2006/07/letter_16.html. Schaeffer-like views were also posted on this blog by Robert Howse, a professor at the University of Michigan Law School who is writing a book about Strauss and neoconservatism: "things had gone so far in an antiliberal direction by the time of that letter that to appeal to liberal principles against Nazism was ridiculous (at least as a matter of political effectiveness). Strauss was probably correct that the only hope—still a hope—was that old style conservatism, even fascism, might displace Hitler (and, yes, he assumed implicitly that even fascism/right wing imperialism would be better than Hitler)."

58. Quoted in Kershaw, *Hitler*, 427; on opposition from other German conservatives (including Franz von Papen) to Hitler, see 136, 508–11. A key Hitlerian response to such grumbling was the "Night of the Long Knives" that tamed the *S.A.*, reassuring the *Reichswehr* and various conservatives.

59. Sheppard's "repulsive monster" (Sheppard, *Leo Strauss*, 61) is close to Horton's translation; it is also used by Steven Smith and William H. F. Altman.

60. Xenos may have good reasons for his decisions, but he neither specifies the original words (*das meskine Unwesen*) nor acknowledges the translation challenges that the letter poses.

61. In a letter he wrote to Löwith just three months earlier, Strauss contrasted the "progressivist and Marxist" Left with the Right of Nietzsche, Kierkegaard, and Dostoevsky (2 February 1933 [#7], *GS* 620); on Kierkegaard and Nietzsche, cf. the undated Strauss to Löwith letter #16 (*GS* 631–32); Strauss also sketches the left-right spectrum in a 1932 letter to Gerhard Krüger (19 August 1932 [#17], *GS* 399). In a letter to Krüger written just two months after the 19 May 1933 letter to Löwith, Strauss cites Mussolini while suggesting, somewhat abstractly, that fascism shares certain faults with the liberal-democratic presuppositions (*liberal-demokratischen Wissens*) that dominated Strauss's generation and that point toward something like Bolshevism. As Strauss continues, he links his "option" for the political Right with his lack of knowledge, and directs Krüger's attention to old and "unmodern" solutions (22 July 1933 [#17], *GS* 433). In a 1935 letter to Löwith, Strauss makes an analogous point about Nietzsche: that, despite his intention to repeat antiquity (*seiner Intention, die Antike zu wiederholen*), Nietzsche perhaps failed to do so because he continued to be conditioned by "modern presuppositions" (*modernen Voraussetzungen*) or by polemics against them (23 June 1935 [#26], *GS* 650). Earlier in this letter comes Strauss's claim that during his twenties he had been profoundly "dominated and bewitched" (*beherrscht und bezaubert*) by Nietzsche (*GS* 648); Altman relies very heavily on this statement in arguing that the young Strauss was a German nihilist (Altman, "Leo Strauss," 590).

62. Apart from restoring "absolutely" (*schlecterdings*) before "nothing," my translation—"the fact that the new right-wing Germany does not tolerate us says absolutely nothing against the principles of the right"—follows Horton's. Here is the complete clause in German: "daraus, dass das rechts-gewordene Deutschland uns nicht toleriert, folgt schlecterdings nichts gegen die rechten Prinzipien" (*GS* 625).

63. Kershaw, *Hitler*, 452–84. In his letter to Jacob Klein of 27 March 1933, Strauss had stressed both the impotence/demise of the Social-Democratic Party and Germany's difficult economic circumstances, particularly the intractable levels of unemployment. Strauss went on to predict that

German parliamentary democracy was doomed (*Es wird niemals mehr in Deutschland eine parlamentarische Demokratie geben—das ist sicher*) [Strauss to Klein, 27 March 1933 (#5), *GS* 461]. In the 1962 Preface to *SCR*, Strauss claimed that Weimar's doom was signaled as early as 1925, when Hindenburg was elected president: "the old Germany was stronger—stronger in will—than the new Germany" (*SCR* 1; cf. Strauss, "Re-education of Axis Countries," 533). Hindenburg's election (in April 1925) occurred after the death of President Friedrich Ebert in February 1925, when the Nazi Party had barely begun its reorientation from bullets to ballots and its meteoric political rise; as late as the Reichstag elections in May 1928, the Nazis received less than 3 percent of the vote (Kershaw, *Hitler*, 302–3, 333). The first volume of *Mein Kampf* was published a few months *after* Hindenburg's election, and the second volume did not appear until the following year. If half of the Communists had forsaken the doomed campaign for their leader Thälmann and had voted in 1925 for Wilhelm Marx, the Social-Democratic candidate, the latter would have defeated Hindenburg (Eyck, *History*, 336). On the occasional harmonization of right-wing and left-wing attacks on Weimar, see Roger Woods, *The Conservative Revolution in the Weimar Republic* (New York: St. Martin's Press, 1996), 70, 100, 101.

64. Horton may exaggerate in asserting that Strauss "could just as easily have quoted the American Declaration of Independence." Our Declaration speaks about natural rights in a crisper and more modest fashion, and Strauss later celebrated the "weight" and "elevation" that immunize the relevant passage from "the degrading effects" of both "excessive familiarity" and misuse (*NRH* 1). By invoking the French Declaration, in any case, Strauss has left Straussians in a less precarious position insofar as Strauss-bashers are likely to find many objectionable items in it. Consider, for example, these three planks: the preamble's claim that "ignorance, forgetting or contempt" of the rights are "the sole causes of public misfortunes (*malheurs*)"; the designation of a natural right to property in Article 2 (Article 17 calls property "an inviolable and sacred right"); and the claim in Article 3 that all authority "resides essentially in the Nation" (neither an individual nor a body can exert authority that does not "emanate expressly" from the nation's).

65. Strauss, "Re-education of Axis Countries," 532–33. As Nathan Tarcov, who edited this New School lecture (along with the earlier-cited 1942 one), sagely notes: "Strauss seems to have erred in the direction of underestimating, not overestimating, the prospects for the spread of liberal democracy—exactly the opposite fault from that with which he has recently been charged." See Tarcov, "Will the Real Leo Strauss Please Stand Up?" *The American Interest* 2, no. 1 (September–October 2006), http://www.the-american-interest.com/ai2/article.cfm?Id=166&MId=5.

66. FDR was inaugurated approximately four months earlier, on 4 March 1933, and his "First 100 Days" ran until mid-June.

67. Anne O'Hare McCormick, "Hitler Seeks Jobs for All Germans," *New York Times*, 10 July 1933.

68. When Sheppard says that "[i]n the light of recent events Strauss turned to read Caesar's *Commentaries* with a newfound comprehension," he implies, without warrant, that Strauss cites the recent events to explain *why* he was reading Caesar (Sheppard, *Leo Strauss*, 61).

69. This literal translation is misleading because of the excised words. The Latin original is "tu regere imperio populos, Romane, memento / (hae tibi erunt artes), pacisque imponere morem, / parcere subjectis et debellare superbos." Here is a translation I have modified from one provided by my colleague, John Dunlap: "As to you, Roman, remember to rule the peoples in (your) dominion / (these will be *your* arts), and to impose the rule of peace, to spare the vanquished and to crush the proud." For the Latin original, I am using *Virgil: Aeneid VI*, ed. Sir Frank Fletcher (Oxford: Clarendon Press, 1968). The words are stated by Anchises, the dead father of Aeneas, after Aeneas had been summoned to the underworld by his father's phantom. Anchises points out a "vast murmuring throng" (VI 871) of "shades" who will go on to become Romans. After naming roughly twenty men—including Romulus, Numa, Caesar, and Fabius Maximus (VI 974–75)—Anchises offers a general reflection about Rome's destiny. Whereas "others" (obviously, the Greeks) excel

at forging bronze, sculpting marble, pleading cases, and charting the stars, Anchises exhorts Aeneas to remember that, as a Roman, his "arts" are to govern "peoples" (*tu regere imperio populos*), to impose/establish the ways of peace (*pacisque imponere morem*), to spare the vanquished (*parcere subjectis*), and to crush (*debellare*—literally, to break down via war) the proud; I am now citing the translation of the *Aeneid* by Robert Fagles (New York: Viking/Penguin, 2006).

70. The reference to the *Hakenkreuz* also echoes the first sentence of the paragraph: *Aber hier liegt der Haken* ("But here's the catch").

71. For Horton, for example, the letter is one that Strauss "consciously marks as a political confession"; Horton is convinced that it is "a very candid statement of Strauss's politics at the time he wrote it." According to Sheppard, Strauss "bitterly plays on the penitential ritual whereby believers enact their complete humility in turning to the symbol of the Cross as the sole source of salvation." In 1077 at Canossa, Henry IV (the Holy Roman Emperor) begged Pope Gregory VII to lift his excommunication. In commenting on the *Kulturkampf*, Bismarck proclaimed in May 1872 that "[w]e are not going to Canossa either physically or morally" (Sheppard, *Leo Strauss*, 62–63). Sheppard offers other helpful observations: Nietzsche speaks of "crawling back to the cross" in *Zarathustra*, part III, "On Apostates"; the *Dixi* phrase evokes Ezekiel 3:18–19 and was employed by Marx in the epilogue to the 1875 *Critique of the Gotha Program* (Sheppard, *Leo Strauss*, 157n28).

72. The *LAM* version leaves out the dash in "pre-modern."

73. The chapter that provides the most thorough discussion of esotericism, furthermore, was substantially completed in 1931 (*PL* 145n1). According to Tanguay, Strauss's understanding of Plato, Maimonides, and esoteric writing was transformed in the years 1935–1940 with the help of Farabi (Tanguay, *Leo Strauss*, 98, 127–28, 147, 179, 360). According to Heinrich Meier, Strauss in 1935 changed his views about both "the political dimension of the philosophical confrontation with revealed religions" and what Strauss called "philosophical politics" (Meier, "How Strauss Became Strauss," in *Enlightening Revolutions*, ed. Svetozar Minkov, 369). Rémi Brague places the decisive turn in roughly 1938 (Brague, "Leo Strauss and Maimonides," in *Leo Strauss's Thought: Toward a Critical Engagement*, ed. Alan Udoff [Boulder, CO: Lynne Rienner Publishers, 1991], 94–97). David Janssens traces certain changes to 1935 (*Between Athens and Jerusalem* 73, 93–94, 107–8), but otherwise touts the continuity in Strauss's focus on the theological-political problem, that is, "the tension between the philosophic life and the theological-political authority of the city" (178).

74. For the quoted phrase, see *PPH* 4, 98, 100, 102, 136. According to Meier, the manuscript was finished in 1935 (Meier, *Leo Strauss*, 4).

75. Like *PL*, furthermore, *PPH* associates Plato's *Republic* with "the ideal State" (148) and also, it seems, with "the eternally immutable prototype" of "the perfect State" (106); cf. *NRH* 138 on "ideal," *CM* 30–32 on city/state, and Batnitzky, *Leo Strauss*, 146–47. Strauss does argue that "political considerations" (*PPH* 74) often caused Hobbes to conceal his true views about religion. The word "exoteric" also appears in one of the book's discussions of Plato (*PPH* 147). David Janssens, however, implies that the word was an embellishment by the translator (Elsa M. Sinclair). As presented by Janssens, drawing on *GS* 168 for the original German, the *PPH* 147 sentence should read thus: "In itself wisdom (*die Einsicht*) stands supreme, for man (*für den Menschen*), however, justice" (Janssens, *Between Athens and Jerusalem*, 230n49). The German original was first published in 1965 as *Hobbes politische Wissenschaft in ihrer Genesis* (Neuwied am Rheim und Berlin: Hermann Luchterland Verlag).

76. The rationales for esoteric writing that Strauss proffers in *PL* differ from those of his 1939 "Spirit of Sparta" article partly because of the latter's poignant accounts of intergenerational communication (534), literary "charm" (534–35), and the masks behind which Xenophon hid his "royal soul" (536). Cf. pp. 71–72 and 124 above; also see *OT* 197/*WIPP* 103, where Strauss argues that readers must undergo "a change of orientation" in order to fathom Xenophon's *Hiero*. Xenos offers a methodical, imaginative, and illuminating elaboration of what Strauss's "change of orientation" might have entailed (*CV* 19–21, 29–32, 53–59, 65–66, 70–71, 101), but I think he underestimates what Strauss learned from classical political philosophy after 1931; cf. pp. 151–53 and 173n61

above on Strauss's posture toward Nietzsche. I'll respond to Xenos's claim that the reorientation hinged on the premodern view that human beings are naturally "evil"—a view Strauss allegedly adopted or adapted from Carl Schmitt—in the next chapter, when I'll also assess Drury's interpretation of Strauss's article on Schmitt.

77. According to a note of Strauss's dated 11 August 1946 (from box 11, folder 11 of the Leo Strauss Papers), Strauss was determined to "strike out everything I have done so far"; the key dilemma, apparently, was "whether the right and the necessity of philosophy are completely evident" (quoted in Meier, *Leo Strauss*, 29n1). Here again, Strauss's primary concern has nothing to do with Left and Right. The "shipwreck" sentence appears in *GS* 660; a German/English version is also available in "Correspondence Concerning Modernity: Karl Löwith and Leo Strauss," *Independent Journal of Philosophy* 4 (1983): 105–6.

78. In his reply, Löwith asks why one should always attempt to put new things into world-historical perspectives and be edified by Caesar and Rome, when Christianity had already undermined (*zersetzt*) this Roman spirit (*Geist*) (Löwith to Strauss, 28 May 1933 (#12), *GS* 627).

79. Cf. Smith, "Skeptical Friend": by refusing to kneel before liberalism's cross and its "unwritten rights," Strauss shows "his awareness of the failure of Weimar to protect the Jews and a proud refusal to accept assimilation as the price for survival."

80. This piece originated as a Hillel lecture Strauss delivered on 4 February 1962, and was transcribed from a tape recording (Kenneth L. Deutsch and Walter Nicgorski, eds., *Leo Strauss: Political Philosopher and Jewish Thinker* [Lanham, MD: Rowman & Littlefield, 1994], 43).

81. Cf. *CM* 211. In arguing that Strauss had an "imperialist orientation," Altman skillfully incorporates the Nietzsche-flavored remark about Churchill that Strauss offers at GN 363 (Altman, "Leo Strauss," 597–99; cf. 590 on "blood, sweat, and tears").

82. Strauss, "What Can We Learn," 519–20, 518. Hermann Rauschning similarly extolled the English: "No one can deny that the British Empire, with its methods of government based on freedom and consent, and with the moral authority of its center, comes very close to an almost spiritual conception of the State and social order" (Rauschning, *Revolution of Nihilism*, 292). Recall Strauss's claim in 1958 that "[w]hile freedom is no longer a preserve of the United States, the United States is now the bulwark of freedom" (*TM* 13).

83. Although even a city is too big for everyone to know everyone else, everyone can know "at least an acquaintance of every other member" (*NRH* 130). In the final chapter, Strauss describes the *polis* as "that complete association which corresponds to the natural range of man's powers of knowing and of loving" (*NRH* 254n2). Behnegar mentions none of these passages when, drawing on *WIPP* 65, he suggests that Strauss probably preferred "the modern state of the nineteenth century" to the ancient city (Behnegar, *Leo Strauss*, 3). Pangle contrasts Strauss's firm embrace of classical political philosophy with his "more qualified endorsement of the superiority of ancient to modern practice" (Pangle, *Leo Strauss*, 124); cf. Holmes's complaint about Strauss's "studied neglect of ancient society and culture" (*Anatomy* 83).

84. See pp. 179–82 below.

85. Strauss's 1964 warning about the permanence of human "malice, envy and hatred" (*CM* 5) appears even more prescient in the aftermath of the Iraq War, not to mention Biafra, Bangladesh, Cambodia, Bosnia, Rwanda, Darfur, and 9/11.

86. See Sheppard, *Leo Strauss*, 58, 73–76, 82 on his career struggles and his family's financial plight, which continued on through the 1940s, when serious health problems also surfaced. On Strauss's struggles in the 1930s, also see Charles E. Butterworth, "Leo Strauss in His Own Write: A Scholar First and Foremost," http://www.bsos.umd.edu/gvpt/Theory/Transcript_Butterworth_pdf. In a letter to Kojève (3 June 1934), written roughly a year after the infamous letter to Löwith, Strauss said this: "If I had a modest income, I could be the happiest man in the world" (*OT* 227 [Gourevitch and Roth]).

87. With a view to clarity, I assume, Horton created two sentences and replaced Strauss's odd dash-semicolon pairing with a period. In an earlier letter, Löwith had specifically asked whether Strauss was still searching painfully in French for the correct words and sentences (Löwith to Strauss, 21 November 1932 [#4], *GS* 611). And in his reply of 28 May 1933 to Strauss's letter, Löwith echoes Strauss's lament on the language issue: Löwith was seeking an academic position in Switzerland because "for me being able to speak and write in German is decisive" and particularly in philosophy is it "impossible to use an alien language" (*GS* 626).

88. Horton seems unaware that, when lamenting "the extent to which he [Strauss] is prepared to play with fascist thoughts, which now belong on history's dust heap," Horton summons to mind the *autoritären,* nay totalitarian, impulse to condemn an individual who has entertained certain "thoughts" for which history has somehow provided a definitive refutation. Must not a philosopher play with any thoughts that might expand or deepen his/her understanding?

89. Strauss to Gershom Scholem, 6 September 1972 (#67), *GS* 762.

90. Smith, "Skeptical Friend."

91. Daniel J. Flynn, *Intellectual Morons: How Ideology Makes Smart People Fall for Stupid Ideas* (New York: Crown Forum, 2004). If Flynn's earlier book, *Why the Left Hates America,* was insufficient to establish his conservative credentials, the Random House author site reports that he has been "booted out of lecture halls for his beliefs."

92. They met in 1938, and taught two joint seminars in 1944–1945 (Sheppard, *Leo Strauss,* 149n122). In his letter to Eric Voegelin of 8 August 1950, Strauss describes Riezler as a friend (Peter Emberley and Barry Cooper, eds., *Faith and Political Philosophy: The Correspondence between Leo Strauss and Eric Voegelin, 1934–1964* [University Park: Pennsylvania State University Press, 1993], 69). The Riezler essay was first published in 1956 (in *Social Research*).

93. Strauss does conclude his essay with an observation about Riezler—"he felt more at home in the thought of ancient Greece than in the thought of his time"—that also seems to describe Strauss. In the same passage, Strauss adds that Riezler was "a liberal, a lover of privacy," whose kinship with Greece reflected his basic view that "[n]ot anguish but awe is 'the fundamental mood' which discloses being as being" (*WIPP* 260).

94. On the other hand, Riezler also stressed that there remained "sufficient room for the parallel, not conflicting, expansion of the white race in Asia and Africa" (*WIPP* 239).

95. Riezler's view, by contrast, was (according to Strauss) that one must choose between a nationalist framework—in which the nation is the highest form of human association and there is "eternal, absolute enmity" among nations—and a cosmopolitan framework in which "humankind as a whole stands above the nations assigning them their role and place and legitimately limiting their aspirations" (Strauss does not here quote Riezler). Riezler "without hesitation" went with nationalism (*WIPP* 235).

96. *NRH* 130–31; Citing *Politics* 1325b23–32, Strauss elsewhere notes that Aristotle "goes so far as to visualize a perfectly good city which has no 'foreign relations' whatever" (*CM* 239). As early as 1936, Strauss highlighted Plato's prioritizing of domestic arrangements over foreign policy (*PPH* 161). Emphasizing the above-quoted passage from *WIPP* 84, Thomas G. West characterizes the Socratic approach to foreign policy as amoral but moderate; Strauss and the classics would pursue *neither* benevolence nor hegemony in the international arena (West, "Leo Strauss and American Foreign Policy," *Claremont Review of Books,* Summer 2004, 14–15). Drawing on Strauss's Thucydides, Howse suggests that West has exaggerated: "No political community can safely exempt itself from the unstable world where the striving for empire and hegemony bumps up against the equally natural impulse to resist foreign domination. . . . Imitating Spartan caution, and narrow self-interest in foreign policy, is not a course of safety." See Robert Howse, "Leo Strauss—Man of War?" http://faculty.law.umich.edu/rhowse/Drafts_and_Publications/strauss iraq.pdf, 79.

97. One encounters a similar pattern in Strauss's *RCPR* lecture on "political history" in Thucydides. Political history, Strauss maintains, "presupposes that freedom and empire are, not unreasonably, mankind's great objectives." His interjection ("not unreasonably") imparts approval to this articulation of the "great objectives." His elaboration, however, returns to the vision of freedom and empire as "massive and popular" goals that do *not* represent the peak of excellence or happiness. Freedom and empire, Strauss continues, "elicit the greatest efforts of large bodies of men. That greatness is impressive. That greatness can be seen or felt by everyone, and it is a greatness which affects the fate of everyone. The theme of political history is massive and popular" (*RCPR* 73). Wise men, by contrast, will "always be inclined to look down on political life, on its hustle and bustle, its glitter and glory" (74). In the opening section of his "What Is Political Philosophy?" essay, Strauss pairs "government or empire" with freedom when sketching "mankind's great objectives," objectives that are "capable of lifting all men beyond their poor selves" (*WIPP* 10). For an idiosyncratic perspective on Strauss's posture toward freedom and empire, see Robert Devigne, *Recasting Conservatism: Oakeshott, Strauss, and the Response to Postmodernism* (New Haven, CT: Yale University Press, 1994), 44–45.

98. *NRH* 134; emphases added. Although the paragraph mentions no proper names, it concludes with a footnote that cites Thucydides, Plato, Xenophon, Aristotle, Cicero, and Aquinas. The Thucydides citation is to III.45.6, where Diodotus calls freedom and empire "the greatest things." On *CM* 239 (one of the three pages Flynn cites to document Strauss's attitude toward empire), Strauss invokes III.45.6 after suggesting that "the omnipresence of War" left Thucydides more pessimistic than Plato and Aristotle were about the levels of self-sufficiency, justice, and virtue that a city might achieve. Wrapping up a detailed analysis of Diodotus, Orwin claims that freedom and empire for Thucydides ultimately "figure in context less as the greatest goods than as tending to the greatest evils"—because they "madden men and plunge them into incurable folly" (Clifford Orwin, "The Just and the Advantageous in Thucydides: The Case of the Mytilenaian Debate," *American Political Science Review* 78, no. 2 [June 1984]: 494). Cf. pp. 261–66 below.

99. For the classics, it seems, the tribe possessed freedom or "public spirit" but lacked civilization or the "high development of the arts and sciences," while Eastern monarchy possessed civilization but lacked freedom (*WIPP* 65). Cf. Aristotle, *Politics* 1327b19–37 and *CM* 30.

100. *WIPP* 65; emphases added. Strauss also concedes that the emergence of "modern democracy" reflects and/or has caused a "reinterpretation" of both freedom and civilization that "could not have been foreseen by classical political philosophy" (*WIPP* 65). Behnegar relies on these passages to emphasize Strauss's friendliness toward modern politics: Strauss "did not return to classical political philosophy because he preferred classical politics to modern democratic politics but because he regarded a return to classical political philosophy as a necessary step in achieving clarity about preferences of any kind." The latter challenge was aggravated later in the nineteenth century by Nietzsche's success in discrediting *civilization* as a standard (Behnegar, *Leo Strauss*, 3). *WIPP* 65 should be compared with *NRH* 143, where Strauss maintains that the nineteenth century occasioned a pivotal shift in philosophy's "meaning" and in how philosophy was regarded by the "common people."

101. Cf. *AAPL* 180–81 on "the fact that the common good has a ceiling (the genuine virtue of all citizens who are capable of it) and a flooring (survival), and that these two ends may make opposite demands on the statesman."

Chapter Five

"Mired in Perpetual War"

Confrontations with Cyber-Age Vilification

To jaw-jaw is always better than to war-war.

— Winston Churchill

I. "FASCISTIC GLORIFICATION OF DEATH AND VIOLENCE"

Although the materials recounted in previous chapters include diverse exemplars of denunciation, the Iraq War has given Shadia Drury a global audience primed for rage, and she has correspondingly adapted and escalated her diatribe. Her longest and most heavily cited web piece is the interview that Danny Postel conducted in October 2003, for openDemocracy.net (this interview ranked fourth among the Google links my July 2007 search for "Leo Strauss" yielded). Drury now accuses Strauss of a "fascistic glorification of death and violence" that "springs from a profound inability to celebrate life, joy, and the sheer thrill of existence."[1]

Drury here links Strauss with Alexandre Kojève, Carl Schmitt, and perhaps Heidegger; the view they allegedly shared is that "man's humanity depended on his willingness to rush naked into battle and headlong to his death. Only perpetual war can overturn the modern project, with its emphasis on self-preservation and 'creature comforts.'" If something like the Bush doctrine leaves America "mired in perpetual war, then all is well. Man's humanity, defined in terms of struggle to the death, is rescued from extinction."[2] I cannot even imagine what type of evidence Drury could offer for these mind-boggling accusations about Strauss.[3]

In her longest discussion of Carl Schmitt, which Drury presents in her 1997 book on Strauss, Drury both exaggerates the bellicosity Schmitt conveys in *The*

Concept of the Political and distorts Strauss's response to it. In elaborating the centrality of the friend/enemy distinction to the "political" realm, Schmitt does describe the "political enemy" as being "the other, the stranger . . . existentially something different and alien";[4] after quoting these words, Drury correctly adds that "[t]he foe is one who threatens one's own existence and way of life" (*LSAR* 88). When Schmitt proceeds immediately to explain that the relevant otherness entails that "in the *extreme* case conflicts with him [the political enemy] are *possible*" (emphases added), however, he softens the militaristic message. Drury acknowledges the possibility that Schmitt tried "to purify the enemy from all moralistic contamination" and thus created a "clean enemy" who would undermine the "venomous hatred" morality and religion often impart to political disputes (*LSAR* 88–89). But in saying that Schmitt's text confirms this interpretation "partially," she is probably too grudging, and she goes further astray when she maintains that, for Schmitt, "political enmity is a self-sufficient reason to kill the other for the simple reason that he is other, different, or alien" (*LSAR* 89).[5] Drury ignores Schmitt's claim that unless political killing is motivated by "an existential threat to one's own way of life, then it cannot be justified"; a state is by definition "internally peaceful, territorially enclosed, and impenetrable to aliens."[6] We may infer that neither the mere existence of foreigners with "alien" ways nor the insults/criticisms such foreigners might convey justifies warfare; otherwise, indeed, most societies would be obliged to conquer the globe in order to end the political divisions that Schmitt exalts.[7] Michael Ignatieff, whom no one has called a Schmittean, emphasizes the spur to genocide that the "fantasy of a world *without* enemies" provides.[8]

Drury's embellishment of Schmitt provides additional ammunition against Strauss when she asserts that Strauss's view of politics is "much harsher and more radical than Schmitt's. By linking faith and politics, Strauss makes the latter more dangerous and more bloody."[9] But when Drury attempts to document her claim that Strauss "proposes . . . to re-theologize the political"—because only an "alliance with religion and morality" will allow politics to unite people and make them "willing to lay down their lives for the collective" (*LSAR* 93)— the only pages she cites (paragraphs 10–11 and the latter portions of 26) are completely silent about both theology and religion.[10] Throughout his book, indeed, Schmitt highlights religious terminology and themes that Strauss in NCS ignores—for example, "the thousand-year struggle between Christians and Moslems," the Bible's injunction to love one's enemy (29), religious communities (37), "the medieval controversy between church and empire," Catholic doctrine/theory (41–42n17), Bismarck's *Kulturkampf* against the church, divine omnipotence (42), martyrs, salvation, holy wars, crusades (48), the necessity that a theologian "considers man to be sinful or in need of redemption" (64), "the fundamental theological dogma of the evilness of the world and man," original sin (65), and Oliver Cromwell's religious fulminations against Spain (67–68).[11]

Needless to say, Drury also passes over the passages in which Strauss seems to condemn Schmitt by noting that "a nation in danger wants its own dangerousness not for the sake of dangerousness, but for the sake of being rescued from danger," by suggesting that Schmitt grounds his "affirmation of the political" merely in "warlike morals" (NCS 24), by observing how odd it is to affirm "fighting as such, wholly irrespective of *what* is being fought *for*" (NCS 32), and by protesting the "polemical meaning" Schmitt attaches to "all political concepts, ideas, and words."[12] As Meier argues, "[w]hereas the political does have central significance for the thought of Leo Strauss, the enemy and enmity do not"; Strauss's greatest worry about an entertainment-oriented world state was that "a life that does not subject itself to the danger of radical questioning and the exertion of self-examination appears to him to be not worth living";[13] citing *Euthyphro* 7b–d and *Phaedrus* 263a, Strauss states that "agreement at all costs is possible only if man has relinquished asking the question of what is right" (NCS 28). Drawing on chapter IV of *Natural Right and History*, furthermore, Robert Howse sketches how "classic natural right" for Strauss "provides a basis in justice for patriotism, but not for bellicose nationalism."[14]

In fairness to Drury, we must also acknowledge two potentially hawkish complaints that Strauss directs at Schmitt: first, because of the powerful contemporary movement "striving for the total elimination of the real possibility" of war, "one cannot—least of all can Schmitt himself—take relief in the fact that the depoliticized state '*for the time being* does not exist'" (NCS 17); and second, the "radical critique of liberalism that Schmitt strives for" requires that human evil be conceptualized in "moral" rather than Hobbesean terms (evil that is "animal and thus innocent") [NCS 26]. But given Strauss's suggestion that the decisive battle, for Schmitt, would pit "the 'spirit of technicity,' the 'mass faith that inspires an antireligious, this-worldly activism'" against "the opposite spirit and faith" (NCS 33), one might infer that it is Schmittian rather than Straussian principles that would require us "to re-theologize the political." As the Zuckerts point out, furthermore, Strauss's critique of cosmopolitanism is softer than Schmitt's because Strauss regards philosophers as being "in effect, fellow citizens of a universal human society" (*TALS* 193). In his essay on Thucydides, Strauss touts "the genuine universalism of understanding" (*CM* 228), which he associates with the love of "beauty and wisdom" (230); and as early as 1939, he sketched a multigenerational form of cosmopolitanism when he suggested that the classical philosophers wrote in order to communicate with posterity.[15]

Many Strauss-bashers eagerly quote the last paragraphs of NCS, where Strauss states that to provide a truly "radical critique of liberalism" Schmitt would need to acquire "a horizon beyond liberalism." To do this, Strauss concludes, one must first fathom how Hobbes "completed the foundation of liberalism," and the "principal intention" of Strauss's notes was to show "what can be learned from Schmitt in order to achieve that urgent task" (35). When we turn to the 1936 book in which Strauss attempts to provide the necessary appraisal of Hobbes, it becomes still easier to discard Drury's assertion that Strauss's view of politics is bloodier and "much harsher" than Schmitt's.[16]

In *The Political Philosophy of Hobbes: Its Basis and Its Genesis*, Strauss elaborates his view that Hobbes pioneered the ideals of modern civilization, both "bourgeois-capitalist" and socialist (introduction), develops Hobbes's protocapitalist material in great detail (*PPH* 117–21, 125), and explains how Hobbes (over the course of his career) moved toward a rejection of courage and aristocratic virtue (49–50, 113–16). In articulating the "horizon beyond liberalism," however, Strauss celebrates not Nietzsche, Heidegger, Spengler, Schmitt, or Jünger, but Plato and Aristotle. Strauss appeals to Plato's and Aristotle's critiques of courage/warrior virtue (146–47),[17] their emphasis on "the eternal order,"[18] and their promotion of the "grateful contemplation of nature" (125). In a chapter published just a year after the Hobbes book, Strauss notes how much less belligerent Plato and Aristotle were than Islamic philosophers and even Maimonides: "his stressing the importance of military virtue in his philosophic prophetology was influenced by the prophetology of the Islamic philosophers, who attach a much higher value to war and to the virtue of courage than Plato and Aristotle had done."[19]

When Strauss in *PPH* addresses the Aristotelian regions of the horizon beyond liberalism, he particularly impugns the harshness of . . . Hobbes. Unlike Hobbes, Aristotle acknowledged the blessings as well as the burdens that good fortune brings to human beings (*PPH* 124); Hobbes "distrusts good fortune and the fortunate, distrusts their gratitude and their gaiety" (125). Once Hobbes had displayed the horror of the human condition, moreover, "joy and laughter are over" (124), and it is "the fearfulness of death rather than the sweetness of life which makes man cling to existence" (124–25).[20] For Aristotle, finally, "everything which one can do without compulsion and exertion, with ease and convenience, counts as pleasant, among other things, freedom from care, idleness, sleep, play, jesting, laughter." Hobbes, by contrast, excludes these from the list of pleasures he provides in *De Homine* (*PPH* 134, 40).[21] Yet Drury manages to complain that *Strauss* had "a profound inability to celebrate life, joy, and the sheer thrill of existence" and thus conveyed/imparted a "fascistic glorification of death and violence."

For Strauss, even Hobbes has a gentle side. Like the aristocratic virtue touted by Castliglione—who added "letters" to "armes" and whose courtier "is to know that the object of war is peace, defence and not conquest"—Hobbes's bourgeois virtues are "the virtues of civilized men" (*PPH* 126). In this respect, both Castiglione and Hobbes are "heirs of the tradition of classical antiquity"; both "feel the deepest repugnance for the baseness of provocative arrogance and cruelty" (127).

II. NICHOLAS XENOS ON NATURAL EVIL

In fleshing out the "deeply reactionary . . . political position" (*CV* xi) that, according to Xenos, Strauss trumpeted in his 1933 letter to Löwith—and communicated esoterically during subsequent decades—Xenos emphasizes the accounts of Schmitt and Hobbes that Strauss offered in NCS (1932) and *PPH* (1936). Xenos hammers relentlessly on the notion that Strauss's devotion to authoritarianism (and its fascist and imperialist accoutrements) follows from his attachment, inspired or provoked by Schmitt, to a certain "premodern" conception of nature and human nature (*CV* 70, 101): "the evil nature of the human being" (*CV* 57, 58, 66, 67–68), "the human being as naturally evil" (60), "the evil nature of human beings," "the essentially evil character of the human being" (65), "the human being's evil nature" (66), "the essential evil of the human being" (71).[22] Xenos acknowledges that when Strauss in NCS and *PPH* speaks about "natural" evil, he is sometimes depicting the "dangerousness" in human beings that precludes anarchistic or libertarian political arrangements (*CV* 55–56). Xenos's above-listed barrage of phrases, however, creates a misleading impression, especially given the cheerfulness Strauss attributes to Plato and Aristotle in the above-cited passages from *PPH*.[23]

Xenos does better with his earlier-mentioned formulation about imposing peace on "a recalcitrant human nature" (*CV* 69), but he still seems to be suggesting that no *liberal* would fret about the threat that recalcitrance poses to peace.[24] The enormity of the evils that human beings are capable of inflicting, moreover, can readily be marshaled against the swollen governmental agendas that authoritarianism, fascism, and imperialism promote. As Locke noted in the seventeenth century, "he that thinks absolute power purifies men's blood and corrects the baseness of human nature need read but the history of this or any other age to be convinced of the contrary" (*ST* 92). In contemplating how the mature Strauss drew on premodern conceptions of human nature, we must also appreciate Aristotle's famous claims—rejected emphatically by Hobbes—that human beings are naturally political.[25] I suspect, finally, that the vast majority of Straussians would join me in embracing the following sorts of nonfascist views: that man is "essentially an 'in-between' being—between the brutes and the gods" (*NRH* 152);[26] that "man's being is revealed . . . by the stars for which his soul longs" (*WIPP* 260); that "constant intercourse with the greatest minds" yields "training in the highest form of modesty, not to say of humility" (*LAM* 8); that "man is so built that he can find his satisfaction, his bliss, in free investigation, in articulating the riddle of being" (*NRH* 75); that human beings are "constantly attracted and deluded by two opposite charms: the charm of competence which is engendered by mathematics . . . and the charm of humble awe, which is engendered by meditation on the human soul" (*WIPP* 40). "Let us also never forget that while there is a philosophic *eros*, there is no philosophic indignation, desire for victory, or anger" (*CM* 110–11).

Xenos has hardly succeeded in demonstrating how Strauss understood human nature during the 1930s, let alone during subsequent decades. One could likewise dispute Xenos's presumption that Strauss's writing (and presumably also his teaching) in the United States was primarily intended to implement a simplistic political "position" (*CV* 29)—based on "political views" that "remained roughly unchanged from the 1930s on" (*CV* 28)—rather than to help his students and readers see more clearly, think more deeply, and write more carefully. Even the classical/premodern "legislator," according to Strauss, is "strictly limited in his choice of institutions and laws by the character of the people for whom he legislates, by their traditions, by the nature of their territory, by their economic conditions," and by other circumstances (*WIPP* 86).[27] To back up his claim that Strauss had aligned himself with the fascists of Italy and perhaps France—who welcomed the use of technology for "premodern notions of corporate identity and heroic glory" but did not adopt Nazi-like racism (*CV* 68, 17)—Xenos invokes Strauss's early interest in Paul de Lagarde and Charles Maurras, and cites Han Jonas's comment that Strauss had temporarily supported Mussolini.[28] For the record, Mussolini was a widely popular figure throughout the 1920s and at least half of the 1930s. In the United States, his "autobiography" was serialized in the 1928 *Saturday Evening Post*, and he was celebrated in magazines as diverse as the *New Republic*, *Commonweal*, and *Social Justice*.[29] In a 1933 letter to Ambassador Henry Breckenridge Long, President Roosevelt stated that he was "deeply impressed" by Mussolini's accomplishments; FDR elsewhere noted that he was "keeping in fairly close touch with that admirable Italian gentleman."[30]

Although Xenos asserts, implausibly, that Strauss's writings are "easy to figure out in the whole," he admits that the particulars can be "frustratingly clumsy to untangle" (*CV* xi; cf. 101). Because of the coherence with which Xenos lays out his larger thesis and the subtlety with which he addresses many of the particulars, *Cloaked in Virtue* is relatively free of the slander and sloppiness that pervade the anti-Straussian works of Drury and Norton.[31] But one sixty-second "deed" might suffice to refute Xenos's entire account of Strauss's American agenda. If we can believe Walter Berns, Strauss voted for Adlai Stevenson rather than Dwight Eisenhower in the 1952 presidential election; Clifford Orwin too states that Strauss voted for Stevenson,[32] but does not specify the year[s] (Stevenson ran against Eisenhower in both 1952 and 1956). To appreciate the "egghead" Stevenson's reputation as a liberal in the early 1950s, consider that vice presidential candidate Richard Nixon mocked him as a graduate of the "Cowardly College of Communist Containment" run by Dean Acheson, Truman's secretary of state;[33] according to Susan Jacoby, "the entire left-of-center intellectual community was devastated" by Stevenson's 1952 defeat.[34] If you're inclined to think that Strauss lied about his 1952 vote in order to arm his supporters against leftist critics, you need to explain why he later revealed his support for Goldwater's 1964 candidacy.[35] In 1972, the year before he died, Strauss indeed took a conspicuously public stand by signing a letter that endorsed Nixon over George McGovern.[36] Xenos, in any case, traces Strauss's "change of orientation" to the 1930s, not the 1960s.

Given Xenos's emphasis on Allan Bloom's role in propelling Strauss's Rightist agenda (*CV* 2–5, 139–42), we must also fathom Bloom's political commitments. Orwin, his friend and former student, reports that Bloom was "a lifelong Democrat who revered Roosevelt's New Deal as the peak of modern American politics" and who exhorted Orwin to vote for Bill Clinton in 1992 (Bloom died roughly two months before the election).[37] In the last seven presidential elections, I voted for Mondale, Dukakis, Clinton, Clinton, Gore, Kerry, and Obama, which should exclude me from the ranks of the extreme reactionaries, however slowly I punched the chad.

III. "TO RUSH NAKED INTO BATTLE"

In assessing Drury's claims about perpetual war and the "willingness to rush naked into battle," there are additional considerations we must contemplate. Most of the people killed in twentieth-century wars were civilians, including millions of children, who were *not* rushing into battle. If Strauss denounced the murder of some Greek schoolchildren by Thracian mercenaries as "[t]he most savage and murderous barbarism" (*CM* 156–57), what words would he have used to express his reaction to the violence perpetrated in Nanking, Hiroshima, My Lai, Srebrenica, Rwanda, and the Beslan Middle School? In a world with bioengineered pathogens and tens of thousands of nuclear weapons, furthermore, perpetual war multiplies the chances that "humanity" will face literal "extinction."[38] And why must one be a soldier for one's life to qualify as a "struggle to the death"?

Despite Drury's interest in *On Tyranny*, she passes over the warning Strauss there provides about "permanent revolution, i.e., permanent chaos in which life will be not only poor and short but brutish as well." If he found permanent revolution horrifying, why would he be a zealot for permanent war, especially in the nuclear age? Wars are also notorious triggers of bloody revolutions, and we know how Strauss felt about the Bolshevik and Nazi revolutions prepared if not precipitated by World War I. The *OT* passage is even more reliable because Strauss laments permanent revolution while touting the virtues of alternatives— the "absolute rule of the wise" and "open or disguised" aristocracy—that would be unpalatable to most of his readers (*OT* 207).[39]

Strauss once describes Communist Russia and Hitler's Germany as "[c]atastrophes and horrors of a magnitude hitherto unknown, which we have seen and through which we have lived" (*SPPP* 168). Could he have thought that Stalinist

Russia, having lost over 26 million citizens in the Second World War and having demonstrated enormous virtue in expelling and crushing the invading Nazis, had been elevated to a new plane of moral excellence? Would he have celebrated the manliness the Red Army displayed as its soldiers raped their way to the Elbe in 1945, sparing neither girls nor grandmothers?[40] Would he have exulted at the elitism that military officers and secret police showed during the war by killing over 150,000 Soviet troops for "cowardice" and desertion-type offenses? Would he have unearthed magnanimity and civic spirit in the decision to send several hundred thousand returning prisoners of war to the gulag because they ended up captured rather than dead—or because they might have been politically contaminated while suffering egregiously in Nazi prison camps?[41] Would he celebrate the multigenerational bonding of modern warfare via the buried artillery shells from World War I that are still killing people, or the birth defects that Agent Orange continues to cause in Vietnamese babies? Would he cherish the added *frisson* that land mines and cluster bombs pose on multiple continents to children at play?

Strauss lived through other horrors that might likewise have been unprecedented—for example, unrestricted submarine warfare, Verdun, phosgene, the Armenian genocide, the Cultural Revolution, the massive civilian slaughters of the Second World War—and the decades since his death have housed many rivals. Also pertinent is Strauss's explicit and implicit disparagement of Ernst Jünger, one of the above-discussed German nihilists. Although Jünger was "much more intelligent and much more educated than Hitler," he penned an antiphilosophical paean to World War I that Strauss holds up for ridicule. Jünger asked, "What kinds of minds are those who do not even know this much that no mind *can* be more profound and more knowing than that of *any* soldier who fell anywhere at the Somme or in Flanders?" Strauss answers that war is "a destructive business. And if war is considered more noble than peace, if war, and not peace, is considered *the* aim, the aim is for all practical purposes nothing other than destruction" (GN 369).[42]

Justin Raimondo, who delivered the nomination speech for Pat Buchanan at the Reform Party convention in 2000, adapts Drury's accusation by attributing a more circumscribed goal to the bloodthirsty Bush administration Straussians: "perpetual war in the Middle East and the pulverization of the existing Arab and Muslim states, all of it lorded over by a rising American empire." For Raimondo, the emphasis on regime change was simply "guff about 'democracy'" delivered "for the benefit of a Western audience, while, on the ground in Iraq, the Straussians in the administration had another agenda—civil war, the atomization of the country, and, perhaps, a regional religious conflict that tears the Muslim world asunder."[43]

During Strauss's less than four-decade residence here, the United States was hardly a paragon of pacifism. We fought the Nazis in Africa, Italy, France, and

Germany, not to mention the battle against the U-boats; we fought the Japanese all across the Pacific; and we put hundreds of thousands of soldiers into both Korea and Vietnam. In the eight months between the fall of the Berlin Wall and Saddam's invasion of Kuwait (2 August 1990), did America's Straussians become transfixed by the prospect of perpetual peace? As I have previously intimated, the twenty-first century will *not* yield "a pacified planet" in which "everyone would be happy and satisfied" and "blood, sweat, and tears" will be obsolete. Despite the monumental successes of the United States in "production and consumption" (GN 360), including food and medicine, even in a peaceful year we lose upwards of 70,000 civilians to automobiles and firearms, in violent deaths, and hundreds of thousands are maimed. Our ensnarement by creature comforts is also counter-balanced by the danger and/or brutality of recreational activities such as football, boxing, mixed martial arts, hockey, auto racing, soccer, downhill skiing, rock climbing, binge drinking, and methamphetamine use.

Did Strauss think that he inhabited the era of the "last man" in which no one had "any ideals and aspirations" and everyone was "well fed, well clothed, well housed," and "well-medicated by ordinary physicians and by psychiatrists" (TWM 97)?[44] There is no reason to suppose that Strauss joined Nietzsche in over-estimating "the tameness of modern Western man"; nor did Strauss use all the "power of passionate and fascinating speech" that he possessed to make his read-ers "loathe, not only socialism and communism, but conservatism, nationalism, and democracy as well" (*WIPP* 54–55).[45] Strauss lived through an unparalleled outburst of humanly inflicted destruction: the bloodiest battles in history (e.g., Caporetto, Verdun, the Somme, Passchendaele, Gallipoli, Tannenburg, Mos-cow, and Stalingrad); the rapid aerial obliteration of major cities (e.g., Dresden, Hamburg, Tokyo, Hiroshima, and Nagasaki); and civil wars in which millions of civilians perished (e.g., in Russia, China, Greece, Nigeria, Indonesia, the Congo, and the India-Pakistan partitioning). He knew of the *Lusitania*, Guernica, Nan-king, Barbarossa, the Bataan Death March, the siege of Leningrad, the Warsaw uprising, Omaha Beach, Iwo Jima, Okinawa, kamikazes, and the Algerian War of Independence. He also knew of the "domestic" equivalents: pogroms, gulags, the massive Ukraine famine, the Great Terror, the Cultural Revolution, *Kristallnacht*, and the Holocaust. If he craved "perpetual war" to remedy modernity's ills, he might have been the twentieth century's biggest fan. And if modern man is "a blind giant" (*RCPR* 239), modern war will not improve his vision.

IV. "THEIR CULT-LIKE QUALITIES":
REPUTABLE AUTHORS JOIN THE CRUSADE

Many of the jolting criticisms I relayed in my introduction were issued before the U.S. invasion of Iraq. Insofar as Straussians are being blamed for this war, we now appear to have blood on our hands. One primary architect (Paul Wolfowitz) was indeed a friend (and former student) of Allan Bloom's who took two courses with Strauss at Chicago, and one journalist (Bill Kristol) who had long pushed for military action against Saddam is a professed Straussian. As was elaborated above, however, many commentators fail to comprehend that Wolfowitz's doctoral work launched him along a different trajectory.

However vile and nonsensical many of her claims are, Shadia Drury has at least invested formidable intelligence, imagination, and time into reading and interpreting Strauss. In the Cyber-Age, however, various commentators are adopting her tone without her training. We have already reviewed the tirades of Tony Papert, Lyndon Larouche, Eugene McCarraher, Al Cronkrite, Brian Leiter, Will Hutton, Francis Boyle, John Walsh, Justin Raimondo, Brent Staples, and others. To fathom the threat to diversity that Straussophobia poses, however, we need to confront additional denunciations that were issued by impressively credentialed scholars and/or published in prestigious venues.

Before writing *Cloaked in Virtue*, Nicholas Xenos published an online article claiming that Strauss in 1933 had wanted to revive "imperial domination," "authoritarian rule," and "pure fascism."[46] Not content to condemn the ideas of Strauss, Xenos also invoked demeaning stereotypes about Strauss's disciples: "Long before attaining public attention, the Straussians were often ridiculed for their cult-like qualities: they speak and write the same way, they write the same books on the same themes over and over again, they dress alike, they are almost all men, they went to the same schools."[47] Professor Paul Gottfried tempers his own critique by allowing the existence of exceptions, but coins an awkward new label ("urban Jewish Scoop Jackson Democrats") and unchivalrously invokes the religion of our spouses:

> Most of his disciples who invoke his works, and in most cases studied with him or his students, bear a sociological and ideological resemblance to each other that must strike any honest commentator. The prominent Straussians who are not urban Jewish Scoop Jackson Democrats (or, today, neocon Republicans), preoccupied with Israeli "security" and American support for the Israeli right, are the exceptions. And some of those who do not entirely fit the stereotype have Jewish spouses and express the same enthusiasm and concerns.[48]

Even as friendly a commentator as Professor Mark Lilla—who was an editor at *The Public Interest* in the early 1980s and went on to study with Harvey C. Mansfield while earning his PhD at Harvard—laments the "lack of curiosity and independence" of Straussians in America. He also joins the bandwagon of those who protest a "Straussian habit of forming dogmatic cliques with students and hiring one another," which makes "potential colleagues wary of hiring them." Their dissertations and books "range from impenetrable exercises in esoteric analysis to solid interpretations of well-known classics"; but even their best interpretations of the classics "rarely display originality or a willingness to stray beyond convention." One puts most of them down, says Lilla, thinking: "just another brick in the wall."[49] Let my book shatter these stereotypes! According to Drury, Lilla is rightly "ashamed of Straussian scholarship" but absurdly tries to distance Strauss from "all the dreadful scholarship and equally dreadful policies he has inspired in America."[50] On the jacket of Steven Smith's book, Lilla offers this praise: "At last: a book on Leo Strauss for the rest of us." Unlike Lilla, I include myself within the *Straussian* "us."

To show that he was not seeking to demonize Straussians, Xenos offered the paltriest disclaimer: "I do not want to leave the impression that I think that Straussians are the root cause of all of [*sic*] contemporary political problems."[51] I only wish that the specters of persecution and stereotype threat could be lifted from my consciousness by the prospect that this group of mine is not responsible for *all* of the world's political failings. How often would an American professor think to deny believing that a group she or he criticizes—for example, feminists, Marxists, jihadists, gay activists, members of the NAACP or NARAL, even hosts of right-wing talk shows—is responsible for everything that plagues contemporary politics?

Xenos's concession is less surprising given the accusation educator/author Earl Shorris—who received the National Humanities Medal in 2000—made in a 2004 issue of *Harper's*.[52] According to Shorris, there "appears to be no end to the damage that is being done in the name of Leo Strauss" (there is a link to this article on the *Embedded* website, and the play ups the ante with its photos, chants, shouts, and orgasms).[53]

To this astounding accusation I would first invoke the example of Bill Kristol, the Straussian who has had the greatest impact on political debate in this country over the past decade or two. In his 25 October 2004 appearance on Neal Conan's "Talk of the Nation" on NPR, Kristol emphasized the gulf that separates Strauss's writings from the practical issues of contemporary politics, and insisted even more strongly that he does not "claim Strauss's authority" for his own political beliefs and recommendations, including the efforts he had made to promote U.S. military intervention in Bosnia, Kosovo, and Iraq. Based on my own experiences—I have read everything Kristol has written in the *Weekly Standard* since its founding in 1995, and much of what he has written elsewhere—Kristol's self-description is accurate: he is judicious about invoking "the name of Leo Strauss." When he proceeded to sketch the political "impulse" that might emerge from taking Strauss seriously, furthermore, he likewise pointed away from endless damage (Shorris) and perpetual war (Drury). Strauss, in Kristol's view, could lead one to harbor "a little more suspicion about notions that everything is moving in a progressive direction; a great suspicion of Utopianism, a great suspicion of the notion that politics can solve all human problems."[54] When Kristol discusses Strauss's legacy in "The Power of Nightmares," he again speaks in moderate and irenic terms:

> For Strauss, liberalism produced a *decent* way of life, and one that he thought was worth defending, but a dead end where nothing could be said to be true; one had no guidance on how to live, everything was relative. Strauss suggested that maybe we didn't just have to sit there and accept that that was our fate, that politics could help shape the way people live, teach them some good lessons about living *decent* and *noble* human lives. And can we think about what cultures, or what politics, what social orders, produce more admirable human beings? I mean, that whole question was put back on the table by Strauss, I think.[55]

This is hardly an invitation to wreak havoc in the name of Leo Strauss. Paul Wolfowitz, the formerly mighty neocon who disavows the Straussian "name," has rarely if ever appealed to Strauss in policy-oriented writings or speeches.

Thinking about destructive things done with an appeal to a name, we should contemplate other phenomena. For every baby named Leo after Strauss, many thousands have been named Osama after bin Laden; and whereas Tim Robbins hatefully displayed a photo of Strauss above his imaginary Office of Special Plans, millions of T-shirts lovingly display Osama's face. No one, moreover, has crashed a hijacked airplane while chanting "Strauss is great!" Nor is the Straussian Army of Iraq using car bombs or explosive vests to slaughter civilians in markets and mosques. Nor has any twentieth-century tyrant responsible for massive bloodshed had "Strauss Is Great" inscribed on his nation's flag. Nor did the Straussian People's Party destroy a sixteenth-century mosque and incite the lynching of a thousand or more Muslims in Gujarat. Nor does the Philosopher's Resistance Army kidnap children to serve as soldiers or sex slaves. Nor have millions of little colored books filled with Strauss's sayings been circulated at home to bolster a brutal regime and abroad to inspire and guide revolutionaries. Nor did Strauss at the ripe age of thirty compose a party manifesto, published in six languages, that called for the abolition of private property, the "forcible overthrow of all existing social conditions," and ten centralization-rich steps that would be applicable in "most advanced countries."

The main things that have been *done* in the name of Leo Strauss over the past half-century involve the revivification of long-dead philosophers: classes were taught, scholarly pieces were published, and writings received literal translations. Among the texts that Straussians have translated are over twenty-five Platonic dialogues, including the *Republic* and the *Laws*; Xenophon's *Memorabilia*, *Education of Cyrus*, *Hiero*, and *Oeconomicus*; Aristotle's *Politics* and *Ethics*; Aristophanes' *Clouds*; Farabi's *Enumeration of the Sciences*, *Book of Religion*, and *Philosophy of Plato and Aristotle*; all of Machiavelli's and Rousseau's major works; Spinoza's *Theological-Political Treatise*; Montesquieu's *The Greatness of the Romans and Their Decline* (a Straussian also contributed to the 1989 Cambridge University Press translation of *The Spirit of the Laws*); and Tocqueville's *Democracy in America*.[56] The time and effort needed to produce translations would seem to confirm the high priority of scholarship among Straussian agendas. Perhaps Drury could scour these books to uncover Nietzschean aphorisms smuggled into the prose and imperialistic exhortations lurking in the footnotes.

In addition to claiming, in one of America's oldest monthlies, that there is "no end to the damage that is being done in the name of Leo Strauss," Shorris makes other accusations that demonstrate his lack of journalistic integrity. To call Grover Norquist—"a man who publicly compared the inheritance tax to the Holocaust"—a Straussian displays shocking confusion about both Norquist and Strauss.[57] Norquist, who has a large portrait of Lenin in his Washington living room, is indeed a serious student of Antonio Gramsci.[58]

Shorris proceeds to offer this scurrilous denunciation: "In his [Strauss's] view, the active life of the citizen of Periclean Athens suffered by comparison with the contemplative life of the philosopher. The Straussians in the Department of Defense and in the think tanks took this to mean that they could kill on principle. And they did."[59] Let us leave aside the facts that Shorris deploys the "Straussian" label loosely and that neither Abram (not Abraham) Shulsky nor various "think-tank" Straussians set the course of U.S. foreign policy. The huge embarrassment is the non sequitur. How does the preferability of the *philosophical* life justify *killing*? Shorris seems to get it backward; among many pertinent examples are those sections of *Politics*, book VII, in which Aristotle invokes the preferability of philosophy to political activity as he justifies the preferability of peace to war.[60] As Strauss puts it in *TM*, "[t]he superiority of peace to war or of leisure to business is a reflection of the superiority of thinking to doing or making" (*TM* 295).

In my opinion, the greatest accomplishment of assembled Straussians is not a war, but a textbook: despite their alleged hostility to democracy, it is Straussians who took an unprecedented collectivist approach in producing the *History of Political Philosophy* edited by Strauss and Cropsey. The latest edition incorporates twenty-eight authors.

Xenos published his essay online. Shorris published in *Harper's*, which is not a peer-reviewed scholarly journal. Will an article in *International Politics*, a venerable peer-reviewed academic journal published by Palgrave Macmillan, provide a more careful, sober, and impartial discussion of Strauss and Iraq? Professor Jim George of Australian National University, alas, provides little redemption.[61]

George draws heavily on Drury. Although less inclined to be invective—for example, he forthrightly concedes that the Straussians operate without a manifesto or even "a strategic outline for practical action" (182)—he too is sloppy with his textual interpretations and citations. And he too sometimes accuses with reckless abandon. For example, George joins the chorus who promiscuously apply the "Straussian" label to Jewish activists/authors with hawkish leanings: George errs by including Robert Kagan, Elliot Abrams, Douglas Feith (183), Richard Perle (186), Donald Kagan (189), and Lewis Libby (188).[62] George adds that the "loyalty of the neoconservative Jews seems to be exclusively related to the Likud Party and the extreme right factions of Israeli politics" (188). The "seems" introduces a small measure of caution, but scarcely tempers the severe and sweeping character of the generalization.[63] I would be surprised to read such a far-fetched accusation in the *Nation*, let alone in a mainstream academic journal. If the loyalty of an American public figure were "exclusively" directed to Israel, let alone to the Likud, most people would regard him or her as a traitor.[64]

When George discusses the orientation of Paul Wolfowitz, he introduces another parade of errors. Early in the article, for example, George cites Gary Dorrien's 2004 book, *Imperial Designs*, for confirming "the deep significance of Strauss for figures such as Paul Wolfowitz" (175). On the page George cites, however, Dorrien concludes that Wolfowitz "was never much of a Straussian" (44). On the very next page, George again cites *Imperial Designs*, and this time provides details in a footnote (198n1). Drawing on Anne Norton, the footnote eventually describes Wolfowitz and the Kristols as being "deeply embedded Straussians, both by training and/or [*sic*] professed inclination." Along the way, George sensibly praises Dorrien for tackling the "complex 'why' questions regarding neoconservative motivations and intent," but George then serves up the slop:

> Dorrien's, [*sic*] *Imperial Designs* (2004) does engage these questions in a sophisticated and provocative manner. Indeed Dorrien's (1993) work (see also *The Neconservative Mind*) is in my opinion the best body of scholarship on the neoconservatives in the available literature. But nowhere in Dorrien's work does he explore the Straussian connection, concentrating instead (plausibly) on the influences of figures such as James Burnham. (George, "Leo Strauss," 198n1)

George here refers to a 1993 work and then recommends that we "also" consult *The Neoconservative Mind*, but this book *is* the 1993 work. George goes much further astray, however, when he here complains that Dorrien's "work," despite being "the best body of scholarship" on the neoconservatives, *nowhere* explores "the Straussian connection." George in fact began his article by invoking Dorrien to document "the deep significance of Strauss for figures such as Paul Wolfowitz" (175). Thus, George both misreads Dorrien by overlooking the claim that Wolfowitz "was never much of a Straussian," and later *erases* Dorrien's discussion of how Wolfowitz was influenced by both Strauss and Allan Bloom. George's complaint about Dorrien is additionally refuted by Dorrien's subsequent discussion of Bill Kristol's debts to both Strauss and Mansfield.[65]

In his conclusion, George starts by distinguishing two different interpretations of Strauss, only one of which is chilling. The milder interpretation emerges if one were "to read Strauss as a profound but distressed old-world intellectual, effectively out of his cultural time and place, who sought to warn his adopted homeland of the dangers of thinking frivolously about matters of life and death"; on such a reading, Strauss's "contribution . . . was to train a disciplined and classically educated American elite in the knowledge of the ancients, those who knew best how to confront such threats" (196). The alternative is to read Strauss "in the way that he insists we must read philosophical texts—skeptically and always aware of esoteric strategies"; on this reading, Strauss is "very much what his detractors claim he is, a cynical manipulator of young minds, a right wing fundamentalist seeking to undermine liberal freedoms in the U.S. and instigate an old world 'war culture' at the core of U.S. foreign policy" (197).

Straussians (and several alarmed critics) tirelessly repeat Strauss's suggestions that an author's manner of reading can supply decisive guidance about how that author wants to be read, so George is here inviting us to *embrace* the harsh accusations we are currently enduring: that Strauss is a "right wing fundamentalist seeking to undermine liberal freedoms in the U.S." and to militarize the world. Has George studied Strauss, and even a sampling of the philosophers Strauss wrote about, carefully enough to issue a proclamation about Strauss's "esoteric strategies"?[66] Or is he simply following the incantations offered by Drury and her Internet-based fans?

Given the numerous blunders George makes, his concluding denunciation—that Straussian neoconservatism is "particularly dangerous" because of its "contemptuous attitudes towards other ways of thinking and other ways of solving complex problems" and its "consequent lack of understanding of major contemporary issues of IR theory and practice" (197)—seems hypocritical, since George himself is so quick to pronounce and denounce on flimsy foundations.

V. TO LILLIPUT—AND BEYOND!

Regarding the alleged Straussian use of militarism to "undermine liberal freedoms," one can trace sloppiness, confusion, and stupidity all the way from Drury's first book to a scene in *Embedded*, making stops along the way on multiple websites. With assistance from Drury, the views of Leo Strauss and Allan Bloom have been grossly misrepresented, and a globe-trotting scholar has invoked *Gulliver's Travels* to portray the United States as a pyromaniac.

Let us commence our strange journey with *Embedded*. After hearing that Europeans were spreading photos of civilian casualties in Iraq, Pearly White (the Richard Perle character) offers the following analogy to illuminate "the Straussian dilemma":

> When Lilliput was on fire, Gulliver urinated over the entire city, including the palace. In so doing he saved all of Lilliput from catastrophe, but the Lilliputians were outraged and appalled at such a show of disrespect.[67]

This version of the incident lazily distorts the original. Gulliver urinated only over the area—the queen's apartment—that was enflamed, not over "the entire city" (Pearly White's phrase). Gulliver indeed congratulates himself for having "applied" the stream "so well to the proper places."[68] Accentuating the hilarious premise that the entire island of Lilliput was on fire, *Embedded* further embellishes when Pearly White says that Gulliver "saved all Lilliput from catastrophe." In fact, Gulliver specifies that he saved only the "magnificent palace," that is, "the rest of that noble pile, which had cost so many ages in erecting."

Even when pronouncing on something as grand as *the* Straussian dilemma, *Embedded* builds on a foundation of sand that originated with our favorite mudslinger. In her 1988 book (*PILS*), Drury invokes Swift to illustrate the following point: Strauss considered "the gap between the vulgar and the wise to be so great, that one of his students, Allan Bloom, likened it to the difference between Gulliver and the Lilliputians." She proceeds to mention the urination incident—to illuminate a "hidden" message she previously discussed—but proclaims confidently that "neither Strauss nor Bloom brings this example to our attention." She then offers the following elaboration:

> When Gulliver urinates all over the palace, the Lilliputians are shocked and horrified. But they soon realize that Gulliver's scandalous conduct was the salvation of the city, for it saves not only the palace from being engulfed in flames, but all of Lilliput! The moral of the story is that the rules that apply to the Lilliputians do not apply to Gulliver. Strauss seduces us into thinking that morality is akin to taboo: there is nothing intrinsically despicable about it [*sic*] when viewed from the point of view of nature and reason. . . . By reflection on the plight of Gulliver we are led to surmise that acting immorally for the sake of the public good is necessary, reasonable and even merciful. So if we are in a position to condemn an innocent man to appease a lynch mob threatening to destroy our society, we can congratulate ourselves on our mercifulness. (*PILS* 195–96)

Here we see the original source of the *Embedded* errors: Gulliver urinates "all over" the palace and thus saves "all of Lilliput!" from the flames. Much graver is Drury's attempt to associate lynching and illegal urination with Strauss's teaching about morality; the "it" in her fourth sentence, furthermore, is hopelessly obscure. Drury is correct that Strauss never brings the incident to "our attention." Bloom, however, does discuss it, and his account is accurate.[69] In the annotated bibliography of her 1997 book, Drury returns to the incident and retains her initial mistakes: "What is absolutely sacrilegious and forbidden to the Lilliputians—urinating over the great palace—is appropriate for Gulliver and beneficial to the Lilliputians because it saved all of Lilliput from being engulfed by the flames!" (*LSAR* 218).[70]

In her capacity as a guru of the left-wing countermedia, Drury has further distorted the Gulliver incident, and the hallucinations have continued to intensify via the independent work of Internet-oriented scholars and journalists. Consider first what happened when Drury's version was picked up by Jim Lobe in a widely cited online article in *Asia Times* (posted on 9 May 2003) that draws heavily on a Lobe-Drury telephone interview.[71] After quoting Drury's statement that Straussians extol "perpetual war," Lobe proceeds to Gulliver:

> As for what a Straussian world order might look like, Drury said the philosopher often talked about Jonathan Swift's story of Gulliver and the Lilliputians. "When Lilliput was on fire, Gulliver urinated over the city, including the palace. In so doing, he saved all of Lilliput from catastrophe, but the Lilliputians were outraged and appalled at such a show of disrespect."[72]

Whereas her earlier inaccurate discussions focused on Strauss's alleged view of the relationship between the wise and "the vulgar" (*PILS* 195) or between "the elite and the masses" (*LSAR* 218), Drury now offers the urination to illuminate a Straussian vision of "world order." In the aftermath of the war in Iraq, Drury has clearly raised the stakes—suggesting an image of America pissing on the world—via an example Strauss did *not* employ (as she admitted in 1988).

Lobe, however, proceeds to offer his own extrapolation that speaks confidently of Strauss: "For Strauss, the act demonstrates both the superiority and the isolation of the leader within a society and, presumably, the leading country vis-à-vis the rest of the world." Who knows what Strauss thought about the urination, or whether he ever spoke of it? For Bloom, the incident is a metaphor for the threat that philosophers pose to society;[73] it is not, as Lobe alleges, a metaphor for the superiority and isolation of "the leader" within a society, and it is certainly not a metaphor for "the leading country" within the world. What Straussian could think that the United States is to the world as Socrates was to "the many"? If Strauss harbored anything like the contempt for America that Drury repeatedly alleges, indeed, he would have regarded our global "superiority" as the problem, not the solution.

When Lobe expanded his article for the version that appeared ten days later (19 May 2003) on the Alternet, his wording diminishes his debt to Drury:

> As to what a Straussian world order might look like, the analogy was best captured by the philosopher himself in one of his—and student Allen [*sic*] Bloom's—many allusions to Gulliver's Travels.[74]

Although he proceeds to quote (with a trivial change) Drury's account of the urination, in the above-quoted sentence Lobe himself pronounces its relevance: "the analogy was best captured. . . ."[75] In his earlier piece, Lobe simply relays what Drury said—that Strauss often discussed Swift—before quoting *her* summary of the urination story. By here referring to Strauss's "many allusions" to Swift, indeed, Lobe now implies that Strauss himself invoked the urination story, perhaps repeatedly. Lobe's expanded article occupied the fifth spot in my 15 July 2007 Google search for Strauss.

Strauss's career as an American professor started in 1938 (he was at the New School from 1938 to 1949 before he started teaching at Chicago). Is Lobe aware that Strauss was born in 1899? If so, it is difficult to imagine what Lobe was thinking when he attributed to Strauss a "Gulliver in Lilliput" model of the U.S. role in the world. Who ever confused the *Wehrmacht*, the Red Army, or the Imperial Navy with the micro-archers of Lilliput, a nation that lacked firearms? A single 1960s-era Soviet ICBM would devastate even Lorbrulgrud, the great metropolis of Brobdingnag.

Instead of proceeding, on his own authority, to claim (unsoundly) that the incident captures what Strauss thought about the United States in the world, Lobe next attributes the model to neoconservatives: "The image captures the neoconservative vision of the United States' relationship with the rest of the world." The urination metaphor conveys Lobe's strong animus against the neocons, but not the vision of "world order" held by any competent neoconservative. For starters, it is clear that the U.S. advantage in power falls short of Gulliver's. Russia remains capable of launching a nuclear attack that would exterminate over a hundred million Americans. Perhaps the biggest military challenge Gulliver faced in Lilliput, by contrast, was the "several thousand" arrows shot by the warriors from Blefuscu, the enemies of Lilliput whose fleet Gulliver captured; by putting on his spectacles to protect his eyes, he averted all threat of serious injury.[76] What in our world, moreover, corresponds to the fire, the castle, and the proscription against urination?[77]

By the time the rumor about Straussian world order is presented by Professor John Mason in an online journal with high academic pretensions, it has evolved still further. Although the only source for Drury that Mason cites is the interview she gave with Danny Postel, Mason seems to be borrowing the Gulliver story from Lobe (Gulliver is nowhere mentioned in the Postel interview). Here is Mason's version:

Dury [*sic*] states that whenever he discussed contemporary international relations, Strauss was fond of repeating the story of Gulliver and the Lilliputians. And more precisely of how: "When Lilliput was on fire, Gulliver urinated over the city, including the palace. In so doing, he saved all of Lilliput from catastrophe, but the Lilliputians were outraged and appalled by such a show of disrespect."

Starting from Drury's claim in 1988 that Strauss failed to mention the urination incident, we now confront Mason's moronic claim that, according to Drury, Strauss *repeatedly* mentioned it and invoked Swift *whenever* he discussed "contemporary international relations." Mason proceeds to add that the urination is an "apt image" for an American Gulliver today who "shows strong exhibitionist tendencies" and whose "militarist urges" cause it to play the "pompier pyromane" around the world. "Pompier pyromane" (pyromaniac fireman) is clever, but I have no idea what Mason means by "exhibitionist tendencies."[78]

Given these attempts to trace the allegedly imperialistic, jingoistic, fascistic, and crusading tendencies of the neocons and the Bush administration to Strauss's and Bloom's enthusiasm for *Gulliver's Travels*, we must fathom three additional points that Bloom makes. First, Bloom states that the urinating Gulliver "did not behave as a good citizen; he did not identify what is good with what is Lilliputian," just as Strauss's denouncers typically do not identify what is good with what is American. Second, Bloom points out that Gulliver is "willing to help his country, but only for its self-defense; he has no crusading fervor."[79] Third, regarding the third article of impeachment—that Gulliver "did, like a false traitor, aid, abet, comfort" the ambassadors from Blefuscu who arrived in Lilliput to sue for peace[80]—Bloom infers that Gulliver does not "accept the distinction between friend and enemy defined by the limits of the nation. Once again, common humanity is what he sees,"[81] as Strauss's critics appeal to common humanity when they accuse him of malevolently overrating the distinction between friends and enemies.

One may additionally fault the critics for speaking as if Strauss and Bloom were interested only in part I of the book. Bloom's essay also emphasizes Gulliver's experiences among the other strange peoples he encounters: for example, the peaceful and public-spirited giants of Brobdingnag (Bloom suggests that their realm combines ancient Sparta with ancient Rome, and says that they embody the moral virtues of Aristotle's *Ethics*); the arrogant and unpoetic Cartesian scientists of Laputa (who serve food shaped as geometrical figures and musical instruments);[82] the "projectors" of Lagado whose hare-brained schemes cover all realms of human endeavor; and the angelically honest, rational, and benevolent Houyhnhnms, whom Swift juxtaposes with the greedy, violent, and lustful Yahoos (Bloom analogizes the former to trans-Platonic utopians, with the latter representing human nature as portrayed by Hobbes).[83] In addition, Bloom's discussion of Swift in *The Closing of the American Mind* barely acknowledges Lilliput, and focuses almost entirely on Laputa.[84]

In her new introduction, Drury intensifies the crudity of her critique. On "the Straussian reading," she insists, *Gulliver's Travels* is a "justification of the immoralist point of view" (*PILS*-05 xl): Strauss and Bloom were "fascinated with the story of Gulliver—not just because sheepish intellectuals tend to have machismo fantasies, but also because the story seemed conducive to their radical elitism" (xxxix–xl). Does Gulliver's horrified viewing of the pimples, spots, and freckles on a six-foot breast qualify as a machismo fantasy?[85] Would devotees of radical elitism identify with Gulliver's status in Brobdingnag vis-à-vis the flies who left their "loathsome excrement or spawn behind" on his food, the lice whose limbs and snouts he could observe so "distinctly," the spaniel who with wagging tail snatched him and conveyed him to its master, the frog who smeared his face and clothes with its "odious slime" and almost sank his boat, or the "frolicsome" monkey who kidnapped Gulliver from his box?[86] Although the greatest danger came from the monkey, who at one point held him "as a nurse doth a child she is going to suckle" and later tried to feed him by cramming "filthy stuff" down his throat, it was the dog incident that left Gulliver the most worried about the effect on his reputation if "the story should go about."[87]

VI. DOSTOEVSKY AND "DELUSIONAL ELITISM"

Drury's habit of wrenching text out of context to pillory Strauss and Straussians for elitism and warmongering is also evident in her recent use, or rather misuse, of Dostoevsky's Grand Inquisitor.[88] Drury struggled for almost two decades to grasp aspects of Swift's lengthy and intricate novel, and now she is struggling to handle a *chapter* from *The Brothers Karamazov*.

Drury lauds the brilliance with which Dostoevsky has captured the mentality of people who have "deluded themselves into thinking that they were akin to gods who are entitled to rule over ordinary mortals." After elaborating many alleged similarities between Strauss and the Inquisitor, Drury ups the ante by asserting that "the Straussian position surpasses the Grand Inquisitor in its delusional elitism as well as in its misanthropy." In terms of misanthropy, even the casual reader of Dostoevsky should recall that the tale—a prose "poem" that Ivan Karamazov wrote and then shared, roughly a year later, with his brother Alyosha—was set in sixteenth-century Spain. Before we hear a word from the Inquisitor, Ivan describes the Seville setting as "the most terrible time of the Inquisition, when fires were lighted every day to the glory of God" and "the flames were crackling round the heretics." The day before the encounter, moreover, the Inquisitor had himself burned almost 100 heretics "in the presence of the king, the court, the knights, the cardinals, the most charming ladies of the court, and the whole population of Seville."[89]

Drury's account excises all reference to the Inquisition, and seems to suggest that the encounter took place during the author's time: "Dostoevsky imagined that Jesus has returned to face a decadent and corrupt Church." By failing to mention the Inquisition, Drury detaches the Inquisitor's remarks from their setting, as if to facilitate *her* anti-Straussian crusade. If she had acknowledged or even remembered the burning of the heretics, would she still have written that "the Straussian elite makes the Grand Inquisitor look compassionate and humane in comparison"?[90] Whereas her initial denunciation focused on the "delusional elitism" and "misanthropy" of "the Straussian position," her reference to "the Straussian elite" suggests that she means to pillory Strauss's followers and not merely his views.[91] She likewise seems to adopt a broad target when she describes "the Olympian laughter of the Straussian gods" that would greet "all the human carnage and calamity" that will flow from "perpetual war, death, and catastrophe."[92] It is also reasonable to assume that most readers will think of *Straussians* when they encounter the adjective "Straussian." As her article approaches its conclusion, Drury focuses explicitly on "self-proclaimed disciples of Leo Strauss"—for example, Paul Wolfowitz, Abram Shulsky, and Bill Kristol—who are among "the most powerful men in America." She claims that she is inclined to give them "the benefit of the doubt by assuming that they have no idea of the sinister depths to which Strauss's political thought descends"; by illuminating these depths, she thinks she "may dissuade some of them from following Strauss too blindly into the abyss." As we have seen, however, the accusations of depravity, mendacity, militarism, and so on, that she elsewhere levels at "Straussians"—without even distinguishing us bibliophilic professors from our activist brethren in DC—presume that most Straussians have already taken the plunge.[93]

When I turn my "critical intellect" (Burnyeat's phrase) upon it, Drury's claim about dissuasion dissolves. From her point of view, has not Bill Kristol been *enthusiastically* shoving the United States toward what she regards as the abyss? If she wants to pacify hawkish Straussians, why accuse Strauss of pathological hawkishness? Drury argues that Strauss was abusing old books by seeding a political platform within his unsound interpretations of them. If she persuades Straussians of this, we would be less interested in the old books, but how would her success promote peace? The effectual truth—and, doubtless, the intended result—of Drury's campaign is to portray Straussians as academically incompetent and politically malevolent: she is *not* attempting to rescue or redeem us by opening our eyes to a slippery slope under our feet. Reading Drury diabolically—the way she reads Strauss—one would infer that, regarding her rescue mission, she is telling a lie that she regards as noble. Given the widespread smugness, laziness, and volatility I perceive in her work, however, I can imagine that she sometimes thinks she is trying to promote our safety. Her claims about the Straussian "position" and the "abyss" wherein his thoughts reside, finally, also require the nonsensical inference that Strauss would have exalted Passchendaele, Auschwitz, Hiroshima, the gulag, and other above-mentioned horrors of the twentieth century.[94]

The errors in Drury's brief discussion of Dostoevsky pile up as she claims that the Inquisitor "condemns Jesus to death, but not before having a long and interesting conversation with the condemned man." Although she apparently overlooked the killing of the heretics, she exaggerates the brutality the Inquisitor inflicts on Jesus. In his opening comments the Inquisitor does promise to burn Him "to-morrow" at the stake as "the worst of heretics" (297),[95] and he later repeats the threat (309).[96] But after Jesus kisses him, he simply opens the door and orders Jesus to leave, and Jesus walks away unharmed (311). Since Jesus utters not a single word during the entire encounter, moreover, it is absurd to describe the encounter as a *conversation*; a careful reader would quickly notice that the Inquisitor is formulating answers on behalf of Jesus and that the only actual conversation in the chapter occurs between Ivan and Alyosha. Dostoevsky could hardly do more to convey the reticence of Jesus.[97]

Drury compounds the distortion when she elaborates the "conversation," asserting that "Jesus naively clings to the belief that what man needs above all else is freedom from the oppressive yoke of the Mosaic law, so that he can choose between good and evil freely according to the dictates of his conscience." Since Jesus provides neither words nor gestures, it is an absurd and offensive insult to say that He "naively clings" to any of the views the Inquisitor attributes to him.[98] One must also protest Drury's specification and elaboration of the fetter—"the oppressive yoke of the Mosaic law"—from which, in Jesus's view, mankind "above all else" needed to be liberated. In the Garnett translation that Drury used, the Inquisitor attributes to Jesus an agenda that is less hostile toward Moses and Judaism: "In place of the rigid ancient law, man must hereafter with free heart decide for himself what is good and what is evil" (302).[99] To Drury I reply that laws may be rigid without being oppressive. In addition, Drury's opening phrase—"what man needs above all else" is freedom from the ancient law—also inflates the Inquisitor's wording ("man must hereafter" replace the law with conscience). Drury thus goes further than Dostoevsky—a man not known for lauding Jews—in discarding Jesus's claim that He came to complete the law not to abandon it (Matthew 5:17).[100]

Despite the article's brevity, its serious interpretive breakdowns, and its failure to acknowledge or discuss *anything* Strauss actually wrote about Dostoevsky, Glenn Greenwald of *Salon* thinks the case is closed: Drury's article has "documented" that, in Strauss's view, "those in power must invent noble lies and pious frauds to keep the people in the stupor for which they are supremely fit."[101]

In another article from 2004, "The Making of a Straussian," Drury supplies a hypothetical case-study—in *Philosophers' Magazine*—of how Straussians acquire the "delusional elitism" she derides in her discussion of the Grand Inquisitor. In her often elegant and witty portrayal of the plight of a Straussian pursuing an academic career, Drury emphasizes that her focus is not on "your average Straussian graduate student," but on one from "the highest echelons of wisdom" who has moved beyond Strauss's bland surface teachings.[102] Personality-wise, the picture is dire: the student blends paranoia with a pomposity that will become "positively overbearing." In Drury's view, there are no intellectually redeeming features even for this exemplary Straussian; within academic circles, apparently, it is now common knowledge that "the Straussian is poorly trained."[103]

Drury first presented the "poorly trained" charge—accompanied by additional invective—in an online article posted in the previous year (2003): Straussians are "compulsive liars," they are "ill-equipped to handle philosophical debate," and they form a "cultish clique" whose members are "comfortable only when preaching to the converted and consorting with the like-minded."[104] Also posted on her web page is a review of Saul Bellow's *Ravelstein* in which she says we are infused with animosity toward "freedom, justice and equality before the law"; we reject even equality of *opportunity* because it would diminish the "pathos of distance" that enables us "to look down on the inferior rabble."[105]

Stephen Holmes conveys a comparably ominous portrait of elitism: Strauss, says Holmes, maintains that the lives of "[m]ost people" are "utterly valueless and unjustifiable" unless they serve to "make philosophers more comfortable and secure."[106] Michael L. Frazer, no Strauss-basher, falls into a similar trap when he suggests that, for Strauss, philosophy is "the *only* thing of value in the world."[107] Let me offer three quick replies to Holmes and Frazer. First, the world created the philosophers, not vice versa, and philosophers investigate innumerable phenomena that *they* lacked the power to create. Second, the existence of a best life does not preclude the existence of other good lives. Third, Strauss managed to articulate reverential appreciation for the birth of a puppy.[108] He conveys a similar thought in a prominent published work: nature is "the ancestor of all ancestors," and "[m]an's 'creative' abilities, which are more admirable than any of his products, are not themselves produced by man: the genius of Shakespeare was not the work of Shakespeare" (*NRH* 92). Although these claims appear in the chapter on the origin of "the idea of natural right," the reference to Shakespeare vaults Strauss into the present.

VII. FROM THE GRAND INQUISITOR TO THE *BASIJI*: ANNE NORTON STRAFES THE STRAUSSIANS

In this chapter, we have examined inquisitorial abuses from Drury and other contemporary authors with credentials that are more than solid. Among the anti-Straussian excesses that tarnish the highest realms of contemporary scholarship, Anne Norton's *Leo Strauss and the Politics of American Empire* is in a class by itself. Although this book was published by Yale University Press and has been celebrated in several major reviews, it is disgracefully unscholarly. The book contains nary a citation or a footnote (there is also no bibliography). Drury is understandably offended by this lacuna, by the absence of "scholarly rigor"—Norton provides "no analysis or philosophical engagement with

Strauss's work"—and by Norton's corresponding reliance on "gossip."[109] As I have previously demonstrated, of course, the mere presence of footnotes, citations, quotation marks, and bibliographies does not ensure that a book embodies academic rigor.

An Interpreter of Evil

Reviewing Norton's book in *Political Theory*, Larry N. George celebrates her "enormous range of references,"[110] despite the absence of all reference material. Because Norton's longest discussion of a single text (*LSPAE* 130–40) addresses Carnes Lord's book on Machiavelli—*The Modern Prince* (hereafter, *MP*)—one can without great difficulty track down the original passages she quotes and see how heinously she abuses them.[111] Why would someone so irresponsible in textual interpretation dare to publish such inflammatory accusations without taking the trouble to document them? Norton is completely unworthy of the trust she presumes. As Schaeffer protests, "misquotation is a far more egregious offense when one avoids even providing references to the pages one is borrowing from."[112] Unlike Drury, however, Norton does not regularly warp the quotations themselves.

Norton commences by quoting Lord's general statement (*MP* 138) that political leaders have the right to express judgments about "the teaching of national history and to take action to shape public school curriculums in this area" (*LSPAE* 136). When she proceeds to address what Lord says about higher education, however, she presents a *1984*-like scenario that departs wildly from Lord's text: instead of being "places of unhindered learning and free speech" (*LSAPE* 136–37), universities "should be held 'politically accountable' for leftist professors and other 'lunatic and sinister' faculty. They should be required to track students for the federal government" (137).

Lord's entire discussion of higher education occupies two paragraphs. The first does include the phrase "politically accountable," but Lord's thrust is much more modest than what Norton concocts. Here is what he says about political accountability: "In many countries, certain major universities, whether public or private, are virtually integral components of the regime by the fact that they create or validate a national elite: consider Oxford and Cambridge in England or Tokyo University (particularly its law school) in Japan. Yet it is hard to hold them politically accountable" (*MP* 139). Lord, obviously, is addressing institutions in England and Japan that have no equivalent in the United States (Norton will spin out an elaborate nightmare about the future of the United States). And saying that it is "hard" to hold such institutions "politically accountable" falls *vastly* short of Norton's version—that universities in general *should be* held politically accountable for "leftist professors and other 'lunatic and sinister' faculty." The "lunatic and sinister" phrase appears only in Lord's second paragraph, where his focus is indeed on the United States. After stating that our university administrators are typically "free from political interference or even scrutiny," Lord provides these three sentences:

> The alternately lunatic and sinister pursuit of the agenda of political correctness that pervades contemporary university life in America raises fundamental issues, including ones of legal due process. Universities have suffered little from abolishing the Reserve Officers' Training Corps (ROTC) presence on campus or barring recruiters from the military or the Central Intelligence Agency. And at least until recently, they have resisted cooperation with the federal government in tracking foreign students who are in the country illegally or may be pursuing dubious courses of study (such as nuclear physics). (*MP* 139)

Contra Norton, Lord does not identify *any* faculty as "lunatic and sinister," and he makes *no* reference to "leftist professors" (in Norton's version, such professors are among the "lunatic and sinister" faculty for whom universities should be held "politically accountable"). It is rather the pursuit of the PC "agenda" which, for Lord, *alternates* between being lunatic and being sinister. Although these two adjectives are conspicuously harsh, in his very next sentence Lord seems to identify the PC agenda with *exclusion*—the abolition of ROTC and the barring of CIA/military recruiters—and not with a certain subset of the faculty. Immediately after suggesting that Lord favors the harassment if not the persecution of leftist professors, Norton states ominously that he would require universities "to track students for the federal government." In reality, he simply points out—although with an obvious air of discontent—that U.S. universities had tended to resist the government's efforts to track *foreign* students who either are here *illegally* or are pursuing "dubious courses of study" like nuclear physics. I concede that a foreign student might have perfectly wholesome reasons for studying nuclear physics.

Norton's reference to tracking in effect prepares the bombshells she launches in her next paragraph as she sketches how Lord's agenda would play out:

> Like the enforcers of virtue in Iran who roam the streets, looking for the woman whose veil has slipped and shown a lock of hair, whose chador is not quite large enough, Lord's moral police, his American *basiji*, would be on the prowl. With each classroom once open to any opinion, however errant, with free speech a common practice, it would be necessary to exercise constant and intense vigilance. There are, Lord tells us, no small number of leftists, "lunatic and sinister" professors, and not all of them are visible. They would have to be identified. All classes would have to be supervised, and, out of class, books and articles checked to ensure that their opinions were neither lunatic nor sinister. These books and articles would have to accord with the standards set by the leader. . . . If we are

to protect ourselves from danger, then we must track foreign students, or any students who might pose a threat to national security. How are they to be found? Here too, vigilance would be required. Perhaps students of a certain ethnicity, or students who study certain languages, or students who chose certain books to read or classes to take might be examined first. Their meetings would also have to be supervised. (*LSPAE* 137–38)

All of this is grounded in the brief passages from Lord that I have already quoted and paraphrased. Lord said nothing about "constant and intense vigilance."[113] Nor, as previously explained, did he identify any professors as being "lunatic and sinister." So he implies nothing about identifying such professors, supervising classes, checking "books and articles" for opinions that are lunatic/sinister, accommodating books and articles to the standards set by "the leader," or tracking all foreign students. From this last fantasy Norton spins a new scenario, admittedly hypothetical ("perhaps"), about identifying and supervising students based on ethnicity, languages studied, books read, and classes taken. Norton does not restrict this paranoid excursus to the university realm. Her next paragraph takes us all the way to totalitarianism:

Perhaps the constant supervision of opinions, the always-present, always-listening ear of the state, would be open [*sic*] only to teachers and students. Perhaps the recording of what is written and read, who meets with whom, and where and for what purpose, who travels abroad and where and why and with whom they meet, would be confined to the universities. Perhaps not. (*LSPAE* 138)

Do not be misled by the cute conclusion ("perhaps not"). The three uses of "perhaps" in the above quotation leaven only the ultimate nightmare that Norton sketches: the prospect of Lord's *basiji* engaging in "constant" supervision outside as well as inside academia. By emphasizing the hypothetical nature of the societywide supervision, she insinuates that her sketch of the narrower arena— "constant and intense vigilance" directed against students, professors, and publications to ensure compliance with "the leader"—is not itself a fantasy.

To fathom the alarmism of Norton's accusation about Lord's "American *basiji*," one should recall the human wave attacks—and the use of teenagers as marching minesweepers—that the Iranian *basiji* pioneered in the Iran-Iraq War.[114] Norton, of course, envisions a less suicidal side of their operations. Perhaps she knew that in 2002, just two years before her book was published, marauding *basiji* killed a betrothed Iranian couple who were accused of engaging in the "morally corrupt" behavior of walking together in public. Although the perpetrators were subsequently tried and convicted of murder, the conviction was overturned by Iran's Supreme Court in April 2007. According to the Islamic penal code that coexists with Iran's civic code, even killers who *mistakenly* regard their victims as "morally corrupt" may be exonerated.[115]

"Identity Pluralizing"

Larry George's fawning review of Norton—which describes her as a "superb cultural observer and semiotician" (401) with a "generously agonistic spirit" (408) who previously excelled at championing "serious, historically pivotal feminist, postcolonial, antiracist, and other identity-pluralizing political strategies" (405)—suggests that Straussophobia is widespread in mainstream political philosophy. Going beyond Norton, who reports that "there were no secret teachings; it was all done in the open" (*LSPAE* 23), George is even willing to relay "the possibility, long rumored, of a 'secret Straussian teaching'" that could be "guarded by some sect of his surviving disciples" (405). Were I reading *Executive Intelligence Review*, I would expect to encounter rumors about "surviving disciples" who guard Straussian secrets. Book reviews in *Political Theory* are usually blander.

George's celebration of Norton's virtuosic contributions to "antiracist, and other identity-pluralizing strategies" is doubly ironic because of the uniquely lazy, incoherent, and presumptuous stratagems she employs in assessing *Straussian* identities. As Drury diagnoses, Norton's overall evaluation of Strauss is positive; Drury differs from Norton by holding Strauss responsible for the highly diverse and destructive evils that his followers have allegedly inflicted on the world. In the prelude to her book, Norton distinguishes "the story of Leo Strauss" (*LSPAE* 1–2) from "the story of the Straussians" (2). Norton also departs from Drury in telling "two stories" about the Straussians, distinguishing Strauss's "philosophical lineage" from the "lesser" Straussians defined by "a distinctly and distinctively conservative politics." Norton further characterizes the lesser Straussians as "a set of students taking that name, regarded by others—and regarding themselves—as a chosen set of initiates into a hidden teaching" (2).

Turning to Norton's first chapter, "Who Is Leo Strauss? What Is a Straussian?" (*LSPAE* 5–20), the reader would expect to find a clear distinction between the two types of Straussians. Although her prelude distinguished the "philosophical lineage" from "a set of students taking that name," her first chapter seems to elaborate the *lineage* when it refers to "students" (e.g., Joseph Cropsey, Ralph Lerner, Harvey Mansfield, Stanley Rosen, and Stephen Salkever) who "read texts with the same care and skill and grace they say Strauss brought to them" (6). The confusion expands in her sequel:

> Strauss also has disciples. These are the people who call themselves Straussians. . . . I will distinguish between the students of Strauss, political theorists interested in Strauss's work (some of whom were and others were not students of Strauss), and these disciples. (*LSPAE* 6–7)

Despite the interpretive challenges the last sentence poses, it is safe to conclude that Norton intended to specify three groups: the disciples, the students, and the "interested" political theorists.[116] The fatal problem is her insistence on severing the Cropsey-like "students" who read carefully (and who presumably comprise the "philosophical lineage") from the disciples, "the people who call themselves Straussians" (*LSPAE* 6), "a set of students taking that name" (2). Stanley Rosen insists that he has never called himself a Straussian, but I detect no such reluctance in the other four careful readers (Cropsey, Lerner, Mansfield, and Salkever). And into which category should we place other well-known scholars who sometimes "call themselves" Straussians (6) and are typically "regarded by others" (2) as Straussians? Many names come quickly to mind: for example, Mary Nichols, Arlene Saxonhouse, Vickie Sullivan, Catherine and Michael Zuckert, Peter Berkowitz, Michael Gillespie, Roger Masters, Arthur Melzer, Clifford Orwin, Thomas Pangle, Steven Smith, and Jerry Weinberger. Norton freely identifies Diana Schaub as a Straussian when lamenting the politicization of President Bush's Council on Bioethics—she even stops to note Schaub's affiliation with a "minor" academic institution (Loyola College of Maryland)—but would she dare to suggest that Schaub's brilliant book, *Montesquieu's Erotic Liberalism*, is unworthy of Strauss's "philosophical lineage" and should instead be lumped with writings by Dinesh D'Souza (68), William Bennett (174, 198) and Frum and Perle (210–12)?[117]

Norton's typology also fails to clarify whether individuals trained by Strauss's students may be counted among "the students of Strauss."[118] When Norton acknowledges the difficulty of differentiating students from disciples, she manages to introduce additional obfuscation: "There is sometimes an element of discipleship in a student, so there is some overlap between these categories. There is very little overlap between the two conditions" (*LSPAE* 6). Perhaps Larry George can refer me to a "semiotician" who will explain how the terms "disciple" and "student" overlap as *categories* more than they do as *conditions*. In the real university, if you interpret texts in the ways associated with Strauss you will be sometimes be called a Straussian even if you do not take "that name" for yourself.

Norton once apologizes for using "Straussian" as a label—but only because it "implicates Strauss in views that were not always his own." She deploys the label because one should "call people what they call themselves" and Straussian is "the name these disciples have taken" (*LSPAE* 7). Her approach further grates because although the disciples (in her account) are "the people who call themselves Straussians" (6), she applies the Straussian label to prominent neoconservatives—Wolfowitz (16), Robert Kagan (16), Donald Kagan (47), and perhaps Richard Perle (17)—who do *not* refer to themselves as Straussians.[119] Since the distinction between "lesser" Straussians (the right-wing "disciples") and the fuzzily described alternative specifies an axis for the entire book, which proceeds to demonize the former, Norton's terminological shortcomings express viciousness as well as incompetence.

Statements such as the following, in any case, fail to promote the "generously agonistic spirit" of "identity-pluralizing" that George attributes to Norton: "From the time I first came to Chicago to the present day, I have seen Arabs and Muslims made the targets of unrestrained persecution, *especially among the Straussians*" (*LSPAE* 210, emph. added); "Perle and Frum and their Straussian colleagues have abandoned reason and study, democratic ideals and philosophical principle" (212); because of "the stubborn ignorance of the Straussians," who "take pride in their narrowness," they have "not kept faith with learning" (226). When she describes Harvey Mansfield, Cropsey (who "rarely mentions politics in class"), Harry Jaffa, Thomas West, Nathan Tarcov, Charles Fairbanks, Francis Fukuyama, Robert Goldwin, William Kristol, Carnes Lord, Leon Kass, James Nichols, Mark Blitz, Walter Berns, and Allan Bloom as *Straussians* (7, 8, 15, 16, 19, 47), could she intend to tar them all with "stubborn ignorance" and the other vices? The status of Bloom is particularly important for Norton because Bloom, "far more than Strauss, has shaped the Straussians who govern in America" (58). Did no one whisper in Norton's ear about Bloom's Democratic affinities?

Norton's use of "unrestrained" to describe the three decades of persecution she has continually witnessed against Arabs and Muslims, especially in connection with Straussian persecutors, is breathtaking.[120] Even on a generous estimate of Straussian numbers, Muslims outnumber us by at least 100,000 to 1, so I dread the day that Norton's book is translated into Arabic, Urdu, or Farsi. Straussians, in any case, are not circulating anti-Muslim texts analogous to the *Protocols of the Elders of Zion*, which the Hamas Charter touts and which remains widely available around the world. Norton was presumably aware, moreover, of the persecutions that Muslims have had to endure in recent decades from their fellow Muslims, for example, what Saddam Hussein did to Iraqi Shi'ites and Kurds; perhaps even the million-plus body count of the Iran-Iraq War can supply some perspective.

Norton does not accuse Wolfowitz of Islamophobia, but she offers a comparably malicious and inane charge about his essay in Kagan's and Kristol's *Present Dangers*.[121] Norton's initial error is her claim that Wolfowitz's essay is titled, "How We Learned to Stop Worrying and Love the *Pax Americana*" (this is rather the title of his first subheading). After unveiling the allusion to the Stanley Kubrick movie—*Dr. Strangelove, or How I Learned to Stop Worrying and Love the Bomb*—and reminding us of the emphasis Straussians place on "slightly altered" quotations, Norton offers this elaboration:

Wolfowitz argues that the Pax Americana is to be best secured by the use of a particular type of arms: tactical nuclear weapons. If the classical interpretive schematic holds, Wolfowitz is suggesting that the Pax Americana is dependent on the willingness and ability to use nuclear weapons. This interpretation is supported by the course of Wolfowitz's career. (*LSPAE* 192)

As always, Norton provides no citations. Here too, there is no citation to provide, since Wolfowitz's essay *never* mentions tactical nuclear weapons; nor does it recommend that they, or any other type of nuclear weapon, be used. The actual title of the essay, "Statesmanship in the New Century," invites no one to deploy "the classical interpretive schematic"—or to love the bomb.

The disciple/student distinction Norton tries to establish within Strauss's legacy blurs additionally when she refers to professors "who read texts and teach in the Straussian manner" (*LSPAE* 10), when she describes certain universities and foundations as Straussian (10–11), and when she offers flippant generalizations: for "the Straussians, though not for the students of Strauss," *Natural Right and History* "seems to stand apart" because it "casts America as the site of modernity's redemption" (118); "Straussians are conservative," and any "liberal and left Straussians" that might have existed "have become extinct" (161); "Strauss's *followers* have been exclusively conservative in my time" (162); "[a]s Strauss's *students* became outnumbered by his *disciples*, politics—the politics of the moment—overcame philosophy."[122] With categories so poorly defined, how could one even think of making a quantitative comparison? When Norton asserts that Baghdad is now "occupied by those who call themselves his [Strauss's] students" (222), the reality community can only groan.[123]

Although Norton rarely blames Strauss for the pernicious aspects of his legacy, she does so in connection with *NRH*: "For Straussians, for Strauss in *Natural Right and History*, the world is full of nihilists" (*LSPAE* 120).[124] Drawing on a sentence from the introduction that she slightly misquotes ("The contemporary rejection of natural right leads to nihilism—nay, it is identical with nihilism" [*NRH* 5]), Norton builds to this uncharitable complaint about Strauss (and Kojève): "Anyone who acknowledges the presence of different standards, the possibility of different forms of moral life, the need to weigh the actions of different people by different standards, is called a nihilist by these anxious men" (*LSPAE* 121). Even *NRH*, however, includes a passage that refutes Norton's sweeping claim: "A very imperfect regime may supply the only just solution to the problem of a given community" (*NRH* 140). Norton, I admit, says nothing about *NRH* that remotely approaches the ignorance Drury conveyed via the following question: "Does not the bulk of *Natural Right and History* consist in the most virulent expansions of the most virulent utterances of the holy book of the ruling party?"[125]

Muslims Everywhere

Despite the numerous and egregious shortcomings of Norton's book, Professor Corey Robin pronounces it to be "short but splendid." I would have hoped that the author of *Fear: The History of a Political Idea* (Oxford University Press)—a widely and wisely celebrated tome—would be less indulgent of such confused and crude scapegoating. But sanity often succumbs when Strauss is discussed, and Robin puts forward his own awkward and unconscionable summary: "A Jewish intellectual from Europe teaches intellectuals in America how to read Muslim intellectuals from the Middle East—and the *result* is a legion of *intellectuals . . . fighting a war against Muslims everywhere.*"[126] Perhaps Robin should show more concern about the legion of intellectuals traducing Straussians everywhere.

Norton, who studied Farabi and Ibn Tufayl during her Chicago days (*LSPAE* 202), strains to distinguish the Islamophobic Straussians from their Islamophilic mentor. She even credits Strauss for having "revived the study of Islamic philosophy among political theorists in the West" (225). She highlights the excerpts from Farabi, Averroes, Avicenna, and Tufayl that were incorporated twenty-five years ago into the *Medieval Political Philosophy* collection edited by Strauss's students, Ralph Lerner and Muhsin Mahdi.[127] To this, let me add that Strauss lamented the absence of tolerable editions (even Arabic editions) of some of Farabi's work (FP 358). Strauss once wrote about "the superhuman beauty of the Qur'an" (*PL* 59), and his 1957 *WIPP* article on Farabi first appeared in a book that was published in Damascus. Drury acknowledges Strauss's profound debt to Farabi (*PILS* 21–23), and Xenos highlights his "deep knowledge of Arabic" as well as his "love and respect for the rationalism of medieval Islamic philosophy" (*CV* 144). Also pertinent is Pangle's assessment (in the introduction to *RCPR*) in 1989, before the emergence of Al-Qaida and before the first Iraq War. Although the Middle Ages are generally regarded as the Dark Ages, Strauss "insisted that one small corner, if you will, of the medieval experience reached a peak of rational illumination that has not been rivaled since"; that corner is medieval political philosophy, "especially in the Muslim world" (*RCPR* xxxiii).

Given the widespread perception that Paul Wolfowitz stood at the vanguard of a Likudnik effort to vanquish the Arab Middle East by getting the United States to invade Iraq, we should also appreciate the gracious speech he delivered—"Bridging the Dangerous Gap between the West and the Muslim World"—on 3 May 2002, when the memory of 9/11 was quite fresh and grievous:

> As salaamu alaykum wa rahmatullahi wa barakatuh. For those of you who don't speak Arabic, and for those of you who do, but don't understand how I speak Arabic, that means, "peace be upon you and the mercy of God and his blessings." It is a traditional Muslim greeting, but it is one that speaks to all people of all religions.

The rest of the speech maintains the same irenic tone. Wolfowitz commends the "equal status" that the Indonesian state grants to "the five major religions of its people"; he also celebrates Indonesia's "many rich cultures and its tradition of tolerance." He invokes the Muslim sultan of Turkey (Beyazit), who welcomed the Jews whom King Ferdinand had expelled from Spain and thus showed that the *Dar al-Islam* was then "one of the most tolerant and progressive parts of the world." He quotes a *hadith* about religious tolerance, and praises "great Muslim thinkers" like Alfarabi and Avicenna for helping to stimulate the Renaissance (by sustaining classical Greek thought during centuries when it had "largely disappeared" from Europe). He extols the commercial, architectural, administrative, scientific, mathematical, and poetical achievements of Islam's "golden age." He even extends his encomium into the twenty-first century:

> I am convinced that the vast majority of the world's Muslims have no use for the extreme doctrines espoused by groups such as al Qaeda or the Taliban. Very much to the contrary. They abhor terrorism. They abhor terrorists who have not only hijacked airplanes, but have attempted to hijack one of the world's great religions. They have no use for people who deny fundamental rights to women or who indoctrinate children with superstition and hatred.[128]

I seek in vain for bellicosity, jingoism, or hatred in these words. Turning to Wolfowitz's deeds, finally, one must acknowledge his attempts in the 1990s to procure assistance for the Muslims of Bosnia and Kosovo.[129]

A Kinder and Gentler Lord

Given Norton's diatribe and the rampant accusations about secret tyranny, I expected an applied-Machiavelli book, published in 2003 by a power Straussian (Carnes Lord), to resonate with the Bush administration's approach to executive power, and so forth. My expectations were quickly dashed, however, when Lord wrote that he was "deeply concerned with the growth of executive power and the trend toward plebiscitary leadership in the advanced democracies, and related phenomena such as the weakening of parties and the erosion of constitutional forms and the rule of law" (*MP* xv).[130] Regarding twentieth-century presidents, Lord does seem to place two Republicans (Eisenhower and Reagan) at the summit, and he does offer sharp criticisms of FDR. The bulk of the latter discussion, however, focuses on Roosevelt's failure to *accommodate* Japan prior to WWII. How could a Straussian enthusiast for empire and perpetual war fail to celebrate the vast carnage inflicted in the Pacific theater and the major bases we left behind? Lord instead offers the following complaints: the United States could perhaps have achieved "a satisfactory settlement of its outstanding disputes with Japan in order to address the more serious Nazi threat"; even in hindsight, it is difficult to reconstruct Roosevelt's policy toward Japan, which was both provocative and inconsistent (195); and Roosevelt seemed to underestimate how formidable an adversary Japan would make. Lord is not as opposed to multiculturalism as Norton assumes:

> perhaps the most serious flaw in FDR's prewar statecraft was his failure to understand, or to make an effort to understand, the adversary. In fact, Roosevelt had little

regard for the Japanese and tended to see them in broad caricature. He was tone-deaf when it came to Japanese cultural sensitivities. He made no apparent effort to appreciate the delicate internal politics of the Japanese cabinet and the exposure (to assassination, among other things) of ministers who tried to accommodate American interests. (*MP* 196–97)

Lord, it should be emphasized, teaches military strategy at the Naval War College, served previously as Dan Quayle's national security advisor, and condemned "the agenda of political correctness that pervades contemporary university life in America" (139). But I am confident in proclaiming that "leftist professors" should be more worried about their blood pressure than they are about "Lord's moral police."

NOTES

1. Danny Postel, "Noble Lies." Drury alleges a Straussian commitment to "perpetual war" in yet another interview that has been widely circulated online: Jim Lobe, "Neocons Dance a Strauss Waltz," *Asia Times*, 9 May 2003, http://www.atimes.com/atimes/Middle_East/EE09Ak01.html. A printable PDF file for this Lobe piece is available at http://www.fpif.org/fpiftxt/817, under the title "The Strong Must Rule the Weak: A Philosopher for an Empire."

2. Drury also posited a direct link between perpetual war and abortion policy. Behind President Bush's stated concern to create a "culture of life" that would eventually outlaw abortion, Drury detected a "grand plan" to "keep women busy having babies—lots of babies. In this way, women will become useful once again; they will return to their vocation as factories for soldiers" (*PILS*-05 xxvi).

3. In her 2005 introduction, Drury commits such allegations about perpetual war to print. Although her initial formulation here—"the prospect of perpetual war is one that the Straussian neoconservatives are more than willing to embrace" (*PILS*-05 xlviii)—is careful and calm by Druryean standards, she concludes the introduction with some of her foulest fantasies. In an unpublished manuscript quoted by Joe Conason, Alan Gilbert—with whom Condoleezza Rice studied extensively at Denver—likewise maintains that militarism suffused Strauss's career. According to Gilbert, Strauss "remains mesmerized by Heidegger's and Schmitt's politics," including their "hatred for international peace, their love of militarism and war"; Strauss's "core political beliefs seem to have frozen in the late 1920s in a way that no subsequent experience would markedly affect" (Conason, *It Can Happen Here*, 44). Gilbert provides two Balkinization postings that stand out for their sloppiness (http://balkin.blogspot.com/2006/07/letter_16.html).

4. Carl Schmitt, *The Concept of the Political*, trans. George Schwab, with a new foreword by Tracy B. Strong (Chicago: University of Chicago Press, 1996), 27. This work began as a 1927 article in the *Archiv für Sozialwissenschaft und Sozialpolitik*, and a revised version was published in book form in 1932. The German-language original of Strauss's review, "Notes on Carl Schmitt, *The Concept of the Political*" (hereafter NCS) was first published in a 1932 issue of the same journal (Schmitt may have helped secure its publication). Elsa M. Sinclair's English translation of NCS was published as an appendix to *SCR* in 1965, and was reprinted in the 1976 edition of Schmitt's *Concept*, translated and edited by George Schwab. The above-described 1996 edition of *Concept* includes a new English translation of NCS; this translation, by J. Harvey Lomax, first appeared in Heinrich Meier, *Carl Schmitt and Leo Strauss: The Hidden Dialogue* (Chicago: University of Chicago Press, 1995), 91–119. I shall cite this translation by *paragraph* number (both versions of the

Lomax translation provide paragraph numbers). On the complex publication history of these works by Schmitt and Strauss, see Meier, *Carl Schmitt*, 6n5, 8n7, 120; also see Schwab's translator's note and p. 5n8. Note, finally, that NCS at times addresses a 1929 lecture by Schmitt—"The Age of Neutralizations and Depoliticizations"—that was reprinted in the 1932 edition of Schmitt's book but does *not* appear in the above-cited Schwab editions of 1976 and 1996. This lecture, however, is included in the expanded Schwab/Strong edition of *The Concept of the Political* published in 2007; an English translation by Matthias Konzett and John P. McCormick was previously published in *Telos* 96 (Summer 1993): 130–42.

5. Did Drury rather mean to say that, for Schmitt, it is right to kill the other/alien when specific actions and/or circumstances create "political enmity"? In any case, she proceeds to offer Adolph Eichmann's lack of animus or hatred in "exterminating the Jews" as an example of how a Schmittian might confront a "clean enemy" (*LSAR* 90). Drury preposterously adds that Strauss was "unable to liberate himself from the conception of the political by which his people were so tragically victimized" (91). Recall Jeet Heer's allegation that she described Strauss as a "Jewish Nazi."

6. Schmitt, *Concept*, 49, 47.

7. Strauss in fact highlights "the resolution with which Schmitt refuses to come on as a belligerent against the pacifists" (NCS 25). For the record, Drury does an admirable job in capturing Schmitt's insistence that the designating of enemies is a purely *political* function (*LSAR* 89), in acknowledging his concern that liberalism (because of its globalizing/universalizing tendencies) "introduces a more intense and unclean politics" (*LSAR* 84), and in emphasizing his insistence on distinguishing the political categories of friend and enemy from the moral categories of good and evil (*LSAR* 87–89, 93–94). Cf. Schmitt, *Concept*, 66 on the horrible "confusion" that ensues when justice and freedom are invoked "to legitimize one's own political ambition and to disqualify or demoralize the enemy"; in the same spirit, Schmitt protests both the conversion of the enemy into "an outlaw of humanity" and the danger that war-ending crusades entail (79); such wars are "unusually intense and inhuman" because the enemy is degraded into "moral and other categories" and must be destroyed rather than be merely forced to "retreat in his borders" (36).

8. Emphasis added. Michael Ignatieff, "The Death That Will Not Die," *New Republic*, 8 October 2007, 52.

9. *LSAR* 93. The stakes are even higher because Drury suggests that "Strauss's American followers" are basically . . . Schmittians (87). In a recent article, Drury makes Schmitt, Strauss, and the latter's allegedly "neoconservative" disciples still more bloodthirsty. For Schmitt, politics was "the business of exterminating the enemy," and anyone who even "challenge[s]" national "stability" is an enemy; Strauss brought religion into the mix because it is "much easier to exterminate the enemy if the enemy is defined as evil, immoral, and ungodly" (Drury, "Exterminating the Enemy," *Free Inquiry* 27, no. 2 [February/March 2007]: 22). Cf. *LSAR* 177–78.

10. Drury cites pages 87 and 97 of the 1976 Schwab edition of NCS, which is differently paginated than the Lomax translations from 1995 (in Meier's *Carl Schmitt*) and 1996 (in Schwab's edition of Schmitt's *Concept*). The pagination of Schmitt's portion does not vary between the two Schwab editions (1976 and 1996).

11. Commenting on "the political theology that Strauss discretely brings to light underneath Schmitt's position," David Janssens observes that Schmitt's approach to politics and revealed religion made him a defender of both of the "challenging alternatives to the philosophic life" that Strauss was "trying to recover" (Janssens, "A Change of Orientation: Leo Strauss's 'Comments' on Carl Schmitt Revisited," *Interpretation* 33, no. 1 [Fall/Winter 2005]: 97–98, 101). Cf. Janssens, *Between Athens and Jerusalem*, 8, 127, 138–39, 144, 160, 173, 178; Meier, *Carl Schmitt*, 48, 68–69, 83; Susan Shell, "Meier on Strauss and Schmitt," *Review of Politics* 53, no. 1 (Winter 1991): 219–23; Gunnell, "Strauss before Straussism," 95–99; and Gregory Bruce Smith, "Athens and Washington: Leo Strauss and the American Regime," in Deutsch and Murley, *Leo Strauss*, 115, 120–22.

12. Schmitt uses these phrases on p. 30 (Schwab edition) and Strauss quotes them (italicizing "polemical") in his thirty-fourth paragraph. Situating *Concept* in earlier writings of Schmitt, including *Political Theology* (1922) and *The Crisis of Parliamentary Democracy* (1923), Richard Wolin provides a militaristic interpretation of *Concept* that Drury cites (*LSAR* 197n78) and presumably endorses (Richard Wolin, "Carl Schmitt: The Conservative Revolutionary Habitus and the Aesthetics of Horror," *Political Theory* 20, no. 3 [August 1992]: 424–47). But Wolin's accounts of Schmitt's anti-rationalist decisionism, Schmitt's rejection of "the good life" as a political goal, and his Jünger-indebted enthusiasm for total war/mobilization make it easy to grasp the gulf between Schmitt and Strauss.

13. Meier, *Carl Schmitt*, 87, 47. Cf. Meier, *Leo Strauss*, 79–87, and Janssens, *Between Athens and Jerusalem*, 100, 104, 106, 127, 144, 160, 163, 170, 178, 190, 214–15n91.

14. Robert Howse, "From Legitimacy to Dictatorship—and Back Again: Leo Strauss's Critique of the Anti-Liberalism of Carl Schmitt," *Canadian Journal of Law and Jurisprudence* 10, no. 1 (1997): 95. Addressing other notorious themes in Schmitt, Howse also notes that "Strauss's classical perspective accepts the critical importance to statecraft of correctly identifying the exception but for the opposite reason—i.e., so that one reduces to the essential *minimum* those cases where public safety is the highest law and where the decision must forget the concern with those principles of justice that point to human perfection" (99); classic natural right therefore *resembles* "the hesitant and uncomfortable liberal disposition toward the exception that is held in contempt by Schmitt" (100).

15. Strauss, "Spirit of Sparta," 534. See pp. 71–72, 124 above.

16. Strauss cites NCS at *PPH* 122n3.

17. Cf. *PPH* 161 on Plato's prioritizing of domestic arrangements rather than foreign policy; also see 162 on peace as the aim of the statesman. In his conclusion, Strauss specifically faults Nietzsche, for whom "the ideal is not the object of wisdom, but the hazardous venture of the will" (165). At *SPPP* 185, Strauss invokes Plato's praise of gentleness to disparage Nietzsche's praise of cruelty.

18. *PPH* 90, 91; cf. 106, 128, 143. According to Janssens, the horizon beyond liberalism was the horizon—shared by both revealed religion and Socratic-Platonic philosophy—of "*nomos* or law as a 'concrete binding order of life'" (Janssens here quotes from Strauss's 1931 lecture, "Cohen and Maimonides"). Strauss's "change of orientation," correspondingly, was his "overcoming of the historicist prejudice" and his "rediscovery of original Platonic philosophy, its Socratic program, and its particular art of writing" (Janssens, *Between Athens and Jerusalem*, 115, 146, 147, 219n33).

19. Leo Strauss, "On Abravanel's Philosophical Tendency and Political Teaching," in *Isaac Abravanel*, ed. J. B. Trend and H. Loewe (Cambridge: Cambridge University Press, 1937), 107n2. In later publications, Strauss identifies manliness as "the virtue of war" (*XSD* 89) and emphasizes that Xenophon omits manliness/courage from the two lists he provides of Socrates' virtues (*OT* 73, 126n6, 203; *XS* 126, 177); cf. Strauss, "Spirit of Sparta," 520–21 on the connection Xenophon perceived between manliness and madness.

20. A few pages later, Strauss again invokes this sweetness: for Hobbes, "the frightfulness of death rather than the sweetness of life reveals the value of living" (*PPH* 132–33).

21. Cf. *CM* 31. For a careful assessment of *PPH*, see Devin Stauffer, "Reopening the Quarrel between the Ancients and the Moderns: Leo Strauss's Critique of Hobbes's 'New Political Science,'" *American Political Science Review* 101, no. 2 (May 2007): 223–33.

22. Xenos does not pause to consider how individuals who allegedly regard themselves as "beyond good and evil" (*CV* 26, 106) could characterize either nature or human nature in such terms. For Schmitt, as sketched above, "the evilness of the world and man" is a "fundamental theological dogma" linked also to original sin (Schmitt, *Concept*, 65). Cf. Machiavelli's well-known pronouncements in chapters 17 and 18 of *The Prince* that men are wicked (*tristi*).

23. *PPH* 90–91, 124–27, 132–33, 147, 161–62; cf. *CV* 62–63. Another pertinent text, from which Xenos quotes extensively (*CV* 58), is a 4 September 1932 letter from Strauss to Schmitt that

highlights "the natural evil of man" (the letter is now widely quoted on the Internet). In explaining why Schmitt, in attacking the Left, draws on "two incompatible or at least heterogeneous lines of thought"—authoritarianism and "bellicose nationalism"—Strauss offers a hypothesis for Schmitt to consider. Strauss asks whether it accords with *Schmitt*'s understanding to link the two elements in this way: "The ultimate foundation of the Right is the principle of the natural evil of man; because man is by nature evil, he therefore needs *dominion*. But dominion can be established, that is, men can be unified, only in a unity *against*—against other men" (hence "the grouping of humanity into friends and enemies" would be "given with human nature"). In attempting to specify the degree to which *Strauss* aligned himself with the Right, we must rely on other sources; we may even question whether these brief remarks about evil capture his mature understanding of the political spectrum (cf. p. 173n61 above). For a complete English translation of the letter, see Meier, *Carl Schmitt*, 124–26; Strauss kept a carbon copy that is now housed among the Leo Strauss Papers (129).

24. It is not liberals who predict that the state will "wither away," allowing everyone to determine how his or her day will be divided among hunting, fishing, herding, and criticizing.

25. Among other passages, cf. *NRH* 129, 168–69, 183, and *CM* 41–43. Insofar as Hobbes "ascribes to the sovereign prince or to the sovereign people an unqualified right to disregard all legal and constitutional limitations according to their pleasure" (*NRH* 193)—and equates foreigners with enemies who may be exterminated without the slightest moral inhibition—Hobbes can readily be appropriated by fascists, authoritarians, and imperialists.

26. Cf. *WIPP* 35, *TM* 254–55, and Aristotle's *Politics* 1253a31–32: "just as man is the best of the animals when completed, when separated from law and adjudication he is the worst of all" (translated by Carnes Lord [Chicago: University of Chicago Press, 1984]).

27. See *NRH* 191–92 on the "doctrinarism" Strauss associates with Hobbes; cf. pp. 274–77 below on Strauss's posture toward political recipes.

28. *CV* 68, 17, 149n55. For Strauss's 1924 essay on Lagarde, see Michael Zank, ed., *Leo Strauss: The Early Writings (1921–1932)* (Albany: SUNY Press, 2002), 90–101. In a casual comment that Xenos accurately paraphrases, Jonas states that Strauss had been an early supporter of Mussolini (*frühzeitig Mussolini-Anhänger*). The only thing Jonas says to delimit the adjective "early" is that Mussolini was not yet anti-Semitic (Hans Jonas, *Erinnerungen* [Frankfurt on Main: Insel Verlag, 2003], 262). Italy did not adopt its racial laws (the *Carta della Razza*) until July 1938. On Jonas's experiences and reflections concerning Strauss, also see *Erinnerungen* 92–95, 261–62, 314; he traces their friendship to the year 1921 (475).

29. John P. Diggins, *Mussolini and Fascism: The View from America* (Princeton, NJ: Princeton University Press, 1972), 27, 183, 187, 233.

30. Diggins, *Mussolini and Fascism*, 279. On Mussolini's popularity among prominent Americans, also see 61–62, 171, 185–86, 196–99, 204, 227, 230–31, 276, 280.

31. Xenos, commendably, also faults Drury for fixating upon Strauss's elitism and for depreciating his concern to promote "the interest of the ruled" (*CV* 88), but he fails to give the devil her due. However poorly Drury sometimes argues, Xenos should assign her more credit for arguing, a decade or two before Xenos did, that we should dismiss large chunks of Strauss's scholarship as smokescreens for his authoritarian agenda, that he was pervasively indebted to Carl Schmitt, that he was encouraging "the inculcation of perpetual fear" (*CV* 66), and that he abhorred the Weimar Republic. It might appear that Xenos cites *The Political Ideas of Leo Strauss* in seven consecutive footnotes (*CV* 157nn2–8), but the last four are citations to *TALS* that Xenos mistakenly presents as Ibids to Drury.

32. Clifford Orwin, "Straussians," 15. For the remark from Berns, who escorted Strauss to register for the 1952 election, see the letter he wrote to the *New Republic* (11 and 18 September 2006, 37).

33. John Foster Dulles, who later served as Eisenhower's secretary of state, called for "rollback" and "liberation" to replace containment. See Norman Podhoretz, "World War IV: How It Started,

What It Means, and Why We Have to Win," in *The Right War? The Conservative Debate on Iraq*, ed. Gary Rosen (Cambridge: Cambridge University Press, 2005), 163. This chapter was first published in the September, 2004 issue of *Commentary*.

34. Susan Jacoby, *The Age of American Unreason*, revised and updated (New York: Vintage Books, 2009), 288.

35. My information about Strauss's 1964 vote comes from Dannhauser, "Leo Strauss," 359.

36. See p. 279 below.

37. Orwin, "Straussians," 15. David Schaefer provides other important details: Bloom supported Carter in 1976, and "publicly boasted of never having voted for a Republican until Ronald Reagan's 1980 presidential candidacy" (Schaeffer, "Ass," 289, 288). For Drury, "Straussians are conservatives without exception" (*PILS* 16).

38. Recall Strauss's dry words from his 1961 critique of Isaiah Berlin: "In the age of thermonuclear weapons the positive relation of science to human survival has lost all the apparent evidence that it formerly may have possessed" (*RCPR* 22–23). Cf. *LAM* 5–6 on "our thoughts concerning thermonuclear wars," and WWRJ 65 on modern technology, which "has also made it possible for the first time, or is about to make possible, the destruction of the human race. The most wicked and vicious human beings who ever were—Nero himself—could not, even if they wished, think of such devices as the atomic bomb." Despite the "fascistic celebration of violence" that Fukuyama allegedly "displays" (Drury, *AK* 179), he offers a moving depiction of the "horrendous consequences" of modern war: "By the twentieth century, the risk of life in a bloody battle had become thoroughly democratized. Rather than the mark of exceptional character, it became an experience forced on masses of men, and ultimately women and children as well. It led not to the satisfaction of recognition, but to anonymous and objectless death" (Fukuyama, *End of History*, 335). In explaining why German cities should be reduced to a maximum of 100,000 inhabitants each, Alfred Rosenberg emphasizes that technology, which had once "drawn a steel wall around an entire State," had "broken through again and restored the age-old organic relationship between people and war" (Rosenberg, *Myth*, 349).

39. In his next sentence Strauss offers his widely cited remark that "liberal or constitutional democracy comes closer to what the classics demanded than any alternative that is viable in our age" (*OT* 207). In trying to accentuate the antidemocratic dimensions of liberal democracy, Xenos seems to overlook the ways that abundance (*OT* 207) can promote stability and spread educational opportunities (*CV* 121–22); on democracy and education, see *WIPP* 36–38, *CM* 36–37, *LAM* 4–5, 12, 21. Drury does acknowledge Strauss's worries about "turmoil and disorder" (*PILS* 112) as well as his emphasis on the unprecedented destructiveness that modern technology can unleash (*PILS* 131, 139, 140, 178).

40. See Giles MacDonogh, *After the Reich: The Brutal History of the Allied Occupation* (New York: Basic Books, 2007), 25–27, 33–34, 42–43, 46, 48–49, 52, 55–57, 98–101, 170, 180, 210, 301, 303.

41. Punishment was also inflicted on the families of soldiers who had surrendered or were MIA. On prisoners and repatriation, see Evan Mawdsley, *Thunder in the East: The Nazi-Soviet War, 1941–1945* (London: Hodder Arnold, 2005), 78, 104–5, 231–32; and Ronald H. Bailey, *Prisoners of War* (Chicago: Time-Life Books, 1983), 123, 170, 177–81.

42. This disparagement of Jünger is among the comments Altman ignores in presenting his neo-Nazi reading of GN.

43. Justin Raimondo, "The Imperial Delusion: Neoconservatism and the Cult of Empire," 16 September 2005, http://www.antiwar.com/justin/?articleid=7294. Raimondo is the editorial director at antiwar.com, and comments regularly on the dangers that Straussians pose.

44. Roughly 800 million people suffer from chronic hunger, and widespread misery is also inflicted by malaria, AIDS, cholera, tuberculosis, trypanosomiasis, typhoid fever, and other diseases that rage even among the young.

45. As Pangle puts it, Nietzsche's "reckless rhetoric" signaled "his willingness to risk or foment any and all upheavals that might derail present civilization." See Thomas Pangle, "Nihilism and Modern Democracy in the Thought of Nietzsche," in *The Crisis of Liberal Democracy: A Straussian Perspective*, ed. Kenneth L. Deutsch and Walter Soffer (Albany: SUNY Press, 1987), 207. Cf. Levine, *Nietzsche*, 159.

46. Xenos, "Leo Strauss," 4–5.

47. Xenos, "Leo Strauss," 11.

48. Paul Gottfried, "Strauss and the Straussians," *Humanitas* 18, nos. 1 & 2 (2005): 29, http://www.nhinet.org/18-1&2.htm.

49. Mark Lilla, "The Closing of the Straussian Mind," *New York Review of Books* 51, no. 17 (4 November 2004): 57. Lilla is here reviewing Norton's *LSPAE* and Lord's *Modern Prince*.

50. *PILS* lii–liii n10. Like Xenos and Lilla, Drury highlights Straussian banality: there is an "overwhelming unanimity readily observable among Straussian interpreters. Indeed the most persistent complaint against Straussian scholars is that they are almost never surprising; they can always be relied on not to be original" (*PILS* 11).

51. Xenos, "Leo Strauss," 17.

52. The medal placed Shorris in august company: Toni Morrison, Robert N. Bellah, Ernest J. Gaines, Quincy Jones, Barbara Kingsolver, Edmund S. Morgan, Judy Crichton, and four others won the award that year.

53. Earl Shorris, "Ignoble Liars: Leo Strauss, George Bush, and the Philosophy of Mass Deception," *Harper's*, June 2004, 65. In a similar spirit, Claude Polin asserts that "in the highest places of American society, Strauss's name seems to be an open sesame for power and influence" (Polin, "Enigmatic Professor," 47). James Atlas, in one of his many puerile remarks about Strauss, asks about "the policies being carried out in his name" (Atlas, "Classicist's Legacy").

54. Later in the session, Kristol concedes that Strauss "seems to have been generally of a conservative bent" and might favor a "tough foreign policy."

55. Kristol speaks these words roughly thirty-five minutes into part II, "The Phantom Victory"; for a transcript, see http://www.daanspeak.com/TranscriptPowerOfNightmares2.html. The documentary aired in late 2004.

56. Shorris admits that Strauss's "core idea" is to "read old books carefully" ("Ignoble Liars" 65); in his book, he also lauds Strauss's formidable intellect and his brilliant interpretations of Plato (Earl Shorris, *The Politics of Heaven: America in Fearful Times* [New York: W. W. Norton & Company, 2007], 168, 175).

57. Shorris, "Ignoble Liars," 69. Although Shorris subsequently interviewed Norquist and wrote about him in greater detail (*Politics of Heaven* 86–88, 133, 206, 227, 236, 241–44), Shorris continues to call him a Straussian (178). For an overview of Norquist's life and agenda, see Easton, *Gang of Five*, 70–88 (on his harsh clashes with Bill Kristol, see 73, 360). Hutton seems to include Norquist (and his anti-tax crusades) as a "direct heir" of Strauss (Hutton, *Declaration*, 92). Cf. John Micklethwait and Adrian Wooldridge, *The Right Nation: Conservative Power in America* (New York: Penguin Press, 2004), 175, 195–96.

58. David Brock, *Blinded*, 66, 331.

59. Shorris, "Ignoble Liars," 70. In a later article, Shorris presents a different angle on Wolfowitz, claiming that his "disposition to evil" is a fact that "cannot be denied" (Shorris, "The National Character," *Harper's*, June 2007, 60). In his book, Shorris suggests that this disposition—"[d]oing evil as part of one's character" (314n9)—is obvious only in "a person like Wolfowitz or Cheney who promotes war and takes the food from the mouths of hungry children" (Shorris, *Politics of Heaven*, 318). For Shorris—as for Drury—Strauss's embrace of "perpetual war" paved the way for the Iraq War (*Politics of Heaven* 21, 58, 170, 175, 197–98, 235, 260, 265, 267). Shorris also suggests, however, that Strauss would have "detested" or "despised" Cheney, Wolfowitz, and Bill Kristol—because he would have joined Shorris in regarding the war as a catastrophic product of

American stupidity (173, 199). Although reviewer Tim Rutten cleverly skewers some of Shorris's idiosyncrasies, he is impressed by Shorris's account of Strauss (Rutten, "No Faith in a Thesis on Politics," *Los Angeles Times*, 15 August 2007, E1).

60. Aristotle, *Politics* 1324a5–1325b31; cf. *Nichomachean Ethics* 1177b1–10.

61. Jim George, "Leo Strauss, Neoconservatism and U.S. Foreign Policy: Esoteric Nihilism and the Bush Doctrine," *International Politics* 42, no. 2 (June 2005): 174–202.

62. George merely describes Abrams and Feith as having a "direct Straussian pedigree" (George, "Leo Strauss," 183). Shorris not only designates Feith, Perle, and Libby as Straussians; he describes Perle and Bill Kristol as President Bush's "prophets," and he states that Feith was "reputed to have sold the war and Straussian thinking" to Vice President Cheney (Shorris, *Politics of Heaven*, 198, 190–91). I. Lewis "Scooter" Libby was an undergraduate at Yale, where in 1972 he took a course on strategic policy with Wolfowitz, who taught international relations there for three years after completing his graduate-school course work. Journalist Anthony David, drawing on a conversation he had with Libby's college girlfriend, maintains that Wolfowitz put Libby into a neocon "trance" at Yale via a secret doctrine originated by *Wohlstetter*: that nuclear-armed tyrannies were intolerable (David, "The Apprentice"). Foolishly assuming that Wolfowitz introduced Libby to "the world of Strauss," Halper and Clarke include Libby on their very inaccurate, Steinberg-indebted list of Strauss's "disciples" (Halper and Clarke, *America*, 67); John Dickerson, *Slate*'s chief political correspondent, likewise maintains that Libby entered "that conservative club" via Wolfowitz (Dickerson, "Who Is Scooter Libby?" *Slate*, 21 October 2005, http://www.slate .com/id/2128530/). After Yale, in any case, Libby went to Columbia Law School, became a lawyer in Philadelphia, married a prominent Democrat, and did volunteer work for Senator Abraham Ribicoff of Connecticut and Governor Michael Dukakis of Massachusetts, both Democrats. Recalling the outstanding paper Libby had written for his course, Wolfowitz recruited Libby in 1981 to do speechwriting with the Policy Planning Staff at the State Department. (I have taken many of these details about Libby from the letters by Wolfowitz and Stan Crock that were posted on the *New York Times* website in connection with Libby's sentencing in 2007 ["Letters to Judge Reggie Walton," 62, 361].) Drury too now labels Libby a Straussian (Shadia Drury, "Gurus of Endless War," *New Humanist* 122, no. 3 [May/June 2007], http://newhumanist.org.uk/1463). In addition to holding two high-level posts—chief of staff and national security adviser—under a powerful vice president, Libby served simultaneously as an assistant to President Bush (see Gellman, *Angler*, 41, 44, 50, 364, 376, and Woodward, *Plan of Attack*, 48–49).

63. Recall Gottfried's claim that most "prominent Straussians" (not "neoconservative Jews") are preoccupied with "American support for the Israeli right."

64. Even an Israeli who put his party above his country would reasonably be chastised. See *WIPP* 80–81, *CM* 47, and Epilogue 310/*LAM* 206 on how the classical political philosopher differs from the partisan; cf. *NRH* 192.

65. Gary Dorrien, *Imperial Designs: Neoconservatism and the New Pax Americana* (New York: Routledge, 2004), 132 (cf. 16); Dorrien even notes Wolfowitz's cameo in *Ravelstein* (64).

66. As recounted above, George includes "Thrasymacus" [*sic*] when attempting to designate the ancient authors Strauss regarded as sources of "foundational and universally valid meaning" (George, "Leo Strauss," 178). Perhaps George was groping for Thucydides.

67. Scene 6, "The Road to Babylon." As Pearly continues, he worries about how "the masses" will respond to the American deaths that the battle against "evil" will cause.

68. Jonathan Swift, *Gulliver's Travels* (New York: Penguin Books, 1977), 92.

69. See Allan Bloom, *Giants and Dwarfs* (New York: Simon & Schuster, 1990), 39, 44–46.

70. Urinating "within"—not *over*—the palace was proscribed as "high treason" (Swift, *Gulliver's Travels*, 92, 104), but not as sacrilege. Seventeen years after her original error, Drury—in the introduction to the 2005 reprinting of *PILS*—finally provides an accurate specification of the fire's location (the queen's apartment). She also speaks more carefully about the danger: "When

Gulliver realized that fire could destroy the whole palace, and *maybe even* all of Lilliput . . . he acted quickly" (*PILS*-05 xxxix; emph. added). Swift, however, never suggests that all of Lilliput was threatened; perhaps Drury added the "maybe even" phrase, consciously or unconsciously, to conceal the more flagrant errors that marred her earlier discussions.

71. The Hong Kong based *Asia Times* averages almost three million readers per month, most of them in North America (http://atimes01.atimes.com/mediakit/readership.html). It pitches itself to movers and shakers, not to fringe activists: "Our readers are people of influence—investors, company executives, decision makers, academics and journalists—who need to know about Asian political, economic and business affairs. We have become a 'must read' for Westerners and Asians who do business with each other" (http://atimes01.atimes.com/mediakit/index.html).

72. Jim Lobe, "Neocons Dance a Strauss Waltz," *Asia Times*, http://www.atimes.com/atimes/Middle_East/EE09Ak01.html; a more elegant version (dated 12 May 2003) is available at http://www.fpif.org/fpiftxt/817.

73. "The condemnation of this comic Socrates is not to be blamed on the prejudices of the Lilliputians; it is a necessity that no amount of talk or education will do away with" (Bloom, *Giants and Dwarfs*, 45).

74. Jim Lobe, "Leo Strauss's Philosophy of Deception," http://alternet.org/story/15935. Lobe's presumptuous proclamations, however, are less embarrassing than some of the blunders in an *Asia Times* article to which Lobe provides a link. According to the long exposé that Pepe Escobar published shortly after the invasion of Iraq commenced, Strauss "died in 1999 as a 100-year old" (http://www.atimes.com/atimes/Middle_East/EC20Ak07.html). Since Escobar has exaggerated Strauss's lifespan by roughly a third, it is less surprising that he links Strauss with neoconservative agendas for the Middle East.

75. Lobe's wording seems to suggest that "Straussian world order" is an analogy, though the dominant analogy here involves Gulliver's urinating on the palace.

76. Swift, *Gulliver's Travels*, 87–88. Also significant is a plan sketched by Lilliput's Treasurer and Admiral to have 20,000 archers shoot Gulliver with poisoned arrows (106). Drury's 2005 introduction to *PILS* prudently emphasizes that the need to sleep renders Gulliver more vulnerable (xxxiv).

77. In his 1968 book, *Gulliver's Troubles*, Stanley Hoffmann used Gulliver's adventures in Lilliput as a metaphor in addressing U.S. foreign policy; for an application to queer studies, see Yoshino, *Covering*, 61.

78. John Mason, "Leo Strauss and the Noble Lie: The Neo-Cons at War," *Logos* 3.2 (Spring 2004), http://www.logosjournal.com/mason.htm. Mason consistently leaves work for the reader in translating his French interjections as well as in penetrating his innumerable misspellings and garbled sentences. For the record, his article was first published by the magazine *Critique* (March 2004) in French; Mason is a political scientist at William Paterson University in New Jersey and a Visiting Scholar at the NYU Center for European Studies. The editorial board of *Logos* includes such luminaries as Stephen Eric Bronner, Dick Howard, Douglas Kellner, and Francis Fox Piven.

79. Bloom, *Giants and Dwarfs*, 46, 42.

80. Swift, *Gulliver's Travels*, 105.

81. Bloom, *Giants and Dwarfs*, 45.

82. Bloom, *Giants and Dwarfs*, 47; Swift, *Gulliver's Travels*, 202–3, 206–7.

83. Bloom, *Giants and Dwarfs*, 51.

84. Bloom, *The Closing of the American Mind* (New York: Basic Books, 1987), 294 (on Lilliput) and 293–98 (on Laputa). In his introduction to the 1952 translation of his book on Hobbes, Strauss says that Lilliput and Brobdingnag serve to represent modern and ancient (*PPH* xv); at *TM* 309n51, Strauss says that the same relation is "imitated on a different plane" (on a philosophical level, I presume) in parts III and IV. Strauss elsewhere highlights the Houyhnhnms (*PAW* 23).

85. Bloom, *Giants and Dwarfs*, 40; Swift, *Gulliver's Travels*, 130.

86. Swift, *Gulliver's Travels*, 148, 152, 155–56, 160, 161–62.

87. Swift, *Gulliver's Travels*, 161–62, 156.

88. Shadia B. Drury, "Leo Strauss and the Grand Inquisitor," *Free Inquiry* 24, no. 4 (June/July 2004), http://www.secularhumanism.org/index.php?section=library&page=drury_24_4.

89. Fyodor Dostoevsky, *The Brothers Karamazov*, trans. Constance Garnett (New York: Vintage Books, 1955), 295; cf. 297. The more meticulous translation by Richard Pevear and Larissa Volokhonsky (San Francisco: North Point Press, 1990) suggests that the heretics were burned "at once," that is, simultaneously (248).

90. When Strauss sketches the "variety of phenomena" that constitute persecution, he identifies the Spanish Inquisition as representing "the most cruel type" (*PAW* 32), and he elsewhere credits Machiavelli for having diagnosed its "inhuman and cruel" character (*WIPP* 44; cf. *TM* 157, 186–88). In his essay on Plato in *HPP*, Strauss does suggest that we "consider Dostoyevsky's *Grand Inquisitor* in the light of Plato's *Statesman*" (*HPP* 47); Drury, however, does not stoop to consider what Strauss actually wrote, in a prominent place, about the key text.

91. Recall Drury's repeated warnings about "Strauss's followers" at the conclusion of her entry in the *Routledge Encyclopedia*.

92. Drury staked out this terrain in 1997 when she elevated Nietzsche's supermen, who are "bewitched" by their own "illusions," above "Strauss's liars who fancy themselves gods playing pranks on mere mortals" (*LSAR* 80).

93. Drury's condescension grates further because of her repeated exaggeration in including Wolfowitz among Strauss's "self-proclaimed disciples."

94. Cf. pp. 68–69 above on the "the most fearful depths of depravity" inhabited by anyone who views morality the way that Strauss did.

95. When Drury says that the condemnation followed rather than preceded the exposition, she overlooks the initial condemnation.

96. These citations and (unless otherwise noted) my remaining in-text and footnote citations reference the above-described Garnett translation of *The Brothers Karamazov* (Drury uses an excerpted version of this translation).

97. Before even introducing the Inquisitor, Ivan points out that Jesus "comes on the scene in my poem, but He says nothing, only appears and passes on" (293). Alyosha later asks about the silence, and Ivan explains as well as confirms it (297). The Inquisitor too comments on it (296–97); in addition, he twice commands Jesus to speak (305, 307) and at the end he waits painfully for Jesus to offer a reply (311). Before encountering the Inquisitor and being arrested, Jesus did say two words—"Maiden arise!"—when He miraculously revived a dead child on the steps of the cathedral (296).

98. Except at the conclusion, where Jesus simply approaches the Inquisitor "in silence" and kisses him, the chapter never portrays Jesus as making any kind of movement (e.g., nodding, blinking, or closing/rolling His eyes). At one point, the Inquisitor comments, "Thou lookest meekly at me and deignest not even to be wroth with me" (298); he later asks, "Why dost Thou look silently and searchingly at me with Thy mild eyes?" (305), and Ivan eventually tells Alyosha that, throughout the encounter, Jesus had listened intently with a gentle facial expression (311). According to Thomas G. West, the kiss means that Jesus forgave the Inquisition (West, "Sins of the Father," *Claremont Review of Books*, Fall 2002, 28–31).

99. Pevear and Volokhonsky supply a still milder translation: "firm ancient law" (255) rather than Garnett's "rigid ancient law." Cf. Drury, *Aquinas and Modernity*, 64–66, 118, 164.

100. Within *The Brothers Karamazov*, chapter 3 of book XI includes a particularly dramatic scene in which Alyosha's quasi-fiancée, Lise Hohlakov, asks him whether the Jews "steal a child and kill it" at Easter. She proceeds to describe a book about the trial of a Jew who took a four year old and "cut off the fingers from both hands, and then crucified him on the wall, hammered nails into him and crucified him." During the trial, furthermore, the Jew "said the child died soon, within

four hours. That was 'soon'! He said the child moaned, kept on moaning and he stood admiring it" (710).

101. Glenn Greenwald, "The President Receives 'Lessons' from His Neoconservative Tutors," posted on 14 March 2007 at http://www.salon.com/opinion/greenwald/2007/03/14/roberts_luncheon/index.html.

102. Drury, "Making," 24. I do not find the surface bland, and I hope Drury is not humiliated that her work is being deconstructed by a lower-tier acolyte. Since my "academic career" has yet to collapse, Drury could not even allow that I am "a schmuck with a mind" (25). The article is posted on Drury's website (http://phil.uregina.ca/CRC/).

103. Drury, "Making," 25.

104. Shadia Drury, "Saving America."

105. Shadia B. Drury, "Gurus of the Right," *Literary Review of Canada* 8, no. 10 (Winter 2000/2001): 19–22. Drury makes a similar accusation against Francis Fukuyama in her 1994 book: Fukuyama "cannot see anything worthy in the quest for equal and mutual recognition" and "regards even the most modest demands for equality as having no legitimate foundation whatsoever" (*AK* 191). What stands out here, and elsewhere, is how Drury starts with a manifestly false slur and then piles on intensifiers—"anything," "even the most modest," "no . . . whatsoever." The *End of History* is long, but even a quick reading suffices to undermine Drury's hasty and hostile interpretation: on Fukuyama's appreciation of egalitarian concerns, see 155, 193–200, 203–5, 292, 338 ("liberal democracy in reality constitutes the best possible solution to the human problem"). Some of these passages focus on Hegel, a key source for Fukuyama's approach to history and recognition: for Hegel, argues Fukuyama, "liberal society is a reciprocal and equal agreement among citizens to mutually recognize each other," and Fukuyama seems to regard such liberalism as "the pursuit of *rational recognition*" (200).

106. Stephen Holmes, *Anatomy*, 80 (1323 of the *TLS* version).

107. Frazer, "Esotericism," 54.

108. Only the moderns are so "crazy" as to believe that the creation of work of art is "more worthy of wonder and more mysterious than the reproduction of a dog" (Strauss to Löwith, 20 August 1946 [#36], *GS* 668; the line also appears on pp. 112–13 of the German-English version published in the *Independent Journal of Philosophy*).

109. *PILS*-05 liii, note 10. After suggesting implausibly that Norton is a Straussian, albeit of the "Academy" rather than the "activist" stripe, Drury provides this dismissive distillation: "The whole point of the book is to distance Strauss from the belligerent political Straussians in the Bush administration, whom she claims were trained by Allan Bloom—the real villain in her story." If only Norton had confined her invective to this tiny cohort.

110. Larry N. George, review of *Leo Strauss and the Politics of American Empire*, by Anne Norton, *Political Theory* 34, no. 3 (June 2006): 401.

111. Carnes Lord, *The Modern Prince: What Leaders Need to Know Now* (New Haven, CT: Yale University Press, 2003).

112. David Schaeffer, "Ass," 293. For other sharp critiques of Norton, see Orwin, "Straussians," and James Costopoulos, "Anne Norton and the 'Straussian' Cabal: How *Not* to Write a Book," *Interpretation* 32, no. 3 (Summer 2005): 269–81. Although Schlesinger laments the effect that Strauss's "German windbaggery" has had on "more empirical thinkers," he is suckered into thinking that Norton's book is "well informed" (Arthur Schlesinger Jr., "The Making of a Mess," *New York Review of Books* 51, no. 14 [23 September 2004]: 40).

113. Schaeffer touches on the "tracking" issues, and provides a thorough rebuttal of several other accusations Norton levels at Lord, including the following: Lord has "argued that American statesmen should take authoritarian leaders as their models, and that the American people should develop a taste for a more authoritarian regime" (*LSPAE* 208); and Lord "can't find a good word to say about the redoubtable Maggie Thatcher" (*LSPAE* 64). For Lord's encomia to Thatcher, see *MP* 6, 10, 138.

114. Matthias Küntzel, "Ahmadinejad's Demons," *New Republic*, 24 April 2006, 15–16.

115. If it is shown that the victims were not corrupt, however, the killer[s] are obliged to pay financial restitution to the families of the victims. The *basiji* are proud to count President Mahmoud Ahmadinejad, who often appears wearing a black-and-white *basiji* scarf, among their alumni. See Küntzel, "Ahmadinejad's Demons," 15; and Nazila Fathi, "Iran Exonerates Six Who Killed in Islam's Name," *New York Times*, 19 April 2007.

116. The tripartite rubric that Earl Shorris offers in summarizing Strauss's "work and legacy" accommodates the admirable books that Strauss's "wondrously scholarly mind" helped generate (Shorris, *Politics of Heaven*, 172), but Shorris also spews slander. Seth Benardete, Shorris concedes, was "a scholar who inspired scholars"; but "the others, whom we know as Straussians, were concerned with power and inspired war" (Shorris highlights Bloom and Mansfield); Benardete also stands out from "the other Straussians" because he could . . . laugh (175, 176). Shorris adds that Bloom was "quite simply, an indefensible man" (182) and that academic Straussians, at least those in "positions of power," survive via "invective and tenure" (172n4).

117. On Schaub, see *LSAPE* 87–91; cf. Costopoulus, "Anne Norton," 272.

118. Although Norton extols Cropsey and Lerner, two "students of Strauss" (*LSPAE* 23) with whom she studied, she would presumably place herself primarily among the "political theorists interested in Strauss's work" (6).

119. Norton's error about Robert Kagan was apparently absorbed and amplified by Arthur Schlesinger Jr., who counts him among "the students of Strauss and Bloom" (Schlesinger, "Making," 40). In specifying Straussians who "regularly surface" in the news and are "open and frank about their intellectual heritage," Workman includes Perle and Wolfowitz while citing Norton's "compelling account of the Straussian connections to the Bush administration" (Workman, "When Might Is Right," 137, 160n2). One should compare Norton's confusing initial account of Perle's Straussian lineage (*LSPAE* 17) with her later move from a slanderous paragraph alleging "Straussian" persecution and vilification of Arabs and Muslims to a slanderous paragraph alleging such vilification in *An End to Evil* (*LSPAE* 210–11). Cf. pp. 33–34 above.

120. In a 2 March 2005 lecture at Columbia University, Norton states that she has heard "anti-Semitic slurs" directed against Muslims and/or Arabs "virtually every day since the day I went to college" (http://www.earthinstitute.columbia.edu/events/foreignpolicy/video.html). Although she thus increases the frequency by suggesting a *daily* phenomenon, she does not blame Straussian persecutors and she confines herself to auditory "slurs" rather than the "unrestrained persecution" she claims (in her book) to have "seen."

121. Wolfowitz's essay, "Statesmanship in the New Century," appears on pp. 307–36 of *Present Dangers: Crisis and Opportunity in American Foreign and Defense Policy*, ed. Robert Kagan and William Kristol (San Francisco: Encounter Books, 2000).

122. *LSPAE* 162; emphases added.

123. For a Straussian's reflections on his nine-month employment in Bagdhad, see John Agresto, *Mugged by Reality: The Liberation of Iraq and the Failure of Good Intentions* (New York: Encounter Books, 2007). Despite Norton's pervasive terminological confusion, the reviewer in *Ethics* exults that her book "explicates the core meaning of the term 'Straussian'" (Bart Schultz, *Ethics* 115, no. 4 [July 2005]: 838).

124. Lilla too scapegoats *NRH*, complaining that its "effects on Strauss's American disciples have been stultifying" (Mark Lilla, "Closing," 56).

125. Drury, "Esoteric Philosophy," 323. This is the only *question* on my list of Drury's most foolish formulations.

126. Emphases added. See Corey Robin, "In the Shadow of Tyranny," *New Statesman*, 13 June 2005, http://www.newstatesman.com/200506130041; Robin is reviewing *LSPAE*.

127. The Free Press hardcover edition of the book was published in 1963. Sari Nusseibeh, the Palestinian scholar and activist who has been both imprisoned and widely slandered in Israel,

describes Mahdi as "one of the world's great authorities on Islamic political philosophy." After Mahdi had persuaded him to read Strauss's "brilliant commentary" on Farabi in *PAW*, Nusseibeh almost wrote his PhD thesis on Farabi (Nusseibeh, *Once Upon a Country*, 145). In 1991, Amnesty International declared Nusseibeh a Prisoner of Conscience (325). In 2002, a scholar at Hebrew University criticized him in a noxiously titled newspaper article: "Sari Nusseibeh—Arafat's Mouth, but Saddam's Eyes and Ears" (469).

128. Paul Wolfowitz, "Bridging the Dangerous Gap between the West and the Muslim World," 3 May 2002, http://www.defenselink.mil/speeches/speech.aspx?speechid=210. The speech was delivered at a conference in Monterey, California.

129. See, for example, http://www.newamericancentury.org/balkans_pdf_04.pdf; Dorrien, *Imperial Designs*, 36, 63–64; Halper and Clarke, *America*, 89–90; Douglas Murray, *Neoconservatism: Why We Need It* (New York: Encounter Books, 2006), 76; and Eric Schmitt, "The Busy Life of Being a Lightning Rod for Bush," *New York Times*, 22 April 2002.

130. See *MP* 12 on plebiscites, 58 on term limits, 67 on the rule of law, 72/82 contra Locke's "godlike princes," 214 on the need for executives to be good listeners, 218 on the "politics of individual performance and publicity seeking," 84 on parties, 131 defending the Constitution against legal positivism, 139 defending due process, and 228 decrying the decay of "political engagement" and "deliberative processes." As will be elaborated below, Strauss once complained that President Kennedy was making an end-run around the Senate Foreign Relations Committee.

Chapter Six

"Untold Mischief" and "Enigmatic Works"

Appreciating Strauss on Machiavelli and Modernity

What other thinker has presented so many facets to the students of his ideas?

—Isaiah Berlin

I. "PERILOUSLY CLOSE TO INSANITY": FLYNN ON SPINOZA AND MACHIAVELLI

We have previously examined Daniel Flynn's attempt to depict Strauss as moron, on political grounds, for praising imperialism; Flynn likewise protested the "Straussian reading of intelligence" that helped propel the United States into Iraq. Flynn, however, also wants to ridicule Strauss's core enterprise as a scholar. Even in attacking Strauss's hermeneutics, Flynn accuses its followers of having "stirred up untold mischief" and of making their students "ignorant" (136). After responding to Flynn's charges with special emphasis on Spinoza and Machiavelli, the bulk of this chapter will highlight Drury's critique of Strauss's Machiavelli. *Thoughts on Machiavelli* is Strauss's longest book, and it has aroused endless controversy. In discussing it I shall do more than I have done in other chapters to contrast Strauss's interpretations with those of other scholars, and to show how far Strauss goes in pursuing an author's "indications."

Flynn thinks he nails Strauss by presenting the following statement, allegedly drawn from *PAW* 161, about interpreting Spinoza: "one is at liberty, and even under the obligation, to disregard Spinoza's own indications."[1] Anyone who has seriously studied Strauss and the history of philosophy—even an inveterate critic of Strauss—would quickly recognize that the quoted clause *clashes* with the common principles of Straussian hermeneutics. To present Strauss as a disrespectful reader, Flynn had to switch the first two words, to omit the qualifying words that commence the sentence, and to ignore its place in Strauss's argument.

Although Strauss's exposition in part I of the relevant essay is complex and often dialectical, he had just spent pages *condemning* the common historicist interpretations that blithely disregard Spinoza's own indications. Along the way, Strauss recommends that one proceed from *Spinoza's* view that "the whole 'history' of his works, the whole historical procedure as employed by the modern students of his works, is superfluous; and therefore, we may add, rather a hindrance than a help to the understanding of his books" (*PAW* 149); for those books to "disclose their full meaning," the reader must "devote all his energy to the understanding of Spinoza" (152); we can understand Spinoza only "if we open our minds, if we take seriously the possibility that he was right" regarding his belief that he had provided "*the* true account of the whole" (154); the "books of men like the mature Spinoza, which are meant as possessions for all times, are primarily addressed to posterity" (160).[2] According to Strauss's account, one possesses the liberty and duty to "disregard Spinoza's own indications" only *after* ascending from Spinoza's statements and completing the arduous—and I should add, much ridiculed—process of painstaking reading.

Let me offer only a selection of additional warnings that Strauss issues in preparing the conclusion Flynn quotes. All knowledge that Spinoza "did not supply directly" must be "integrated into a framework authentically or explicitly supplied by Spinoza himself." Any "extraneous" knowledge—for example, knowledge about Spinoza's life, his character, his interests, his sources, the occasion and time that framed his composition, or the addressees of his books—"can never be permitted to supply the clue to his teaching except *after* it has been *proved* beyond any reasonable doubt that it is *impossible* to make head and tail [*sic*] of his teaching as he presented it." As always, Strauss warns the reader against trying to understand the author "better than he understood himself" before one has understood him "as he has understood himself" (*PAW* 159). The interpreter "must follow the signposts erected by Spinoza himself," beginning from a clear vision, "based on *Spinoza's explicit statements,* of Spinoza's predecessors *as seen by Spinoza.*" One must likewise do one's "utmost" not to "go beyond the boundaries drawn by the terminology of Spinoza and of his contemporaries" (161). After this meticulous build-up, Strauss presents a thirty-six-word sentence from which Flynn misquotes the final fourteen words: "Only *after* one has *completed* the interpretation of Spinoza's teaching, when one is confronted with the *necessity of passing judgment on it,* is one at liberty, and even under the obligation, to disregard Spinoza's own indications."[3] Had Flynn not reversed the phrase "is one," he would have been forced to confront the conditional tone of Strauss's suggestion that one "disregard" Spinoza's indications.

Flynn likewise stumbles embarrassingly when he draws on Strauss's attention to chapter numbers in Machiavelli to assert that, as a general matter, "[s]ome numbers, such as seven and thirteen, alert Strauss to a text's hidden meaning."[4] To regard seven and thirteen as *general* keys to hidden meanings would be moronic, but no interpreter who is even moderately well-informed would attribute such an approach to Strauss. Before the Iraq War, counting was perhaps the primary activity for which Straussians were mocked, so Flynn's complaint warrants a response.

Flynn cites no evidence for Strauss's alleged concern for the number seven. Strauss does emphasize seven in interpreting Maimonides, who in fact divides many of his works using multiples of seven. The *Guide of the Perplexed* has seven sections, which are in turn divided into seven subsections or chapters (*WIPP* 166, *LAM* 142); the *Treatise on the Art of Logic* has fourteen chapters (in addition, it implicitly divides philosophy/science into seven parts, it explains 175 [7 X 25] terms, and its seventh chapter discusses fourteen rules of valid syllogisms); and the *Misneh Torah* is divided into fourteen books (although the content of the two groups differs, both the *Misneh Torah* and the *Guide* also divide the commandments into fourteen groups) [*WIPP* 165].[5]

Regarding thirteen, Flynn quotes—with two errors—the following passage from *HPP* 286 (Flynn omits the "of" in the third sentence and the comma before *fortuna* in the last sentence):

> The *Prince* consists of 26 chapters. Twenty-six is the numerical value of the letters of the sacred name of God in Hebrew, the Tetragrammaton. But did Machiavelli know of this? I do not know. Twenty-six equals 2 times 13. Thirteen is now and for quite sometime has been considered an unlucky number. So "twice 13" might mean both good luck and bad luck, and hence altogether: luck, *fortuna*.

Flynn then unleashes a paragraph full of unwarranted indignation:

> This borders perilously close to insanity. What evidence is there that Machiavelli paid any attention to the precise number of chapters in *The Prince*, let alone included that many chapters to deliver an encrypted message about luck or God?[6]

Flynn's boldness is especially ludicrous because he does not appear to have read any of Strauss's writings on Machiavelli; Flynn draws the key quotation from McAllister's book about Strauss and Voegelin. Flynn brings the reader to the precipice of "insanity" and then asks the question about evidence while being oblivious to the fact that Strauss has answered it.

In discussing chapter numbers in Machiavelli, Strauss's chapter on Machiavelli in *HPP* starts with the *Discourses on the First Ten Books of Titus Livy*.[7] The *Discourses* presents itself as a commentary on Livy's *History of Rome*, and it turns out that the number of "books" in this *History* (142) is identical to the number of chapters in the *Discourses* (*HPP* 279).[8] Strauss proceeds to sketch how, in his opinion, Machiavelli's "use and non-use of Livy is the key to the understanding of the work" (*HPP* 280), a work that perhaps every serious reader regards as puzzling.[9] A few pages later, in the paragraph Flynn attempts to quote, Strauss reminds us that "the number of chapters of the *Discourses* is meaningful and has been deliberately chosen" (*HPP* 286); Strauss proceeds immediately to ask about *The Prince*. Strauss's answer starts with the quoted passage about the numbers twenty-six and thirteen. The paragraph eventually asks "whether we cannot get some help from looking at the twenty-sixth chapter of the *Discourses*." Lo and behold, this chapter bears an uncanny and momentous resemblance to *The Prince*: both highlight the new prince in the new principality, and both avoid using the words "tyrant" or "tyranny." The prior chapter (I.25) indeed indicates that absolute power (*una potestà assoluta*), "which the writers *call* tyranny" [emph. added], will be the theme of the next chapter.[10] Elsewhere in the *Discourses*, Machiavelli does refer to tyrants and tyranny, disparage them, and argue that republics are superior to principalities. So it is eminently sane to speculate about a connection between twenty-six and "prince." The twenty-sixth chapter of the *Discourses*, moreover, contains the only quotation from the New Testament that Machiavelli provides in either book: *qui esurientes implevit bonis, et divites dimisit inanes* ("who filled the hungry with good things and sent the rich away empty"). By applying the quoted words to David—rather than to God as Mary does in Luke 1:53—Machiavelli manages to convey "a most horrible blasphemy": that God is a tyrant whom human princes should imitate (*HPP* 287). The insult is aggravated because Mary is speaking the quoted words as a prayer to God after the angel Gabriel has revealed that she will bear God's Son, mankind's redeemer.[11] Whereas David makes this memorable *Discourses* appearance in the twenty-sixth chapter, he makes his sole *Prince* appearance in the thirteenth chapter, which also includes the book's sole explicit reference to the Bible. As Strauss sketches in a footnote (*TM* 329–30n10), Machiavelli *inverts* the message of the David and Goliath story by omitting David's reliance on divine assistance. To conquer the luck/fortune often associated with the number thirteen, readers may infer, we should rely upon our "own arms" rather than God.[12]

II. THE MACHIAVELLIAN MOUTHPIECE

Although we cannot blame Flynn's major blunders on Drury, she is one of the main secondary sources he relies upon, and she has certainly helped propagate the "Straussian equals Machiavellian" equation on a global scale. In the course of assessing Drury's discussion of Strauss's Machiavelli, I shall argue that its shortcomings also tarnish her approach to Strauss's account of the ancient/modern "quarrel."

When addressing and assessing Strauss on Machiavelli, Drury is less outrageous than she is with Strauss's Plato, Xenophon, and Thucydides.[13] Fewer misquotations and citation errors leap off the page; nor does she seem to yank passages out of context. But the contradictions and accusatory exaggerations remain abundant, and the topic is of special importance given Machiavelli's alleged role as the founder of modernity—and given Drury's claims that Strauss and his disciples are Machiavellian in the old-fashioned and simple sense.

It is in her chapter titled "Machiavelli's Subversion of Esotericism" that Drury renews the fateful interpretive decision that guides *PILS* (and her later studies): "Here, as throughout this book, I will continue to ignore any serious contribution Strauss might have made to the history of political thought" (114).[14] As elsewhere, her neglect of the text compromises her interpretation of the commentator.

Drury begins by addressing the scholarly reaction to Strauss's *Thoughts on Machiavelli*, which appeared in 1958. She attempts to boil the common view of Strauss's agenda down to two themes: although Machiavelli "writes boldly and without any technical language" and his writing "appears transparent and easy to read," Machiavelli has hidden his "true meaning"; and the thing Machiavelli is trying to hide is "the extent to which he is violently anti-Christian, morally unscrupulous and diabolical"; Strauss's Machiavelli is a teacher of evil, "far more Machiavellian than anyone ever dreamed possible." Drury diagnoses two "serious difficulties" with these interpretations of Strauss, but I find serious difficulties in her diagnosis, especially in her first objection: that as a writer Machiavelli is "regarded as one of the boldest and 'one of the most honest of all time'" (*PILS* 115).[15]

Drury acquired the claim about Machiavelli's honesty from Gaetano Mosca, via the scholarly "arms" of Dante Germino (*PILS* 231n5), who in turn is quoting James Meisel.[16] As Drury notes, Germino endorses Mosca's view, and she is also correct in claiming agreement from Pocock. Contra Drury, however, neither Herbert Butterfield nor Felix Gilbert invokes Machiavelli's alleged frankness against Strauss.[17] Drury elaborates her objection by posing several questions, including these two: "How much more boldly could Machiavelli have expressed himself? What more could he have said?" (*PILS* 115).

These questions point to a pivotal matter. As Drury knows, Machiavelli generally writes unpretentiously and without the notorious encumbrances of scholasticism; his major works are brimming with discussions of years, places, individuals, and other concrete phenomena. When Drury elaborates the consequences of his style, however, she distorts them: "As Strauss has told us, Machiavelli's books are esoteric in a way that is particularly ingenious and difficult to detect because Machiavelli *appears* to write so simply, clearly and openly, that everyone believes they understand them" (*PILS* 116). Drury correctly quotes Mansfield's claim that "almost all readers, and especially scholarly readers, believe they understand" *The Prince* and the *Discourses*.[18] Mansfield, however, is not Strauss, and Drury has no business here speaking of what Strauss "has told us."

I myself think that Mansfield exaggerates, having forgotten how challenging Machiavelli's twists, turns, and long accounts of forgotten people and places are for the vast majority of contemporary readers. Few individuals who scrutinize the original Italian or any literal translation are likely to describe the prose as consistently simple, clear, and open; the disjunctions between the titles and content of Machiavelli's chapters, especially in the *Discourses*, constitute another obstacle. Consider the description that translator Robert Adams offers of the Italian text of *The Prince*: although there are "epigrams and aphorisms with the brief, cruel point of a stiletto," more typical are "complex sentences overburdened by modifiers, laden with subordinate clauses, and serpentine in their length" (xvii).[19]

The scholarly readers who think they have understood Machiavelli with less than painstaking study typically deprecate Machiavelli's virtue as an author (he's sloppy with facts and especially with quotations, he's lax about consistency, his grammar is poor, etc.).[20] For better or worse, however, every time I read Machiavelli, I perceive problems, puzzles, allusions, jokes, and, especially in the *Discourses*, long sequences of "zig-zag" sentences that change course midstream. The jargon-free but detail-laden surface, of course, can make such maneuvers more difficult to notice. To someone corrupted by Straussian studies of Machiavelli, many of the conventional interpretations seem embarrassingly glib.

In Strauss's "What Is Political Philosophy?" essay, we encounter a different assessment from the one—Machiavelli appears to write "so simply, clearly, and openly"—Drury asserts that "Strauss has told us" (*PILS* 115). Strauss here states that the "honest and plain-spoken" founder of modernity is Thomas Hobbes, an Englishman who "lacked the fine Italian hand of his master," that is, Machiavelli (*WIPP* 48). For Drury, by contrast, the puppeteer is Strauss. If Machiavelli is just an honest and plain-spoken Italian, Drury can more plausibly claim that, rather than conveying a genuine interpretation, Strauss is using Machiavelli as a vehicle for articulating his *own* teaching of evil. In Drury's words, Strauss uses Machiavelli as a "mouthpiece" to "avoid pronouncing unpleasant, unsalutary and dangerous truths in his own name"; for Strauss, Machiavelli's "conception of the relationship between politics and morality" is the "true account" (*PILS* 117). Given her flippancy in dismissing Strauss's scholarship about Machiavelli, she thus insinuates that Strauss is inserting evil into the mouth of an innocent man.[21] Drury can indeed take credit for helping the label "Straussian" displace the label "Machiavellian"—and perhaps even "racist"—as a term of reproach in contemporary American politics. The controversy Strauss initiated by treating Machiavellianism as a clue to Machiavelli now pales before the controversy about Strauss's responsibility for Straussianism. Shakespeare's Machevil and Marlowe's Machiavel have yielded to Robbins's "Leonardo."

"The Tradition of Machiavelli"

In responding to Drury's questions about Machiavelli's boldness, I begin by pointing out the ignorance of Machiavelli displayed even by a literate, articulate, cagey, seasoned, and internationally celebrated scholar who has studied *TM*: Shadia Drury. In *PILS*, she writes that (according to Strauss) Marsilius of Padua "follows the tradition of Machiavelli" (218n89); perhaps she was merely unaware of when *Marsilius* lived (he was born roughly two centuries before Machiavelli). This "top ten" error is even more embarrassing coming from the hands of the widely acclaimed prince of Strauss studies. Every time one opens the second or third editions of *HPP*, there sits the chapter by Strauss on Marsilius right before the chapter by Strauss on Machiavelli; the chapter on Marsilius even ends with the word "Machiavelli," as Strauss looks ahead from the anticlericalism of Marsilius to the acute "antitheological passion" that induced Machiavelli to break with the classical tradition by questioning the supremacy of contemplation.[22] In a later chapter, Drury manages to identify Marsilius as a medieval, but proceeds to invoke Machiavelli while offering one of the most pathetic of her many inflammatory readings:

> Deferring to Aristotle in a rather scholastic manner, Strauss remarks . . . that a natural law that would suffer deformed children to live is certainly not natural, being contrary to Aristotle's judgment on the matter. It seems that Strauss cannot help agreeing with Machiavelli and Nietzsche that Christianity is inferior to pagan religion because it has the effect of rendering the world weak. (*PILS* 109)

Here is what Strauss actually wrote: "Among the rules which can metaphorically be called 'natural rights' Marsilius mentions the rule that human offspring must be reared by the parents up to a certain time; he may have regarded this rule as not unqualifiedly rational since Aristotle had held that no deformed child should be reared" (*HPP* 267/*LAM* 200). Drury herself emphasizes the importance, for Strauss, of distinctions between natural law and natural right[s], and this difference is accentuated by Strauss's use here of the adverb "metaphorically." Drury's error about natural law, however, is dwarfed by the transgression she commits in conflating Strauss with Marsilius. After pointing out that Drury's citation to *HPP* is erroneous (by more than thirty-five pages, in fact), Jaffa offers the following critique:

> Strauss does not, deferring to Aristotle, say that by the natural law deformed children should not live. He does not even say that Marsilius says this. What he says is that Marsilius *may* have thought the rule that commands parents to raise their children to a certain age was not unqualifiedly rational, because Aristotle had said that deformed children should not live. There is no justification for saying or implying that either Marsilius or Strauss advocated infanticide for deformed children,

or that in this either of them deferred to Aristotle. But Marsilius may indeed have doubted—because of Aristotle—the unqualified rationality of this precept. Whether Strauss agreed with Marsilius cannot in any way be decided from this passage.[23]

The gross inadequacy of Drury's sentence about Strauss and Aristotle itself erodes the credibility of the inflammatory sentence about Christianity that follows it; recall her chronological confusion in including Plato within the "secular alliance" Strauss associated with Farabi, Marsilius, and Machiavelli.[24]

As we have seen before, Drury often starts with a blatant mistake and then races into fantasy. How could any sober commentator read *HPP* 267 and presume to proclaim that Strauss was here "deferring to Aristotle in a rather scholastic manner"? What distinguishes this particular fiasco, however, is that Jaffa published his critique in August 1987, at least four months before *PILS* came out. Jaffa's article appeared immediately following Drury's own article ("Leo Strauss's Classic Natural Right Teaching") in the same issue of *Political Theory*,[25] based on a copy of a paper she had delivered in March of 1986. The phrasing in the book version differs slightly from the phrasing in the article. But every morsel of error, bluster, and silliness is preserved. Now, it is possible that *PILS* was published so early in 1988 that Drury did not have time to draw on Jaffa to make any corrections, however embarrassing her mistakes. But based on the opening of Jaffa's article,[26] it is also possible that she received it as an actual letter as early as April of 1986.[27]

Preservation Preeminence

The sympathy Drury conveys for the opinion that Machiavelli is "transparent and easy to read" (*PILS* 115) is further discredited by the superficial interpretation of Machiavelli that *she* provides in her 2004 book, *Terror and Civilization*. When she here summarizes his teaching, she trots out the most hackneyed of Machiavelli clichés: "In politics, the preservation of the state is the only good" (*TC* 48). The matter is particularly urgent because of her earlier insistence that for Strauss, Machiavelli's "conception of the relationship between politics and morality" is the "true account" (*PILS* 117). Her recent privileging of preservation is even more pitiable because she is addressing Machiavelli's entire corpus, not just *The Prince*. Now it is my turn to ask contemptuous questions (all of the italics are mine).[28]

- Wouldn't Machiavelli's maxim that war is "deferred to the advantage of others" (*Prince* III, 12–13) imperil the *preservation* of states that are persuaded by it to launch continual and indiscriminate attacks?
- How are states *preserved* when confronted by men like Moses and Cyrus who are "forced" to introduce "new orders and modes" to "found *their* state and *their* security" (*Prince* VI, 23)?

- How does the effort to *preserve* the state compare to the effort to *"regain* the state" by reinstilling "that terror and that fear in men that had been put there in *taking* it" (*Discourses* III.1.3)?
- Where is Machiavelli's decision elevating the Roman state/republic "that wishes to make an *empire*" over the Spartan one "for whom it is enough to maintain itself" (I.5.3)?
- Where are *"glories* and *riches*,*"* the "end that each has before him" (*Prince* XXV, 99)?
- Where is the prospect that "two virtuous princes in succession are sufficient to *acquire the world*" (*Discourses* I.20)?
- Where is the population growth needed by "[t]hose who plan for a *city* to make a great *empire*" via "love" and/or "force" (II.3.1)?
- Where are the domestic "tumults" that were necessary for Rome's *"expansion"* (I.6.3)?
- Where is the "public *freedom*" that followed in Rome from "those tumults that many inconsiderately damn" (I.4.1)?
- Where is the *"free* way of life" that enables states to *expand* in dominion and/ or riches (II.2.1)?
- Where are the "golden times when each can hold and defend the opinion he wishes" (I.10.5)?
- Where is the supreme praise/glory available only to "those who have been heads and orderers of *religions*" (I.10.1)?
- Where, finally, is the Machiavellian instruction that will help men "learn to be *content* to live under the empire that has been proposed to them by *fate*" (III.6.1)?

You see, Professor Drury, we Straussians are typically willing to spend copious time and energy trying to figure out how, in Machiavelli's mind, these and innumerable other passages mesh. We believe that Strauss's writings offer invaluable assistance in that endeavor. And if such passages cohere, we too are compelled to acknowledge the "graceful subtlety of his speech" (*TM* 13) however much we are troubled by particular statements and perhaps also by Machiavelli's larger project.

The example of Agathocles is especially significant regarding Drury's recent claim that for Machiavelli, "the preservation of the state is the only good." In an early footnote, Strauss straightforwardly explains how the criticisms of Agathocles in *The Prince*, chapter VIII that make Machiavelli's thematic discussion so contradictory (*TM* 47) are implicitly retracted in succeeding chapters. In the preceding chapter, Machiavelli had claimed that the direct and indirect killings Cesare Borgia engineered in the Romagna helped restore "peace and good government" to a chaotic region. But in depicting how Agathocles eliminated the elites of Syracuse to become king, chapter VIII does not even hint that

Syracuse was better off—that any preexisting "state" was "preserved"—by the slaughter of thousands that Machiavelli also offers as the model for "well-used" cruelty.[29]

Regarding Strauss's constantly ridiculed tendency to portray Machiavelli as a teacher of evil, finally, we must note that the core message of *The Prince*, according to Strauss, is about creating a state, not preserving it. "The chief theme of the *Prince* is the wholly new prince in a wholly new state, that is, the founder" (*HPP* 277). By reverting in 2004 to the crudest default reading of Machiavelli, Drury confirms that he provided fertile terrain for Strauss to plow.

"His Other Virtues"

I shall offer two more examples of the many one could marshal concerning how Strauss illuminated the depths of Machiavelli's boldness. First, on the basis of subtle attention to the wording of *Prince* chapter XVII, Strauss notes that Machiavelli does not merely defend the "inhuman cruelty" of Hannibal; Machiavelli calls it a "virtue" (*HPP* 275–76). In explaining why Hannibal was able to wage war in "alien" lands with "a very large army, mixed with infinite kinds of men" without dissension, Machiavelli identifies the cause with these words: *sua inumana crudeltà, la quale, insieme con infinite sua virtù, lo fece sempre, nel conspetto de' suoi soldati, venerando e terrible*. In English, thus: "his *inhuman cruelty*, which, together with *his infinite virtues*, always made him venerable and terrible in the sight of his soldiers." When the sentence concludes after a semicolon, however, Machiavelli casually identifies the cruelty *as* a virtue: *e sanza quella, a fare quello effetto, le altre sua virtù non li bastavano* ("and without it, his *other virtues* would not have sufficed to bring about this effect").[30] Machiavelli's boldness on this matter can easily be overlooked by readers who are lulled by the apparent repetition and/or who fail to ascertain the antecedent of *quella*. And the vast numbers who rely on several widely used English translations are condemned to obliviousness by the translators who summon the word "qualities" instead of "virtues" because they assumed it would be inconceivably bold for Machiavelli to allege that inhuman cruelty is a form of human excellence redolent of the moral virtues that Machiavelli is deconstructing in chapters XV–XIX of *The Prince*.[31] In the framework that chapter XV provides, Machiavelli famously contrasts the "vices" that can help the prince "save his state" (*salvare lo stato*) with liberality, mercy (*pietà*), faith, humanity, honesty (*integrità*), religiosity, chastity and other "qualities" (*qualità*) that are "held good" (*tenute buone*). The only references to *virtù* in chapter XVII are the three above-discussed references to Hannibal.

Machiavelli makes it easy for his readers to grasp the morally neutral aspects of Renaissance "virtue" when—in I, VI, and VII—he highlights the polarity between virtue (paired with relying on one's "own arms") and fortune (paired with relying on the arms of others). Additional elaboration comes when Machiavelli invokes the virtue of an archer's bow (VI), the bodily virtue of Agathocles (VIII), and the analogy between virtue and flood control (XXV). So readers are robbed when a translator deploys a variety of morally neutral terms (e.g., ability, prowess, skill, quality) to translate *virtù* and thus prevents them from reading with Machiavellian eyes.

The issues about wording in chapter XVII of *The Prince* are even more compelling because of Machiavelli's earlier equivocations about the virtue of Agathocles. His strongest criticism of Agathocles is that "one cannot call it virtue to kill one's citizens, betray one's friends, to be without faith, without mercy, without religion" (VIII, 35). As Strauss has suggested, however, Machiavelli proceeds to dilute if not abandon all of these constraints on what he will describe as virtue. Within the batch of chapters about the moral virtues, for example, Machiavelli emphasizes that princes often need to act "against faith, against charity, against humanity, against religion" (XVIII, 70). And whereas Machiavelli earlier protests that Agathocles' "savage cruelty and inhumanity, together with his infinite crimes" (*efferata crudeltà e inumanità, con infinite scelleratezze*) preclude him from being considered an "excellent" man (VIII, 35), he later celebrates Hannibal's *inumana crudeltà* as a virtue; the phrase *con infinite scelleratezze* ("with infinite crimes") about Agathocles likewise yields to *con infinite sua virtù* ("with his infinite virtues") about Hannibal. The first two sentences of the Agathocles chapter (VIII) impart ambiguity about the relationship between evil—acquisition modes that are *scellerata e nefaria* ("criminal and nefarious")—and virtue, and Strauss has provided the essential clue about how Machiavelli later resolves that ambiguity.[32] Needless to say, translators of *The Prince* tend to dilute its praise of both Agathocles and Hannibal.

Drury acknowledges Strauss's suggestions that enlisting the reader to solve such puzzles can be a strategy of persuasion, not just of concealment: "When the truth is kept hidden, it can only be discovered by effort. But once discovered, it is believed to be one's own." Drury suggests, not implausibly, that Strauss's "seductive method of teaching" is "modeled after the method he attributes to Machiavelli" (*PILS* 121). But credit should also go to Thucydides, Plato, and Xenophon.

"Against Faith"

My second example of the depths of Machiavelli's boldness is the "horrible blasphemy" Strauss unmasks in *Discourses* I.26. The blasphemy remains undigested by several scholars who have studied *TM* carefully and openmindedly. Such individuals, joined by countless others unfamiliar with or unpersuaded by Strauss, often remain under the spell of the strongly religious language that appears in writings for which Machiavelli did *not* claim comprehensiveness, particularly the Exhortation to Penitence;[33] many readers are also swayed by accounts of Machiavelli's receiving the last rites.[34]

The Exhortation, which was found in Machiavelli's handwriting among his papers, was never even given a title by Machiavelli, and there is huge uncertainty about both when and for whom he wrote it. Machiavelli had joined a religious confraternity, the Company of Piety, in 1495, but the sermon could have been delivered for some other group—or not at all. According to Robert Adams, furthermore, such performances did "not necessarily imply an unusual measure of religious devotion in the speaker; they were part of the complex and long-continued initiation rituals by which a society in which money, family, and seniority counted overwhelmingly, prepared young men for formal positions of leadership and decision" (119).[35] Although the document is not bereft of "Machiavellian" maneuvers, let me put the essential question to rest. No one who is even moderately persuaded by Strauss's reading of *The Prince* and the *Discourses* can regard the Exhortation as an expression of Machiavelli's actual views about God, the Holy Spirit, creation, gratitude, charity, liberality, mercy, usury, repentance, mortification, heaven, hell, blasphemy, lust, angels, worldly pleasure, the "hands of the devil" (*mani del diavolo*), the "snares of sin" (*lacci del peccato*), and "our Emperor Jesus Christ" (*imperadore nostro Cristo Iesù*).[36]

Those who regard Machiavelli as a pious Christian also cite various passages in *The Prince* (especially in XXVI) and the *Discourses* in which Machiavelli deploys religious language. They presume that in such passages Machiavelli is not simply pretending to be religious and thus following the forceful and highly irreverent advice he offers in chapter XVIII: that although the prince must stand ready to act "against faith, against charity, against humanity, against religion," he should strive to "appear all mercy, all faith, all honesty, all humanity, all religion," and "nothing is more necessary to appear to have than this last quality" (70–71). Christians, Muslims, and Jews are united in thinking that God is offended by individuals who, for the sake of worldly benefit, merely simulate piety.

Even if Machiavelli had not written the prefaces that mark off the special knowledge-claims of *The Prince* and the *Discourses*, I do not see how a sincere Christian could write either book.[37] On this matter, the burden falls on the scholars who perceive piety. Machiavelli's celebration of feigned religiosity is one key clue. And because that celebration presumes that people in general are religious—otherwise the pretense would be useless and would only serve to offend God—it is vastly easier to conceive why an atheistic Machiavelli would present numerous passages that seem religious than to conceive why a devout Machiavelli would present numerous passages that discredit religion.[38] If one adds the Inquisition to the equation, the burden of proof shifts still further.

I doubt that any post–World War II edition of the *Encyclopedia Britannica* contains a sentence more misleading than this one, from its article on Machiavelli by Roberto Ridolfi, the esteemed biographer: "there is hardly a page of his writings and certainly no action of his life that does not show him to be . . . basically religious."[39] Contra Drury, highly accomplished scholars continued to be swayed—dare I say suckered?—by Machiavelli's efforts to appear religious. Among the many available examples of naïve readings, let me offer two that were published in a prestigious journal by individuals who have paid serious and respectful attention to the studies produced by Strauss, Mansfield, Clifford Orwin, Vickie Sullivan, other skilled Straussian interpreters, and a variety of non-Straussian scholars who find Machiavelli irreligious.

Marcia L. Colish's Machiavelli exudes a Providentialism that embraces the ancient Romans as well as the modern ones: "For Machiavelli, God acts in history and His intervention and providence are forces to be reckoned with, along with fortune and necessity"; "God sent great leaders, like Numa and Scipio Africanus, to the Romans" (602); God "manifests His will through signs and portents" (indeed, "nothing important happens without them"); God also "manifests His power in His saints through their holy lives" (603); and Moses was of course "divinely commissioned" (605).[40] Cary J. Nederman, who wrote the Machiavelli entry for the *Stanford Encyclopedia of Philosophy*, stands out for the peaks of piety he detects in *The Prince*. Especially this book, says Nederman, teaches that God "decides who is to do His bidding" and that "perpetual political success is a sign of the divine gift"; Moses is the archetype "precisely because he was chosen by God but simultaneously used his own abilities to advance and fulfill God's plan" (621); virtue cannot be "realized without a supernatural gift" (625); "[t]hat some plan or wisdom stands behind fortune forms an article of faith in Machiavelli's thought" (628); "Machiavelli's God is one who has bestowed upon humankind every favor—from material goods and resources to speech and reason" and it is *The Prince* that "provides the key evidence for Machiavelli's Christian orientation" (629); "[t]he whole thrust of Machiavelli's political theory is the promotion of preparation for divine ordination" (637). Nederman is even sold on the sincerity of the book's concluding allegations that God was ready to assist the would-be liberator of Italy: "the sea has opened; a cloud has escorted you along the way; the stone has poured forth water; here manna has rained" (633).[41] Strauss, by contrast, notices that Machiavelli describes these events as extraordinary things "without example" and does *not* call them miracles. From such considerations Strauss infers that Machiavelli wishes to *deny* "the reality of those Biblical miracles and therewith . . . the reality of all Biblical miracles" (*TM* 73). How many brilliant and learned twentieth-century scholars have to flounder before we can admit that Strauss provided an urgently needed tutorial concerning the deviousness and depth with which Machiavelli addressed religion?

Even if you side with Ridolfi, Colish, Nederman, and their numerous allies, we can all marvel that 500 years of study and debate leave us with such diametrically opposed readings of the man who wrote the world's most famous political treatise. Whatever else one concludes, it should be obvious that Strauss gave Machiavelli maximal credit for having the subtlety of thought and expression that could yield such a bizarre legacy. Many academic titans conclude that Machiavelli is sloppy in both his thinking and his writing, but who will be scouring *their* works in the twenty-sixth century? Drury's skimpy appreciation of Machiavelli, coupled with her vendetta against Strauss, has left large parts of her argument marred by trivialization.

"Extreme Situations"

Drury's superficiality and carelessness also surface when she elsewhere impugns Strauss in the name of . . . Machiavelli. In interpreting the brief discussion in Aristotle's *Ethics* that presents all natural right as changeable, Strauss infers that "in extreme situations the normally valid rules of natural right are justly changed, or changed in accordance with natural right; the exceptions are as just as the rules" (*NRH* 160).[42] According to Drury, it is Machiavelli rather than Strauss who impugns such exceptions by calling them unjust. For Machiavelli, the prince must often "commit injustice for the greater good of the state or its preservation," and thus Machiavelli is sometimes "commended for daring to call injustice by its name" (*PILS* 102). As we have seen regarding Agathocles, Hannibal, and other examples, however, Machiavelli's daring more typically expresses itself when he *omits* concern for the welfare of "the state" and/or links slaughter and a variety of cruel actions with *virtue*. As Strauss emphasizes (*TM* 236), furthermore, Machiavelli fails in *The Prince* XV even to include justice among the "qualities that are held good" (the moral virtues that everyone finds "praiseworthy" in a prince); and whereas Machiavelli in XVI "could have contented himself with saying that the virtue of justice requires the sacrifice of the virtue of liberality," Machiavelli developed a thesis—the vice of stinginess is "preferable to the virtue of liberality"—that "seems to be unnecessarily shocking" (*TM* 239). In comparing Strauss and Machiavelli, finally, Drury fails to address the sequel paragraph in *NRH* where Strauss contrasts Aristotle with Machiavelli. It is Machiavelli who simply "denies" natural right because he "takes his bearings by the extreme situations," who "seems to derive no small enjoyment from contemplating" the deviations, and who is "not concerned with the punctilious investigation of whether any particular deviation is really necessary" (*NRH* 162).

"The Lowly but True Principles"

"How much more boldly could Machiavelli have expressed himself" (*PILS* 115)? Had Machiavelli not presented a variety of novel ideas in *stages*, readers would have quickly approached the summit of shock and his books might have been burned as well as banned.[43] Although Strauss in both *TM* (173) and

WIPP (46) dubs Machiavelli the founder of the Enlightenment, other comments highlight a contrary impetus. Because he is "a rebel against everything that is respected," Machiavelli "must certainly adapt himself to the taste of the vulgar, if he desires to get a posthumous hearing for his new modes and orders" (hence the "bias" he displays toward "the extreme and spectacular"). The "true opinion about the most general, the most comprehensive things can never become popular opinion," so Machiavelli faces a daunting challenge in attempting to "train his readers" to discover "the lowly but true principles which he can only intimate" (*TM* 132). In elaborating this challenge, Strauss presents his most clear and complete statement about how Machiavelli's boldness coexists with a deeper realm of his thinking that has escaped generations of readers. Machiavelli, says Strauss, appeals on different occasions to different principles that are "publicly defensible but which contradict one another":

> Thus he mitigates his attack on the Roman church by appealing to original Christianity. He mitigates his attack on Biblical religion by praising religion in general. He mitigates his attack on religion by praising humanity and goodness. He mitigates his analysis of the bad and inhuman conditions of goodness and humanity by cursing tyranny and by blessing liberty and its prize, the eternal prudence and generosity of a senate. He mitigates the impact of his unsparing analysis of republican virtue at its highest by paying homage to the goodness and religion of the common people and to the justice of their demands. He mitigates the impact of his unsparing analysis of the defects of the common people by his appeal to a patriotism which legitimates the policy of iron and poison pursued by a most ferocious lion and a most astute fox or which legitimates the kind of rule known traditionally as tyranny. (*TM* 132)

By skillfully investigating such contradictions—and by equipping us to conduct our own explorations—Strauss helps us see less of what Machiavelli *appears* to be, and more of what he *is*.[44]

In connection with Machiavelli's use of staging, mitigating, and related devices, we should consider another aspect of the rhetoric Strauss claims to have discovered: that Machiavelli "expresses with the greatest boldness such views as are tolerable to one party but he is very cautious in regard to views which have no respectable support whatever. More precisely, he conceals the ground on which he partly agrees with one party" (*TM* 34). Strauss later suggests that the sympathetic party within "the Christian republic" could be described as the Ghibellines, the "men who would have gone with Frederick the Second of Hohenstaufen." Speaking "more precisely," Strauss asserts that these individuals, who were ready to "attack ecclesiastical authority with more than masculine courage," would be subsumed under one or more of the following three descriptions: they "esteem the fatherland more than the soul"; "driven and perhaps blinded by passion for the liberty of their fatherland," they are "more attached to their earthly fatherland than to the heavenly fatherland"; they are "lukewarm Christians" (172).[45] In his "What Is Political Philosophy?" essay, Strauss provides a simpler overview. Machiavelli expected to succeed in influencing many "lukewarm Christians" who would choose fatherland over soul if the two came into conflict; they could "guarantee that his books would get some hearing" by making those books "publicly defensible" (*WIPP* 45–46). For "reliable allies in his war to the finish," however, Machiavelli was counting on a tiny group who would undergo a "full conversion" and would "gradually inspire, in favorable circumstances, the formation of a new ruling class . . . comparable to the patriciate of ancient Rome" (46). These "reliable allies" are presumably the high-level officers described in *TM*—but even they "inspire" rather than rule. To put it plainly, Machiavelli had to mitigate his campaign against religion not only by appearing to be religious on numerous occasions; in Strauss's account, he also had to exaggerate his patriotism—Strauss even notes the possible tensions between Tuscany and Italy—his admiration for Roman antiquity, and his zeal for republican liberty.[46] In the background are the conundrums posed by the prospect that Machiavelli hoped for a future in which princes could continue to manipulate the sentiments of believers.

Drury's blind spot regarding boldness is reflected in the title of her chapter, "Machiavelli's Subversion of Esotericism." She plunges further overboard when she links Strauss with the thesis that Machiavelli's "work . . . contains no exoteric philosophy, no salutary teaching, no noble lies, no pious frauds" (*PILS* 116). As the quotation about the "lowly but true principles" (*TM* 132) amplifies, however, Strauss argues that Machiavelli's work is pervaded by such doctrines, however much the surface teachings and lies/frauds ultimately fall short in being salutary, noble, or pious. Drury has bequeathed to the Web the claim that Strauss describes religion as a pious fraud, which he never does, but overlooks his statement that *Machiavelli* "has no moral or other objections to pious fraud" (*TM* 168). In *The Prince*, XXVI, indeed, Machiavelli pours on the piety and patriotism so profusely that the chapter was often described as rhetorical even before Strauss joined the debate. Mansfield's introduction even suggests that the infamous advice—about beating and subduing Lady Fortune—with which Machiavelli concludes the previous chapter is a fraud intended to exploit his hypermanly readers (xxiv).

III. ESOTERICISM, ANCIENT AND MODERN

Drury also flounders when she proceeds to claim that, for Strauss, "[t]he single most fundamental difference between the ancients and moderns is that the latter no longer believe in the need or the necessity of esoteric writing" (*PILS* 55); for Strauss, furthermore, "esotericism is identical to classical philosophy or ancient wisdom" (149) and Hobbes is "quintessentially modern precisely because he drops all decorum, all appearances and all esotericism" (142). Although Strauss describes him as "honest and plain-spoken" in comparison with Machiavelli (*WIPP* 48), Strauss elsewhere stresses the difficulties of unraveling Hobbes's "fundamental obscurities" (*WIPP* 182), particularly the challenge posed by his having provided four or five competing versions of his political philosophy—*De Cive*, the *Elements of Law*, the second half of *De Homine*, and the English and Latin versions of *Leviathan*.[47] If Drury were correct, furthermore, Strauss must have thought that Hobbes was sincere in all of his innumerable utterances about religion: for example, his claim that he is *certain* that his principles follow from the "Authority of Scripture," and his suggestion that he might seek to "preach Jesus Christ" to the native "Idolaters of America."[48] In fact, Strauss depicts Hobbes as an exemplar of "dry atheism" (*WIPP* 171) who had "no reason for believing in the authority of the Bible" (185). That Strauss regards Hobbes as an esoteric writer is additionally confirmed when Strauss plays with the prospect that each chapter of *Leviathan*'s third part—"Of a Christian Commonwealth"— refutes "one particular orthodox dogma while leaving untouched all other orthodox dogmas" (*PAW* 184n22). Strauss elsewhere suggests that contemporary scholars simply fail to grasp "the degree of circumspection or of accommodation to the accepted views that was required, in former ages, of 'deviationists' who desired to survive or to die in peace" (*NRH* 198–99n43).

Strauss explicitly and eloquently denies that key moderns regarded esotericism as obsolete when he laments the "common misunderstanding of the intention, not only of Machiavelli but also of a whole series of political thinkers who succeeded him":

> We no longer understand that in spite of great disagreements among those thinkers, they were united by the fact that they all fought one and the same power—the kingdom of darkness, as Hobbes called it; that fight was more important to them than any merely political issue. This will become clearer to us the more we learn again to understand those thinkers as they understood themselves and the more familiar we become with *the art of allusive and elusive writing which all of them employ*, although to different degrees. (*TM* 231, emph. added)

Although Strauss goes on to suggest that esotericism declined after the French Revolution, he finds powerful strands of it in Rousseau, as we shall soon discuss.

Drury in *PILS* seems to be groping to convey something Strauss explained lucidly in his famous essay, "Persecution and the Art of Writing": that "[a]fter about the middle of the seventeenth century an ever-increasing number" of philosophers who had suffered from persecution—*but not all modern philosophers*, we must infer—wished "to contribute to the abolition of persecution as such" (*PAW* 33). Because they sought "to enlighten an ever-increasing number of people who were not potential philosophers," it is "comparatively easy to read between the lines of their books" (34).[49] Although one of Strauss's footnotes offers Hobbes as a model of this new type of esotericism, another note places Spinoza among the practitioners of the older type.[50] The invocation of the "kingdom of darkness" at *TM* 231 echoes the claim in *PAW* about enlighteners who believed that "suppression of free inquiry" had been "accidental, an outcome of the faulty construction of the body politic, and that the kingdom of general darkness could be replaced by the republic of universal light" (*PAW* 33). In the words of Arthur Melzer, we should distinguish the "full-blown" esotericism that classical and medieval authors employed—partly or largely out of concern that "philosophic rationalism would harm society"—from the "relatively loose kind of concealment" characteristic of the Enlightenment thinkers who were concealing "primarily to avoid persecution and to ensure the survival and effectiveness of their writings."[51]

As we have seen, Drury tosses out accusations with such zeal that she often contradicts herself. She does so also regarding esotericism. On the one hand, she denies that, according to Strauss, Machiavelli and his modern successors perceived a "necessity" or even a "need" to write between the lines;[52] modernity for Strauss "is characterized above all else by its openness" (*PILS* 142). This denial reinforces her crude attempt to dismiss Strauss's scholarship as a screen for *his* corrupting teaching. Later in her book, however, she acknowledges that the "thoroughly modern" Locke, according to Strauss, retains "the moderation of speech characteristic of the ancient philosophers" and "thought it legitimate to use noble prejudices for a good cause" (*PILS* 144–45).[53] Insofar as "economism is Machiavellianism come of age" (*WIPP* 49), Locke obviously qualifies as a pivotal "modern" in Strauss's typology.

Regarding Strauss's alleged horror at the modern abandonment of esoteric writing, we should also note his attributions of evasiveness to two other influential moderns. "What Montesquieu's private thoughts were will always remain controversial" (*NRH* 164). And after quoting Rousseau's question about "la distinction des deux doctrines, si avidement reçu du *tous* les philosophes, et par laquelle ils professaient en secret des sentiments contraires à ceux qu'ils enseignaient publiquement" (*NRH* 258n15),[54] Strauss adds that Rousseau felt compelled to present his "philosophic or scientific" teaching with "a great deal of reserve" (*NRH* 260). Strauss also states that, according to Rousseau, "one may not only suppress or disguise truths devoid of all possible utility but may even be positively deceitful about them by asserting their contraries, without thus committing the sin of lying" (*NRH* 261n20).[55] Rousseau, furthermore, opposes the Enlightenment by reasserting "the crucial importance of the natural inequality of men in regard to intellectual gifts" and by reintroducing "Socratic wisdom" (262)—despite the novel forms of egalitarianism he conveys in the

Second Discourse and the *Social Contract*.[56] And surely Montesquieu is no less "allusive and elusive" than Rousseau.[57]

Although it contradicts her thesis that Strauss identifies modernity with the evisceration of esotericism, Drury does eventually concede that, for Strauss, Rousseau "followed the ancients" in thinking that political health "requires the support of religion" (*PILS* 153) and that science "must be kept secret from the common man" (*PILS* 154, quoting *NRH* 260).[58] Perhaps she forgot that just a few pages earlier she stated that for Strauss, "the moderns, following Hobbes, no longer believe that religion is necessary to the peace, order and stability of political society" (*PILS* 142).

Let us focus finally on *Beyond Good and Evil*, in which Nietzsche (says Strauss) "platonizes" by deploying "graceful subtlety as regards form, as regards intention, as regards the art of silence" (*SPPP* 175). When Drury asserts that, for Strauss, Nietzsche restores the noble lie (*PILS* 175) and "returned to the mendacity of the ancients" (*LSAR* 72), she amplifies her accusation of Strauss's mendacity at the expense of her attempt to expose Strauss's hidden critique of Machiavelli—that Machiavelli's main sin was initiating the openness that *defines* modern philosophy.[59] Nietzsche, after all, "inaugurated" the third wave of modernity (*WIPP* 54) that quickly hatched the "culmination" or "highest self-consciousness" of "[m]odern" thought (55)—and Nietzsche proclaimed that God was dead. Turning to the fruit that fell from the poisonous tree, I must also highlight the boundless grief that Straussians have received for attempting to extract secret teachings from the above mentioned thinkers (Machiavelli, Spinoza, Hobbes, Locke, Montesquieu, Rousseau, Nietzsche, etc.) along with other modern authors such as Montaigne, Bacon, Shakespeare, Descartes, Grotius, Shaftesbury, Hume, Smith, Franklin, Tocqueville, Mill, and various novelists.

IV. "VILIFIED FOR ALL TIME"?

Drury's flailings regarding esotericism are not coupled with the caustic denunciations I have been protesting in earlier chapters. But they reinforce her oft-stated and now widely echoed claim that the primary agenda of Strauss and his followers is to promote lies and the lying liars who tell them.

Contra Drury (*PILS* 115), the "results" of Strauss's inquiries into Machiavelli are far from commonplace. "Commonplace" also fails to acknowledge Strauss's sustained and rigorous critique of the influential scholarly attempts to define Machiavelli as "a passionate patriot or a scientific student of society or both" (*TM* 10).[60] George Mosse, whom Drury cites to illustrate how *TM* was criticized for ignoring both recent scholarship on Machiavelli and "the whole intellectual life of Italy at the time" (*PILS* 114, 231n3), likewise criticizes Strauss for defying "modern scholarship" by removing "the distinction between Machiavelli and Machiavellianism."[61] Strauss, however, has enhanced this distinction by differentiating among the Machiavellianisms of at least three separate groups: the lukewarm Christians (*TM* 172); the existing princes who can be freed from guilt (283–84); and the "highest officers" whom Machiavelli will recruit among the philosophers of the future (168, 297). "Commonplace" is a joke when applied to the agenda that Strauss adumbrates and Straussians (e.g., Mansfield, Tarcov, Sullivan, Christopher Lynch, and Leo Paul S. De Alvarez) have elaborated concerning Machiavelli's recruiting enterprise. Is it not *shocking* to claim that Machiavelli between the lines provided a sketch of Christian theology and how it could be politically "appropriated" during future centuries to advance human power and glory in *this* world?[62] Strauss hypothesizes that the theme of book 2 of the *Discourses* is the "critical analysis" of Christianity, an analysis that builds on "a certain similarity between warfare proper and spiritual warfare" (*TM* 102). Also remarkable is Strauss's claim that from III.35 on, Machiavelli's "own intention" becomes his "chief theme" (*TM* 153), conveying his "strategy and tactics" (106) and his efforts as a "captain" to recruit an army via books (154).[63] And who prior to Strauss highlighted the distinct groups that Machiavelli on different occasions meant to invoke with the pronoun "we," or suggested that Machiavelli sometimes used the words "prince" and "princes" to designate superhuman powers (47–48, 130)?

Comprehending Machiavelli is more than difficult, in Strauss's view: "Machiavelli expects his reader less to have read Livy and other writers than to read them in conjunction with the *Discourses* after he has read the *Discourses* once or more than once" (*TM* 121–22). Regarding the *Discourses*, Strauss even asserts that at best he has only "pointed the way which the reader must take in studying Machiavelli's work" (174); he has not provided a full interpretation of any of the 142 chapters (303–4n48). Drury is correct to conclude that Strauss showed "daring" in arguing that "only the most meticulous scholarship and the most laborious attention to detail can begin to uncover the arcane thoughts of Machiavelli" (*PILS* 115). But such daring pales before Drury's presumption in presuming to unmask Strauss—via *sloppy* scholarship and via *inattention* to key details—as an evil captain with a rampaging posthumous army.

Reading Strauss as he reads Machiavelli and others, the conspiracy buffs should carefully scrutinize *TM*, the works of Machiavelli and Livy, and other texts to uncover perhaps how *Strauss* recruits, spreads out his criticisms of current modes and orders, boldly attacks positions when he can appeal to some public support, and so forth. And they should contemplate how hard it is, according to Strauss, to understand Machiavelli: "to achieve clarity about his use of Livy is an infinite task: its completion would require complete understanding of every sentence of the *Discourses* and of Livy" (*TM* 104).[64] Maybe, as Drury implies, activist Straussians treat this as a pious fraud and feel confident in abandoning such studies so they can proceed in hypnotizing leaders to promote religious fundamentalism, oppress minorities, subordinate women, and foment world wars. But most Straussians are professors minding their own business: teaching, reading, and writing.

To imitate Machiavelli, whose project allegedly began at home—with the "Italian-reading youth" (*TM* 171)—would have been particularly daunting for an émigré like Strauss writing in a foreign language. If Strauss were seeking captaincy along Machiavellian lines, in any case, he has employed many more "sites" (*TM* 155) than did Machiavelli, whose primary text was Livy. Drury makes a point of not applying to Strauss the controversial techniques he deploys as an interpreter.[65] There is room here for an interesting debate, but Drury's decision is fatal because of *her* manifest and numerous failures to provide accurate citations and quotations, to acknowledge the context of quotations, and to eschew ungrounded invective.

V. "UNDER THE SPELL OF CHRISTIANITY"?

Consistent with her unsound claim that Strauss's Machiavelli eschews "pious frauds" (*PILS* 116)—and with her unforgivable assertion that Strauss had "little or no appreciation of the inner dimension of faith" (*LSAR* 56)—is Drury's attempt to ridicule Strauss for concluding that Machiavelli "is very much under the spell of Christianity" (*PILS* 123–24). Taken literally, this lazily worded claim is outlandish, since Strauss's Machiavelli is basically an atheist. Drury presumably intended to say that, according to Strauss, Machiavelli was overly impressed by the worldly successes that Christianity achieved via doctrines, ceremonies, and institutions—and *without* help from God.[66] But in presuming that Machiavelli managed, without divine assistance, to create posthumously *his* unprecedented modes and orders, how could Strauss complain that Machiavelli overestimated the successes of Christianity?

By exaggerating Machiavelli's attachment to Christianity, furthermore, Drury mischievously or inadvertently provides additional support for her thesis that, according to Strauss, "what Machiavelli hides is not so much the extent to which he is anti-Christian, but the extent to which he is opposed to the pagan tradition of Greek philosophy" (*PILS* 118). Does Drury think that Strauss was unaware that while almost no one calls Machiavelli a Platonist, generations of learned scholars have been seduced into thinking he was a Christian?[67]

Because of the numerous occasions in *The Prince* and the *Discourses* when Machiavelli invokes God and praises religion, the atheistic Machiavelli Strauss portrays is energetically hiding his true views. On the whole, Machiavelli's opposition to Greek philosophy is *more* obvious because of the thoroughness with which he erases as well as defies it. He neither pretends to favor the Greek classics, nor counsels princes to do so. Nowhere in his books does he mention

Socrates and other landmarks of Plato's dialogues.[68] In *The Prince* and *Discourses*, Plato appears only as failed teacher of conspirators (*TM* 327n187), and Aristotle too is mentioned but once.[69] Befitting the Roman focus of the *Discourses*, Cicero is more prominent, making three appearances. On only one of them (I.4.1), however, does Machiavelli address Cicero as a thinker/author rather than as a political actor; as Strauss points out, it is ironic that Cicero's *On Friendship* is invoked to conclude Machiavelli's praise of the "violent strife" between the Roman plebs and nobles (*TM* 95).[70] Despite Machiavelli's interest in Rome, he never mentions Polybius, and the latter's views are warped when Machiavelli silently appropriates them in *Discourses* I.2 (*TM* 290–91). The *Art of War*, we may add, never mentions Plato, Aristotle, Cicero, or even Xenophon. In both *HPP* (291) and *TM*, Strauss emphasizes the relative respect with which Machiavelli cites and characterizes Xenophon: Machiavelli "may be said to start from certain observations or suggestions made by Xenophon and to think them through while abandoning the whole of which they form a part" (*TM* 293). Preparing this claim about abandonment, however, Strauss highlights Machiavelli's decision to ignore Xenophon's Socrates and to limit himself to the *Hiero* and especially the *Cyropaedia* (*TM* 291).[71]

Despite these obvious facts about Machiavelli's treatment of Socrates, Plato, Xenophon, and Aristotle, Professor Benedetto Fontana indignantly elevates Machiavelli, who intended "to use the ancients in order to educate the newly emergent people to self-rule and to self-government," above Strauss, who intended "to use *these very same texts* in order to maintain the people in their condition of disaggregation and fragmentation" (emph. added). Fontana here not only fails to grasp Machiavelli's belittlement or abandonment of Socrates, Plato, Aristotle, Polybius, and Cicero; he also depreciates Machiavelli's overwhelming attention to Livy among the ancient "texts." Has Strauss in any way used *Livy* to "maintain" popular "disaggregation and fragmentation"? Fontana embarrasses himself further when he proceeds to assert that Machiavelli "teaches the necessity of lying, of 'simulation and dissimulation,' openly and truthfully to the people, while Strauss teaches secretly and esoterically the necessity of the 'noble lie.'"[72] As the Zuckerts have so amusingly elaborated, Strauss is a veritable whistleblower when it comes to unmasking centuries of noble lies. And it is Strauss who first demonstrated how Machiavelli systematically failed to "openly and truthfully" discuss his main resource (Livy) among the ancient texts that Fontana invokes. Needless to say, Strauss also cites and quotes his sources vastly more truthfully than most of the critics I have been confronting.

Although Strauss emphasizes the diverse devices Machiavelli used to conceal his real views, Strauss pronounces that Machiavelli made a "complete break with the Biblical tradition" (*TM* 142). His break with classical political philosophy, however profound, was tempered in at least two respects. First, argues Strauss, Machiavelli was the "heir" to its great art of writing (120). Second, Machiavelli also adopted its public-spirited and "politically responsible" orientation against classical hedonism (291–92).

Why would Machiavelli, in Strauss's opinion, do more to conceal his opposition to Christianity than his opposition to the Greek philosophers? Insofar as religion was an infinitely more dangerous enemy, Machiavelli had compelling reasons, contra Drury, to conceal his antireligious side more than his anticlassical side. The "hazardous character of Machiavelli's campaign," writes Strauss, is illustrated by his explicit and implicit emphasis in *Discourses* II.5 on the contrast between the pagan Romans—who, as Machiavelli had earlier indicated, adopted Juno from the conquered Veientes (I.12.1)—and "the Biblical religion," which attempted to destroy paganism, particularly in connection with images and idols (*TM* 143). Islam "conquered by force" (*TM* 144) and, we may add, was thereby able to impose Arabic. But Christians, as Machiavelli says, were impelled to retain the Latin language because "they had to write this new law with it." Given "the other persecutions they made," a new language would have allowed them to eliminate all records of "things past." Machiavelli highlights the contributions of Saint Gregory (i.e., Pope Gregory I) in "burning the works of the poets and the historians, ruining images, and spoiling every other thing that might convey some sign of antiquity" (*Discourses* II.5.1).[73]

In thinking about Gregory, we are indebted to Strauss's reminder that Savonarola praised him for having burned the works of Livy; hence, Machiavelli's "first task" in the *Discourses* was to "establish the authority of Livy and, prior to this, the authority of classical Rome" (*TM* 92).[74] By later highlighting Machiavelli's opening promise to address "all those books of Livy that have not been intercepted by the malignity of the times" (*Discourses*, Preface), Strauss (at *TM* 143) reminds us that Livy's *Histories* had powerful *human* enemies.[75]

Pocock concedes merit to Strauss's efforts to unearth a hidden critique of the Bible, yet remains unconvinced that Machiavelli harbors "full-fledged paganism or atheism";[76] by invoking paganism, Pocock reveals another failure in his effort to understand Strauss, who emphasizes that the enthusiasm for Roman polytheism that Machiavelli displays is merely a stage (*TM* 175). Like so many others attached to a middle way, Pocock even clings to the possibility Machiavelli thought the Christian ethos was "valid" yet inaccessible in "a historical and political world."[77]

According to Drury, Strauss blames Machiavelli for having "accelerate[d] the Christian revolt against the aristocratic tradition of Greek philosophy" (*PILS* 118). Here again, alas, Drury ignores Strauss's far-reaching elaborations of the ground that Christianity shares with the ancients. "The classics," according to Strauss, "demand that the end of civil society be the practice of moral virtue" (*TM* 255); they refuse to "accept as authoritative the end which all or the most respectable states pursue" (256). Did Christianity rebel against such attempts to elevate justice, wisdom, and the common good above worldly wealth, power, and glory? In abandoning concern for the soul and its "proper order" (*TM* 294), Machiavelli abandons both Christianity and classical political philosophy. Whereas the latter "understood the moral-political phenomena in the light of man's highest virtue or perfection" (295), and Christians look up to God, Jesus, and heaven, Machiavelli ridicules *ozio* (idleness/leisure) and directs our attention to the fox and the lion. Departing from both traditions, Machiavelli "understands man in the light of the sub-human rather than of the super-human," giving "free rein" to "the passionate concern with the goods of chance and the goods of the body."[78] With his path-breaking abandonment of "fixed ends," Machiavelli renders man "as it were infinitely malleable" (297); in departing from understandings of nature that give man "a definite place within the whole, a very exalted place" (TWM 85), Machiavelli tramples on both Jerusalem and Athens. Despite their antagonism, biblical "righteousness is obedience to the divinely established order, just as in classical thought justice is compliance with the natural order" (TWM 86).[79] The pernicious forms of utopianism that Strauss traces to Machiavelli likewise defy both orientations:

> The philosophers advise us to love fate, stern fate. The Bible promises us God's mercy. But the comfort which comes from God is as little pleasant to the flesh as is the love of fate.[80]

However much the Greek philosophers agreed with Machiavelli about the harshness of "human conditions"—and however much Jerusalem and Athens ultimately wrestle within "the Great Tradition"—the classics unite with the Biblical religions by combating acquisitiveness, inculcating self-restraint, and summoning self-improvement.[81] As Strauss observes in his "Restatement" with an obvious eye to both Machiavelli and Kojève, "[n]either Biblical nor classical morality encourages us to try, solely for the sake of our preferment or our glory, to oust from their positions men who do the required work as well as we could" (*OT* 205). Strauss acknowledges that Plato "does not hesitate to make his founder of a good society, the wise legislator, demand that he be supported by a tyrant." Other considerations aside, however, such a tyrant is "merely" a "helper or a tool for the wise and virtuous legislator." Plato thus "states with great caution the case for a tyrant preparing a republic in which moral virtue can be practiced," while Machiavelli substitutes republican virtue for moral virtue, emancipates acquisitiveness, and "even argues for tyranny pure and simple" (*TM* 293).[82]

Machiavelli, finally, also departs palpably from both traditions in his zeal to understand the low in terms of the high:

> Machiavelli is our most important witness to the truth that humanism is not enough. Since man must understand himself in the light of the whole or of the origin of the

whole which is not human . . . he must transcend humanity in the direction of the subhuman if he does not transcend it in the direction of the superhuman. (*TM* 78)

When Strauss used the identical phrase ("humanism is not enough") in a lecture published in 1956, he added that "[e]ither man is an accidental product of a blind evolution or else the process leading to man, culminating in man, is directed toward man" (*RCPR* 7).[83] Strauss elsewhere provides the following variation: "It is safer to try to understand the low in the light of the high than the high in the light of the low. In doing the latter one necessarily distorts the high, whereas in doing the former one does not deprive the low of the freedom to reveal itself fully as what it is" (*SCR* 2/*LAM* 225).[84] As the Zuckerts note, society is "both a means to bodily existence and a manifestation of the whole that transcends the individual"; despite their differences, philosophy and morality "share the concern with the noble, that is, with transcendence toward the whole" (*TALS* 175).[85]

Let me highlight one final failing in Drury's treatment of esotericism. For Strauss, Drury alleges, Machiavelli's esotericism "hides his conscious intention to subvert the wisdom of antiquity and to introduce 'new modes and orders'" (*PILS* 126). But Strauss *emphasizes* Machiavelli's recurring if sometimes muted boldness in proclaiming novelty. As Strauss observes in a particularly prominent place—the second paragraph of the *WIPP* section on "The Modern Solutions"—Machiavelli "compared his achievement to that of men like Columbus," claiming to have "discovered a new moral continent." Strauss adds that Machiavelli's claim to novelty is "well founded" (*WIPP* 40). In *Natural Right and History*, Strauss treats Hobbes as the founder of modern natural right, and acknowledges Hobbes's "astonishing claim" to be the founder of "political philosophy or political science" simply (*NRH* 166–67). Strauss nonetheless describes Machiavelli as "that greater Columbus, who had discovered the continent on which Hobbes could erect his structure" (*NRH* 177).[86] On the first page of his long chapter on the *Discourses* in *TM*, Strauss notes that at the beginning of the work Machiavelli "appears to proclaim the daring character of his enterprise without any reserve" (*TM* 85); Strauss then refers to Machiavelli as "a new Columbus" (87).[87] Even earlier in *TM*, furthermore, Strauss points out that "[t]he body of the *Discourses* opens with a challenge to tradition, with a statement proclaiming the entire novelty of Machiavelli's enterprise" (24), that is, his "boldness" in "questioning the established modes and orders and in seeking new modes and orders" (34). The parallel revelation in *The Prince*, by contrast, is "hidden away somewhere in the center" (24), although Strauss emphasizes its rhetorical impact: "No one, I believe, questions the common opinion that Machiavelli did doubt the common view regarding the relation between morality and politics, for every one has read chapters 15ff. of *The Prince*" (*TM* 43).[88]

VI. "THE INTREPIDITY OF HIS THOUGHT"

Strauss's obvious respect for Machiavelli's status as a thinker and a writer can also help us resolve the second puzzle Drury perceives in the standard view of *TM*: the admiration Strauss "seems to have for the man he has so unconditionally castigated" (*PILS* 115). We must first note how Drury yet again fails to follow the elementary rules of quoting and citing. According to Drury, Strauss "considers Machiavelli to have a spirit so 'intrepid' and a mind so 'noble' that they could not possibly be fathomed by the modern scientists of society who would claim him as their own" (*PILS* 115–16). For evidence, her footnote (231n6) cites *TM* 121 and 201. The second page is completely irrelevant, and the first merely distinguishes the "rules of noble rhetoric" from those of "vulgar rhetoric" (Strauss is lamenting that the translations of Machiavelli and other "great writers" have been so loose). Perhaps Drury was thinking of Strauss's claim in the introduction that what is "truly admirable" in Machiavelli is "the intrepidity of his thought, the grandeur of his vision, and the graceful subtlety of his speech" (*TM* 13).[89] Even on this page, however, there is no reference to the nobility of Machiavelli's mind or to social scientists. The citation errors are particularly significant because of the extreme language Drury uses to characterize Strauss's assessments of Machiavelli: Strauss applies "his severest condemnation as well as his most exalted praise."[90] In complaining that neither citation supports Drury's claim about the noble, the Zuckerts presumably dismiss the relevance of the discussion of noble rhetoric on *TM* 121. Seeking "the passage most praising of Machiavelli nearest to her citation," the Zuckerts charitably offer Strauss's claim on *TM* 120 that Machiavelli is a "not unworthy" heir of the "supreme art of writing" that the Great Tradition "manifested at its peaks" (*TALS* 294n66). Apart from this instance, the Zuckerts provide their potent critique of Drury without unmasking any of her ubiquitous errors in quoting and citing. The error they catch proves to be the spearhead of a whole column.

Strauss's praise of Machiavelli's thought, vision, and speech also reduces the temptation to demonize Machiavelli in reaction to Strauss's notorious criticisms.[91] Strauss designates him as the prince of the modern world, and concludes his book by "wondering as to what essential defect of classical political philosophy could possibly have given rise to the modern venture as an enterprise that was meant to be reasonable" (*TM* 298). Although it is likely that no prior scholar did as much to show how much the "evil" teachings of *The Prince* pervade the *Discourses,* we must also credit Strauss for suggesting that *The Prince* includes deliberate exaggerations. Because the "true addressees of *The Prince* have been brought up in teachings which . . . reveal themselves to be much too confident of human goodness, if not of the goodness of creation, and hence too gentle or effeminate," Machiavelli's "pupils must go through a process of brutalization in order to be freed from effeminacy" (*TM* 81–82). And just as soldiers often train with heavier bayonets, "one learns statecraft by seriously playing with extreme courses of action which are rarely, if ever, appropriate in actual politics."[92] Regarding several different issues, therefore, Drury exaggerates in saying that Strauss's Machiavelli is "far more Machiavellian than anyone ever dreamed possible" (*PILS* 115). As Mansfield and Tarcov suggest concerning Machiavelli's deconstruction of morality, Machiavelli seems to have anticipated that over the course of centuries many readers would revert to default positions.[93]

According to Vickie Sullivan, Machiavelli intended to become a scapegoat. Drawing on the discussion in *Discourses* II.5 of the man who would pervert the records of antiquity in order to acquire "a reputation and a name," Sullivan argues that Machiavelli "must have been aware that the notorious maxims" of *The Prince* and the *Discourses* "would certainly earn him a name from posterity"; neither book was published while Machiavelli was alive; he "willingly sacrificed himself for the benefit of humanity."[94] I suspect, finally, that even Drury admires Strauss for the cleverness with which he induced generations of scholars to dismiss him because of the moralism he conveyed in suggesting that Machiavelli was a "teacher of evil" (*TM* 9).[95]

To critics of Strauss's work on Machiavelli, I offer several concessions. As stated or implied by Strauss and by Straussians such as Mansfield and De Alvarez, the true Machiavelli is buried under such a mountain of marginalia that the burden falls on *us* to explain things clearly if we expect mainstream scholars to embrace our contributions. If we confine ourselves to hints because we doubt you are fit to handle the truth—or because we want you to have the exhilarating opportunity to solve the puzzles on your own—it would be ignoble to condemn your irritation.

There remains first the large task of elaborating the deeply buried "long-range" suggestions to the "young" about appropriating Christianity, and there also remains the gargantuan burden of fleshing out the historical processes by which Machiavelli's books were allegedly converted into the politics and culture of the modern world.[96] Along these lines, Strauss often speaks oracularly—for example, concerning Frederick II, the Ghibellines, the revival among Italian-reading youth, the possible destruction of West from Scythian irruption (*TM* 171), and the need to secularize the papal states (68)—in a way that invites further inquiry. And we Straussians would need assistance from conventional historians concerning these and many other points. Pocock's question is reasonable and deserves an answer: in Strauss's mind, did any earlier reader understand Machiavelli as thoroughly as he did?[97] If comprehending Machiavelli is almost an infinite task, however, there is no time for conspiracies. Fathoming philosophy and the permanent questions or problems is one thing. But to understand a detailed political agenda (e.g., Machiavelli's appealing to the followers of Frederick II or preparing for an eruption of Scythians), one must spend abundant time outside of the typical Straussian canon.

I cannot speak for the "great minds," but the rest of us face a dilemma when confronting Strauss. He repeatedly addresses textual puzzles and connections that would escape our notice, and suggests ever deeper levels of esoteric teachings. Many readers quickly become alienated and decide that their lives will not be scarred by a failure to dig any further; many readers react similarly to works such as the *Peloponnesian War*, Plato's *Laws*, the *City of God*, the *Summa Theologica*, the *Discourses on Livy*, Locke's *Essay Concerning Human Understanding*, the *Wealth of Nations*, the *Critique of Pure Reason*, the *Phenomenology of the Spirit*, *Das Kapital*, *Being and Time*, and the Hebrew Scriptures, not to mention lengthy classics in literature, history, and science. Only a few readers of Strauss are both able and willing to continue indefinitely on the paths that he sketches, which include lengthy detours into long-dead authors who wrote in many different languages. Once you step on the train, you may have trouble deciding when it is prudent to step off.[98] Individuals such as Paul Wolfowitz, in any case, exited early in the journey.

NOTES

1. Flynn, *Intellectual Morons*, 135. Shorris memorably invokes Spinoza while echoing Flynn's complaint about intelligence: "The Straussian method is to see what does not exist except to a Straussian. . . . The Straussians in the Bush Administration read the world as Strauss read Spinoza. They whispered what they divined into the ear of the president, and the president went to war" (Shorris, *Politics of Heaven*, 193).

2. The key interpretive difficulty is that Spinoza's own books fall between the two extremes—"hieroglyphic" or "essentially unintelligible" books like the Bible (*PAW* 148) and intelligible or "self-explanatory" ones like Euclid's (149–51)—for which he formulates rules of reading. In correcting his "insufficient rules of reading," the reader would still be guided by the "fundamental principles" of *Spinoza* (154) and "remain faithful to the spirit of his injunction" (159).

3. *PAW* 161; emphases added throughout.

4. Flynn, *Intellectual Morons*, 137.

5. Also see *LAM* 158, 172; on *LAM* 158, where Strauss discusses I.26 of Maimonides' *Guide of the Perplexed*, he comments that 26 is "the numerical equivalent of the secret name of the Lord, the God of Israel; 26 may therefore also stand for His Torah."

6. Flynn, *Intellectual Morons*, 137.

7. Strauss prioritizes the *Discourses* and *The Prince*—and strives to generate an interpretation that does justice to each of them—because only in these two books does Machiavelli begin with an epistle claiming that the respective book contains "everything that Machiavelli knows" (*TM* 17). In the short introduction to the new Modern Library collection, Albert Russell Ascoli honors Strauss by highlighting his and Arendt's critiques of Machiavelli. But Ascoli errs pathetically when he includes Strauss among the interpreters who deserve blame because they allegedly "identify Machiavelli with one text—usually *The Prince*, sometimes the *Discourses*." See *The Essential Writings of Machiavelli*, edited and translated by Peter Constantine (New York: Modern Library, 2007), xi. Even *TM*'s table of contents should suffice to refute Ascoli's charge.

8. Cf. *TM* 48–49. Also see *HPP* 284 on how the absence of a "proem" to book III calls attention to the distinction between chapters and proems and therefore to the number of chapters. On how and why Machiavelli discusses the entirety of Livy's *History* beyond the "first ten books" (*la Prima*

Deca) specified in Machiavelli's full title, see *TM* 49, *TM* 88–89, and *HPP* 279. Only 35 of the 142 books survive intact, though some of the lost books are available in summary form. In one of his three references to named scholars, Strauss invokes a Cambridge professor (and cites Petrarch) for the claim that it was "common knowledge that Livy's *History* consisted of 142 books" (*TM* 305n66). According to Adams, Machiavelli grew up with a copy because his father had prepared an index for a new edition (*The Prince*, 2nd edition, translated and edited by Robert M. Adams [New York: W. W. Norton & Company, 1992], 89–90). In belittling Strauss's "bizarre" numerological approach to the *Discourses*, Xenos skeptically mentions that work's "alleged correspondences" to Livy's *History* (*CV* 116). For Robert J. McShea and many others, 142 is merely a "curious" coincidence, though McShea concedes Strauss's point that Machiavelli deals with the whole of Rome's history, "far past the time of Augustus" (Robert J. McShea, "Leo Strauss on Machiavelli," *Western Political Quarterly* 16, no. 4 [December 1963]: 792). Some of Strauss's insights seem to have been incorporated into the mainstream: Peter Constantine opens his lengthy excerpts from the *Discourses* by pronouncing that Machiavelli is "mirroring" the 142 books of Livy (*Essential Writings of Machiavelli* 101).

9. Strauss elaborates Machiavelli's employment of Livy at great length in the third chapter of *TM* (e.g., at 90–91, 93, 96–104, 121–22, 141, 153–58).

10. *HPP* 286. As Strauss points out in *TM* 48, I.26 is also the only chapter in the *Discourses* whose title identifies the new prince as its theme. On the possible implications of I.26–27 for chapter XXVI of *The Prince*, see *TM* 67–69.

11. Strauss elaborates this Machiavellian view of God at *TM* 187–89. At least one scholar not hampered by Straussophobia has tried to refute the charge of blasphemy. See Dante Germino, "Blasphemy and Leo Strauss's Machiavelli," in Deutsch and Nicgorski, *Leo Strauss*, 297–307.

12. Strauss provides a detailed analysis of Machiavelli's understanding of fortune at *TM* 209–23. Also see *TM* 52 on how Machiavelli in *Discourses* I.10 goes out of his way to mention that there were twenty-six Roman emperors from Caesar to Maximinus, without explaining why he is addressing this particular collection. At *TM* 312n22, Strauss points out that there are thirteen chapters in the *Discourses* that begin with word "I" (*Io*); 315n37 notes that twenty-six of the forty-nine chapters in book III contain references to Livy.

13. On Thucydides, see pp. 261–66 below.

14. Drury first articulates this claim in her preface: "I shall ignore altogether Strauss's contribution to the study of the history of ideas" (*PILS* ix).

15. Drury's second objection concerns "the deep and apparently genuine admiration that Strauss seems to have for the man he has so unconditionally castigated" (*PILS* 115), and I shall respond to it below.

16. Dante Germino, "Second Thoughts on Leo Strauss's Machiavelli," *Journal of Politics* 28, no. 4 (November 1966): 816.

17. Felix Gilbert, "Politics and Morality," review of *Thoughts on Machiavelli*, by Leo Strauss, *Yale Review* 48 (1958–1959): 465–69. By describing Machiavelli as a "writer who has set one critic against another for a number of centuries" (728), Butterfield moves *toward* Strauss's orbit (Herbert Butterfield, review of *Thoughts on Machiavelli*, by Leo Strauss, *Journal of Politics*. 22, no. 4 [November 1960]: 728-30).

18. Harvey C. Mansfield, "Strauss's Machiavelli," *Political Theory* 3, no. 4 (November 1975): 372. As sketched above, Drury asserts that "[c]ommentators" generally attribute to Strauss the thesis that because Machiavelli "writes boldly and without any technical language, his writing appears transparent and easy to read" (*PILS* 115). Although Isaiah Berlin's well-known essay, "The Originality of Machiavelli," shares Drury's thesis that Machiavelli is stylistically straightforward, Berlin highlights the "violent" disparity among the interpretations, the "startling degree of divergence about the central view, the basic political attitude of Machiavelli." See Isaiah Berlin, *Against the Current* (New York: Viking Press, 1980), 25–36, 63–64, 79.

19. For recent non-Straussian discussion of how difficult it is to pin down basic Machiavellian terminology—for example, the fox, the lion, mercenaries, auxiliaries, and republics—see two articles by my colleague Timothy J. Lukes: "Lionizing Machiavelli," *American Political Science Review* 95, no. 3 (September 2001): 561–75; and "Martialing Machiavelli: Reassessing the Military Reflections," *Journal of Politics* 66, no. 4 (November 2004): 1089–108.

20. A particularly smug pronouncement issues from McShea: Machiavelli was not well educated, he had an "impatient and passionate character," and there are "numerous grammatical and spelling errors in the original manuscripts" (McShea, "Leo Strauss," 791). The translator of the new Modern Language collection, Peter Constantine, here aligns with Strauss: Machiavelli's manuscripts "reveal how carefully he edited his own work" (xviii); the "powerful, multilayered texture" of Machiavelli's masterpieces helps explain why his works have spawned so much debate and disagreement (xix); and *The Prince* is "one of the most enigmatic works in history" (this quotation comes from an unnumbered page preceding the translation).

21. On how Drury thus abandons her shortcut—attributing to Strauss "the ideas he attributes to the wise *ancients*" (*PILS* 15; emph. added)—see *TALS* 119 and Schaeffer, "Shadia Drury's Critique," 84. On the immunity of the commentator, see p. 120 above.

22. *HPP* 269; cf. *WIPP* 44, on "antitheological ire," and *TM* 327n187.

23. Harry Jaffa, "Dear Professor Drury," *Political Theory* 15, no. 3 (August 1987): 322.

24. See pp. 114–16 above.

25. Shadia B. Drury, "Leo Strauss's Classic Natural Right Teaching," *Political Theory* 15, no. 3 (August 1987): 299–315.

26. Jaffa, "Dear Professor Drury," 316.

27. In the book's preface, she warmly thanks Jaffa for his "long and untiring but always fascinating and open-minded correspondence" (*PILS* xv). *PILS* was reprinted in 2005 "as is" save for its appalling new introduction, which neither corrects nor acknowledges any of the book's errors.

28. Here, as elsewhere, I am using the University of Chicago Press editions of *The Prince* (1985) and the *Discourses* (1998). The former is translated by Mansfield, the latter by Mansfield and Tarcov.

29. There is no basis in either *The Prince* or the *Discourses* for Caranfa's claim that without this slaughter Agathocles "would not have been able to defend his city from the invading Carthaginians" (Angelo Caranfa, *Machiavelli Rethought: A Critique of Strauss's Machiavelli* [Washington, DC: University Press of America, 1978], 69). Agathocles in fact rose through the military to become the "praetor" of Syracuse *before* he killed "all the senators and the richest of the people" (*Prince* 34). Among the prominent neoconservatives mislabeled as Straussians is Michael Ledeen, whose book on Machiavelli—*Machiavelli on Modern Leadership* (New York: St. Martin's Press, 1999)—was highlighted on the floor of the House by Congressman Ron Paul (see http://www.house.gov/paul/congrec/congrec2003/cr071003.htm and Paul, *Foreign Policy*, 261, 265–68). If you are familiar with Strauss's Machiavelli, however, even a quick reading of Ledeen's book should enable you to dismiss the alleged association. Among the many tell-tale signs is Ledeen's claim that Machiavelli "denounces" Agathocles because he "maintained his personal tyranny by the continuous use of evil measures" (101). Near the end of chapter VIII, Machiavelli does attribute "infinite betrayals and cruelties" to Agathocles (*Prince* 37). But Machiavelli proceeds immediately to designate Agathocles as the exemplar of well-used cruelty, which is committed "at a stroke" and is *not* "persisted in"; "badly used" cruelties, by contrast, are few in the beginning but "grow with time." As Strauss explains at *TM* 309–10n53, the ambiguity-laden criticisms Machiavelli presents in his initial account of Agathocles are in effect retracted by his subsequent praise of Nabis (IX), good arms (XIV), Cyrus (XIV), Hannibal (XVII), and Severus (XIX). When Ledeen asserts that Machiavelli "spares no epithet in denouncing" tyrants (173), moreover, he displays his ignorance of the fact, loudly and widely conveyed by Strauss, that *The Prince* abandons the distinction between princes and tyrants. Even regarding the *Discourses*, Strauss articulates grim news: although the *Discourses* powerfully

states the "case for republics," it also instructs "potential tyrants in how to destroy republican life" (*HPP* 289; cf. *TM* 111, 266, 275, 282–83). For a detailed account of Ledeen's academic training, see http://www.frontpagemag.com/articles/Printable.asp?ID=11512. For adjacent photos of Strauss and Ledeen, see www.albionmonitor.com/0306a/index.html.

30. *The Prince* XVII, p. 67; emphases added. Two sentences later, Machiavelli repeats the reference to "his [Hannibal's] other virtues" (*l'altre sua virtù*). In *Discourses* III.22.6, Machiavelli moves from the "severity" of Manlius Torquatus, who killed his own son (III.22.4), to the suspicion that "your other virtues" (*l'altre tue virtù*) bring upon you (III.22.6). Livy includes "inhuman cruelty" when lamenting Hannibal's "great vices"; see Livy's *History of Rome*, XXI.4, http://mcadams.posc.mu.edu/txt/ah/Livy/Livy21.html; the posted version is from volume III of the Everyman's Library edition (London: J. M. Dent, 1905), translated by Rev. Canon Roberts.

31. See, for example, Peter Constantine, ed., *Essential Writings of Machiavelli*, 66; *The Prince*, trans. George Bull (New York: Penguin Books, 1975), 97–98; *The Prince*, trans. Russell Price (Cambridge: Cambridge University Press, 1988), 60; *The Prince*, trans. T. G. Bergin (Arlington Heights, IL: Crofts Classics, 1947), 49.

32. Also note *Discourses* II.18.2, where Hannibal is described as a "very excellent man" (*uomo eccellentissimo*). On other instances of staging between chapters VIII and XVII of *The Prince*, see *TM* 304–5n58.

33. Machiavelli, "Exhortation to Penitence," in *The Prince*, ed. Robert M. Adams, 119–22; for the Italian quotations, I am using Machiavelli, *Il teatro e tutti gli scritti letterari*, a cura di Franco Gaeta (Milano: Feltrinelli Economica, 1965), 209–13.

34. Regarding the rites, Strauss offers a quotation from Fichte: departing with all of the sacraments "no doubt was very good for the children whom he left behind as well as for his writings" (*TM* 329n2).

35. Sebastian De Grazia describes the piece as "carefully composed, probably late in life, for delivery to a confraternity" (De Grazia, *Machiavelli in Hell* [Princeton, NJ: Princeton University Press, 1989], 59).

36. Even Pocock regards the Exhortation as inconsistent with what "we know from non-esoteric statements": that Machiavelli was "profoundly at variance" with an "ethos of sin and repentance" (Pocock, "Prophet," 395). Mansfield may go too far in stating that the piece "is not quite an exhortation, but it is an invitation to do the things for the doing of which one must be exhorted to penitence" (Mansfield, "Strauss's Machiavelli," 375); Machiavelli neither generated the title nor speaks of exhortation anywhere in the text.

37. I would not even dream, however, of saying that Machiavelli—despite the inhuman cynicism of his main religious plank—had "little or no appreciation of the inner dimension of faith that is at the heart of religious experience," as Drury says of Strauss (*LSAR* 56). In my view, which has been profoundly shaped by Strauss, Machiavelli could not have provided such a devastating critique of religion, nor provided skillful simulations or parodies such as the Exhortation, had he been ignorant in this way.

38. Germino asks an important question regarding the Exhortation: "why would a zealous and committed atheist, aiming at the destruction of Christianity—the picture of Machiavelli we find in Strauss's pages—be willing to appear as a believer, indeed a fervent and pious believer?" (Dante Germino, "Second Thoughts," 799). As Machiavelli emphasizes, however, to "appear as a believer" can be an urgent political necessity, and it seems that Machiavelli delivered the Exhortation in a somewhat political setting. Nor did Strauss insist that Machiavelli intended to destroy Christianity. Consider what Strauss says about how "the imitation of ancient Rome would consist in using Christianity as a civil religion"; in departing from what Livy had written concerning the "chicken men" in *Discourses* I.14, for example, Machiavelli intended "to facilitate the imitation of the ancient Romans by modern men, an imitation which is compatible with the formal maintenance of the Christian religion" (*TM* 110). Cf. p. 242 above on "appropriation."

39. *Encyclopedia Britannica*, Macropedia, vol. 11 (Chicago: Helen Hemingway Benton, 1974), 230. Regarding Machiavelli's actions, one gets a different impression from Paul Rahe: "Among his associates, he was notorious as a scoffer. He so rarely attended mass that it was a subject of comment" (Paul A. Rahe, "In the Shadow of Lucretius: The Epicurean Foundations of Machiavelli's Political Thought," *History of Political Thought* 28, no. 1 [Spring 2007]: 44).

40. The quotations are all from Colish's above-cited 1999 "Republicanism" article. Colish also provides a long list of articles and books that posit genuine religiosity on Machiavelli's part (see 599n5–7).

41. All of these citations are from Cary J. Nederman, "Amazing Grace: Fortune, God, and Free Will in Machiavelli's Thought," *Journal of the History of Ideas* 60 no. 4 (1999): 617–38.

42. As she does so often, Drury leaps to identify Strauss with a doctrine that he is attributing to a text he is interpreting. Although I concede that Strauss is probably sympathetic toward positions he attributes to the "wise ancients," there is no excuse for her saying that Strauss here "insists" that the exceptions are as just as the rules (*PILS* 102). Her maneuver is even more problematic because Strauss is threading among three distinct "types of *classic* natural right teachings"—"Socratic-Platonic-Stoic," Aristotelian, and Thomistic (*NRH* 146; emph. added)—and because his discussion of the extreme situations unfolds only from a "suggestion" that he was "tempted to make" to resolve the clashing interpretations of Aristotle offered by Averroës and Aquinas (159).

43. On Machiavelli's use of stages, see *TM* 43–45; cf. 143 on Juno, and 226–27 on the modification of "first statements" about Rome's debt to Numa; Machiavelli even retracts his initial praise of religion's utility in combating the Terentillian law (see *TM* 228 on *Discourses* I.13 and I.39). For a sketch of the differences between first and later statements concerning morality, see *TM* 231–34 and cf. *PAW* 185.

44. Strauss also argues along mitigation lines in interpreting Spinoza's *Theologico-Political Treatise*: "To exaggerate for the purposes of clarification, we may say that each chapter of the *Treatise* serves the function of refuting one particular orthodox dogma while leaving untouched all other orthodox dogmas. Only a minority of readers will take the trouble of keeping firmly in mind the results of all chapters and of adding them up" (*PAW* 184). In a footnote after the first sentence, Strauss adds that "[f]undamentally the same procedure" is followed by Hobbes in *Leviathan*, part III (*PAW* 184n82).

45. The first two descriptions draw on the accusation Machiavelli relays in the *Florentine Histories* (VII.6, 283) that Cosimo de Medici was someone who "loved himself more than his fatherland and who loved this world more than the next" (*WIPP* 41).

46. Drury acknowledges how, in Strauss's account, Machiavelli often appeals insincerely to Livy to exploit the "prejudice in favour of antiquity" (*PILS* 123, quoting *TM* 136).

47. Strauss asserts that none "can be regarded as simply superior" and adds that Hobbes "never said or indicated that one of those different versions is the most authentic" (*WIPP* 173).

48. Hobbes, *Leviathan*, chap. 30, 378; chap. 46, 701. It is also easy to unmask noble lies that Hobbes proffers in nonreligious contexts: for example, that men are equal in wisdom because "every man is contented with his share" (chap. 13, 184); that nothing a sovereign does can be an "injury to any of his Subjects" (chap. 18, 232); that "in Monarchy, the private interest is the same with the publique" (chap. 19, 241); and that a parent's dominion over his or her child arises only from "the Childs Consent" (chap. 20, 253).

49. Given Pocock's insistence that the intricacy Strauss depicts in modern esotericism is laughably "occult" (Pocock, "Prophet," 392) one can only imagine how he would evaluate the methods Strauss claims to unearth in Maimonides.

50. *PAW* 34n15, 35n17. The longest chapter in *PAW*, furthermore, is the one that addresses Spinoza the modern, rather than the chapters on Maimonides and Halevi.

51. Arthur M. Melzer, "Esotericism and the Critique of Historicism," *American Political Science Review* 100, no. 2 (May 2006): 280, 289n6. For an illuminating historical overview, see

Paul J. Bagley, "On the Practice of Esotericism," *Journal of the History of Ideas* 53, no. 2 (1992): 231–47; also see Pangle, *Leo Strauss*, 72–74, and Rafael Major, "The Cambridge School and Leo Strauss: Texts and Context of American Political Science, *Political Research Quarterly* 58, no. 3 (September 2005): 477–85. Robert Howse emphasizes the distinction between exotericism and esotericism. An exoteric teaching is an "obscure or brief presentation of the truth" that is, "in principle, accessible to all thoughtful readers in all times and places," once they have penetrated the camouflaging "paradoxes, contradictions, and ambiguities." Whereas exotericism may be found in modern as well as ancient works, only the ancients (according to Howse's Strauss) also practice esotericism. The latter takes two forms, private *oral* instruction (see *PAW* 34–35) and the use of noble lies within largely exoteric books; it aims at "enlisting an army of nonphilosophical students and disciples in the political project of protecting philosophy and its reputation in the political community" (Robert Howse, "Reading between the Lines: Exotericism, Esotericism, and the Philosophical Rhetoric of Leo Strauss," *Philosophy and Rhetoric* 32, no. 1 [1999], 61). Lenzner, finally, maintains that Strauss "restricted his discussion of the distinction between exoteric and esoteric teachings almost exclusively to his work on the medievals"; he never speaks "in his own name" of an esoteric teaching provided by Plato, Aristotle, or Machiavelli (Steven J. Lenzner, "A Literary Exercise in Self-Knowledge: Strauss's Twofold Interpretation of Maimonides," *Perspectives on Political Science* 31, no. 4 [Fall 2002]: 229).

52. *PILS* 55, 116; cf. 149 on "why modernity can dispense with esotericism."

53. See p. 65 above on how Drury's mentor John Yolton condemned Strauss for alleging that Locke conveyed hidden teachings.

54. Here is my translation of Rousseau's phrase: "the distinction between the two doctrines [i.e., teachings], so avidly embraced by *all* the philosophers, and by which they secretly professed sentiments contrary to those they were publicly teaching." Strauss here cites the Hachette edition of Rousseau's collected works; as recently reported, Strauss is quoting from *Observations (Réponse au Roi de Pologne)*, which can be found in the third volume of the *Pléiade* edition of Rousseau. See Fabrice Paradis Beland, "An Update of Strauss's Notes and References in the First Part of the Chapter 'The Crisis of Modern Natural Right' in *Natural Right and History*," *Interpretation* 35, no. 2 (Spring 2008): 183, 187.

55. What Strauss states here in a footnote he addresses in the text of an earlier article in which he also cites—and draws key evidence from—the fourth promenade of Rousseau's *Reveries d'un promeneur solitaire* (Strauss, "On the Intention of Rousseau," *Social Research* 4, no. 4 [December 1947]: 469–70). Also see *NRH* 267n32 on Rousseau's equivocations concerning the "hypothetical" character of the state of nature and *NRH* 277n44 on "the moderate character of most of Rousseau's proposals which were meant for immediate application."

56. Cf. *WIPP* 53 on "the insoluble antagonism between the large majority who in the best case will be good citizens and the minority of solitary dreamers who are the salt of the earth." On Rousseau's pivotal contributions to modern thought, also see *NRH* 263, 281, 292–93; *WIPP* 51–52; *TWM* 89; *PILS* 157–58, 168.

57. On Montesquieu, also see *WIPP* 265 (*L'Esprit des lois* is "voluntarily obscure") and *PAW* 28–29. Perhaps Strauss would exclude Montesquieu and Rousseau from the category of "comparatively easy to read" philosophers who wrote after "about the middle of the seventeenth century" (*PAW* 33–34). In his posthumously published essay on Lessing, Strauss identifies Descartes, Leibniz, and Spinoza ("even so bold a writer as Spinoza") along with Lessing as men who had been "initiated" into the "tradition of exotericism" (*RCPR* 71).

58. On Locke's case for the utility of religion, see the passages that Strauss quotes at *NRH* 204n49 (from the *Second Reply to the Bishop of Worcester*) and 221 (from the *Reasonableness of Christianity*). It is reasonable to presume, furthermore, that Strauss was aware of Locke's famous condemnation of atheists in the *Letter on Toleration*: "the taking away of God, though but even in thought, dissolves all." Cf. *WIPP* 202 and 208 on Locke's criticisms of atheistic nations.

59. *PILS* 55, 116, 142, 149. Drury does appreciate the Platonism Strauss attributes to *Beyond Good and Evil* (*PILS* 179).

60. Did Machiavelli not say "enough to have himself vilified for all time?" (*PILS* 115). The above-mentioned scholars did not and do not vilify Machiavelli.

61. George L. Mosse, *American Historical Review* 64, no. 4 (July 1959): 954.

62. For an overview of Mansfield's approach, see Minowitz, "Political Philosophy and the Religious Issue." Kim Sorensen, regrettably, fails to provide a thorough discussion of the appropriation angle.

63. Strauss adds that each of the final chapters of the first two books (I.60 and II.33) comprises a distinct section that likewise sketches Machiavelli's own enterprise (*TM* 106; at 304n56, Strauss implies that he regards I.60 as the final section of book I, and he confirms this at 314–15n36). Cf. *TM* 22 and 72 on the "long range project" of the *Discourses*, 107 on Machiavelli's "exploration of hitherto unknown territory" to prepare its conquest by "his brothers," and 168 and 297 on the posthumous recruitment of the "highest officers."

64. Although Strauss hammers on the necessity of grasping Machiavelli's "use and nonuse of Livy" in order to fathom the *Discourses* (*HPP* 280; *TM* 90–91, 93, 96–104, 121–22, 141, 153–58), the allegedly Straussian Ledeen draws heavily on the *Discourses* without ever mentioning Livy (he does find time to discuss Patrick Riley, Michael Jordan, Roberto Baggio, Vince Lombardi, Leo Durocher, Bill Gates, Warren Buffet, Malcolm Forbes, Pope John Paul II, Federico Fellini, Bob Dole, Silvio Berlusconi, and Shaka Zulu). See Michael Ledeen, *Machiavelli.*

65. *PILS* ix; Drury, "Reply to My Critics," 2.

66. Drury initially asserts that Strauss criticizes Machiavelli for having been "seduced by Christianity" (*PILS* 117), and soon acknowledges that Strauss's Machiavelli deployed a "secular model" of Christianity (118). Cf. *TM* 84 on the great difficulty of understanding how Machiavelli can, "on the basis of his principles, account for the victory of Christianity." Also note the distinction Strauss draws between the "purely political" explanation offered by certain successors of Machiavelli (84) and the deeper but still secular explanations that Strauss thinks Machiavelli secretly provides (52). Cf. Larry Peterman, "Approaching Leo Strauss: Some Comments on *Thoughts on Machiavelli*," *Political Science Reviewer* 16 (Fall 1986): 339–48; and Thomas L. Pangle and Peter J. Ahrensdorf, *Justice among Nations: On the Moral Basis of Power and Peace* (Lawrence: University Press of Kansas, 1999), 138–39, 142–43.

67. In listing the various categories of men who are celebrated or praised, *Discourses* I.10 is silent about philosophers and even includes "the idle" among the individuals who are "infamous and detestable." Cf. the critique of philosophy Machiavelli delivers in a central chapter of the *Florentine Histories* (V.1, 185).

68. One may contrast Machiavelli (1469–1527) with his contemporary Thomas More (1478–1535); book I of *Utopia* (1516) celebrates Plato and paraphrases Socrates (28, 35–37), even though it dramatizes various forms of evil that pervade politics (Thomas More, *Utopia*, rev. ed., trans. Robert M. Adams [Cambridge: Cambridge University Press, 2002]). More also makes his character Peter Giles elevate ancient Greek contributions to philosophy above those of the ancient Romans, who "left us nothing very valuable except certain works of Seneca and Cicero" (10). Drury does acknowledge Strauss's emphasis on Machiavelli's erasure of "ancient philosophy" (*PILS* 130).

69. At *Discourses* III.26.2, Machiavelli casually notes that among the causes of "the ruin of tyrants," Aristotle includes "having injured someone on account of women." Even on this issue, Strauss suggests, Machiavelli does not fully endorse Aristotle's teaching (*TM* 343n192); cf. Sorensen, *Discourses*, 133. Plato's only appearance in the *Florentine Histories* comes at VII.6 (283), when Machiavelli describes Marsilio Ficino—the president of the Platonic Academy that the Medici founded in Florence—as a "second father of Platonic philosophy."

70. Strauss also notes that Cicero's status drops with each succeeding reference (I.33.4, I.52.3); in the final one, Machiavelli portrays him as having "ruined himself and his party by a grave error of judgment which could easily have been avoided" (*TM* 125).

71. It is difficult to understand why Xenos regards the *TM* 291 overview of Cyrus and Socrates as "cryptic" (*CV* 116). Janssens, meanwhile, exaggerates in asserting that Machiavelli was unaware of Xenophon's interest in Socrates (Janssens, *Between Athens and Jerusalem*, 237n72). On Xenophon's anticipations of Machiavelli, start with the indices of *XSD* and especially *OT*; also see *RCPR* 147. On this topic Drury does an admirable job (*PILS* 119).

72. Benedetto Fontana, "Reason and Politics: Philosophy Confronts the People," *Boundary 2* 33, no. 1 (Spring 2006): 34, 35. Cf. pp. 227–28 above on Drury's attempt to use Machiavelli as the exemplar of straight talk.

73. Although Machiavelli here also accuses "the Gentile sect" of attempting to persecute its predecessors, he had already acknowledged the Romans' embrace of Juno; as Mansfield and Tarcov note, furthermore, Livy abundantly documented the survival of the Etruscan language, writings, and religions (*Discourses* 139n4). In Strauss's words: "If we read somewhat more carefully Machiavelli's remarks concerning what the Romans did to the Tuscans, we see that the Romans did not destroy, and did not even attempt to destroy, the religion of the Tuscans; for instance, instead of destroying the image of the Tuscan Juno they made it their own. Hence Machiavelli's 'belief' that the pagan religion did to the preceding religion what 'the Christian sect desired to do to the pagan sect' is not more than a stage of his argument, a provisional thought which he discards almost immediately after he expresses it. . . . What remains as undeniable truth is the fact that Judaism and Christianity attempted to destroy every vestige of the pagan religion" (*TM* 143). In a footnote, Strauss adds that Machiavelli "could not help being aware of the fact that the Roman Church persecuted Judaism as well as paganism" (322n140). Cf. p. 219n90 above on the Inquisition.

74. In "On the Intention of Rousseau" (472n50), Strauss quotes (in French) from a provocative remark about Gregory that the final footnote of Rousseau's *First Discourse* offers while adumbrating the dangers of the printing press: "It is said that Caliph Omar, consulted on what should be done with the library of Alexandria, replied in these terms: If the books in this library contain things opposed to the Koran, they are bad and must be burned. If they contain only the doctrine of the Koran, burn them anyway—they are superfluous. Our learned men have cited this reasoning as the height of absurdity. However, imagine Gregory the Great in place of Omar, and the Gospel in place of the Koran, the library would still have been burned, and it would be perhaps the finest deed in the life of that illustrious pontiff" (*The First and Second Discourses*, trans. Roger D. Masters and Judith R. Masters [New York: St. Martin's Press, 1964], 61n).

75. At *HPP* 288–89, Strauss makes the connection between the Christian "persecutions" and "the malignity of the times" even easier to see. L. J. Walker, S.J., translates *de' tempi* in the key phrase (*che dalla malignità de' tempi*) as "of time" rather than "of the times"—one of the many mistakes he makes in failing to understand how bold, and how careful, Machiavelli really was. See Machiavelli, *Discourses on Livy*, trans. L. J. Walker, S.J. (Harmondsworth, UK: Penguin Books, 1976), 99. Walker properly translates *la malignità de' tempi* in the preface to book II, where it appears in a different context (268–69).

76. Pocock, "Prophet," 398.

77. Pocock, "Prophet," 397; cf. 395.

78. *TM* 297; cf. 167 on "the perfection envisaged by both the Bible and classical philosophy." Strauss elsewhere lauds "a Christian saint," Thomas More (*CM* 61), for being "one of the profoundest students of Plato's *Republic*" (*NRH* 139). Also consider the following passages: *WIPP* 41–42, *HPP* 273, *NRH* 178 on "the substitution of patriotism or merely political virtue for human excellence," and *NRH* 315 on the "love of lucre."

79. As early as 1936, Strauss criticized Hobbes in similar terms (*PPH* 90, 91, 106, 125, 128, 143); cf. *RCPR* 100–101. Strauss even likens the "elusive chance" that obstructs realization of the classical best regime to "inscrutable providence" (TWM 86).

80. Strauss, "What Can We Learn," 528–29. As Janssens notes, furthermore, both Jerusalem and Athens maintain that *human beings* are "incapable of creating the perfect society" (Janssens, *Between Athens and Jerusalem*, 194).

81. Adherents of the political philosophy tradition "founded by Socrates, Plato, and Aristotle" agreed about "the fundamentals"; that tradition was "transformed, but not broken under the influence of the biblical virtues of mercy and humility"; and it "still supplies us with the most needful guidance as regards the fundamentals" (Strauss, "What Can We Learn," 527). By using strategies Drury eschews, such as counting paragraphs, Larry Peterman deconstructs the Great Tradition more carefully than Drury does (Peterman, "Approaching Leo Strauss," 326–30). On the relationships among antiquity, modernity, and Christianity, also see Tanguay, *Leo Strauss*, 208–10, 251, 254, 292–94, 302–4, 343, 353.

82. *TM* 345n215 cites *Laws* 709d10–710b2, 711a6–7, 735d2–e5; cf. 690a1–c4.

83. In his essay on Aristotle, Strauss invokes modern speculation that the world has emerged from "a blind necessity which is utterly indifferent as to whether it and its product ever becomes known" (*CM* 43).

84. Cf. *NRH* 128–29, where Strauss criticizes the "materialistic or crypto-materialistic view" that "forces its holders to understand the higher as nothing but the effect of the lower": such a view precludes "the possibility that there are phenomena which are simply irreducible to their conditions." Although the paragraph starts by elaborating the response of "the classics"—and the concluding footnote cites Plato, Xenophon, Aristotle, and Cicero—Strauss imparts his own voice when he employs the terms "strategic genius," "freedom from calculation," "*ad hoc* hypotheses," "crypto-materialistic," "utilitarian," and "empirical science of man." Also see Epilogue 311/*LAM* 207, where Strauss criticizes "the new political science" for trying "to understand the higher in terms of the lower."

85. Sorensen's thorough assessment of such matters reinforces his larger thesis about Strauss's openness to revelation (Sorensen, *Discourses*, 38, 78, 95, 109, 111).

86. In the preface to 1952 American edition of *PPH*, Strauss says that the original 1936 version erred in identifying Hobbes as the "originator" of modern political philosophy. The "immediate and perhaps sufficient cause" of the error was inadequate reflection on the opening of Machiavelli's *Discourses*. All the authorities agreed that this book was Machiavelli's magnum opus, and the *Discorsi* "present themselves at first glance as an attempt to restore something lost or forgotten rather than as an attempt to open an entirely new vista." Only later did Strauss realize that Machiavelli "still exercised a kind of reserve which Hobbes disdained to exercise" (*PPH* xv).

87. For the controversy about the publication status of Machiavelli's preface, contrast Felix Gilbert, "Politics," 467 with the Mansfield and Tarcov *Discourses* 5n2, xxvi; Mansfield, "Strauss's Machiavelli," 374; and Mansfield, *Machiavelli's New Modes and Orders* (Ithaca, NY: Cornell University Press, 1979), 25n1.

88. A bit later, Strauss articulates a vivid summary of the agenda of the fifteenth chapter: "Right at the beginning of the third part (chaps. 15–23) Machiavelli begins to uproot the Great Tradition. . . . All ancient or traditional teachings are to be superseded by a shockingly new teaching" though Machiavelli is "careful not to shock anyone unduly" (*TM* 59; cf. 36, 56); also cf. *PPH* xvi on the "clarion call" of the fifteenth chapter.

89. When Strauss contrasts Machiavelli to the new political science at the conclusion of the epilogue, he praises his "teaching" as "graceful, subtle, and colorful" (Epilogue 327/*LAM* 223). Despite her claim that Strauss elevated Machiavelli above "the modern scientists of society" (*PILS* 115–16)—and despite a passage that she quotes at *PILS* 123 (actually, she misquotes it, but only by turning "peaks" into "peak") in which Strauss describes Machiavelli as the "heir" of the "supreme

art of writing" (*TM* 120)—Drury elsewhere forgets these passages that highlight Machiavelli's subtlety. In her 2004 denunciation of Strauss and Straussians as heirs to Dostoevsky's Grand Inquisitor, Drury asserts that Machiavelli was "much admired by Strauss for everything except his lack of subtlety" ("Leo Strauss and the Grand Inquisitor"; see pp. 198–200 above).

90. *PILS* 126. In the passage with the errant citation, Drury says Strauss "so unconditionally castigated" Machiavelli but also expresses a "deep admiration of his genius" (115); near the end of the chapter she says that Strauss issued both "the most severe condemnation" and "the most exalted praise" (132).

91. Within the past decade, Michael Lind in the *New York Times* (reviewing Daniel Boorstin's *The Seekers* on 6 September 1998) commended Boorstin for skillfully opposing the "blackened" reputation that American Straussians had allegedly created for Machiavelli.

92. Particularly pertinent among the examples Strauss offers is the way that *The Prince* elevates good arms at the expense of prudence (*TM* 82). Along these lines Strauss also denies that Machiavelli vulgarly worships success (*TM* 253; cf. 132, 287). The *TM* 82 remark about the "merely pedagogic function" that some of Machiavelli's "most outrageous statements"—as well as some of his "most comforting" ones"—were intended to serve should be compared with several remarks by Strauss about Xenophon's *Hiero*: the circumstances that impel someone (even "a perfectly just man") advising a tyrant to *appear* "utterly unscrupulous" might explain "the most shocking sentences" in *The Prince* (*OT* 56–57). In diagnosing in Strauss the "assumption that everything Machiavelli says, he means," Angelo Caranfa errs laughably (Caranfa, *Machiavelli*, 51). On training with heavier weapons, see Machiavelli, *Art of War*, translated, edited, and with a commentary by Christopher Lynch (Chicago: University of Chicago Press, 2003), II.112–15, 121, 125; Strauss cites these passages at *TM* 310n56.

93. *Discourses*, introduction, xxxiii: Machiavelli directs attention away from the *words* people use in political situations to "the necessities they face. The prince must adjust his words to his deeds, not the other way around. Most people do not or cannot accept that necessity—a failing that is *their* necessity. They will continue in their moralizing habits because they are too weak to face a world in which necessity decides."

94. Vickie B. Sullivan, *Machiavelli's Three Romes: Religion, Human Liberty and Politics Reformed* (Dekalb: Northern Illinois University Press, 1996), 143, 144; cf. Leo Paul S. De Alvarez, *The Machiavellian Enterprise* (DeKalb: Northern Illinois University Press, 1999), 78–79. For a study that takes the self-sacrificing aspects of Machiavelli to their ultimate conclusion, see Philip J. Kain, "Niccolò Machiavelli—Adviser of Princes," *Canadian Journal of Philosophy* 25, no. 1 (March 1995): 33–55. According to Kain, Machiavelli firmly believes in damnation ("If you do evil, you go to hell. Period.") and persuades his princely readers to commit the politically necessary actions that will damn them. Machiavelli himself, as "the adviser who serves the common good . . . finally accepts his own condemnation to hell" (50–54).

95. Perhaps Strauss's firmest condemnation concludes the first paragraph of *TM*: "If it is true that only an evil man will stoop to teach maxims of public and private gangsterism, we are forced to say that Machiavelli was an evil man" (*TM* 9).

96. Paul Rahe had done the most to discharge the latter task. See his three-volume series, *Republics Ancient & Modern* (Chapel Hill: University of North Carolina Press, 1994).

97. Pocock, "Prophet," 388. Note Strauss's claim that both Spinoza and Rousseau erred in regarding *The Prince* as a satire (*TM* 26). For sketches of how Bacon, Hobbes, Spinoza, and Rousseau might have appropriated Machiavelli, see *TM* 176, 294, 318–19n71, 343n189, 344n194; *NRH* 61n, 177–80; *WIPP* 47–48, TWM 87–89, *HPP* 273–74, and *PPH* 88.

98. Cf. *WIPP* 72 on the historicism "cab."

Chapter Seven

From the Peloponnesus to Iraq— and Michigan

PART 1: BALLISTIC DRURY

What I am guilty of in the eyes of my critics is the original crime, the crime of crimes—philosophy.

—Shadia Drury

I. "HER PHILOSOPHICAL LOVE OF TRUTH"?

The major new text of Strauss's that Drury elaborates in her introduction to the 2005 reprinting of *PILS* is his essay on Thucydides in *The City and Man*. Given her recent emphasis on Straussian warmongering, it is fitting that she discusses Strauss's interpretation of this classic/classical text about war and peace.[1] In the space of a few pages, alas, she again manages to introduce a plethora of distortions and outright errors. Strauss's 102-page essay on Thucydides' mammoth book is the longest of the three essays that comprise *CM*, and it is mutilated when Drury tries to press one of her crude templates upon it. The stakes are further heightened because Irving Kristol, in a widely cited passage, credits Strauss (along with Donald Kagan) for having made the *History of the Peloponnesian War* "the favorite neoconservative text on foreign affairs."[2]

The biggest flaw in Drury's new introduction is her poorly supported and ridiculously simplistic thesis that, like Thucydides and Plato, "Strauss admired Sparta, not Athens" (xxxvi).[3] Drury offers no citations to support this claim about Strauss's preference. She does, however, prepare the claim by asserting that Strauss did *not* object to the Athenian massacre at Melos; he objected rather to Athens's "candid veracity." Thus, Strauss "preferred Spartan brutality over Athenian brutality because the former was dressed in sacred myths" (xxxvi). To support these odd interpretations, Drury here cites two pages from *CM* (214, 217), but there is nothing on either page that suggests criticism of Athenian veracity, and there is much that suggests criticism of Spartan brutality.[4] Regarding Cleon, an atypical Athenian whom Strauss earlier described as "abominable" (201), Strauss observes: "Like a Spartan he condemns the generous desire of the Athenians to spare the lives of the Mytileneans"; Cleon in effect appeals to "unchangeable laws of questionable goodness." After pointing out that Cleon ends up being "severely punished for his contempt of speeches," Strauss adds that he is "reasonableness itself" compared to the Spartan Alcidas, who stupidly killed prisoners out of slavish adherence to Spartan custom (214).

When Drury manages to provide a more detailed elaboration of Strauss's alleged Spartanism, she uses language that would alarm many present-day readers: "The root of Strauss's antipathy to Athens was her philosophical love of truth, which freedom promotes."[5] Returning to her assertion concerning the Melian dialogue, Drury adds that both it and "the Athenian discussion about the policy regarding Mytilene were deeply troubling to Strauss" because faith in gods had yielded to *realpolitik*: "a philosophical embrace of the world as it is— without myths or illusions" (*PILS-05* xxxvii). Her assault reaches a peak when she later states that neoconservatives are "convinced that the fanatical values of their Islamic foes are the right values: the values of Sparta, the values that are necessary for military success" (xliii–xliv).

Drury's interpretation about Melos and Mytilene founders immediately because nowhere in his long essay does Strauss criticize Athenian veracity regarding either Melos or Mytilene. How could she possibly conclude that the Athenian discussion about Mytilene was "deeply troubling" to him? Strauss *celebrates* the debate in which the exemplary Diodotus convinced an assembly to overturn the harsh anti-Mytilene decision previously reached at the behest of Cleon, the Athenian demagogue who embodies a *Spartan* orientation.[6] Whereas the Mytileneans, who had unsuccessfully revolted from an Athenian ally, were not put to the sword, the Spartans—in a parallel case elaborated just a few pages later (III.52–68)—slaughtered the Plataeans, indulging the longstanding Theban hatred of the Plataeans in order to promote something "immediately profitable" to Sparta. Strauss stresses that there was no one in the Peloponnesian camp "to oppose the killing of the helpless Plataeans" (*CM* 190). As Strauss puts it in a later section of his essay, the Plataeans were "condemned and executed without a single voice except their own being raised in their favor before the Spartan tribunal" (215). In the Athenian episode, by contrast, the Mytileneans end up surviving because the case for them was "as powerfully stated by an Athenian [Diodotus] as was the case against them." The Athenians also differ from the Spartans by virtue of their assumption that "killing must serve a purpose other than the satisfaction of the desire for revenge" (215). Because Drury attributes the preference for Sparta to Thucydides as well as to Strauss, she would have trouble explaining Strauss's striking claim that the speech of Diodotus "reveals more of Thucydides himself than does any other speech" (231); according to Strauss, moreover, this speech expresses an "act of humanity" that is "the only action recorded by Thucydides which properly reflects his thought on the political plane" (231–32). Correspondingly, Thucydides "loathes" Cleon (213) and "strongly disapproved" of Cleon's posture toward the Mytileneans (220).[7]

Although Drury's assertions that Strauss condemned Athens for its veracity in the Melian dialogue are less far-fetched, they remain erroneous. First, Strauss stresses that the relevant conversation took place behind closed doors (*CM* 184, 200) and that the ambassadors were speaking only with the "leading men" of Melos (whom they mistakenly presumed would share their view of right's feebleness when it confronts a palpable superiority in might) [184–85]. And although Strauss describes the Athenian speeches as "shocking" (210) and surprisingly frank (152, 193), he also claims that they represented not all of Athens but only "modern, innovating, daring Athens whose memory barely extends beyond Salamis and Themistocles" (200);[8] the speakers on Melos in fact differed from the "large majority" (204) of Athenians. One reason the atrocity on Melos—as opposed to the speeches—is "so shocking," finally, is that "the Athenians are men superior to the Spartans" (211). As we shall see, this is one of many passages that undermine Drury's bizarre declaration that Strauss "admired Sparta, not Athens."

When Strauss directly contrasts Athens and Sparta concerning veracity, furthermore, his language seems to favor the Athenians. Regarding the speech about Athens that its ambassadors improvised in Sparta, Strauss says the following:

> What distinguishes their exercise of imperial power from that of all others is the singular fairness in their dealings with their subjects. It is above all by the amazing frankness with which they defend the Athenian acquisition of empire that they reveal Athenian power, for only the most powerful can afford to utter the principles which they utter. (*CM* 172)

The Spartans who speak in Athens, by contrast, are "underhanded and grudging," and their "lack of frankness and of pride is not redeemed by graciousness" (173). Where in such words is the "antipathy to Athens" Strauss allegedly felt because of "her philosophical love of truth" (*PILS*-05 xxxvii)?

To illuminate the earlier-cited statement, articulated clearly as Strauss's verdict, that "the Athenians are men superior to the Spartans," Strauss again invokes the explanations the Athenian ambassadors supplied in Sparta: because of her concern for honor beyond fear and profit, Athens "exercises her imperial rule in a juster, more restrained, less greedy manner than her power would permit her to do and the same power will lead others in her place in fact to do" (*CM* 211). The invocation of the future in the last clause confirms that Strauss is introducing an evaluation of his own, not merely paraphrasing the ambassadors (he does not here provide a citation to Thucydides, who presents the ambassadors' speech at I.72–78). When, to amplify Athenian superiority, Strauss goes on to paraphrase Pericles' funeral speech (here too he does not provide a fresh citation), he begins by inserting his own judgment that the "qualities which distinguish her [Athens] are those which Sparta above all others lacks": [9]

> generosity without pettiness or calculation, freedom, generous gaiety and ease, courage in war which stems not from compulsion, dictation, and harsh discipline but from generosity, in brief, a well-tempered love of the noble and the beautiful. (*CM* 211)

Even more than most of the statements I addressed in previous chapters, Drury's blunt summary—"Strauss admires Sparta, not Athens"—defiles both the spirit and the letter of Strauss's writings. There is no need to dwell upon the fact that Strauss devoted such a vast amount of his time to studying, teaching, and writing about Athenian authors. Does he ever discuss a Spartan text?

Despite posing for two decades as Strauss's definitive interpreter, Drury seems oblivious to the subtle dialectic concerning Sparta and Athens that Strauss attempts to unearth in Thucydides, that "great Athenian" (*CM* 151)—a dialectic that clearly infuses Strauss's own discussion. Strauss could hardly be more explicit: the second section of his essay is "The Case for Sparta: Moderation and the Divine Law," the third section is "The Case for Athens: Daring, Progress, and the Arts," and the eighth section is "The Spartan Manner and the Athenian Manner." It is also obvious that Strauss's Thucydides interweaves the Athens/Sparta comparison into historical and cosmological dialectics concerning war and peace, brutality and gentleness, motion and rest, civilization and barbarism, the divine and the natural. [10]

As best I can determine, the following overarching assessments of the two cities express the views of both Strauss and Strauss's Thucydides:

> The rise from original and universal insecurity, weakness, and poverty . . . became in certain places the rise from original and universal barbarism to what one may call Greekness, the union of freedom and love of beauty. (*CM* 156)

> Just as humanity divides itself into Greeks and barbarians, Greekness in its turn has two poles, Sparta and Athens. . . . Sparta cherishes rest whereas Athens cherishes motion. The peak of Sparta and Athens was reached at the outbreak of the Peloponnesian war. In that greatest motion, power, wealth, and Greekness, built up during a long rest, are used and used up. . . . The greatest motion weakens, endangers, nay destroys, not only power and wealth but Greekness as well. . . . The most savage and murderous barbarism, which was slowly overcome by the building up of Greekness, reappears in the midst of Greece: Thracian mercenaries in the pay of Athens murder the children attending a Greek school. (*CM* 156–57)

Sparta may have been a better city than Athens; Athens surpassed her by far by natural gifts, by her individuals.[11] (*CM* 212)

Sparta and Athens were worthy antagonists not only because they were the most powerful Greek cities but because each was in its own way of outstanding nobility. (*CM* 217)

The third passage above echoes the title of Strauss's book and innumerable other passages in his corpus. At one point, indeed, Strauss proceeds to reconsider "our first impression, according to which Thucydides' horizon is the horizon of the city" (153), a horizon that seems to favor Sparta. The reconsideration, by illuminating how "the most important consideration concerns that which transcends the city" (154), will favor Athens.

Even though the "universalism of Athens, the universalism of the city . . . is doomed to failure," it points to and inspires the kind of universalism that the *Peloponnesian War* embodies: "the genuine universalism of understanding" (*CM* 228). It is in Athens, moreover, that

the two heterogeneous universalisms become in a way fused: the fantastic political universalism becomes tinged, colored, suffused, transfigured by the true universalism, by the love of beauty and of wisdom as Thucydides understands beauty and wisdom, and it thus acquires its tragic character; it thus becomes able to foster a manly gentleness. (*CM* 230)

Strauss could hardly be clearer about what he regards as Thucydides' dialectical manner of writing: "Generally speaking, he lets us see the war at each point as it could be seen at the time; he shows us the war from different viewpoints," and there is a "deliberate movement of his thought between two different points of view" (162).[12] Strauss of course provides many passages that convey Thucydides' appreciation of Sparta, especially for its moderation, stability, and piety (e.g., *CM* 146–47, 151); but he also describes Spartan demands, decisions, or attributes as being (at least in Thucydides' eyes) "ridiculous," "inept," or "laughable."[13]

To complete my critique of Drury's thesis, I shall merely highlight some passages I have not already discussed in which Strauss's Thucydides conveys admiration for Athens. Because Drury twice links Strauss and Thucydides as men who admire Sparta *rather than* Athens, her thesis obviously is weakened by passages from *CM* that suggest a preference for Athens on the part of either author.

However highly Thucydides may have thought of Sparta, moderation, and the divine law, his thought belongs altogether to innovating Athens. (*CM* 159)

The highest form of rest is not, like the form represented by Sparta, opposed to daring but presupposes the utmost daring. (*CM* 160)

As Pericles makes clear in the beautiful sentences of his Funeral Speech, Athens more than any other city gave free rein to the individual's development toward graceful manysidedness or self-sufficiency or permitted him to be a genuine individual: so that he could be infinitely superior as a citizen to the citizens of any other city. (*CM* 193)

Insofar as the Spartans and their allies had to adopt Athenian initiative, daring, and inventiveness to defeat her, furthermore, Athens lived up to the role Pericles claimed for her as "the teacher of Hellas."[14] The passage about "graceful manysidedness," incidentally, is only one of the hundreds of passages that undermine Drury's recent declaration about "Strauss's collectivist way of thinking."[15]

Given Drury's claim that enthusiasm for Sparta among "conservatives of every stripe"—including Plato, Thucydides, and Strauss—is rooted in "aristocratic mean-spiritedness" (*PILS*-05 xxxvii), and given Xenophon's well known collaborations with Spartans, Drury would have been well served to elaborate what Strauss says about Sparta in his studies of Xenophon. In the only work Strauss wrote that included Sparta in the title, he presents Xenophon as being a sharp critic of Sparta: "The *Constitution of the Lacedemonians* . . . is actually a most trenchant, if disguised, satire on that city and its spirit."[16] Strauss soon proceeds to add his own anti-Spartan judgments to the mix. As an ably disguised satire on the Spartan lack of education, Xenophon's book is "a most graceful recommendation of education." Because "Sparta and philosophy are incompatible," Sparta became an inviting starting point both for true utopias that ruthlessly idealize politics and for ruthless attacks on politics. Such works satirize "the spirit of Sparta, or the conviction that man belongs, or ought to belong, entirely to the city."[17] Strauss published this article in 1939, before there were Straussians to accuse of Spartanist militarism.[18] In Sparta, Strauss elsewhere notes, Socrates "would have been exposed as an infant" (*OT* 220).

II. INTO THE WILD BLUE YONDER

Given her horrifying accusations that Strauss, because of his "fascistic glorification of death and violence," wished to foment perpetual war, and given her confidence in blaming Straussians for the U.S. invasion of Iraq, it is staggering that Drury does such a poor job in the new introduction to her magnum opus. In previous chapters, I have mentioned several of the offensive passages, but now is the time to give them sustained attention. I shall here focus largely on the deeds and speeches of alleged Straussians rather than those of Strauss himself. It is in foreign policy that Drury unearths the most monstrous of the evils for which she blames us, and she proves to be unreliable in both her empirical claims and her efforts to interpret nonphilosophical texts.

Naming Names

After adding the adjective "rabid" to the long list of demeaning words she has used to describe Strauss (*PILS*-05 ix), Drury quickly turns to elaborate the current political menace posed by Straussians: "those who believe the things that Strauss believed are bound to behave badly when they are in positions of power and influence" (x).[19] I eagerly turned to the relevant footnote (note 2) looking for depictions of "Straussians Gone Wild!" or for citations to accounts of specific abuses. All Drury provides, however, is a reference to her earlier-discussed *Philosophers' Magazine* article in which she sketched a two-page *fantasy* about the fate of a pompous and paranoid high-echelon graduate student; he cannot find an academic job because Straussians are "poorly trained," so he seeks employment in government or a right-wing think tank.[20]

Perhaps social scientists adept at fieldwork can investigate Drury's hypothesis by comparing Straussians and non-Straussians as professors, chairs, deans, parents, and T-ball coaches. Perhaps Drury would reply that not all Straussians "believe the things that Strauss believed," but in the cited article and elsewhere she often refers to Straussians, disciples, acolytes, followers, students, and so on, without bothering to compare their beliefs.[21] And she has the temerity to cite her fantasy article *again* when she asserts that Strauss "created" a "whole class of compulsive and self-righteous deceivers inside and outside the academy" who are "likely to be treacherous and tyrannical" once they find their way into "the corridors of power" (*PILS*-05 xvi and note 18). If we are "bound to behave badly . . . in positions of power and influence," we should presumably be removed from such positions. Unlike Drury, Paul Gottfried suggests that appalling Straussian behavior is summoned even by the ivory tower: "The fact that Strauss's disciples typically behave thuggishly (not to mince words) when put into an academic setting is not at all surprising. Many of them are no more concerned about the life of the mind than were the party officials assigned to German universities under the Third Reich."[22] These are not the sort of generalizations I expect to encounter in an academic journal titled *Humanitas*.

As previously elaborated, Drury often does a terrible job of backing up her interpretations of Strauss's texts. The outrageous accusations she provides in the new introduction are undermined by a different type of carelessness:

> No one represents the daunting political power of the Straussians in the Bush administration more than Paul Wolfowitz, Deputy Minister of Defense and assistant to Vice President Dick Cheney. Wolfowitz was one of the key architects of the war on Iraq and a self-proclaimed follower of Strauss. Wolfowitz was a student of Strauss in Chicago and then a student of Allan Bloom at Cornell. (*PILS*-05 x)

Yes, these are exactly the words Drury wrote. Given the alarm she consistently has conveyed about Straussians in Washington and the horrors of neoconservatism, one would expect Drury to be at least minimally informed about the man she associates with the vanguard of the vast right-wing conspiracy. As we have seen on many occasions, however, Drury is comfortable addressing momentous matters hastily and unreliably. Let me here offer four purely factual corrections: Wolfowitz was not an assistant to Vice President Cheney (Wolfowitz did assist Cheney when Cheney was the secretary of defense under President George H. W. Bush, but Drury's focus is on the administration of George W. Bush); Wolfowitz was the Deputy Secretary of Defense, not the deputy minister (unlike Canada's, our national bureaucracy features secretaries and directors rather than ministers); and Wolfowitz studied with Bloom at Cornell *before* he studied with Strauss at Chicago.[23] It is also objectionable to describe Wolfowitz as a "self-proclaimed" follower of Strauss, since he proclaims that he is *not* a follower of Strauss. As reported by Michael Hirsh of *Newsweek* in 2003, Wolfowitz "mocks the idea that he is a Straussian,"[24] and I have encountered no record of his describing himself as one. In the well-known interview with Sam Tanenhaus of *Vanity Fair*, Wolfowitz maintains that he was not even a disciple of Allan Bloom.[25] Hamid Dabashi, professor of Iranian studies and comparative literature at Columbia University, declares that Wolfowitz was "indoctrinated" by Strauss ("the father of American neoconservatives"), and outdoes Drury by turning Wolfowitz into the secretary of defense.[26]

When Drury rehashes the mishmash in her 2007 essay in *Political Theory*, she repeats her doubly mistaken description of Wolfowitz as "deputy minister of defense" and "assistant to Vice President Dick Cheney," she repeats her dubious description of him as "a self-proclaimed follower of Strauss"—this time she says he *is* (not "was") a follower—and she seems oblivious of the fact that Wolfowitz left the administration two years earlier to become the president of the World Bank.[27]

Drury Abandons the Reality Community

Bill Kristol *is* a self-proclaimed Straussian, and Drury completes a full sentence about him before introducing an error. According to Drury, Kristol wrote his doctoral thesis on Machiavelli, "a topic that was as dear to Strauss as it was to Mansfield" (Harvey Mansfield was Kristol's thesis advisor) [*PILS*-05 xi]. Kristol's thesis, however, was *not* about Machiavelli; titled "The American Judicial Power and the American Regime," it focused on the *Federalist Papers*.[28]

Drury also goes astray when she discusses Irving Kristol, the father of Bill Kristol and "the father of neoconservatism." According to Drury, the elder Kristol "acknowledges Strauss as the greatest influence on his thought" (*PILS*-05 xii); she cites the opening of his 1995 essay, "An Autobiographical Memoir." Drury is wrong. Kristol here singles out *two* thinkers: one of them is Strauss, but the other is Lionel Trilling, the Columbia professor and literary critic who wrote *The Liberal Imagination*.[29] Drury's 2005 misrepresentation is particularly egregious because of the weight she places in *LSAR* and elsewhere on Kristol's channeling of Strauss into neoconservatism.

Drury further fantasizes in her 2007 *Political Theory* essay when she says that Kristol "identifies Strauss as the main influence on neoconservative thought in general and its approach to foreign policy in particular." She here provides no citation, and seems merely to have inflated her already erroneous 2005 claim—that Kristol identifies Strauss as the greatest influence on *Kristol's* thought—to the claim that Kristol identifies Strauss as the greatest influence on "neoconservative thought in general," particularly in foreign policy. Regarding the latter, Drury does provide additional evidence when she cites the *Weekly Standard* article in which Kristol says that, thanks to Strauss and Donald Kagan, *The Peloponnesian War* is "the favorite neoconservative text on foreign affairs."[30] Here again, we confront Druryite distortion. Kristol's claim about "the favorite neoconservative text" does not even imply that *Thucydides* is the "main influence" on the neoconservative approach to foreign policy. Kristol provides the remark about the "text" in parentheses immediately after stating that there is no "set of neoconservative beliefs" concerning foreign policy, but only a set of attitudes "derived from historical experience."[31] It is reasonable to hypothesize that the historical experiences of the past two millennia, especially when coupled with technological developments, would sometimes yield more important lessons than a book written by Thucydides. And whatever Kristol thinks about the impact *The Peloponnesian War* has had on neoconservative foreign policy, Strauss's impact in popularizing Thucydides does not in Kristol's eyes make *Strauss* "the main influence" on neoconservative foreign policy. One should also recall that Kristol attributes equal importance to Donald Kagan as a conduit of Thucydides to neoconservatism.

Douglas Massey, the world-renowned sociologist, is an apt follower of Drury—he emphasizes *LSAR*—as he flounders with this material. He shows great creativity, however, in the way that he butchers the Kristol passage by misquoting it to eliminate Kagan and to leave Strauss with sole credit for making Thucydides a neocon favorite: "The favorite neoconservative text on foreign affairs, thanks to professor Leo Strauss of Chicago . . . is Thucydides." As if to cover his crime in excising "and Donald Kagan," Massey changes "professors" to "professor."[32] Anne Norton, meanwhile, mislabels Kagan a Straussian and then credits him for having "made Thucydides the architect of American empire."[33] Who knew?

As I have attempted to demonstrate, Drury does a dreadful job in addressing Strauss's Thucydides, and she churns out falsehoods when she tries to trace Strauss's influence through the likes of Wolfowitz and the Kristols. The travesty is completed when she attempts to assess a text that is seminal for the contemporary controversy about Iraq.

Drury's Nuclear Option

To elaborate her critique of neoconservative foreign policy, Drury relies heavily on a report posted on the website of PNAC (Project for a New American Century),[34] an organization in which Bill Kristol played a prominent leadership role (the report was issued in late 2000). Since such texts tend to be more straightforward than a typical work by Strauss, I thought that Drury might interpret the report accurately. It did not take long, however, to stumble on a preposterous passage. According to Drury, the report "recommends . . . a global monopoly over weapons of mass destruction. The aim is to remove all adversarial, unfriendly, or undemocratic regimes from power."[35] For the barest fraction of a second, I wondered if any of the twenty-seven project participants—including Stephen Cambone, Donald Kagan, Robert Kagan, Gary Schmitt, Kristol, Libby, Shulsky, and Wolfowitz—could have been insane enough to recommend that the United States pursue a monopoly over nuclear weapons, including the thousands currently under Russian control. It turns out that there is *nothing* on any of the document's ninety pages about pursuing a monopoly over nuclear weapons (or other weapons of mass destruction). In fact, various passages presume that other countries will continue to possess such weapons, that China will modernize and expand its arsenal (8), and that new countries may acquire them; hence the importance of developing defenses against ballistic missiles (v, 6, 12, 51–53). The following early passage seems unambiguous:

> smaller adversarial states, looking for an equalizing advantage, are determined to acquire their own weapons of mass destruction. Whatever our fondest wishes, the reality of the [*sic*] today's world is that there is no magic wand to eliminate these weapons (or, more fundamentally, the interest in acquiring them).[36]

The United States will thus continue to rely upon deterrence against WMDs (chemical and biological as well as nuclear), and it will presumably continue to forswear building its own chemical or biological arsenals (8). Yes, the authors call on the United States to *maintain* nuclear *superiority* (iv, 7), but this falls vastly short of a monopoly, which they recognize would be impossible.

Drury's specification of the "aim" of the alleged nuclear policy—"to remove all adversarial, unfriendly, or undemocratic regimes from power"—may be equally farfetched. There is nothing on any page about removing all undemocratic regimes, or even removing all unfriendly and adversarial regimes. In their most extensive and pertinent discussion of regime change, the authors do fault the 1997 Quadrennial Defense Review because it "assumed that Kim Jong Il and Saddam Hussein each could begin a war—perhaps even while employing chemical, biological, or even nuclear weapons—and the United States would make no effort to unseat militarily either ruler." Consequently, future war games should probably consider "the force requirements necessary not only to defeat an attack but to remove these regimes from power and conduct post-combat stability operations" (10). Drury's departure from the reality-based community is again dramatic. According to Drury, the report promotes the removal of "all adversarial, unfriendly, or undemocratic regimes"; the actual report only *suggests* that future war games include *scenarios* whereby the United States would remove *two* undemocratic, hostile regimes. I and many others would condemn the Bush administration because it did *not* devote sufficient attention to the PNAC recommendation about planning for "post-combat stability operations" in Iraq.

"The Straussian Ideal"?

As was previously mentioned, Drury uses her absurd thesis that Strauss was a Spartanist to support her claim that the neoconservatives exalt the Spartan virtues of our Islamist enemies. In her vivid words, "[n]othing represents the Straussian ideal of political health more than the crazed Islamic youths we see on television—young men ready to immolate themselves on a moment's notice" (*PILS*-05 xliii). From here, she reaches a new summit of vitriol. The triumph of the "jihadist mentality" would "no doubt please Strauss and his misanthropic philosophers"; in a world "full of catastrophe and carnage," Strauss's "monstrous elite . . . will not lack for entertainment" (li).[37] As I have previously suggested, on such a view the two World Wars would have made Strauss the happiest man of his time—happier than Socrates, who could relish only the snail-paced killing of antiquity. And what happened to the stereotype that Straussians are pedants enthralled by the process of dissecting footnotes?

Elaborating earlier material—her 1990 insinuation that Straussians comically imagine themselves as gods, her 1997 reference to "Strauss's liars who fancy themselves gods playing pranks on mere mortals" (*LSAR* 80), and her 2004 statement about "the Olympian laughter of the Straussian gods"[38]—Drury highlights the tragic angle when she concludes her new introduction: "If America is mired in endless wars in the name of God and nation, the Straussians (or noble liars) . . . will imagine that they are gods entertaining themselves with the mutual slaughter of the mortals on their television screens" (*PILS*-05 li). Drury's 1990 rendition conveyed a modicum of taste and humor. But I can find nothing to redeem the shameful viciousness of this last image, and the time has come for scholars and other commentators to disown her pernicious nonsense.

PART 2: CONCLUSION

Man's being is revealed by the broad character of his life, his deeds, his works, by what he esteems and reveres not in word but in deed—by the stars for which his soul longs if it longs for any stars.

—Leo Strauss

I. THE POLITICIZATION OF PHILOSOPHY

What lessons should we draw from the cacophony and contempt that surround recent discussions of Leo Strauss and his legacy? First, Strauss deserves credit for his decades-long hammering on the inevitable tension between society and thought; he particularly lamented the modern tendency toward the "politicization" of philosophy, including its emergence as a "weapon" in political struggle.[39] When Strauss in a 1962 lecture complained about "a general victory of mediocrity" (WWRJ 59), he could not have anticipated the parade of disgracefully flawed quotations, paraphrases, citations, attributions, associations, interpretations, and speculations that I have been recounting. In trying to explain this sorry record, I would attribute the corruption of inquiry to these causes, among others: impatience, partisan zeal, the propensity to scapegoat, the complexity of Strauss's posture as a commentator, the time shortages that afflict political deliberation and action, the professional concerns that impel academics and others to publish, and perhaps also the very ease of writing and publishing in the cyber-age. Regarding the latter, we are witnessing a desperate race between the capacity of the Web to generate error, deformation, and slander and its capacity to correct them. Strauss and Straussians have worked miracles in counteracting the postmodernist declaration of "the death of the author"; perhaps the next step is the resurrection of the editor.

In the course of paraphrasing Burke, Strauss elucidates the problem of time pressure: "Practice lacks the freedom of theory" partly because "it cannot wait"; while practical thought operates "with a view to some deadline" and actions are irreversible, theory "can and must ever again begin from the beginning" (NRH 309). Speaking solely in his own name, Strauss observes that because anyone who offers "comprehensive reflections on the political situation which lead up to the suggestion of a broad policy" must appeal "in the last resort to principles accepted by public opinion or a considerable part of it," the comprehensive reflections dogmatically assume principles that "can well be questioned" (WIPP 13)—and *should* be questioned, we may infer, by a philosopher. In reflecting on Aristotle, Strauss goes farther: because there is no "unqualified transcending, even by the wisest man as such, of the sphere of opinion . . . the beginning or the questions retain a greater evidence than the end or the answers," and the return to the beginning "remains a constant necessity" (CM 20–21). By itself, this passage almost suffices to refute Drury's allegations of Straussian brainwashing: Strauss offers the "converts . . . ready-made answers to all the difficult questions" (PILS 193), and "Strauss's philosopher is free of all the doubts and devils that plague a truly wise man" (AK 150).[40] As Strauss elaborates in a recently published 1948 lecture, finally, philosophy in its "original sense" could be only be pursued by "people who are not concerned with decisions, who are not in a rush, for whom nothing is urgent except disputation."[41] Almost every human being has to be "concerned with decisions"—and deadlines—but precision should rule for scholars.

As I have demonstrated, the chief culprit in distorting and demonizing Strauss and Straussians has been Shadia Drury, despite her prestigious chair, her international reputation, her extensive reading, her obvious talents (acuity, imagination, industriousness, verve, and concision), and the intriguing vistas she opens up. She has functioned for decades as a unique combination of professor and prosecutor; I cannot think of another celebrated scholar who has contributed so much misinformation on the prime subject of his or her expertise. How might one explain this? Condemnation suffuses what Drury writes; her eagerness to combat the political evils she perceives, and to attract attention, apparently contributed to the pervasive overstatements I have documented. In her 2004 book, Drury was willing to proclaim that "feeling is the thing, and that reason has serious limitations" (*TC* x), and she certainly lacks the interpretive fastidiousness for which Straussians are often ridiculed. Given the magnitude of her accusations and the easy access she presumably had to Strauss's books, one cannot excuse her failures in checking her quotations and citations. Her contradictions and repeated exaggerations additionally undermine her professed commitment to spreading the truth.

II. RECIPES FOR TODAY'S USE

Overconfidence and misrepresentation helped create the Iraq disaster—and they continue to mar efforts to explain it. Socratic humility is never obsolete. In a 1949 letter to Kojève, Strauss wrote that "the older one grows, the more clearly one sees how little one understands."[42]

It is now obvious that serious intellectual shortcomings—especially a paltry understanding of political and cultural realities in Iraq—helped generate the failures of the aggressive agenda that was so enthusiastically promoted by Bill Kristol, Paul Wolfowitz, and others.[43] However much these two men learned from Strauss, and however much we can learn from their consistently thoughtful and incisive prose, as "statesmen" they displayed grave defects in prudence, even if the "surge" and the Sunni Awakening have pulled Iraq away from the abyss. As previously mentioned, Kristol and Steven Lenzner in 2003 credited Strauss's "rehabilitation of the notion of regime" for enabling President Bush to advocate regime change in a manner that avoids both "the pitfalls of a wishful global universalism" and "a fatalistic cultural determinism."[44] Subsequent events suggest that the United States stumbled into the first of these pitfalls. Strauss noted that "[g]enerally speaking, even the lowliest men prefer being subjects to men of their own people rather than to any aliens" (*CM* 239). In addition, he proclaimed that, according to classical political philosophy, a "very imperfect regime may supply the only just solution to the problem of a given community" (*NRH* 140) and that a "given community may be so rude or so depraved that only a very inferior type of order can 'keep it going'" (*WIPP* 87).

Before the war, several key players issued warnings that would prove prophetic. In 1994, Wolfowitz wrote that MacArthur's "disastrous experience in Korea after the stunning victory at Inchon should be warning enough against the assumption that the occupation of Iraq would be as easy as the liberation of Kuwait. Even if easy initially, it is unclear how or when it would have ended."[45] In 2000, Wolfowitz presented a broader view, after noting the "uncomfortable fact" that "economic and social conditions may better prepare some countries for democracy than others":

> Promoting democracy requires attention to specific circumstances and to the limitations of U.S. leverage. Both because of what the United States is, and because of what is possible, we cannot engage either in promoting democracy or in nation-building simply as an exercise of will. We must proceed by interaction and indirection, not imposition. In this respect, post–World War II experiences of Germany and Japan offer misleading guides to what is possible now, even in a period of American primacy. What was possible following total victory and prolonged occupation—in societies that were economically advanced but, at the same time, had profoundly lost faith in their own institutions—does not offer a model that applies in other circumstances.[46]

Also noteworthy is the 1994 declaration by Schmitt and Shulsky (the latter notorious now for his role in the Office of Special Plans) that "the CIA serves the president best when it 'tells it like it is,' not like the president wants it to be."[47]

We needed neither Strauss nor his critics to transmit the venerable wisdom of Humpty Dumpty's fall; both the unpredicted demise of the Soviet Union and its subsequent struggle to produce humane but effective institutions display another memorable lesson about how intricate—and resistant to top-down management—contemporary societies typically are. Despite what one of Bush's "senior advisor[s]" told Ron Suskind in the summer of 2002 while belittling "judicious study," not even an empire can create its own reality.[48] Strauss warns us that we must operate with "the greatest possible care" to counteract "the specific fallacies to which our judgment on political things is exposed" (*WIPP* 15), and he admits the explosion of decentralized knowledge that the scientific method promotes.[49] Turning back to Iraq, we may assume that the slaughter, the maimings, the refugees, and the monetary costs—Gore in 2007 stated that U.S. expenditures had already topped 700 billion dollars[50]—will discourage future U.S. adventures in regime change, even without book burnings or a purge of Straussians.[51]

Throughout his career, Strauss interpreted the history of political philosophy as a quest for the standards or goals that should guide human life. Whereas "[t]he classical solution supplies a stable standard by which to judge of any actual order," the modern solution "eventually destroys the very idea of a standard that is independent of actual situations" (*OT* 225). But even though Strauss suggests that Plato and Aristotle supplied a "universally valid hierarchy of ends" (*NRH* 162) that is "sufficient for passing judgment on the level of nobility of individuals and groups and of actions and institutions," he stresses that this hierarchy is "insufficient for guiding our actions" beforehand (*NRH* 163).[52] Despite his sharp and extensive critiques of historicism, he highlighted the dynamism and "immense complexity" of twentieth-century societies (*WIPP* 15),[53] he asserted that there can never be "a perfectly lucid and unambiguous connection . . . between a general teaching and a contingent event" (*OT* 67), he acknowledged or at least implied that classical political philosophy could not provide "recipes for today's use" (*CM* 11),[54] and he offered no recipes of his own.

Although the justices of the U.S. Supreme Court are occasionally likened to philosopher-kings, Strauss (as far as I know) never published a single sentence that attempted to shape a major Court decision on issues that may be presumed to have interested him while he lived in the United States.[55] Nor did Strauss write his books and his essays to sway voters in a U.S. election, to influence American policies in Korea or Vietnam, or to address the concerns of Rachel Carson. Strauss in 1941 praised R. H. S. Crossman's *Plato Today* for its five chapters that show "how Plato would have judged, or might have judged, of the most important political facts of our time" (*WIPP* 264), but Crossman has his Plato discuss details involving elections, committees, hereditary privilege, commerce, unions, diplomacy, political parties, sex roles, the Constitution, the New Deal, slavery, plutocrats, and other matters with a British M.P. (134–53), an Educationalist in an American "brain trust" (154–80), and President Franklin Roosevelt himself (180–90).[56]

In his essay, "On Classical Political Philosophy," Strauss does stress the geographical portability of statesmanship, at least in the ancient world. On the classical understanding, an individual who possesses political science does not merely "deal properly with a large variety of situations in his own community; he can, in principle, manage well even the affairs of any other political community, be it 'Greek' or 'barbarian.'"[57] When Strauss adds that Themistocles was "admired and listened to" among the barbarians after he had to flee from Athens, Strauss appears to add his own voice to the claim about universalizing (*WIPP* 82). It seems appropriate to object that Themistocles would have floundered if transported to a place such as China, India, Japan, or Peru.[58] And in modern times, various factors that Strauss acknowledges—population size, industrialization, nuclear weapons, and the extreme complexity and pace of scientific/technological change—further enhance the challenges of statesmanship. Could Strauss have thought that either he or Martin Heidegger—the "only great thinker in our time" (*RCPR* 29) and "the only man who has an inkling of the dimensions of the problem of a world society" (*RCPR* 43)—possessed the capacity to "manage well" the "affairs" of either Germany or the United States?

Even if we were utterly confident in specifying political standards and the best regime, prudence would oblige us to be cautious in proposing radical changes. Strauss links "the spirit of statesmanship" with "moderate courses" as opposed to extremism and "narrow obstinacy" (*NRH* 67); for the arena of *action*, Strauss was willing to extol "muddling through."[59] Regarding most if not all of the major challenges America faces in the twenty-first century, the world will not provide cakewalks, slam dunks, or bulletproof evidence. Strauss faulted "the new political science" for fiddling while Rome burns (Epilogue 327/*LAM* 223), and some of his disciples have been playing with fire. I admit that we paragraph-counting Straussians stand accused of fiddling.

When Strauss diagnoses "the crisis of our time, the crisis of the West" (*CM* 1) or "the crisis of modernity" whose existence is "obvious to the meanest capacities" (TWM 81), he might seem to be inviting rash conduct, as certain critics (e.g., Drury, Gunnell, and Holmes) have suggested; with such language, Strauss departs from the "serenity or sublime sobriety" he lauds in classical political philosophy.[60] In a published 1963 lecture, Strauss offers this confident elaboration:

> The assertion that we are in the grip of a crisis is hardly in need of proof. Every day's newspapers tell us of another crisis, and all these little daily crises can easily be seen to be parts, or ingredients, of the one great crisis, the crisis of our time.[61]

When he specifies the components of the crisis in *CM*, however, Strauss seems to be addressing ideas and values rather than institutions or policies. Neither the obvious decline in the West's power nor the possible destruction of the West would prove that a crisis exists (*CM* 2–3).[62] The crisis is rather "the West's having become uncertain of its purpose" (*CM* 3)—that modern man "no longer believes that he can know what is good and bad, what is right and wrong" (TWM 81).[63] In an essay published in 1961, Strauss suggested that Berlin's famous article, "Two Concepts of Liberty," was a "characteristic document of the crisis of liberalism." Strauss was particularly incensed by Berlin's concluding claim that to "realize the relative validity of one's convictions and yet stand for them unflinchingly, is what distinguishes a civilized man from a barbarian" (*RCPR* 17).[64] In his oft-cited conclusion of TWM, finally, Strauss locates the crisis in liberal democracy (rather than in the West), identifies its deepest cause as the power of Nietzsche's critique of modern rationalism, and infers that this cause precludes a return to the first two waves of modernity, which spawned liberal democracy and communism. In this rendition, however, Strauss explicitly denies that the "theoretical crisis" inevitably produces a "practical" one. We can avoid a practical crisis for two reasons: first, because of liberal democracy's "obvious" superiority to communism; and second, because liberal democracy, unlike fascism as well as communism, derives "powerful support" from "premodern" thought (TWM 98).[65]

Has Strauss's claim that "liberal or constitutional democracy comes closer to what the classics demanded than any alternative that is viable in our age" (*OT* 207) become obsolete with the demise of communism and the rise of Islamism? Perhaps Xenos would say that certain Straussians, in pushing the United States to promote liberal democracy abroad, are also hoping to modify it at home, a reform that is less dangerous now that global communism is no longer a threat.[66] To temper exaggerated, premature, or vague declarations about crises, in any case, we can employ the Socratic/phenomenological principles Strauss did so much to revive, particularly his explanations of how classical philosophers began on the ground of ordinary political experience and worked their way up the "ladder" that runs "from common sense to science."[67]

III. WHAT WOULD STRAUSS SAY?

There were professed Straussians who pushed the invasion of Iraq, there were some who opposed it—for example, George Anastaplo, William Galston, Nathan Tarcov, and Michael Zuckert—and there were some who equivocated (e.g., me). Imagine two Straussians having engaged in a vigorous debate about whether the United States should invade Iraq in 2003. Among the contested issues could have been these. Will our soldiers have to fight Stalingrad-like battles in Iraqi cities? Will Saddam initiate large-scale chemical attacks? How many troops will be needed to occupy the country, and whom will they employ as interpreters? Will the war weaken us militarily and politically in ways that make it harder to address the WMD dangers that Iran and North Korea pose? If Saddam stays in power because we do not invade, what sorts of regional and/or global havoc might he promote—and what toll will the UN sanctions continue to take on the Iraqi people? What would be the prospects for regime improvement after Saddam died a natural death? How trustworthy is Ahmad Chalabi? How large are the hidden caches of weapons, and what are our prospects for finding them? What is the condition of Iraq's oil infrastructure, and how vulnerable would it be to insurgent attacks? If Saddam is defeated, will his operatives set the wells on fire? And what are the chances that Iraq would collapse into civil war or that Iran would conduct a major intervention into a weakened Iraq? Could such developments spawn a regional war between Sunnis and Shiites?[68] Would our military and/or economic resources, finally, be more fruitfully employed in other tasks: for example, in stabilizing Afghanistan, preparing for trouble in Pakistan, developing a ballistic-missile shield, securing loose Soviet nukes, improving port security, preserving biodiversity, reducing carbon emissions, prosecuting the war on drugs—and regulating credit-default swaps? Confronted by such questions, neither party would have found answers in Strauss's texts.

Let me suggest another thought experiment to dramatize the tension between theory and practice. Provisionally assume that the giants of classical political philosophy dwelled at the peaks of human wisdom, and that Behnegar is correct in maintaining that knowledge of the whole enriches observations about parts;[69] in addition, imagine that Plato, Aristotle, and Xenophon were revived in 2002 and that we had interpreters fluent in ancient Greek. Before seeking their guidance about Iraq, wouldn't we need to spend a decade or more tutoring them about history, science, technology, economics, religion, and other matters? Now imagine reviving Strauss from 1973. There would be vastly less ground to cover. But we would still be compelled to address many complex topics: the subsequent evolution of the Cold War, the demise of the Soviet Union, and China's capitalistic turn; the Khomeini revolution and its aftermath; a variety of other Middle East developments, including the 1973 war, the Camp David Accords, the assassination of Anwar Sadat, turbulence in Lebanon, the Iran-Iraq War, the Islamist uprising in Algeria, the Persian Gulf War, and the failed Shiite uprising that followed it; the development of Al-Qaida, the Taliban, Al Jazeera, Londonistan, information technology, and the global petroleum business; the Internet's uses as a tool of terrorist recruitment and training; the technology of producing and storing nuclear, biological, and chemical weapons; the stability of the Saudi monarchy, Mubarak's Egypt, and Musharraf's Pakistan; relationships among Iraqi Shiites, Sunnis, and Kurds; Russian and Chinese engagements in the Middle East; the prospect of eliciting assistance from American allies; the prospect of Turkish moves against the Kurds; the equipment, personnel, and training of land, sea, and air forces in Iraq, the United States, Britain, other potential allies, and other potential adversaries; Iraq's geography and climate; the costs of weapons, supplies, transport, and military medicine; basic facts about the U.S. economy and the federal budget; the backgrounds and dispositions of Baathist officials and of non-Baathist Iraqi leaders (e.g., Grand Ayatollah Ali al-Sistani and Muqtada al-Sadr); and other matters. Can we even hazard a guess about what conclusions or recommendations Strauss would proffer? Would he remember Paul Wolfowitz? And how many weeks of briefings would he tolerate before he returned, say, to complete his study of Plato's *Gorgias* (see *SPPP* vii)?

In the same decade that Hannah Arendt (who died in 1975) was writing in detail about the Pentagon Papers, the Viet Cong, civil disobedience, the Fourteenth Amendment, the New Left, Black Power, John F. Kennedy, Lyndon Baines Johnson, Richard Nixon, Robert McNamara, Frantz Fanon, Noam Chomsky, and James Forman, Strauss was producing his most remote works (*SA, XSD, XS, AAPL*);[70] in the year of his death, Strauss returned to refine his discussion of Thucydides on the gods and to write an essay on Xenophon's *Anabasis*.[71] As far as I can recall, in none of Strauss's published writings does he mention the

WPA, the TVA, the FBI, the stock market, inflation, deflation, the gold standard, protective tariffs, tax shelters, deficit spending, mortgages, alcoholism, J. Edgar Hoover, John Foster Dulles, George Kennan, Dean Acheson, Harry Truman, Henry Kissinger, LBJ, Fidel Castro, Ho Chi Minh, Maoism, the Marshall Plan, the Korean War, the Suez Canal, Anthony Eden, Konrad Adenauer, Gamal Adbel Nasser, Golda Meier, Moshe Dayan, the Berlin Wall, NATO, the Warsaw Pact, ICBMs, radar, computers, the Bay of Pigs, the Cuban Missile Crisis, Mexico, prison recidivism, the National Recovery Administration, the minimum wage, Social Security, Medicare, the AFL-CIO, the American Federation of Teachers, power plants, oil refining, highway construction, lead poisoning, coal mining, nuclear waste, water pollution, pesticides, deforestation, Martin Luther King, Malcolm X, migrant labor, the Black Panthers, the 1967 War, or the Civil Rights Act.

I know of only five interventions by Strauss (during his decades in America) that one could plausibly characterize as "political." As previously noted, in 1943 he delivered a lecture about the reeducation of Germany. Second, in 1957 he wrote a long letter to the *National Review* defending Israel.[72] Third, he wrote a 1961 memo to Charles H. Percy, the Republican CEO of Bell & Howell, about the desirability of reaching a *modus vivendi* with the Soviet Union (Percy served as the U.S. Senator from Illinois from 1967 to 1985 and wrote the foreword for Jaffa's 1965 *Equality and Liberty*, which was dedicated to Strauss).[73] Fourth, he joined the University Center for Rational Alternatives (UCRA) founded in 1969 by Sidney Hook, Oscar Handlin, Lewis Feuer, and others. This group, which by 1973 had roughly 3,000 members, opposed the "academic disruption and violence" associated with the student revolts of the late 1960s.[74] Fifth and finally, Strauss joined Hook, Handlin, and forty other professors in signing a *New York Times* ad that endorsed Nixon over McGovern in 1972.[75] To the ever-expanding group of individuals who identify Straussianism with the imperial presidency, however, I would commend the complaint Strauss offered concerning an episode of presidential aggrandizement that pales before the maneuvers of either Nixon or George W. Bush. As conveyed in a personal letter to Willmoore Kendall, Strauss was irate about President Kennedy's efforts to promote the 1963 limited test-ban treaty: "I know nothing of constitutional law but I cannot believe that 'advice and consent of the Senate' means that the Senate can be confronted with a fait accompli like the test ban treaty: is there no possibility that some representatives of the foreign relations committee who are in the opposition must be called in for this kind of negotiations long before any treaty is initialed?"[76]

It is difficult to imagine that even the most ardent Straussians in 2002 and 2003 were worrying about what Strauss would have recommended concerning Iraq. Someone blessed with total clarity about the divine, the good, and the soul would still need abundant and diverse information to succeed in politics, as

Strauss himself emphasizes.[77] If you insist on designating an offbeat scapegoat for the war, try Albert Wohlstetter—or Ralph Nader, whose third-party candidacy contributed to the defeat of Al Gore in 2000.

IV. LIAR, LIAR

The "noble lie," which has become the chief identifying mark of Straussianism, deserves vastly more space than I can here allocate to it. Let me offer only four points to counteract the burgeoning infamy. First, leaders and lovers all over the world have been lying for millennia without any help from Leo Strauss.[78] The infamous line from Schmitt and Shulsky about the deception integral to politics was, ironically, *supported* by Saddam's success in pretending to have hidden WMDs;[79] Saddam was *more* devious than people realized. Many prominent critics have conceded that, however flagrantly the Bush administration distorted the evidence about the aluminum tubes, the Niger "yellowcake" uranium, and the mobile bioweapons labs, it had excellent reasons for believing that WMDs would turn up in Iraq.[80] The 2008 SSCI report—issued under a Democrat-controlled Senate by a committee that Senator John D. Rockefeller IV chaired—emphasized that several key allegations from the Bush administration were "substantiated" by the then-available estimates from U.S. intelligence agencies.[81] Almost everyone failed to consider that Saddam Hussein was hiding a lack of weapons, not weapons. In her Senate remarks of 10 October 2002, Hillary Clinton stated that Saddam "has worked to rebuild his chemical and biological weapons stock, his missile-delivery capability and his nuclear program"; she even accused him of giving "aid, comfort, and sanctuary to terrorists, including Al Qaeda members."[82] Just a month earlier, furthermore, Al Gore spoke still more forcefully: "We *know* that he [Saddam] has stored away secret supplies of biological weapons and chemical weapons *throughout* his country."[83]

Second, as the Zuckerts deftly convey, Strauss emphasized the noble, not the lie; "insofar as philosophical reticence or accommodation is justified, it is justified by the public good" (*TALS* 127). In the *Republic*, Socrates tells his interlocutors, and Plato thus tells his readers, that the relevant tale about the "city in speech"—that its guardians were fashioned together under its territory by the god, who also set up the infamous hierarchy of souls (gold, silver, iron/bronze)—is a lie.[84] Plato and Socrates are here communicating an important *truth*: "the ways in which nature falls short in supplying a perfectly just foundation for political life." In a similar spirit, observe the Zuckerts, Strauss in the *TM* introduction questions America's lies about its origins—by highlighting the Louisiana Purchase and "the fate of the Red Indians" after citing Thomas Paine's suggestion that the United States was built on freedom and justice—and he elsewhere proclaims the "injustices" and "hypocrisy" of traditional aristocracies (*LAM* 21).[85] Arthur Melzer adds that for the classical philosophers, esotericism was also a way to "protect and preserve the commonsense, pretheoretical awareness of the city."[86]

Third, lying can be highly imprudent, as we all learned from Chicken Little and the Boy Who Cried Wolf. Francis Boyle loves to quote Machiavelli's commendation of deception—"he who deceives will always find someone who will let himself be deceived"—but even Machiavelli never suggests that you can keep deceiving the same people in the same way on any topic you choose.[87] The Bush administration suffered a grievous loss of credibility at home and abroad. Having embarrassed itself by issuing the most confident proclamations about Saddam's WMDs, the U.S. government may have a harder time dealing with genuine proliferation problems. Having disgraced itself by its predictions of a glorious post-invasion Iraq and by its inadequate planning for the occupation, the administration damaged its capacity to summon other difficult endeavors (e.g., addressing the financial meltdown of 2008).

Fourth, erring is different from lying.[88] There is also a difference between lying and exaggerating, especially when the latter entails emphasizing the considerations that are most suitable for persuading the relevant audience. As has been widely discussed, Wolfowitz admitted to Sam Tanenhaus that the WMD argument was trumpeted because the administration thought it would sell better than would appeals to the administration's other "fundamental concerns," including the plight of the Iraqi people.[89]

V. DIVERSITY DISHONESTY

To help skeptical readers fathom "the possibility that political life may be closely linked to deception" (Schmitt and Shulsky), I shall now offer examples of rhetorical "targeting" from the annals of affirmative action. What one could call the "first wave" in combating segregation and Jim Crow in postwar America pursued colorblindness via antidiscrimination laws and policies.[90] As late as 1965, affirmative action (in President Johnson's Executive Order 11246) retained its intimate association with color-blindness: federal contractors were instructed to "take affirmative action to ensure that applicants are employed, and that employees are treated during employment, without regard to their race, creed, color, or national origin";[91] to this day, there is extensive support for outreach programs, the publicizing of job openings, the gathering of racial/ethnic data, and other steps designed to prevent discrimination against the relevant groups. By the 1970s, however, institutions routinely used the term "affirmative action" to describe color-conscious programs intended to reduce the effects of discrimination that had been pervasive in the *past*. In the words of Justice Ginsburg from her dissent in *Gratz v. Bollinger* 539 U.S. 244 (2003), "[a]ctions designed to burden groups long denied full citizenship stature are not sensibly ranked with measures taken to hasten the day when entrenched discrimination and its after effects have been extirpated."[92]

Professor Randall Kennedy of Harvard Law School admits that the early crusade to dismantle the legacy of Jim Crow may have included deception: "insofar as widespread trauma accompanied the demand that blacks simply be treated the same as whites, it made perfect tactical sense not to raise additional issues that could result only in increased resistance."[93] The constant packaging of affirmative action with equal opportunity ("an AA/EO employer") helps to obscure the discrimination, however limited in scope and intensity, that preferential treatment entails. In the 1979 *Weber* case (*United Steelworkers of America, AFL-CIO v. Weber* [443 U.S. 193]), when the Supreme Court upheld a job-training program that reserved half of the slots for black employees, the Court had to reject the "literal interpretation" of the 1964 Civil Rights Act. Title VII (Section 703a) of that act forbids an employer "to discriminate against any individual with respect to his compensation, terms, conditions, or privileges of employment, because of such individual's race, color, religion, sex, or national origin"; an employer is even forbidden "to limit, segregate, or classify his employees or applicants for employment in any way which would deprive any individual of employment opportunities or otherwise adversely affect his status as an employee" because of the designated traits.[94] Insofar as EO/antidiscrimination laws prevent one from asking an applicant about his or her racial or ethnic identity, of course, "diversity"-seeking employers must often read between the lines to determine whether an applicant falls into a targeted category.

Strauss himself noted that legal/formal equality in the United States coexisted with a pervasive type of inequality: "a social hierarchy at the bottom of which are the Negroes (or colored people in general)."[95] While drawing out the logic of what he provisionally calls the "Socratic-Platonic-Stoic natural right teaching" (*NRH* 146), Strauss identifies justice with "equality of opportunity" (every citizen has "the opportunity, corresponding to his capacities, of deserving well of the whole and receiving the proper reward for his deserts") that precludes discrimination based on sex, beauty, and other irrelevant characteristics (*NRH* 148).[96] In retrospect, however, he was too pessimistic about the prospects for fighting discrimination in the United States and Europe: because liberalism "stands or falls by the distinction between state and society, or by the recognition of a private sphere, protected by the law but impervious to the law," Strauss argues, the liberal state is "constitutionally unable and even unwilling to prevent 'discrimination' against Jews by individuals or groups."[97] A legal prohibition would abolish the private sphere and therefore destroy the liberal state (*SCR* 6/*LAM* 230). It seems to me that his thinking here about the private sphere was too rigid or abstract. Justice Thomas, the alleged Straussian, has many allies in thinking that natural rights protect individuals, even in the private sphere, from arbitrary treatment based on their race, ethnicity, sex, and analogous traits.

The final turning point for diversity was the 1978 *Bakke* case (*Regents of the University of California v. Bakke* [438 U.S. 265]). Because the UC–Davis Medical School was a public institution, the Court's attention focused on the equal protection clause of the Fourteenth Amendment, whose language is much vaguer than that of the Civil Rights Act.[98] The Court, applying its "strict scrutiny" standard, struck the medical school's admissions plan, which reserved sixteen seats in each class for designated minority groups (Blacks, Chicanos, Asians, and American Indians). In his plurality opinion, Justice Powell concluded that several goals the UC Regents had invoked to justify the preferences—increasing the number of minority doctors, countering the general effects of societal discrimination, and increasing the number of physicians serving minority communities—were not "substantial enough to support the use of a suspect classification" (IV A–C). In section IVD of his opinion, however, Powell argued that "the attainment of a diverse student body . . . clearly is a constitutionally permissible goal for an institution of higher education." Diversity thereafter became America's most capacious and tendentious mantra. In *Grutter v. Bollinger* (539 U.S. 306 [2003]), a Court majority finally ruled that student diversity could reconcile appropriately configured preferential treatment with the "strict scrutiny" standard.

Despite the history I have sketched above, many ardent friends, or at least flatterers, of democracy expressed outrage that referenda in California (Proposition 209 in 1996), Washington (Initiative 200 in 1998), and Michigan (Proposal 2 in 2006) appropriated the phrase "civil rights initiative" when attempting to ban preferential treatment (in public institutions) based on "race, sex, color, ethnicity, or national origin."[99]

The largest, and least noble, lie that surfaced in the debate over the Michigan cases was this claim: without the relevant plans—the twenty-point bump the undergraduate college allotted to targeted groups and the more "holistic" treatment that the law school adopted to ensure that it would enroll a "critical mass" of said groups—the respective student bodies would include no "meaningful diversity." Our first defendant will be Jeffrey S. Lehman, the president of Cornell University. Although his warm-up was more nuanced, Lehman built to the claim that "without affirmative action pedagogically meaningful diversity could not be achieved."[100] On its face, this claim is absurd. Since no Bokanovsky groups from *Brave New World* might enroll, even an all-white student body—not to mention one that was, say, 4 percent rather than 8 percent African American—would probably include vast realms of "pedagogically meaningful diversity." Students would differ in age, sex, sexual orientation, marital status, religion, health, wealth, nationality, region of origin, cultivated talents (e.g., art, music, drama, and athletics), political ideology, undergraduate major, family background, drug/alcohol usage, career plans, and other qualities relevant to the educational experience. What Lehman meant to say, I believe, is that without a critical mass of the targeted racial/ethnic groups, the standard "multicultural" benefits of diversity would be fatally compromised. A cruder version of Lehman's claim appears in an *amicus* brief filed by a group of organizations including the American Jewish Committee, the Central Conference of American Rabbis, and Hadassah: disallowing consideration of race "would have the effect of eliminating meaningful diversity on American campuses,"[101] as if having a batch of Jewish or Muslim students on a Christian campus would represent a meaningless form of diversity. My final example comes from the brief issued by thirty-eight private institutions including Brandeis, Cal Tech, Carnegie Mellon, Emory, Johns Hopkins, Notre Dame, NYU, Northwestern, and Rochester. After acknowledging the roughly 200-point combined-SAT gap between whites and African Americans in 2002, and adding that high-school grades are another "seemingly race race-neutral factor" that can "disadvantage qualified minority applicants," the authors offer this presumptuous claim: we are "acutely aware that such allegedly race-neutral factors tend to skew admissions against meaningful diversity."[102] Are the members of a group an undifferentiated blob unless that group includes a critical mass of African Americans and Latinos?

Perhaps the most pathetic abuse of diversity-language in the Michigan briefs comes when the American Sociological Association summons the allegedly rock-solid findings of "sociological research." The brief asserts that "growing up nonwhite" is "an experience that sociological research *demonstrates* transcends *every other* life experience."[103] Could there possibly exist studies proving, say, that being a child in a typical Chinese American family is more traumatizing than being a child in a white household plagued by alcoholism, drug addiction, spousal abuse, or pedophilia? Are there studies equating the struggle of a typical Latino child with the struggles of white children afflicted by blindness, deafness, leukemia, diabetes, autism, cerebral palsy, or quadriplegism? Are there even studies demonstrating that growing up African American shapes one's identity more than the experience of growing up Amish, Hasidic, or Wahabi?

By converting "diversity" into a political/policy slogan, the academic world (joined by other powerful sectors of American society) has wielded its influence to eviscerate a noble word. The points I have made in the preceding seven paragraphs have little if any bearing on whether affirmative action and "diversity" policies are just and/or socially beneficial.[104] I would insist, however, that the corrupting effects of politics on language and thought are not limited to the right half of the political spectrum.

For the foreseeable future, Straussians of all stripes will confront layers of acute suspicion. Anyone who is unfamiliar with a "critical mass" of Straussians should refrain from generalizing about them. And anyone who wants to explain the foreign policy of the Bush administration should be skeptical when considering the assessments offered by Robbins, Hersh, Norton, Drury, Shorris, Massey,

Jim George, and comparable figures. Given the anger and prejudice that Strauss and his followers routinely summon, finally, academics have even more reason to avoid touting diversity without specifying the types (e.g., racial/ethnic and sexual) they mean to address.

VI. WINKS, NODS, AND DISGUISES

Although I have hardly refuted the proposition that Irving and Bill Kristol are pursuing a political "realignment" inspired by Leo Strauss, I would like to offer additional reasons for proceeding cautiously in making such charges. Hints, intimations, and deeply buried teachings can operate powerfully in provoking thought, liberating inhibitions, enticing philosophical effort, and inculcating patience; as Drury and others have noted, such devices can also serve to give the reader an "investment" in various conclusions. The devices, however, are less useful for riling up revolutionary passions, imparting dogma, or laying out a program.[105] According to Strauss, Machiavelli's *Prince* and *Discourses* include a hidden agenda that is detailed, comprehensive, and radical, but Drury ignores or at least depreciates Strauss's account of Machiavelli's campaign. Nothing in Strauss's corpus, in any event, approaches the ubiquitous ridicule Machiavelli directs against current "modes and orders" and their underpinnings, a ridicule that continually weakens the "respect" that would deter revolution and other forms of violence. Nor does Strauss provide a constant parade of errors, contradictions, and puzzles that undermine the explicit arguments and assertions he provides. Strauss's observations about the antidogmatic essence of Plato's dialogues apply also to his own writings. How could one impart slogans between the lines of a commentary? The more lengthy and convoluted a text is, the less suited it is for conveying practical guidance. Persuasion via esoteric teachings cannot appeal to crude prejudice, provoke wrath, or guide action as ordinary discourse can.[106] Someone might think God has commanded him to exterminate infidels, but a teaching must be rational or at least persuasive. I was drawn to Strauss by the penetrating and meticulous reading, writing, and thinking that I believe he models. For recipes and rabble-rousing, one should look elsewhere.

Although it cannot serve as the last word on the subject, the Zuckerts provide a thorough, thoughtful, and witty overview of the literary maneuvering that Strauss practiced in the course of his unprecedented campaign to *expose* esoteric teachings from Thucydides and Aristophanes through Nietzsche. Given the crisis into which historicism had propelled modernity, the Zuckerts argue, Strauss generated a new kind of enlightenment that could revive the prospect of natural right and "save the possibility of philosophy by showing its true nature, its real worth, and its content freed from its exoteric accoutrements." By highlighting esotericism, he was presumably making it *more* difficult to deploy (*TALS* 127–28, 132, 134)—at least in countries where his writings were readily accessible.[107] To the extent that he wrote as he read (*PAW* 144), requiring readers to penetrate various obscurities and to dot some *i*'s, he was primarily aiming at two goals: to address playfully the widespread skepticism with which his esoteric *readings* were greeted; and to promote "philosophic education" by enticing his readers to scrutinize the original texts and to exercise their skills upon his puzzles (*TALS* 138–39, 135–36, 140).[108] Such pursuits, obviously, leave Straussians with less time for lobbying, pamphleting, and campaigning, not to mention insurrectionary plotting.[109] As early as 1939, Strauss commended classical authors as "the most efficient teachers of independent thinking."[110] Although Steven Lenzner has done more than any author I have encountered to diagnose contradictions, ambiguities, and interpretive errors in Strauss, Lenzner unearths carefully constructed pedagogical lessons rather than invitations to political action. Xenos makes a serious effort to uncover the latter, but he has only scratched the surface. Apart from the numerous objections I have already articulated, I would pose this question to Xenos: how exactly does Strauss entice his American readers to cherish a "deeply reactionary" (*CV* xi) agenda?

As previously mentioned, the hyperscholarly pages of *Political Theory* recently highlighted the "long rumored" possibility of a secret Straussian teaching that has been "guarded by some sect of his surviving disciples."[111] Strauss himself acknowledges that various premodern philosophers hid their opinions by "limiting themselves to oral instruction of a carefully selected group of pupils" (*PAW* 34–35). On the other hand, Strauss published extensively, and also spoke at great length to the crowds who took or audited his classes.[112] Drury boasts that her momentous 1988 allegations about Strauss were based "exclusively" on an analysis of his published works (*PILS-05* ix). Many of Strauss's classes at Chicago and St. John's were tape-recorded, transcribed, and copied, but Drury never cites or addresses these transcripts. The transcription of his 1959 class on the *Symposium* was, with Strauss's permission, edited by Seth Benardete and eventually published.[113]

From a professor who possesses transcripts for roughly thirty-three courses, I acquired the following account. Most of Strauss's classes in the 1960s were seminars devoted to a single text and/or author; there were also lecture classes, such as "Natural Right and History." The seminars began with a student reading a seven-page (double-spaced) paper on the assigned portion of text; after commenting on the paper, Strauss would launch a discussion of that portion; typically, a designated student would read aloud various passages that Strauss wanted to address. The transcripts were routinely distributed to PhD students once they had been appointed to teaching positions.[114] Since the transcripts have been around for decades, I assume that some critic would have sounded the alarm about any subliminal exhortations to fascist revolution or nihilistic destruction. The acute political controversies that divided leading first-generation

Straussians such as Jaffa, Bloom, Martin Diamond, and Walter Berns provide additional evidence that no "sect" is guarding a secret oral teaching.[115]

Heinrich Meier, the editor of Strauss's *Gesammelte Schriften*, neither met Strauss nor studied with any of his students.[116] Peter Berkowitz, who has contributed numerous articles to both the *Wall Street Journal* and the *New Republic*, was inspired by Marx-indebted professors during his undergraduate days at Swarthmore, where he majored in English; after living in a kibbutz, he earned a master's degree in philosophy at the Hebrew University of Jerusalem, where he simply "stumbled upon" *Spinoza's Critique of Religion* in the library.[117] In the introduction to his recent study, Meier provides a persuasive overview of the phenomena that constrain and distort verbal transmission:

> The founding of the school will be successful only if the teacher adapts his oral teaching to his students' ability to understand. It is very likely that he will entrust his farthest-reaching reflections, his most profound thoughts, and his most challenging considerations to his carefully written books. Members of a school, however, are inclined to value the oral tradition more highly. They tend to overestimate or to regard as absolutely indispensable what for them was of enormous significance.[118]

These considerations reinforce the obvious mandate that one treat Strauss's published writings as being more authoritative than his correspondence and lectures. Most people who find themselves intoxicated by Strauss, in any case, would presumably be inclined to spend decades learning languages, mastering his multimillennial set of sources, and dissecting his commentaries. "Historicism is not a cab which one can stop at his convenience" (*WIPP* 72), and the same may apply to Straussianism.[119]

Drury, by contrast, seems to imply that certain students quickly flash to the esoteric teaching presented in—not between—the lines (*PILS* ix) and then haunt "the corridors of power" (*PILS*-05 xvi) in order to renovate politics by whispering magical charms against peace, freedom, and equal opportunity. Even if there were a conspiratorial message along the lines that Drury suggests, I would condemn the way she attempts to unearth it via misquotation, exaggeration, slander, oracular proclamation, and a shortcut—attributing to Strauss the views he attributes to the wise ancients—that she frequently fails to follow.

I acknowledge that none of Strauss's scholarship is immune to criticism, and that extremely painstaking work would be required to demonstrate his thesis that the books of Machiavelli and others have had the world-transforming influence he alleges; ironically, this thesis may now be better received because of the widespread allegations of a *Straussian* conspiracy. I also acknowledge that Strauss and his followers often cut corners in addressing the secondary literature when they write about past authors (many stereotypes have *some* foundation in reality). I would nevertheless exhort the scholarly mainstreams to open themselves to his "diverse" contributions. Consider the praise recently issued by two non-Straussians free of neoconservative taint. For Perry Anderson, "Strauss's range and subtlety as a master of the canon of political philosophy had no equal in his generation"; for George Kateb, Strauss was a great reader who "revivifies what he touches" and a thinker "through whose mind every idea passed, from the most radical to the most reactionary."[120]

If Strauss, within so many interpretive studies that I find compelling, smuggled in intricate plans for Machiavelli-scale innovation, then I would regard him as the greatest writer who ever lived—even if I were horrified by the hidden plans. George Sabine and others would have to abandon the claim that Strauss's readings were an invitation to "perverse ingenuity," and concede that Strauss had deployed an almost superhuman ingenuity that brought a perverse future into being.

Imagine that you were confident you could identify Strauss's deepest teaching within the chorus of views he reconstructs: if you are inspired by him to cherish independent thinking, there is little reason to adopt his views unless you find them more persuasive than the numerous contrary views he elaborates as a commentator—and other alternatives you encounter elsewhere.[121] "Since the greatest minds contradict one another regarding the most important matters, they compel us to judge of their monologues; we cannot take or trust what any one of them says" (*LAM* 7). By his relentless efforts to reconstruct the teachings of the authors he interprets, Pangle suggests, Strauss "experiments with (and tries to seduce his readers to follow him in experimenting with) becoming a convert, if you will, to each great thinker's argumentative power and revelatory insight into the phenomena."[122]

By explaining European and Middle Eastern traditions of esotericism to Americans, Strauss contributed to a new Enlightenment, however many puzzles he left for his readers to solve. As the transmitter of a heritage that otherwise might have remained buried for centuries, Strauss is a conservative, or at least a conserver.[123] That heritage also provides a common ground with the religion that is now inspiring America's most inveterate enemies.[124] After quoting Strauss's claim that "human beings will never create a society which is free from contradictions" (*SCR* 6/*LAM* 230), Pangle suggests that, regarding foreign policy, Strauss would promote a "liberal outlook that, in a spirit ready to learn and to argue, holds open the door to a dialogue with decent and thoughtful critics emerging from alien and especially more traditional sorts of social and religious outlooks."[125] For these and other reasons, Strauss is a friend, but not a flatterer, of diversity. In seeking a "counterpoison" to the "mass culture" (*LAM* 5) that increasingly dominates our world, Strauss has exposed Baby Boomers and surrounding generations to philosophical peaks from many times and places that otherwise could seem alien and repulsive. By enticing his students and readers to appreciate the "still and small voices" (*LAM* 25) that can reside beneath the surfaces of discourse, furthermore, Strauss equips both feminists and "multiculturalists" to combat hegemony. With the help of the Internet, DVDs, and the traumas of the Iraq War, study of Strauss will doubtless spread. Will he wither under the light of exposure, or will legions of historicists wilt under assault from harsher and younger Straussians?

No one has done more than Leo Strauss to illuminate the depths of Enlightenment and pre-Enlightenment political philosophy. Applying the insights he uncovered is our challenge, not his.

NOTES

1. The first edition of Drury's book, published in 1988, briefly addressed Thucydides (*PILS* 196–97). Though the discussion is hardly unproblematic, I shall respond only to the material she added in 2005, which is more detailed and provocative.

2. Irving Kristol, "The Neoconservative Persuasion," *Weekly Standard*, 25 August 2003, 24.

3. A Crooked Timber blogger named "Henry"—who I assume is Henry Farrell, a political science professor at George Washington University—shares Drury's general contempt for Strauss, but reverses Drury regarding Strauss's approach to Thucydides' civic preferences. Whereas most interpreters read the *History* as a "step-by-step dissection of Athenian arrogance," claims Henry, Strauss "sees it as a celebration of Athens' love for the noble and the beautiful" (http://crooked timber.org/2003/10/03/what-was-leo-strauss-up-to). For Strauss and his followers, adds the author, the United States is "the closest thing going in the modern world to the grandeur that was classical Athens." Strauss's "tortured" reading thus promoted America's efforts in the Cold War. This article appears under the title, "What Was Leo Strauss Up To?" (it was posted on 3 October 2003). Henry Farrell is the only "Henry" among the sixteen individuals specified in the "Who Are We" section of the blog. I directed multiple queries to Professor Farrell but received no reply.

4. To appreciate how Drury abuses Strauss's discussion of Spartan *piety*, consider the way *PILS*-05 xxxvi misquotes (by adding "because they"), and additionally embellishes, what Strauss wrote about Spartan "adversity in the first part of the war" (*CM* 182).

5. Drury here contradicts one of her concluding claims in *PILS*: "democratic society provides the sort of freedom that is necessary to the unhampered pursuit of the philosophical life," and Strauss thus "makes it clear that he is not an enemy of democracy" (*PILS* 194). As was previously discussed, however, Drury's new introduction relays an even more egregious contradiction when it asserts that her original volume "showed" that Strauss was "a sworn enemy of freedom and democracy" (*PILS*-05 ix).

6. *CM* 215, 231–34; on Cleon's Spartan characteristics, see 213–14; Thucydides presents the debate between Cleon and Diodotus at III.35–50.

7. In the essay on Thucydides that appears in the third edition of the Strauss and Cropsey textbook, *The History of Political Philosophy* (Chicago: University of Chicago Press, 1987), David Bolotin similarly extols both Diodotus and the denouement of the Mytilenaian debate (21–22, 28–31). Cf. Orwin, "The Just and the Advantageous," and Howse, "Leo Strauss—Man of War?" 74–77.

8. Cf. pp. 122–23 above.

9. In one of the twelve paragraphs of his speech (II.39), Pericles does contrast Athens with Sparta.

10. Cf. Workman, "When Might Is Right," 141–42. In the words of Seth Benardete: "The structure of the whole is plainly designed to let each of the various aspects of Thucydides' history come to light by itself, so that one will both be tempted to see and be checked from seeing each aspect as the whole of Thucydides' meaning" (Benardete, "Leo Strauss's *The City and Man*," 14).

11. Note that only the Spartan superiority is voiced conditionally ("may have been"), and that the Athenian superiority is larger ("by far").

12. To counteract Drury's crude allegations of Spartanism, one must also fathom Strauss's claim that Thucydides sometimes presented incomplete judgments touting Sparta because he was adopting "the point of view of those on whom he passes judgment" (*CM* 208). Analogously, after observing that the Spartan Brasidas is the only Thucydidean character "praised by the author for his mildness," Strauss explains that although Nicias and Demosthenes were no less mild, Thucydides highlights Brasidas primarily because "mildness was so rare among Spartans as distinguished from Athenians" (*CM* 213).

13. *CM* 180, 221, 224; cf. 225 on Spartan "ineptness" and "comedy." On 180, Strauss also seems to refer in his own name to the "ridiculous features of Sparta," and his judgment likewise seems to surface within the other cited references.

14. *CM* 206, 226; Thucydides presents Pericles' remark in the first sentence of II.41.

15. Shadia B. Drury, "Leo Strauss and the American Imperial Project," *Political Theory* 35, no. 1 (February 2007): 64.

16. Strauss, "Spirit of Sparta," 528.

17. Strauss, "Spirit of Sparta," 531.

18. Cf. *XSD* 119 on "the critique of Sparta that is implicit in the *Oeconomicus* as a whole." To the extent that Xenophon's writings had a "pro-Spartan bias," Strauss suggests, that bias was—at least in part—an exoteric accommodation to the reality Xenophon articulates at *Anabasis* IV.6.9: "at that time the Spartans ruled all Greeks" (*SPPP* 130, 133; cf. the discussions of Xenophon's exile on *SPPP* 122, 136).

19. Drury adds that Strauss educated "an elite of callous ruffians unfit for political power" (*PILS*-05 xvii).

20. The subtitle to this article—"Shadia Drury *imagines* the progress of a disciple . . . from graduate student to Washington"—properly highlights the fantasy element (emph. added). If only there were subtitles to warn the reader about the flights of fancy in her other works.

21. As previously discussed (p. 96n106, Drury did once state that Strauss taught some of his students to be "statesmen and gentlemen" while teaching others to be philosophers (*PILS* 188).

22. Gottfried, "Strauss," 28.

23. Abella errs similarly when he claims that Wolfowitz became a student of Bloom's at Chicago (*Soldiers of Reason* 198n).

24. Hirsh, "Welcome to the Real World," 32.

25. See pp. 24–25 above on Wolfowitz's debt to Strauss and Bloom.

26. Hamid Dabashi, "Native Informers and the Making of the American Empire," *Al-Ahram Weekly*, 1–7 June 2006 (#797), http://weekly.ahram.org.eg/2006/797/special.htm.

27. Drury, "Leo Strauss and the American Imperial Project," 62.

28. Easton, *Gang of Five*, 47, 409n47. For an illuminating overview of Bill Kristol's influence in pushing for the U.S. invasion of Iraq, see Gary Dorrien, "'Benevolent Global Hegemony': William Kristol and the Politics of American Empire," *Logos* 3.2 (Spring 2004), http://www.logosjournal.com/dorrien.htm.

29. In the 1995 essay, Kristol (b. 1920) also highlights Sidney Hook as an early influence and links the impact of Trilling and Strauss (on Kristol) with later decades (the 1940s and the 1950s, respectively); in another essay, Kristol states that Trilling and Reinhold Niebuhr were his "two intellectual godfathers" in the late 1940s (Irving Kristol, *Neoconservatism: The Autobiography of an Idea* [New York: The Free Press, 1995], 6, 484; also see 13–15 and 483 on the chronology). For the record, Kristol elsewhere includes Strauss—along with Milton Friedman, Friedrich Hayek, and "the cultural conservatives"—in sketching the intellectual roots of neoconservatism (Irving Kristol, *Reflections of a Neoconservative* [New York: Basic Books, 1983], xii). For additional comments by Kristol on Strauss, see *Reflections*, 76, and *Neoconservatism*, 6–9, 145, 158, 187–88, 380.

30. "Drury, "Leo Strauss," 62.

31. Irving Kristol, "Neoconservative Persuasion," 24. Kristol elsewhere claims that political philosophers, from Thucydides on, found the international realm to be "so radically affected by contingency, fortune and fate" that they saw "little room for speculative enlightenment"; ideology, says Kristol, "can obtain exasperatingly little purchase over the realities of foreign policy" (*Neoconservatism* 78–79).

32. Massey, *Return*, 129–30.

33. *LSPAE* 47. Shorris invokes biology rather than architecture: Strauss and his followers carry "the imperialism of Pericles in the DNA of their political philosophy" (Shorris, *Politics of Heaven*, 260). Workman too reaches a sweeping conclusion—"Straussian thought on empire is virtually indistinguishable from its reading of Thucydides" ("When Might Is Right" 144)—but offers illuminating reflections as he compares Strauss and Orwin with competing interpreters of Thucydides.

34. Thomas Donnelly, principal author, *Rebuilding America's Defenses: Strategy, Forces and Resources for a New Century*, http://www.newamericancentury.org/RebuildingAmericasDefenses. pdf (September 2000). As Drury's discussion commences, she fails both to relay the four recommendations the 1997 PNAC Statement of Principles provides (http://www.newamericancentury .org/statementof principles.htm) and to distinguish that statement from the organization (PNAC) that issued it (*PILS*-05 xxxviii); Drury's note 43 on p. lv conveys additional errors. In the summer of 2008, both PNAC and its website appeared to be defunct, but the website later revived. Cf. Paul Reynolds, "End of the Neo-con Dream," *BBC News*, 21 December 2006, http://news.bbc.co.uk/2/ hi/middle_east/6189793.stm.

35. *PILS*-05 xxix. Drury also here provides the common and more impressionistic accusations that the authors are "intoxicated with power and the glorification of war" and write "as if the world were clay or putty."

36. Donnelly et al., *Rebuilding*, 7.

37. Whereas I included Drury's above-mentioned claim about Strauss's "antipathy" for Athens on my "top ten" list for *foolish* comments, these new statements summon the *demonizing* label. Both labels might be needed to characterize this recent outburst: Straussians "pretend that fighting to augment American interests around the world is the same as fighting for God's own justice, truth, and freedom against satanic foes" (*AM* 129). Cf. p. 212n9 above on Strauss and Carl Schmitt.

38. See p. 145 above on "To My Critics" and pp. 198–99 above on the Grand Inquisitor.

39. *CM* 44; *NRH* 34, 192; Socratic rhetoric is "based on the premise that there is a disproportion between the intransigent quest for truth and the requirements of society, or that not all truths are always harmless" (*OT* 26). When Adam Curtis argues that in "an age when all the grand ideas have lost credibility," the "fear of a phantom enemy is all the politicians have left to maintain their power," it doesn't occur to him that he and others are making a phantom enemy of Strauss and Straussians. See part 3, "The Shadows in the Cave," http://www.daanspeak.com/TranscriptPower OfNightmares3.html.

40. For other illustrations of Strauss's "zetetic" approach, see *LAM* 7; *WIPP* 11, 39; *CM* 62; *OT* 37, 105 (cf. 218), 210, 215–16; *RCPR* 235–36, 260, 267; *MITP* 223. The Zuckerts maintain that Strauss "never retreats from his conclusion that philosophy, Socratic or otherwise, can never complete the circle of knowledge" (*TALS* 153). In attributing "a closed mind" to Strauss, Sheldon Wolin joins Drury (Wolin, *Democracy Incorporated*, 312n23).

41. Cf. Plato's *Theatetus* 172c–e. Strauss delivered the lecture, "Reason and Revelation," at Hartford Theological Seminary on 8 January 1948. The full text is included in Heinrich Meier, *Leo Strauss*, 141–80; the above quotation appears on 148.

42. *OT* (Gourevitch and Roth) 242.

43. After disparaging predictions that ethnic turmoil would plague post-invasion Iraq, Kaplan and Kristol argued that U.S. forces "could probably be drawn down to several thousand soldiers after a year or two" and that Iraq was "ripe for democracy" (Kaplan and Kristol, *War over Iraq*,

97–99). Even in the pages of the *Claremont Review*, one now reads that for both the Iraq and Afghanistan wars the planning was "conducted with an astonishing indifference to the entirely foreseeable need to create a secure political environment after conventional military operations had ceased" (Colin Dueck, "Arms and the Man," *Claremont Review of Books* [Spring 2007]: 20). The indictment from Mark Helprin, a widely published Claremont Institute fellow, is still more sweeping: "The United States has fought the war in Iraq as if history, strategy, maneuver, preparation, foresight, fact, integrity and common sense did not exist" (Mark Helprin, "Forced to Get Along," *New York Times*, 19 July 2007).

44. Kristol and Lenzner, "What Was Leo Strauss," 38.

45. Paul Wolfowitz, "Victory Came Too Easily," review of *Crusade: The Untold Story of the Persian Gulf War*, by Rick Atkinson, *National Interest* 35 (Spring 1994): 91–92.

46. Paul Wolfowitz, "Statesmanship in the New Century," in Kagan and Kristol, *Present Dangers*, 320–21. A modified version of this essay was published as "Remembering the Future" in *National Interest* 59 (Spring 2000): 35–45. The more I read Wolfowitz, the less he resembles Arianna Huffington's description of him as "one of the most fanatical of the fanatics" (Huffington, *Fanatics and Fools* [New York: Hyperion, 2004], 51).

47. Gary J. Schmitt and Abram N. Shulsky, "The Future of Intelligence," *National Interest* 38 (Winter 1994/1995): 63–73 (the quoted passage is from the eighth paragraph of the section titled "To Centralize or Not?"). Shulsky also supplied an early warning (in a book first published in 1991) about the challenges that defectors pose: "it is difficult to be certain that they are genuine," and the "conflicting information provided by several major Soviet defectors . . . bedeviled U.S. intelligence for a quarter of a century" (Abram N. Shulsky and Gary J. Schmitt, *Silent Warfare: Understanding the World of Intelligence*, 3rd ed. [Dulles, VA: Potomac Books, 2002], 22; Schmitt joined Shulsky to produce the second edition, published in 1993). The artifices of Chalabi and Curveball may endure as long, and with more devastating consequences. Cf. Laura Rozen, "Con Tract: The Theory Behind Neocon Self-Deception," *Washington Monthly* 35, no. 10 (October 2003): 11–13.

48. Ron Suskind, "Faith, Certainty and the Presidency of George W. Bush," *New York Times Magazine*, 17 October 2004.

49. "[M]athematical problems which formerly could not be solved by the greatest mathematical geniuses are now solved by high-school students" (*RCPR* 237); cf. *WIPP* 15–16, "On the Intention of Rousseau" 486, and *LAM* 20, 23.

50. Al Gore, *Assault on Reason*, 117, 188.

51. Cf. Brian Danoff, "Leo Strauss, George W. Bush, and the Problem of 'Regime Change,'" *Social Policy* 34, no. 2–3 (Winter 2003/Spring 2004): 35–40; Francis Fukuyama, "After Neoconservatism," *New York Times*, 19 February 2006; and Zbigniew Brzezinski, *Second Chance: Three Presidents and the Crisis of American Superpower* (New York: Basic Book, 2007), 157.

52. Cf. Strauss on Burke: "Knowing the proper ends of government, one does not know anything of how and to what extent those ends can be realized here and now, under these particular circumstances both fixed and transitory" (*NRH* 305).

53. Cf. TWM 83 on the "immense variety" of "radical change" in modernity.

54. "The teaching of the classics can have no immediate practical effect, because present-day society is not a *polis*" (Strauss, "New Interpretation," 332). Xenos might try to get around such passages by asserting that Strauss proffers fascist imperialism.

55. The relevant cases would include *West Coast Hotel Co. v. Parrish* (1937), *United States v. Carolene Products Co.* (1938), *United States v. Darby* (1941), *West Virginia State Board of Education v. Barnette* (1943), *Korematsu v. United States* (1944), *Everson v. Board of Education* (1947), *Shelly v. Kraemer* (1948), *Dennis v. United States* (1951), *Youngstown Sheet & Tube Co. v. Sawyer* (1952), *Zorach v. Clauson* (1952), *Terry v. Adams* (1953), *Brown v. Board of Education* (1954), *Roth v. United States* (1957), *Mapp v. Ohio* (1961), *Baker v. Carr* (1962), *Engel v. Vitale* (1962), *Sherbert v. Verner* (1963), *School District of Abington Township v. Schempp* (1963), *Reyn-*

olds v. Sims (1964), *Heart of Atlanta Motel, Inc. v. United States* (1964), *Griswold v. Connecticut* (1965), *Harper v. Virginia Board of Elections* (1966), *Miranda v. Arizona* (1966), *United States v. Seeger* (1965), *United States v. O'Brien* (1968), *Brandenburg v. Ohio* (1969), *Welsh v. United States* (1970), and even *Roe v. Wade* (handed down on 22 January 1973, eight months before Strauss died).

56. R. H. S. Crossman, *Plato Today* (Oxford: Oxford University Press, 1939). Crossman's Plato also addresses Nazism and Soviet Communism. Although Strauss commends several chapters for displaying "the common sense and moderation" of Plato, he faults the earlier chapters in which Crossman interpreted "the *Republic* of the dead Plato quite literally" (*WIPP* 264). In 1945, Crossman was elected to a seat in the House of Commons; he served for almost three decades.

57. In his "What Is Political Philosophy" essay, Strauss stated that "political science . . . in the original meaning of the term" would be a defining feature of "the great statesman" (*WIPP* 14).

58. Cf. *LAM* 7, where Strauss laments the "unfortunate necessity which prevents us from listening to the greatest minds of India and of China: we do not understand their languages, and we cannot learn all languages."

59. Patrice Higonnet nevertheless characterizes Straussianism as "a duplicitous Wilsonianism gone mad," hostile to compromise as well as world government (Higonnet, *Attendant Cruelties*, 303). In attempting to sketch a path from Strauss to President Bush's emotionalism, "resoluteness," and indifference to facts and nuance, Patricia Owens misidentifies a statement from *LAM* 22—that only a good intention can be "held to be unqualifiedly good"—as expressing Strauss's views (rather than those of Rousseau or Kant) (Owens, "Beyond Strauss, Lies, and the War in Iraq: Hannah Arendt's Critique of Neo-Conservatism," *Review of International Studies* 33 [2007]: 279; cf. 271). And although Sheldon Wolin emphasizes that Strauss's "teaching" involves principles or values rather than policies and programs, he asserts that "Straussian ideology outfits its adherents . . . with grandiose ambitions, like 'democratizing' the Middle East" (Wolin, *Democracy Incorporated*, 170, 171; cf. 168). On the inevitability of muddling through, see p. 86 above.

60. *WIPP* 28; cf. *OT* 198, *LAM* 6, and *XSD* 83 (quoting Winckelmann on Xenophon).

61. Leo Strauss, "The Crisis of Our Time," in Harold J. Spaeth, ed., *The Predicament of Modern Politics* (Detroit: University of Detroit Press, 1964), 43.

62. In his 1946 article about Plato, Strauss both asserted the existence of a practical crisis— "[t]he test of extreme severity which modern civilization is undergoing before our eyes on the plane of action"—and stated that this crisis was "accompanied by an increasingly insistent attack of a theoretical character on the principles of modern civilization" (Strauss, "New Interpretation," 327). He says nothing to specify the severe "test"; perhaps he wanted his readers to think of the Holocaust, the Second World War, and Stalinism. In a 1956 lecture, Strauss did say that "the decline of Europe, the danger to the West, to the whole Western heritage" constitutes a menace comparable to "that which threatened Mediterranean civilization" in roughly 300 A.D. As the paragraph continues, however, Strauss's attention focuses on the cultural or spiritual realm: the replacement of the morning prayer by the morning newspaper (Strauss here cites Nietzsche), "the stimulation of all kinds of interests and curiosities without true passion," and "the danger of universal philistinism and creeping conformism" (*RCPR* 31). Hannah Arendt too speaks casually and confidently of "[t]he general crisis that has overtaken the modern world everywhere and in almost every sphere of life" (Arendt, *Between Past and Future* [New York: Penguin Books, 1977], 170).

63. On the foreign-policy guidelines one might derive from such critiques, see Michael C. Williams, "What Is the National Interest? The Neoconservative Challenge in IR Theory," *European Journal of International Relations* 11, no. 3 (2005): 307–37.

64. Berlin was quoting an unnamed "admirable writer of our time"; that writer is Joseph Schumpeter, in *Capitalism, Socialism, and Democracy* (New York: Harper Torchbooks, 1975), 243. On the crises, also see the following: Gunnell, "Political Theory," 122–34, "Myth," 123–27, and *Between Philosophy and Politics*, 108, 115; André Liebich, "Straussianism and Ideology," in

Ideology, Philosophy, and Politics, ed. Anthony Parel (Waterloo, Canada: Wilfrid Laurier Univ. Press, 1983), 231; and Deutsch and Soffer, *Crisis*, 1–13. To read about the death of liberalism, one should consult not Strauss but Professor Wendy Brown of UC–Berkeley, who argues that "the institutions as well as the political culture comprising liberal democracy are passing into history" (Brown, "American Nightmare: Neoliberalism, Neoconservatism, and De-Democratization," *Political Theory* 34, no. 6 [December 2006]: 691). Given the demise of the Soviet Union and the horrifying rise of Islamic terrorism, Behnegar maintains that "there is so little sense of a crisis of liberal democracy that it seems to be the only game in town, at least in the West" (Behnegar, *Leo Strauss*, 4).

65. As previously discussed, Xenos instead weds premodern thought to authoritarianism, leaving Strauss as the esoteric but enthusiastic promoter of nonracist fascism and imperialism (see pp. 77, 154–57 above).

66. Cf. Xenos, "Neocon Con Game," 243, and *CV* 144.

67. Epilogue 308/*LAM* 204. Also see Dannhauser, "Becoming Naïve Again," 637–41, and the following passages from Strauss: *CM* 11–12 on the primacy of "the common sense understanding of political things" (cf. *CM* 25); *TM* 237 on proceeding "in an orderly and convincing manner from the primarily given, from what can be known by everybody in broad daylight, to the hidden center"; *TM* 13 ("There is no surer protection against the understanding of anything than taking for granted or otherwise despising the obvious and the surface"); and *WIPP* 23–25. According to Stanley Rosen, by contrast, Strauss shared in the "common agreement of ancients and moderns" that philosophy's task is "to create the present by an act of will." See Stanley Rosen, *Hermeneutics as Politics,* 2nd ed. (New Haven, CT: Yale University Press, 2003), 181, cf. 17, 105, 110, 125, 180; by the end of the book, Rosen proclaims himself a Maoist (15, 178, 190–93).

68. On the "Parade of Horribles" memos (Feith's phrase) that Rumsfeld drafted and then shared with key decisionmakers, see Feith, *War and Decision*, 332–35, and David Von Drehle, "Wrestling with History," *Washington Post Magazine*, 13 November 2005, W12. One may grant to Wolfowitz, furthermore, that several major fears he mentioned to Sam Tanenhaus concerning the invasion — for example, "an environmental disaster resulting from huge hydrogen sulfide fires in the north," a "fortress Baghdad," a Turkish intervention, and the collapse of Arab governments — proved to be misplaced.

69. "Since individual events carry the stamp of the whole, those who have reflected on the whole can see the evidence presented by individual events much more clearly than others" (Behnegar, *Leo Strauss*, 208–9).

70. See Hannah Arendt, *Crises of the Republic* (New York: Harcourt Brace Jovanovich, 1972). As Lewis Coser notes, there was "hardly a political controversy, from the civil rights movement to the Vietnam War and Watergate, on which she did not take a passionate stand" (Lewis A. Coser, *Refugee Scholars in America* [New Haven, CT: Yale University Press, 1984] 193).

71. See Lampert, *Leo Strauss*, 10.

72. An online version of Strauss's letter to *National Review*, which appeared on page 23 of the 5 January 1957 issue (vol. 3, no. 1), is available at http://www.claremontmckenna.edu/salvatori/publications/pdf/LeoStrauss.pdf (see appendix A, pp. 43–46).

73. For excerpts from the memo, see the paper Nathan Tarcov posted at http://ptw.uchicago.edu/Tarcov02.pdf, 7, 9. The key step, wrote Strauss, was to convince the Russians that "the free West is here to stay" (9n12).

74. George H. Nash, *The Conservative Intellectual Movement in America: Since 1945* (New York, Basic Books: 1976), 322; cf. 429n7. On UCRA, also see William K. Stevens, "Strategy for Campus," *New York Times*, 7 August 1970. The "academic disruption and violence" phrase is attributed to Sidney Hook in "Rational Alternatives," an article from the 31 August 1970 issue of *Time Magazine*; my estimate of UCRA's membership comes from "Crisis Amid the Calm," *Time Magazine*, 8 October 1973, which also notes Hook's alarm about "the galloping movement

for the abolition of curricular requirements" and the prospect that students will fail to develop "a permanent defense against gullibility." On the reaction of Strauss and/or Straussians to the excesses of the 1960s, also see *TALS* 229–30, Devigne, *Recasting Conservatism*, 55, and Tanguay, "Neo-conservatisme," 316–17.

75. "Of the two major candidates for the Presidency of the United States, we believe that Richard Nixon has demonstrated the superior capacity for prudent and responsible leadership. Consequently, we intend to vote for President Nixon on November 7th and we urge our fellow citizens to do the same." Among the other signers were Donald Fleming, Lon Fuller, Milton Friedman, Gertrude Himmelfarb, Irving Kristol, Robert Nisbet, Edward Shils, Ithiel de Sola Pool, W. V. O. Quine, William Riker, Myron Rush, and Paul Seabury. The advertisement appeared on page E7 of the *Times* on 15 October 1972.

76. John A. Murley and John E. Alvis, *Willmoore Kendall: Maverick of American Conservatives* (Lanham, MD: Lexington Books, 2002), 247. The letter is dated 18 September 1963. Writing their epilogue on Strauss for the 1987 edition of *HPP*, Pangle and Tarcov identified Marxism's most grievous flaw as its failure "adequately to recognize the permanent need to devise institutional checks against the abuse of power" (933).

77. See *WIPP* 61, 83 on "individual situations"; cf. *NRH* 191–92, 305 and *RCPR* 99; and consider Socrates' deflation of Glaucon in Xenophon's *Memorabilia* 3.6 (cf. *CM* 65).

78. Hannah Arendt pulls no punches as she opens her 1954 "Truth and Politics" essay: "No one has ever doubted that truth and politics are on rather bad terms with each other, and no one, as far as I know, has ever counted truthfulness among the political virtues. Lies have always been regarded as necessary and justifiable tools not only of the politician's or the demagogue's but also of the statesman's trade" (Arendt, *Between Past and Future*, 223). Cf. Owens, "Beyond Strauss," 268–69, 281–82.

79. See Daalder and Lindsay, *America Unbound*, 146, 152–53, 155, 159–60; Feith, *War and Decision*, 329–31, 614n; Alfonsi, *Circle in the Sand*, 396–97, 402–4, 408–9; Daniel J. Kevles, "The Poor Man's Atomic Bomb," *New York Review of Books*, 12 April 2007: 63; and Gordon and Trainor, *Cobra II*, 64–66, 118–20, 124–26 (cf. 80–84 and 135–36 on how U.S. military plans were shaped by the perceived need to anticipate chemical and/or biological attacks). Also relevant are these two articles from the *New York Times*: Gordon and Trainor, "Even as U.S. Invaded, Hussein Saw Iraqi Unrest as Top Threat," 12 March 2006; and Nathaniel Fick, "Worries Over Being Slimed," 16 March 2008.

80. The testimony of Brian Urquhart that "hardly anyone" believed the Iraqi denials— "[i]nterminable Iraqi obstructions and deceptions made no sense to the Western powers and Western observers if in fact the WMDs were already destroyed"—might itself suffice (Urquhart, "Disaster: From Suez to Iraq," *New York Review of Books*, 29 March 2007, 35). One can also appeal to numerous other authorities—for example, Dorrien, *Imperial Designs*, 189–91—in addition to the sources cited in the previous note. On the profound impact that anticipation of anthrax and/or smallpox attacks had on Bush, Cheney, Libby, and other decision-makers, see Weisberg, *Bush Tragedy*, 188–97, 200, 205, 209. On the dubious claims regarding the tubes, labs, and yellowcake, see Isikoff and Corn, *Hubris*, 38–41, 165–66, 306–7 (on the tubes); 85–100, 144, 147–48, 162–64, 202–5 (on the yellowcake); 117–19, 124–25, 130–32, 182–84, 226–29, 307–9 (on the mobile labs). Also see Thomas Powers, "What Tenet Knew," *New York Review of Books*, 19 July 2007, 72; Woodward, *Plan of Attack*, 173–74, 197–99, 208, 249, 289–91, 298 312, 327, 331–32, 395–96, 404, 437–39; and Woodward, *State of Denial*, 92–102, 115, 121, 159–60, 165, 214–17, 235–37, 242–43, 278–79, 303–4.

81. U.S. Senate Select Committee on Intelligence, *Report on Whether Public Statements Regarding Iraq by U.S. Government Officials Were Substantiated by Intelligence Information*, June 2008. See the following conclusions: no. 1 (on the possibility of a nuclear program), no. 2 (on possession of biological weapons, production capability, and mobile labs), and no. 3 (on possession

of chemical weapons). The report nevertheless criticizes various pronouncements for having failed to convey, among other things, the "substantial disagreements" among the intelligence reports (no. 1); the report also declares unequivocally that Rumsfeld's Senate testimony about "deeply buried" WMD facilities was "not substantiated by available intelligence information" (no. 6) (see pp. 15, 28, 37, 47, 50 of the document posted at http://intelligence.senate.gov/080605/phase2a.pdf). In addition, the report unequivocally denies that intelligence information supported allegations that Iraq had provided weapons training for Al-Qaida, that the two entities were linked in a "partnership" (no. 12, p. 71), and that Saddam had been "prepared" to equip terrorist groups with WMDs for attacks against the United States (no. 15, p. 82). For a sample of the administration's most embarrassing pronouncements, see pp. 17–19 ("There can be no doubt that Saddam Hussein has biological weapons"), 29–30 ("Our conservative estimate is that Iraq today has a stockpile of between 100 and 500 tons of chemical weapons agent"), and 47–48 ("Intelligence . . . leaves no doubt that the Iraq regime continues to possess and conceal some of the most lethal weapons ever devised").

82. Jeff Gerth and Don Van Natta Jr., "Hillary's War," *New York Times*, 29 May 2007. Although Suskind's latest book emphasizes the back-channel denials, concerning WMDs, that were conveyed by Saddam Hussein's foreign minister (Naji Sabri) and by his head of intelligence (Tahir Jalil Habbush), one of Suskind's chief American sources—Rob Richer, a veteran CIA official who became the head of its Near East Division in late 2002—told Suskind that "[e]veryone was sure" that Iraq possessed proscribed weapons (Ron Suskind, *The Way of the World: A Story of Truth and Hope in an Age of Extremism* [New York: HarperCollins, 2008], 361). Perhaps Suskind's most alarming accusation is that the White House arranged for Habbush—after he had fled to Jordan with U.S. help (369)—to write and sign a fake letter (dated 1 July 2001) addressed to Saddam. The letter, which Ayad Allawi allegedly handed to British journalist Con Coughlin in December 2003, presented two momentous fabrications: that Mohammed Atta had trained in Iraq to "lead the team which will be responsible for attacking the targets" and that Al-Qaida had helped Iraq obtain a shipment from Niger (371, 374–75). Richer, who may have been Suskind's only source for the claim that the White House composed the letter and instructed the CIA to have Habbush rewrite it, subsequently issued this denial: "I never received direction from George Tenet or anyone else in my chain of command to fabricate a document from Habbash [*sic*] as outlined in Mr. Suskind's book." Suskind has posted this statement, and excerpts from his interviews with Richer, at http://www.ronsuskind.com/thewayoftheworld/transcripts/.

83. Emphases added; see http://www.washingtonpost.com/wp-srv/politics/transcripts/gore_text092302.html.

84. Socrates also commends benevolent dishonesty at *Republic* 331c, 378a, 389b, and 459c–460a. Given the tendency to associate Straussianism with the tycoonery of the Bush administration, one should recall the severe economic and other deprivations that await the *Republic*'s gold-soul rulers and silver-soul auxiliaries (416d–417a, 457d).

85. Zuckerts, *TALS* 130–31. Cf. *TALS* 44–45 on the difference between a refusal to challenge views that sustain social order and "a 'manipulation' of the masses to get them to think what philosophers wanted them to think or to enable the philosophers to rule." Drawing on the title essay of *PAW*, Robert Howse elaborates a variation on the latter, whereby philosophers use "noble lies" not to rule but to inspire certain individuals to protect philosophy (Howse, "Reading between the Lines," 61, 69–72; cf. pp. 254–55n51 above). Howse provides cynical but illuminating observations (70–71) about *Republic* 539c, a passage Strauss cites when claiming that a "mature" philosopher would write an "exoteric" book—one that combines an "edifying" popular teaching with a hidden philosophical teaching concerning "the most important subject"—because of his "love . . . for the puppies of his race" (*PAW* 36). Howse, building on his assertion that Strauss never gives "an adequate account of nonmercenary love," regards the claim about the puppies as a noble lie (76n18). To this I respond: what sorts of *mercenary* purposes could have motivated Strauss to labor so assiduously as a teacher and an author? Surely he did not expect *XSD* or *AAPL* to be best-sellers.

Howse acknowledges that "direct political activity would divert the philosopher's time and energy from philosophizing" (75n14), but seems to overlook the contrast between Strauss and Socrates: as a professional educator and prolific writer, Strauss (like Plato) presumably had less time and energy for philosophizing.

86. Melzer, "Esotericism," 293.

87. When Machiavelli adds that Alexander VI "never did anything, nor ever thought of anything, but how to deceive men" (*The Prince* 70), he conveys one of his most comical exaggerations (cf. *TM* 306n14).

88. At some point, of course, being lazy in finding the truth imparts an odor of dishonesty to one's mistakes, as I have complained concerning Drury, Norton, and others.

89. "The truth is that for reasons that have a lot to do with the U.S. government bureaucracy we settled on the one issue that everyone could agree on which was weapons of mass destruction as the core reason, but . . . there have always been three fundamental concerns. One is weapons of mass destruction, the second is support for terrorism, the third is the criminal treatment of the Iraqi people. Actually I guess you could say there's a fourth overriding one which is the connection between the first two" (Sam Tanenhaus, "Interview with Deputy Secretary Wolfowitz"). As Bill Kristol has noted, Tanenhaus's article distorts these comments when it describes them as an admission that the WMDs had never been "the most important *casus belli*" (Kristol, "What Wolfowitz Really Said," *Weekly Standard*, 9 June 2003); see Sam Tanenhaus, "Bush's Brain Trust," 168. Readers of Bob Woodward, in any case, are unlikely to doubt the depth of Cheney's worries concerning Iraq's presumed WMDs and linkages with terrorists (Woodward, *Plan of Attack*, 4, 25, 132, 164, 175–76, 182, 237–39, 292, 419–20, 429; Woodward, *State of Denial*, 120, 135, 234–35, 237–38, 259–60); cf. Weisberg, *Bush Tragedy*, 209, and Gellman, *Angler*, 53, 156, 185–86, 227–28, 233–36, 343–44. On the administration's fears about WMDs, also see Feith, *War and Decision*, 224–28, 238–39, 311–12, 325–32, 338–40, 470–74, 591–92n, 614n.

90. In successfully challenging the constitutionality of the exclusion of blacks by the University of Oklahoma law school, Thurgood Marshall of the NAACP argued in 1950 that "classifications and distinctions based on race and color have no moral or legal validity in our society." In the landmark 1954 case, *Brown v. Board of Education* 347 U.S. 483, which proscribed government-mandated educational segregation, the NAACP had argued broadly that "[d]istinctions drawn by state authorities on the basis of color or race violate the 14th Amendment." Quoted in Terry Eastland, *Ending Affirmative Action* (New York: Basic Books, 1996), 31–33.

91. Quoted in John David Skretny, *The Ironies of Affirmative Action* (Chicago: University of Chicago Press, 1996), 134.

92. See page 4 of the PDF file posted at http://www.law.cornell.edu/supct/pdf/02-516P.ZD2. Note the two major obfuscations that this sentence yields under strict scrutiny. First, insofar as the "after effects" of entrenched discrimination will never be "extirpated," one might infer that Ginsburg welcomes the transformation of affirmative-action benchmarks and targets into informal but persistent quotas. Second, policies like Michigan's, because they grant preferences to Latinos, extend eligibility for preferential treatment to millions of immigrants who were *not* subjected to decades of discrimination in the United States. On immigration, see Schuck, *Diversity*, 75–133, and Hugh Davis Graham, *Collision Course: The Strange Convergence of Affirmative Action and Immigration Policy in America* (Oxford: Oxford University Press, 2002). In highlighting the difference between "racial distinctions that redress social disparities and those that keep people in their place," Nunberg ridicules the "brazen audacity" with which American conservatives have allegedly co-opted color-blindness in order to "defend the privileges of their strongest constituency, white male Americans" (Geoffrey Nunberg, *Talking Right*, 153, 155, 156).

93. From the 1940s through the 1960s, "against the backdrop of laws that used racial distinctions to exclude Negroes from opportunities available to white citizens, it seemed that racial subjugation could be overcome by mandating the application of race-blind law" (Randall Kennedy,

"Persuasion and Distrust: A Comment on the Affirmative Action Debate," *Harvard Law Review* 99 [1986]: 1335, 1335n32).

94. Justice Rehnquist's *Weber* dissent famously begins by invoking the *1984* scene in which an Inner Party official inflaming a London crowd against the Eurasian enemy during Hate Week is handed a note and then switches seamlessly to identifying the enemy as Eastasia. Although Amy Gutmann resolutely defends preferential treatment, she acknowledges that it includes preferring "some *basically* qualified candidates over other *more* qualified candidates because of their color (or gender, or some other characteristic that is not tied to superior job performance)." See "Responding to Racial Injustice," in *Color Conscious*, ed. Amy Gutmann and K. Anthony Appiah, (Princeton, NJ: Princeton University Press, 1996), 122, 130, 132.

95. *LAM* 264; cf. "Crisis of Our Time" 47 and WWRJ 49.

96. A very similar passage, presented as an interpretation of Kojève's views, appears in the 1954 French translation of Strauss's "Restatement on Xenophon's *Hiero*" but was not included in the subsequent English versions. See Patard, "'Restatement' by Leo Strauss," 51–52.

97. Speaking through his "fictional alter ego," Rodrigo Crenshaw (721n1), legal theorist Richard Delgado is even more dogmatic: "Liberal democracy and racial subordination go hand in hand, like the sun, moon, and stars"; if you are black or Mexican, "you should flee Enlightenment-based democracies like mad, assuming you have any choice" (Delgado, "Rodrigo's Seventh Chronicle: Race, Democracy, and the State," *UCLA Law Review* 41, no. 3 [February 1994]: 734).

98. Title VI of the Civil Rights Act is also relevant to preferential treatment practiced by private educational institutions: Title VI extends the ban against discrimination based upon race, color, or national origin to "any program or activity receiving federal financial assistance." Invoking what he argued was "the clear legislative intent," however, Justice Powell in *Bakke* concluded that Title VI "must be held to proscribe only those racial classifications that would violate the Equal Protection Clause or the Fifth Amendment" (II C, end). Key civil rights statutes are posted online at http://www.eeoc.gov/policy/vii.html, http://www.justice.gov/crt/cor/coord/titlevistat.htm, and http://www.eeoc.gov/policy/cra91.html; for an overview of Title VI, see http://www.justice.gov/crt/cor/coord/titlevi.htm.

99. On the efforts of Secretary of State Robin Carnahan to hamper the Missouri Civil Rights Initiative by warping the summary language for the measure's title, see Peter Schmidt, "Foes of Affirmative-Action Preferences Say Missouri Official's Edits Changed Meaning of Ballot Measure," *Chronicle of Higher Education*, 30 July 2007.

100. Jeffrey S. Lehman, "The Evolving Language of Diversity and Integration in Discussions of Affirmative Action from *Bakke* to *Grutter*," in *Defending Diversity: Affirmative Action at the University of Michigan*, ed. Patricia Gurin, Jeffrey S. Lehman, and Earl Lewis (Ann Arbor: University of Michigan Press, 2004), 72.

101. See http://www.vpcomm.umich.edu/admissions/legal/gru_amicus-ussc/um/AJC-both.doc, 24. The University of Michigan posted a vast trove of documents, including the briefs I am citing, at http://www.vpcomm.umich.edu/admissions/.

102. See http://www.vpcomm.umich.edu/admissions/legal/gra_amicus-ussc/um/Carnegie M-both.pdf, 14. One wonders whether the numerous commentators who condemn Straussian secrecy and "whispering" are similarly alarmed about the well-known difficulty of getting colleges, universities, and professional schools to share data about racial/ethnic differences regarding incoming students (GPAs and scores on standardized tests) and subsequent performance (e.g., passage rates on the bar exam).

103. Emphases added (http://www.vpcomm.umich.edu/admissions/legal/gru_amicus-ussc/um/ ASA-gru.pdf, 28).

104. I say this partially for the benefit of Richard King, who maintains that Straussians are reluctant to "take broadly shared white racial prejudice seriously as a historical and political force" (King, "Rights and Slavery," 74).

105. Meier wisely emphasizes Strauss's efforts to make "the dignity of political life visible once again" (Meier, *Leo Strauss*, 9). Meier nevertheless denies that Strauss proposed a "political counterproject" against modernity (11): Strauss's "theologico-political treatises" make "no attempt to draw persistently to themselves the attention of politically promising and ambitious readers by inspiring their political idealism or by feeding their will to rule"; nor do these treatises sketch a perfect city capable of "inducing identification and devotion" (14). Strauss's chief endeavor, according to Meier, was to *justify* the philosophical life (15). Meier does attribute antibourgeois "political counterproject[s]" to Rousseau, Hegel, and Nietzsche (11); cf. 23–24, 98, 100, 109.

106. Strauss elevates the classical political philosophers who cherish "education or liberation" above both the "the social 'engineer' who thinks in terms of manipulating or conditioning" and the prophet who "believes that he knows the future" (*WIPP* 90; cf. Epilogue 310/*LAM* 206 on the engineer).

107. Drawing on Strauss's remark that "every book is accessible to all who can read the language in which it was written" (*PAW* 187), Xenos helpfully observes that only a small number of individuals—whether philosophic or "vulgar"—could have read Spinoza's *Theologico-Political Treatise* when it was published (*CV* 77, 80). Strauss, by contrast, wrote in the paperback age. Cf. pp. 190–91 above on the barrage of Straussian translations.

108. Cf. Ferrari, "Strauss's Plato," 36–38, 58, 61, 64; Melzer, "Esotericism," 292; and McAllister, *Revolt Against Modernity*, 86–87, 97–98. The Zuckerts also credit Larry Peterman's intricate study of *TM* ("Approaching Leo Strauss") with having "dotted an *i*" (*TALS* 140; cf. *OT* 27). Steven Lenzner, in addition to correcting some quotations, complains that the Zuckerts have underestimated Strauss's literary complexity (Lenzner, "Guide for the Perplexed," *Claremont Review of Books*, Spring 2007, 55–57). For examples of what Lenzner can do with minutia, see Lenzner, "Literary Exercise," 228–29, 233n17–18, 234n41, and "Author as Educator," http://www.claremont .org/publications/pubid.255/pub_detail.asp. Although Lenzner elsewhere suggests that Strauss "had an enterprise on the scale of the one he attributed to Machiavelli," that enterprise was merely to revive "classical political philosophy" so as to "ensure that it would not once again be 'blurred or destroyed'" (Steven J. Lenzner, "Leo Strauss and His Contemporaries," *Political Science Reviewer* 22 [1993]: 146; Lenzner here quotes *TM* 174–75). Cf. Michael Frazer's suggestion that Strauss might have hoped to nourish a "broad community of philosophically literate nonphilosophers" who preserve past insights and encourage free inquiry (Frazer, "Esotericism," 51); even if the experience of "many centuries in greatly different natural and moral climates" showed that the "urban patriciate" was the only class "habitually sympathetic to philosophy" (*NRH* 143), perhaps things are different now.

109. According to Janssens, a single "classic text" that has been "composed and polished with exceeding care over a long period of time" only yields its "full meaning to a sustained and protracted study that may take years, perhaps a lifetime" (Janssens, *Between Athens and Jerusalem*, 174).

110. Strauss, "Spirit of Sparta," 535.

111. Larry George, review of *LSPAE*, 405.

112. Cf. *LAM* 9 on his commitment to nonregistered students. As reported by Clifford Orwin, Strauss's classes were "always open to whoever wished to attend them, regardless of whether they could afford to enroll in them." Orwin, letter to the *International Herald Tribune*, 9 December 1994, http://www.iht.com/articles/1994/12/09/edlet_15.php.

113. Leo Strauss, *On Plato's Symposium* (Chicago: University of Chicago Press, 2001). See page vii for a description of the circuitous path that finally yielded the published text. In *RCPR*, Pangle includes several of Strauss's lectures, at least one of which ("An Introduction to Heideggerian Existentialism") Pangle derived from a transcript (xxix), but these were apparently formal lectures rather than class sessions.

114. In listing the classes Strauss taught at Chicago, Anastaplo also indicates the availability of transcripts ("Leo Strauss at the University" 13–18). For a description of Strauss's pedagogy, see

the Hadley Arkes article ("Strauss on Our Minds" 69, 79–80) in the same volume (Deutsch and Murley, *Leo Strauss*); Dannhauser, "Becoming Naïve Again"; and Heilbrunn, *They Knew*, 91.

115. Eugene Sheppard is clever but also arrogant and hostile when he attributes the rifts among Strauss's disciples merely to disagreement about "what truths can be openly discussed without violating propriety" (Sheppard, *Leo Strauss*, 1). For an informed and frank overview of these rifts, see *TALS* 197–259.

116. Heinrich Meier, "Pourquoi Leo Strauss?" *Commentaire* 29, no. 114 (Summer 2006): 308.

117. Peter Berkowitz, "The Longer Way," in *Why I Turned Right: Leading Baby Boom Conservatives Chronicle Their Political Journeys*, ed. Mary Eberstadt (New York: Threshold Editions, 2007), 247–54. Berkowitz later earned his JD and his PhD in political science at Yale (257), where he interacted with Steven B. Smith, who had recently joined the Yale faculty.

118. Meier, *Leo Strauss*, xix. Cf. Ferrari, "Strauss's Plato," 61–64; Howse, "Reading between the Lines," 61, 67, 70, 75n11; and Batnitzky, *Leo Strauss*, 163–65.

119. Strauss here appears to be borrowing a metaphor from Max Weber: "the materialist interpretation of history is no cab to be taken at will" (see "Politics as a Vocation," in *From Max Weber: Essays in Sociology*, ed. H. H. Gerth and C. Wright Mills [Oxford: Oxford University Press, 1946], 125). Engagement with Strauss would presumably differ for those who fulfill his definition of "the great minds" (or perhaps "the greatest minds"): "teachers who are not in turn pupils" (*LAM* 3); in a 1956 lecture, Strauss described "the great thinkers" as "men who faced the problems without being overpowered by any authority" (*RCPR* 29).

120. Anderson, *Spectrum*, 27; George Kateb, *Perspectives on Politics* 5, no. 2 (June 2007): 356, 358; Kateb is here reviewing *TALS* along with the recent books on Strauss by Pangle and Smith.

121. Xenos, however, exaggerates in stating that Strauss "cannot simply be quoted on a topic, because there is *always* a quote available that apparently says the opposite" (*CV* xi; emph. added). And although the dazzling diversity of the ideas that Strauss has planted on his pages does equip his defenders to summon "plausible deniability" (*CV* xi), it also helps immunize them "gegen die rechten Prinzipien" (*GS* 625).

122. Pangle, *Leo Strauss*, 45. Cf. *TALS* 46, Mansfield, "Timeless Mind," 25, and Sheppard, *Leo Strauss*, 66–67, 108–9. Meier argues that Strauss's "deepest response to the challenge of radical historicism" included his "movement" from the history of philosophy to the intention of the philosopher (Meier, *Leo Strauss*, 64). Sketching the differences between Strauss's *Social Research* (1947) essay on Rousseau and his subchapter on Rousseau in *NRH* (1953), Meier suggests that "[s]hifts in emphasis, obfuscations, and reductions" are the price Strauss sometimes paid when attempting "to situate a philosophy in the narrative logic of a comprehensive course of history" (Meier, *Leo Strauss*, 67; cf. Pippin, "Modern World," 459–64). Because the *NRH* section (260–63) does emphasize the doctrine of natural inequality, which Meier correctly diagnoses as a major theme of the 1947 article's account of Rousseau's *First Discourse*, I would quibble with Meier's use of this example. I nevertheless commend Meier's attempt to distinguish occasional "teachings" (e.g., the "three waves of modernity") from Strauss's persistent efforts to move from "the history of philosophy to the intention of the philosopher." In trying to understand an author (including Strauss) as she or he understood herself or himself, the interpreter may enter "a plain on which the arguments take the lead and the alternatives visibly emerge that, beyond the 'historical embeddedness' of both the author and the interpreter, determine the issue towards which the thought of both is directed" (Meier, *Leo Strauss*, 71). Regarding *NRH*'s treatment of Burke, Lenzner offers complaints similar to the one Meier makes about its treatment of Rousseau (Lenzner, "Strauss's Three Burkes," *Political Theory* 19, no. 3 [August 1991]: 372–77).

123. In explaining why Maimonides chose to convey "the secrets of the Torah" in writing, Strauss stresses Maimonides' fear that the "external conditions for oral communication" might soon disappear (*PAW* 50–51). Cf. Sheppard, *Leo Strauss*, 110.

124. According to Adam Curtis and others, indeed, Straussians and Islamists are de facto allies in the war against liberalism.

125. Pangle, *Leo Strauss*, 87; cf. Howse, "From Legitimacy to Dictatorship," 95. Peter Levine, by contrast, concludes that Strauss "sees no possibility of communication among cultures, which he imagines as completely discrete entities. One integrated set of values defines each culture precisely and serves as the foundation of all its members' lives" (Levine, *Nietzsche*, 166).

Works Cited: Select List

Abella, Alex. *Soldiers of Reason: The RAND Corporation and the Rise of the American Empire.* Orlando: Harcourt, 2008.

Agresto, John. *Mugged by Reality: The Liberation of Iraq and the Failure of Good Intentions.* New York: Encounter Books, 2007.

Alfarabi, Abu Nasr Muhammad. *See Farabi.*

Alfonsi, Christian. *Circle in the Sand: Why We Went Back to Iraq.* New York: Doubleday, 2006.

Alterman, Eric. "Kristolizing the (Neoconservative) Moment." *Nation,* 12 February 2007, 10.

Altman, William H. F. "Leo Strauss on 'German Nihilism': Learning the Art of Writing." *Journal of the History of Ideas* 68, no. 4 (October 2007): 587–612.

Anastaplo, George. "Leo Strauss at the University of Chicago." In *Leo Strauss, the Straussians, and the American Regime,* edited by Kenneth L. Deutsch and John A. Murley, 3–30. Lanham, MD: Rowman & Littlefield, 1999.

———. "On Leo Strauss: A Yahrzeit Remembrance." *University of Chicago Magazine* 67 (Winter 1974): 30–38.

Anderson, Perry. *Spectrum: From Right to Left in the World of Ideas.* London: Verso, 2005.

Arendt, Hannah. *Between Past and Future.* New York: Penguin Books, 1977.

———. *Hannah Arendt–Karl Jaspers Correspondence, 1926–1969.* Edited by Lotte Kohler and Hans Saner. Translated by Robert and Rita Kimber. New York: Harcourt Brace Jovanovich, 1992.

———. *Letters 1925–1975: Hannah Arendt and Martin Heidegger.* Translated by Ursula Ludz. Orlando: Harcourt, 2004.

Atlas, James. "Chicago's Grumpy Guru." In *Essays on the Closing of the American Mind,* edited by Robert L. Stone, 68–72. Chicago: Chicago Review Press, 1989. Originally published in *New York Times Magazine,* 3 January 1988.

———. "A Classicist's Legacy: New Empire Builders." *New York Times,* 4 May 2003.

Batnitzky, Leora. *Leo Strauss and Emmanuel Levinas: Philosophy and the Politics of Revelation.* Cambridge: Cambridge University Press, 2006.

Behnegar, Nasser. *Leo Strauss, Max Weber, and the Scientific Study of Politics.* Chicago: University of Chicago Press, 2003.

Benardete, Seth. "Leo Strauss's *The City and Man.*" *Political Science Reviewer* 8 (1978): 1–20.

Berlin, Isaiah. "The Originality of Machiavelli." In *Against the Current,* edited by Henry Hyde, 25–79. New York: Viking Press, 1980.

Bernstein, Richard. "A Very Unlikely Villain (or Hero)." *New York Times,* 29 January 1995, E4.

Blackburn, Simon. *Plato's Republic: A Biography.* New York: Atlantic Monthly Press, 2006.

Blitz, Mark. "Strauss's Laws." *Political Science Reviewer* 20 (Spring 1991): 186–222.

Bloom, Allan. *The Closing of the American Mind.* New York: Basic Books, 1987.

———. *Giants and Dwarfs.* New York: Simon & Schuster, 1990.

Bobonich, Christopher. *Plato's Utopia Recast: His Later Ethics and Politics.* Oxford: Oxford University Press, 2002.

Boyle, Francis A. *Destroying World Order: U.S. Imperialism in the Middle East Before and After September 11.* Atlanta: Clarity Press, 2004.

———. "My Alma Mater Is a Moral Cesspool." *Counterpunch,* 2 August 2003, http://www .counterpunch.org/boyle08022003.html.

Brague, Rémi. "Athens, Jerusalem, Mecca: Leo Strauss's 'Muslim' Understanding of Greek Philosophy." *Poetics Today* 19, no. 2 (Summer 1998): 235–59.

Brown, Wendy. *Regulating Aversion: Tolerance in the Age of Identity and Empire.* Princeton, NJ: Princeton University Press, 2006.

Bumiller, Elisabeth. *Condoleezza Rice: An American Life.* New York: Random House, 2007.

Burnyeat, Myles. "Sphinx without a Secret." *New York Review of Books* 32, no. 9 (30 May 1985): 30–36.

Butterfield, Herbert. Review of *Thoughts on Machiavelli,* by Leo Strauss. *Journal of Politics* 22, no. 4 (November 1960): 728–30.

Butterworth, Charles E. "Leo Strauss in His Own Write: A Scholar First and Foremost," posted at http://www.bsos.umd.edu/gvpt/Theory/Transcript_Butterworth_pdf.

Buttigieg, Joseph A. "Straussism and the 'Habits of Civilized Discourse.'" *Boundary* 33, no. 1 (Spring 2006): 2–6.

Caranfa, Angelo. *Machiavelli Rethought: A Critique of Strauss's Machiavelli.* Washington, DC: University Press of America, 1978.

Chait, Jonathan. "Substandard: The Thuggery of William Kristol." *New Republic,* 27 August 2007, 5.

Cockburn, Andrew. *Rumsfeld: His Rise, Fall, and Catastrophic Legacy.* New York: Scribner, 2007.

Cohen, Hermann. *Religion of Reason out of the Sources of Judaism.* Translated by Simon Kaplan. New York: Frederick Ungar, 1972.

Colish, Marcia L. "Republicanism, Religion, and Machiavelli's Savonarolan Moment." *Journal of the History of Ideas* 60, no. 4 (1999): 597–616.

Colmo, Christopher. "Theory and Practice: Alfarabi's *Plato* Revisited." *American Political Science Review* 86, no. 4 (December 1992): 966–76.

Conason, Joe. *It Can Happen Here: Authoritarian Peril in the Age of Bush.* New York: Thomas Dunne Books/St. Martin's Press, 2007.

Continetti, Matthew. "Scenes from the Gingrich Campaign." *Weekly Standard,* 19 March 2007, 18–23.

Costopoulos, James. "Anne Norton and the 'Straussian' Cabal: How *Not* to Write a Book." Review of *Leo Strauss and the Politics of American Empire,* by Anne Norton. *Interpretation* 32, no. 3 (Summer 2005): 269–81.

Cronkrite, Al. "Judeo-Christian Decadence: At the Fount of Power." *Ether Zone,* 15 May 2003, http://etherzone.com/2003/cron051503.shtml.

Crossman, R. H. S. *Plato Today.* Oxford: Oxford University Press, 1939.

Curtis, Adam, "The Power of Nightmares." BBC Documentary. Transcript posted at http://www .daanspeak.com/TranscriptPowerOfNightmares1.html.

Daalder, Ivo H., and James M. Lindsay. *America Unbound: The Bush Revolution in Foreign Policy,* rev. ed. Hoboken, NJ: John Wiley & Sons, 2005.

Dabashi, Hamid. "Native Informers and the Making of the American Empire." *Al-Ahram Weekly,* 1–7 June 2006 (#797), http://weekly.ahram.org.eg/2006/797/special.htm.

Dannhauser, Werner J. "Becoming Naïve Again." *American Scholar* 44, no. 4 (Autumn 1975): 636–42.

——. "Leo Strauss in His Letters." In *Enlightening Revolutions: Essays in Honor of Ralph Lerner*, edited by Svetozar Minkov, 355–61. Lanham, MD: Lexington Books, 2006.

Danoff, Brian. "Leo Strauss, George W. Bush, and the Problem of 'Regime Change.'" *Social Policy* 34, no. 2–3 (Winter 2003/Spring 2004): 35–40.

David, Anthony. "The Apprentice." *American Prospect*, 5 June 2007, http://www.prospect.org/cs/articles?article=the_apprentice.

De Grazia, Sebastian. *Machiavelli in Hell*. Princeton, NJ: Princeton University Press, 1989.

Deutsch, Kenneth L., and John A. Murley, eds. *Leo Strauss, the Straussians, and the American Regime*. Lanham, MD: Rowman & Littlefield, 1999.

Deutsch, Kenneth L., and Walter Nicgorski, eds. *Leo Strauss: Political Philosopher and Jewish Thinker*. Lanham, MD: Rowman & Littlefield, 1994.

Deutsch Kenneth L., and Walter Soffer, eds., *The Crisis of Liberal Democracy: A Straussian Perspective*. Albany: SUNY Press, 1987.

Devigne, Robert. *Recasting Conservatism: Oakeshott, Strauss, and the Response to Postmodernism*. New Haven, CT: Yale University Press, 1994.

Donnelly, Thomas, principal author, *Rebuilding America's Defenses: Strategy, Forces and Resources for a New Century* (September 2000). Posted at http://www.newamericancentury.org/RebuildingAmericasDefenses.pdf.

Dorrien, Gary. *Imperial Designs: Neoconservatism and the New Pax Americana*. New York: Routledge, 2004.

——. *The Neoconservative Mind: Politics, Culture, and the War of Ideology*. Philadelphia: Temple University Press, 1993.

Dostoevsky, Fyodor. *The Brothers Karamazov*. Translated by Constance Garnett. New York: Vintage Books, 1955.

——. *The Brothers Karamazov*. Translated by Richard Pevear and Larissa Volokhonsky. San Francisco: North Point Press, 1990.

Draper, Robert. *Dead Certain: The Presidency of George W. Bush*. New York: The Free Press, 2007.

Drew, Elizabeth. "The Neocons in Power." *New York Review of Books*, 12 June 2003, 20–22.

Dreyfuss, Robert, and Jason Vest. "The Lie Factory." *Mother Jones*, January/February 2004, http://www.motherjones.com/news/feature/2004/01/12_405.html.

Drury, Shadia B. *Alexandre Kojève: The Roots of Postmodern Politics*. New York: St. Martin's Press, 1994.

——. *Aquinas and Modernity: The Lost Promise of Natural Law*. Lanham, MD: Rowman & Littlefield, 2008.

——. "The Esoteric Philosophy of Leo Strauss." *Political Theory* 13, no. 3 (August 1985): 315–37.

——. "Exterminating the Enemy," *Free Inquiry* 27, no. 2 (February/March 2007): 22–23.

——. "Gurus of Endless War." *New Humanist* 122, no. 3 (May/June 2007), http://newhumanist.org.uk/1463.

——. "Gurus of the Right." *Literary Review of Canada* 8, no. 10 (Winter 2000/2001): 19–22.

——. "The Hidden Meaning of Strauss's *Thoughts on Machiavelli*." *History of Political Thought* 6, no. 3 (Winter 1985): 575–90.

——. "Leo Strauss." In *Routledge Encyclopedia of Philosophy*, edited by E. Craig. London: Routledge, 1998, http://0-www.rep.routledge.com.sculib.scu.edu:80/article/S092. Also available at http://phil.uregina.ca/CRC/encyc_leostrauss.html.

——. "Leo Strauss and the American Imperial Project." *Political Theory* 35, no. 1 (February 2007): 62–67.

——. *Leo Strauss and the American Right*. New York: St. Martin's Press, 1997.

——. Leo Strauss and the Grand Inquisitor." *Free Inquiry* 24, no. 4 (June/July 2004), http://www .secularhumanism.org/index.php?section=library&page=drury_24_4.

——. "Leo Strauss's Classic Natural Right Teaching." *Political Theory* 15, no. 3 (August 1987): 299–315.

——. "Locke and Nozick on Property." *Political Studies* 30, no. 1 (1982): 28–41.

——. "The Making of a Straussian." *Philosophers' Magazine* 25 (1st quarter 2004): 24–25. Posted (under a different title) at http://www.republic-news.org/archive/84-repub/84_drury.htm.

——. *The Political Ideas of Leo Strauss*. New York: St. Martin's Press, 1988.

——. "Saving America: Shadia Drury Unpacks Neoconservatism," 11 September 2004. Posted at http://evatt.labor.net.au/news/254.html and http://evatt.org.au/publications/papers/112.html.

——. "Straussians in Power: Secrecy, Lies, and Endless War." In *PILS-2005*, ix–lvii.

——. *Terror and Civilization: Christianity, Politics, and the Western Psyche*. New York: Palgrave Macmillan, 2004.

——. "To My Critics." *Vital Nexus* 1, no. 1 (May 1990): 119–34. Posted as "Reply to My Critics" at http://phil.uregina.ca/CRC/vitalnexus.html.

Easton, Nina. *Gang of Five*. New York: Simon & Schuster, 2000.

Eyck, Erich. *A History of the Weimar Republic*, vol. 1. New York: John Wiley & Sons, 1962.

Farabi. *Alfarabi: Philosophy of Plato and Aristotle*. Translated and with an introduction by Muhsin Mahdi. Ithaca, NY: Cornell University Press, 2001.

——. *Alfarabi: The Political Writings*. Translated by Charles E. Butterworth. Ithaca, NY: Cornell University Press, 2001.

Feith, Douglas J. *War and Decision: Inside the Pentagon at the Dawn of the War on Terrorism*. New York: HarperCollins, 2008.

Felix, Antonia. *Condi: The Condoleezza Rice Story*. New York: Pocket Books, 2002.

Ferrari, G. R. F. "Strauss's Plato." *Arion* 5, no. 2 (Fall 1997): 36–65.

Ferry, Luc. *Political Philosophy 1: Rights—the New Quarrel between the Ancients and the Moderns*. Translated by Franklin Philip. Chicago: University of Chicago Press, 1990.

Flynn, Daniel J. *Intellectual Morons: How Ideology Makes Smart People Fall for Stupid Ideas*. New York: Crown Forum, 2004.

Foer, Franklin. "Great Escape: How Bill Kristol Ditched Conservatism." *New Republic*, 28 May 2001, 17–21.

Fontana, Benedetto. "Reason and Politics: Philosophy Confronts the People." *Boundary 2* 33, no. 1 (Spring 2006): 7–35.

Ford, Richard Thompson. *The Race Card: How Bluffing about Bias Makes Race Relations Worse*. New York: Farrar, Straus, and Giroux, 2008.

Fortin, Ernest. "Between the Lines: Was Leo Strauss a Secret Enemy of Morality?" *Crisis*, December 1989, 19–26.

Foskett, Ken. *Judging Thomas: The Life and Times of Clarence Thomas*. New York: HarperCollins Publishers, 2004.

Frazer, Michael L. "Esotericism Ancient and Modern: Strauss Contra Straussianism on the Art of Political-Philosophical Writing." *Political Theory* 34, no. 1 (February 2006): 33–61.

Frohnen, Bruce, Jeremy Beer, and Jeffrey O. Nelson, eds. *American Conservatism: An Encyclopedia*. Wilmington, DE: ISI Books, 2006.

Frum, David, and Richard Perle. *An End to Evil*. New York: Ballentine Books, 2004.

Fukuyama, Francis. *America at the Crossroads*. New Haven, CT: Yale University Press, 2006.

——. *The End of History and the Last Man*. New York: Free Press, 2006.

Gellman, Barton. *Angler: The Cheney Vice Presidency*. New York: Penguin Press, 2008.

George, Jim. "Leo Strauss, Neoconservatism and U.S. Foreign Policy: Esoteric Nihilism and the Bush Doctrine." *International Politics* 42, no. 2 (June 2005): 174–202.

George, Larry N. Review of *Leo Strauss and the Politics of American Empire*, by Anne Norton. *Political Theory* 34, no. 3 (June 2006): 401–8.

Germino, Dante. "Blasphemy and Leo Strauss's Machiavelli." In *Leo Strauss: Philosopher and Jewish Thinker*, edited by Kenneth L. Deutsch and Walter Nicgorski, 297–307. Lanham, MD: Rowman & Littlefield, 1993.

———. "Second Thoughts on Leo Strauss's Machiavelli." *Journal of Politics* 28, no. 4 (November 1966): 794–817.

Gilbert, Felix. "Politics and Morality." Review of *Thoughts on Machiavelli*, by Leo Strauss. *Yale Review* 48 (1958–1959): 465–69.

Gordon, Michael R., and General Bernard E. Trainor. *Cobra II: The Inside Story of the Invasion and Occupation of Iraq.* New York: Pantheon Book, 2006.

Gore, Al. *The Assault on Reason.* New York: Penguin Press, 2007.

Gottfried, Paul. "Strauss and the Straussians." *Humanitas* 18, nos. 1 & 2 (2005): 26–30, http://www.nhinet.org/18-1&2.htm.

Gourevitch, Victor. "Philosophy and Politics I." *Review of Metaphysics* 22 (1968): 58–84.

———. "Philosophy and Politics II." *Review of Metaphysics* 22 (1968): 280–328.

Gunnell, John G. *Between Philosophy and Politics.* Amherst: University of Massachusetts Press, 1986.

———. "The Myth of the Tradition." *American Political Science Review* 72 (March 1978): 122–34.

———. "Political Theory and Politics: The Case of Leo Strauss," *Political Theory* 13, no. 3 (August 1985): 339–61.

———. "Strauss Before Straussism: The Weimar Conversation." *Vital Nexus* 1, no. 1 (May 1990): 74–104. Also in Deutsch and Nicgorski, *Leo Strauss: Political Philosopher and Jewish Thinker*, 107–28.

Halper, Stefan, and Jonathan Clarke. *America Alone: The Neo-Conservatives and the Global Order.* Cambridge: Cambridge University Press, 2004.

Hayes, Stephen F. *Cheney: The Untold Story of America's Most Powerful and Controversial Vice President.* New York: HarperCollins, 2007.

Heer, Jeet. "The Mind of the Administration, Part One: The Philosopher." *Boston Globe*, 11 May 2003, http://www.boston.com/news/globe/ideas/articles/2003/05/11/the_philosopher/.

Heilbrunn, Jacob. *They Knew They Were Right: The Rise of the Neocons.* New York: Doubleday, 2008.

Hersh, Seymour M. *Chain of Command.* New York: HarperCollins Publishers, 2004.

———. "Selective Intelligence." *New Yorker*, 12 May 2003, 44–51.

Hesiod. *Theogony, Works and Days, Testimonia.* Translated by Glenn W. Most. Cambridge, MA: Harvard University Press, 2006.

Higonnet, Patrice. *Attendant Cruelties: Nation and Nationalism in American History.* New York: Other Press, 2007.

Hirsh, Michael. "Welcome to the Real World." *Newsweek*, 23 June 2003, 32.

Hitler, Adolf. *Mein Kampf.* Translated by Ralph Mannheim. Boston: Houghton Mifflin, 1999.

Hobbes, Thomas. *Leviathan.* Edited by C. B. Macpherson. Harmondsworth, England: Pelican Books, 1968.

Holmes, Stephen. *The Anatomy of Antiliberalism.* Cambridge, MA: Harvard University Press, 1993.

———. "Plato's Dogs: Reflections on the University after 9/11." In *To Restore Democracy*, edited by Robert E. Calvert, 185–204. Lanham, MD: Rowman & Littlefield, 2006.

Howse, Robert. "From Legitimacy to Dictatorship—and Back Again: Leo Strauss's Critique of the Anti-Liberalism of Carl Schmitt." *Canadian Journal of Law and Jurisprudence* 10, no. 1 (1997): 77–103.

——. "Leo Strauss—Man of War?" (2006). Posted at http://faculty.law.umich.edu/rhowse/ Drafts_and_Publications/straussiraq.pdf.

——. "Reading between the Lines: Exotericism, Esotericism, and the Philosophical Rhetoric of Leo Strauss." *Philosophy and Rhetoric* 32, no. 1 (1999): 60–77.

Hutton, Will. *A Declaration of Interdependence: Why America Should Join the World*. New York: W. W. Norton & Company, 2003.

Isikoff, Michael, and David Corn. *Hubris: The Inside Story of Spin, Scandal, and the Selling of the Iraq War*. New York: Crown Publishers, 2006.

Jaffa, Harry V. "The Achievement of Leo Strauss." *National Review* 25 (7 December 1973): 1353–55.

——. *The Conditions of Freedom*. Baltimore: Johns Hopkins University Press, 1975.

——. "Dear Professor Drury." *Political Theory* 15, no. 3 (August 1987): 316–26.

Janssens, David. *Between Athens and Jerusalem: Philosophy, Prophecy and Politics in Leo Strauss's Early Thought*. Albany: SUNY Press, 2008.

——. "A Change of Orientation: Leo Strauss's 'Comments' on Carl Schmitt Revisited." *Interpretation* 33, no. 1 (Fall/Winter 2005): 93–104.

Kagan, Robert William. "God and Man at Yale—Again." *Commentary* 73, no. 2 (February 1982): 48–51.

Kagan, Robert William, and William Kristol, eds. *Present Dangers: Crisis and Opportunity in American Foreign and Defense Policy*. San Francisco: Encounter Books, 2000.

Kaplan, Lawrence F., and William Kristol. *The War over Iraq: Saddam's Tyranny and America's Mission*. San Francisco: Encounter Books, 2003.

Kateb, George. Review of *Leo Strauss: An Introduction to His Thought and Intellectual Legacy*, by Thomas Pangle, *Reading Leo Strauss*, by Steven B. Smith, and *The Truth about Leo Strauss*, by Catherine and Michael Zuckert. *Perspectives on Politics* 5, no. 2 (June 2007): 355–59.

Kelley, Norman. *The Head Negro in Charge Syndrome: The Dead End of Black Politics*. New York: Nation Books, 2004.

Kendall, Willmoore. Review of *Thoughts on Machiavelli*, by Leo Strauss. *Philosophical Review* 75, no. 2 (April 1966): 247–54.

Kenneally, Ivan. "The Use and Abuse of Utopianism: On Leo Strauss's Philosophic Politics." *Perspectives on Political Science* 36, no. 3 (Summer 2007): 141–47.

Kershaw, Ian. *Hitler: 1889–1936 Hubris*. New York: W. W. Norton, 1998.

Kesler, Charles R. "Is Conservatism Un-American?" *National Review*, 22 March 1985.

King, Richard H. "Intellectuals and the State: The Case of the Straussians." *Comparative American Studies* 4, no. 4 (2006): 395–408.

——. "Rights and Slavery, Race and Racism: Leo Strauss, the Straussians, and the American Dilemma." *Modern Intellectual History* 5, no. 1 (2008): 55–82.

Klein, Joe. "Neither Here nor There." *Guardian Unlimited*, 3 July 2002, http://www.guardian .co.uk/eu/story/0,,748364,00.html.

Kojève, Alexandre. *Introduction to the Reading of Hegel*. Translated by James H. Nichols. New York: Basic Books, 1969.

Kristol, Irving. *Neoconservatism: The Autobiography of an Idea*. New York: The Free Press, 1995.

——. "The Neoconservative Persuasion." *Weekly Standard*, 25 August 2003, 23–25.

Kristol, William, Anne Norton, and Nicholas Xenos. "Leo Strauss's Lasting Influence on U.S. Policy." Interview on Neal Conan's "Talk of the Nation," National Public Radio, 25 October 2004, http://www.npr.org/templates/story/story.php?storyId=4125689.

Lampert, Laurence. *Leo Strauss and Nietzsche*. Chicago: University of Chicago Press, 1996.

Larmore, Charles. "The Secrets of Philosophy." *New Republic*, 3 April 1989, 30–35.

LaRouche, Lyndon H., Jr. "Insanity as Geometry." In *Children of Satan*, 6–28, 2004. Posted at http://www.larouchepac.com/files/pdfs/child_satan_book.pdf.

Ledeen, Michael. *Machiavelli on Modern Leadership*. New York: St. Martin's Press, 1999.

Lenzner, Steven J. "Author as Educator." 2002. Posted at http://www.claremont.org/publications/pubid.255/pub_detail.asp.

——. "Guide for the Perplexed." Review of *Leo Strauss: An Introduction to His Thought and Intellectual Legacy*, by Thomas Pangle, *Reading Leo Strauss*, by Steven B. Smith, and *The Truth about Leo Strauss*, by Catherine and Michael Zuckert. *Claremont Review of Books*, Spring 2007, 53–57.

——. "Leo Strauss and His Contemporaries." *Political Science Reviewer* 22 (1993): 124–56.

——. "A Literary Exercise in Self-Knowledge: Strauss's Twofold Interpretation of Maimonides." *Perspectives on Political Science* 31, no. 4 (Fall 2002): 225–34.

——. "Strauss's Fârâbî, Scholarly Prejudice, and Philosophic Politics." *Perspectives on Political Science* 28, no. 4 (Fall 1999): 194–202.

——. "Strauss's Three Burkes." *Political Theory* 19, no. 3 (August 1991): 364–90.

Lenzner, Steven J., and William Kristol. "What Was Leo Strauss Up To?" *Public Interest* 153 (Fall 2003): 19–39.

Lerner, Ralph, and Muhsin Mahdi, eds. *Medieval Political Philosophy*. Ithaca, NY: Cornell University Press, 1972.

Levine, Peter. *Nietzsche and the Modern Crisis of the Humanities*. Albany: SUNY Press, 1995.

Levinson, Sanford. *Wrestling with Diversity*. Durham, NC: Duke University Press, 2003.

Lilla, Mark. "The Closing of the Straussian Mind." Review of *The Modern Prince*, by Carnes Lord, and *Leo Strauss and the Politics of American Empire*, by Anne Norton. *New York Review of Books* 51, no. 17 (4 November 2004): 55–59.

——. "The End of Philosophy." *Times Literary Supplement*, 5 April 1991, 3–5.

——. "Leo Strauss: The European." *New York Review of Books* 51, no. 16 (21 October 2004): 58–60.

Lind, Michael. "The Weird Men behind George W. Bush's War." *New Statesman*, 7 April 2003, http://www.newstatesman.com/200304070003.

Linker, Damon. "The Philosopher and Everyone Else." Review of *Leo Strauss and the Theologico-Political Problem*, by Heinrich Meier, and *Reading Leo Strauss*, by Steven B. Smith. *New Republic*, 31 July 2006, 26–33.

Lobe, Jim. "Leo Strauss's Philosophy of Deception" (19 May 2003). Posted at http://alternet.org/story/15935.

——. "Neocons Dance a Strauss Waltz." *Asia Times*, 9 May 2003, http://www.atimes.com/atimes/Middle_East/EE09Ak01.html.

Locke, John. *The Reasonableness of Christianity: As Delivered in the Scriptures*. Edited by George W. Ewing. Washington, DC: Regnery Gateway, 1965.

——. *The Second Treatise of Government*. Edited by Thomas P. Peardon. Indianapolis: Bobbs-Merrill, 1952.

Lord, Carnes. *The Modern Prince: What Leaders Need to Know Now*. New Haven, CT: Yale University Press, 2003.

Luban, David. Letter to the *New York Times*, 11 May 2003, Week in Review,12.

Machiavelli, Niccolò. *Discourses on Livy*. Translated by Harvey C. Mansfield and Nathan Tarcov. Chicago: University of Chicago Press, 1998.

——. *The Essential Writings of Machiavelli*. Edited by Albert Russell Ascoli and Peter Constantine. New York: Modern Library, 2007.

——. "Exhortation to Penitence." In *The Prince*, 2nd ed., translated and edited by Robert M. Adams, 119–22. New York: W. W. Norton & Company, 1992.

———. *The Florentine Histories*. Translated by Laura F. Banfield and Harvey C. Mansfield. Princeton, NJ: Princeton University Press, 1988.

———. *Il Principe e Discorsi*, 2nd ed. Edited by Sergio Bertelli. Milan: Giangiacomo Feltrinelli, 1981.

———. *The Prince*. Translated by Harvey C. Mansfield. Chicago: University of Chicago Press, 1985.

Mahdi, Muhsin S. *Alfarabi and the Foundation of Islamic Political Philosophy*. Chicago: University of Chicago Press, 2001.

Mann, James. *Rise of the Vulcans: The History of Bush's War Cabinet*. New York: Viking, 2004.

Mansfield, Harvey C. *Machiavelli's New Modes and Orders*. Ithaca, NY: Cornell University Press, 1979.

———. "Strauss's Machiavelli." *Political Theory* 3, no. 4 (November 1975): 372–84.

———. "Timeless Mind." Review of *Leo Strauss and the Politics of Exile*, by Eugene Sheppard, and *Leo Strauss: An Intellectual Biography*, by Daniel Tanguay. *Claremont Review of Books* 8, no. 1 (Winter 2007/2008): 23–26.

Marsilius of Padua. *Defensor Pacis*. Translated by Alan Gewirth, with a new afterword and bibliography by Cary J. Nederman. New York: Columbia University Press, 2001.

Mason, John. "Leo Strauss and the Noble Lie: The Neo-Cons at War." *Logos* 3.2 (Spring 2004), http://www.logosjournal.com/mason.htm.

Massey, Douglas. *Return of the "L" Word*. Princeton, NJ: Princeton University Press, 2005.

———. "Return of the 'L' Word: An Interview with Douglas Massey." *Mother Jones*, 13 May 2005, http://www.motherjones.com/news/qa/2005/05/douglas_massey.html.

McAllister, Ted V. *Revolt Against Modernity: Leo Strauss, Eric Voegelin, and the Search for a Postliberal Order*. Lawrence: University Press of Kansas, 1996.

McCarraher, Eugene. "The Incoherence of Hannah Arendt: Breaking the Marriage between Heaven and Earth." *Christianity Today*, March–April 2006, http://www.christianitytoday.com/bc/2006/002/8.32.html.

McCormick, John P. "Fear, Technology, and the State: Carl Schmitt, Leo Strauss, and the Revival of Hobbes in Weimar and National Socialist Germany." *Political Theory* 22, no. 4 (November 1994): 619–52.

McShea, Robert J. "Leo Strauss on Machiavelli." *Western Political Quarterly* 16, no. 4 (December 1963): 782–97.

Meier, Heinrich. *Carl Schmitt and Leo Strauss: The Hidden Dialogue*. Translated by J. Harvey Lomax. Chicago: University of Chicago Press, 1995.

———. "How Strauss Became Strauss." In Minkov, *Enlightening Revolutions*, 363–82.

———. *Leo Strauss and the Theologico-Political Problem*. Translated by Marcus Brainard. Cambridge: Cambridge University Press, 2006.

———. "Pourquoi Leo Strauss?" *Commentaire* 29, no. 114 (Summer 2006): 307–14.

Melzer, Arthur M. "Esotericism and the Critique of Historicism." *American Political Science Review* 100, no. 2 (May 2006): 279–95.

Merida, Kevin, and Michael A. Fletcher. *Supreme Discomfort: The Divided Soul of Clarence Thomas*. New York: Doubleday, 2007.

Merrill, Clark A. "Leo Strauss's Indictment of Christian Philosophy." *Review of Politics* 62, no. 1 (Winter 2000): 77–105.

Michaels, Walter Benn. *The Trouble with Diversity*. New York: Metropolitan Books, 2006.

Micklethwait, John, and Adrian Wooldridge. *The Right Nation: Conservative Power in America*. New York: Penguin Press, 2004.

Milich, Klaus J. "Fundamentalism Hot and Cold: George W. Bush and the 'Return of the Sacred.'" *Cultural Critique* 62 (Winter 2006): 91–125.

Minowitz, Peter. "Machiavellianism Come of Age? Leo Strauss on Modernity and Economics." *Political Science Reviewer* 22 (1993): 157–97.

———. "Political Philosophy and the Religious Issue: From the Ancient Regime to Modern Capitalism." In *Educating the Prince: Essays in Honor of Harvey Mansfield*, edited by William Kristol and Mark Blitz, 142–75. Lanham, MD: Rowman & Littlefield, 2000.

More, Thomas. *Utopia*. Rev. ed. Translated by Robert Adams. Cambridge: Cambridge University Press, 2002.

Muravchik, Joshua. "The Neoconservative Cabal." *Commentary*, September 2003, 26–33.

Myers, David N. *Rewriting History: Historicism and Its Discontents in German-Jewish Thought*. Princeton, NJ: Princeton University Press, 2003.

Nadon, Christopher. "From Republic to Empire: Political Revolution and the Common Good in Xenophon's *Education of Cyrus*." *American Political Science Review* 90 (June 1996): 361–74.

Nash, George H. *The Conservative Intellectual Movement in America: Since 1945*. New York, Basic Books: 1976.

Nederman, Cary J. "Amazing Grace: Fortune, God, and Free Will in Machiavelli's Thought." *Journal of the History of Ideas* 60, no. 4 (1999): 617–38.

Newell, W. R. "Tyranny and the Science of Ruling in Xenophon's 'Education of Cyrus.'" *Journal of Politics* 45, no. 4 (November, 1983): 889–906.

Norton, Anne. *Leo Strauss and the Politics of American Empire*. New Haven, CT: Yale University Press, 2004.

Nunberg, Geoffrey. *Talking Right: How Conservatives Turned Liberalism into a Tax-Raising, Latte-Drinking, Sushi-Eating, Volvo-Driving, New York Times–Reading, Body-Piercing, Hollywood-Loving, Left-Wing Freak Show*. New York: Public Affairs, 2006.

Nusseibeh, Sari, with Anthony David. *Once Upon a Country: A Palestinian Life*. New York: Farrar, Straus & Giroux, 2007.

Orr, Susan. *Jerusalem and Athens: Reason and Revelation in the Work of Leo Strauss*. Lanham, MD: Rowman & Littlefield, 1995.

Orwin, Clifford. "The Just and the Advantageous in Thucydides: The Case of the Mytilenaian Debate." *American Political Science Review* 78, no. 2 (June 1984): 485–94.

———. "The Straussians Are Coming!" *Claremont Review of Books*, Spring 2005, 14–16.

Owens, Patricia. "Beyond Strauss, Lies, and the War in Iraq: Hannah Arendt's Critique of Neo-Conservatism." *Review of International Studies* 33 (2007): 265–83.

Packer, George. *The Assassin's Gate*. New York: Farrar, Straus, and Giroux, 2005.

Pangle, Thomas L. *Leo Strauss: An Introduction to His Thought and Intellectual Legacy*. Baltimore: Johns Hopkins University Press, 2006.

———. "A Platonic Perspective on the Idea of the Public Intellectual." In *The Public Intellectual*, edited by Arthur M. Melzer, Jerry Weinberger, and M. Richard Zinman, 15–26. Lanham, MD: Rowman & Littlefield, 2003.

———. "Nihilism and Modern Democracy in the Thought of Nietzsche." In Deutsch and Soffer, *Crisis of Liberal Democracy*, 180–211.

Papert, Tony. "The Secret Kingdom of Leo Strauss." *Executive Intelligence Review*, 18 April 2003, http://www.larouchepub.com/pr/site_packages/2003/leo_strauss/3015secret_kingdom_ap_.html (also available at http://www.larouchepac.com/files/pdfs/child_satan_book.pdf, 47–55).

Patard, Emmanuel. "'Restatement' by Leo Strauss (Critical Edition)." *Interpretation* 36, no. 1 (Fall 2008): 3–100.

Paul, Ron. *A Foreign Policy of Freedom: "Peace, Commerce, and Honest Friendship."* Lake Jackson, TX: Foundation for Rational Economics and Education, 2007.

Peterman, Larry. "Approaching Leo Strauss: Some Comments on *Thoughts on Machiavelli*." *Political Science Reviewer* 16 (Fall 1986): 317–51.

Pfaff, William. "The Long Reach of Leo Strauss." *International Herald Tribune*, 15 May 2003.

Pippin, Robert B. "Being, Time, and Politics: The Strauss-Kojève Debate." *History & Theory* 32, no. 2 (May 1993): 138–61.

———. "The Modern World of Leo Strauss." *Political Theory* 20, no. 3 (August 1992): 448–72.

Plato. *Gorgias.* Translated by James H. Nichols Jr. Ithaca, NY: Cornell University Press, 1998.

———. *Laws.* Translated by Thomas L. Pangle. New York: Basic Books, 1980.

———. *Republic.* 2nd ed. Translated by Allan Bloom. New York: Basic Books, 1991.

———. *Statesman.* Translated by Seth Benardete. Chicago: University of Chicago Press, 1986.

Pocock, J. G. A. "Prophet and Inquisitor." *Political Theory* 3, no. 4 (November 1975): 385–401.

Podhoretz, Norman. "World War IV: How It Started, What It Means, and Why We Have to Win." In *The Right War? The Conservative Debate on Iraq*, edited by Gary Rosen, 102–69. Cambridge: Cambridge University Press, 2005.

Polin, Claude. "The Enigmatic Professor Strauss, Part I." *Chronicles*, July 2007, 47–51.

Postel, Danny. "Noble Lies and Perpetual War: Leo Strauss, the Neo-Cons, and Iraq." *openDemocracy*, 16 October 2003, http://www.opendemocracy.net/faith-iraqwarphilosophy/article_1542 .jsp.

Raimondo, Justin. "The Imperial Delusion: Neoconservatism and the Cult of Empire" (16 September 2005). Posted at http://www.antiwar.com/justin/?articleid=7294.

Rauschning, Hermann. *The Revolution of Nihilism: Warning to the West.* New York: Alliance Book/Longmans, 1939.

Risen, James. "How Pair's Finding on Terror Led to Clash on Shaping Intelligence." *New York Times*, 28 April 2004, A1, A19.

Robbins, Tim. *Embedded Live.* DVD. Directed by Tim Robbins. New York: Havoc Inc., 2003.

Robin, Corey. "In the Shadow of Tyranny." Review of *Leo Strauss and the Politics of American Empire*, by Anne Norton. *New Statesman*, 13 June 2005, http://www.newstatesman.com/ 200506130041.

Rosen, Stanley. *Hermeneutics as Politics.* 2nd ed. New Haven, CT: Yale University Press, 2003.

Rosenberg, Alfred. *The Myth of the Twentieth Century.* Translated by Vivian Bird. Torrance, CA: Noontide Press, 1982. The German original of this edition was published in 1937.

Roston, Aram. *The Man Who Pushed America to War: The Extraordinary Life, Adventures, and Obsessions of Ahmad Chalabi.* New York: Nation Books, 2008.

Ryn, Claes G. *America the Virtuous: The Crisis of Democracy and the Quest for Empire.* New Brunswick, NJ: Transaction Publishers, 2003.

Saxonhouse, Arlene W. "Democracy, Equality, and *Eidē*: A Radical View from Book 8 of Plato's *Republic*." *American Political Science Review* 92 (June 1998): 273–83.

Schaar, John H., and Sheldon S. Wolin. "*Essays on the Scientific Study of Politics*: A Critique." *American Political Science Review* 57, no. 1 (March 1963): 125–50.

Schaeffer, David Lewis. "The Ass and the Lion." Review of *Leo Strauss and the Politics of American Empire*, by Anne Norton. *Interpretation* 32, no. 3 (Summer 2005): 283–305.

———. "Shadia Drury's Critique of Leo Strauss." *Political Science Reviewer* 23 (1994): 80–127.

Schlesinger, Arthur, Jr. "The Making of a Mess." *New York Review of Books* 51, no. 14 (23 September 2004): 40–43.

Schmitt, Carl. *The Concept of the Political.* Translated by George Schwab, with a new foreword by Tracy B. Strong. Chicago: University of Chicago Press, 1996.

Schmitt, Gary J., and Abram N. Shulsky. "Leo Strauss and the World of Intelligence (By Which We Do Not Mean *Nous*)." In Deutsch and Murley, *Leo Strauss*, 407–12.

———. "The Future of Intelligence." *National Interest*, 1 December 1994.

Schuck, Peter H. *Diversity in America: Keeping Government at a Safe Distance.* Cambridge, MA: Harvard University Press, 2003.

Sheppard, Eugene R. *Leo Strauss and the Politics of Exile: The Making of a Political Philosopher.* Waltham, MA: Brandeis University Press, 2006.

Shorris, Earl. "Ignoble Liars: Leo Strauss, George Bush, and the Philosophy of Mass Deception." *Harper's Magazine*, June 2004, 65–71.

——. *The Politics of Heaven: America in Fearful Times.* New York: W. W. Norton & Company, 2007.

Singh, Aakash. *Eros Turannos: Leo Strauss and Alexandre Kojève Debate on Tyranny.* Lanham, MD: University Press of America, 2005.

Smith, Gregory Bruce. "Athens and Washington: Leo Strauss and the American Regime." In Deutsch and Murley, *Leo Strauss*, 103–27.

Smith, Steven B. *Reading Leo Strauss.* Chicago: University of Chicago Press, 2006.

——. "A Skeptical Friend of Democracy." *New York Sun*, 14 March 2007, http://www.nysun .com/article/50399.

Solomon, Lewis D. *Paul D. Wolfowitz: Visionary Intellectual, Policymaker, and Strategist.* Westport, CT: Praeger Security International, 2007.

Sorensen, Kim A. *Discourses on Strauss: Revelation and Reason in Leo Strauss and His Critical Study of Machiavelli.* South Bend, IN: University of Notre Dame Press, 2006.

Stauffer, Devin. "Reopening the Quarrel between the Ancients and the Moderns: Leo Strauss's Critique of Hobbes's 'New Political Science.'" *American Political Science Review* 101, no. 2 (May 2007): 223–33.

Steele, Claude M. "Thin Ice: 'Stereotype Threat' and Black College Students." *Atlantic Monthly*, August 1999, 44–54.

——. "A Threat in the Air: How Stereotypes Shape Intellectual Identity and Performance." *American Psychologist* 52, no. 6 (June 1997): 613–19.

Steinberg, Jeffrey. "Leo Strauss, Fascist Godfather of the Neo-Cons." *Executive Intelligence Review*, 21 March 2003, http://www.larouchepub.com/other/2003/3011profile_strauss.html.

Sullivan, Vickie B. *Machiavelli's Three Romes: Religion, Human Liberty and Politics Reformed.* Dekalb: Northern Illinois University Press, 1996.

Strauss, Leo. Also see pp. xi–xiii above.

——. "Correspondence Concerning Modernity: Karl Löwith and Leo Strauss." *Independent Journal of Philosophy* 4 (1983): 105–19.

——. "The Crisis of Our Time" and "The Crisis of Political Philosophy." In *The Predicament of Modern Politics*, edited by Harold J. Spaeth, 41–54 and 91–103. Detroit: University of Detroit Press, 1964.

——. *Jewish Philosophy and the Crisis of Modernity: Essays and Lectures in Modern Jewish Thought.* Edited by Kenneth Hart Green. Albany: SUNY Press, 1997.

——. "On Abravanel's Philosophical Tendency and Political Teaching." In *Isaac Abravanel*, edited by J. B. Trend and H. Loewe, 93–129. Cambridge: Cambridge University Press, 1937.

——. "On Collingwood's Philosophy of History." *Review of Metaphysics* 5, no. 4 (June 1952): 559–86.

——. "On the Intention of Rousseau." *Social Research* 14, no. 4 (December 1947): 455–87.

——. "On a New Interpretation of Plato's Political Philosophy." *Social Research* 13, no. 3 (September 1946): 326–67.

——. "The Re-education of Axis Countries Concerning the Jews." *Review of Politics* 69, no. 4 (Fall 2007): 530–38. Lecture delivered in 1943.

——. "The Spirit of Sparta or the Taste of Xenophon." *Social Research* 6, no. 4 (November 1939): 502–36.

——. "What Can We Learn from Political Theory?" *Review of Politics* 69, no. 4 (Fall 2007): 515–29. Lecture delivered in 1942.

Swidey, Neil. "The Mind of the Administration, Part Two: The Analyst." *Boston Globe*, 18 May 2003, http://www.boston.com/news/globe/ideas/articles/2003/05/18/the_analyst/.

Swift, Jonathan. *Gulliver's Travels*. New York: Penguin Books, 1977.

Tanenhaus, Sam. "Bush's Brain Trust." *Vanity Fair*, July 2003, 114–18, 164–65, 168.

———. "Interview with Deputy Secretary Wolfowitz." *Vanity Fair*, 10 May 2003, http://www.defenselink.mil/transcripts/2003/tr20030509-depsecdef0223.html.

Tanguay, Daniel. *Leo Strauss: Une biographie intellectuelle*. Paris: Grasset & Fasquelle/Brodard & Taupin, 2003. Available, in an English translation by Christopher Nadon, as *Leo Strauss: An Intellectual Biography*. New Haven, CT: Yale University Press, 2007.

———. "Neoconservatisme et religion democratique." *Commentaire* 29, no. 114 (Summer 2006): 315–24.

Tarcov, Nathan. "Philosophy & History: Tradition and Interpretation in the Work of Leo Strauss." *Polity* 16, no. 1 (Fall 1983): 5–29.

———. "On a Certain Critique of 'Straussianism.'" *Review of Politics* 53, no. 1 (Winter 1991): 3–18. Also in Deutsch and Murley, *Leo Strauss*, 259–74.

———. "Will the Real Leo Strauss Please Stand Up?" *The American Interest* 2, no. 1 (September/October 2006), http://www.the-american-interest.com/ai2/article.cfm?Id=166&MId=5.

Thomas, Andrew Payton. *Clarence Thomas: A Biography*. San Francisco: Encounter Books, 2001.

Thompson, Michael J., ed. *Confronting the New Conservatism: The Rise of the Right in America*. New York: New York University Press, 2007.

Thucydides. *The Peloponnesian War*. Translated by Steven Lattimore. Indianapolis: Hackett Publishing Company, 1998.

Udoff, Alan, ed. *Leo Strauss's Thought: Toward a Critical Engagement*. Boulder, CO: Lynne Rienner Publishers, 1991.

Unger, Craig. *The Fall of the House of Bush: The Untold Story of How a Band of True Believers Seized the Executive Branch, Started the Iraq War, and Still Imperils America's Future*. New York: Scribner, 2007.

Vlastos, Gregory. Review of *On Tyranny*, by Leo Strauss. *Philosophical Review* 60, no. 4 (October 1951): 592–94.

Walsh, John. "The Philosophy of Mendacity." *Counterpunch*, 2 November 2005, http://counterpunch.org/walsh11022005.html.

Weisberg, Jacob. *The Bush Tragedy*. New York: Random House, 2008.

Weisman, Alan. *Prince of Darkness: Richard Perle*. New York: Union Square Press, 2007.

Weitz, Eric D. *Weimar Germany: Promise and Tragedy*. Princeton, NJ: Princeton University Press, 2007.

West, Thomas G. "Leo Strauss and American Foreign Policy." *Claremont Review of Books*, Summer 2004, 13–16.

Wolfowitz, Paul. "Bridging the Dangerous Gap between the West and the Muslim World." Speech presented at the World Affairs Council, Monterey, California, 3 May 2002, http://www.defenselink.mil/speeches/2002/s20020503-depsecdef.html.

———. "The Man Who Saved the Day—Sort Of . . ." Review of *To End a War*, by Richard Holbrooke. *National Interest* 53 (Fall 1998): 102–8.

———. "Remembering the Future." *National Interest* 59 (Spring 2000): 35–45.

———. "Statesmanship in the New Century." In Kagan and Kristol, *Present Dangers*, 307–36.

———. "Victory Came Too Easily." Review of *Crusade: The Untold Story of the Persian Gulf War*, by Rick Atkinson. *National Interest* 35 (Spring 1994): 87–92.

Wolin, Richard. "Carl Schmitt: The Conservative Revolutionary Habitus and the Aesthetics of Horror." *Political Theory* 20, no. 3 (August 1992): 424–47.

———. *The Heidegger Controversy*. Cambridge, MA: MIT Press, 1993.

——. *Heidegger's Children: Hannah Arendt, Karl Löwith, Hans Jonas, and Herbert Marcuse.* Princeton, NJ: Princeton University Press, 2001.

——. "Leo Strauss, Judaism, and Liberalism." *Chronicle of Higher Education* 52, no. 32 (14 April 2006): B13–14.

Wolin, Sheldon S. *Democracy Incorporated: Managed Democracy and the Specter of Inverted Totalitarianism.* Princeton, NJ: Princeton University Press, 2008.

Wood, Gordon S. "The Fundamentalists and the Constitution." *New York Review of Books* 35, no. 2 (18 February 1988): 33–40.

Wood, Peter. *Diversity: The Invention of a Concept.* San Francisco: Encounter Books, 2003.

Woodward, Bob. *Bush at War.* New York: Simon & Schuster, 2002.

——. *Plan of Attack.* New York: Simon & Schuster, 2004.

——. *State of Denial.* New York: Simon & Schuster, 2006.

Workman, Thom. "When Might Is Right: Ancient Lamentations, Straussian Ministrations, and American Dispensations." In *The New Imperialists: Ideologies of Empire*, edited by Colin Mooers, 137–65. Oxford: Oneworld Publications, 2006.

Wurmser, David. *Tyranny's Ally: America's Failure to Defeat Saddam Hussein.* Washington, DC: AEI Press, 1999.

Xenophon. *The Education of Cyrus.* Translated by Wayne Ambler. Ithaca, NY: Cornell University Press, 2001. In the text, I usually refer to this work as the *Cyropaedia.*

——. *Hiero* or *Tyrannicus.* Translated by Marvin Kendrick, revised by Seth Benardete. In Leo Strauss, *On Tyranny*, edited by Victor Gourevitch and Michael S. Roth, 3–21. New York: Free Press, 1991.

——. *Memorabilia.* Translated by Amy L. Bonnette, with an introduction by Christopher Bruell. Ithaca, NY: Cornell University Press, 1994.

——. *Oeconomicus.* Translated by Carnes Lord. In Leo Strauss, *Xenophon's Socratic Discourse*, 3–80. Ithaca, NY: Cornell University Press, 1970.

Xenos, Nicholas. *Cloaked in Virtue: Unveiling Leo Strauss and the Rhetoric of American Foreign Policy.* New York: Routledge, 2008.

——. "Leo Strauss and the Rhetoric of the War on Terror." *Logos* 3.2, Spring 2004, http://www.logosjournal.com/xenos.pdf.

——. "The Neocon Con Game: Nihilism Revisited." In Thompson, *Confronting the New Conservatism*, 225–46.

Yolton, J. W. "Locke on the Law of Nature." *Philosophical Review* 67 (1958): 477–98.

Yoshino, Kenji. *Covering: The Hidden Assault on Our Civil Rights.* New York: Random House, 2006.

Young-Bruehl, Elisabeth. *Hannah Arendt, for Love of the World.* New Haven, CT: Yale University Press, 1982.

Zuckert, Catherine H. *Postmodern Platos.* Chicago: University of Chicago Press, 1996.

Zuckert, Catherine H., and Michael Zuckert. *The Truth about Leo Strauss: Political Philosophy and American Democracy.* Chicago: University of Chicago Press, 2006.

Index of Names

Abella, Alex, 25, 27, 28, 45n47, 290n23
Abrams, Elliot, 29, 192, 217n62
Adams, Robert A., 228, 234, 251n8
Adeimantus, 154, 168n15, 169n16
Agathocles, 231–32, 233, 236, 252n29
Agresto, John, 109, 221n123
Alfarabi, Abu Nasr Muhammad. *See* Farabi
Alterman, Eric, 17n33, 42n27
Altman, William, 84–85, 98n130, 98n132, 98n134, 99n139, 99n143, 173n61, 176n81, 215n42
Anastaplo, George, 27–28, 51n112, 55, 69, 87n7, 87n11, 91n62, 125, 277, 299n114
Anderson, Perry, 288
Andocides, 78–79, 96n108
Aquinas, Thomas, 178n98, 254n42
Arendt, Hannah, 10–11, 36–38, 50n100, 51n104, 51nn105–6, 51nn110–11, 163, 250n7, 278, 293n62, 294n70, 295n78
Aristophanes, 58, 102, 108, 130n27, 161, 190, 285
Aristotle, 23, 26, 97n118, 101–2, 115, 116–18, 132n52, 133n66, 139n119, 160, 161, 165, 171nn37–38, 172n55, 177n96, 178nn98–99, 182, 183, 191, 197, 214n26, 229–30, 236, 244, 254n42, 254–55n51, 256n69, 258n81, 258nn83–84, 272, 275, 278

Aronowitz, Stanley, 3
Ascoli, Albert, 250n7
Ashbrook, Tom, 29, 46n58
Ashcroft, John, 64
Astyages, 94n93, 94n95
Atlas, James, 10, 27, 28–29, 30, 31–32, 46n52, 46n54, 107, 109, 216n53
Austin, Dorothy, 15–16n18
Averroës, 101–2, 128n16, 209, 254n42

Bagley, Paul, 254–55n51
Batnitzky, Leora, 128n15
Beatty, Jack, 46n58
Behnegar, Nasser, 4, 129n18, 155, 176n83, 178n100, 278, 294n64, 294n69
Bellow, Saul, 25, 201
Benardete, Seth, 70, 125, 138n109, 221n116, 286, 289n10
Bennett, William, 11, 109, 111, 112, 130nn29–30, 130n34, 131n46, 206
Berkowitz, Peter, 15n8, 87n5, 206, 287, 300n117
Berlin, Isaiah, 215n38, 223, 251n18, 276, 293n64
Berns, Walter, 51n113, 125, 184, 207, 214n32, 286–87
Bernstein, Richard, 111–12
Blackburn, Simon, 138n111, 139n120, 146, 169n17

317

About the Author

Peter Minowitz is associate professor of political science at Santa Clara University in California. In addition to his publications discussing Leo Strauss and Harvey Mansfield, he has written about Woody Allen's *Crimes and Misdemeanors*, Frank Herbert's *Dune* series, Karl Marx, and Adam Smith. His works on Smith include a 1993 book, *Profits, Priests, and Princes: Adam Smith's Emancipation of Economics from Politics and Religion*, and "Adam Smith's Invisible Hands," an online article in *Econ Journal Watch* (http://www.econjournalwatch.org/pdf/MinowitzComment1December2004.pdf).